SUBSTANCE USE: INDIVIDUAL BEHAVIOUR, SOCIAL INTERACTIONS, MARKETS AND POLITICS

ADVANCES IN HEALTH ECONOMICS AND HEALTH SERVICES RESEARCH

Series Editors: Michael Grossman and Björn Lindgren

ADVANCES IN HEALTH ECONOMICS AND HEALTH
SERVICES RESEARCH   VOLUME 16

SUBSTANCE USE: INDIVIDUAL BEHAVIOUR, SOCIAL INTERACTIONS, MARKETS AND POLITICS

EDITED BY

BJÖRN LINDGREN

Lund University Centre for Health Economics, Sweden

MICHAEL GROSSMAN

City University of New York Graduate Center and National Bureau of Economic Research, USA

2005

ELSEVIER
JAI

Amsterdam – Boston – Heidelberg – London – New York – Oxford
Paris – San Diego – San Francisco – Singapore – Sydney – Tokyo

ELSEVIER B.V.	ELSEVIER Inc.	ELSEVIER Ltd	ELSEVIER Ltd
Radarweg 29	525 B Street, Suite 1900	The Boulevard, Langford	84 Theobalds Road
P.O. Box 211	San Diego	Lane, Kidlington	London
1000 AE Amsterdam	CA 92101-4495	Oxford OX5 1GB	WC1X 8RR
The Netherlands	USA	UK	UK

© 2005 Elsevier Ltd. All rights reserved.

This work is protected under copyright by Elsevier Ltd, and the following terms and conditions apply to its use:

Photocopying
Single photocopies of single chapters may be made for personal use as allowed by national copyright laws. Permission of the Publisher and payment of a fee is required for all other photocopying, including multiple or systematic copying, copying for advertising or promotional purposes, resale, and all forms of document delivery. Special rates are available for educational institutions that wish to make photocopies for non-profit educational classroom use.

Permissions may be sought directly from Elsevier's Rights Department in Oxford, UK: phone (+44) 1865 843830, fax (+44) 1865 853333, e-mail: permissions@elsevier.com. Requests may also be completed on-line via the Elsevier homepage (http://www.elsevier.com/locate/permissions).

In the USA, users may clear permissions and make payments through the Copyright Clearance Center, Inc., 222 Rosewood Drive, Danvers, MA 01923, USA; phone: (+1) (978) 7508400, fax: (+1) (978) 7504744, and in the UK through the Copyright Licensing Agency Rapid Clearance Service (CLARCS), 90 Tottenham Court Road, London W1P 0LP, UK; phone: (+44) 20 7631 5555; fax: (+44) 20 7631 5500. Other countries may have a local reprographic rights agency for payments.

Derivative Works
Tables of contents may be reproduced for internal circulation, but permission of the Publisher is required for external resale or distribution of such material. Permission of the Publisher is required for all other derivative works, including compilations and translations.

Electronic Storage or Usage
Permission of the Publisher is required to store or use electronically any material contained in this work, including any chapter or part of a chapter.

Except as outlined above, no part of this work may be reproduced, stored in a retrieval system or transmitted in any form or by any means, electronic, mechanical, photocopying, recording or otherwise, without prior written permission of the Publisher.
Address permissions requests to: Elsevier's Rights Department, at the fax and e-mail addresses noted above.

Notice
No responsibility is assumed by the Publisher for any injury and/or damage to persons or property as a matter of products liability, negligence or otherwise, or from any use or operation of any methods, products, instructions or ideas contained in the material herein. Because of rapid advances in the medical sciences, in particular, independent verification of diagnoses and drug dosages should be made.

First edition 2005

British Library Cataloguing in Publication Data
A catalogue record is available from the British Library.

ISBN: 0-7623-1233-5
ISSN: 0731-2199 (Series)

∞ The paper used in this publication meets the requirements of ANSI/NISO Z39.48-1992 (Permanence of Paper).
Printed in The Netherlands.

Working together to grow
libraries in developing countries

www.elsevier.com | www.bookaid.org | www.sabre.org

ELSEVIER   BOOK AID International   Sabre Foundation

CONTENTS

LIST OF CONTRIBUTORS   ix

PREFACE   xv

ACKNOWLEDGEMENTS   xvii

INTRODUCTION
   Björn Lindgren and Michael Grossman   xix

PART I: INDIVIDUAL BEHAVIOUR

THE PSYCHOBIOLOGY OF AGGRESSIVE BEHAVIOUR
   Lil Träskman-Bendz and Sofie Westling   3

INDIVIDUAL BEHAVIOURS AND SUBSTANCE USE: THE ROLE OF PRICE
   Michael Grossman   15

DEMAND FOR ILLICIT DRUGS AMONG PREGNANT WOMEN
   Hope Corman, Kelly Noonan, Nancy E. Reichman and Dhaval Dave   41

THE EFFECT OF ALCOHOL CONSUMPTION ON THE EARNINGS OF OLDER WORKERS
   Henry Saffer and Dhaval Dave   61

DRUGS AND JUVENILE CRIME: EVIDENCE FROM A
PANEL OF SIBLINGS AND TWINS
    H. Naci Mocan and Erdal Tekin   91

ANTIDEPRESSANTS AND THE SUICIDE RATE:
IS THERE REALLY A CONNECTION?
    Matz Dahlberg and Douglas Lundin   121

PART II: SOCIAL INTERACTIONS

CHOICE, SOCIAL INTERACTION AND ADDICTION:
THE SOCIAL ROOTS OF ADDICTIVE PREFERENCES
    Ole-Jørgen Skog   145

THE SPREAD OF DRUG USE: EPIDEMIC MODELS
OR SOCIAL INTERACTION?
    Hans O. Melberg   173

STRUCTURAL ESTIMATION OF PEER EFFECTS IN
YOUTH SMOKING
    Brian Krauth   201

PART III: MARKETS

TRENDS IN WINE CONSUMPTION IN NORWAY:
IS DIFFUSION THEORY APPLICABLE?
    Ingeborg Rossow   215

AN INVESTIGATION OF THE EFFECTS OF
ALCOHOL POLICIES ON YOUTH STDs
    Michael Grossman, Robert Kaestner and   229
    Sara Markowitz

CAN WE MODEL THE IMPACT OF INCREASED DRUG TREATMENT EXPENDITURE ON THE U.K. DRUG MARKET?
Christine Godfrey, Steve Parrott, Gail Eaton, Anthony Culyer and Cynthia McDougall   257

TOBACCO CONTROL POLICIES AND YOUTH SMOKING: EVIDENCE FROM A NEW ERA
John A. Tauras, Sara Markowitz and John Cawley   277

THE FIRES ARE NOT OUT YET: HIGHER TAXES AND YOUNG ADULT SMOKING
Philip DeCicca, Don Kenkel and Alan Mathios   293

COUPONS AND ADVERTISING IN MARKETS FOR ADDICTIVE GOODS: DO CIGARETTE MANUFACTURERS REACT TO KNOWN FUTURE TAX INCREASES?
Dean R. Lillard and Andrew Sfekas   313

PART IV: POLITICS

SYMBOLISM AND RATIONALITY IN THE POLITICS OF PSYCHOACTIVE SUBSTANCES
Robin Room   331

WHAT DOES IT MEAN TO DECRIMINALIZE MARIJUANA? A CROSS-NATIONAL EMPIRICAL EXAMINATION
Rosalie L. Pacula, Robert MacCoun, Peter Reuter, Jamie Chriqui, Beau Kilmer, Katherine Harris, Letizia Paoli and Carsten Schäfer   347

ECONOMIC PERSPECTIVES ON INJECTING
DRUG USE
    David E. Bloom, Ajay Mahal and Brendan O'Flaherty   371

MODELS PERTAINING TO HOW DRUG POLICY
SHOULD VARY OVER THE COURSE OF A DRUG
EPIDEMIC
    Jonathan P. Caulkins   397

ECONOMIC EVALUATION OF RELAPSE
PREVENTION FOR SUBSTANCE USERS:
TREATMENT SETTINGS AND HEALTH CARE
POLICY
    Tetsuji Yamada, Chia-Ching Chen and Tadashi Yamada   431

LIST OF CONTRIBUTORS

David E. Bloom	Department of Population and International Health, Harvard School of Public Health, Harvard University, Boston, MA and National Bureau of Economic Research, Cambridge, MA, USA
Jonathan P. Caulkins	RAND Drug Policy Research Center & Management and H. John Heinz III School of Public Policy, Carnegie Mellon University, Pittsburgh, PA, USA
John Cawley	Department of Policy Analysis and Management, Cornell University, Ithaca, NY and National Bureau of Economic Research, Cambridge, MA, USA
Chia-Ching Chen	Department of Health and Behavioral Studies, Columbia University, USA
Jamie Chriqui	The MayaTech Corporation, Silver Spring, MD, USA
Hope Corman	Department of Economics, Rider University, Lawrenceville, NJ and National Bureau of Economic Research, Cambridge, MA, USA
Anthony Culyer	Institute for Work & Health, Toronto, ON, Canada and Department of Economics and Related Studies, University of York, York, UK

LIST OF CONTRIBUTORS

Matz Dahlberg	Department of Economics, Uppsala University, Uppsala, Sweden
Dhaval Dave	Department of Economics, Bentley College, Waltham, MA and National Bureau of Economic Research, Cambridge, MA, USA
Philip DeCicca	Department of Economics, University of Michigan, Ann Arbor, MI, USA
Gail Eaton	Department of Health, London, UK
Christine Godfrey	Department of Health Sciences and Centre for Health Economics, University of York, York, UK
Michael Grossman	Ph.D. Program in Economics, City University of New York Graduate Center, New York, NY and National Bureau of Economic Research, Cambridge, MA, USA
Katherine Harris	Substance Abuse and Mental Health Administration, Rockville, MD, USA
Robert Kaestner	Institute of Government and Public Affairs and Department of Economics, University of Illinois at Chicago, Chicago, IL and National Bureau of Economic Research, Cambridge, MA, USA
Don Kenkel	Department of Policy Analysis and Management, Cornell University, Ithaca, NY and National Bureau of Economic Research, Cambridge, MA, USA
Beau Kilmer	Department of Public Policy, John F. Kennedy School of Government, Harvard University, Cambridge, MA, USA

List of Contributors

Brian Krauth	Department of Economics, Simon Fraser University, Burnaby, BC, Canada
Dean R. Lillard	Department of Policy Analysis and Management, Cornell University, Ithaca, NY, USA
Björn Lindgren	Lund University Centre for Health Economics, Lund, Sweden
Douglas Lundin	Läkemedelsförmånsnämnden, Solna, Sweden
Robert MacCoun	Goldman School of Public Policy, University of California at Berkeley, Berkeley, CA, USA
Ajay Mahal	Department of Population and International Health, Harvard School of Public Health, Boston, MA, USA
Sara Markowitz	Department of Economics, Rutgers University, Newark, NJ and National Bureau of Economic Research, Cambridge, MA, USA
Alan Mathios	Department of Policy Analysis and Management, Cornell University, Ithaca, NY, USA
Cynthia McDougall	Centre for Criminal Justice Economics and Psychology, Wentworth College, The University of York, Heslington, UK
Hans O. Melberg	Norwegian Institute for Alcohol and Drug Research (SIRUS), Oslo, Norway
Naci H. Mocan	Department of Economics, University of Colorado, Denver, CO and National Bureau of Economic Research, Cambridge, MA, USA

Kelly Noonan	Department of Economics, Rider University, Lawrenceville, NJ and National Bureau of Economic Research, Cambridge, MA, USA
Brendan O'Flaherty	Department of Economics, Columbia University, New York, NY, USA
Rosalie L. Pacula	RAND Corporation, Santa Monica, CA and National Bureau of Economic Research, Cambridge, MA, USA
Letizia Paoli	Max Planck Institute for Foreign and International Criminal Law, Freiburg, Germany
Steve Parrott	Centre for Health Economics, Alcuin College, University of York, York, UK
Nancy E. Reichman	Department of Pediatrics, Robert Wood Johnson Medical School of the University of Medicine and Dentistry of New Jersey, New Brunswick, NJ, USA
Peter Reuter	School of Public Policy, University of Maryland, College Park, MD, USA
Robin Room	Centre for Social Research on Alcohol and Drugs, Stockholm University, Stockholm, Sweden
Ingeborg Rossow	Norwegian Institute for Alcohol and Drug Research, Norway
Henry Saffer	Department of Economics, Kean University, Union, NJ and National Bureau of Economic Research, Cambridge, MA, USA
Carsten Schäfer	Max Planck Institute for Foreign and International Criminal Law, Freiburg, Germany

List of Contributors xiii

Andrew Sfekas   Centre for Health Industry Market
                        Economics, Northwestern University,
                        Evanston, IL, USA

Ole-Jørgen Skog   Department of Sociology, University of
                        Oslo, Oslo, Norway

John A. Tauras   Department of Economics, University of
                        Illinois at Chicago, Chicago, IL and
                        National Bureau of Economic Research,
                        Cambridge, MA, USA

Erdal Tekin   Department of Economics, Georgia State
                        University, Atlanta, GA and National
                        Bureau of Economic Research, Cambridge,
                        MA, USA

Lil Träskman-Bendz   Department of Clinical Neurosciences,
                        Lund University, Lund, Sweden

Sofie Westling   Department of Clinical Neurosciences,
                        Lund University, Lund, Sweden

Tadashi Yamada   Department of Economics, University of
                        Tsukuba, Tsukuba-City, Japan

Tetsuji Yamada   Department of Economics, Rutgers
                        University, Camden, NJ, USA

PREFACE

This book marks the resumption of an annual series of research in health economics previously published by JAI Press Inc. and entitled *Advances in Health Economics and Health Services Research*. Fifteen volumes in that series appeared in the years from 1979 through 1995. The continuation of the series is being published by JAI, an imprint of Elsevier Ltd.

This volume contains a selection of papers presented at the 24th Arne Ryde Symposium entitled "Economics of Substance Use: Individual Behaviour, Social Interactions, Markets, and Politics" and held at the Lund University Center for Health Economics on August 13 and 14, 2004. We wish to thank all the participants, especially those who discussed the papers, for their extremely helpful comments. We also wish to thank Mats Berglund, Kristian Bolin, Stig Larsson, Petter Lundborg, and Agneta Öjehagen for joining us on the committee, chaired by Björn Lindgren, that organized the symposium. Special thanks are due to Mats, Agneta, and especially to Kristian and Petter for helping us to review the revised papers after the symposium. In addition, we are indebted to Inger Lindgren who served as administrative assistant for the symposium and the volume. We could not have held the symposium or produced the volume without her.

We are deeply grateful to the Arne Ryde Foundation for financing the symposium. Arne Ryde was a promising doctoral student in economics at Lund University. He died tragically in a road accident in the spring of 1968 when he was only 23 years old. In his memory, his parents Valborg and Sven Ryde established the Arne Ryde Foundation for the advancement of economic research at Lund University. Since 1973, the foundation has generously supported international symposia, workshops, and lectures in a variety of areas of economics. Finally, we wish to thank the Swedish Council for Working Life and Social Research and the Health Economics Program of the National Bureau of Economic Research for additional financial support.

Björn Lindgren
Lund, Sweden

Michael Grossman
New York, USA

ACKNOWLEDGEMENTS

All chapters were peer-reviewed. Special thanks go to:

Mats Berglund	Lund University, Lund, Sweden
Kristian Bolin	Lund University, Lund, Sweden
Jonathan Caulkins	RAND Drug Policy Research Center and Carnegie Mellon University, Pittsburgh, PA, USA
Hope Corman	Rider University, Lawrenceville, NJ and National Bureau of Economic Research, Cambridge, MA, USA
Dhaval Dave	Bentley College, Waltham, MA and National Bureau of Economic Research, Cambridge, MA, USA
Philip DeCicca	University of Michigan, Ann Arbor, MI, USA
Björn Ekman	Lund University, Lund, Sweden
Sören Höjgård	Lund University, Lund, Sweden
Robert Kaestner	University of Illinois at Chicago, Chicago, IL and National Bureau of Economic Research, Cambridge, MA, USA
Brian Krauth	Simon Fraser University, Burnaby, BC, Canada
Petter Lundborg	Lund University, Lund, Sweden
Ajay Mahal	Harvard School of Public Health, Boston, MA, USA

Sara Markowitz	Rutgers University, Rutgers, NJ and National Bureau of Economic Research, Cambridge, MA, USA
Kerry Anne McGeary	Drexel University, Philadelphia, PA, USA
Paul Nystedt	Linköping University, Linköping, Sweden
Agneta Öjehagen	Lund University, Lund, Sweden
Rosalie Liccardo Pacula	RAND Corporation, Santa Monica, CA and National Bureau of Economic Research, Cambridge, MA, USA
Damien de Walque	World Bank, Washington, DC, USA
Kenneth Warner	University of Michigan, Ann Arbor, MI, USA
Peter Zweifel	University of Zürich, Zürich, Switzerland

INTRODUCTION

The economics of substance use and abuse deals with the consumption of goods that share two properties. First, they are addictive in the sense that an increase in past consumption of the good leads to an increase in current consumption. Second, their consumption harms the consumer and others. This second property makes them of interest from policy, legal, and public health perspectives. Clearly, not every addictive good harms the user and others. A person can be addicted to jogging, classical music, detective novels, attending church, and other activities that do not harm others and may yield future benefits to the individual in addition to increases in current utility. But the consumption of such substances as cigarettes, alcohol, cocaine, marijuana, and heroin can harm the consumer and others. The existence of external costs (harm to others) and ignored internal costs (harm to self) suggests a possible justification for government intervention in the market for these goods. This intervention may be regulation in the form, for example, of taxation, minimum purchase ages, and restrictions on advertising. It may also take the form of bans on consumption and the provision of treatment for users.

Studies of the determinants and consequences of the consumption of addictive substances shed light on the relative effectiveness of alternative interventions and on the benefits of these interventions. Until the late 1970s, most economists did not pay much attention to these issues. Instead, they accepted the conventional wisdom that the demand for addictive substances is unlikely to be very responsive to price. Empirical studies by Cook and Tauchen (1982) in the case of excessive alcohol consumption and by Lewit, Coate, and Grossman (1981) and Lewit and Coate (1982) in the case of cigarette smoking challenged that proposition. Using data for states of the United States, Cook and Tauchen (1982) reported that a $1 increase in the state excise tax on distilled spirits lowered the age-adjusted cirrhosis mortality rate – a standard measure of excessive alcohol consumption – by approximately the same percentage as it lowered per capita consumption of distilled spirits. Using data for teenagers residing in different states of the US, Lewit et al. (1981) estimated a price elasticity of demand for cigarettes of -1.45. Using similar data for adults, Lewit and Coate (1982) reported price elasticities of −0.74 for young adults, −0.44 for middle-aged adults, and −0.15 for older adults.

With the publication of Becker and Murphy's seminal paper on rational addiction in 1988, a theoretical framework became available that could explain why forward-looking consumers might choose to consume harmfully addictive substances. Rational or farsighted consumers take account of the negative future effects of current consumption when they determine the optimal quantity of an addictive good in the current period. Contrary to conventional wisdom, Becker and Murphy stress that the demand for addictive goods may be quite responsive to price in the long run. Thus, their theory is appealing from an empirical perspective because it can explain results in the studies on the demand for cigarettes and excessive alcohol use mentioned above. Their theory also is appealing from an empirical perspective because it contains a testable prediction: namely, the quantity demanded of an addictive good should be negatively related not only to the current price of the good but also to the past and future price.

Since the late 1980s, research on substance use by economists has mushroomed. Part of this has been due to attempts to test the Becker–Murphy model and to refine and challenge it. A number of studies published in the 1990s and summarized in Grossman's paper in this volume confirmed the key prediction of that model for cigarettes, alcohol, and cocaine. Other studies pointed out that addiction models with hyperbolic discounting yield similar predictions as the Becker–Murphy model, which assumes exponential discounting. The former set of models, however, has very different normative implications (e.g., Gruber & Köszegi, 2001). Additional research has capitalized on the increasing availability of individual panel datasets or long panels of area cross-sections to examine the robustness of the price effects in earlier studies. The results of these studies have not been uniform. Some report fairly large price effects (for example, Gruber & Zinman, 2001 for teenage smoking). Others report much smaller effects (e.g., DeCicca, Kenkel, & Mathios, 1998 for teenage smoking; Dee, 1999 for teenage alcohol use).

The appearance of new and rich datasets and new econometric techniques also has led to research on the adverse consequences of substance use. Relationships such as that between excessive alcohol consumption shortly before driving and motor vehicle crashes clearly imply causality from substance abuse to the outcome issue. But other positive correlations, such as that between the use of alcohol and marijuana and risky sexual behaviour, may be traced to an omitted "third variable" or to reverse causality (e.g., Rees, Argys, & Averett, 2001). At the same time, more definitive

Introduction xxi

estimates of the determinants and consequences of substance use have elicited cost–benefit comparisons of alternative ways to control abuse.

The tremendous expansion in research in the economics of substance use and abuse and the presence of many unresolved issues motivated the conference on which this volume is based. While most of the papers are by economists, the disciplines of medicine, political science, and psychology also are represented. Any successful attempt to address substance use must adopt an interdisciplinary perspective. The aim of the conference to cover issues pertaining to individual behaviour, social interactions, markets, and politics made this all the more necessary.

INDIVIDUAL BEHAVIOUR

Six papers on individual behaviour are included in this volume. The first three are devoted to the determinants of individual consumption behaviour, the next two analyse the impact of individual substance use on labour market performance and criminal activities, respectively, while the last one challenges recent research, which claims that the increase in the prescription of antidepressants is the major factor behind the observed reduction in suicide rates during the 1990s.

Substance use is often associated with aggressive behaviour and violence. Certainly, economists tend to analyse aggression in game-theoretical models (hawk- and dove-games), in which each player has a capability of being aggressive, which would be chosen and used in a specific situation if the player believes that it would be to his or her advantage. Psychiatrists *Lil Träskman-Bendz and Sofie Westling*, however, present a survey of the psychobiology of aggressive behaviour. They conclude that monoaminergic genes, childhood misconduct, and environmental stress predispose aggression and violence later in life. Steroids and carbohydrates are also present in aggressive behaviour.

Michael Grossman discusses economic approaches to the demand for harmfully addictive substances with an emphasis on the role of money prices. He examines trends in real prices and in the use of cigarettes, alcohol, and drugs in the US and presents estimates of time-series demand functions. He discusses how economists have extended their traditional model of consumer behaviour to incorporate addictive aspects and concludes with some implications for tax policy and for the debate on the legalization of marijuana, cocaine, and heroin.

Pregnant women can invest in the health of their unborn children through the use of prenatal inputs such as nutrition and prenatal care and by avoiding unhealthy behaviours such as smoking cigarettes and using drugs. *Hope Corman, Kelly Noonan, Nancy Reichman, and Dhaval Dave* use survey data from a US national birth cohort study linked to respondents' medical records and city-level drug prices to estimate the demand for illicit drugs among pregnant women. They find that a US$ 10 increase in the retail price of a gram of pure cocaine decreases illicit drug use by 12–15%. The estimated price effects for heroin are lower than for cocaine and less robust across alternative model specifications.

Studies have shown that heavy alcohol consumption is negatively related to wages and earnings, while moderate levels of drinking raise wages and earnings. *Henry Saffer and Dhaval Dave* analyse the effects of alcohol consumption on the labour market outcomes of older individuals, using a longitudinal data set consisting of five waves of the US Health and Retirement Study. Contrary to prior studies, their results indicate that alcohol use has a non-positive effect on earnings and wages of older workers.

Despite the strong evidence that drug use and criminal activity are positively correlated, causality has not been conclusively established. *Naci Mocan and Erdal Tekin* investigate the impact of individual drug use on robbery, burglary, theft, and damaging property for juveniles. Using data from the US National Longitudinal Study of Adolescent Health and a variety of fixed-effects models that exploit variations over time and between siblings and twins, they find that drug use has a significant impact on the propensity to commit crime.

In the early 1990s, a new kind of antidepressants, the selective serotonin reuptake inhibitors, was introduced. The introduction was followed by a large increase in the prescription rates of antidepressants. *Matz Dahlberg and Douglas Lundin* challenge the claims from recent research that this increase in prescription rates is the major factor behind the observed decline in suicide rates, using relatively detailed, though aggregate, data on suicides and sold quantities of antidepressants in Sweden 1990–2000. After controlling for a number of covariates, they do not find any statistically significant effect on the suicide rate from the sales of antidepressants.

SOCIAL INTERACTIONS

Economic analysis can account for social interactions in several ways. The three papers that are included all stress different aspects. The first paper

Introduction xxiii

emphasizes the social roots of individual preferences, the second observational learning and social stigma in drug user behaviour, and the third the influences of peers in young people's smoking decisions.

Ole-Jørgen Skog challenges the Becker–Murphy theory of rational addiction. He argues first that the attempts to test the theory by econometric methods have been misguided. Then he takes his critique a few steps further by discussing the Becker–Murphy definition of addiction and by presenting empirical evidence, which contradicts the results of econometric tests. He emphasizes the social roots of individual preferences and argues that a proper understanding of addictive phenomena cannot be obtained unless they are seen in their proper socio-cultural context.

Some people claim that drug use is contagious and suggest that the spread of drug use can be analysed with the same standard epidemiological models, which are used to analyse the spread of infectious diseases. *Hans Olav Melberg* challenges this view. He argues that its main weakness is its lack of attention to micro foundations and puts forward an alternative approach, based on social interaction and the two mechanisms of observational learning and social stigma. Simulation model results are reported, and the problems of testing the predictions of the model are discussed.

Whether young persons are influenced by their peers in their decisions to smoke cigarettes is of great policy relevance, and the consensus in the literature seems to be that peers are quite influential. *Brian Krauth* outlines a new approach to measuring peer influence, a structural model that allows for positive correlation in observable and unobservable characteristics among peers. Using data for Canada, California, and the US in general, he finds that close friend smoking is substantially less influential than is generally found in previous studies.

MARKETS

Six papers analyse the behaviour of markets for alcohol, drugs, and cigarettes.

Ingeborg Rossow presents trends in wine consumption in Norway over the four-decade period 1960–2002 and investigates whether they can be explained by diffusion theory. Using eight cross-sectional national Norwegian surveys on adults, the results of her analysis are partly affirmative. Early adopters were certainly characterized by high social status and by being more "cosmopolite." The typical S-shaped curve for adoption rate was not found, however, nor the expected association between wine consumption and social network.

Using US state-level data for 1982–2001, *Michael Grossman, Robert Kaestner, and Sara Markowitz* examine the role of alcohol policies (beer taxes and statuses pertaining to alcohol sales and drunk driving) in reducing the incidence of sexually transmitted diseases among teenagers and young adults. Their results indicate that higher beer taxes are associated with lower rates of gonorrhoea for males and are suggestive of lower AIDS rates. Strict drunk driving policies in the form of zero tolerance laws may also lower the gonorrhoea rate among males under the legal drinking age.

Christine Godfrey, Steve Parrott, Gail Eaton, Anthony Culyer, and Cynthia McDougall develop a simple dynamic model of the impact of changing the number of problem drug misusers in treatment in England and Wales on the social costs of drug misuse. In their model, consequences are divided into five domains: health, crime, social care, work, and driving. Social costs are estimated to be around GBP 12 billion. An increase in the numbers in treatment is estimated to reduce social costs by between GBP 3 and GBP 4.4 billion across a 5-year period.

The years 1997–2001 were a period in the US characterized by significant changes in cigarette prices and in tobacco control policies. *John Tauras, Sara Markowitz, and John Cawley* take advantage of this variation to provide new estimates of the impact of cigarette prices, taxes, and tobacco control policies on youth and young adult smoking propensity and intensity. Employing a fixed-effects technique, they find a strong negative impact of cigarette prices and taxes on youth and young adult smoking prevalence and conditional demand. They also find that purchase, use, and possession laws are inversely related to youth and young adult smoking prevalence.

Philip DeCicca, Don Kenkel, and Alan Mathios challenge the apparently conventional wisdom that adolescent smoking is substantially more tax- or price-responsive than adult smoking. Using the 1992 and 2000 waves of the US National Education Longitudinal Survey, they extend previous research (a) by exploring the role of past taxes and (b) by focusing on young adults who face different cigarette taxes because they moved to a different state between 1992 and 2000. They find that only the 1992 tax is significantly associated with smoking participation in 2000. Moreover, when the sample is restricted to movers, the estimated relationship between current taxes and smoking participation becomes weak and statistically insignificant.

In most studies of smoking behaviour and cigarette demand, researchers assume that cigarette manufacturers do not have market power. In a market as highly concentrated as the cigarette industry, this assumption may be inappropriate. *Dean Lillard and Andrew Sfekas* develop a pricing model for a monopolist that sells an addictive good and show under which conditions the

Introduction   xxv

monopolist lowers the price he charges when a future tax is imposed. Using US household data, they investigate whether individuals use cents-off coupons in a way consistent with the price discrimination implied by the model. They find evidence that all smokers, not just the young, are more likely to use coupons prior to tax increase, if they are exposed to more advertising.

POLITICS

To a larger or lesser extent, all papers above contain implications for policy-making. The five papers included in this final section are more directly concerned with policy-making and with the policy-making environment.

Robin Room first discusses some of the properties of psychoactive substances, which lie behind their symbolic power at both the personal and the political level. He then considers several analyses of symbolism and rationality and their relationship in the politics of psychoactive substances and argues that values-based rationality must be considered alongside instrumental rationality in understanding human actions. Science-based arguments are often used in values-based as well as in instrumentally oriented policy arguments, and he concludes by analysing some of the implications of this with examples from the Swedish policy context.

"What does it mean to decriminalize marijuana?" *Rosalie Liccardo Pacula, Robert MacCoun, Peter Reuter, Jamie Chriqui, Beau Kilmer, Katherine Harris, Letizia Paoli, and Carsten Schäfer* provide an answer to that question by examining liberalization policies being adopted in various Western countries. They highlight distinct elements about particular policies that are important for analysis and interpretation and discuss some of the environmental factors that also shape these policies, using data from the US as an example. The authors conclude that researchers should be careful, when conducting intra- or international comparisons of policies, since important aspects are easily ignored.

Injecting drug use has for long been treated as a law enforcement problem and a stain on society. With the emergence of HIV/AIDS, the discourse on injecting drug use has widened to include crucial public health and human rights concerns. *David Bloom, Ajay Mahal, and Brendan O'Flaherty* address how economic analysis can contribute to the understanding of injecting drug use and HIV transmission. By focusing on incentives and examining the costs and benefits of drug use from the perspective of the individual injecting drug user, they derive insights into behaviour that should be useful for policy-makers. The authors also present new results on the economics of needle-exchange programmes.

Drug use and associated problems are not stable but vary dramatically over time. In his paper, *Jonathan Caulkins* outlines some broad regularities concerning how drug problems evolve over time. He then sketches some plausible mechanisms for ways in which aspects of that variation might be endogenous and not just exogenous. He finally reviews two classes of dynamic models of drug use – the one-state "A-models" and the two or more state "LH" models – and derives the implications for how policy should vary over a drug epidemic.

Tetsuji Yamada, Chia-Ching Chen, and Tadashi Yamada examine the effectiveness of treatment settings for 13,775 substance users in New Jersey Drug and Alcohol Abuse Treatment between October 2002 and February 2004. They also identify factors that are associated with substance users' recurrence to the treatment centre. Educational attainment, counselling services from healthcare providers, mental agency services, and detoxification treatments all had a significant impact on preventing relapse behaviour.

REFERENCES

Becker, G. S., & Murphy, K. M. (1988). A theory of rational addiction. *Journal of Political Economy, 96*, 675–700.

Cook, P. J., & Tauchen, G. (1982). The effect of liquor taxes on heavy drinking. *Bell Journal of Economics, 13*, 379–390.

DeCicca, P., Kenkel, D., & Mathios, A. (1998). Putting out the fires: Will higher taxes reduce the onset of youth smoking? *Journal of Political Economy, 110*, 144–169.

Dee, T. (1999). State alcohol policies, teen drinking, and traffic fatalities. *Journal of Public Economics, 72*, 289–315.

Gruber, J., & Köszegi, B. (2001). Is addiction "rational"? Theory and evidence. *Quarterly Journal of Economics, 116*, 1261–1303.

Gruber, J., & Zinman, J. (2001). Youth smoking in the United States: Evidence and implications. In: J. Gruber (Ed.), *Risky behaviour among youths: An economic analysis* (pp. 69–120). Chicago: University of Chicago Press.

Lewit, E. M., & Coate, D. (1982). The potential for using excise taxes to reduce smoking. *Journal of Health Economics, 1*, 121–145.

Lewit, E. M., Coate, D., & Grossman, M. (1981). The effects of government regulation on teenage smoking. *Journal of Law and Economics, 24*, 545–569.

Rees, D., Argys, L. M., & Averett, S. (2001). New evidence on the relationship between substance use and adolescent sexual behaviour. *Journal of Health Economics, 20*, 835–845.

Björn Lindgren
Michael Grossman
Editors

PART I:
INDIVIDUAL BEHAVIOUR

THE PSYCHOBIOLOGY OF AGGRESSIVE BEHAVIOUR

Lil Träskman-Bendz and Sofie Westling

ABSTRACT

Among psychiatric illnesses, genetically determined disorders usually have an early onset and a severe and complicated course. Gene–environmental interaction is of importance for aggressive impulsive behaviour. For example, alcoholism type II has a high family loading, a severe course, and is often associated with antisocial behaviour. In order to gain further understanding of aggressive and impulsive behaviour, genes determining serotonin metabolism, neurosteroids and carbohydrate metabolism should be of interest to investigate. Furthermore, modern brain-imaging studies will reveal the site of action of aggressiveness and impulsivity. Within brain regions of interest, biological studies will promote our knowledge of this deleterious behaviour.

INTRODUCTION

Aggressive behaviour is one of the many mammal instincts for survival. Among humans, advanced psychological functions contribute to several expressions of aggression. One example is suicidal aggression. There are reports on murderers who later committed suicide, or on patients with severe psychiatric illness, who committed extended suicide. About 25% of violent psychiatric patients have harmed themselves, while about 10% of suicide attempters have a history of assault (Plutchik & Van Praag, 1989). These researchers also reported a high correlation between ratings of suicide risk and ratings of violence. Furthermore, Engström, Persson, and Levander (1999) found temperamental similarities between suicide attempters and violent offenders.

Swedish studies show a high premature mortality in criminal populations. Lidberg (1993) reported that violent deaths were common among delinquents, and about 50% of these deaths were suicides.

According to Gray (1987) and Barrat (1991), hostility and anxiety are signs of brain arousal, and individuals with high arousal are sensitive to external stressful events. Their psychic tension disappears only after a destructive break-through. Another aspect of aggression is an inherent inability to control impulses. Schalling (1993) suggested impulsivity to be the link between psychopathology and biological vulnerability as similar, or even the same, as biological deviations could be seen in impulsive, self-destructive, and antisocial persons. Impulsive and aggressive traits might contribute significantly to the risk of attempting suicide among alcoholics (Koller et al., 2002).

Male alcoholic individuals could be classified into type I (late onset) or type II alcoholics (early onset with antisocial traits) according to criteria described by Cloninger (1987). Finnish alcoholic, impulsive offenders have personality profiles like type II alcoholics (Virkkunen & Linnoila, 1993). According to Cloninger (1987), type II alcoholics have high family loading, less ability to abstain from alcohol, little guilt or fear associated with drinking, and more frequent alcohol-related antisocial behaviour.

Mulder (2001) performed a cross-sectional review on alcoholism and personality, and concluded that there is a clear association between antisocial behaviour and alcoholism, and antisocial behaviour seems to start before alcoholism. Childhood conduct disorder and hyperactivity have also been mentioned as factors predisposing alcoholism and antisocial behaviour (Söderström, 2002). Interestingly, this typology of childhood risk factors is not specific for alcoholism, as it is generally accepted in psychiatry that early onset of disorders means that they are most probably genetically determined, and that their life course becomes increasingly severe and complicated (Mulder et al., 1994).

NEUROBIOLOGICAL ASPECTS OF AGGRESSIVE BEHAVIOUR

Brain regions of importance for aggression are, e.g., the sensory cortical areas, amygdala, hippocampi, hypothalamus, brain stem, prefrontal cortex, and corpus callosum. The site of action determines the impact of various functions (Table 1). The regulatory monoaminergic systems play an important role in this organization.

Monoamines (Fig. 1)

There is a well-known association between aggressive behaviour and low function of the monoamine serotonin (Valzelli, 1981). Depue and Spoont (1986) concluded that there are two behavioural systems, one inhibiting and the other facilitating. The former is sensitive to environmental stimuli and is linked with serotonergic pathways in the septum–hippocampus area. The latter is activated during goal-oriented behaviour and is linked with the mesolimbic dopamine paths. This two-system model, in which dopamine and serotonin modulate each other, might explain personality features such as impulsivity and mood fluctuations.

Levels of the serotonin metabolite 5-hydroxyindoleacetic acid (5-HIAA), analysed in lumbar cerebrospinal fluid (CSF), are often low in patients who make violent suicide attempts, as well as in impulsive violent offenders, impulsive arsonists, and people with a history of aggressive acts (Åsberg,

Table 1. The Role of Different Brain Regions for Aggressive Behaviour.

Brain Region	Main Function Related to Aggression
Sensory cortical areas	Input becomes conscious
Amygdala	Colouring of input by memories, emotions, and urges from the limbic system
Hippocampi	Associative learning
Hypothalamus	Connects to autonomic input and output
Brain stem	Stereotyped responses to emotions and urges
Prefrontal cortex	Executive functions such as planning, impulse control, and strategies
Corpus callosum	Connections between the dominant, language-steering hemisphere, and the subordinate hemisphere responsible for interpretation of emotions on non-verbal information

Source: Söderström (2002).

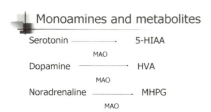

Fig. 1. Monoamines are Degradated by Use of the Enzyme Monoamine Oxidase (MAO) to 5-Hydroxyindoleascetic Acid (5-HIAA), Homovanillic Acid (HVA), and 3-Methoxy-4-Hydroxyphenyl Glycol (MHPG), which are Found in the Brain as well as in the Rest of the Body.

Träskman, & Thorén, 1976; Brown et al., 1979; Lidberg et al., 1985b; Träskman et al., 1981; Virkkunen et al., 1987). Ågren et al. (1986) suggested low CSF levels of both serotonin and dopamine metabolites among impulsive violent or suicidal individuals. Söderström et al. (2003) reported a strong association of the CSF HVA–5-HIAA ratio with psychopathic traits.

In alcoholic criminal offenders, low CSF 5-HIAA was associated with irritability and impaired impulse control (Virkkunen et al., 1994b).

Platelets could be regarded as neurone models. Activity of the degradating enzyme monoamine oxidase (MAO) in platelets might be used for subtyping alcoholics (Demir et al., 2002). There are many studies which show low-platelet MAO activity in impulsive and/or sensation-seeking persons, individuals with type II (early onset) alcoholism, and in recurrent criminality (Buchsbaum, Coursey, & Murphy, 1976; Lidberg et al., 1985a; Oreland et al., 2002). Suicidal impulsive patients with alcoholism had low-platelet MAO activity according to our studies (Engström, Nyman, & Träskman-Bendz, 1996). Psychotic violent offenders had lower-platelet MAO activity than other criminal persons according to another study (Belfrage, Lidberg, & Oreland, 1992).

Deviances in serotonin receptor function, or abnormal binding to platelet-membrane receptors, or receptor binding in Single-Photon Emission Computerized Tomography (SPECT) studies of the brain, have also been reported in depressed suicidal, violent, and/or impulsive patients with or without alcoholism (Simonsson et al., 1991; Pandey et al., 2002; Tiihonen et al., 1997; Lindström et al., 2004; Audenaert et al., 2001; Heinz et al., 2001).

Blunted responses after serotonin challenge reflect decreased serotonin function in the limbic system and hypothalamus. Associations between such blunted responses and impulsivity, irritability, aggression, suicidal behaviour and antisocial behaviour have been reported by several researchers

(Coccaro, Gabriel, & Siever, 1990; Manuck et al., 2002). Similarly, Fishbein et al. (1989) reported blunted reactions in impulsive and aggressive substance users. Low serotonin function was also seen in children with a familial type of aggression (Halperin et al., 2003).

Gerra et al. (2004) observed impaired serotonin function in heroin addicts, which in combination with certain temperamental traits, could increase the proneness for addiction, and probably complicated clinical pictures, e.g. co-morbidity, as well.

King (1981) reviewed the role of catecholamines for aggressiveness, and reported that several studies showed that mesolimbic dopamine causes an impairment of the behavioural response threshold, which in turn results in increased aggression.

Neuroactive Steroids (Fig. 2)

Higley et al. (1992) studied aggressive rhesus monkeys and found low CSF 5-HIAA and high CSF noradrenaline as well as high levels of corticotrophin (adrenocorticotropic hormone, ACTH) and cortisol in plasma. This indicates that these monkeys not only were aggressive (serotonin) but also had a high arousal (noradrenaline and steroids).

Deviances in steroid metabolism have been proven in relation to both suicidal and violent behaviour. High corticosteroid concentrations as well as non-suppression of cortisol in the dexamethasone suppression test have been observed in depressed suicidal patients (Coryell & Schlesser, 2001). In contrast, suicidal individuals with impulsive personality disorders have low 24-h urinary and plasma concentrations (Westrin, Frii, & Träskman-Bendz, 2003).

High serum testosterone was seen in male delinquents of different ages (Mattsson et al., 1980; Rasanen et al., 1999). In violent and alcoholic offenders, high free CSF testosterone was associated with aggressiveness, monotony avoidance, sensation-seeking, suspiciousness, and reduced socialization (Virkkunen et al., 1994a). These findings are in contrast to results reported by Gustavsson, Träskman-Bendz, and Westrin (2003), where depressed males had significantly lower CSF testosterone than others. CSF 5-HIAA did not correlate significantly with CSF testosterone in this study. The reason for this is probably that 5-HIAA is related to impulsivity rather than to aggressiveness (Linnoila et al., 1983; Virkkunen & Linnoila, 1993).

At present, there are interesting discussions concerning the possible role of low cholesterol in violent behaviour. Originally, epidemiological

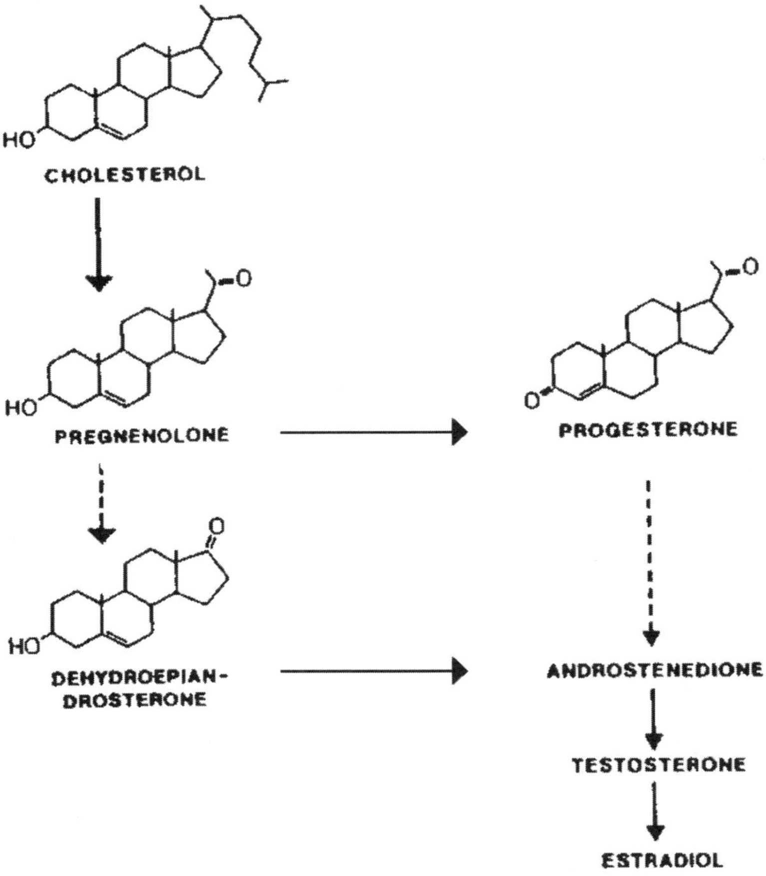

Fig. 2. Parts of Steroid Metabolism of Relevance for Aggressive Behaviour.

investigations found an association between low cholesterol and violent death in the county of Värmland, Sweden (Lindberg et al., 1992). Later, studies on suicidal patients and aggressive primates have shown relationships between low serotonergic function and low cholesterol, which probably could be explained by disrupted cellular membranes due to shortage of cholesterol, and hence receptors becoming increasingly weak or sensitive (Scanlon, Williams, & Schloss, 2001). Golomb, Stattin, and Mednick (2000) reported low cholesterol in violent criminals. A recent study by

Repo-Tiihonen et al. (2002) showed that low levels of another lipid, triglyceride, were associated with childhood onset of conduct disorder and premature death.

Carbohydrates

Low blood glucose has been noticed in aggressive individuals, probably due to high insulin levels (Linnoila, DeJong, & Virkkunen, 1989; Virkkunen et al., 1994b). In our group, Westling et al. (2004) have shown high CSF insulin in patients who made violent suicide attempts, and this was regardless of psychiatric diagnosis.

In one study of alcoholics, a 5-h oral glucose tolerance test, in which glucose, prolactin, and cortisol responses were measured, was performed by Fishbein et al. (1992). Low nadir cortisol and blunted prolactin response to glucose were linked with antisocial personality and aggressiveness.

Virkkunen et al. (1994b) reported that type II alcoholics were vulnerable to hypoglycaemic reactions after an oral load of glucose.

Genes and the Family

Delinquent behaviour can be seen across generations. Long-term studies have shown that conduct disorder during childhood may predispose school problems, deviant peers, antisocial criminal adult behaviour, and/or alcoholism (Olweus, 1980). Much of this effect is genetically determined (Heath et al., 1997). When healthy individuals, who had alcoholic fathers, were subject to stress tests with and without alcohol, it was found that alcohol given to these subjects attenuated the stress response, which was not the case concerning subjects without alcoholic fathers (Zimmerman et al., 2004).

Recent investigations reveal that a functional polymorphism in the gene coding for MAO-A (high MAO-A expression) could moderate the effect of maltreatment during childhood (Caspi et al., 2002).

Genetic factors are supposed to contribute to about 40% of personality variance.

Among monoaminergic genes, MAO-A gene polymorphisms, e.g. the low-activity 3-repeat allele, confer increased susceptibility of antisocial and aggressive behaviour (Samochowiec et al., 1999; Manuck et al., 2002). Behavioural deviances often seen in people with low-platelet MAO-B activity could be explained by the presence of two long alleles of the transcription factor AP-2 beta gene (Oreland et al., 2002).

Serotonin transporter genes have also been studied in various populations, and the 5-HTTLPR polymorphism might contribute to early onset alcoholism and violent behaviour rather than to suicidal behaviour (Hallikainen et al., 1999; Zalsman et al., 2001). According to Manuck et al. (1999), an aggressive disposition is associated with an intronic polymorphism of the tryptophan hydroxylase (TPH) gene.

CONCLUSION

So far, psychobiological research suggests that monoaminergic genes, childhood conduct disorders as well as environmental stress predispose deviant behaviour such as antisocial aggressive behaviour or type II alcoholism later in life. Excitatory and inhibitory biochemical and psychosocial powers are constantly acting in consort. Apart from monoamines, steroids and carbohydrates are involved in aggression and violence. Current research using brain-imaging techniques will certainly offer further understanding of biological events and hopefully a chance to invent specific treatment tools for this behaviour, socio-economically deleterious for the individual, his/her immediate surroundings, and society at large.

ACKNOWLEDGEMENTS

Our studies are supported by the Swedish Research Council, the Sjöbring Foundation, the Skåne County Research Foundation, and the Lund University ALF (government funds to support the research of medical doctors). Ulla Persson is greatly acknowledged.

REFERENCES

Ågren, H., Mefford, I. N., Rudorfer, M. V., et al. (1986). Interacting neurotransmitter systems. A non-experimental approach to the 5HIAA–HVA correlation in human CSF. *Journal of Psychiatric Research, 20,* 175–193.

Åsberg, M., Träskman, L., & Thorén, P. (1976). 5-HIAA in the cerebrospinal fluid – A biochemical suicide predictor? *Archives of General Psychiatry, 33,* 1193–1197.

Audenaert, K., Van Laere, K., Dumont, F., et al. (2001). Decreased frontal serotonin 5-HT 2a receptor binding index in deliberate self-harm patients. *European Journal of Nuclear Medicine*, *28*, 175–182.
Barrat, E. S. (1991). Measuring and predicting aggression within the context of personality theory. *Journal of Neuropsychiatry Clinical Neuroscience*, *3*(Suppl. 1), 35–39.
Belfrage, H., Lidberg, L., & Oreland, L. (1992). Platelet monoamine oxidase activity in mentally disordered violent offenders. *Acta Psychiatrica Scandinavica*, *85*, 1–4.
Brown, G. L., Goodwin, F. K., Ballenger, J. C., et al. (1979). Aggression in humans correlates with cerebrospinal fluid amine metabolites. *Psychiatry Research*, *1*, 131–139.
Buchsbaum, M. S., Coursey, R. D., & Murphy, D. L. (1976). The biochemical high-risk paradigm: Behavioural and familial correlates of low platelet monoamine oxidase activity. *Science*, *194*, 339–341.
Caspi, A., McClay, J., Moffitt, T. E., et al. (2002). Role of genotype in the cycle of violence in maltreated children. *Science*, *297*, 851–854.
Cloninger, C. R. (1987). Neurogenetic adaptive mechanisms in alcoholism. *Science*, *236*, 410–416.
Coccaro, E. F., Gabriel, S., & Siever, L. J. (1990). Buspirone challenge: Preliminary evidence for a role for central 5-HT 1A receptor function in impulsive aggressive behaviour. *Psychopharmacology Bulletin*, *3*, 393–405.
Coryell, W., & Schlesser, M. (2001). The dexamethasone suppression test and suicide prediction. *American Journal of Psychiatry*, *158*, 748–753.
Demir, B., Ucar, G., Ulug, B., et al. (2002). Platelet monoamine oxidase activity in alcoholism subtypes: Relationship to personality traits and executive functions. *Alcohol*, *37*(6), 597–602.
Depue, R. A., & Spoont, M. R. (1986). Conceptualizing a serotonin trait. A behavioural dimension constraint. *Annals of New York Academic Science*, *487*, 47–62.
Engström, G., Nyman, G. E., & Träskman-Bendz, L. (1996). The Marke–Nyman temperament (MNT) scale in suicide attempters. *Acta Psychiatrica Scandinavica*, *94*, 320–325.
Engström, G., Persson, B., & Levander, S. (1999). Temperament traits in male suicide attempters and violent offenders. *European Psychiatry*, *14*(5), 278–283.
Fishbein, D. H., Dax, E., Lozovsky, D. B., et al. (1992). Neuroendocrine responses to a glucose challenge in substance users with high and low levels of aggression, impulsivity, and antisocial personality. *Neuropsychobiology*, *25*(2), 106–114.
Fishbein, D. H., Lozovsky, D., & Jaffe, J. H. (1989). Impulsivity, aggression, and neuroendocrine responses to serotonergic stimulation in substance abusers. *Biological Psychiatry*, *25*(8), 1049–1066.
Gerra, G., Garofano, L., Bosari, S., et al. (2004). Analysis of monoamine oxidase A (MAO-A) promoter polymorphism in male heroin-dependent subjects: Behavioural and personality correlates. *Journal of Neural Transmission*, *111*(5), 611–621.
Golomb, B. A., Stattin, H., & Mednick, S. (2000). Low cholesterol and violent crime. *Journal of Psychiatric Research*, *34*(4–5), 301–309.
Gray, J. A. (1987). *The psychology of fear and stress*. New York: Cambridge University Press.
Gustavsson, G., Träskman-Bendz, L., & Westrin, Å. (2003). CSF testosterone in 43 male suicide attempters. *European Neuropsychopharmacology*, *13*, 105–109.
Hallikainen, T., Saito, T., Lachman, H. M., et al. (1999). Association between low activity serotonin transporter promoter genotype and early onset alcoholism with habitual impulsive violent behavior. *Molecular Psychiatry*, *4*(4), 385–388.

Halperin, J. M., Schulz, K. P., McKay, K. E., et al. (2003). Familial correlates of central serotonin function in children with disruptive behavior disorders. *Psychiatry Research, 119*(3), 205–216.
Heath, A. C., Bucholz, K. K., Madden, P. A., et al. (1997). Genetic and environmental contributions to alcohol dependence risk in a national twin sample: Consistency of findings in women and men. *Psychological Medicine, 27*, 1381–1396.
Heinz, A., Mann, K., Weinberger, D. R., et al. (2001). Serotonergic dysfunction, negative mood states, and response to alcohol. *Alcoholism: Clinical and Experimental Research, 25*, 485–486.
Higley, J. D., Mehlman, P. T., Taub, D. M., et al. (1992). Cerebrospinal fluid monoamine and adrenal correlates of aggression in free-ranging rhesus monkeys. *Archives of General Psychiatry, 49*, 436–441.
King, R. B. (1981). Neuropharmacology of depression, anxiety and pain. *Clinical Neurosurgery, 28*, 116–136.
Koller, G., Preuss, U. W., Bottlender, M., et al. (2002). Impulsivity and aggression as predictors of suicide attempts in alcoholics. *European Archives of Psychiatry and Clinical Neuroscience, 252*(4), 144–160.
Lidberg, L. (1993). Criminality – A fatal disease? *Läkartidningen, 90*, 918, 923.
Lidberg, L., Modin, I., Oreland, L., et al. (1985a). Platelet monoamine oxidase activity and psychopathy. *Psychiatry Research, 16*, 339–343.
Lidberg, L., Tuck, J. R., Åsberg, M., et al. (1985b). Homicide, suicide and CSF 5-HIAA. *Acta Psychiatrica Scandinavica, 71*, 230–236.
Lindberg, G., Rastam, L., Gullberg, B. et al. (1992). Low serum cholesterol concentration and short term mortality from injuries in men and women. *British Medical Journal, 305*, 277–229.
Lindström, M. B., Ryding, E., Bosson, P., et al. (2004). Impulsivity related to brain serotonin transporter binding capacity in suicide attempters. *European Neuropsychopharmacology, 14*, 295–300.
Linnoila, M., Virkkunen, M., Scheinin, M., et al. (1983). Low cerebrospinal fluid 5-hydroxyindoleacetic acid concentration differentiates impulsive from nonimpulsive violent behavior. *Life Sciences, 33*, 2609–2614.
Linnoila, M., DeJong, J., & Virkkunen, M. (1989). Monoamines, glucose metabolism and impulse control. *Psychopharmacology Bulletin, 25*, 404–406.
Manuck, S. B., Flory, J. D., Ferrell, R. E., et al. (1999). Aggression and anger-related traits associated with a polymorphism of the tryptophan hydroxylase gene. *Biological Psychiatry, 45*(5), 603–614.
Manuck, S. B., Flory, J. D., Muldoon, M. F., et al. (2002). Central nervous system serotonergic responsivity and aggressive disposition in men. *Psychological Behaviour, 77*(4–5), 705–709.
Mattsson, A., Schalling, D., Olweus, D., et al. (1980). Plasma testosterone, aggressive behavior, and personality dimensions in young male delinquents. *Journal of the American Academy of Child Psychiatry, 19*, 476–490.
Mulder, R. T. (2001). Alcoholism and personality. *Australian and New Zealand Journal of Psychiatry, 36*, 44–52.
Mulder, R. T., Wells, J. E., Joyce, P. R., et al. (1994). Antisocial women. *Journal of Personality Disorders, 8*, 279–287.
Olweus, D. (1980). The consistency issue in personality psychology revised – With special reference to aggression. *British Journal of Social and Clinical Psychology, 19*, 377–390.

Oreland, L., Damberg, M., Hallman, J., et al. (2002). Risk factors for the neurohumoral alterations underlying personality disturbances. *Neurotoxicity Research*, *4*(5–6), 421–426.

Pandey, G. N., Dwivedi, Y., Rizavi, H. S., et al. (2002). Higher expression of serotonin 5-HT(2A) receptors in the post-mortem brains of teenage suicide victims. *American Journal of Psychiatry*, *159*, 419–429.

Plutchik, R., & Van Praag, H. M. (1989). The measurement of suicidality, aggressivity and impulsivity. *Progress in Neuro-psychopharmacology and Biological Psychiatry*, *13*, 23–34.

Rasanen, P., Hakko, H., Visure, S., et al. (1999). Serum testosterone levels, mental disorders and criminal behaviour. *Acta Psychiatrica Scandinavica*, *99*, 348–352.

Repo-Tiihonen, E., Halonen, P., Tiihonen, J., et al. (2002). Total serum cholesterol level, violent criminal offences, suicidal behavior, mortality and the appearance of conduct disorder in Finnish male criminal offenders with antisocial personality disorder. *European Archives of Psychiatry and Clinical Neuroscience*, *252*(1), 8–11.

Samochowiec, J., Lesch, K. P., Rottmann, M., et al. (1999). Association of a regulatory polymorphism in the promoter region of the monoamine oxidase A gene with antisocial alcoholism. *Psychiatry Research*, *86*(1), 67–72.

Scanlon, S. M., Williams, D. C., & Schloss, P. (2001). Membrane cholesterol modulates serotonin transporter activity. *Biochemistry*, *40*(35), 10507–10513.

Schalling, D. (1993). Neurochemical correlates of personality impulsivity, and disinhibitory suicidality. In: S. Hodgins (Ed.), *Mental disorder and crime* (pp. 208–226). New York, NY: Sage Publications.

Simonsson, P., Träskman-Bendz, L., Alling, C., et al. (1991). Peripheral markers in patients with suicidal behavior. *European Neuropsychopharmacology*, *1*, 503–510.

Söderström, H. (2002). Neuropsychiatric background factors to violent crime. Göteborg dissertations, Kompendiet.

Söderström, H., Blennow, K., Sjödin, A.-K., et al. (2003). New evidence for an association between the CSF HVA:5-HIAA ratio and psychopathic traits. *Journal of Neurology Neurosurgery and Psychiatry*, *74*, 918–921.

Tiihonen, J., Kuikka, J. T., Bergstrom, K. A., et al. (1997). Single-photon emission tomography imaging of monoamine transporter in impulsive violent behaviour. *European Journal of Nuclear Medicine*, *24*, 1253–1260.

Träskman, L., Åsberg, M., Bertilsson, L., et al. (1981). Monoamine metabolites in cerebrospinal fluid and suicidal behaviour. *Archives of General Psychiatry*, *38*, 631–642.

Valzelli, L. (1981). Psychopharmacology of aggression: An overview. *International Pharmacopsychiatry*, *16*, 39–48.

Virkkunen, M., Kallio, E., Rawlings, R., et al. (1994a). Personality profiles and state aggressiveness in Finnish alcoholic, violent offenders, fire setters, and healthy volunteers. *Archives of General Psychiatry*, *51*(1), 28–33.

Virkkunen, M., & Linnoila, M. (1993). Brain serotonin, type II alcoholism and impulsive violence. *Journal of Studies on Alcohol*, *11*(Suppl), 163–169.

Virkkunen, M., Nuutila, A., Goodwin, F. K., et al. (1987). Cerebrospinal fluid monoamine metabolite levels in male arsonists. *Archives of General Psychiatry*, *44*, 241–247.

Virkkunen, M., Rawlings, R., Tokola, R., et al. (1994b). CSF biochemistries, glucose metabolism, and diurnal activity rhythms in alcoholic, violent offenders, fire setters, and healthy volunteers. *Archives of General Psychiatry*, *51*, 20–27.

Westling, S., Ahrén, B., Träskman-Bendz, L., et al. (2004). High CSF-insulin in violent suicide attempters. *Psychiatry Research*, *129*, 249–255.

Westrin, Å., Frii, K., & Träskman-Bendz, L. (2003). The dexamethasone suppression test and DSM-III-R diagnoses in suicide attempters. *European Psychiatry, 18*, 350–355.

Zalsman, G., Frisch, A., Bromberg, M., et al. (2001). Family-based association study of serotonin transporter promoter in suicidal adolescents: No association with suicidality but possible role in violence traits. *American Journal of Medical Genetics, 105*(3), 239–245.

Zimmerman, U., Spring, K., Wittchen, H. U., et al. (2004). Arginine vasopressin and adrenocorticotropin secretion in response to psychosocial stress is attenuated by ethanol in sons of alcohol-dependent fathers. *Journal of Psychiatric Research, 38*(4), 385–393.

INDIVIDUAL BEHAVIOURS AND SUBSTANCE USE: THE ROLE OF PRICE

Michael Grossman

ABSTRACT

I discuss economic approaches to the demand for harmfully addictive substances with an emphasis on the role of money prices. First, I examine trends in the real prices and in the prevalence of the use of cigarettes, alcohol, cocaine, heroin, and marijuana in the U.S.A. Then I present estimates of time-series demand functions. Next, I discuss how economists have modified their traditional model of consumer behaviour to incorporate the addictive aspects of illegal substances. I conclude with implications for tax policy and for the lively and contentious debate concerning the legalization of marijuana, cocaine, and heroin.

1. INTRODUCTION

The economics of substance use and abuse deals with the consumption of goods that share two properties. First, they are addictive in the sense that an increase in past consumption of the good leads to an increase in current consumption. Second, their consumption harms the consumer and others.

This second property makes them of interest from policy, legal, and public health perspectives. Clearly, not every addictive good harms the user and others. A person can be addicted to jogging, classical music, detective novels, attending church, and other activities that do not harm others and may yield future benefits to the individual in addition to increases in current utility. But the consumption of such substances as cigarettes, alcohol, cocaine, marijuana, and heroin can harm the consumer and others. For example, cigarette smoking has been labelled as the largest preventable cause of death by the last three annual U.S. Surgeon General's Report on Smoking and Health. Motor vehicle accident mortality is the leading cause of death of persons between the ages of 1 and 35 years in the U.S.A., and alcohol is involved in almost 50 per cent of these fatal accidents. The consumption of cocaine and other illicit substances results in deaths due to drug overdoses and the violence that accompanies the purchase and sale of illegal drugs. The existence of external costs (harm to others) and ignored internal costs (harm to self) suggests a possible justification for government intervention. This policy may not, however, be justified if it generates substantial external costs, or if the costs of eliminating the harms are greater than the costs arising from the harms.

The U.S. Government and those of many other countries have chosen to regulate some addictive substances (e.g., cigarettes and alcohol) via taxation; minimum purchase age laws; restrictions on consumption in schools, the workplace, and public places; and stiff fines for driving under the influence of alcohol. They have chosen to outlaw other substances (e.g., cocaine, heroin, opium, and marijuana). Taxation, other forms of regulation, and bans raise the prices of these substances. In addition, bans create black markets and encourage criminal activities that may harm innocent victims.

The full price of addictive goods can be defined broadly to include not only the money price but such indirect cost elements as the monetary value of the travel and waiting time required to obtain the good, the monetary value of the expected penalties for possession of illegal drugs or conviction of drunk driving, and the monetary value of the adverse health effects. The responsiveness of these substances to full price is an important parameter in determining the optimal level of taxation and the impacts of legalization. The economics of substance use and abuse is very relevant to these issues because recent theoretical advances predict that addictive goods should be more sensitive to price than previously believed. A growing body of empirical studies confirms this prediction.

2. PRICE AND CONSUMPTION TRENDS IN THE U.S.A.

To keep this chapter manageable, the research that I will be discussing deals with the effects of money price on consumption and abuse, and on interactions between money price and other components of full price. It is natural to focus on money price given the preeminence of the law of the downward-sloping demand function. Moreover, money price is a convenient variable for governments to manipulate via excise taxation. Taxes are "blunt instruments" because they impose welfare cost on non-abusers. But the enforcement and administrative costs of such policies as minimum purchasing ages are likely to be much higher than those associated with taxation (Grossman, Chaloupka, Saffer, & Laixuthai, 1994). Taxation also is very relevant in the case of illegal drugs because policy proposals to legalize these substances can be combined with taxation (e.g., Becker, Murphy, & Grossman, 2004).

Given my emphasis on money price and on U.S. data and policy, it is instructive to examine trends in the real prices of cigarettes, alcohol, cocaine, heroin, and marijuana (the money price of each substance divided by the Consumer Price Index for all goods) and corresponding trends in the prevalence of the use of these substances. Fig. 1 shows trends in real cigarette, beer, wine, and distilled spirits prices from 1975 to 2003. This period encompasses most of the U.S. anti-smoking campaign, which dates to the issuance of the first Surgeon General's Report on Smoking and Health in 1964. It includes the entire campaign to reduce deaths from motor vehicle accidents by discouraging alcohol abuse. This campaign began in the mid-1970s and has been expanded to include other outcomes of alcohol abuse.

The figure shows that the real prices of alcohol and cigarettes have declined significantly for certain periods during which the anti-smoking and anti-drinking campaigns have been in effect. These declines can be traced in part to the stability in nominal terms of the Federal excise tax rates on cigarettes and alcohol. In the case of cigarettes, the real price fell by 14 per cent between 1975 and 1980 (and by 20 per cent between 1965 and 1980) before rising by 88 per cent between 1980 and 1992. This large increase resulted in part from the three Federal tax hikes. The 12 per cent decline in price between 1992 and 1997 was generated by a cut of 40 cents in the nominal price of a pack of Marlboro cigarettes by the Philip Morris Companies in April 1993, which was matched by competitors of other name brands soon after. This price cut represented an attempt to ward off

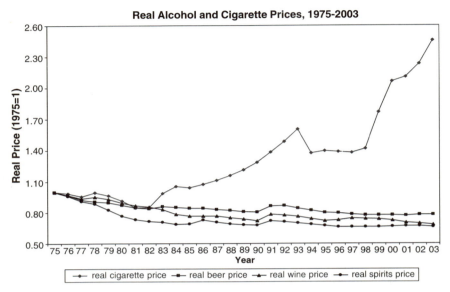

Fig. 1. Real Alcohol and Cigarette Prices (1975–2003). Nominal Cigarette Prices are taken from Orzechowski and Walker (2004). Nominal Annual Beer, Wine, and Distilled Spirits Prices are taken from the Bureau of Labour Statistics Home Page (www.bls.gov). The Consumer Price Index (CPI) is taken from the Same Source.

competition from generic brands of cigarettes. Since 1997, the real price has risen by 72 per cent in response to the settlement of the lawsuits filed by 46 state attorneys general against cigarette makers to recover Medicaid funds spent treating diseases related to smoking (the Master Settlement Agreement or MSA), two Federal tax increases, and a number of state tax increases.

The downward trends in real price for beer, wine, and distilled spirits are much more dramatic. These reductions between 1975 and 1990 were 20, 28, and 32 per cent, respectively. Since the Federal tax rates on all three beverages were raised in 1991, real price declines amounted to 9 per cent for beer, 13 per cent for wine, and 8 per cent for spirits.

Trends in the real prices of cocaine, heroin, and marijuana for the period from 1975 to 2003 are shown in Fig. 2. Despite large allocations of resources to interdiction and criminal justice as part of the Federal War on Drugs, the real price of one pure gram of cocaine fell by 89 per cent, and the real price of one pure gram of heroin fell by 87 per cent between 1975 and 2003. Most

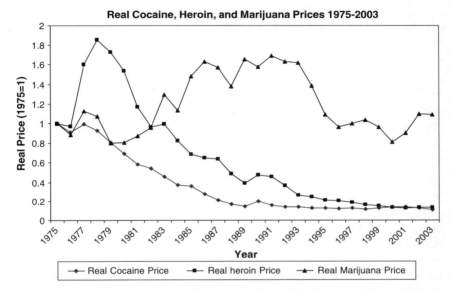

Fig. 2. Real Cocaine, Heroin, and Marijuana Prices (1975–2003). Prices are Based on Purchases made by Drug Enforcement Agents to Apprehend Drug Dealers as Recorded in the System to Retrieve Information from Drug Evidence (STRIDE) Maintained by the Drug Enforcement Administration (DEA) of the U.S. Department of Justice. Nominal Prices are Computed Based on Methodologies Developed by Grossman and Chaloupka (1998).

of the cocaine price decline took place between 1975 and 1985. On the other hand, the price of heroin was fairly stable until 1983 and declined thereafter.

The real price of marijuana shows a somewhat different trend. It increased by almost 10 per cent during the period as a whole. This overall upward trend can be decomposed into an expansion from 1975 to 1991, followed by a decline until 1996, and an increase after that year. The price rose by 70 per cent in the earliest period, declined by 40 per cent in the middle period, and increased by 13 per cent in the latest period. Marijuana prices are not adjusted for purity, but Pacula, Grossman, Chaloupka, O'Malley, and Farrelly (2001) report that purity fell between 1982 and 1992, and rose between 1992 and 1998. Hence, the price swings in Fig. 2 may understate the changes in the price of one pure gram of marijuana.

The decline in the real price of cocaine has attracted the most attention in the popular press. Basov, Jacobson, and Miron (2001) point to a number of causal factors. One was the development of the production sector and the results of learning-by-doing that followed the reintroduction of cocaine into the U.S. market in the early 1970s after a long period of absence. A second was vertical integration, which reduced the number of levels in the chain of distribution, and the cost of wholesaling and retailing. In addition, there was a shift to low-cost labour as the professionals who dealt cocaine in the 1970s were replaced by unemployed residents of urban ghettos in the 1980s. Finally, the degree of competition in the illegal cocaine industry may have increased over time, and technologic progress in evading law enforcement may have taken place. While there is little "hard" empirical evidence to support these explanations, Basov et al. (2001) find that the 25 per cent decline in the relative wage of low-skilled labour since 1979 can account for approximately 20 per cent of the decline in the real price of cocaine since that year.

The downward trend in the real price of cocaine that has accompanied the upward trend in resources allocated to enforcement does not mean that the War on Drugs has been a failure. By using data for cities over time for the years 1985 through 1996, Kuziemko and Levitt (2004) find that cocaine prices are positively related to the certainty of punishment as measured by per capita drug-offence arrests and the severity of punishment as measured by the fraction of drug arrests that result in the criminal being sentenced to prison. On balance, however, the rise in enforcement has been swamped by other factors.

Trends in cigarette smoking participation, alcohol consumption, and binge drinking among high-school seniors for the years from 1975 to 2003 are shown in Fig. 3. These data come from the cross-sectional surveys conducted by the Institute of Social Research of the University of Michigan each year since 1975 as part of the Monitoring The Future (MTF) project. Cigarette smoking is defined as the percentage who smoked in the past 30 days, alcohol use is the percentage who consumed beer, wine, or distilled spirits in the past year, and binge drinking is the percentage who had five or more drinks in a row on at least 1 day in the past 2 weeks. There are several reasons to focus on MTF and on teenagers in examining trends in cigarette smoking and alcohol use. MTF data for high-school seniors provide the longest consistent time series on these behaviours. Moreover, there is a good deal of evidence that cigarette smoking and excessive alcohol use are habits that begin early in life (e.g., Grossman et al., 1994). Hence, policies to reduce their prevalence among youths may be the most effective tools to discourage them in all segments of the population. Finally, studies reviewed in Section 5 conclude that substance use by teenagers and young adults is more sensitive to price than is substance use by older adults.

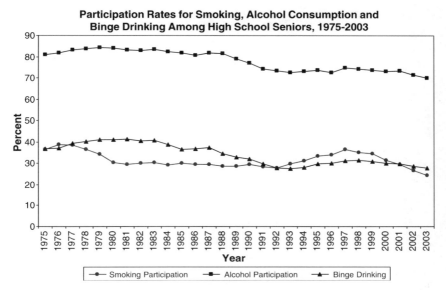

Fig. 3. Participation Rates for Smoking, Alcohol Consumption and Binge Drinking Among High-School Seniors (1975–2003).

All three outcomes shown in Fig. 3 declined between 1975 and 2003. The reduction in smoking participation is consistent with the dramatic increase in the real price of cigarettes shown in Fig. 1, but the reductions in alcohol use and in binge drinking are not consistent with the reductions in the real prices of alcoholic beverages. It is difficult, however, to make causal inferences from the data in Figs. 1 and 3 because of developments in the anti-smoking and anti-drinking campaigns that occurred during this time and lagged responses to these developments. They include the diffusion of knowledge about the harmful effects of cigarette smoking, increases in the minimum legal ages required to purchase alcohol and cigarettes, the requirement of warning labels on alcoholic beverage containers and cigarette packages, the enactment of restrictions on advertising and bans on cigarette smoking in public places and in the workplace, and the passage of legislation to increase the likelihood of apprehending and convicting drunk drivers.

Trends in annual (past year) marijuana, cocaine, and heroin participation as percentages for high-school seniors from 1975 to 2003 are presented in Fig. 4. The focus on high-school seniors is particularly relevant here because illegal drug use is a young person's habit, at least for most segments of the

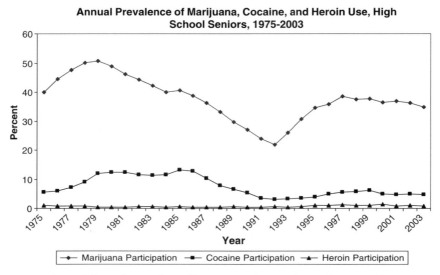

Fig. 4. Annual Prevalence of Marijuana, Cocaine, and Heroin Use: High-School Seniors (1975–2003).

population. Trends in marijuana use suggest that the number of youths who use this substance rises as its real price falls. Marijuana participation fell from 40.0 per cent in 1975 to 21.9 per cent in 1992 while price was rising. Participation then grew to 38.5 per cent in 1997 while price was falling, before falling to 34.9 per cent in 2003 while price was rising.

With a participation rate that ranges between 0.4 and 1.5 per cent, heroin use by high-school seniors is extremely rare. The series for cocaine is somewhat more revealing. Participation grew from 5.6 per cent in 1975 to 13.1 per cent in 1985 at the same time as the real price fell by approximately 64 per cent. Of course, the real price of cocaine continued to fall after the prevalence of its use peaked. Grossman and Chaloupka (1998) attribute this to such developments as the "just say no" to drugs campaign begun by Nancy Reagan shortly after Ronald Reagan became President in 1981, efforts by the Partnership for a Drug-Free America to publicize the harmful effects of cocaine, and the dramatic cocaine-related deaths in June 1986 of the basketball star Len Bias and the football star Don Rogers. They also summarize evidence suggesting that cocaine was viewed as a benign illicit drug from the early 1970s to the early 1980s.

Individual Behaviours and Substance Use: The Role of Price 23

The MTF surveys from which the data in Fig. 4 were obtained contain imperfect measures of chronic drug use and obviously exclude certain groups of heavy users such as the homeless and criminals. Therefore, rates of hospital emergency room mentions for marijuana, cocaine, and heroin per 100,000 population for the period from 1978 to 2002 are plotted in Fig. 5, and the percentages of arrestees testing positive for these three substances for the period from 1989 to 2003 are plotted in Fig. 6. The hospital emergency room data cover persons of all ages and pertain to episodes in which one or more of the three drugs was mentioned as a cause of the episode. Hence there can be more mentions than episodes. The data in Fig. 6 are based on urine tests and pertain to persons 18 years of age and older.

According to Fig. 5, drug-related hospital emergency room episodes have trended upward at rapid rates, especially for cocaine. The shorter time series in Fig. 6 reveal declines in the percentages of arrestees who tested positive for cocaine and marijuana, but an increase in the percentage who tested positive for marijuana. As is the case with the outcomes in Figs. 3 and 4,

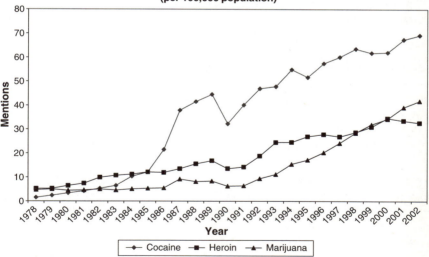

Fig. 5. Rates of Hospital Emergency Room Mentions for Marijuana, Cocaine, and Heroin (1978–2002, per 100,000 Population). Data are taken from the Drug Abuse Warning Network (DAWN) Maintained by the Substance Abuse and Mental Health Services Administration.

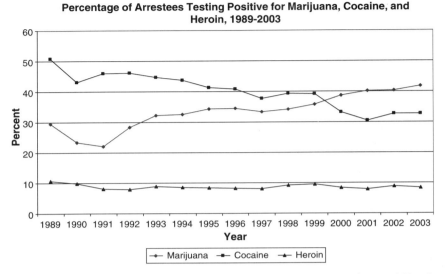

Fig. 6. Percentage of Arrestees Testing Positive to Marijuana, Cocaine, and Heroin (1989–2003). Data are taken from Arrestee Drug Abuse Monitoring Network (ADAM), Formerly Termed Drug Use Forecasting (DUF), and Maintained by the National Institute of Justice.

definitive statements about the relationship between price and participation in heavy use of illegal drugs or consumption by chronic users cannot be made because trends in other determinants are not held constant.

3. TIME-SERIES DEMAND FUNCTIONS

To examine the relationship between price and the substance use outcomes in Figs. 3–6, I fit time-series demand functions using 10 of the 12 indicators of use in the figures as outcomes. My procedure is to regress each outcome on a measure of its real price and a time trend. In the cases of alcohol use and binge drinking, I use the real beer price as a measure of the cost of alcohol since beer is the drink of choice among youths who consume alcoholic beverages (e.g., Grossman, Chaloupka, & Sirtalan, 1998). I do not consider heroin participation by high-school seniors as an outcome because of its very low prevalence rate. I do not show results for cocaine participation by seniors because the real price of cocaine always had an insignificant regression coefficient. That does not necessarily mean that the demand function for cocaine is perfectly inelastic because studies reviewed in Section 5 that capitalize on cross-sectional price variation or within city variation over time do find evidence in favor of a downward-sloping demand function.

Given the high correlations between real substance use prices and time, the estimation of demand functions for the remaining 10 items is perhaps more of an art than a science. My procedure is to experiment with three alternative trend specifications. The first includes a linear time trend; the second adds time squared to the first model; and the third adds time cubed to the second model. All three models contain the real price of the dependent variable. I then select the model with the lowest residual variance and obtain Newey–West (1987) t-ratios for the regression coefficients of that model. The standard errors on which these t-ratios are based allow for heteroscedasticity and for autocorrelation up to and including a lag of three. Standard errors based on longer lags were very similar to those presented. When small differences in residual variances produce large differences in the real price coefficient, I present the results of more than one specification.

Compared to the use of repeated cross sections or panels to estimate demand functions, the use of national time series has certain advantages. First, one can cover a longer period of time and include the most recent data. Second, one can examine whether price changes in the period at issue have the potential to account for a significant share of the observed changes in the corresponding measures of use over time. This analysis does not have to employ price effects obtained from data that do not cover the entire period. The disadvantages of the time series are that there are a small number of observations and a considerable amount of intercorrelation among the variables. In addition, price effects are biased downward in absolute value if the price variables contain random measurement error or if supply functions slope upward and are biased upward in absolute value if price is a predetermined variable whose current value is positively correlated with lagged shocks that increase past consumption.

Table 1 contains regressions for cigarette smoking participation in the past 30 days, alcohol use in the past year, binge drinking in the past 2 weeks, and marijuana participation in the past year by high-school seniors in MTF. When alcohol use and binge drinking are the dependent variables, I add a regression that includes a population weighted average of the effective legal age for the purchase of beer with an alcoholic content of 3.2 per cent or less by weight in each state of the U.S.A. in a given year. I include the drinking age because it is a readily available and widely cited policy instrument of the

Table 1. Cigarette Smoking, Alcohol Use, Binge Drinking, and Marijuana Regressions, High-School Seniors.

	Cigarette Smoking	Alcohol Use[c]		Binge Drinking[c]		Marijuana Participation
Price[a]	−0.122	−0.335	−0.430	−0.684	−0.525	−0.098
	(−5.23)	(−2.86)	(−7.30)	(−5.47)	(−15.11)	(−3.65)
Time	−3.289	−0.070	−0.669	−1.279	−0.462	1.115
	(−6.09)	(−0.11)	(−5.35)	(−1.90)	(−8.13)	(1.03)
Time squared	0.227	−0.062		−0.117		−0.134
	(5.83)	(−1.42)		(−0.26)		(−1.58)
Time cubed	−0.004	0.001		0.008		0.003
	(−4.52)	(1.57)		(0.82)		(1.58)
Legal drinking age			−1.937		−4.612	
			(−2.00)		(−8.58)	
R^2	0.822	0.939	0.939	0.950	0.972	0.792
F-statistic	27.71	92.15	128.49	115.13	294.58	22.85
Price elasticity[b]	−0.464	−0.428	−0.549	−1.985	−1.525	−0.459

Note: Sample size is 29 in each regression. Newey–West (1987) t-statistics are given in parentheses. Standard errors on which they are based allow for heteroscedasticity and for autocorrelation up to and including a lag of three. Intercepts are not shown.

[a]Price pertains to the real price of cigarettes, beer, and marijuana, respectively. The cigarette price is the price as of November 1 of year $t-1$ adjusted for Federal tax increases as of January 1 of year t and for the 45-cent increase in the nominal price in late November of 1998. The beer price in the alcohol use equation is the annual price lagged 1 year. Similarly, the marijuana price in the marijuana participation equation is the annual price lagged 1 year. The beer price in the binge drinking equation is a simple average of the prices in the fourth quarter of year $t-1$ and the first quarter of year t.

[b]Evaluated at sample means.

[c]In model with legal drinking age, specification without time squared and time cubed has lowest residual variance.

anti-drinking campaign. Moreover, its effects have been studied extensively in previous research (e.g., Grossman et al., 1994).

Except when the legal drinking age is employed as a regressor, the cubic time specification minimizes the residual variances of the outcomes in Table 1. Each real price coefficient is negative and statistically significant in that table. In addition, small changes in residual variances are not associated with large changes in these estimates. At the point of sample means, the price elasticities of cigarette smoking participation and marijuana participation are both equal to −0.46. The price elasticity of alcohol use is −0.43 in the model without the drinking age and −0.55 in the model with this variable. The price elasticity of binge drinking is quite large: −1.98 when the drinking age is excluded and −1.52 when it is included. This large estimate is not a function of the manner in which the trend is specified. The elasticity is −1.46 in a regression that simply includes a linear trend and −0.93 in a regression that contains the drinking age but no trend terms.

The regressions in Table 1 can be used to examine whether price changes in the period at issue have the potential to account for a significant share of the observed changes in the corresponding measures of use over time. First, consider cigarette participation; between 1992 and 1997 the real price of cigarettes fell by 12 per cent due mainly to a cut of 40 cents in the nominal price of a pack of Marlboro cigarettes by the Philip Morris companies in April 1993. At the same time, smoking participation rose from 29.9 per cent in 1993 to 36.5 per cent in 1997. The cigarette participation equation predicts a decline in participation of 2.5 percentage points. This amounts to 38 per cent of the observed 6.6 percentage point decline. Since 1997, the real price has grown by 72 per cent, while participation declined to 24.4 per cent in 2003. The predicted decline from the regression is 11.8 percentage points or approximately 98 per cent of the observed 12.1 percentage point fall.

Next consider alcohol use and binge drinking; between 1990 and 1992, the real price of beer rose by 7 per cent due to the Federal excise tax hike in 1991. At the same time, alcohol use fell by 3.6 percentage points from 77.1 to 73.5 per cent, and binge drinking dropped by 4.3 percentage points from 32.2 to 29.9 per cent. For the former outcome, the predicted decline of 2.7 percentage points from the regression with the drinking age accounts for 75 per cent of the observed reduction. For the latter outcome, the predicted decline of 3.7 percentage points accounts for 86 per cent of the observed decline.

Finally, consider the predicted impacts of the wide swings in the real price of marijuana; between 1975 and 1992, price increased by approximately 100 per cent, while participation fell from 40.0 to 21.9 per cent. The predicted decline of 12.4 percentage points explains 69 per cent of the observed 18.1 percentage point reduction. The real price proceeded to fall by 40 per cent through 1997, while participation expanded to 38.5 per cent. The predicted increase of 9.8 percentage points accounts for 60 per cent of the 16.6 percentage point growth. The most recent period was characterized by a 14 per cent price increase and a 3.6 percentage point reduction in participation. The regression explains approximately 56 per cent of this reduction.

Table 2 contains the regressions for rates of hospital emergency room mentions for marijuana, cocaine, and heroin; and Table 3 contains the regressions for the percentages of arrestees testing positive for each of these

Table 2. Regressions for Rates of Hospital Emergency Room Mentions for Marijuana, Cocaine, and Heroin.

	Marijuana		Cocaine		Heroin	
Price[a]	−0.021	−0.093	−0.198	−0.015	−0.004	0.001
	(−1.79)	(−5.67)	(−5.20)	(−1.21)	(−2.03)	(2.34)
Time	0.570	1.425	−28.533	2.723	−4.663	1.461
	(1.10)	(9.21)	(−5.51)	(6.67)	(−1.83)	(15.25)
Time squared	−0.556		1.705		0.308	
	(−1.28)		(7.00)		(2.41)	
Time cubed	0.004		−0.031		−0.005	
	(3.77)		(−7.74)		(−2.37)	
R^2	0.988	0.918	0.985	0.948	0.979	0.959
F-statistic	416.03	122.87	337.22	210.53	234.07	254.59
Price elasticity[b]	−0.265	−1.188	−1.732	−0.133	−0.614	0.095

Note: Sample size is 25 in each regression. Newey–West (1987) t-statistics are given in parentheses. Standard errors on which they are based allow for heteroscedasticity and for autocorrelation up to and including a lag of three. Intercepts are not shown.
[a]Price pertains to the real price of marijuana, cocaine, and heroin, respectively, in year t.
[b]Evaluated at sample means.

three substances. Since the outcomes in these two tables are collected throughout the year, prices are not lagged as they are in Table 1. Unlike the estimated price effects in Table 1, those in Tables 2 and 3 are sensitive to small changes in residual variances due to alternative trend specifications. Therefore, I present two models for each outcome – one with the best-fitting trend specification and a second with a simple linear trend. Changes in reporting practices and in survey design may account for some of the instability in the results (e.g., Reuter, 1999).

Eleven of the twelve price coefficients in Tables 2 and 3 are negative. The exception occurs in the heroin mention equation with a linear trend. Seven of the eleven negative price coefficients are significant at the 5 per cent level of confidence on a one-tailed test (the relevant test since the alternative hypothesis is that the coefficient is negative). The exceptions occur in the cocaine mention equation with a linear trend, in the two marijuana arrestee equations, and in the heroin arrestee equation with a linear trend.

Price elasticities in the arrestee data are all less than 0.20 in absolute value except when cocaine is the outcome. Then the elasticity is estimated in a range between −0.41 and −0.35. The elasticities in the mentions data are very sensitive to the trend specification. The cubic trend model produces elasticities of −0.26 for marijuana, −1.73 for cocaine, and −0.61 for heroin.

Table 3. Regressions for Percentages of Arrestees Testing Positive for Marijuana, Cocaine, and Heroin.

	Marijuana[c]		Cocaine		Heroin	
Price[a]	−0.019	−0.012	−0.111	−0.096	−0.001	−0.0001
	(−0.65)	(−0.99)	(−8.40)	(−7.11)	(−2.06)	(−0.18)
Time	0.729	1.074	−2.580	−1.538	0.160	−0.074
	(0.59)	(8.72)	(−3.81)	(−23.96)	(3.69)	(−0.71)
Time squared	0.018		0.109		0.160	
	(0.29)		(1.08)		(3.69)	
Time cubed			−0.003		−0.005	
			(−0.79)		(−2.71)	
R^2	0.840	0.838	0.970	0.963	0.638	0.116
F-statistic	19.18	30.97	79.81	155.44	4.40	0.78
Price elasticity[b]	−0.106	−0.068	−0.406	−0.353	−0.175	−0.016

Note: Sample size is 15 in each regression. Newey–West (1987) *t*-statistics are given in parentheses. Standard errors on which they are based allow for heteroscedasticity and for autocorrelation up to and including a lag of three. Intercepts are not shown.
[a]Price pertains to the real price of marijuana, cocaine, and heroin, respectively, in year *t*.
[b]Evaluated at sample means.
[c]Inclusion of time cubed raises residual variance.

The linear trend model yields corresponding elasticities of −1.18 for marijuana, −0.13 for cocaine, and 0.09 for heroin. Given the short-time series, especially in the arrestee data and changes in reporting and design, the results in Tables 2 and 3 suggest that the outcomes at issue are negatively related to price.

4. BASIC CONCEPTS

In the previous section, I approached the demand for a harmful addiction from the perspective of a conventional model of consumer behaviour, which ignores addiction. I simply allowed the outcome at issue to depend on its real price, trend terms, and for alcohol the legal drinking age (a positive correlate of the indirect costs borne by underage youths when they attempt to purchase alcohol). One can employ two other approaches to this topic: A myopic model of addictive behaviour, which ignores the future consequences of current consumption and a rational model of addictive behaviour, which incorporates future consequences. The latter approach is developed by Becker and Murphy (1988) in their seminal treatment of the economics of addiction. Since the first two approaches are nested within the

Becker–Murphy framework, I emphasize this perspective. Given its somewhat controversial nature, I indicate at the outset that, in my view, Becker and Murphy's main contribution is to suggest that it is a mistake to assume that addictive goods are not sensitive to price. Even if one does not accept all the aspects of their model, one can examine this proposition in the context of the standard theory of consumer behaviour.

An increase in past consumption of an addictive good raises current consumption because it increases the marginal utility of current consumption of that good (the increase in satisfaction or utility caused by an increase in consumption of the good). This is the reinforcement property of an addictive good stressed by psychologists. A harmful addiction, the focus of my discussion, is one in which past consumption has detrimental effects on current utility, such as reductions in health and, therefore, in utility caused by cigarette smoking, excessive alcohol use, and the use of cocaine. Harmful addictions exhibit the physiologic property of tolerance in the sense that the utility from a given amount of current consumption is lower when past consumption is higher. Note that I follow most of the literature in using the terms addiction and habit as synonyms. Consumers are myopic if they ignore the effects of current consumption on future utility when they determine the optimal or utility-maximizing quantity of an addictive good in the present period. On the other hand, they are rational or farsighted if they take account of future effects of current consumption when they determine the optimal quantity of an addictive good in the present period.

In sharp contrast to the myopic addiction approach, Becker and Murphy (1988) assume that consumers take account of future effects of current consumption when they determine the optimal amount of an addictive good in the current period. They use this notion to construct a model of rational addiction that among other things contains the first explicit derivation of long- and short-run demand functions for addictive goods in the case of farsighted consumers. The conventional wisdom is that addictive goods are not sensitive to price possibly because small changes in the consumption of these goods cause large changes in the marginal benefit of consumption. Contrary to this conventional wisdom, Becker and Murphy stress that the demand for addictive goods may be responsive to price in the long run. They also stress that the quantity demanded of an addictive good is negatively related not only to the current price of the good but also to its past and future price. Economists define a set of goods to be complements if a reduction in the price of one good causes consumption of all of them to rise. In the Becker–Murphy model of rational addiction, the quantities of an addictive good consumed in different periods are complements.

Becker, Grossman, and Murphy (1994) show that the Becker–Murphy model generates a demand function for consumption of an addictive good in period $t(C_t)$ of the form:

$$C_t = \alpha C_{t-1} + \beta \alpha C_{t+1} + \theta P_t \qquad (1)$$

Here, P_t is the price of C_t. Other determinants of current period consumption are suppressed. Since α and β (the time discount factor) are positive and θ is negative, current consumption is positively related to past and future consumption (C_{t-1} and C_{t+1}, respectively) and negatively related to current price. In particular, α measures the effect of an increase in past consumption on the marginal benefit of current consumption. This parameter also measures the effect of an increase in future consumption on the marginal benefit of current consumption. The larger the value of α the greater is the degree of reinforcement or addiction. Eq. (1) highlights the source of intertemporal complementarity in the rational addiction model. It arises because increases in past or future consumption (caused by reductions in past or future prices) cause current consumption to rise.

Eq. (1) also implies that the short-run price elasticity, which holds past consumption constant, must be smaller than the long-run price elasticity, which allows past consumption to vary. This property does not hold in general for a non-addictive good. Hence, comparisons between the price elasticities of the two types of goods may be misleading if they are not based on long-run price elasticities. Put differently, since past consumption reinforces current consumption, the price response grows over time in the case of an addictive good. For example, a price increase in 2004 would reduce consumption in 2004, which in turn would cause consumption in 2005 and in all future years to fall ceteris paribus. Indeed, the long-run price response is greater the higher the degree of addiction or reinforcement.

Extensions of the above framework imply differential price responses by age, income, and education in the case of addictive goods (Becker, Grossman, & Murphy, 1991). The total cost of addictive goods to consumers equals the sum of the good's price and the money value of the future adverse effects, such as the negative effects on earnings and health from smoking, heavy drinking, or heavy dependence on cocaine. Future costs tend to be less important to poorer, less educated, and younger consumers because they generally place a smaller monetary value on health and other harmful future effects than richer, more educated, and older consumers who have higher wage rates. Moreover, the poor, youths, and the less educated are likely to have lower time discount factors (higher rates of time preference for the present) than the rich, adults, and the more educated (Grossman, 2001).

It follows that the poor, youths, and the less educated are more sensitive to changes in money prices of addictive goods, whereas the middle- or upper-income classes, adults, and the more educated respond more to changes in the perceived or actual harmful consequences that take place in the future. Becker (1992) also shows that interactions between peer pressure, which is much more important for youths than for adults, and addiction predict greater price sensitivity by youths.

Differences in discount rates as a function of age are related to modifications of the rational addiction model by Gruber and Köszegi (2001). They assume that consumers are forward looking but behave in a time-inconsistent manner because the discount factor that they apply between the current period and the next one is smaller than the discount factor that they apply to consecutive future periods. Consumers still respond to future consumption or prices in their model, but the scope for government intervention in markets for addictive goods is greater because ignored internal costs are much bigger than in the Becker–Murphy model.

5. EMPIRICAL EVIDENCE

In this section, I summarize empirical evidence that highlights the importance of money price as a determinant of the demand for harmful substances. Compared to the estimates that I presented in Section 3, this evidence is based on large cross sections, repeat cross sections, or panels. I begin with studies that obtain price effects in the context of the Becker–Murphy (1988) rational addiction model and then consider evidence that emerges from research using myopic or conventional approaches.

The rational model has been applied successfully to the demand for cigarettes by Chaloupka (1991); Keeler, Barnett, and Manning (1993); and Becker et al. (1994). It also has been applied successfully to the demand for alcohol by Grossman (1993) and Grossman et al. (1998), and to the demand for cocaine by Grossman and Chaloupka (1998). All these studies report negative and significant price effects, positive and significant past and future consumption effects, and larger long-run than short-run price elasticities. Typical short-run and long-run price elasticities of demand in these studies are -0.40 and -0.75 for cigarettes; -0.41 and -0.65 for alcohol measured by the number of drinks in the past year; -0.79 and -1.00 for alcohol measured by cirrhosis mortality (a standard index of excessive alcohol consumption); and -0.70 and between -0.67 and -1.35 for cocaine consumption.

Gruber and Köszegi (2001) also present evidence in support of forward-looking behaviour by estimating reduced form demand function for cigarette consumption by pregnant women (number of cigarettes smoked per day by these women). They find that this outcome is negatively related to the past and future state-specific cigarette excise tax as well as to the current tax. These are the complementary price effects stressed by Becker and Murphy.

The studies just mentioned and others contain additional support in favour of the economic approach to addictive behaviour. Grossman (2001) summarizes nine studies which show that youths respond more to cigarette prices than adults. By contrast, the information that began to emerge in the early 1960s about the harmful long-run effects of smoking has had a much greater effect on smoking by the rich and more educated than by the poor and less educated (Grossman, 2001).

I have stressed the importance of the negative effect of price on youth participation in the consumption of harmful substances because changes in participation by youths primarily reflect start behaviour. At older ages, changes in participation are due mainly to decisions to cease consumption. Quits are key outcomes because most of the health effects at issue are reversible. Colman, Grossman, and Joyce (2003) and Douglas (1998) provide evidence on the role of price in the decision to stop smoking in U.S. data. Douglas (1998) approaches the quit decision in the context of the rational addiction model. Despite high correlations among the current price, the price next year (future price), and the price last year (past price), he finds positive and significant future price coefficients in his quit equations. This indicates that smokers in his sample are forward looking. The current and past price coefficients are not significant, but Douglas includes the number of cigarettes smoked per day at a peak period in his hazard equations. Clearly, past price may operate through this variable, suggesting that it should be omitted from the equations.

Colman et al. (2003) study the effects of cigarette excise taxes on the decision to quit smoking by pregnant women. This is a particularly important decision since smoking by these women accounts for one in five low-weight babies and is the most important modifiable risk factor for poor pregnancy outcomes. They have data on smoking 3 months prior to conception and 3 months prior to delivery. Since rarely there is a change in the tax on cigarettes in this brief period, they focus on the current tax effect. They find that pregnant women living in states that raised cigarette taxes between 1993 and 1999 were more likely to quit smoking once they became pregnant than women residing in other states. The magnitude of the effect at issue is substantial. If a 1-cent increase in taxes increases price by 1 cent, then a 10 per cent increase in price would increase the probability that a pregnant woman quits smoking by 10 per cent. Over one-quarter of the 9 percentage point increase in quit rates that occurred over the sample period can be explained by increases in cigarette taxes during that period. Colman et al. (2003) estimate that a 30-cent increase in taxes in constant dollars would have the same effect on quit rates as enrolling women in prenatal smoking cessation programmes.

As in the case of cigarettes, cocaine consumption by teenagers and young adults appears to be more price sensitive than consumption by adults (Chaloupka, Grossman, & Tauras, 1999; Grossman & Chaloupka, 1998; Saffer & Chaloupka, 1999). These three studies do not consider consumption by the homeless and by prison inmates, who may behave very differently from the population at large. Recall, however, that I find negative and in most cases significant cocaine price effects in the mentions and arrestee regressions in Tables 2 and 3.

Marijuana has been the most widely used illicit substance in the U.S.A. since data first became available in the early 1970s. Marijuana price elasticity estimates are particularly important in light of the swings in participation documented in Section 2. Pacula et al. (2001) present a fairly wide range of estimates of marijuana participation price elasticities for high-school seniors but indicate that a conservative lower-bound figure is −0.30. Their upper-bound figure of −0.69 may be too small given the measurement error in price discussed in the study. They also show that the upward trend in price between 1982 and 1992, and the downward trend between 1992 and 1998 can explain at least part of the "1980s marijuana recession" and the "1990s expansion".

Excessive alcohol consumption is perhaps the most common example of a legally addictive good next to cigarette smoking. The two goods are not, however, linked to adverse health outcomes and to addiction in the same way. There is overwhelming evidence that smoking has detrimental health effects. One can usually focus on whether and how much an individual smokes since these measures are highly correlated with the smoking-related costs of interest. With alcohol, the situation is more complex. Unlike cigarettes, many persons regularly consume small quantities of alcohol. Most individuals who consume alcohol do not harm themselves or others; indeed, moderate alcohol consumption has been shown to lower the risk of coronary heart disease in men. Instead, the adverse effects of alcohol spring from the overuse or misuse of this substance. Examples include cirrhosis of the liver, drunk driving crashes, workplace accidents, various forms of violent behaviour, risky sexual behaviour, and failure to complete college.

Given this, it is notable that all of these outcomes are inversely related to the cost of alcohol (see Grossman, 2001, for a comprehensive review).

6. POLICY IMPLICATIONS

Since harmful addictions are sensitive to price, the government can discourage these behaviours by taxation or by bans. In the U.S.A., Federal and state excise taxes account for approximately 30 per cent of the price of cigarettes (40 per cent if the 45-cent price increase due to the settlement of the Medicaid lawsuits is treated as a tax) and approximately 20 per cent of the price of alcohol. Cocaine may sell for as much as 10–40 times its free market price (see the studies summarized by Miron (2003)). My discussion implies that cigarette smoking, alcohol abuse, and the consumption of illicit substances would rise substantially if tax rates were lowered or cocaine, marijuana, and heroin were legalized. But this observation does not justify the current policies. Revenue considerations aside, taxation of harmful addictions is justified only if there are external costs or ignored internal costs associated with these behaviours. Bans can be viewed in a similar manner. Moreover, legalization with taxation is an alternative to bans.

I have considered these issues with respect to cigarette and alcohol taxation elsewhere (Grossman et al., 1994; Grossman, 2001). Here I note that the primary unresolved issue in determining the optimal taxes on these goods relates to which harmful consequences should be treated as external. This is especially complicated if smokers, for example, are forward looking but behave in the time-inconsistent manner described by Gruber and Köszegi (2001). In their model, even if the discount factor that consumers apply to consecutive future periods is reasonable, the smaller discount factor used in comparing the current period and the next one creates the potential for large ignored internal costs. They then show that the optimal tax may be much higher than the one that offsets purely external costs because the tax acts as a self-control mechanism that makes smokers better off. What I can conclude is that permanent increases in price caused by excise tax increases will have substantial effects on the consumption of cigarettes and alcohol. These strong price effects have been proven over and over in the literature and should not be ignored in the policy debate.

If illicit substances such as cocaine were legal and taxed, the factors just discussed would enter into the determination of the optimal tax. Clearly that is not the case, and the main policy debate is whether in fact the consumption of cocaine as well as that of marijuana and heroin should be legalized.

At first glance, it appears as if I have added "fuel to the fire" of the anti-legalization advocates. After all, the weight of the empirical evidence is that demand functions for illegal drugs, like demand functions for other goods, slope downward. Youths and young adults appear to be more responsive to price than older adults. This is troubling since the former groups may discount the future most heavily and may be most susceptible to the type of time-inconsistent behaviour described by Gruber and Köszegi (2001).

There are two factors, however, that add a good deal of "fuel to the fire" of the pro-legalization advocates. The increase in consumption that accompanies legalization depends on the price elasticity of demand and on the magnitude of the price reduction caused by the removal of penalties for production and distribution. Published studies reviewed by Miron (2003) suggest an extremely large cocaine price reduction of between 10- and 40-fold.

Miron's extremely careful and detailed empirical analysis indicates, however, that these estimates of price reductions due to legalization are overstated. He compares the markup from raw material (which he terms "farmgate") to retail for cocaine to such legal products as chocolate, coffee, tea, beer, spices, tobacco, and potatoes. While the retail cocaine price is many times the costs of the raw materials required to produce it, markups also are large for these legal goods, although smaller than those for cocaine. These data suggest that the black market price of cocaine is 2–4 times larger than the price that would prevail if it were legalized. Miron reaches similar conclusions based on the price of cocaine used for legal purposes. He attributes these results to evasion of costs by black market suppliers. These costs include taxes on labour and capital, costs associated with environmental, safety, health, and labour market regulation, and costs due to advertising. The avoidance of these costs by black market suppliers offsets some but not all of the expected penalties imposed by the government on these suppliers. While the impact on price is smaller than suggested by previous analysts, Miron's estimates still imply that legalization would result in significant reductions in price and, consequently, large increases in cocaine use.

A second factor that "throws even more water on the fire" built by anti-legalization advocates is that a regime in which cocaine production and consumption are fully legal, but cocaine use is discouraged by excise taxes on production or consumption has not been and should be evaluated. Monetary taxes have been considered a poor substitute for a drug war because excise taxes have been assumed to be unable to reduce drug use by as much as a War on Drugs. The argument is that producers could always choose to go "underground" and sell illegally if a monetary tax made legal prices higher than underground prices.

Becker et al. (2004) show, however, that the market price of cocaine with a monetary excise tax could be greater than the price induced by a War on Drugs, even when producers could ignore the monetary tax and produce illegally underground. The reason is that the government could allocate resources to preventing production in the illegal market. In effect it imposes a non-monetary tax in this market whose expected value exceeds the tax in the legal market. In certain circumstances, they conclude that the threat of imposing a cost on illegal producers that is above the excise tax if they produce legally is sufficient to discourage illegal production. Hence, the threat does not have to be carried out on a large scale and is much less costly to implement than a War on Drugs in a regime in which drugs are illegal.

Excise taxes imposed on producers or consumers of drugs play the same role in a regime in which drugs are legal as expected penalties imposed on producers and consumers when drugs are illegal. Both raise the full price of consumption and reduce the quantity demanded. But excise taxes are simply transfers, while penalties and efforts to enforce and evade them use real resources. Hence, social welfare potentially is greater in a regime in which drugs are legal and taxed. Tax revenue could be redistributed to the population in a lump sum fashion or used to fund drug treatment and prevention programmes. In the long-run legalization might lead to a lower level of consumption than the present situation. To address the problem of consumption by youths, legalization and taxation could be combined with minimum purchase age laws already in place for alcohol and cigarettes.

I have not provided enough evidence to conclude in a definitive manner whether the use of cocaine, marijuana, and other illicit substances should be legalized. I have, however, highlighted three factors that have been ignored or not emphasized in the debate concerning legalization. The first is that legalization is likely to have a substantial positive effect on consumption if prices fall by as much as that suggested by many contributors to the debate. The second is that these price reductions, while almost certainly sizable, may have been greatly overestimated. The third is that legalization and taxation – the approach that characterizes the regulation of cigarettes and alcohol – may be better than the current approach.

Clearly, more research on the characteristics of the taxation and legalization regime is required before it can be recommended. I hope, however, that I have convinced the reader to treat with a significant amount of scepticism propositions such as the demand for illegal drugs is not sensitive to price; tremendous price reductions will occur if drugs are legalized; and legalization and taxation is not a feasible policy option.

ACKNOWLEDGEMENTS

This chapter was presented at the *24th Arne Ryde symposium* entitled "*Economics of substance use: Individual behaviour, social interactions, markets, and politics*" at Lund University, Lund, Sweden, 13–14 August, 2004 and at "*Drug abuse: A workshop on behavioural and economic research*" organized by the National Institute on Drug Abuse, Bethesda, Maryland, 18–20 October, 2004. I wish to thank Mats Berglund, Henry Brownstein, Siddharth Chandra, Dhaval Dave, Inas Rashad, Peter Zweifel, and the participants in the symposium and workshop for helpful comments. I also wish to thank Austin Henkel, Silvie Colman, Robert Raphael, and Jennifer Tennant for research assistance. An expanded version of the chapter containing details on the construction of the time-series data that I employ and a more detailed survey of the literature is available on request. This chapter has not undergone the review accorded official National Bureau of Economic Research (NBER) publications; in particular, it has not been submitted for approval by the Board of Directors. Any opinions expressed are mine and not those of the NBER.

REFERENCES

Basov, S., Jacobson, M., & Miron, J. A. (2001). Prohibition and the market for illegal drugs: An overview of recent history. *World Economics*, 2, 133–157.
Becker, G. S. (1992). Habits, addictions and traditions. *Kyklos*, 45, 327–346.
Becker, G. S., & Murphy, K. M. (1988). A theory of rational addiction. *Journal of Political Economy*, 96, 675–700.
Becker, G. S., Grossman, M., & Murphy, K. M. (1991). Rational addiction and the effect of price on consumption. *American Economic Review*, 81, 237–241.
Becker, G. S., Grossman, M., & Murphy, K. M. (1994). An empirical analysis of cigarette addiction. *American Economic Review*, 84, 396–418.
Becker, G.S., Murphy, K.M., & Grossman, M. (2004). *The economic theory of illegal goods: The case of drugs*. Working paper, Department of Economics, University of Chicago, Chicago.
Chaloupka, F. J. (1991). Rational addictive behaviour and cigarette smoking. *Journal of Political Economy*, 99, 722–742.
Chaloupka, F. J., Grossman, M., & Tauras, J. A. (1999). The demand for cocaine and marijuana by youth. In: F. J. Chaloupka, M. Grossman, W. K. Bickel & H. Saffer (Eds), *The economic analysis of substance use and abuse: An integration of econometric and behavioral economic research* (pp. 133–155). Chicago: University of Chicago Press.
Colman, G., Grossman, M., & Joyce, T. (2003). The effect of cigarette excise taxes on smoking before, during, and after pregnancy. *Journal of Health Economics*, 22, 1053–1072.
Douglas, S. (1998). The duration of the smoking habit. *Economic Inquiry*, 36, 49–64.

Grossman, M. (1993). The economic analysis of addictive behaviour. In: M. E. Hilton & G. Bloss (Eds), *Economics and the prevention of alcohol-related problems* (pp. 91–123). National Institute on Alcohol Abuse and Alcoholism Research Monograph No. 25. Washington, DC: U.S. Government Printing Office.

Grossman, M. (2001). The economics of substance use: The role of price. In: C. R. Hsieh & M. Grossman (Eds), *Economic analysis of substance use and abuse: The experience of developed countries and lessons for developing countries* (pp. 1–30). Cheltenham, England: Edward Elgar Limited.

Grossman, M., & Chaloupka, F. J. (1998). The demand for cocaine by young adults: A rational addiction approach. *Journal of Health Economics, 17*, 427–474.

Grossman, M., Chaloupka, F. J., Saffer, H., & Laixuthai, A. (1994). Effects of alcohol price policy on youth: A summary of economic research. *Journal of Research on Adolescence, 4*, 347–364.

Grossman, M., Chaloupka, F. J., & Sirtalan, I. (1998). An empirical analysis of alcohol addiction: Results from the Monitoring The Future panels. *Economic Inquiry, 36*, 39–48.

Gruber, J., & Köszegi, B. (2001). Is addiction "rational"? Theory and evidence. *Quarterly Journal of Economics, 116*, 1261–1303.

Keeler, T. E., Hu, T., Barnett, P. G., & Manning, W. G. (1993). Taxation, regulation, and addiction: A demand function for cigarettes based on time-series evidence. *Journal of Health Economics, 12*, 1–18.

Kuziemko, I., & Levitt, S. (2004). An empirical analysis of imprisoning drug offenders. *Journal of Public Economics, 88*, 2043–2066.

Miron, J. A. (2003). The effect of drug prohibition on drug prices: Evidence from the markets for cocaine and heroin. *Review of Economics and Statistics, 85*, 522–530.

Newey, W. K., & West, K. D. (1987). A simple positive semi-definite heteroscedasticity and autocorrelation consistent covariance matrix. *Econometrica, 55*, 703–708.

Orzechowski, W., & Walker, R. (2004). The tax burden on tobacco (Vol. 38, 2003). Arlington, VA: Orzechowski and Walker.

Pacula, R. L., Grossman, M., Chaloupka, F. J., O'Malley, P. M., & Farrelly, M. C. (2001). Marijuana and youth. In: J. Gruber (Ed.), *Risky behaviour among youths: An economic analysis* (pp. 271–326). Chicago: University of Chicago Press.

Reuter, P. (1999). Drug use measures: What are they telling us? *National Institute of Justice Journal, April*(239), 12–19.

Saffer, H., & Chaloupka, F. J. (1999). The demand for illicit drugs. *Economic Inquiry, 37*, 401–411.

DEMAND FOR ILLICIT DRUGS AMONG PREGNANT WOMEN

Hope Corman, Kelly Noonan, Nancy E. Reichman and Dhaval Dave

ABSTRACT

We use postpartum survey data linked to medical records and city-level drug prices to estimate the demand for illicit drugs among pregnant women. We find that a $10 increase in the retail price of a gram of pure cocaine decreases illicit drug use by 12–15%. The estimated price effects for heroin are lower than for cocaine and are less robust across alternative model specifications. This study provides the first estimates of the effects of drug prices on prenatal drug use and yields important information about the potential of drug enforcement as a tool for reducing illicit drug use among pregnant women.

1. INTRODUCTION

Pregnant women can invest in the health of their unborn children through the use of prenatal inputs such as nutrition and prenatal care, and by avoiding unhealthy behaviours such as smoking cigarettes and using drugs. Economists have been modelling the demand for prenatal care as an input into the production of infant health for about 20 years (see, e.g., Corman,

Joyce, & Grossman, 1987). Several economists have modelled the demand for cigarettes among pregnant women (see, e.g., Evans & Ringel, 1999) and have estimated the price elasticity to be about −0.50. From this result, they have concluded that higher taxes on tobacco have the potential to improve birth outcomes.

Less is known about the demand for non-prescribed drugs among pregnant women. The paucity of knowledge stems from a lack of data. Due to the illegal nature of drug transactions and stigma related to usage, pregnant women are especially likely to under-report drug usage in surveys. In this chapter, we use survey data from a national birth cohort study that have been linked to respondents' medical records and city-level drug prices to estimate the demand for illicit drugs among pregnant women. Our results provide the first estimates of the effects of drug prices on prenatal drug use and yield important information about the potential of drug enforcement as a tool for reducing illicit drug use among pregnant women.

2. BACKGROUND

We know of no study that has estimated the demand for illicit drugs among pregnant women, although there are two sets of studies in the economics literature that are related to this topic. One set focuses on the demand for tobacco by pregnant women. The other examines the demand for illicit drugs within the overall population and estimates price elasticities or policy effects. Our study bridges these two literatures by estimating the demand for illicit drugs among pregnant women and calculating elasticities of participation with respect to drug prices.

Studies of the demand for tobacco products by pregnant women have been motivated by the fact that smoking is a behaviour known to be harmful to both the mother and the developing foetus. Although much less is known about the effects of using illicit drugs (such as cocaine) during pregnancy, there is reason to believe that such substances also have detrimental effects on the foetus. The medical literature on this topic is extensive but not conclusive; a recent study (Singer et al., 2004) indicates that prenatal cocaine exposure can increase the risk of certain cognitive impairments among offspring, particularly those raised in cognitively non-stimulating environments. One of the few studies by economists (Kaestner, Joyce, & Wehbeh, 1996) found that illicit drug use during pregnancy reduces birth weight by 5–10%. Overall, the evidence, though limited, squares with the common sense notion that illicit drug use during pregnancy is harmful to the foetus.

We first discuss the literature on the demand for illicit drugs and then go over the relevant literature on prenatal cigarette smoking. Grossman, Chaloupka, and Shim (2002), in a recent comprehensive literature review, and Grossman, Kaestner, and Markowitz (2002) reported that most studies examining the demand for illicit drugs are based on two surveys – the National Household Survey on Drug Abuse (NHSDA) and the national Monitoring the Future Survey. Both of these data sets contain measures of drug use that are self-reported and therefore likely under-reported. It is possible that the accuracy of reports is correlated with the intensity of drug use (i.e., the lightest users may be the most or the least likely to report having used drugs). According to Grossman, Chaloupka, and Shim (2002), the existing literature indicates that the demand for cocaine among teens and young adults is more price elastic than that among older adults.

Grossman and Chaloupka (1998) estimated the demand for cocaine using data from the Monitoring the Future Survey. They focused on cocaine because it was the second most frequently reported drug (after marijuana) in that data set and because good estimates of its price were available. Using a rational addiction specification that controlled for past and future participation, they found that the short-run participation elasticity among youths in grades 8 through 12 was about −1.0.

Saffer and Chaloupka (1999a), using the NHSDA, found that annual participation elasticities varied between −0.30 and −0.60 for cocaine and between −0.60 and −0.90 for heroin. In contrast to Monitoring the Future, which is a youth sample, the NHSDA sample represents the overall population. It is therefore not surprising to find lower participation elasticities in the NHSDA. In another study using the NHSDA, Saffer and Chaloupka (1999b) found that cocaine elasticities were higher for women and youth than for the overall sample. Given these patterns, we would expect that urban unmarried women (a broad characterization of the sample we use in this chapter) have relatively high cocaine participation elasticities. Finally, also using the NHSDA, Saffer, Chaloupka, and Dave (2001) found, in both structural and reduced-form models, that illicit drug use varies inversely with state expenditures for drug control. This result indicates that it may be important to control for state policies when examining variations in the demand for illicit drugs.

Cigarette smoking among pregnant women has received a great deal of attention in the public health arena. Economists have examined the role that cigarette prices play in determining the demand for this risky behaviour. A recent article by Colman, Grossman, and Joyce (2003) provides an excellent review of recent literature on the demand for cigarette smoking by pregnant women. They cited studies by Evans and Ringel (1999), Ringel and Evans (2001), Gruber and Koszegi (2001), and Ebrahim, Floyd, Merritt, Decoufle, and Holtzman (2000), among others. Based on vital statistics data, these studies reveal participation elasticities ranging from about −0.2 to −0.7. Colman et al. (2003) addressed the issue of quit rates during pregnancy, and explored the possibility that pregnant women may be more sensitive to price changes than non-pregnant women. Using Pregnancy Risk Assessment Monitoring System (PRAMS) data, they found high sensitivities of pregnant and pre-pregnant women to increases in cigarette prices (elasticities much closer to −1.0 than those found in studies of the broader, mostly non-pregnant, population). They offer convincing evidence that women who are pregnant are more sensitive to price changes than non-pregnant women, who bear additional costs of smoking (in terms of the health of the unborn child).

Overall, the literature indicates that both drug users and pregnant cigarette smokers are fairly sensitive to variations in price. We know of no previous study that has examined variations in drug prices as a factor in affecting drug use among pregnant women. The main reason for the dearth of research on this topic is the lack of accurate data on prenatal drug use. We combine high-quality individual-level data on prenatal drug use obtained from medical records and maternal interviews with city-level data on drug prices to conduct the first ever study of the price responsiveness of prenatal drug use.

3. DATA

We use data from a recent national birth cohort survey that have been linked to medical records of mother respondents and their babies. The Fragile Families and Child Wellbeing (FFCWB) survey follows a cohort of parents and their newborn children in 20 U.S. cities (in 15 states). The study was designed to provide information about the conditions and capabilities of new (mostly unwed) parents; the nature, determinants, and trajectories of their relationships; and the long-term consequences for parents and children of welfare reform and other policies. The survey data are rich in sociodemographic characteristics of both mothers and fathers, as well as parents' relationships and living arrangements.

The FFCWB study randomly sampled births in 75 hospitals between 1998 and 2000. By design, approximately three quarters of the mothers interviewed were unmarried. Face-to-face interviews were conducted with 4898 mothers while they were still in the hospital after giving birth.[1] Additional data were collected from the hospital medical records (from the birth) for a sub-sample of 1867 births in 10 cities (in 7 states). The medical record data contain information on prenatal drug use from laboratory tests of the mother or baby and in notes by physicians or social workers (more detail is given below, under Section 4).

In this chapter, we examine prenatal use of illicit drugs within this cohort of urban, mostly unmarried women who have just given birth. We use data on the 1748 births that have medical records data as well as complete data on all analysis variables from the baseline survey. The sample is not representative of the population new births in the U.S.A. for two reasons – (1) non-marital births are over-represented and (2) births were sampled exclusively in large cities. It also represents only a subset of the FFCWB sample. Nevertheless, it represents an important group to study from a public policy standpoint in that it is likely to include chronic or heavy users who may impose some of the heaviest costs on infants and society.

4. MEASURES

4.1. Prenatal Drug Use

Risky behaviours are notoriously under-reported. New mothers may be particularly likely to under-report prenatal drug use because of the illegal nature and stigma associated with that behaviour and fear of child protective services involvement. Kaestner et al. (1996) modelled the measurement error in self-reported drug use by combining data on self-reports with "actual use" based on urine tests. They found that only 17% of women who tested positive for illicit drug use at the time their children were born reported that they had used drugs.

Arendt, Singer, Minnes, and Salvator (1999) compared the sensitivity of different sources of data on prenatal cocaine use (medical records, urine screens, meconium analyses, and postpartum interviews) for 323 births. They assumed no false positives from any source. Surprisingly, the clinical measures (urine and meconium screens, together) revealed fewer cases of cocaine use than medical records in conjunction with postpartum interviews. They concluded that a combination of medical records analysis and postpartum interview is the best way to ascertain prenatal cocaine use.

Although the Fragile Families interview was far less detailed on the issue of illicit drug use than that used by Arendt et al., we adopt the strategy of combining responses to a postpartum survey with a detailed review of the mothers' and babies' medical records. During the mother's interview in the hospital after giving birth, she was asked whether she had used any illicit drugs during her pregnancy, but not about the specific types of drugs she may have used.[2] In our sample 100 mothers reported that they had used drugs (at all) during pregnancy.

The medical records contain information about the mother's drug use during pregnancy from laboratory tests of the mother or baby and in notes by physicians, nurses, or social workers. In our sample, 44% of the 1748 mothers had results from urine toxin screens in their charts;[3] of these 99 (13%) tested positive for cocaine, heroin, marijuana, other drugs (including amphetamines, methadone, and barbiturates/benzioazepines) or unspecified drugs, or a combination of drugs. Another 91 cases of prenatal drug use were picked up from notes in various places in the mothers' and babies' charts. Overall, 190 (10.9%) of the mothers in our sample had some indication of prenatal drug use recorded in their own or their baby's chart; of these, 17% used cocaine, 4% used heroin, 47% used marijuana, 4% used other drugs (including amphetamines, methadone, and barbiturates/benzioazepines) or unspecified drugs, and 28% used a combination of drugs.

We constructed three measures of prenatal drug use: Whether the mother indicated in the postpartum interview that she had used illicit drugs at all during the pregnancy (5.7%), whether there was any indication of prenatal drug use in the mother's or baby's medical record (10.9%), and whether there was indication of prenatal drug use from the interview *or* medical records (11.5%). The percentages based on medical records are high and in the range presented in a review of 16 studies by Howell, Heiser, and Harrington (1999). They also are consistent with the rates found in a recent survey that asked individuals whether they were pregnant, and if they were, whether they had used any illicit drug in the past year (about 14%) or in the past month (about 5%) (SAMHSA 2000).[4]

Table 1 shows the levels of agreement between the two sources of reports. Of the 100 mothers who reported having used drugs in the interview, 89 had evidence of prenatal drug use in the medical records. Of the 190 mothers with evidence of prenatal drug use in the medical records, less than half reported in the interview that they had used drugs. It is thus clear that the interviews missed a large number of cases of actual drug use. As it is unlikely that mothers would report that they had used drugs during pregnancy when they actually had not and because the medical record evidence of drug use also is unlikely to be incorrect, we base most of our analyses on the measure of whether the mother reported in the interview that she used drugs *or* there

Table 1. Mothers' Use of Any Illicit Drug during Pregnancy, by Source of Report.

Interview	Medical Records		Total
	No	Yes	
No	1,547	101	1,648
	0.885	0.058	0.943
Yes	11	89	100
	0.006	0.051	0.057
Total	1,558	190	1,748
	0.891	0.109	1.00

was evidence in the medical records that she had done so (11.5% of sample). We refer to this measure as the "either/or" measure.

4.2. Drug Prices

An advantage of our analysis is that we use drug prices at the city level. Many prior studies on the demand for illicit drugs have used state-level prices despite the fact that drug prices vary widely from city to city. While it is possible that there is also within-city variation in drug prices at any given time, measurement error is likely to be much smaller using city-level than state-level prices.

Data on cocaine and heroin prices for the 10 metropolitan areas in this study were computed from purchases made by under-cover drug enforcement agents.[5] The System to Retrieve Information from Drug Evidence (STRIDE), maintained by the Drug Enforcement Agency (DEA), records the total cost, amount, and potency of these drug purchases. Since these data are based on actual transactions, they directly reflect street-level prices. These prices are expected to be relatively accurate because any unreasonable price offered by a DEA agent may raise suspicion on the dealer's part and endanger the agent. However, because the transactions are of varying quantity and quality, the cost of each drug must be standardized.[6]

Standardized prices of one pure gram of cocaine and heroin in a given metropolitan area for a given year were derived in the following manner:

$$\log Cost_{ijt} = \pi_0 + \pi_1 \log Potency_{ijt} + \pi_2 \log Amount_{ijt} + \pi_{3j} \sum MSA_j + \pi_{4t} Year_t + \pi_{5jt} \sum MSA_j \times Year_t + v_{ijt} \quad (1)$$

The subscripts denote the ith transaction in the jth metropolitan area (MSA) for year t. *Cost* refers to the total cost of the purchase, *Amount* is the total gram weight of the purchase, and *Potency* is the percent of the total amount that represents pure drug. MSA and *year* refer to dichotomous indicators of each, and $MSA \times Year$ refers to indicators of the interaction between the two. As we are interested in the retail prices of cocaine and heroin, we included only buys of 40 g or less. The price of one pure gram of the drug in MSA_j for year t was then imputed as:

$$\exp(\pi_0 + \pi_{3j} + \pi_{4t} + \pi_{5jt}) \qquad (2)$$

In order to maximize the sample size for estimation, we imputed prices that were missing in any given metropolitan area for any given year by assigning the mean price for all other available metropolitan areas in that particular state.[7]

The strong addictive properties of cocaine and heroin imply an intertemporal reinforcement effect wherein current consumption is positively affected by past consumption.[8] Thus, current drug use will be affected by past drug prices in addition to the current price. In order to maximize the variation in drug prices and minimize collinearity in our small sample, 3-year average cocaine and heroin prices were used in the analysis, based on the year of birth and the 2 preceding years.[9] This measure allowed for both contemporaneous and lagged effects of prices on prenatal drug use.[10]

Several studies have shown that the drug price measures from STRIDE are strongly correlated with the cost of supplying drugs to the retail market. Kuziemko and Levitt (2001) found that STRIDE cocaine prices from 1986 through 1996 are positively related to state-level indicators of the certainty of punishment, measured by the per capita number of drug arrests, and the severity of punishment, measured by the fraction of drug arrests resulting in imprisonment. Basov, Jacobson, and Miron (2001) argued that due to the illicit, secretive nature of the drug trade, both production and sales are labor intensive compared to legal markets and most jobs are likely to be filled by low-skilled employees, youths, or others with limited outside opportunities. They showed that cocaine and heroin prices from STRIDE are positively related to the state-specific relative unskilled wage in a time series of states from 1974 to 1999. The results from these two studies confirm that STRIDE-based drug prices reflect the costs of retailing, which include both labor costs and expected penalties.

4.3. Control Variables

One of the advantages of the FFCWB data is that they include a rich set of characteristics on the mother and father, as well as on their relationship status. Table 2 shows the means of the variables used in our analyses. We include a basic set of covariates that are typically available in birth certificate data – maternal age (years), education (which we code as high school graduate, some college but not college graduate, or college graduate, compared to less than high school), race/ethnicity (non-Hispanic Black, Hispanic, or other non-White non-Hispanic, compared to non-Hispanic White), nativity (whether the mother was foreign-born), marital status (whether the mother was married at the time of the birth),[11] and parity (whether it was the mother's first birth). In certain models, we also include insurance information (whether the birth was covered by Medicaid or other government program, henceforth referred to as "Medicaid"), whether the mother lived with both of her parents at age 15, whether she reported that she attends religious services regularly (several times per month), whether she was married at the time of conception (instead of at the time of the birth),[12] whether she knew the father at least a year prior to conception,[13] the number of pregnancies the mother ever had (including the current one), the father's age (expressed as the number of years the father's age exceeded the mother's age), and the father's education (whether he was a high school graduate).

In certain models we include city-level median family income to account for factors at the city level that may affect both city-level drug prices and drug use. In other models, we include state fixed effects to control for state-level policies, such as the funding of drug prevention programs, or the strictness of drug laws and enforcement, which as discussed earlier also may be correlated with both drug prices and drug use.[14]

Our analyses focus on the effects of retail drug prices on illicit drug use during pregnancy. As shown in Table 2, the mean retail price of one pure gram of cocaine is about $90 with a standard deviation of $22, and the mean price of one pure gram of heroin is about $214 with a standard deviation of $66. These prices are deflated by the national Consumer Price Index and reported in constant "Year 2000" dollars (in $10 denominations). Both price series move together with a simple correlation of 0.63 (not shown in table).

As is clear from Table 2, the mothers in the sample are predominantly minority, unmarried (as indicated earlier, this was by design), and poor or near-poor (two-thirds of births were covered by Medicaid). The 3rd and 4th columns show the characteristics of the sample by whether or not the

Table 2. Sample Characteristics ($N = 1,748$).

	All Mothers Mean (Standard Deviation)	Drug Users[a] Mean (Standard Deviation)	Non-drug Users Mean (Standard Deviation)
Mother's characteristics			
Age (years)	24.99	24.70	25.02
	(5.98)	(6.04)	(5.98)
High school graduate	0.30	0.35	0.30
Some college (but not graduate)	0.23	0.16	0.24
College graduate	0.10	0.02	0.11[b]
Medicaid birth	0.67	0.85	0.64[b]
Hispanic	0.37	0.19	0.39[b]
Non-Hispanic Black	0.41	0.65	0.38[b]
Other non-White non-Hispanic	0.05	0.02	0.05
Immigrant	0.19	0.02	0.21[b]
Lived with both parents at age 15	0.44	0.31	0.45[b]
Attends religious services several times/month	0.39	0.26	0.40[b]
First birth	0.37	0.27	0.39[b]
Number of pregnancies ever	0.75	0.84	0.74[b]
Father's characteristics			
High school graduate	0.63	0.56	0.64
Age difference (years) (father minus mother)	2.57	3.52	2.44[b]
	(5.12)	(6.27)	(4.93)
Parents' relationship			
Married at time of birth	0.24	0.08	0.26[b]
Mother knew father 12 months prior to conception	0.85	0.83	0.85
Married at time of conception	0.23	0.08	0.25[b]
City economy			
Median yearly family income (thousands of dollars)	46.607	42.487	47.143[b]
	(12.801)	(92.17)	(13.10)
Drug prices			
3-year average price of 1 g of cocaine (tens of dollars)	8.80	8.33	8.86[b]
	(2.18)	(2.06)	(2.18)
3-year average price of 1 g of heroin (tens of dollars)	21.36	20.19	21.51[b]
	(6.56)	(5.62)	(6.66)

[a] Prenatal drug use according to interview *or* medical records.
[b] Difference between users and non-users significant at 1% level.

mothers used drugs during pregnancy (based on the either/or measure). Although both users and non-users had about the same mean age (25 years), they differed with respect to race/ethnicity, poverty (as proxied by Medicaid), marital status, and whether the mother was an immigrant. Over one-quarter (26%) of the non-users were married at the time of the birth, compared to only 8% of the users. There was a larger mean age difference between the mother and the father among the users than the non-users. Users were less likely than non-users to attend religious services regularly and to have lived with both parents at age 15. Drug users lived in cities with lower median family incomes than did non-users to live in cities with low median family incomes. Non-users were more likely than the drug users to be having their first birth. Importantly, the mean city-level drug prices of both cocaine and heroin were higher for the non-users than for the drug users. In order to control for potential confounding influences of the covariates on this association (between drug prices and prenatal drug use), we turn to multivariate models.

5. MULTIVARIATE ANALYSIS

We estimate the use of drugs during pregnancy based on parents' individual and relationship characteristics, either city-level median family income or state fixed effects, and 3-year average cocaine or heroin price in the metropolitan area where the baby was born.[15] As is typically done in studies of the demand for drugs, we assume that drug prices are exogenous to the women in our sample.[16]

In Table 3, we present estimates from probit models. Each cell represents a different equation in which the dependent variable is equal to one if the mother used any illicit drugs according to the either/or measure.[17] Each column corresponds to a different model specification. The 1st row represents five different specifications which all included the price of cocaine, and the 2nd row represents the five different specifications where we included the price of heroin. For each cell, we present the probit coefficient, the standard error (in parentheses), and the marginal effect of a one-unit change on the probability that the mother used drugs during the pregnancy (in square brackets).

Model 1 includes a basic set of covariates that are typically found in birth records, plus the real average retail cocaine (or heroin) price per pure gram (expressed in $10 denominations for the base year of 2000). Our basic covariates include – mother's age; mother's age squared; mother completed

Table 3. Any Illicit Drug Use during Pregnancy (from Interview or Medical Records) ($N = 1,748$).

Drug Price	Model 1 Coefficient (Standard Error) [Marginal Effect]	Model 2 Coefficient (Standard Error) [Marginal Effect]	Model 3 Coefficient (Standard Error) [Marginal Effect]	Model 4 Coefficient (Standard Error) [Marginal Effect]	Model 5 Coefficient (Standard Error) [Marginal Effect]
3-year average price of 1 g of cocaine (tens of dollars)	−0.103 (0.037) [−0.015]	−0.119* (0.036) [−0.017]	−0.103* (0.037) [−0.015]	−0.113* (0.035) [−0.015]	−0.103* (0.037) [−0.014]
3-year average price of 1 g of heroin (tens of dollars)	−0.036* (0.013) [−0.005]	0.008 (0.051) [0.001]	−0.042* (0.012) [−0.006]	0.006 (0.049) [0.001]	−0.040* (0.012) [−0.006]

Note: In row 1 we present results from five different models for prenatal drug use according to interview or medical records. All include cocaine price as the drug price variable. In row 2 we present results from comparable models with heroin, rather than cocaine, price. The model different specifications are discussed in the text.
*Significant at 1%.

high school, some college, is a college graduate; mother was born outside the U.S.A.; mother is Black; mother is Hispanic; mother is neither White, Black, nor Hispanic; first birth; number of pregnancies the mother ever had (including the current pregnancy as well as induced and spontaneous abortions); mother's marital status at the time of the birth; and the drug (cocaine or heroin) price. Model 2 includes the same set of covariates plus state fixed effects. Model 3 includes the covariates in Model 1, plus city-level median yearly family income rather than state fixed effects.[18] Model 4 includes additional or more refined measures of maternal characteristics (whether the birth was covered by Medicaid, whether the mother lived with both parents when she was 15 years of age, whether the mother reported that she attends religious services on a regular basis, the age difference between the father and the mother, whether the father had at least a high school education, whether the mother was married at the time of conception rather than at the time of the birth, and whether she knew the father for at least 1 year before the baby was conceived), as well as cocaine (or heroin) prices and state fixed effects. Finally, Model 5 includes all of the covariates in Model 4, plus city-level median yearly family income rather than state fixed effects.

From Table 3, we find that cocaine prices have consistent and significant effects on mothers' use of drugs during pregnancy. The marginal effects vary between −0.014 and −0.017, which means that a $10 increase in the price of 1 g of pure cocaine decreases illicit drug use by 12–15%.[19] We find that heroin prices also have a significant effect on illicit drug use in models that do not include state fixed effects,[20] with a $10 increase in price decreasing prenatal drug use by 4–5%.[21]

We take advantage of having different sources of data on mothers' prenatal drug use to examine how much of a difference the choice of measure makes. Table 4 shows "Model 5" estimates using three different measures of prenatal drug use, for cocaine and heroin, respectively: The measure based only on the interview reports (columns 1 and 2), that based only on the medical records (columns 3 and 4), and the either/or measure (columns 5 and 6). The last set of results (columns 5 and 6) is identical to Model 5 shown in Table 3. Thus, the 1st row represents three different equations with drug use as the dependent variable, with cocaine prices and the other Model 5 covariates, and the 2nd row includes results from the same three model specifications but with heroin prices. We would expect the marginal effects in column 2 to be lower than those in column 6, since less than half of the women who used drugs (according to the either/or measure) responded affirmatively to the interview question. Indeed, for either cocaine or heroin, the marginal effect of a $10 increase in price on the proportion of pregnant

Table 4. Any Illicit Drug Use during Pregnancy, Using Alternative Measures of Drug Use ($N = 1,748$).

Drug Price	Interview Coefficient (Standard Deviation)	Interview Marginal Effect	Medical Records Coefficient (Standard Deviation)	Medical Records Marginal Effect	Interview or Medical Records Coefficient (Standard Deviation)	Interview or Medical Records Marginal Effect
3-year average price of 1 g of cocaine (tens of dollars)	−0.074** (0.036)	−0.005	−0.106*** (0.037)	−0.014	−0.103*** (0.037)	−0.014
3-year average price of 1 g of heroin (tens of dollars)	−0.024* (0.014)	−0.002	−0.044*** (0.012)	−0.006	−0.040*** (0.012)	−0.006

Significant at *10%, **5% and ***1%.

Note: In row 1 we present results which use the "Model 5" covariates from Table 3 plus cocaine prices to estimate prenatal drug use measured three different ways – mother used drugs during pregnancy based on interview response, mother used drugs during pregnancy based on medical records, and mother used drugs during pregnancy based on either interview or medical records. In row 2 we present comparable results using heroin prices instead of cocaine prices.

women using drugs was about three times greater when using data from medical records *or* interviews than when using the interview data alone. The statistical significance also was higher when using the either/or measure. The differences in effect size indicate that relying solely on self-reported drug use would lead one to under-estimate the responsiveness of prenatal drug use to variations in price.[22] The differences in statistical significance suggest that analyses based on self-reported drug use are prone to Type II errors (incorrectly "accepting" the null hypothesis of no price effect).

Table 5 indicates the ranges of the demand elasticities implied by the results of Models 1–5 in Table 4, using the three different drug use measures – maternal interview, medical records, and either/or. The elasticities are based on mean values of drug usage and drug prices. For cocaine prices, elasticities range between -0.77 and -1.37. Though higher than those from studies cited earlier, these elasticities are credible in light of past research indicating that women and youth have higher drug and cigarette participation elasticities than other groups and that pregnant women are more responsive to cigarette prices than non-pregnant women. Heroin price elasticities vary more than cocaine prices across specifications with and without state fixed effects. However, the highest estimates of heroin price elasticity are close to the price elasticities of cocaine.

We examined several alternative specifications to test the robustness of our results. First, we took into consideration that our measure of drug use is somewhat imprecise in that we combined all illicit drugs together. In our sample, as in the SAMHSA survey discussed earlier, many women used marijuana, a less powerful and addictive drug than cocaine and most others. In addition, a few women in the sample used methadone, which may not be illegal. As a sensitivity test, we ran models excluding women who we know used only methadone or marijuana. The results (not shown) were highly consistent with those in Table 3 and the elasticities were very similar to those in Table 5. Additionally, since many of the covariates other than drug prices may be endogenous (as discussed earlier), we ran models that included only age, race, education, and drug prices (plus state fixed effects or city-level median family income); variables unlikely to be influenced by drug use or

Table 5. Elasticities of Prenatal Drug Use with Respect to Drug Prices.

	Interview	Medical Records	Interview or Records
Cocaine	-0.77	-1.13 to -1.37	-1.07 to -1.30
Heroin	0.75 to -0.75	0 to -1.18	0.19 to -1.11

unobserved individual-level characteristics. Estimates of the effects of drug prices on drug use in these models were similar to those found in Table 3 (results not shown), indicating that the inclusion of potentially endogenous covariates did not bias our estimates. The consistency of the price effects across alternative specifications also suggests that they do not reflect unobserved factors. Finally, we ran models that also included two prenatal behaviours other than drug use — smoking cigarettes at all during the pregnancy (from the survey) and first-trimester initiation of prenatal care (from the medical record). These variables may reflect a taste (or distaste) for risky behaviours, but are endogenous in that they could be "caused" by drug use or correlated with risk factors that are unobserved. To the extent that these behaviours are exogenous to drug use, they may proxy the mother's taste for risky behaviours during the pregnancy. Holding these other risky behaviours constant, the effects of drug prices on drug use were within the range of those presented in Tables 3 and 4 (results not shown).

6. CONCLUSION

We found that the demand for illicit drugs among pregnant women is quite responsive to drug prices. This is an important finding because impacting prices is one of the key methods by which the public sector can affect the demand for illicit, unhealthy substances and is potentially a potent weapon in the war on drugs. As we expected based on the literature reviewed earlier, the participation elasticities with respect to price for our sample are much higher than those that have been found for the general population, for three reasons:

1. Our sample is exclusively urban and over-represents unmarried, young, minority women. For this group, the monetary price of drugs represents a larger portion of the full price of drugs (since their opportunity cost of time is lower). Thus, a given change in the monetary price represents a large change in the full price, yielding a larger consumption response and a larger elasticity.
2. Our sample consists exclusively of pregnant women, who are likely more rational/forward looking than non-pregnant women. Thus, they may have a lower reservation price for using drugs, since they are also taking into account the future consequences for their babies of their current behaviour. As pregnant women have a lower reservation price than non-pregnant women, a given increase in drug price will be more likely to cause the former group to stop consuming drugs, yielding a higher elasticity.

3. We used an objective measure of drug use that likely captured casual (more elastic) drug use not picked up in the interviews. The fact that measures of prenatal drug use based on both self-reports and medical records yield higher participation elasticities than those based on just self-reports from postpartum interviews suggests that results based only on self-reported drug use should be interpreted with caution.

NOTES

1. Additional background on the research design of the FFCWB study is available in Reichman, Teitler, Garfinkel, and McLanahan (2001).

2. The exact question asked was: "During your pregnancy, about how often did you use drugs such as marijuana, crack cocaine, or heroin – nearly everyday, several times a week, several times a month, less than once a month, or never." When coding prenatal drug use based on the interview responses, those answering anything but "never" were considered prenatal drug users.

3. Unlike the Arendt et al. study, the FFCWB study did not conduct urine screens. Thus, we rely on reports of screens found in the mothers' or babies' medical records.

4. SAMHSA (Substance Abuse and Mental Health Services Administration) http://webapp.icpsr.umich.edu/cocoon/SAMHDA-STUDY/03262.xml

5. Due to the small numbers of DEA marijuana purchases, we did not have enough data to compute marijuana prices. Thus, our analyses are based exclusively on cocaine and heroin prices.

6. See Dave (2004) and Saffer and Chaloupka (1999a) for further discussion of STRIDE.

7. Results were not sensitive to this imputation.

8. See Chaloupka, Tauras, and Grossman (2000) and Dave (2004).

9. The births took place over a 3-year period, from 1998 to 2000. As we employed 3-year averages, the drug prices span 1996–1998 for the women interviewed in 1998, the years 1997–1999 for the women interviewed in 1999, and 1998–2000 for the women interviewed in 2000. In order to ensure that our results are not affected by changes in drug prices over time, we examined trends from 1996 to 2000. For both cocaine and heroin, we found no clear trends in real prices per pure gram over this period. As data from more cities and years become available, we will be able to distinguish between short- and long-run price effects.

10. Using 2-year average drug prices did not materially change the results.

11. In the FFCWB survey, the mother was asked whether she was married to the baby's father rather than whether she was married at all. Thus, information from the survey question may be slightly different than that reported on birth certificates.

12. This variable is based on marriage dates, birth dates, and the baby's gestational age. Again, this variable reflects whether the mother was married to the baby's father rather than whether she was married at all.

13. This variable is based on the baby's birth date and gestational age, as well as the mother's report of how long she knew the father.

14. As our sample includes data from 10 cities located in only 7 states, we face certain limitations. First, we could not investigate the effects of state policy variations. Instead, in certain models, we included state fixed effects to hold constant the entire state policy regime. Second, because of limited variation in both the number of states and city-level drug prices, particularly for heroin, there may be collinearity between state fixed effects and drug prices. For this reason, we estimated models both with and without state fixed effects. Finally, there was insufficient city variation within states to include both state fixed effects and city-level variables in the same models.

15. Due to the high degree of correlation between the two drug price measures, we did not run models that included both cocaine and heroin prices.

16. One reason researchers make this assumption is that cocaine and heroin are basically agricultural goods that cost little to produce. The supply price is then a function of the supply of workers willing to risk penalties to engage in the production and sale of the retail product, and the expected penalties imposed by local governments.

17. For the full results, see Corman, Noonan, Reichman, and Dave (2004).

18. In another specification not shown, we substituted city-level unemployment rate for city-level income. Results were similar to those presented here. Data limitations did not allow us to include state fixed effects and more than one city-level variable in the same model.

19. We divide the marginal effects by 0.115, the proportion of the sample that used drugs during pregnancy.

20. As discussed earlier, that there is collinearity between the state fixed effects and heroin prices.

21. The estimates pertain to models 1, 3, and 5.

22. The rate of drug use based either/or measure is about twice as high as that based on the interviews alone and the coefficients of drug prices are about three times as large. Thus, relying on the interviews alone would under-estimate the price responsiveness of prenatal drug use due to both the under-reporting of drug use and the greater price sensitivity among those who used drugs (based on the either/or measure) but indicated in the interview that they had not.

ACKNOWLEDGEMENTS

The medical records data collection was funded by Grant no. R01-HD-35301 from the National Institute of Child Health and Human Development (NICHD) and Grant no. 030978 from the Robert Wood Johnson Foundation. The analysis was funded by Grant no. R01-HD-45630 from NICHD. We are grateful for the valuable assistance of Ofira Schwartz-Soicher, Jennifer Borkowski, Brian Tokar, Andrew Shore, and Jennifer Marogi.

REFERENCES

Arendt, R. E., Singer, L. T., Minnes, S., & Salvator, A. (1999). Accuracy in detecting prenatal drug exposure. *Journal of Drug Issues, 29*(2), 203–214.

Basov, S., Jacobson, M., & Miron, J. (2001). Prohibition and the market for illegal drugs: An overview of recent history. *World Economics, 2*(4), 133–158.

Chaloupka, F. J., Tauras, F. J., & Grossman, M. (2000). The economics of addiction. In: P. Jha & F. Chaloupka (Eds), *Tobacco control in developing countries*. New York: Oxford University Press.

Colman, G., Grossman, M., & Joyce, T. (2003). The effect of cigarette excise taxes on smoking before, during, and after pregnancy. *Journal of Health Economics, 22*(6), 1053–1072.

Corman, H., Joyce, T., & Grossman, M. (1987). Birth outcome production function in the United States. *The Journal of Human Resources, 22*(3), 339–360.

Corman, H., Noonan, K., Reichman, N. E., & Dave, D. (2004). *Demand for illicit drugs by pregnant women*. Working Paper no. w10688. National Bureau of Economic Research Working Paper.

Dave, D. (2004). *Illicit drug use among arrestees and drug prices*. Working Paper no. w10648. National Bureau of Economic Research Working Paper.

Ebrahim, S. H., Floyd, R. L., Merritt, R. K., Decoufle, P., & Holtzman, D. (2000). Trends in pregnancy-related smoking rates in the United States, 1987–1996. *Journal of the American Medical Association, 283*(3), 361–366.

Evans, W. N., & Ringel, J. S. (1999). Can higher cigarette taxes improve birth outcomes? *Journal of Public Economics, 72*(1), 135–154.

Grossman, M., & Chaloupka, F. J. (1998). The demand for cocaine by young adults: A rational addiction approach. *Journal of Health Economics, 17*(4), 427–474.

Grossman, M., Chaloupka, F. J., & Shim, K. (2002). Illegal drug use and public policy. *Health Affairs, 21*(2), 134–145.

Grossman, M., Kaestner, R., & Markowitz, S. (2002). *Get high and get stupid: The effect of alcohol and marijuana use on teen sexual behavior*. Working Paper no. 9216. National Bureau of Economic Research Working Paper.

Gruber, J., & Koszegi, B. (2001). Is addiction "rational"? Theory and evidence. *Quarterly Journal of Economics, 116*(4), 1261–1303.

Howell, E. M., Heiser, N., & Harrington, M. (1999). A review of recent findings on substance abuse treatment for pregnant women. *Journal of Substance Abuse Treatment, 16*(3), 195–219.

Kaestner, R., Joyce, T., & Wehbeh, H. (1996). The effect of maternal drug use on birth weight: Measurement error in binary variables. *Economic Inquiry, 34*(4), 617–629.

Kuziemko, I., & Levitt, S. (2001). *An empirical analysis of imprisoning drug offenders*. Working Paper no. w8489. National Bureau of Economic Research Working Paper.

Reichman, N. E., Teitler, J. O., Garfinkel, I., & McLanahan, S. S. (2001). Fragile families: Sample and design. *Children and Youth Services Review, 23*(4/5), 303–326.

Ringel, J. S., & Evans, W. N. (2001). Cigarette taxes and smoking during pregnancy. *American Journal of Public Health, 91*(11), 1851–1856.

Saffer, H., & Chaloupka, F. (1999a). The demand for illicit drugs. *Economic Inquiry, 37*(1), 401–411.

Saffer, H., & Chaloupka, F. (1999b). Demographic differentials in the demand for alcohol and illicit drugs. In: F. Chaloupka, W. Bickel, M. Grossman & H. Saffer (Eds), *The economic analysis of substance use and abuse. An integration of econometric and behavioral economic research* (pp. 187–211). Chicago: University of Chicago Press.

Saffer, H., Chaloupka, F., & Dave, D. (2001). State drug control spending and illicit drug participation. *Contemporary Economic Policy, 19*(2), 150–161.

Singer, L. T., Minnes, S., Short, E., Arendt, R. E., Farkas, K., Lewis, B., Klein, N., Russ, S., Min, M. O., & Kirchner, H. L. (2004). Cognitive outcomes of preschool children with prenatal cocaine exposure. *Journal of the American Medical Association, 291*(20), 2448–2456.

THE EFFECT OF ALCOHOL CONSUMPTION ON THE EARNINGS OF OLDER WORKERS

Henry Saffer and Dhaval Dave

ABSTRACT

This study analyses the effects of alcohol consumption on the labour market outcomes of older individuals. The data set used consists of five waves of the Health and Retirement Study. The results from models with a limited number of covariates indicate that there is a wage and earnings premium associated with alcohol use. This premium progressively diminishes as more individual-level controls are added to the standard earnings function. The data set is longitudinal which allows for estimation of individual-fixed-effects specifications. These results indicate that alcohol use does not have a positive effect on earnings and wages.

1. INTRODUCTION

Research by economists on the relationship between alcohol consumption and earnings of older individuals has been very limited. This is surprising given that older individuals are the fastest growing segment of the population. Although alcohol consumption generally declines with age, younger cohorts have increasing levels of alcohol consumption at older ages (NIAAA, 2000). Older individuals also have many of the same alcohol-related problems common in the general population in addition to other aging-related problems, including an age-related decrease in the physical ability to tolerate alcohol. Furthermore, the use of prescription drugs by older individuals has been increasing, which raises the risk of adverse drug and alcohol interactions. Although older individuals consume less alcohol, their reduced ability to tolerate alcohol can result in the onset of problems at a lower level of consumption.

The relationship between alcohol consumption and labour market outcomes has been the focus of a number of prior studies. Studies of the effects of alcohol consumption on earnings, wages and employment, using various methodologies, have been conducted with the Epidemiological Catchment Area data, the National Household Survey of Drug Abuse, the National Longitudinal Survey of Youth 1979 (NLSY 79) and the Canadian General Social Survey. The empirical results tend to show that heavy alcohol consumption is negatively related to wages and earnings. However, prior studies also show that moderate levels of drinking raise wages and earnings relative to abstention. One explanation for this counterintuitive finding relies on the U-shaped relationship between alcohol consumption and mortality (Shaper, 1990; Doll, Peto, Hall, Wheatley, & Gray, 1994; Thun et al., 1997). Moderate alcohol consumption may improve health and in turn raise productivity and wages, while heavy alcohol consumption adversely affects health and thus lowers productivity and earnings.[1] Others have argued that alcohol use may enhance social interactions, which may help moderate alcohol consumers to make contacts and augment their work-related network, and thus improve their earnings. These explanations suggest a positive causality from moderate alcohol consumption to wages and earnings.

The purpose of this study is to investigate the relationship between alcohol consumption and earnings for older workers. The data set used in the analysis is the Health and Retirement Survey (HRS), and the sample is limited to working individuals between the ages of 40 and 62 years. The HRS is well suited for the estimation of an alcohol–earnings function. It contains an extended set of individual characteristics including several indicators of physical and mental health, tolerance towards risk, and the individual's occupation and industry classification. All of these factors provide important individual-level controls in the earnings profile since they may be confounders in the relationship between drinking and wages or earnings.

2. PRIOR STUDIES

The human capital–earnings equation developed by Mincer (1974) is the basis of the empirical work underlying the literature examining the effects of alcohol consumption on earnings. These prior studies are summarized in Table 1. Mullahy and Sindelar (1989, 1991, 1993, 1995, 1996) and Kenkel and Ribar (1994) find that heavy drinking reduces income and employment outcomes. Berger and Leigh (1988), Hamilton and Hamilton (1997), Heien (1996), French and Zarkin, (1995), Zarkin, French, Mroz & Bray (1998), MacDonald and Shields (2001) and van Ours (2004) find that alcohol consumption can increase income or wages, at least in a moderate range of consumption.

Causality is difficult to establish because alcohol use may be correlated with unmeasured personal factors, such as ability or motivation that influence productivity and wages (i.e. statistical endogeneity), and because wage income and earnings directly influence alcohol consumption (i.e. structural endogeneity). Researchers studying the relationship between alcohol use and labour market outcomes have approached these empirical problems by a variety of methodologies. Some studies simply use ordinary least squares (OLS) while others have used instrumental variables (IV).[2] The IV models have typically relied on alcohol prices or taxes, policies affecting the availability of alcohol and other individual-level variables as identifying instruments. The efficacy of the instrumental variables procedure depends critically on the quality of the instruments. One key criterion is the validity of the exclusion restrictions – the identifying instruments for alcohol consumption must not have any direct effect on labour market outcomes. In this case, alcohol prices, taxes and other policies are considered ideal, and the validity of their exclusion from the earnings function is generally accepted. However, the validity of the exclusion restrictions for some of the other identifying variables used in prior studies is questionable. For instance, Mullahy and Sindelar (1996) also use early family history of alcoholism, and van Ours (2004) uses the individual's own early consumption of alcohol in their instrumental sets. It is difficult to justify the assumption that an individual's early home environment and lagged alcohol use do not directly affect the current labour market outcomes.

The quality of the instruments also depends on their power to move the dependent variable. That is, the instruments must be strongly correlated with alcohol consumption. The biases resulting from weak instruments are well documented.[3] In this regard, alcohol prices and taxes are not ideal. Since the demand for alcohol, particularly among heavy drinkers,

Table 1. Prior Studies of the Effect of Alcohol Use on Earnings.

Study Author(s)	Data	Estimation Method	Primary Conclusion
Studies which find that heavy drinking reduces earnings			
Mullahy and Sindelar (1989)	Epidemiological Catchment Area	Single-equation model	Heavy drinking reduces earnings
Mullahy and Sindelar (1991)	Epidemiological Catchment Area	Single-equation model	Heavy drinking reduces earnings
Mullahy and Sindelar (1993)	Epidemiological Catchment Area	Single-equation model	Heavy drinking reduces earnings
Mullahy and Sindelar (1995)	Epidemiological Catchment Area	Single-equation model	Heavy drinking reduces earnings
Mullahy and Sindelar (1996)	National Health Interview Survey	IV model	Heavy drinking reduces employment
Studies which find that moderate drinking increases earnings			
Zarkin et al. (1998)	National Household Survey Drug Abuse	Single-equation model	Drinking increases wages
Berger and Leigh (1988)	Quality of Employment Survey	Selection model	Drinking increases wages
Heien (1996)	National Household Survey on Alcohol Use	IV model	Moderate drinking increases earnings
MacDonald and Shields (2000)	Health Survey for England	IV model	Moderate drinking increases average wage
van Ours (2004)	Dutch Survey	IV model	Moderate drinking increases wage for men
Barrett (2002)	Australian National Health Survey	Selection model	Moderate drinking increases earnings

Studies which find that heavy drinking reduces earnings and that moderate drinking increases earnings		
Hamilton and Hamilton (1997)	General Social Survey of Canadians	Selection model	Moderate drinking increases earnings; heavy drinking reduces earnings
French and Zarkin (1995),	Data from four worksites	Single-equation model	Moderate drinking increases wages; heavy drinking reduces wages
Studies which find that drinking has no effect on earnings		
Kenkel and Ribar (1994)	NLSY 79	Single-equation model, sibling-fixed-effects model and IV model	Heavy drinking reduces earnings; sibling models show no effect of drinking
Dave and Kaestner (2002)	Current Population Survey (CPS)	Reduced-form Model	Alcohol has no effect on wage
Peters (2002)	NLSY 79	Single-equation model and fixed-effects	No effect of alcohol in fixed-effects model

is relatively inelastic, a large number of observations are necessary to obtain credible IV estimates.

Studies that do not find a discernible effect of alcohol consumption on earnings or wages have relied on other methodologies. Dave and Kaestner (2002) estimate reduced-form models of the effect of alcohol taxes on employment, weekly hours worked and wages. Their analysis is based on outgoing rotation files from the Current Population Survey (CPS) from 1979 to 1995, yielding sample sizes in excess of those required to reliably detect small effects. They do not find any adverse effect of alcohol use on labour market outcomes. However, their study does not directly test the effect of light drinking on earnings and wages. Peters (2004) estimates individual-fixed effects models from waves of the NLSY and finds that alcohol consumption does not have any statistically significant effect on earnings. Her analysis is based on young adults ages 17–37 years.

This study is the first to examine the relationship between alcohol consumption and labour market outcomes among older workers. By relying on the longitudinal nature of the HRS, it controls for unmeasured individual factors that may confound this relationship by estimating individual-fixed-effects specifications, and bypasses the use of questionable instruments for identification.

3. DATA

This analysis relies on the HRS, conducted by the Institute for Social Research at the University of Michigan. The HRS is an ongoing longitudinal study of over 7,000 individuals, which began in 1992 and is repeated every other year. Data are currently available up through 2000. The original sample frame included individuals born between 1931 and 1941. In 1998 the study was expanded by including cohorts born between 1924 and 1930, and those born between 1942 and 1947. For this project, the sample is restricted to older adults between 40 and 62 years of age, in order to minimize selection bias associated with retirement or partial retirement. This yields a sample size of about 45,000 observations to test the effects of drinking on working status. In order to analyse the effects of drinking on wages or earnings, the sample is further restricted to working individuals, yielding about 25,000 observations.

The labour force outcome variables include working status, the log of earnings, the log of wage and hours worked. *Working status* is defined as a dichotomous indicator for whether the respondent is currently doing any work for pay. *Individual earnings* refer to employment income in the past year including wages, salary, overtime, bonuses, tips and military income. The log of earnings can be decomposed into the log of wages and the log of hours worked. The wage refers to the current hourly wage rate, and hours worked refer to total weekly hours worked for pay.

Alcohol consumption is measured by average number of drinks per day. Questions on alcohol consumption are not perfectly uniform across all waves. In the first two waves, the survey question asks about the number of drinks that the respondent generally has daily. The categorical responses of zero, less than one, one to two, two to three, and five or more are recoded as 0, 0.5, 1.5, 3.5 and 5, respectively. In the third, fourth and fifth waves, the questions are more specific. The first survey question asks the respondent about intensity of use, which is the number of drinks per day on the days that the respondent consumes alcohol. The follow-up question asks about drinking frequency in the past 3 months, which is the number of days per week that the respondent drinks on average. Both are continuous variables. To create a variable which is comparable to waves one and two, these variables on intensity and frequency are multiplied together and then divided by seven. This variable represents the average number of drinks per day. In addition, the responses from waves three, four and five are converted into the same interval categories used in waves one and two. The square of average drinks per day is also defined to capture the inverted U-shaped relationship between alcohol consumption and earnings. In order to control for the break in the survey questions between the first two waves and the subsequent waves, spline regression functions are estimated. The spline regression function includes interaction terms between alcohol consumption variables and a dichotomous indicator for the first two waves.[4]

Another variable measuring drinking participation is also defined. This is a dichotomous indicator of positive consumption, up to and including two drinks per day. A limit of two drinks is chosen for this definition since subsequent models suggest that the inflection in the quadratic relation between alcohol use and labour market outcomes occurs around this level of consumption.[5] When this variable is used the individuals who drink more than two drinks per day are dropped from the sample. This is only about 3% of the HRS data set. With the heavier consumers dropped, the coefficient of moderate consumption can then be interpreted as the marginal effect of moderate consumption over abstention.

Several measures of human capital are included in the earnings and wage equations. Data on years of education are used to construct a continuous variable for years of schooling completed, which ranges from 0 to 17.

Indicators are also defined for whether the respondent's father and mother completed at least 8 years of schooling. Tenure is defined as years worked on the current job. Another variable measuring total number of years in the labour force is also included in the models.

Other forms of human capital that may affect labour force outcomes include physical and mental health. A set of three dichotomous self-rated health variables are defined. These are indicators of excellent health, very good health and good health. Another variable that measures any work-limiting disability is also defined. Indices of physical health and mental health conditions are also constructed. The physical health index includes eight diagnosed conditions during the respondent's lifetime including high blood pressure, diabetes, cancer, lung disease, heart problems, stroke, psychiatric problems and arthritis. The index of mental health includes up to eight symptoms of mental illness. These are feeling depressed, feeling as if "everything was an effort", sleep problems, being unhappy, feeling lonely, feeling sad, inability to "get going" and not enjoying life.

Tolerance toward risk may also act as a confounding factor in the relationship between drinking and labour-force outcomes. Individuals with a greater tolerance for risk may partake in more risky activities, including drinking, and work in riskier, higher-paying occupations. A categorical index of risk preference can be defined based on hypothetical scenarios where the respondent is asked to choose between a current steady income stream and another higher-paying job with varying probabilities.[6] An indicator for individuals who identify themselves to be the most risk averse is included in the models.

Dichotomous demographic variables indicating male, married, black, race other than white or black, and Hispanic are also included in the specifications. Continuous variables measuring age and its square are defined to capture the quadratic age–earnings profile.

Other variables affecting wages or earnings are included in alternate models. As a measure of non-labour income, assets are calculated as total wealth in the form of home equity and other real plus financial assets net of all debt. A dichotomous indicator of full-time working status is also defined for individuals who report working for 35 h or more per week. A set of 13 dichotomous indicators for the industry of the respondent's current job and a set of 17 occupation codes are also defined. Weighted sample means for all working older adults are reported in Table 2. Means are also presented by drinking status, for abstainers and moderate drinkers. All variables measured in dollars are adjusted for yearly changes in the overall price level using the national consumer price index (CPI).

Table 2. Weighted Sample Means.

Variable	Definition	All	Workers	Abstainers	Drinkers	No Dental Visit	Dental Visit
Work	Dichotomous indicator for whether respondent is currently working for pay	0.681	—	—	—	—	—
Earnings	Individual earnings from all sources including wages, salary, tips, overtime, bonuses and military income, adjusted by annual consumer price index (CPI), in dollars	14344.630	21089.750	17598.480***	24786.120	15427.570***	22904.400
Log earnings	Natural logarithm of earnings	—	9.702	9.558***	9.845	9.491***	9.821
Wage	Current hourly wage rate, adjusted by annual CPI, in dollars	9.039	13.867	11.026***	16.473	9.047***	14.681
Log wage	Natural logarithm of wage	—	2.129	1.991***	2.268	1.887***	2.240
Hours worked	Total hours worked per week for pay	28.846	42.622	41.856***	43.382	42.855	42.678
Log hours worked	Natural logarithm of hours worked	—	3.672	3.649***	3.696	3.680	3.672
Full time	Dichotomous indicator for whether respondent works at least 35 h per week and 36 weeks per year	0.543	0.799	0.783***	0.813	0.796	0.801
Drinking participation	Dichotomous indicator for whether the respondent consumes two or fewer drinks on average per day	0.407	0.447	—	—	0.268***	0.384

Table 2. (Continued).

Variable	Definition	All	Workers	Abstainers	Drinkers	No Dental Visit	Dental Visit
Average drinks per day	Average number of drinks consumed per day by the respondent	0.453	0.488	0.000***	0.717	0.378**	0.418
Education	Years of schooling completed	12.630	13.066	12.672***	13.542	11.913***	13.698
Age	Age of respondent	56.492	56.113	56.232***	55.992	56.576***	56.103
Age squared	Square of age	3202.125	3158.943	3172.326***	3145.279	3210.765***	3157.998
Tenure	Current job tenure in years	13.820	13.820	13.375***	14.151	12.456***	14.135
Years worked	Total number of years worked	29.539	32.980	32.476***	33.235	33.746*	33.401
Male	Dichotomous indicator for males	0.476	0.535	0.458***	0.585	0.566***	0.517
Black	Dichotomous indicator for black	0.100	0.088	0.110***	0.068	0.134***	0.071
Other race	Dichotomous indicator for race other than white or black	0.038	0.035	0.045***	0.024	0.050***	0.032
Hispanic	Dichotomous indicator for Hispanic	0.071	0.063	0.070***	0.054	0.103***	0.055
Married	Dichotomous indicator for respondents who are married	0.729	0.739	0.725***	0.756	0.670***	0.753
Mother's education	Dichotomous indicator for whether respondent's mother attended 8 or more years of schooling	0.733	0.768	0.733***	0.805	0.671***	0.822
Father's education	Dichotomous indicator for whether respondent's father attended 8 or more years of schooling	0.657	0.689	0.647***	0.734	0.586***	0.738

Net assets	Net household wealth equal to all assets, including housing, vehicles, business, individual retirement annuity(IRA), and savings, minus all debt, including home loans, mortgage or other debt, adjusted by annual CPI, in dollars	192600.800	200639.500	156946.200***	250614.700	100474.900***	248883.100
Health excellent	Dichotomous indicator for whether respondent self-reported health as excellent	0.199	0.236	0.191***	0.289	0.159***	0.245
Health very good	Dichotomous indicator for whether respondent self-reported health as very good	0.312	0.354	0.337***	0.376	0.306***	0.381
Health good	Dichotomous indicator for whether respondent self-reported health as good	0.279	0.289	0.316***	0.255	0.341***	0.272
Work limiting health	Dichotomous indicator for whether health problems limit kind or amount of paid work	0.226	0.098	0.115***	0.078	0.123***	0.088
Physical health index	Number of conditions that respondent has been ever diagnosed with, including high blood pressure, diabetes, cancer, lung disease, heart problems, stroke, psychiatric problems and arthritis	1.273	1.042	1.158***	0.914	1.230***	1.052

Table 2. (Continued).

Variable	Definition	All	Workers	Abstainers	Drinkers	No Dental Visit	Dental Visit
Mental health index	Number of self-reported symptoms of mental illness in the past week, including feeling depressed, everything was an effort, restless, unhappy, lonely, sad, could not get going and not enjoying life	1.249	0.978	1.151***	0.769	1.423***	1.048
Risk tolerance	Dichotomous indicator for the most risk averse individuals in the sample	0.619	0.612	0.634***	0.587	0.630***	0.572
Agriculture and forestry	Dichotomous indicators for whether respondent currently works in these industries	0.029	0.029	0.029	0.028	0.037***	0.022
Mining and construction		0.062	0.062	0.057	0.062	0.080***	0.051
Non-durable manufacturing		0.071	0.071	0.076**	0.065	0.078*	0.067
Durable manufacturing		0.108	0.108	0.103	0.110	0.125***	0.099
Transportation		0.072	0.072	0.067*	0.076	0.086***	0.067
Wholesale		0.042	0.042	0.036***	0.049	0.041	0.044
Retail		0.106	0.106	0.111***	0.099	0.123***	0.095
Finance, insurance and real estate		0.070	0.070	0.062***	0.079	0.055***	0.077
Business repair services		0.067	0.067	0.067	0.066	0.068	0.076
Personal services		0.041	0.041	0.051***	0.030	0.066***	0.030
Entertainment and recreation		0.015	0.015	0.011***	0.017	0.014	0.015
Professional services		0.269	0.269	0.284***	0.265	0.194***	0.301
Public administration		0.050	0.050	0.046**	0.054	0.032***	0.057

	Dichotomous indicators for respondent's current type of occupation					
Managerial specialty			0.164	0.126***	0.202	0.100***	0.184
Professional or technical specialty	0.181	0.181	0.162***	0.208	0.101***	0.224
Sales	0.103	0.103	0.098***	0.110	0.101	0.105
Clerical	0.157	0.157	0.171***	0.150	0.115***	0.174
Household and building services	0.011	0.011	0.018***	0.005	0.024***	0.006
Protection	0.015	0.015	0.012***	0.018	0.019**	0.012
Food preparation	0.025	0.025	0.032***	0.019	0.037***	0.018
Health services	0.020	0.020	0.029***	0.011	0.031***	0.017
Personal services	0.055	0.055	0.069***	0.040	0.071***	0.044
Farming and forestry	0.026	0.026	0.029**	0.023	0.037***	0.019
Mechanics and repair	0.038	0.038	0.033*	0.038	0.047**	0.035
Construction trade	0.039	0.039	0.038	0.036	0.056***	0.037
Precision production	0.034	0.034	0.034	0.030	0.044***	0.028
Machine operator	0.058	0.058	0.070***	0.045	0.089***	0.046
Transport operator	0.051	0.051	0.056***	0.045	0.087***	0.038
Handler or operator	0.022	0.022	0.024***	0.018	0.042***	0.013
Armed forces	0.0004	0.0004	0.0001**	0.0007	0.0000*	0.0003
Observations	46,224	25,838	13,054	11,532	3,984	9,765

Notes: Means are reported for individuals ages 40 to 62 years. Number of observations listed represents the maximum number. For some variables, the actual sample size is less due to missing information. Asterisks indicate that the difference between the two groups is statistically significant as follows:***significant at 0.01 level, **significant at 0.05 level and *significant at 0.10 level.

4. EMPIRICAL STRATEGY

The empirical strategy must consider both statistical endogeneity and structural endogeneity. Consider the following specifications of the structural models for earnings (Y_{it}) and alcohol consumption (A_{it}):

$$Y_{it} = b_1 A_{it} + b_2 X_{it} + b_3 U_i + \varepsilon_{it} \tag{1}$$

$$A_{it} = c_1 Y_{it} + c_2 Z_{it} + c_3 U_i + \eta_{it} \tag{2}$$

Eq. (1) is the earnings profile based on Mincer (1974), modified to include the effect of drinking. It states that earnings for individual i in period t are a function of alcohol consumption (A_{it}), observable characteristics including age, age squared, other demographics, human capital and job-specific factors (X_{it}), and unobservable characteristics such as personality traits, time preference, motivation or family history (U_i). Eq. (2) is a demand for alcohol, which is a function of earnings (Y_{it}). The vector Z_{it} represents observed characteristics that determine alcohol demand including price, demographics and other factors, which in turn may be the same as some of the observed determinants of earnings (X_{it}). Similarly, alcohol use may also depend on the same unmeasured individual-specific factors (U_i) that also influence earnings. Finally, ε_{it} and η_{it} are random disturbance terms.

The parameter of interest is b_1, the structural effect of alcohol use on earnings. A simple estimation of Eq. (1) may be biased because of two reasons. This is reflected in Eq. (3), the reduced form alcohol demand function, obtained by substitution of Eq. (1) into Eq. (2):

$$A_{it} = \left(\frac{b_2 c_1}{1 - b_1 c_1}\right) X_{it} + \left(\frac{c_2}{1 - b_1 c_1}\right) Z_{it} + \left(\frac{c_3 + b_3 c_1}{1 - b_1 c_1}\right) U_i$$

$$+ \left(\frac{c_1}{1 - b_1 c_1}\right) \varepsilon_{it} + \left(\frac{1}{1 - b_1 c_1}\right) \eta_{it} \tag{3}$$

or

$$A_{it} = \pi_1 X_{it} + \pi_2 Z_{it} + \pi_3 U_i + \pi_4 \varepsilon_{it} + \pi_5 \eta_{it}$$

First, if there are common unmeasured factors (U_i) that determine both earnings and alcohol use ($b_3 \neq 0$ and $c_3 \neq 0$), then these unmeasured factors are likely to be correlated with alcohol use ($\pi_3 \neq 0$). This correlation between U_i and A_{it} will lead to biased and inconsistent estimates of the structural effect b_1. Since the sign of π_3 is indeterminate, the direction of this bias is generally unknown. A second reason for correlation between alcohol use and the error term in Eq. (1) is structural endogeneity or reverse causality. Since alcohol use may in turn depend on earnings due to an income or wealth effect ($c_1 \neq 0$), A_{it} is correlated with ε_{it} ($\pi_4 \neq 0$). In this case, however, the direction of the bias is known. Prior studies have shown that alcohol is a normal good, and thus the parameter c_1 is positive (see Ruhm & Black, 2002). This implies a positive correlation between A_{it} and ε_{it}.[7] It can be shown that this bias is equal to:

$$E[\Sigma(A_{it} - A)(\varepsilon_{it})/\Sigma(A_{it} - A)^2] \qquad (4)$$

which is positive if A_{it} and ε_{it} are positively correlated ($\pi_4 > 0$).[8] As a result, reverse causality will cause the magnitude of the effect of alcohol use on earnings (b_1) to be overestimated.

Initially, Eq. (1) is estimated using OLS with alternate measures of labour market outcomes and with a parsimonious set of demographic and human capital covariates. Subsequent specifications include additional controls as a proxy for a subset of the unmeasured components vector U_i. The next set of specifications includes area-fixed effects to control for unobserved state- and county-specific factors that may simultaneously determine earnings and alcohol use. Assuming that unobserved individual-specific factors are time-invariant (U_i), the most extended set of models are estimated with individual-fixed effects. In this case, the individual-fixed effects purge U_i from the estimation of Eq. (1) and correct for statistical endogeneity.

As a specification check, alcohol consumption is replaced with a dichotomous indicator for any visit to a dentist since the respondent's last interview.[9] While a dental visit may proxy for unmeasured factors such as health or preventive care, it is difficult to argue that a visit to a dentist should have any direct causal effect on wages or earnings. It is more likely that dental visits reflect the influence of omitted variables, in which case the estimation strategy should be able to eliminate any effect of dental visits.

Finally, an instrumental variables methodology, used in prior studies, is followed as an alternate solution to the endogeneity bias. Consistent with the literature, the instrumental set includes alcohol taxes, number of liquor outlets, cigarette taxes, religious affiliation and the diagnosis of diabetes.[10] Prior studies have argued that these variables are plausible instruments, which can be excluded from the earnings function.[11] Since an IV strategy critically depends on the quality of the instruments, which may not necessarily be indicated by standard diagnostics, these results are presented as a caveat to conclusions based on these models.

5. RESULTS

Table 2 presents weighted sample means for the full sample of individuals ages 40–62 years and for those who are working. About 68% of the sample is currently working for pay, with the remainder unemployed or not part of the labour force. The mean annual earnings for workers are $21,090 and the mean hourly wage rate is $13.87. Among workers, about 45% are drinkers who have on average two or fewer drinks a day, 5% have more than two drinks daily and the rest are current abstainers. The average individual consumes about half a drink daily. In the HRS, current alcohol participation for individuals older than 62 years decreases to 31%. While alcohol consumption generally declines with age, newer cohorts have increasing levels of alcohol consumption as they get older (NIAAA, 2000).

Sample means are also provided by drinking status, with the individuals classified as abstainers or drinkers. These figures show the wage and earnings premium associated with drinking. For example, drinkers earn $24,786 compared to $17,598 for abstainers, an increase of about 41%. They also have a significantly higher hourly wage rate of $16.47 compared to $11.03 for abstainers, an increase of almost 50%. The average number of drinks consumed per day by moderate drinkers is less than one.

The figures in Table 2 also show that alcohol use is significantly correlated with other observed characteristics that affect labour-market performance. For example, drinkers have completed more years of schooling and come from more educated families are more likely to be married (white males) and have a higher current job tenure as well as worked more years in general. They also tend to be of better physical and mental health. All of these characteristics possessed by drinkers are consistently associated with higher earnings in the labour economics literature. Higher human capital, in the form of knowledge or health capital, raises productivity, and hence wages and earnings (Ben Porath, 1967; Grossman, 1972). The literature on racial and gender discrimination also shows that males consistently earn more than females, and whites earn more than blacks and other minorities (Altonji & Blank, 1999). A wage premium associated with marriage, on the order of 10–40%, has also been documented for males (Korenman & Neumark, 1991). Drinking is also positively correlated with a higher-risk tolerance. Thus, if drinkers transfer their tolerance for risk to other areas of their life, including choosing occupations with a higher degree of injury risk or unemployment risk, then they may also earn more due to the associated compensating wage differential (Rosen, 1986). The figures further indicate that drinkers are more likely to work in higher-paying jobs and industries, including finance and insurance, and managerial, professional and technical specialties. It is apparent from the data that there is selection on observable factors: individuals who drink are not a random sample. They are also more likely to work in different industries and occupations, and have other characteristics that positively affect their productivity, earnings and wages. This selection on observable factors indicates that selection on unobserved factors may also play an integral role. It may be the case that the relation between drinking and earnings is driven by other unmeasured heterogeneity between drinkers and non-drinkers. The multivariate models address this possibility.[12]

Table 3 presents the results for average drinks per day on working status and hours of work. All specifications include the linear and quadratic form of this variable to capture the inverted U-shaped relationship between alcohol use and earnings. The first panel presents the results for working status. In the basic specification with a sparse set of human capital and demographic controls, the quadratic relation between drinking and working is statistically significant. Consuming up to about an average of two drinks per day raises the likelihood that the individual currently works for pay; over two drinks per day lowers this probability. The effects of other independent variables on working status are similar to prior empirical studies and are not reported. The next specification extends the set of covariates to include other observed factors that may be correlated with labour-force outcomes. Specifically, non-labour income, as proxied by real assets, measures of physical and mental health, and an indicator for the most risk-averse individuals is added. Alcohol use no longer has any statistically significant effect on working status. This implies that physical and mental health, and a tolerance towards risk of drinkers is sufficient to explain the positive correlation between drinking and working. Similar results are found for the next set of models, which controls for state-county-and individual-fixed effects.

The second panel of Table 3 presents the models for the log of total hours worked weekly, conditional on positive-working status. Since this is a conditional labour supply model, the extended specifications control for the log of the wage in addition to the other personal characteristics. While the sample means show that drinkers tend to work slightly more hours, even the most basic controls for human capital and demographics are able to wipe out this correlation. The average number of drinks per day does not have a statistically significant effect on labour supply in any of the specifications.

Table 4 presents the results for log earnings and log wages. Only those individuals currently working for pay are included in the analysis. For both

Table 3. Labour Supply, Average Drinks per Day.

Dependent Variable	Independent Variable	Basic	Extended	State-Fixed Effects	County-Fixed Effects	Individual-Fixed Effects
Work	Average drinks per day	0.070***(7.73)	0.003(0.36)	0.002(0.28)	0.004(0.49)	0.014(1.42)
	Average drinks per day squared	−0.017***(7.10)	−0.003(1.40)	−0.003(1.27)	−0.003(1.37)	−0.004(1.57)
	Years worked	No	Yes***	Yes***	Yes***	Yes***
	Net assets	No	Yes***	Yes***	Yes***	Yes
	Physical health	No	Yes***	Yes***	Yes***	Yes***
	Mental health	No	Yes***	Yes***	Yes***	Yes***
	Risk tolerance	No	Yes	Yes	Yes	No
	State fixed effects	No	No	Yes***	No	No
	County fixed effects	No	No	No	Yes***	No
	Individual fixed effects	No	No	No	No	Yes***
Log hours worked	Average drinks per day	−0.005(0.46)	−0.010(0.86)	−0.007(0.58)	−0.006(0.49)	−0.014(1.02)
	Average drinks per day squared	−0.004(1.41)	−0.003(1.04)	−0.004(1.33)	−0.004(1.31)	0.0002(0.05)

Log wage	No	Yes***	Yes***	Yes***
Years worked and tenure	No	Yes***	Yes***	Yes***
Net assets	No	Yes***	Yes***	Yes***
Physical health	No	Yes***	Yes***	Yes***
Mental health	No	Yes	Yes	Yes*
Risk tolerance	No	Yes*	Yes*	No
Industry	No	Yes***	Yes***	Yes***
Occupation	No	Yes***	Yes***	Yes***
State-fixed effects	No	No	No	No
County-fixed effects	No	No	Yes***	No
Individual-fixed effects	No	No	No	Yes***

Notes: All specifications include education, age, age squared, male, black, other race, Hispanic, married, mother's education, father's education and year indicators. All earnings and wage models also include full-time status. Absolute t-values are shown in parentheses. For other covariates, asterisks indicate the significance of the joint *F*-test. ***significant at 0.01 level, **significant at 0.05 level and *significant at 0.10 level.

Table 4. Earnings, Average Drinks per Day and Dental Visit.

Dependent Variable	Independent Variable	Basic	Extended	State-Fixed Effects	County-Fixed Effects	Individual-Fixed Effects
Log earnings	Average drinks per day	0.157***(7.56)	0.092***(4.23)	0.068***(3.14)	0.036*(1.67)	−0.011(0.41)
	Average drinks per day squared	−0.039***(6.87)	−0.021***(3.35)	−0.017***(2.70)	−0.009(1.49)	0.001(0.17)
	Years worked and tenure	Yes***	Yes***	Yes***	Yes***	Yes***
	Log hours worked	No	Yes***	Yes***	Yes***	Yes***
	Net assets	No	Yes***	Yes***	Yes***	Yes
	Physical health	No	Yes***	Yes***	Yes***	Yes
	Mental health	No	Yes*	Yes***	Yes***	Yes
	Risk tolerance	No	Yes	Yes	Yes	No
	Industry	No	Yes***	Yes***	Yes***	Yes***
	Occupation	No	Yes***	Yes***	Yes***	Yes***
	State fixed-effects	No	No	Yes***	No	No
	County-fixed effects	No	No	No	Yes***	No
	Individual-fixed effects	No	No	No	No	Yes***
	Dental visit	0.165***(10.38)	0.121***(7.27)	0.107***(6.42)	0.101***(5.93)	0.013(0.54)

Log wage						
Average drinks per day	0.171***(10.23)	0.105***(6.07)	0.077***(4.52)	0.056***(3.21)	−0.012(0.56)
Average drinks per day squared	−0.040***(8.80)	−0.023***(4.84)	−0.018***(3.90)	−0.013***(2.69)	0.002(0.34)
Years worked & tenure	Yes***	Yes***	Yes***	Yes***	Yes***
Log hours worked	No	Yes***	Yes***	Yes***	Yes***
Net assets	No	Yes***	Yes***	Yes***	Yes
Physical health	No	Yes***	Yes***	Yes***	Yes***
Mental health	No	Yes	Yes	Yes	Yes
Risk tolerance	No	Yes	Yes*	Yes**	No
Industry	No	Yes***	Yes***	Yes***	Yes***
Occupation	No	Yes***	Yes***	Yes***	Yes***
State-fixed effects	No	No	Yes***	No	No
County-fixed effects	No	No	No	Yes***	No
Individual-fixed effects	No	No	No	No	Yes***
Dental visit	0.165***(11.95)	0.106***(7.37)	0.088***(6.12)	0.076***(5.18)	−0.008(0.38)

Notes: All specifications include education, age, age squared, male, black, other race, Hispanic, married, mother's education, father's education and year indicators. All earnings and wage models also include full-time status. Absolute t-values are shown in parentheses. For other covariates, asterisks indicate the significance of the joint F-test. ***significant at 0.01 level, **significant at 0.05 level and *significant at 0.10 level.

of these dependent variables, the basic models control for full-time working status, and the extended models additionally control for the log of actual hours worked. In the earnings function, this captures any differences in earnings due to hours worked and thus isolates the effect of alcohol use on productivity or wages. The wage rate itself may also be a function of the number of hours worked. In the basic specifications, average number of drinks has a statistically significant effect on log earnings and log wage. The coefficients imply that an average of one drink per day raises earnings by 11.9% and raises wages by 13.7%, relative to abstention. The relation is parabolic however. Drinking raises earnings up to an average of about two drinks per day, and then lowers earnings. With respect to wages, the inflection occurs at about two and a half drinks.[13] In the extended specifications, the quadratic relationship between drinking and earnings is still significant, with the inflection occurring at roughly the same number of drinks as in the basic models. However, this richer group of controls causes the marginal effects of an additional drink to decline in absolute magnitude by about 40%. Individuals who have on average one drink per day now experience a 7.1% increase in earnings and an 8.2% increase in wages. The next set of models controls for unobserved time-invariant state-specific characteristics by including state-fixed effects. Though still statistically significant, the absolute magnitude of the marginal effect of drinking falls by an additional 30%. The next set of models controls for unobserved time-invariant county-specific characteristics by including county fixed effects. Though the linear term is marginally significant, the marginal effect falls by an additional 50%. The progressively diminished marginal effects indicate that there is a large degree of selection on observed factors and that the relation between alcohol use and earnings or wages is sensitive to these additional covariates.

This strongly suggests that there may also be additional selection on unobserved characteristics. Specifically, since drinking and working are individual behavioural choices, it is very likely that there are unobserved individual-specific factors that may be correlated with both the outcomes, such as family background, time preference, motivation, or social environment. The next set of specifications includes individual-fixed effects, which control for all time-invariant individual-specific unobservables. The marginal effect of alcohol use on earnings or wages is statistically insignificant in these models.

The bottom panel in Table 4 presents similar results for the log of wages. The simple means showed that drinkers earned a wage almost 50% higher than non-drinkers. Considerable selection on even the sparsest group of observed characteristics causes this wage premium to decline to 13.1% in the basic specification for one drink versus abstention. In the extended model, the marginal effect, while significant and positive, is substantially reduced to 8.2% and then further to 5.7% when state-fixed effects are added and further reduced to 4.3% when county effects are added. Controlling for time-invariant heterogeneity between individuals completely wipes out this wage premium between drinkers and non-drinkers.[14]

The individual-fixed-effects models in Tables 3 and 4 control for statistical endogeneity, by controlling for all omitted unchanging individual-specific factors. These results show that drinking has no effect on the earnings and wages of older workers. These models do not control for structural endogeneity due to any reverse causality running from earnings or wages to alcohol use. If the income effect is significant, it was shown in Section 4 that any remaining bias due to this reverse causality will be positive. That is, the marginal effect of alcohol use in the individual-fixed-effects specifications will represent an upper bound of the true effect if moderate consumption has a positive income elasticity. Thus, the results from the individual-fixed-effects models suggest that alcohol use has a non-positive effect on wages and earnings.

Table 4 also presents the results from a specification test which uses an indicator for any dental visit since the respondent's last interview. The models in Table 4 estimate the effect of a dental visit on log earnings and log wages based on the same specifications used for drinking. This specification test is similar to the results presented by DiNardo and Pischke (1997). They found that owning a pencil created a wage premium similar to computer use, which cast doubt on the presumed causal effect of computer usage on wages. From the table of weighted means, individuals who visited a dentist exhibit the same kind of wage and earnings premium as drinkers. For example, compared to those who did not report a dental visit, individuals who visited a dentist had 48% higher earnings and 62% higher wages. These two groups also differed significantly along many of the same observed characteristics as drinkers and non-drinkers. Similar to moderate alcohol use, a dental visit is also likely to have a positive-income elasticity. While a dental visit may proxy for unobserved health capital, it is difficult to argue that such a visit should have any direct causal effect on earnings or wages.[15]

The results for dental visits in Table 4 show that the marginal effect on earnings and wages is initially positive but becomes progressively smaller in magnitude as the number of covariates is extended. The coefficient of any dental visit becomes statistically insignificant with the addition of individual-fixed-effects. The pattern of these results is the same as the pattern for drinking. Since there is no causality from dental visits to earnings and wages, this exercise also casts doubt on the presumed causality from drinking to earnings and wages. It appears that both dental visits and drinking proxy for the influence of omitted individual characteristics.

One methodology that has commonly been applied in the prior literature is IV estimation. An IV model can yield consistent estimates by accounting for both structural and statistical endogeneity. However, the efficacy of the IV procedure depends critically on the quality of the instruments. To showcase the caution that must be exercised, results from IV estimation are presented in Table 5. Consistent with various prior studies, the identifying instruments include the state excise taxes on beer and cigarettes, alcohol availability as proxied by the number of liquor outlets in a state, an indicator for any religious affiliation, and an indicator for the diagnosis of diabetes. The Davidson–MacKinnon overidentification test provides a test for the validity of the exclusion restriction.[16] In all of the IV models presented, this test statistic suggests that the instruments satisfy the exclusion restriction and do not belong in the earnings or wage functions. Except for the cigarette tax, all identifying instruments are highly significant and have the correct sign in the first-stage regression. The alcohol participation elasticity with respect to the beer tax is estimated at −0.34, a magnitude consistent with the literature. The joint F-statistic on these excluded instruments is also highly significant, indicating that the instrumental group is strongly correlated with alcohol consumption. By all measures, standard diagnostics indicate that the identifying instruments are valid, and hence the IV procedure should give consistent estimates. However, the results show an implausibly high return to moderate consumption for both earnings and wages. Moderate drinking is shown to raise earnings by 27% and wages by 28%, effects that are four to six times larger than the corresponding single-equation estimates.[17] The standard errors in the IV models are inflated by a factor of nine. It seems that any bias in the single-equation estimates is exacerbated in the IV models. Therefore, even when the IV appear valid, the conclusions from such studies should be interpreted with care in conjunction with the plausibility of the magnitudes.

6. CONCLUSION

This study analyses the effect of alcohol consumption on the earnings of older workers ages 40–62 years. The wage and earnings premium associated with drinking, which has been documented for other samples in prior

Table 5. Earnings, Wages, and Drinking Participation Instrumental Variables[a].

Estimation	OLS	2SLS	OLS	2SLS	First Stage
Dependent variable	Log earnings	Log earnings	Log wage	Log wage	Drinking participation
Drinking participation[b]	0.045***(2.96)[0.015]	0.267**(2.11)[0.127]	0.075***(6.16)[0.012]	0.280***(2.62)[0.107]	—
Excluded Instruments					
Beer tax	—	—	—	—	−0.886***(3.05) $\varepsilon = -0.342$
Liquor outlets	—	—	—	—	0.004***(4.03)
Cigarette tax	—	—	—	—	−0.0003(0.52)
Any religion	—	—	—	—	−0.074***(5.12)
Diabetes	—	—	—	—	−0.117***(10.18)
Joint F-test	—	—	—	—	31.11***
Overidentification test[c]	—	6.44(0.17)	—	5.39(0.25)	—

2SLS: Two Stage Least Squares.
[a] All models include education, age, age squared, tenure, years worked, male, black, other race, Hispanic, married, mother's education, father's education, full time indicator, log hours worked, real assets, indicators of physical and mental health, risk tolerance, indicators of industry and occupation, year indicators, and state-fixed effects. ***significant at 0.01 level, **significant at 0.05 level and *significant at 0.10 level.
[b] Marginal effects are reported. Absolute t-values are in parentheses, and standard errors are in brackets.
[c] Chi-square statistic for Davidson–MacKinnon test of overidentifying restrictions is reported. Associated P-values are in parentheses.

studies, is evident among these older workers from the HRS. The particular concern was to examine whether this positive association between drinking and earnings represented a true causal effect or whether it was driven by unmeasured individual heterogeneity.

To assess the strength and robustness of this association, the marginal effects from parsimonious models are compared with extended specifications that progressively add richer sets of controls. Given that the magnitudes of the marginal effects of alcohol use were significantly diminished when indicators of physical and mental health, risk tolerance, occupation, industry of work, state and county of residence were added to the basic specification, there appears to be a considerable amount of selection along these dimensions. This high degree of sensitivity of the effect to the additional correlates suggests that selection on unobservables may also be important. Specifically, since drinking and working are individual behavioural choices, other unmeasured individual-specific factors may be confounding the link between these two outcomes. The longitudinal nature of the HRS facilitated the estimation of individual-fixed-effects models that controlled for all omitted time-invariant individual characteristics. From these models, alcohol use was found to have no statistically significant effect on any labour market outcome, including working status, weekly hours worked, earnings and wages. Individual-fixed-effects specifications cannot, however, account for bias that may remain due to earnings and wages affecting alcohol consumption through an income effect. Under the likely scenario that the income elasticity of moderate drinking is positive, these estimates should then be interpreted as an upper bound for the true effect of drinking on earnings. The results therefore indicate that alcohol use has a non-positive effect on the earnings and wages of older workers. The positive wage premium associated with drinking is more likely due to systematic differences between drinkers and abstainers that are also correlated with their productivity than due to a true causal productivity gain from drinking.

NOTES

1. The primary health benefit of moderate alcohol use is a decrease in coronary heart disease. Other evidence suggests that moderate alcohol use is associated with greater levels of breast and colorectal cancers, and has negative health effects in the long term (NIAAA, 2000). Dave and Kaestner (2002) argue that the link between moderate alcohol use, heart disease and mortality is not a justification for improved employee health and thus improved employee productivity.

2. For OLS see, for example, French and Zarkin (1995), Zarkin, French, Mroz, and Bray (1998) and Mullahy and Sindelar (1989, 1991). For IV, see for example, Kenkel and Ribar (1994), Heien (1996), Mullahy and Sindelar (1996), Hamilton and Hamilton (1997), MacDonald and Shields (2000) and van Ours (2004).

3. See Nelson and Startz (1990) and Bound, Jaeger, and Baker (1995).

4. These interaction terms are never statistically significant, indicating that the structural break in the survey questions does not materially alter the results. Separate models were also estimated for the first two waves and the subsequent waves. The results for these two samples are virtually identical. All models reported in this chapter are for the full sample and include the spline interaction terms.

5. Changing the threshold to one or three drinks does not qualitatively affect the conclusions.

6. Questions on tolerance towards risk are asked only once to each individual, and thus these variables do not vary over time in the data set. See Barsky et al. (1997) for a detailed analysis of the risk preference module in the HRS.

7. In order to rule out an infinite feedback loop and assure stability of the simultaneous system, it is generally assumed that the denominator $(1-b_1c_1)$ is positive.

8. See Pindyck and Rubinfeld (1998).

9. This variable is not available for the first two waves.

10. The excise tax on beer and the number of liquor outlets in a given state are reported in the *Brewers' Almanac*, published annually by the U.S. Brewers' Association. The state excise tax on cigarettes is from *The Tax Burden on Tobacco*. These variables are appended to the HRS data by the individual's state of residence. Diagnosis of diabetes is measured as a dichotomous indicator for whether the respondent has ever been told by a doctor that he has diabetes. Religious affiliation is defined as a dichotomous indicator for whether the respondent affiliates himself as Catholic, Protestant or some other religion.

11. Just about every study that has relied on an IV strategy has incorporated alcohol prices, taxes or availability laws into the instrumental set. The cigarette excise tax is also included to capture cross-price effects of smoking on drinking. MacDonald and Shields (2001) argue that while a non-acute illness such as diabetes may reduce alcohol consumption since drinking may aggravate this condition, it can typically be controlled and is not "severe enough to inhibit occupational attainment." Religion generally promotes a temperate lifestyle and thus can also affect alcohol consumption, but should not have a direct effect on earnings.

12. Models estimated separately by gender do not show any significant differences in the marginal effects between males and females. Hence, results are presented for the pooled sample.

13. Similar results for both the earnings and the wage equations are reassuring since controlling for hours worked in the earnings function should isolate the effect of alcohol use on productivity and the hourly wage rate. Also, estimating models that exclude full-time status or actual hours worked as independent variables does not significantly alter the marginal effects of alcohol use. As a final specification check, the earnings and wage functions are also estimated via Heckman sample selection models to control for any biases due to selecting only working individuals into the sample. The marginal effects of alcohol use remain highly similar. This is not surprising given that models of working status and weekly hours worked as dependent

variables do not show any significant effect of alcohol use. This suggests that the correlation between alcohol use and wages is not caused by drinkers working more than non-drinkers.

14. This may be due to a lack of variation in the drinking measure for an individual over time. Restricting the sample to only those individuals who are represented in all five waves, so as to maximize the time-series variation, does not alter the results. The insignificance may also be due to errors in self-reported consumption, which may be magnified in fixed-effects specifications. However, the progressive decline in the marginal effects when richer sets of controls are added, even in non-fixed-effects models, adds more confidence to the qualitative conclusions. Furthermore, if the results were completely driven by errors in the variables, then all measures of alcohol consumption should be affected similarly. However, crude measures of heavy or problematic alcohol use based on self-reported attitudinal variables are indeed found to have a statistically negative effect on productivity, even in the individual-fixed-effects specifications.

15. The associated wage premium is implausibly large to be explained by the argument that aesthetically better looking teeth may result in higher earnings.

16. See Davidson and MacKinnon (1993).

17. In Mullahy and Sindelar (1996), the instrumental variables pass the over-identification test in five out of the six cases. However, IV estimates for males are on the order of 6–16 times larger for employment and 3–10 times larger for unemployment, compared to OLS. Similar inflation of the marginal effects in IV models is also reported in van Ours (2004).

ACKNOWLEDGEMENTS

This chapter was funded by Grant No.: R21 AA014334 from the National Institute on Alcoholism and Alcohol Abuse. The authors would like to thank Kerry Anne McGeary and Angela Dills for helpful comments.

REFERENCES

Altonji, J., & Blank, R. (1999). Race and gender in the labour market. In: O. Ashenfelter & D. Card (Eds), *Handbook of labour economics* (pp. 3143–3259). New York: Elsevier Science: North-Holland.

Barrett, G. (2002). The effect of alcohol consumption on earnings. *The Economic Record*, 78(1), 79–96.

Ben Porath, Y. (1967). The production of human capital and the life cycle of earnings. *Journal of Political Economy*, 75, 352–365.

Berger, M., & Leigh, J. (1988). The effect of alcohol use on wages. *Applied Economics*, 20, 1343–1351.

Bound, J., Jaeger, D., & Baker, R. (1995). Problems with instrumental variables estimation when the correlation between the instruments and the endogenous variables is weak. *Journal of the American Statistical Association, 90*, 443–450.

Dave, D., & Kaestner, R. (2002). Alcohol taxes and labour market outcomes. *Journal of Health Economics, 21*(2), 357–371.

Davidson, R., & MacKinnon, J. (1993). *Estimation and inference in econometrics.* New York: Oxford University Press.

DiNardo, J., & Pischke, J. (1997). The returns to computer use revisited: Have pencils changed the wage structure too? *Quarterly Journal of Economics, 112*(1), 291–303.

Doll, R., Peto, R., Hall, E., Wheatley, K., & Gray, R. (1994). Mortality in relationship to consumption of Alcohol: 13 years' observations on male British doctors. *British Medical Journal, 309*, 911–918.

French, M., & Zarkin, G. (1995). Is moderate Alcohol use related to wages? Evidence from four worksites. *Journal of Health Economics, 14*, 319–344.

Grossman, M. (1972). On the concept of health capital and the demand for health. *Journal of Political Economy, 80*, 223–255.

Hamilton, V., & Hamilton, B. (1997). Alcohol and earnings: Does drinking yield a wage premium? *Canadian Journal of Economics, 30*, 135–151.

Heien, D. (1996). Do drinkers earn less? *Southern Economic Journal, 63*(1), 60–68.

Kenkel, D., & Ribar, D. (1994). Alcohol consumption and young adults' Socioeconomic status. *Brookings Papers on Economic Activity: Microeconomics,* 119–175.

Korenman, S., & Neumark, D. (1991). Does marriage really make men more productive? *Journal of Human Resources, 26*(2), 282–307.

MacDonald, Z., & Shields, M. (2001). The impact of alcohol consumption on occupation attainment in England. *Economica, 68*, 427–453.

Mincer, J. (1974). *Schooling, experience and earnings.* New York: National Bureau of Economic Research.

Mullahy, J., & Sindelar, J. (1989). Life-cycle effects of alcoholism on education, earnings and occupation. *Inquiry, 26*, 272–282.

Mullahy, J., & Sindelar, J. (1991). Gender differences in labour market effects of alcoholism. *American Economic Review, 81*(2), 161–165.

Mullahy, J., & Sindelar, J. (1993). Alcoholism, work and income. *Journal of Labour Economics, 11*(3), 494–520.

Mullahy, J., & Sindelar, J. (1995). Health income and risk aversion. *The Journal of Human Resources, 30*(3), 439–459.

Mullahy, J., & Sindelar, J. (1996). Employment, unemployment and problem drinking. *Journal of Health Economics, 15*, 409–434.

NIAAA. (2000). *10th special report to congress on alcohol and health.* Washington, DC: National Institute on Alcohol Abuse and Alcoholism.

Nelson, C., & Startz, R. (1990). The distribution of the instrumental variables estimator and its T-ratio when the instrument is a poor one. *Journal of Business, 63*, s125–s140.

Peters, B. (2004). Is there a wage bonus from drinking? Unobserved heterogeneity and the alcohol/productivity paradox. *Applied Economics, 36*(20), 2299–2315.

Rosen, S. (1986). The theory of equalizing differences. In: O. Ashenfelter & R. Layard (Eds), *Handbook of Labour Economics* (pp. 641–692). Amsterdam: North-Holland.

Ruhm, C. J., & Black, W. E. (2002). Does drinking really decrease in bad times? *Journal of Health Economics, 21*(4), 659–678.

Shaper, A. G. (1990). Alcohol and mortality: A review of prospective studies. *British Journal of Addiction, 85*, 837–847.
Thun, M. J., Peto, R., Lopez, A. D., Monaco, J. H., Henley, S. J., Heath, C. W., & Doll, R. (1997). Alcohol consumption and mortality among middle aged and elderly US adults. *New England Journal of Medicine, 337*, 705–714.
Zarkin, G., French, M., Mroz, T., & Bray, J. (1998). Alcohol use and wages: New results from the national household survey on drug abuse. *Journal of Health Economics, 17*, 53–68.
van Ours, J. (2004). A pint a day raises a man's pay; but smoking blows that gain away. *Journal of Health Economics, 23*(5), 863–886.

DRUGS AND JUVENILE CRIME: EVIDENCE FROM A PANEL OF SIBLINGS AND TWINS

H. Naci Mocan and Erdal Tekin

ABSTRACT

Using data from the U.S. National Longitudinal Study of Adolescent Health, this chapter investigates the impact of individual drug use on robbery, burglary, theft, and damaging property for juveniles. Using a variety of fixed-effects models that exploit variations over time and between siblings and twins, the results indicate that drug use has a significant impact on the propensity to commit crime. We find that the median impact of cocaine use on the propensity to commit various types of crimes is 11 percentage points. The impact of using inhalants or other drugs is an increase in the propensity to commit crime by 7 percentage points, respectively.

1. INTRODUCTION

The analysis of the determinants of juvenile risky behaviour in general, and juvenile crime in particular has become an important research question (Gruber, 2001; Levitt, 1998b; Mocan and Rees, 2005). Drug use is a potentially important determinant of criminal activity, although the extent of the relationship between drugs and crime has not been identified clearly. Despite the strong evidence that drug use and criminal activity are positively correlated, the causal impact of drug use on crime has not been conclusively established (see the literature reviews of Chaiken & Chaiken, 1990; Harrison, 1992). Even though some recent studies using aggregate data provided evidence on the potential causal impact of drug use on crime (Corman & Mocan, 2000; Grogger & Willis, 2000), convincing cause-and-effect evidence from micro-data is missing.[1] The difficulty in identifying the causal impact of drug use on crime stems from the possibility that the observed positive correlation between drug use and crime may be due to the influence of an unobserved variable which has an impact on both drug use and criminal activity. For example, if the degree of risk aversion of the individual has an impact on both his drug use and criminal behaviour, then biased estimates of the impact of drug use on crime would be obtained in analyses that do not take into account the confounding due to risk aversion.

This chapter investigates the link between illicit drugs and juvenile crime using nationally representative individual-level data. To eliminate confounding due to unobservable variables, we exploit the longitudinal aspect of the data which include siblings and twins who live in the same household. The use of longitudinal data to eliminate time-invariant individual heterogeneity is a standard tool in micro-econometrics. As explained below in detail, the longitudinal nature of our data, and an unusually large number of personal and family background variables allow us to examine the impact of illicit drug use on an individual's criminal activity.

Data on twins have been employed by previous research to estimate returns to education, schooling and marriage decisions, and the impact of birth weight on infant health (Ashenfelter & Krueger, 1994; Miller, Mulvey, & Martin, 1995; Behrman, Rosenzweig, & Taubman, 1994, 1996; Almond, Chay, & Lee, 2002). All of these twin studies employed cross-sectional data on twins, and to the best of our knowledge, this is the first study that uses a *panel* of siblings and twins to control for both the impacts of time-invariant and time-varying unobservables.

We analyse four different crimes – robbery, burglary, damaging property, and theft. The four drug use indicators we employ are the use of cocaine, the use of inhalants, the injection of illegal drugs, and the use of other drugs. We address potential measurement error in drug use.

Drug use is found to increase the propensity to commit crime. Using cocaine, inhalants, and other drugs increases the propensity to commit crime from 6 to 11 percentage points; injecting drugs increases the probability of committing crime by 41 percentage points.

In this chapter, Section 2 presents the analytical framework, Section 3 discusses the measurement error in drug use, Section 4 describes the data, Section 5 displays the results, and Section 6 is the conclusion.

2. ANALYTICAL FRAMEWORK

The crime supply equation with the addition of drug use can be presented as follows:[2]

$$CR = f(X, A, F, DR) \qquad (1)$$

where CR stands for a measure of the extent of the criminal activity of the individual; X represents the characteristics of the person, such as age, race and ethnicity, and religious beliefs; A stands for location-specific deterrence and economic variables that impact criminal involvement, such as crime-specific arrest rates, police presence, and the unemployment rate; F is a vector of parent and family characteristics; and DR represents drug use of the individual.[3]

Drug consumption in Eq. (1) is a function of the price of drugs, buyers' income, and tastes for drug use, and specific penalties targeted at drug users. Using Goldstein's (1985) conceptual framework, drug use can affect criminal activity through three channels. First, the "pharmacological" effect is the direct impact of drug use on criminal activity because drug use may increase aggression. The second is the "economic" effect – that higher expenditures on drugs cause some users to finance these expenditures by committing crime. The third is the "systemic" effect – the violence due to the illegality of the drug market, because the participants cannot rely on contracts and courts to resolve disputes. If the "economic" effect is the dominant factor to influence criminal activity, the impact of drug use on crime could be ambiguous. For example, if the demand for drugs is price inelastic, then an increase in drug use, say due to a rightward shift of the supply of drugs, would be associated with an increase in drug consumption which is coupled with a decrease in drug spending. If the economic effect is more important than the pharmacological one, increased drug use would be associated with a reduction in crime.[4]

Empirical specification of the crime supply equation as a function of observable and unobservable personal characteristics (including biological attributes), deterrence measures, economic conditions, as well as the attributes of the family, and the extent of the drug use of the individual is presented by the following equation:

$$CR_{jit} = \alpha + \delta X_{jit} + \gamma F_{jit} + \beta DR_{jit} + \tau A_{st} + \mu_{ji} + \lambda_{jit} + \Omega_{ji}^F + \Psi_{jit}^F + \varepsilon_{jit} \quad (2)$$

where CR_{jit} is the criminal activity measure of the ith individual of the jth sibling (or twin) pair at time t; X_{jit} represents observable individual characteristics such as age, race, gender and religiosity of the person, weekly allowance of the child, and measures of risk aversion such as whether the child wears seatbelt while driving; F_{jit} stands for observable family attributes, including parent characteristics and measures of the extent of supervision at home (the complete list of these variables is given in Section 4); DR_{jit} represents consumption of drugs; A_{st} stands for the deterrence measures faced by the individual, such as the arrest rates and the size of the police force, as well as local economic conditions in location s at time t where the child resides; μ_{ji} captures individual-specific time-invariant unobservables which include intellect; λ_{jit} represents person-specific time-varying unobservables; Ω_{ji}^F captures unobservable time-invariant family attributes; Ψ_{jit}^F is unobservable time-varying family attributes; and ε_{jit} is a standard error term.

Taking the first difference of Eq. (2) across time periods gives:

$$\Delta CR_{jit} = \delta \Delta X_{jit} + \gamma \Delta F_{jit} + \beta \Delta DR_{jit} + \tau \Delta A_{st} + \Delta \lambda_{jit} + \Delta \Psi_{jit}^F + \Delta \varepsilon_{jit} \quad (3)$$

where Δ stands for time differencing. Eq. (3) is a standard fixed-effects model, where time-invariant family and individual characteristics drop out, but time-varying heterogeneity remains.

Note that in Eq. (3), the change in individual's criminal activity between the 2 years depends, among other factors, on the change in local deterrence and economics variables (A_{st}). The values of these variables are not collected beyond the first year of our data; therefore, ΔA_{st} cannot be calculated. However, following Currie and Moretti (2003), and Cook and Ludwig (2002), we include state or county dummies to control for such factors. That is, we replace ΔA_{st} with state- or county-fixed effects for the first-differenced models.

There is variation in the consumption of illicit drugs between sibling pairs. This allows us to eliminate time-varying family effects by taking within-sibling differences of Eq. (3), which gives:[5]

$$\nabla \Delta CR_{jit} = \delta \nabla \Delta X_{jit} + \beta \nabla \Delta DR_{jit} + \nabla \Delta \lambda_{jit} + \nabla \Delta \varepsilon_{jit} \quad (4)$$

where ∇ stands for between-sibling differencing. This specification eliminates all heterogeneity with the exception of time-varying individual-specific unobservables (λ_{jit}). Note that the family environment and location-specific economic, and deterrence variables drop out in Eq. (4) as they are the same for all siblings of the same household.

The analogue of Eq. (4) for twins is:

$$\nabla \Delta CR_{jit} = \delta \nabla \Delta X_{jit} + \beta \nabla \Delta DR_{jit} + \nabla \Delta \varepsilon_{jit} \quad (5)$$

In Eq. (5), time-varying individual-specific heterogeneity is eliminated under the assumption that it is biologically the same between twins. This may particularly be the case for monozygotic (identical, or MZ) twins. Therefore, Eq. (5) is estimated for all twins (monozygotic and fraternal), as well as for MZ twins.

3. MEASUREMENT ERROR

Data collection procedures were designed to minimize concerns about confidentiality, as described in detail in Section 4. For example, respondents were not provided with written questionnaires; rather they listened to sensitive questions on delinquent behaviour and drug use through earphones, and entered their answers directly on laptop computers. Nevertheless, it is still conceivable that drug use is reported with error. Furthermore, it is plausible that the reporting error is not symmetric in the classical sense, but it is one sided.

To demonstrate the impact of non-random measurement error in drug use in first-differenced data, consider the following equation:

$$\Delta CR_{it} = \beta \Delta DR_{it}^* + \Delta \varepsilon_{it} \quad (6)$$

where i stands for the ith individual and t is the time period. The subscript j and other covariates are dropped for ease of exposition. Let ΔDR_{it}^* be the actual drug use, DR_{it} stand for the reported drug use, and v_{it} represent the measurement error. The reported drug use is equal to the actual drug use plus the measurement error; that is, $DR_{it} = \Delta DR_{it}^* + v_{it}$. Note that $DR = 1$ if the individual reports using drugs, and $DR = 0$ if he/she reports no drug use. Similarly, $DR^* = 1$ if the actual drug use is positive and $DR^* = 0$ if actual drug use is zero. Let the probability distribution of v_{it} be:

$$\text{Prob}(DR_{it} = 1, DR_{it}^* = 1) = p_1, \quad \text{Prob}(DR_{it} = 1, DR_{it}^* = 0) = 0,$$

$$\text{Prob}(DR_{it} = 0, DR_{it}^* = 0) = p_2, \quad \text{Prob}(DR_{it} = 0, DR_{it}^* = 1) = q$$

That is:

DRit	DR^*_{it}	vit	Prob(vit)
1	1	0	p1
1	0	1	0
0	0	0	p2
0	1	−1	q

The first row in the table indicates that the probability of using drugs and reporting as such is p_1. The second row indicates that the probability of reporting positive drug use when the person in fact did not use drugs is zero. The probability of telling the truth when actual drug use is zero is p_2, and q stands for the probability of lying when the actual drug use is positive.

The estimated β in Eq. (6) is equal to:

$$\hat{\beta}_\Delta = \frac{\Sigma_i \Delta DR_{it} \Delta CR_{it}}{\Sigma_i \Delta DR_{it}^2} = \frac{\Sigma(\Delta DR^*_{it} + \Delta v_{it})(\Delta DR^*_{it}\beta + \Delta \varepsilon_{it})}{\Sigma \Delta DR_{it}^2}$$

Simplifying and taking the probability limit gives:

$$p\lim \hat{\beta} = \beta \, \frac{\text{var}(\Delta DR^*) + \text{cov}(\Delta v, \Delta DR^*)}{\text{var}(\Delta DR)}$$

It can be shown that (see Appendix A):

$$p\lim \hat{\beta} = \beta \left[\frac{p_1 p_2}{(p_1 - p_1^2)(1 - \rho)} \right] \quad (7)$$

where ρ is the autocorrelation coefficient of reported drug use between the time periods (i.e., $\rho = \text{cov}(DR_{it}, DR_{it-1})/\text{var}(DR_{it})$ assuming a covariance-stationary process for DR).

Following Ashenfelter and Zimmerman (1997), the probability limit of β in Eq. (7) can be substituted into Eq. (6) to obtain:

$$\Delta CR_{it} = \beta \left[\frac{p_1 p_2}{(p_1 - p_1^2)(1 - \rho)} \right] \Delta DR_{it} + \Delta \varepsilon_{it} \quad (8)$$

Note that p_1 is readily available in the data, which is the mean reported drug use. The medical literature contains detailed information regarding the reliability of self-reported substance use. For example, in an analysis the drinking patterns of college students, it has been found that the reliability of reporting in the quantity and frequency of drinking beer, wine, and spirits was high, with a reliability ratio of 0.84.[6] Reliability ratios range from 0.89

to 0.92 for items such as "driven a car while drinking," "missed a class because of hangover," and "damaged property because of drinking" (Weiss et al., 1998). An analysis of out-of-treatment drug users indicated a reliability ratio of 0.72 for self-reported cocaine use, 0.77 for heroin, and 0.82 for crack. The ratio was 0.88 for the number of times the person injected drugs. For both cocaine and opiate use, total agreement between self-reports and urinalysis was over 84 percent (Johnson et al., 2000). Utilizing this literature, we postulate that 80 percent of drug users reported their drug use correctly. This suggests that $p_2 = 1 - (p_1/0.8)$, $q = p_1/4$, and ρ is calculated from the data, separately for each drug use measure.[7] Variations in the reporting rate did not change the results in a meaningful way.

It is well known that classical measurement error in the explanatory variable attenuates its estimated coefficient, and the bias is exacerbated in first-differenced data (Levitt, 1998a; Griliches and Hausman, 1985). In our case, where we entertain the possibility of one-sided measurement error due to differential propensity of telling the truth about the use of illicit drug use, the bias depends on p_1, p_2, and ρ.

In models that employ time and sibling (or twin) differencing, we estimate models (suppressing other covariates) such as:

$$\nabla \Delta CR_{jit} = \beta \nabla \Delta DR^*_{jit} + \nabla \Delta \varepsilon_{jit}$$

The probability limit of the estimated coefficient is equal to (the details are in Appendix A):

$$p \lim \hat{\beta} = \beta \left[\frac{4p_1 p_2}{(p_1 - p_1^2)(4 + \Phi)} \right]$$

where $\Phi = 2(-\rho_{DR_{j22}DR_{j21}} - \rho_{DR_{j22}DR_{j12}} + \rho_{DR_{j22}DR_{j11}} + \rho_{DR_{j21}DR_{j12}} - \rho_{DR_{j21}DR_{j11}} - \rho_{DR_{j12}DR_{j11}})$. Φ is calculated from reported drug use as it depends on observed correlations in reported drug use over time and between siblings or twins. Thus, in models with time and sibling (or twin) differencing we have,[8]

$$\nabla \Delta CR_{jit} = \beta \left[\frac{4p_1 p_2}{(p_1 - p_1^2)(4 + \Phi)} \right] \nabla \Delta DR_{jit} + \nabla \Delta \varepsilon_{jit} \qquad (9)$$

4. DATA

The data used in the analyses are drawn from the two waves of the National Longitudinal Study of Adolescent Health (Add Health).[9] Add Health is a nationally representative study of adolescents in grades 7–12. An in-school questionnaire was administered to every student who attended one of the sampled 132 U.S. schools on a particular day during the period between September 1994 and April 1995. A random sample of approximately 200 adolescents from each high school/feeder school pair was selected for in-home interviews which were conducted from April to December 1995.[10] The in-home interviews constituted the core sample and contained about 12,000 adolescents. In addition to the core sample, several special samples (e.g., ethnic and genetic) were also drawn on the basis of in-school interviews. The core and the special samples provide a total number of 20,745 adolescents for Wave I. The adolescents are interviewed for the second time from April to August 1996 for Wave II. In Wave II, 14,738 adolescents were interviewed.[11] Data are gathered from adolescents, from their parents, siblings, friends, romantic partners and fellow students, and from school administrators. The survey was designed to provide detailed information on teen behaviour, including their criminal and substance use/abuse.

One feature of Add Health that we utilize in this chapter is the genetic oversample. The genetic sample consists of pairs of siblings (full, half, and stepsiblings), identical twins, and fraternal twins. Eligibility for the genetic sample was determined based on the responses provided by adolescents in the in-school questionnaire. All mixed sex twin pairs were classified as fraternal, or dizygotic (DZ). In addition to asking each twin if they were MZ or DZ, each twin was also given a set of questions on confusability of appearance (if they looked like two peas in a pod as young children, and three questions on whether they are confused by strangers, teachers, or family members). A zygosity scale is created, which is an average of the confusability item scores over the reports of both twins. When self-reported data on appearance was missing, mother's report of confusability of appearance was used. If there was conflict between the twins' self-reports of zygosity and the classification based on confusability of appearance, the twins are classified as "uncertain zygosity." Using the responses from Wave I questionnaire, those classified as uncertain zygosity were asked in Wave II for cheek samples for DNA analysis. There are 43 twin pairs that refused to provide a sample for testing, and they are deleted from our sample. After deleting twins with undetermined zygosity, the raw sample of siblings (including twins) consists of 4,030 individuals. Of these, 1,986 are full siblings, 700 are half siblings, 821 are DZ twins, and 523 are MZ twins. The sample of twins contains the DZ and MZ twins; and the sample of identical twins consists of the 523 MZ twins. Twins constitute 7 percent of the sample.[12] There is one set of triplets and no quadruplets. The triplets are coded as three sets of twins.

The survey includes a number of detailed questions about delinquent behaviour of adolescents. Specifically, respondents were asked whether they had committed any of the following acts in the 12 months prior to the interview date – robbery, burglary, damaging property, and theft. Adolescents were also asked about whether they had used different types of illicit drugs such as cocaine, other drugs (heroin, LSD, etc.), inhalants, or ever injected any illegal drugs with a needle. In wave I, the juveniles were asked if they ever used these drugs. In wave II, they were asked if they used these drugs since the last interview. Survey administrators took several steps to maintain data security and to minimize the potential for interviewer or parental influence. First, respondents were not provided with any printed questionnaires. Rather, all data were recorded on laptop computers. Second, for sensitive topics, such as delinquent behaviour and substance use/abuse, the adolescents listened to pre-recorded questions through earphones and entered their answers directly on the laptops.[13]

Definitions of the variables used in empirical analyses based on the siblings and twins samples and their descriptive statistics are reported in Table 1.[14] The first two columns of Table 1 report the weighted means and standard deviations of the sibling sample of Wave I. The next column displays the standard deviations of the first-differenced variables, and the last column presents the standard deviations for the first-and-sibling-differenced variables. Some personal and household characteristics, such as race, ethnicity, gender, and whether parents were born in the U.S.A. do not change between the waves. Therefore, these variables are not reported in Table 1. The deterrence variables in Wave I, such as arrest rates, pertain to 1992, and they were not collected in Wave II. This is not a drawback because sibling or twin differencing eliminates all variables that are the same across twins or siblings. Put differently, siblings of the same household are exposed to the same time-series variation in contextual variables, such as local economic and social conditions, and deterrence measures.

5. RESULTS

In Table 2, we report the estimated coefficients of drug use indicators using the sample of siblings (including twins). The top panel presents results pertaining to Eq. (3), which is the time-differenced model. As noted above these models include state dummies as controls for the change in the local deterrence variables across periods since these variables do not exhibit variation in the data. Models with county-fixed effects did not change the

Table 1. Descriptive Statistics.

	Definition	Wave I Cross Section Siblings and Twins		First Difference Siblings and Twins	First and Sibling Difference
		Mean	Standard deviation	Standard deviation	Standard deviation
Damage	Dummy variable (= 1) if deliberately damaged someone else's property that did not belong to you in the past 12 months, 0 otherwise	0.208	0.406	0.422	0.582
Burglary	Dummy variable (= 1) if went into a house or building to steal something in the past 12 months, 0 otherwise	0.054	0.226	0.254	0.359
Theft	Dummy variable (= 1) if took something from a store without paying for it, or took something worth more than 50 dollars in the last 12 months	0.251	0.434	0.462	0.656
Robbery	Dummy variable (= 1) if used or threatened to use a weapon to get something from someone in the past 12 months, 0 otherwise	0.047	0.211	0.240	0.322
Cocaine	Dummy variable (= 1) if ever used any kind of cocaine (including powder, freebase, or crack cocaine) in life, 0 otherwise	0.027	0.161	0.177	0.222
Inhale	Dummy variable (= 1) if ever used inhalants, such as glue or solvents in your lifetime, 0 otherwise	0.068	0.251	0.230	0.303
Other drugs	Dummy variable (= 1) if ever used any other type of illegal drug, such as lysergic acid diethylamide (LSD), phencyclidine (PCP), ecstasy, mushrooms, speed, ice, heroin, or pills, without a doctor's prescription in your lifetime, 0 otherwise	0.073	0.260	0.248	0.337
Inject	Dummy variable (= 1) if ever injected (shot up with a needle) any illegal drug, such as heroine or cocaine, in your lifetime, 0 otherwise	0.002	0.047	0.075	0.107

Allowance	Allowance per week	4.730	7.872	10.934	13.882
Welfare	Dummy variable (= 1) if any parent is on welfare, 0 otherwise	0.131	0.337	0.312	0.487
Seatbelt	Dummy variable (= 1) if wears seatbelt every time in a car, 0 otherwise	0.863	0.344	0.357	0.402
Tattoo	Dummy variable (= 1) if had a permanent tattoo, 0 otherwise	0.039	0.193	0.203	0.668
Piercing	Dummy variable (= 1) if has both ears pierced, 0 otherwise	0.541	0.498	0.254	0.341
No chance to live until 35[a]	Dummy variable (= 1) if the perceived chance of living until age 35 years is less than 50%, 0 otherwise	0.036	0.187	0.246	0.565
Good chance to live until 35	Dummy variable (= 1) if the perceived chance of living until age 35 years is more than 50%, 0 otherwise	0.871	0.336	0.404	0.823
Gut feeling – Yes[b]	Dummy variable (= 1) if agrees with the statement "I usually go with 'gut feeling' when making decisions without thinking too much about the consequences," 0 otherwise	0.403	0.491	0.600	0.755
Gut feeling – Neutral	Dummy variable (= 1) if neither agrees nor disagrees with the statement "I usually go with 'gut feeling' when making decisions without thinking too much about the consequences," 0 otherwise	0.212	0.409	0.539	0.405
Perceived IQ – Below average[c]	Dummy variable (= 1) if in comparison to other people of the same age, the perceived intelligence is below average, 0 otherwise	0.066	0.248	0.296	0.717
Perceived IQ – Average	Dummy variable (= 1) if in comparison to other people of the same age, the perceived intelligence is about average, 0 otherwise	0.393	0.488	0.523	1.092
GPA	Average GPA from math, science, history, and English classes	2.772	0.865	0.808	0.758
Chooses own friends	Dummy variable (= 1) if parents allow the respondent to decide with whom to hang around, 0 otherwise	0.853	0.354	0.447	

Table 1. (Continued)

	Definition	Wave I Cross Section Siblings and Twins		First Difference Siblings and Twins	First and Sibling Difference
		Mean	Standard deviation	Standard deviation	Standard deviation
Decides television time	Dummy variable (= 1) if parents allow respondent to decide how much television to watch, 0 otherwise	0.817	0.387	0.475	0.840
Decides own curfew on weekends	Dummy variable (= 1) if parents allow the respondent to decide about the time to be at home on weekend nights, 0 otherwise	0.317	0.465	0.546	0.985
Decides own curfew on weeknights	Dummy variable (= 1) if parents allow the respondent to decide about the time to be at home on weeknights, 0 otherwise	0.629	0.483	0.554	0.980
Height	Height in centimetres	168.378	10.600	4.715	6.177
Weight	Weight in kilogrammes	64.083	16.379	5.488	7.180
Alcohol available	Dummy variable (= 1) if alcohol is available at home, 0 otherwise	0.264	0.441	0.590	
Drugs available	Dummy variable (= 1) if illegal drugs are easily available at home, 0 otherwise	0.024	0.154	0.209	
		$n = 3,394$		$n = 3,039$	$n = 1,294$

[a] The omitted category is: Dummy variable (= 1) if the perceived chance of living until age 35 years is 50%, 0 otherwise.
[b] The omitted category is: Dummy variable (= 1) if disagrees with the statement "I usually go with 'gut feeling' when making decisions without thinking too much about the consequences," 0 otherwise.
[c] The omitted category is: Dummy variable (= 1) if in comparison to other people of the same age, the perceived intelligence is above average, 0 otherwise.

Table 2. The Impact of Drug Use on Crime: All Siblings (Including Twins).

	Without Measurement Error Correction				With Measurement Error Correction			
	Robbery	Burglary	Theft	Damage	Robbery	Burglary	Theft	Damage
First-Differenced Data								
Cocaine	0.146***	0.134***	0.140***	0.165***	0.115***	0.106***	0.111***	0.131***
	(0.047)	(0.040)	(0.052)	(0.053)	(0.037)	(0.032)	(0.042)	(0.042)
Inhale	0.168***	0.153***	0.191***	0.181***	0.133***	0.121***	0.152***	0.143***
	(0.036)	(0.033)	(0.043)	(0.042)	(0.029)	(0.026)	(0.034)	(0.033)
Other drugs	0.038	0.051*	0.079**	0.126***	0.024	0.032*	0.050**	0.080**
	(0.032)	(0.030)	(0.041)	(0.041)	(0.020)	(0.019)	(0.026)	(0.026)
Inject	0.199	0.331***	0.497***	0.312*	0.176	0.293***	0.440***	0.276*
	(0.158)	(0.114)	(0.111)	(0.161)	(0.139)	(0.101)	(0.097)	(0.142)
First-and-Sibling-Differenced Data								
Cocaine	0.142**	0.155***	0.154*	0.118	0.098**	0.107***	0.107*	0.082
	(0.062)	(0.058)	(0.086)	(0.086)	(0.043)	(0.04)	(0.06)	(0.06)
Inhale	0.128***	0.168***	0.210***	0.155**	0.094***	0.124***	0.155***	0.114**
	(0.041)	(0.043)	(0.065)	(0.063)	(0.03)	(0.032)	(0.048)	(0.046)
Other drugs	0.004	0.066	0.065	0.093	0.002	0.040	0.039	0.056
	(0.039)	(0.042)	(0.062)	(0.059)	(0.024)	(0.026)	(0.038)	(0.036)
Inject	0.403**	0.511***	0.754***	0.404**	0.357**	0.453***	0.669***	0.358**
	(0.159)	(0.151)	(0.135)	(0.163)	(0.141)	(0.134)	(0.120)	(0.145)

*, **, and *** indicate statistical significance at <10%, <5%, and <1% levels, respectively. Robust standard errors are in parentheses.
In the upper panel of the table, sample sizes range from 3,018 to 3,024 for robbery, burglary, from 3,015 to 3,021 for theft, and from 3,019 to 3,025 for damage. In the lower panel, sample sizes range from 1,304 to 1,307 for robbery, from 1,300 to 1,303 for burglary, from 1,304 to 1,307 for theft, and from 1,303 to 1,306 for damage. All regressions include 21 control variables as described in the text.

results significantly. In addition to drug use measures, the regressions include the following explanatory variables – seatbelt use, height, weight, grade point average (GPA), perceived IQ *below average*, perceived IQ *average*, welfare, alcohol at home, drugs at home, guns at home, allowance, tattoo, piercing, no chance to live until 35, good chance to live until 35, decides own curfew on weekends, decides own curfew on weeknights, decides television time, chooses own friends, gut feeling *yes*, and gut feeling *neutral*.

The bottom panel of Table 2 displays the results obtained from Eq. (4), which involves time differencing as well as sibling differencing. In this specification, variables pertaining to family attributes as well as the state dummies drop out as they do not vary between siblings. Both panels of

Table 2 display two sets of results. The left-hand side presents the results unadjusted for measurement error in drug use, where the right-hand side displays the results with measurement error adjustment. For each drug variable we used specific values of Φ obtained from the data.

As Table 2 demonstrates, drug use coefficients are positive and significantly different from zero in almost all cases in the top panel, and a similar picture emerges in the bottom panel, with the exception of the impact of *other drugs*.[15] We estimated all models with the inclusion of an additional variable which controls for the age difference between the siblings. The results remained the same.

Table 3 presents the results for twins. As in Table 2, the upper panel displays the results of the fixed-effects model (Eq. (3)), while the lower panel contains the results obtained from time and within-twin differencing.[16] We do not analyse injection because of the very small number of twins who injected drugs. To the extent that individual unobserved time-varying heterogeneity is the same between twins, this specification is represented by Eq. (5). Although the sample size goes down to about 450 in case of twins, drug use coefficients remain significant in many cases, even in models with time and twin differencing. For example, in the lower panel, cocaine consumption impacts theft and damage. The use of other types of drugs influences burglary, theft, and damage.

Table 4 displays the results for identical twins. Although there are only 400 observations in the fixed-effects model (top panel), with the exception of theft, we observe statistically significant associations between crime and drug measures. For example, robberies are influenced by using cocaine and inhalants, burglaries are influenced by inhalants, and damage is influenced by using inhalants and other drugs. In the lower panel where the results of fixed-effects and within-twin differences are reported, the sample size goes down to 176, and therefore, the coefficients are not estimated with precision.

The results in Tables 2–4 demonstrate the positive impact of drug use on crime. Although the precision of the estimated coefficients goes down as the sample gets smaller, the point estimates of individual drug variables are stable across specifications. We calculated the median point estimate for each drug category across crime types. In models with first differences, the median impact on crime of using cocaine is 11 percentage points. The impact of using inhalants is 13 percentage points. The median impacts on crime of other drugs and injecting drugs are 5 and 28 percentage points, respectively. In double-differenced models the median impacts are 11 percentage points for cocaine, 7 percentage points for inhalants, 7 percentage points for other drugs, and 41 percentage points for injection.

Table 3. The Impact of Drug Use on Crime: All Twins.

	Without Measurement Error Correction				With Measurement Error Correction			
	Robbery	Burglary	Theft	Damage	Robbery	Burglary	Theft	Damage
First-Differenced Data								
Cocaine	0.173*	0.111*	0.116	0.176**	0.131*	0.084*	0.088	0.133**
	(0.094)	(0.063)	(0.095)	(0.083)	(0.071)	(0.048)	(0.072)	(0.063)
Inhale	0.224***	0.146***	0.175**	0.237***	0.174***	0.113***	0.136**	0.183***
	(0.072)	(0.055)	(0.087)	(0.075)	(0.056)	(0.042)	(0.067)	(0.058)
Other drugs	0.110**	0.054	0.088	0.168**	0.065**	0.032	0.052	0.099**
	(0.057)	(0.044)	(0.066)	(0.070)	(0.034)	(0.026)	(0.039)	(0.042)
First-and-Twin–Differenced Data								
Cocaine	0.183	0.088	0.268**	0.278*	0.119	0.057	0.175**	0.181*
	(0.111)	(0.109)	(0.128)	(0.149)	(0.072)	(0.071)	(0.084)	(0.097)
Inhale	0.078	0.118	0.168	0.081	0.058	0.087	0.124	0.060
	(0.079)	(0.086)	(0.124)	(0.097)	(0.058)	(0.064)	(0.092)	(0.072)
Other drugs	0.082	0.121*	0.174*	0.258***	0.049	0.073*	0.105*	0.155***
	(0.068)	(0.063)	(0.098)	(0.09)	(0.041)	(0.038)	(0.059)	(0.054)

*, **, and *** indicate statistical significance at <10%, <5%, and <1% levels, respectively. Robust standard errors are in parentheses.
In the upper panel of the table, sample sizes are 1,023 or 1,024 for robbery and burglary, 1,022 or 1,023 for theft, and 1,024 or 1,025 for damage. In the lower panel, sample sizes are 452 or 453 for robbery and burglary, 453 or 454 for theft and damage. All regressions include 21 control variables as described in the text.

The results for injection should be taken with caution because of the small number of users in this case.

5.1. Undifferenced Estimates

To investigate the impact of unobserved heterogeneity, we estimated models using cross-sectional data from Wave I. We added a number of additional variables that could not be included in the first- and first-and-sibling-differenced models. These are time-invariant characteristics of the child and the parents, such as child's race, religious affiliation, gender, whether the child is born in the U.S.A., and parent education. We estimated these cross-sectional models with all siblings and twins. We also estimated them using all available observations (all children). The estimates for drug use variables were always positive and 4 to 7 percentage points larger than the ones obtained from first- and first-and-twin-differenced models reported earlier.

Table 4. The Impact of Drug Use on Crime: Identical Twins.

	Without Measurement Error Correction				With Measurement Error Correction			
	Robbery	Burglary	Theft	Damage	Robbery	Burglary	Theft	Damage
First-Differenced Data								
Cocaine	0.418***	0.108	0.055	0.121	0.331***	0.086	0.044	0.096
	(0.123)	(0.107)	(0.181)	(0.127)	(0.098)	(0.085)	(0.144)	(0.101)
Inhale	0.337***	0.167*	0.111	0.280**	0.229***	0.114*	0.076	0.190**
	(0.113)	(0.095)	(0.131)	(0.138)	(0.077)	(0.064)	(0.089)	(0.094)
Other drugs	0.095	0.072	0.016	0.208**	0.059	0.044	0.009	0.128**
	(0.103)	(0.072)	(0.120)	(0.105)	(0.064)	(0.043)	(0.074)	(0.065)
First-and-Twin-Differenced Data								
Cocaine	0.219	0.001	0.219	−0.195	0.16	0.000	0.16	−0.143
	(0.149)	(0.230)	(0.144)	(0.149)	(0.109)	(0.168)	(0.105)	(0.109)
Inhale	0.043	0.080	−0.105	−0.251	0.027	0.050	−0.065	−0.156
	(0.113)	(0.183)	(0.172)	(0.177)	(0.07)	(0.113)	(0.107)	(0.110)
Other drugs	0.043	0.138	0.173	0.249***	0.025	0.080	0.100	0.144***
	(0.088)	(0.1000)	(0.155)	(0.088)	(0.051)	(0.058)	(0.09)	(0.051)

*, **, and *** indicate statistical significance at <10%, <5%, and <1% levels, respectively. Robust standard errors are in parentheses.
Sample size is 397 in the upper panel models and 176 in the lower panel models. All regressions include 21 control variables as described in the text.

This suggests that unobserved propensity to commit crime, which cannot be controlled for in cross-sectional regressions, tends to be positively correlated with drug use.

5.2. Reverse Causality

Although taking first and sibling (or twin) differences eliminates unobserved heterogeneity that would otherwise have been included in the error terms, it can still be argued that drug use may be influenced by reverse causality from property crimes if committing these crimes is associated with increased income. To account for this potential reverse causality, we considered a reduced-form drug use equation, where the instruments that impact the drug use of the juvenile include the following variables – whether at least one of the three best friends smokes at least one cigarette a day, whether at least one of the three best friends drinks alcohol at least once a month, and whether at least one of the three best friends uses marijuana at least once a month. While it can plausibly be argued that friends' consumption of cigarette, alcohol, and marijuana may be correlated with own drug use, it is less obvious that these instruments are uncorrelated with own criminal activity. Unfortunately no better instruments are available. State- or county-level alcohol and drug prices are not viable candidates to identify the effect of drug use as they do not vary between siblings and twins. School-based policy variables are not useful either, because all twins and most siblings attend the same school.[17] Estimation of the double-differenced crime and double-differenced reduced-form drug use equations with full information maximum likelihood revealed that although the magnitudes of the estimated drug use coefficients are similar to those reported in Tables 2–4, most coefficients are not estimated with precision. The imprecision of the estimated coefficients is most likely due to weak instruments, but the data set does not include better instrument candidates. (The explicit specification is reported in Appendix B.)

In Table B1 in Appendix B, we report the coefficients for inhale and inject for siblings, twins, and identical twins. These are the drugs that created the most precise estimates. For siblings, the use of inhalants has a positive impact on burglary, theft, and damage. Injection has an impact on robbery and burglary. In case of all twins, injection has an impact on theft, and in the sample of identical twins injection influences burglary and theft.

6. CONCLUSION

The causal effect of drug use on crime has not yet been credibly established due to statistical difficulties. The propensity to use drugs may be correlated with unobserved attributes and characteristics of the individual. If these attributes, such as risk aversion or intelligence, have an influence on criminal activity, then estimates of drug use on crime are biased because of this confounding.

In this chapter we employ the Add Health data, which is a nationally representative panel data set of high school students in the U.S.A. that contains an oversample of siblings and twins. In addition to an unusually large number of interesting variables that aim to gauge personal characteristics, family background and family supervision, the data set contains detailed information about drug use and criminal activity of the juveniles. In particular, consumption of cocaine, injecting drugs, using inhalants, and using other drugs are measured. The crimes we analyse are robberies, burglaries, and thefts committed by juveniles and whether they damaged property.

The variation of drug use between siblings and twins allows us to exploit within-sibling differences of the first-differenced data. This enables us to filter out time-varying unobservables that are common to each household (therefore to each sibling). In addition, taking the twin differences of the first-differenced data enables us to eliminate the genetic component of criminal activity common to both twins. We adjust for measurement error in drug use with an algorithm that allows for non-symmetric measurement error.

The results indicate that drug use increases the propensity to commit crime. The median impact of injecting drugs on the probability of committing robbery, burglary and theft, and creating property damage is 41 percentage points, although this result should be taken with caution because it is based on small number of individuals who inject drugs. The median impact of cocaine is an increased criminal propensity of 11 percentage points. The use of inhalants generates a (median) 7 percentage point increase in the propensity to commit crime; and other drugs increase the propensity to commit crime by 6 percentage points.

NOTES

1. A few papers analysed micro-data in related context. Markowitz (2000) investigated the impact of alcohol and drug prices on violent crime using the National Crime Victimization Survey, Jofre-Bonet and Sindelar (2002) analysed the impact of drug treatment on criminal behaviour.
2. Theoretical justification of the inclusion of drug use in the crime equation can be found, among others, in Ehrlich (1973).
3. Empirical evidence from aggregate data on the impact on crime of deterrence, economic conditions and drug use can be found, among others, in Corman and Mocan (2002), Corman and Mocan (2000), Levitt (1998b, 1999), and Raphael and Winter-Ebmer (2001).
4. For a more detailed discussion, see Mocan and Corman (1998).
5. Note that this procedure also eliminates time-varying economic and deterrence measures as they do not exhibit variation between the individuals in the same household. Subjective probabilities of apprehension and conviction may differ between siblings. However, to the extent that they are approximated by such measures as arrest and conviction rates in the locality, they do not vary.
6. The reliability ratio is the proportion of individuals who are confirmed to have provided correct information about their drug use. Confirmation is typically based on drug tests.
7. Variations in the reporting rate did not change the results in a meaningful way.
8. It is assumed that $\nabla \Delta DR$ and ΔDR are uncorrelated with other covariates, which is supported by the data. Other covariates are assumed to contain no measurement error.

9. The Add Health project is a programme project designed by J. Richard Udry (PI) and Peter Bearman, and funded by grant P01-HD31921 from the National Institute of Child Health and Human Development to the Carolina Population Center, University of North Carolina at Chapel Hill, with cooperative funding participation by the National Cancer Institute; the National Institute of Alcohol Abuse and Alcoholism; the National Institute on Deafness and Other Communication Disorders; the National Institute on Drug Abuse; the National Institute of General Medical Sciences; the National Institute of Mental Health; the National Institute of Nursing Research; the Office of AIDS Research, NIH; the Office of Behaviour and Social Science Research, NIH; the Office of the Director, NIH; the Office of Research on Women's Health, NIH; the Office of Population Affairs, DHHS; the National Center for Health Statistics, Centers for Disease Control and Prevention, DHHS; the Office of Minority Health, Centers for Disease Control and Prevention, DHHS; the Office of Minority Health, Office of Public Health and Science, DHHS; the Office of the Assistant Secretary for Planning and Evaluation, DHHS; and the National Science Foundation. Persons interested in obtaining data files from The National Longitudinal Study of Adolescent Health should contact Add Health Project, Carolina Population Center, 123 West Franklin Street, Chapel Hill, NC 27516-2524, U.S.A. (e-mail: addhealth@unc.edu).

10. Participating high schools were asked to identify junior high or middle schools that were expected to provide at least five students to the entering class of the high school. These schools are called feeder schools. Their probability of selection was proportional to the percentage of the high school's entering class that came from that feeder.

11. The sample for the Wave II in-home interview was composed of the respondents of the Wave I in-home interview with the following exceptions: A respondent who was in the 12th grade in Wave I and who was not part of the genetic sample was not interviewed in Wave II. Respondents who were only in Wave I's disabled sample were not re-interviewed.

12. The proportion of twins in total births has been rising steadily over the last two decades. When most of the adolescents of the sample were born around 1980, twin births were about 2 percent of total births (*National Vital Statistics Report*, 1999).

13. For less sensitive questions, the interviewer read the questions aloud, and entered the respondent's answers.

14. Questions in Wave II are worded as "Since the last interview...". Therefore, the change in behaviour between the two waves is easily identifiable.

15. Note that the relative sample size of the first- and first-and-sibling-differenced data depends on the number of siblings in households. For example, if a household consists of two siblings, the first-differenced (time-differenced) data will contain two observations, and the first-and-sibling-differenced data will contain one observation. On the other hand, if the household consists of three siblings A, B, and C, the first-differenced data will contain three observations, and the first-and-sibling-differenced data will also contain three observations (it will consist of $\Delta A - \Delta B$, $\Delta A - \Delta C$, and $\Delta B - \Delta C$, where ΔA is a first-differenced variable of sibling A). In case of a household with four siblings, the first-differenced data have four observations and first-and-sibling-differenced data have six observations.

16. The sample size of the first-and-twin-differenced data is not half of the first-differenced twin sample because of missing values in some variables.

17. Grossman, Kaestner, and Markowitz (2002) highlight the same point in their analysis of drug use on teenage sexual activity.

ACKNOWLEDGEMENTS

We thank Kaj Gittings and Norovsambuu Tumennasan for excellent research assistance, and David Blau, Phil Cook, John Donohue, Mike Grossman, Robert Kaestner, Francis Kramarz, Steve Levitt, Donna Stubbs, Jens Ludwig, participants of the *2003 European Summer symposium in labour economics, Spring 2004 NBER children's program meeting, 2004 society of labor economics meetings*, and *24th Arne Ryde symposium on economics of substance abuse*, and especially Karen Kafadar for helpful suggestions.

REFERENCES

Almond, D., Chay, K. Y., & Lee, D. S. (2002). *Does low birth weight matter? Evidence from the U.S. population of twin births*. Center for Labor Economics Working Paper no. 53. University of California, Berkeley.

Ashenfelter, O., & Krueger, A. (1994). Estimates of the economic returns to schooling from a new sample of twins. *American Economic Review, 84*(5), 1157–1173.

Ashenfelter, O., & Zimmerman, D. J. (1997). Estimates of the returns to schooling from sibling data: Fathers, sons, and brothers. *The Review of Economics and Statistics, 79*(1), 1–9.

Behrman, J. R., Rosenzweig, M. R., & Taubman, P. (1994). Endowments and the allocation of schooling in the family and in the marriage market: The twins experiment. *The Journal of Political Economy, 102*(6), 1131–1174.

Behrman, J. R., Rosenzweig, M. R., & Taubman, P. (1996). College choice and wages: Estimates using data on female twins. *The Review of Economics and Statistics, 78*(1), 672–685.

Chaiken, J. M., & Chaiken, M. R. (1990). Drugs and predatory crime. In: M. Tonry & J. Q. Wilson (Eds), *Drug and crime*. Chicago: University of Chicago Press.

Cook, P., & Ludwig, J. (2002). *The effects of gun prevalence on burglary: Deterrence vs. inducement*. NBER Working Paper no. 8926.

Corman, H., & Mocan, H. N. (2000). A time-series analysis of crime, deterrence, and drug abuse in New York city. *American Economic Review, 90*(3), 584–604.

Corman, H., & Mocan, H. N. (2002). *Carrots, sticks and broken windows*. NBER Working Paper no. W9061.

Currie, J., & Moretti, E. (2003). Mother's education and the intergenerational transmission of human capital: Evidence from college openings. *Quarterly Journal of Economics, 188*(4), 1495–1532.

Ehrlich, I. (1973). Participation in illegitimate activities: A theoretical and empirical investigation. *Journal of Political Economy, 81*(3), 521–565.

Goldstein, P. (1985). The drugs/violence nexus: A tripartite conceptual framework. *Journal of Drug Issues, 15*(4), 493–506.
Griliches, Z., & Hausman, J. (1985). Errors in variables in panel data. *Journal of Econometrics, 31*, 93–118.
Grogger, J., & Willis, M. (2000). The emergence of crack cocaine and the rise in urban crime rates. *The Review of Economics and Statistics, 82*(4), 519–529.
Grossman, M., Kaestner, R., & Markowitz, S. (2002). *Get high and get stupid: The effect of alcohol and marijuana use on teen sexual behavior.* NBER Working Paper no. 9216.
Gruber, J. (Ed.) (2001). *Risky behavior among youths.* Chicago and London: University of Chicago Press.
Harrison, L. D. (1992). The drug–crime nexus in the USA. *Contemporary Drug Problems, 19*(2), 203–246.
Jofre-Bonet, M., & Sindelar, J. L. (2002). *Drug treatment as a crime fighting tool.* NBER Working Paper no. W9038.
Johnson, M. E., Fisher, D. G., et al. (2000). Reliability and validity of not-in-treatment drug users' follow-up self-reports. *Aids and Behavior, 4*(4), 373–380.
Levitt, S. D. (1998a). Why do increased crime arrest rates appear to reduce crime: Deterrence, incapacitation, or measurement error? *Economic Inquiry, 36*(3), 353–372.
Levitt, S. D. (1998b). Juvenile crime and punishment. *Journal of Political Economy, 106*(6), 1156–1185.
Levitt, S. D. (1999). The effect of prison population size on crime rates: Evidence from prison overcrowding litigation. *The Quarterly Journal of Economics, 111*(2), 319–351.
Markowitz, S. (2000). *An economic analysis of alcohol, drugs, and violent crime in the National Crime Victimization Survey.* NBER Working Paper no. W7982.
Miller, P., Mulvey, C., & Martin, N. (1995). What do twins studies reveal about the economic returns to education? A comparison of australian U.S. findings. *American Economic Review, 85*(3), 586–599.
Mocan, N. H., & Corman, H. (1998). An economic analysis of drug use and crime. *Journal of Drug Issues, 28*(3), 613–629.
Mocan, N. H., & Rees, D. (2005). Economic conditions, deterrence, and juvenile crime: Evidence from micro data. *American Journal of Law and Economics, 7*(2).
National Vital Statistics Report. (1999). Vol. 47, No. 24. National Center for Health Statistics, Hyattsville, Maryland.
Raphael, S., & Winter-Ebmer, W. (2001). Identifying the effect of unemployment on crime. *The Journal of Law and Economics, 44*, 259–283.
Weiss, R. D., Najavits, L. M., et al. (1998). Validity of substance use self-reports in dually diagnosed outpatients. *American Journal of Psychiatry, 155*(1), 127–128.
Grossman, M., Kaestner, R., & Markowitz, S. (2002). *Get high and get stupid: The effect of alcohol and marijuana use on teen sexual behavior.* NBER Working Paper no. 9216.
Hu, W. Y. (1999). Child support, welfare delinquency, and woman's labor supply. *Journal of Human Resources, 34*(1), 71–103.
Mocan, N. H., & Tekin, E. (2003). Nonprofit sector and part-time work: An analysis of employer–employee matched data of child care workers. *Review of Economics and Statistics, 85*(1), 38–50.
Mocan, N. H., Tekin, E., & Zax, J. S. (2004). The demand for medical care in urban China. *World Development, 32*(2), 289–304.

APPENDIX A

General Framework

$DR_{it} = DR^*_{it} + v_{it}$, where DR^*_{it} is the actual drug use (0 = No, 1 = Yes) and DR_{it} is the reported drug use (0 = No, 1 = Yes).

Let probability distribution of v_{it} be:

$$\text{Prob}(DR_{it} = 1, DR^*_{it} = 1) = p_1$$

$$\text{Prob}(DR_{it} = 1, DR^*_{it} = 0) = 0$$

$$\text{Prob}(DR_{it} = 0, DR^*_{it} = 0) = p_2$$

$$\text{Prob}(DR_{it} = 0, DR^*_{it} = 1) = q$$

In other words:

DR_{it}	DR^*_{it}	v_{it}	$\text{Prob}(v_{it})$
1	1	0	p_1
1	0	1	0
0	0	0	p_2
0	1	−1	Q

$$p_1 + p_2 + q = 1$$

$$E(v) = -q$$

$$E(DR^*) = 1 - p_2$$

$$\text{var}(v) = q - q^2$$

$$\text{var}(DR^*) = p_2 - p_2^2$$

$$\text{cov}(v, DR^*) = -p_2 q$$

$$\text{var}(DR) = p_1 - p_1^2$$

Probability Limit of the Coefficient of Drug Use in First-Differenced Data
The probability limit is:

$$p \lim \hat{\beta} = \beta \frac{\text{var}(\Delta DR^*_t) + \text{cov}(\Delta v_t, \Delta DR^*_t)}{\text{var}(\Delta DR_t)}$$

Drugs and Juvenile Crime

Note that by definition:
$$\text{var}[\Delta DR_t^*] = \text{var}[\Delta DR_t] - \text{var}[\Delta v_t] - 2\text{cov}[\Delta DR_t^*, \Delta v_t]$$

Thus:
$$\text{cov}(\Delta DR_t^*, \Delta v_t) = \frac{1}{2}\text{var}(\Delta DR_t) - \frac{1}{2}\text{var}(\Delta v_t) - \frac{1}{2}\text{var}(\Delta DR_t^*)$$

Substitution for $\text{cov}(\Delta DR^*, \Delta v)$ provides:
$$p\lim \hat{\beta} = \beta \frac{0.5[\text{var}(\Delta DR_t) + \text{var}(\Delta DR_t^*) - \text{var}(\Delta v_t)]}{\text{var}(\Delta DR_t)}$$

Note that:
$$\text{var}(\Delta DR_t) = \text{var}(DR_t - DR_{t-1}) = \text{var}(DR_t) + \text{var}(DR_{t-1}) - 2\text{cov}(DR_t, DR_{t-1})$$

Assuming that DR is covariance stationary, that is:
$$\text{var}(DR_t) = \text{var}(DR_{t-1})$$
$$\text{var}(\Delta DR_t) = 2\sigma_{DR}^2(1 - \rho_{DR_t, DR_{t-1}})$$

where $\sigma_{DR}^2 = \text{var}(DR_t)$.
Similarly:
$$\text{var}(\Delta DR_t^*) = 2\sigma_{DR^*}^2(1 - \rho_{DR_t^*, DR_{t-1}^*}) \quad \text{and} \quad \text{var}(\Delta v_t) = 2\sigma_v^2(1 - \rho_{v_t, v_{t-1}})$$

where $\sigma_v^2 = \text{var}(v_t)$ and $\sigma_{DR^*}^2 = \text{var}(DR_t^*)$.

Substituting the variances of DR, DR^* and v into the probability limit formula, one obtains:

$$p\lim \hat{\beta} = \beta \frac{0.5[2\sigma_{DR}^2(1 - \rho_{DR_t, DR_{t-1}}) + 2\sigma_{DR^*}^2(1 - \rho_{DR_t^*, DR_{t-1}^*}) 2\sigma_v^2(1 - \rho_{v_t, v_{t-1}})]}{2\sigma_{DR}^2(1 - \rho_{DR_t, DR_{t-1}})} \tag{A1}$$

Note that:
$$\text{cov}(DR_t, DR_{t-1}) = \text{cov}(DR_t^* + v_t, DR_{t-1}^* + v_{t-1})$$
$$= \text{cov}(DR_t, DR_{t-1}) = \text{cov}(DR_t^*, DR_{t-1}^*) + \text{cov}(DR_{t-1}^*, v_t)$$
$$+ \text{cov}(DR_t^*, v_{t-1}) + \text{cov}(v_t, v_{t-1}) \tag{A2}$$

Also:
$$\text{cov}(DR_t, DR_{t-1}) = \rho_{DR_t, DR_{t-1}}\sigma_{DR}^2$$
$$\text{cov}(DR_t^*, DR_{t-1}^*) = \rho_{DR_t^*, DR_{t-1}^*}\sigma_{DR^*}^2$$
$$\text{cov}(v_t, v_{t-1}) = \rho_{v_t, v_{t-1}}\sigma_v^2$$

Therefore, one can rewrite Eq. (A2) as:
$$\rho_{DR_t,DR_{t-1}}\sigma^2_{DR} = \rho_{DR^*_t,DR^*_{t-1}}\sigma^2_{DR^*} + \rho_{v_t,v_{t-1}}\sigma^2_v + \text{cov}(DR^*_{t-1},v_t) + \text{cov}(DR^*_t,v_{t-1})$$

As:
$$\text{cov}(DR^*_{t-1},v_t) = \text{cov}(DR^*_{t-1},DR_t - DR^*_t) = \text{cov}(DR^*_{t-1},DR_t) - \text{cov}(DR^*_{t-1},DR^*_t)$$

Assuming $\text{cov}(DR^*_{t-1},DR_t) = 0$, one obtains:
$$\text{cov}(DR^*_{t-1},v_t) = -\rho_{DR^*_t,DR^*_{t-1}}\sigma^2_{DR^*}$$

Similarly:
$$\text{cov}(DR^*_t,v_{t-1} \;\text{cov}(DR^*_t,DR_{t-1} - DR^*_{t-1}) = \text{cov}(DR^*_t,DR_{t-1}) - \text{cov}(DR^*_t,DR^*_{t-1})$$

Assuming $\text{cov}(DR^*_t,DR_{t-1}) = 0$, one gets:
$$\text{cov}(DR^*_t,v_{t-1}) = -\rho_{DR^*_t,DR^*_{t-1}}\sigma^2_{DR^*}$$

Therefore, Eq. (A2) is equivalent to:
$$\rho_{DR_t,DR_{t-1}}\sigma^2_{DR} = \rho_{DR^*_t,DR^*_{t-1}}\sigma^2_{DR^*} + \rho_{v_t,v_{t-1}}\sigma^2_v - \rho_{DR^*_t,DR^*_{t-1}}\sigma^2_{DR^*} - \rho_{DR^*_t,DR^*_{t-1}}\sigma^2_{DR^*}$$

$$\rho_{DR_t,DR_{t-1}}\sigma^2_{DR} = \rho_{v_t,v_{t-1}}\sigma^2_v - \rho_{DR^*_t,DR^*_{t-1}}\sigma^2_{DR^*}$$

Solving for $\rho_{v_t,v_{t-1}}$ yields:
$$\rho_{v_t,v_{t-1}} = \frac{\rho_{DR_t,DR_{t-1}}\sigma^2_{DR} + \rho_{DR^*_t,DR^*_{t-1}}\sigma^2_{DR^*}}{\sigma^2_v} \tag{A3}$$

Substitution of Eq. (A3) into Eq. (A1) gives:
$$p\lim \hat{\beta} = \beta \frac{0.5\left[2\sigma^2_{DR}(1 - \rho_{DR_t,DR_{t-1}}) + 2\sigma^2_{DR^*}(1 - \rho_{DR^*_t,DR^*_{t-1}}) - 2\sigma^2_v\left(1 - \frac{\rho_{DR_t,DR_{t-1}}\sigma^2_{DR} + \rho_{DR^*_t,DR^*_{t-1}}\sigma^2_{DR^*}}{\sigma^2_v}\right)\right]}{2\sigma^2_{DR}(1 - \rho_{DR_t,DR_{t-1}})}$$

Simplification yields:
$$p\lim \hat{\beta} = \beta \frac{\sigma^2_{DR} + \sigma^2_{DR^*} - \sigma^2_v}{2\sigma^2_{DR}(1 - \rho_{DR_t,DR_{t-1}})} = \frac{p_1 p_2}{(p_1 - p_1^2)(1 - \rho_{DR_t,DR_{t-1}})}$$

Drugs and Juvenile Crime 115

Therefore:
$$p \lim \hat{\beta} = \beta \frac{p_1 p_2}{(p_1 - p_1^2)(1 - \rho_{DR_t, DR_{t-1}})}$$

Probability Limit of the Coefficient of Drug Use in Double-Differenced Data

The probability limit is:
$$p \lim \hat{\beta} = \beta \frac{\text{var}(\nabla \Delta DR_{jit}^*) + \text{cov}(\nabla \Delta v_{jit}, \nabla \Delta DR_{jit}^*)}{\text{var}(\nabla \Delta DR_{jit})}$$

By definition:
$$\text{var}(\nabla \Delta DR_{jit}^*) = \text{var}(\nabla \Delta DR_{jit}) - \text{var}(\nabla \Delta v_{jit}) - 2\text{cov}(\nabla \Delta DR_{jit}^*, \nabla \Delta v_{jit})$$

Therefore:
$$\text{cov}(\nabla \Delta DR_{jit}^*, \nabla \Delta v_{jit}) = \frac{1}{2} \text{var}(\nabla \Delta DR_{jit}) - \frac{1}{2} \text{var}(\nabla \Delta v_{jit}) - \frac{1}{2} \text{var}(\nabla \Delta DR_{jit}^*)$$

and
$$p \lim \hat{\beta} = \beta \frac{0.5[\text{var}(\nabla \Delta DR_{jit}) + \text{var}(\nabla \Delta DR_{jit}^*) - \text{var}(\nabla \Delta v_{jit})]}{\text{var}(\nabla \Delta DR_{jit})} \quad (A4)$$

Note that:
$$\text{var}(\nabla \Delta DR_{jit}) = \text{var}(DR_{j2t} - DR_{j2t-1} - DR_{j1t} + DR_{j1t-1})$$
$$= \text{var}(DR_{j2t}) + \text{var}(DR_{j2t-1}) + \text{var}(DR_{j1t}) + \text{var}(DR_{j1t-1})$$
$$- 2\text{cov}(DR_{j2t}, DR_{j2t-1}) - 2\text{cov}(DR_{j2t}, DR_{j1t})$$
$$+ 2\text{cov}(DR_{j2t}, DR_{j1t-1}) + 2\text{cov}(DR_{j2t-1}, DR_{j1t})$$
$$- 2\text{cov}(DR_{j2t-1}, DR_{j1t-1}) - 2\text{cov}(DR_{j1t}, DR_{j1t-1})$$

where the subscripts 1 and 2 represent the first and the second individuals in sibling (twin) pair j, and $t-1$ and t represent the first and the second time periods. Suppressing j for ease of notation, we can rewrite the above equation as follows:
$$\text{var}(\nabla \Delta DR_{it}) = 4\sigma_{DR}^2 - 2\rho_{DR_{2t}, DR_{2t-1}}\sigma_{DR}^2 - 2\rho_{DR_{2t}, DR_{1t}}\sigma_{DR}^2$$
$$+ 2\rho_{DR_{2t}, DR_{1t-1}}\sigma_{DR}^2 + 2\rho_{DR_{2t-1}, DR_{1t}}\sigma_{DR}^2$$
$$- 2\rho_{DR_{2t-1}, DR_{1t-1}}\sigma_{DR}^2 - 2\rho_{DR_{1t}, DR_{1t-1}}\sigma_{DR}^2$$

Assuming constant variances of drug use between siblings and over time, one obtains:
$$\text{var}(\nabla \Delta DR_{it}) = \sigma_{DR}^2(\Phi + 4)$$

where

$$\Phi = -2\rho_{DR_{2t},DR_{2t-1}} - 2\rho_{DR_{2t},DR_{1t}} + 2\rho_{DR_{2t},DR_{1t-1}} + 2\rho_{DR_{2t-1},DR_{1t}} - 2\rho_{DR_{2t-1},DR_{1t-1}} \\ - 2\rho_{DR_{1t},DR_{1t-1}} \tag{A5}$$

Similarly:

$$\text{var}(\nabla\Delta DR^*_{it}) = \sigma^2_{DR^*}(\Psi + 4)$$

where

$$\Psi = -2\rho_{DR^*_{2t},DR^*_{2t-1}} - 2\rho_{DR^*_{2t},DR^*_{1t}} + 2\rho_{DR^*_{2t},DR^*_{1t-1}} + 2\rho_{DR^*_{2t-1},DR^*_{1t}} - 2\rho_{DR^*_{2t-1},DR^*_{1t-1}} \\ - 2\rho_{DR^*_{1t},DR^*_{1t-1}}$$

and,

$$\text{var}(\nabla\Delta v_{it}) = \sigma^2_v(\Omega + 4)$$

where

$$\Omega = -2\rho_{v_{2t},v_{2t-1}} - 2\rho_{v_{2t},v_{1t}} + 2\rho_{v_{2t},v_{1t-1}} + 2\rho_{v_{2t-1},v_{1t}} - 2\rho_{v_{2t-1},v_{1t-1}} - 2\rho_{v_{1t},v_{1t-1}}$$

Substituting the expressions for the variances in Eq. (A4) gives:

$$p\lim \hat{\beta} = \beta \frac{\text{var}(DR^*_{it})(4 + \Psi) + \frac{1}{2}(\text{var}(DR_{it})(4 + \Phi) - \text{var}(v_{it})(4 + \Omega) - \text{var}(DR^*_{it})(4 + \Psi))}{(4 + \Phi)\text{var}(DR_{it})}$$

$$p\lim \hat{\beta} = \beta \frac{1}{2} \frac{(\text{var}(DR_{it})(4 + \Phi) - \text{var}(v_{it})(4 + \Omega) + \text{var}(DR^*_{it})(4 + \Psi))}{\text{var}(DR_{it})(4 + \Phi)}$$

Note that:

$$\text{cov}(DR_{1t}, DR_{2t-1}) = \text{cov}(DR^*_{1t} + v_{1t}, DR^*_{2t-1} + v_{2t-1})$$

$$\text{cov}(DR_{1t}, DR_{2t-1}) = \text{cov}(DR^*_{1t}, DR^*_{1t}) + \text{cov}(DR^*_{1t}, v_{1t}) + \text{cov}(v_{2t-1}, DR^*_{2t-1}) \\ + \text{cov}(v_{2t-1}, v_{2t-1})$$

As

$$\text{cov}(DR_{1t}, DR_{2t-1}) = \rho_{DR_{1t},DR_{2t-1}}\sigma^2_{DR}$$

$$\text{cov}(DR^*_{1t}, DR^*_{2t-1}) = \rho_{DR^*_{1t},DR^*_{2t-1}}\sigma^2_{DR^*}$$

$$\text{cov}(v_{1t}, v_{2t-1}) = \rho_{1t,v_{2t-1s}}\sigma^2_v$$

we obtain

$$\text{cov}(DR_{1t}, DR_{2t-1}) = \rho_{DR_{1t},DR_{2t-1}}\sigma^2_{DR} = \rho_{DR^*_{1t},DR^*_{2t-1}}\sigma^2_{DR^*} + \rho_{v_{1t},v_{2t-1}}\sigma^2_v$$
$$+ \text{cov}(DR^*_{1t}, v_{2t-1}) + \text{cov}(v_{1t}, DR^*_{2t-1}) \quad (A6)$$

The third term in Eq. (A6) is:

$$\text{cov}(DR^*_{1t}, v_{2t-1}) = \text{cov}(DR^*_{1t}, DR_{2t-1} - DR^*_{2t-1})$$
$$= \text{cov}(DR^*_{1t}, DR_{2t-1}) - \text{cov}(DR^*_{1t}, DR^*_{2t-1})$$

Assuming $\text{cov}(DR^*_{1t}, DR_{2t-1}) = 0$, we obtain:

$$\text{cov}(DR^*_{1t}, v_{2t-1}) = -\text{cov}(DR^*_{1t}, DR^*_{2t-1}) = -\rho_{DR^*_{1t},DR^*_{2t-1}}\sigma^2_{DR^*} \quad (A7)$$

The fourth term in Eq. (A6) is:

$$\text{cov}(v_{1t}, DR^*_{2t-1}) = \text{cov}(DR_{1t} - DR^*_{1t}, DR^*_{2t-1})$$
$$= \text{cov}(DR_{1t}, DR^*_{2t-1}) - \text{cov}(DR^*_{1t}, DR^*_{2t-1})$$

Again, assuming $\text{cov}(DR_{1t}, DR^*_{2t-1}) = 0$, we obtain:

$$\text{cov}(v_{1t}, DR^*_{2t-1}) = -\text{cov}(DR^*_{1t}, DR^*_{2t-1}) = -\rho_{DR^*_{1t},DR^*_{2t-1}}\sigma^2_{DR^*} \quad (A8)$$

Substituting Eqs. (A7) and (A8) into Eq. (A6), one obtains:

$$\rho_{DR_{1t},DR_{2t-1}}\sigma^2_{DR} = -\rho_{DR^*_{1t},DR^*_{2t-1}}\sigma^2_{DR^*} + \rho_{v1,v_{2t-1}}\sigma^2_v$$

or

$$\rho_{DR_{1t},DR_{2t-1}} = \frac{-\rho_{DR^*_{1t},DR_{2t-1}}\sigma^2_{DR^*} + \rho_{v_{1t},v_{2t-1}}\sigma^2_v}{\sigma^2_{DR}}$$

One can obtain similar expressions for:

$$\rho_{DR_{2t},DR_{1t}}, \quad \rho_{DR_{2t},DR_{1t-1}} \rho_{DR_{2t-1},DR_{1t}}, \quad \rho_{DR_{2t-1},DR_{1t-1}}, \quad \rho_{DR_{1t},DR_{1t-1}}$$

Substituting each of these correlation coefficients into Eq. (A5) one obtains

$$\Phi = \frac{\sigma^2_v \Omega - \sigma^2_{DR^*}\Psi}{\sigma^2_{DR}}$$

$$\Omega = \frac{\sigma^2_{DR}\Phi + \sigma^2_{DR^*}\Psi}{\sigma^2_v}$$

Substitution of Ω into Eq. (A4) gives:

$$p \lim \hat{\beta} = \beta \frac{1}{2} \frac{\left[\sigma_{DR}^2(4+\Phi) - \sigma_v^2\left(4 + \frac{\sigma_{DR}^2 \Phi + \sigma_{DR*}^2 \Psi}{\sigma_v^2}\right) + \sigma_{DR*}^2(4+\Psi)\right]}{\sigma_{DR}^2(4+\Phi)}$$

which simplifies to:

$$p \lim \hat{\beta} = \beta \frac{2[\sigma_{DR}^2 - \sigma_v^2 + \sigma_{DR*}^2]}{\sigma_{DR}^2(4+\Phi)}$$

Substituting the expressions for variances one obtains:

$$p \lim \hat{\beta} = \beta \frac{4 p_1 p_2}{(p_1 - p_1^2)(4 + \Phi)}$$

APPENDIX B

To address potential reverse causality, we specify Eqs. (B1) and (B2):

$$\nabla \Delta CR_{jit} = \delta \nabla \Delta X_{jit} + \beta \nabla \Delta DR_{jit} + \mu_{jit} \quad \text{(B1)}$$

$$\nabla \Delta DR_{jit} = B \nabla \Delta X_{jit} + \zeta \nabla \Delta Z_{jit} + \eta_{jit} \quad \text{(B2)}$$

In Eq. (B2) Z represents the instruments that impact the drug use of the juvenile which include the following variables – whether at least one of the three best friends smokes at least one cigarette a day, whether at least one of the three best friends drinks alcohol at least once a month, and whether at least one of the three best friends uses marijuana at least once a month. While it can plausibly be argued that friends' consumption of cigarette, alcohol, and marijuana may be correlated with own drug use, it is less obvious that these instruments are uncorrelated with own criminal activity. Unfortunately, no better instruments are available. State- or county-level alcohol and drug prices are not viable candidates to identify the effect of drug use as they do not vary between siblings and twins. School-based policy variables are not useful either, because all twins and most siblings attend the same school.[B1]

Eqs. (B1) and (B2) are estimated jointly using full information maximum likelihood. We allow for a correlation between the error terms in Eqs. (B1) and (B2) using the discrete factor method (DFM). The DFM assumes that the correlation between these two equations is governed by a common factor, the distribution of which can be approximated by a step function. The common

Table B1. The Impact of Drug Use on Crime with Reverse Causality. Full Information Maximum Likelihood Estimates of Drug Use.

		Without Measurement Error Correction				With Measurement Error Correction			
		Robbery	Burglary	Theft	Damage	Robbery	Burglary	Theft	Damage
All Siblings	Inhale	0.136	0.179*	0.196*	0.176*	0.100	0.132*	0.144*	0.130*
		(0.095)	(0.095)	(0.095)	(0.095)	(0.07)	(0.07)	(0.07)	(0.07)
	Inject	0.401*	0.515*	0.768	0.424*	0.356*	0.457*	0.681	0.376*
		(0.264)	(0.264)	(0.264)	(0.264)	(0.234)	(0.234)	(0.234)	(0.234)
All Twins	Inhale	0.064	0.137	0.128	0.096	0.047	0.101	0.095	0.071
		(0.179)	(0.179)	(0.18)	(0.18)	(0.132)	(0.132)	(0.133)	(0.133)
Identical Twins	Inhale	−0.003	0.071	−0.133	−0.206	−0.002	0.044	−0.082	−0.128
		(0.338)	(0.336)	(0.335)	(0.335)	(0.21)	(0.208)	(0.208)	(0.208)

*, **, and *** indicate statistical significance at <10%, <5%, and <1% levels, respectively. Robust standard errors are in parentheses.

discrete factor is then integrated out of the model as in the standard random effects approach. This method is less restrictive than the specifying functional form, such as joint normality. See Hu (1999), Mocan, Tekin, and Zax (2004), and Mocan and Tekin (2003) for applications of the DFM.

NOTE

B1. Grossman, Kaestner, and Markowitz (2002) highlight the same point in their analysis of drug use on teenage sexual activity.

ANTIDEPRESSANTS AND THE SUICIDE RATE: IS THERE REALLY A CONNECTION?

Matz Dahlberg and Douglas Lundin

ABSTRACT

Recent research claims that the major part of the observed reduction in suicide rates during the 1990s can be explained by the increase in the prescription of antidepressants. However, this conclusion is based on research that only looks at raw correlations; confounding effects from other variables are not controlled for. Using a rich Swedish data set, we re-investigate the issue. After controlling for other covariates, observed as well as unobserved, that might affect the suicide rate, we find, overall, no statistically significant effects from antidepressants on the suicide rate; when we do get significant effects, they are positive for young persons. Regarding the latter result, more research is needed before any firm policy conclusion can be made.

1. INTRODUCTION

The introduction of a new kind of antidepressants, the selective serotonin reuptake inhibitors (SSRIs), in the early 1990s has in many countries led to a very large increase in the prescription rate of antidepressants. Recent research claims that the major part of the observed reduction in suicide rates during the same period can be explained by the increase in the prescription of antidepressants. The reason one might expect there to be a negative relation between the suicide rate and antidepressant prescriptions, is the fact that most individuals who commit suicide are depressed (Cheng, 1995), and that very few of these have received adequate treatment (Isacsson, Boethius, & Bergman, 1992; Isacsson, Holmgren, Wasserman, & Bergman, 1994; Isometsä et al., 1994).

Isacsson (2000) finds that the suicide rate decreased by 19% in parallel with the increased use of antidepressants, from 23.3 suicides per 100,000 inhabitants in 1991 to 18.8 in 1996 ($\rho = -0.90$, $P<0.05$). The annual difference in suicide rates and in the use of antidepressants did not correlate with each other, but the differences between the consecutive 3-year periods did. He further finds that there were no demographic groups with regard to age, gender or county in which the suicide rate decreased in the absence of an increased usage of antidepressants. However, for women under 30 and over 75 years of age, and in 4 of the 23 counties, suicide rates remained unchanged despite an increased use of antidepressants. Isacsson (2000) finds similar patterns for Denmark, Norway, and Finland. The author concludes that his naturalistic study is not conclusive, but that the increased use of antidepressants appears to be one of the contributing factors to the decrease in the suicide rate. In another study for Sweden, Carlsten, Waern, Ekedahl, and Ranstam (2001), examined data for the period 1977–1997 and found that suicide rates declined over the whole study period, but the rate of decline accelerated after the SSRIs were introduced in 1990. Rihmer (2001) finds the same to be true in Hungary. Prescriptions of antidepressants rose steeply after the introduction of SSRIs in the early 1990s and rates of suicide declined, despite steep increases in unemployment and alcohol consumption.

Unlike the earlier studies, Hall et al. (2003) do not find the increase in the prescription of antidepressants during the 1990s to be accompanied by a decline in overall suicide rates. There was a marked decrease in suicide rates among older men and women, but this was offset by increases in younger adults. But since the older age groups are the ones having the highest exposure to antidepressants, Hall et al. (2003) also come to the conclusion that there seems to be an association, less suicides if antidepressants are prescribed to more patients.

The only study not coming to this conclusion is Barbui, Campomori, D'Avanzo, Negri, and Garattini (1999), who find no association between suicide rates and antidepressants use in Italy in the period 1986–1996, the period during which the SSRIs were introduced.

All of the above studies base their conclusions on raw correlations between the two variables "suicide rate" and "prescription rate of antidepressants". They do not perform any statistical analysis where they try to control for confounding factors. Ludwig and Marcotte (2004) perform a more careful analysis, using data from 27 different countries collected over nearly 20 years, where they control for covariates. They find that an increased usage of antidepressants translates into less suicide. However, the data they use do not contain information about the prescription rates in different age groups, which does not allow them to investigate whether there are any differences between age groups.

In this chapter we reinvestigate whether the increased prescription of antidepressants can explain the simultaneous reduction in suicide rates using more detailed data that allows us to control for other covariates, observed as well as unobserved, that might affect the suicide rate. We have data available on sold quantity of antidepressants and suicide rates for Sweden disaggregated in the following dimensions – gender, age group, county, and year. The data provides us with enough variation in the two variables to allow us to run multivariate regression models, where we control for unemployment, alcohol sales, as well as unobserved covariates, which are specific to a county, an age group, or a certain year.

We find no statistically significant effects from antidepressants on the suicide rate in Sweden, when assuming that the effects are the same for all age groups. However, when allowing for heterogeneous effects on different age groups, we find a *positive* and statistically significant effect of the sold quantities of antidepressant on the suicide rate of young persons (under the age of 25). The latter result seems to be robust to several alternative model specifications.

2. DATA AND DESCRIPTIVE STATISTICS

2.1. Data

The data set used for this study contains information on suicides and sold quantity of antidepressants in Sweden over the years 1990–2000. The information is available separately for county, gender, and different age groups, that is, an observation in the data set gives the number of suicides and sold quantity of antidepressants – for a specific year, in a specific county, for a specific age group (5-year intervals), and separately for men and women.[1] Data on suicides are taken from the Swedish National Health

Board's mortality register, which registers all deaths by cause. Data on sold quantity of antidepressants are taken from Apoteket AB, the Swedish central government owned retail monopoly for prescription drugs, which collects comprehensive data on drugs sales.

Table 1 gives some summary statistics. Presumed suicides are classified into one of two categories – certain and uncertain. In this study, we will mainly use certain and uncertain suicides added together. According to specialists in the field, approximately 70–80% of those suicides that are classified as uncertain are true suicides, so the convention is to perform the analysis on certain and uncertain added together, rather than only using certain suicides in the analysis with the argument that this will minimize bias.[2] Our measure of sold quantity of antidepressants is defined daily dose (DDD), which is the assumed average daily dose of the drug when it is used by adults in its main indication. The DDD is set by the World Health Organization.

In 1997, the Swedish government introduced a new reimbursement scheme for prescription drugs, which sharply increased the out-of-pocket costs for patients filling their prescriptions. Since the reform was announced in advance, many patients took the opportunity to hoard drugs (fill as many prescriptions as possible) during the last months of 1996 before the new scheme was in place. In the data, one can, therefore, see a sharp peak in the sales statistics for 1996, followed by a decline in 1997, which of course does not reflect the actual pattern of the utilization of drugs. Therefore, in order to get more accurate estimates of the actual utilization of drugs we adjust the data for 1996 and 1997 in the following manner – first the annual growth in sold quantity was calculated for the period 1995–1998, based on the numbers for the two years 1995 and 1998. Then the sold quantity for 1996 was added with the sold quantity for 1997, after which the total sold quantity for these two years was allocated so that the quantity for 1997 was

Table 1. Summary Statistics for Dependent and Main Explanatory Variables.

Variable	Mean	Standard Deviation	Minimum	Maximum
Suicide rate (certain + uncertain)[a]	16.74	16.87	0	153.31
Suicide rate (certain)[a]	11.09	13.35	0	102.18
Sold quantity (in DDDs)[b]	9.77	8.77	0	37.12
Number of observations	4,646			

[a]Per 100,000 inhabitants.
[b]DDDs per capita.

higher than the quantity for 1996 by a factor equal to the calculated annual growth rate.

2.2. Descriptive Statistics

The claim that the increased usage of antidepressants has caused a reduction in suicide rates is usually based on graphs like the ones in Figs. 1–3, which plots the development of the two variables during the 1990s (Figs. 2 and 3 separately for men and women). Here we can see that there has been a substantial growth in the sold quantity of antidepressants during the 1990s for both men and women, although the growth has been much more dramatic for women. While men and women used about the same number of DDDs per capita in 1990, women used twice as many in 2000.

The suicide rate has dropped for both men and women. But here the pattern is reversed: Men have experienced a much steeper decline than

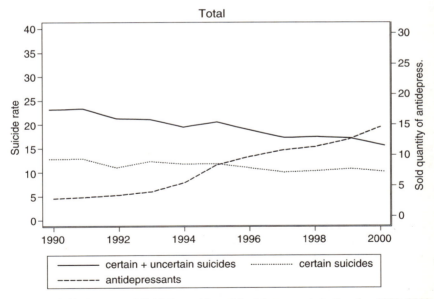

Fig. 1. Suicide Rates and Sold Quantities of Antidepressants in Sweden 1990–2000, Men and Women. *Source*: Own calculations based on the data described in this chapter.

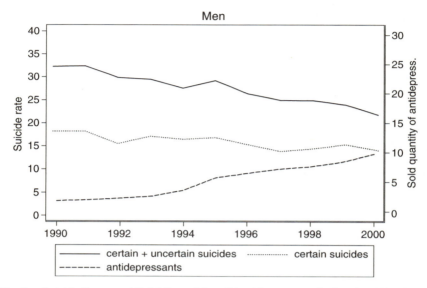

Fig. 2. Suicide Rates and Sold Quantities of Antidepressants in Sweden 1990–2000, Men. *Source*: Own calculations based on the data described in this chapter.

women in absolute terms (−10.5 vs. −4.8). In relative terms, though, it is very close, −32% vs. −34%.

In Table 2 we can see, separately for different age groups, how the suicide rates and prescription rates have changed between the years 1990 and 2000. For all age groups, save 15–19, the suicide rate has declined by some 25–50%. The largest decline in absolute numbers is found in age groups 60–64 and 50–54. Simultaneously the sold quantity of antidepressants has increased dramatically in all age groups; ranging from 270% in age group 15–19 to 1,260% in age group 20–24. The largest growth in absolute figures are in age groups 50–54 and 55–59.

There are interesting differences between some age groups. For instance, although the increase in sold quantity of antidepressants was almost the same in age groups 60–64 and 65–69, the suicide rate in 60–64 declined by half while for 65–69 it only declined by a fourth. In the age group 15–19 the suicide rate stayed roughly the same over the period, although there was a significant increase in the prescription of antidepressants. Both of these observations casts doubt on the hypothesis of a simple negative relation

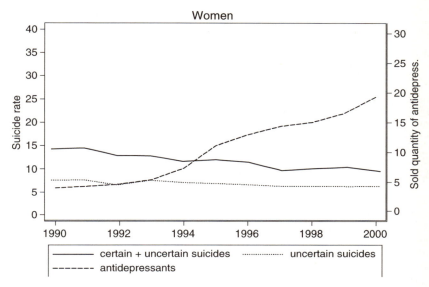

Fig. 3. Suicide Rates and Sold Quantities of Antidepressants in Sweden 1990–2000, Women. *Source*: Own calculations based on the data described in this chapter.

between antidepressant prescriptions and the suicide rate. The correlation between the difference in suicide rate (column 5) and the difference in sold quantity of antidepressants (column 9), although negative, is only −0.05.

Table 3 gives the numbers for the 2 years 1990 and 2000 separately for the counties. All counties have seen a decline, although there are large differences, with the largest decline experienced in the county of Södermanland and the smallest in the county of Värmland. Just like for all age groups, the sold quantity of antidepressants has increased dramatically in all counties; ranging from 279% in the county of Kronoberg to 611% in the county of Stockholm. Also the county-level data provides figures that cast doubt on the hypothesis of a simple relation between the prescribing of antidepressants and the suicide rate. The suicide rates in some counties have declined very little although there has been a substantial increase in the sold quantity of antidepressants, see for example Östergötland, Gotland, and Värmland. The correlation between the difference in suicide rate (column 5) and the difference in sold quantity of antidepressants (column 9) is somewhat larger than in Table 2, but still rather small, −0.22.

Table 2. Suicide Rates and Sold Quantities of Antidepressants in Sweden 1990 and 2000, by Age Group.

Age Group	Suicide Rate[a]				Sold Quantity of Antidepressants[b]			
	1990	2000	Difference	Difference (%)	1990	2000	Difference	Difference (%)
10–14	1.2	0.5	−0.7	−58	0.0	0.5	0.5	∞
15–19	8.0	8.1	0.1	1	0.1	2.8	2.7	270
20–24	18.0	12.6	−5.4	−30	0.5	6.8	6.3	1,260
25–29	19.3	14.2	−5.1	−26	1.3	9.5	8.2	630
30–34	27.9	14.2	−13.7	−49	2.1	12.3	10.2	486
35–39	27.0	19.9	−7.1	−26	3.3	16.2	12.9	391
40–44	30.5	20.0	−10.5	−34	3.7	19.5	15.8	427
45–49	33.0	21.9	−11.1	−34	4.4	21.9	17.5	398
50–54	35.7	21.3	−14.4	−40	5.0	23.6	18.6	372
55–59	35.6	22.8	−12.8	−36	5.6	24.6	19	339
60–64	37.5	18.8	−18.7	−50	5.6	22.4	16.8	300
65–69	31.8	23.3	−8.5	−27	5.6	21.2	15.6	279
70–74	32.7	24.3	−8.4	−26	5.6	23.6	18.0	321
75–79	38.2	25.4	−12.8	−34	6.0	26.4	20.4	340
80+	32.7	25.0	−7.7	−24	5.6	25.6	20.0	357

Source: Own calculations based on the data described in this chapter.
[a]Per 100,000 inhabitants.
[b]DDDs per capita.

A last piece of circumstantial evidence that casts doubt on the hypothesis of a causal relationship between the sold quantity of antidepressants and the suicide rate is the fact that the downturn in the suicide rate seems to have started before the utilization of antidepressants escalated; Fig. 4 shows that there has been a decline in the suicide rate since the early 1980s.

3. STATISTICAL SPECIFICATION

We will assume that there is an underlying process that connects per capita suicide rates, S_{ijt}, and the sold quantity of antidepressants, A_{ijt}, in county $i = 1, \ldots, N$, for age group $j = 1, \ldots, C$ at time $t = 1, \ldots, T$ such that:

$$S_{ijt}(A_{ijt}, \alpha) = e^{\alpha A_{ijt}}$$

where we are interested in estimating the parameter α. Since suicide rates are non-negative, the exponential form is suitable. Furthermore, for the exponential form, any changes are proportional to the suicide rate, which seems

Table 3. Suicide Rates and Sold Quantities of Antidepressants in Sweden 1990 and 2000, by County.

County	Suicide Rate[a]				Sold Quantity of Antidepressants[b]			
	1990	2000	Difference	Difference (%)	1990	2000	Difference	Difference (%)
Stockholm	26.4	15.6	−10.8	−40.1	1.9	13.5	11.6	611
Uppsala	24.2	14.3	−9.9	−40.1	3.3	16.1	12.8	388
Södermanland	16.8	9.4	−7.4	−44.0	2.8	15.5	12.7	454
Östergötland	19.6	17.0	−2.6	−13.3	3.0	15.5	12.5	417
Jönköping	17.5	12.2	−5.3	−30.3	3.5	14.7	11.2	320
Kronoberg	21.9	18.7	−3.2	−14.6	3.9	14.8	10.9	279
Kalmar	17.0	11.5	−5.5	−32.3	2.4	13.6	11.2	467
Gotland	29.8	26.2	−3.6	−12.1	2.3	14.3	12.0	522
Blekinge	21.9	13.3	−8.6	−39.3	2.7	13.9	11.2	415
Skåne	26.7	15.5	−11.2	−41.9	3.4	16.2	12.8	376
Halland	22.8	17.1	−5.7	−25.0	3.0	13.6	10.6	353
Västra Götaland	22.5	15.8	−6.7	−29.8	4.2	15.7	11.5	274
Värmland	21.9	21.1	−0.8	−3.6	3.8	16.1	12.3	324
Örebro	21.3	13.2	−8.1	−38.0	2.0	12.2	10.2	510
Västmanland	24.8	17.1	−7.7	−31.0	2.7	14.3	11.6	430
Dalarna	24.6	19.0	−5.6	−22.8	2.7	14.1	11.4	422
Gävleborg	21.4	16.5	−4.9	−22.9	2.6	14.8	12.2	469
Västernorrland	20.3	15.8	−4.5	−22.2	2.0	12.7	10.7	535
Jämtland	25.0	20.8	−4.2	−16.8	2.4	14.4	12.0	500
Västerbotten	17.1	12.1	−5.0	−29.2	2.2	14.0	11.8	536
Norrbotten	25.4	14.8	−10.6	−41.7	1.8	10.7	8.9	494

Source: Own calculations based on the data described in this chapter.
[a]Per 100,000 inhabitants.
[b]DDDs per capita.

more plausible than, for example, constant changes produced by a linear relation.

Apart from the sold quantity of antidepressants, the suicide rate in a county for a certain age group in a certain year might also be determined by other, observable and unobservable, factors. Therefore, we will also control for other observable variables, x_{it}, that are assumed to affect the suicide rate[3] and for county-specific fixed effects, f_i, age-specific fixed effects (where ages are in 5-year intervals), f_j, and time dummies, τ_t. The county-specific and the age-specific fixed effects control for variables that affect the suicide rate in the same way over time for a certain county and for a certain age group, while the time dummies control for unobservable variables that vary over time but that are assumed to affect the suicide rate in the same way for

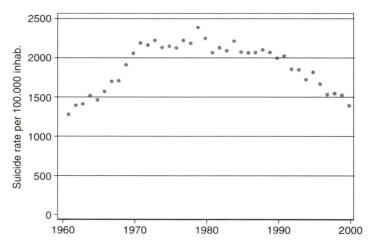

Fig. 4. Suicide Rates in Sweden 1960–2000, Men and Women. *Source*: Own calculations based on the data described in this chapter.

all counties and all age groups in a given year. The fixed effects and the time dummies might be correlated with the observable variables. Furthermore, the suicide rate can also be affected by disturbances, u. Thus, we have the following relationship to be estimated for the suicide rate:

$$S_{ijt}(A_{ijt}, x_{it}, f_i, \tau_t, \alpha, \beta) = \mu_{ijt} e^{\alpha A_{ijt} + x_{it}\beta} v_{ijt} \qquad (1)$$

where $\mu_{ijt} = e^{f_i + f_j + \tau_t}$ is a scaling factor of the county suicide rate for a specific age group in a specific year and $v_{ijt} = e^{u_{ijt}}$ is the disturbance term. The most obvious way to estimate Eq. (1) is perhaps to take the logarithm of it and use ordinary least square (OLS) to estimate the familiar log-linear fixed effect model. However, this is a less suitable estimation strategy in the present case for different reasons related to the characteristics of the data.

A first characteristic of our data is that it contains a substantial amount of zeroes. Suicide is an uncommon event, and it is quite often the case that no suicide is committed in a certain age group, in a certain county, during a particular year. The "zeroes" create two distinct problems. First, the log-linear model cannot handle a "zero" observation.[4] Second, the distribution of the dependent variable will be skewed to the left, and a normal or indeed any other type of symmetrical distribution cannot be assumed. A solution to the "zeroes-problem" is to aggregate the units of analysis so that the dependent variable takes on a number larger than zero for all observations.[5] However, in doing so some interesting questions cannot be investigated; for example, we would not be able to investigate whether there are any heterogeneous effects with respect to age or sex. In addition, we will lose observations, which will yield less precise estimates.

A second characteristic of our data is the discrete nature of them (which, of course, the "zeroes-problem" also is a consequence of). Suicides are discrete events and the number of suicides committed is an integer. While this is not a problem for larger populations, for smaller populations it is, since the discrete nature of the suicides will then transfer to the suicide rate, which is our dependent variable. For a population of 5,000, one additional suicide corresponds to 20 suicides per 100,000 inhabitants. Since the precision of suicide rate estimates as a consequence will depend on the population size, we cannot expect the variance of the regression errors to be homoscedastic, if we estimate Eq. (1) with common methods. The smaller the population is, the larger the variance is.[6] In Figs. 5 and 6, the distribution of number of suicides and the suicide rate, respectively, is shown, illustrating how the distributions are skewed.

Since the Poisson distribution is useful for modelling non-negative integer outcomes, we will in this chapter make use of the fixed effects Poisson (FEP) estimator. The FEP estimator has nice robustness properties. Given that the conditional mean equation is correctly specified, including the strict exogeneity of x_{it}, our estimates are consistent and asymptotically normal, and we can estimate our model without further distributional assumptions (see, Wooldridge, 1999). However, the estimates might not be efficient.[7] Furthermore, the ordinary maximum likelihood standard errors are not valid for inference. The standard errors must be made robust against misspecification, which is straightforward (see, Wooldridge, 1999). The robust standard errors might be larger or smaller than the ordinary standard errors.

4. RESULTS

4.1. Baseline Estimates

In the baseline specification we will use those suicides that are classified as both "certain" and "uncertain". We will elaborate with three specifications. In the first specification, we do not control for anything else that varies over time than the sold quantity of antidepressants.[8] This is in line with what the earlier studies in the field have done. In the second specification, we also

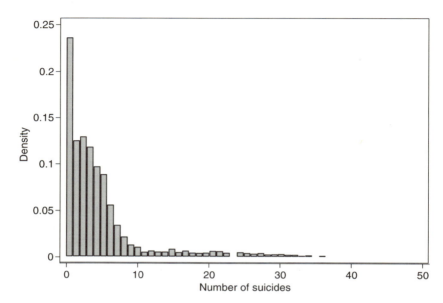

Fig. 5. Distribution for the Number of Suicides. *Source*: Own calculations based on the data described in this chapter.

control for unobserved time effects that affect the suicide rate in the same way in each county in a given year (captured through the time dummies). In the third specification, we also control for socio-economic characteristics.

From the baseline results in Table 4 it is clear that there is a negative and highly statistically significant correlation between the sold quantity of antidepressants and the suicide rate when we do not control for unobserved time effects (cf. the results in the first column). This is what the earlier research has found (see, e.g., Isacsson, 2000). When adding time dummies (second column) and socio-economic characteristics (last column) as covariates in the model specification, the estimated standard errors for the antidepressants variable increases for both specifications, leaving antidepressants insignificant.

Regarding the socio-economic characteristics, it is clear that the unemployment rate and the amount of sold alcohol are important variables (at least in a statistical sense); the higher the unemployment rate is in a county and the more alcohol that is being sold in a county, the higher the suicide rate in the county is.[9] The divorce rate, average income, and population density do, however, not have any statistically significant effects on the suicide rate.[10]

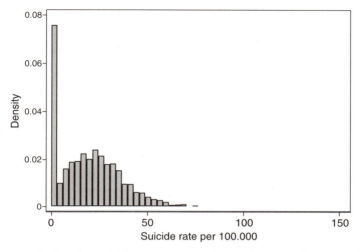

Fig. 6. Distribution for Suicide Rate. *Source*: Own calculations based on the data described in this chapter.

4.2. Are There Different Effects for Men and Women?

The descriptive statistics presented in Section 2 indicated that the connection between the sold quantities of antidepressants and the suicide rate might be different for men and women (cf. Figs. 2 and 3). To examine whether there are different effects of antidepressants on the suicide rate for men and women, we will run separate regressions for the two groups.[11] As is clear from the results presented in Table 5, there are no statistically significant effects of the sold quantity of antidepressants on the suicide rate for any of the groups. For the socio-economic variables, the results are similar as for all persons. The only difference is that the divorce rate seems to be important for the female suicide rate; the higher the divorce rate is the lower the female suicide rate is.

4.3. Are There Different Effects in Different Age Groups?

That the effects might be different for different age groups is heatedly debated in several countries at the moment (especially in the U.S.A. and the U.K.); the debate is mainly concerned with the effects from the new

Table 4. Baseline Estimates: All Individuals.

	First Specification	Second Specification	Third Specification
Antidepressants	−0.020*** (0.0013)	0.0009 (0.0034)	0.0021 (0.0033)
Unemployment			0.00006*** (0.00002)
Income			0.0024 (0.0059)
Divorced			−0.00006 (0.00012)
Alcohol			0.1182*** (0.0428)
Population density			−0.0039 (0.0042)
FE_{county}	Yes	Yes	Yes
$FE_{age\ group}$	Yes	Yes	Yes
Time dummies	No	Yes	Yes
Number of observations	3,465	3,465	3,399

Notes: Robust standard errors are presented in brackets. ***, **, and * denotes significance at the 1%, 5%, and 10% significance level, respectively. FE_{county} denotes county-specific fixed effects, and $FE_{age\ group}$ denotes age-specific fixed effects.

antidepressants on the suicide rate among children and in adolescence since some researchers claim that the effect might be positive for those age groups.

To examine whether there are different effects in different age groups, we will estimate a model in which we interact the antidepressants variable with dummy variables for different age groups; for those under the age of 25 (young), for those in the age interval 25–54 (middle-aged), and for those above 55 (reference group). From the results presented in Table 6, it seems like antidepressants have a positive and statistically significant effect on young people, and the size of the effect seems to be approximately the same for both sexes. There are no significant effects on the suicide rate for the other age groups.

5. ROBUSTNESS CHECKS

We will conduct four robustness checks on the results obtained when the sold quantities of antidepressants are interacted with the age-dummies (i.e., the robustness checks will be made on the results in Table 6). First, we examine how sensitive the results are to an alternative estimation method (the log-linear fixed effects estimator).[12] Second, we examine what happens when we only use those suicides that are classified as certain as the dependent variable. Third, in the baseline analysis, we implicitly assumed that there is no serial correlation in the suicide rate. However, if there is such a correlation in the error process, the resulting standard errors are

Table 5. Separate Regressions for Men and Women.

	Men		Women	
	First Specification	Second Specification	First Specification	Second Specification
Antidepressants	0.0025 (0.0050)	0.0040 (0.0049)	0.0020 (0.0048)	0.0026 (0.0048)
Unemployment		0.00006*** (0.00002)		0.00007** (0.00003)
Income		0.0093 (0.0069)		−0.014 (0.011)
Divorced		0.0001 (0.00015)		−0.0005** (0.00023)
Alcohol		0.1092** (0.0518)		0.143* (0.0774)
Population density		−0.0007 (0.0050)		−0.011 (0.0076)
FE_{county}	Yes	Yes	Yes	Yes
$FE_{age\ group}$	Yes	Yes	Yes	Yes
Time dummies	Yes	Yes	Yes	Yes
Number of observations	3,465	3,399	3,465	3,399

Notes: Robust standard errors are presented in brackets. ***, **, and * denotes significance at the 1%, 5%, and 10% significance level, respectively. FE_{county} denotes county-specific fixed effects, and $FE_{age\ group}$ denotes age-specific fixed effects.

Table 6. Examining Whether There Are Any Idiosyncratic Effects with Respect to Age.

	All	Men	Women
Antidepressants	0.006* (0.0036)	0.0074 (0.0051)	0.0072 (0.0050)
Antidepressants × young	0.048*** (0.0168)	0.060** (0.029)	0.061** (0.0256)
Antidepressants × middle aged	0.002 (0.0026)	0.005 (0.0045)	0.0016 (0.0033)
Unemployment	0.00006*** (0.00002)	0.00006*** (0.00002)	0.00007** (0.00003)
Income	0.0028 (0.0059)	0.0097 (0.0069)	−0.014 (0.011)
Divorced	−0.00005 (0.00012)	0.0001 (0.00015)	−0.0005** (0.00023)
Alcohol	0.1155*** (0.0426)	0.1071** (0.0516)	0.139* (0.0772)
Population density	−0.0039 (0.0042)	−0.0008 (0.0050)	−0.011 (0.0075)
FE$_{county}$	Yes	Yes	Yes
FE$_{age\ group}$	Yes	Yes	Yes
Time dummies	Yes	Yes	Yes
Number of observations	3,399	3,399	3,399

Notes: Robust standard errors are presented in brackets. ***, **, and * denotes significance at the 1%, 5%, and 10% significance level, respectively. FE$_{county}$ denotes county-specific fixed effects, and FE$_{age\ group}$ denotes age-specific fixed effects.

inconsistently estimated and may lead to severely biased estimates in small samples (see, e.g., Kézdi, 2002; Bertrand, Duflo, & Mullainathan, 2004). To examine how sensitive the earlier results are to this, we re-estimate a model in which we allow the errors to be correlated over time within each county.[13] Finally, we control for county-specific time trends to allow for different (county-specific) evolutions over time for the suicide variable. The results are presented in Table 7.[14] Two conclusions can be drawn. First, the baseline result that there are no significantly negative effects of the sold quantity of antidepressants on the suicide rates seems to be robust in relation to those alterations considered in Table 7. Second, when we get a statistically significant effect, it is *positive* and it affects mainly *young* people. Also in this sense the baseline results do seem to be robust to different re-specifications of the model.

6. CONCLUSIONS

In this chapter we have reinvestigated the issue of whether the increased prescription of antidepressants can explain the simultaneous reduction in suicide rates. Using fairly detailed data on suicide rates and sold quantities of antidepressants, we find, after controlling for other covariates, observed as well as unobserved, that might affect the suicide rate, no statistically significant effects from antidepressants on the suicide rate. This result is at odds with recent research claiming that the new type of antidepressants explains the major part of the large reduction in suicide rates in several countries.

However, when we allow for heterogeneous effects on different age groups, we find a *positive* and statistically significant effect of sold quantities of antidepressants on the suicide rate for young persons (under the age of 25). This result seems to be robust to several alternative model specifications.

Are there any caveats with our approach? Well, this chapter uses observational data to study the issue at hand (just like the articles cited in the Introduction). In the medical research community, data from clinical trials are usually preferred over observational data, since selection bias can be avoided. However, when studying the issue at hand, we think there are good reasons why observational data is to be preferred. First, suicides are rare events, and thus most trials have insufficient power to provide clear evidence. Second, most trials are of too short duration, typically 8–12 weeks, to identify the longer-term effects. Third, patients taking part in trials are under more careful scrutiny than ordinary patients, so any signs of suicidal

Table 7. Robustness Checks on Estimation Method and on Classification of Suicides.

	All	Men	Women
Log-linear (with zeros)			
Antidepressants	0.001 (0.0042)	0.001 (0.0050)	0.002 (0.0037)
Antidepressants × young	0.041** (0.0205)	0.082*** (0.0270)	0.007 (0.0203)
Antidepressants × middle aged	−0.002 (0.0034)	0.002 (0.0053)	0.002 (0.0028)
Number of observations	3,024	2,856	2,031
Log-linear (no zeros)			
Antidepressants	−0.0008 (0.0035)	0.0001 (0.0040)	−0.0008 (0.0026)
Antidepressants × young	0.019 (0.0169)	0.036 (0.0246)	0.023** (0.0106)
Antidepressants × middle aged	−0.003 (0.0030)	−0.001 (0.0045)	−0.002 (0.0024)
Number of observations	3,399	3,399	3,399
Only certain suicides			
Antidepressants	0.00002 (0.0067)	−0.002 (0.0089)	0.004 (0.0078)
Antidepressants × young	−0.011 (0.0340)	−0.060 (0.0564)	0.053* (0.0331)
Antidepressants × middle aged	−0.004 (0.0054)	−0.009 (0.0099)	0.002 (0.0065)
Number of observations	3,399	3,399	3,399
Allowing for autocorrelation in the residuals			
Antidepressants	0.006 (0.0047)	0.007 (0.0066)	0.007 (0.0047)
Antidepressants × young	0.048** (0.0207)	0.060 (0.0389)	0.061*** (0.0211)
Antidepressants × middle aged	0.002 (0.0030)	0.005 (0.0049)	0.002 (0.0034)
Number of observations	3,399	3,399	3,399
County-specific time trends			
Antidepressants	0.007 (0.0050)	0.007 (0.0068)	0.010 (0.0048)
Antidepressants × young	0.0519** (0.0215)	0.060 (0.0396)	0.068*** (0.0206)
Antidepressants × middle aged	0.002 (0.0030)	0.005 (0.0049)	0.002 (0.0034)
Number of observations	3,399	3,399	3,399

Notes: Robust standard errors are presented in brackets. ***, **, and * denotes significance at the 1%, 5%, and 10% significance level, respectively. In all specifications we use the same controls as in Table 6.

behaviour could better be detected and given appropriate attention by caregivers.

Having said this, we do not find evidence from randomized trials useless. What is then the evidence from clinical trials on the connection between suicide and antidepressants? In the most comprehensive synthesis of data from randomized trials, Khan, Khan, Kolts, and Brown (2003) found no evidence of a beneficial effect of antidepressants on suicide. Concerning pediatric use, Gunnel and Ashby (2004) summarize the existing body of literature as: "Data from pediatric trials suggest that SSRIs are associated with an increased risk of suicidal behavior and most SSRIs seem to be ineffective for childhood depression". Thus, the evidence from randomized trials seems to be in line with what we find.

Probably the most controversial of our results is that the likelihood of suicide seems to increase for young people when using antidepressants. However, since no policy should be changed based on the results from a single study, we do not want to stress this result too much. More research is needed before any firm conclusion can be made on this very important issue.

Another question that remains to be answered is, if it is not the increased usage of antidepressants, what is it then that explains the reduction in suicide rates? Since the reduction in suicide rates started already before the introduction of the SSRI-type of antidepressants, it is quite likely that there are some other explanations for the downturn in suicide rates. This should be a topic for future research on this issue.

NOTES

1. We do not use the rare cases of suicides for those under the age of 10. The age group intervals are as follows: 10–14, 15–19,...,75–79, and 80–99.
2. The reason it will minimize bias is that there are some suicides that are never classified as suicides, for example, some of the traffic accidents and some of the drowning accidents (see, e.g., the information at NASP's, the Swedish National Centre for Suicide Research and Prevention of Mental Ill-Health, web page, http://www.ki.se/suicide). However, as a robustness check, we will also conduct the analysis only on those suicides that are classified as certain.
3. The x-variables that we will include in the regressions are unemployment rate, average income, divorce rate, sold quantities of alcohol, and population density. These variables are only observed at the county level for each year, not separately for each age group.
4. The usual way of solving this problem is to tamper with the data and add a small number to zero observations.
5. This is typically what the earlier studies have done.
6. See Osgood (2000) for a discussion in a cross-sectional setting.
7. Given that the assumptions for the FEP estimator are satisfied, Hahn (1997) has shown that FEP is the efficient semi-parametric estimator.
8. However, we do control for unobserved county-specific fixed effects that affect the suicide rate in the same way over time in each county and for unobserved age-specific fixed effects that affect the suicide rate in the same way over time within each age group (5-year intervals).
9. The unemployment rate is defined as the open unemployment in a county divided by the population in the county ($\times$ 100,000) and the alcohol variable is the amount of alcohol (measured in 100% ethanol) sold per inhabitant over 14 years of

age at the state-owned company Systembolaget. The latter variable might be a somewhat problematic measure of alcohol consumption in certain counties in Sweden for the later years due to an increased consumption of alcohol from neighbouring countries with a low-tax policy on alcohol.

10. The divorce rate is the total number of divorces in a county in a given year divided by the population in the county (× 100,000), the income variable is average after-tax income (in 1,000 s of Swedish kronor), and the population density is the county-population per square kilometre.

11. We run two regressions for each group – one in which we, in addition to the antidepressants, only control for the unobservable characteristics and one in which we control for both the unobservable and the observable characteristics.

12. We estimate two versions of the log-linear fixed effects estimator; one where we keep the zeroes (implying that we lose observations when taking the logarithm of the suicide variable), and one where we add a one to each suicide before taking the logarithm (not to lose observations when taking the logarithm of the suicide variable).

13. Technically, this is done in STATA by clustering on county.

14. In the table, we only report the results for the antidepressants variable and its interactions with the age-dummies. The other covariates are the same as in Table 6.

ACKNOWLEDGEMENTS

We are grateful to Agneta Öjehagen, Lars Lindvall and seminar participants at Uppsala University, and at the *2004 Arne Ryde symposium on the "economics of substance use"* in Lund for valuable comments and discussions.

REFERENCES

Barbui, C., Campomori, A., D'Avanzo, B., Negri, E., & Garattini, S. (1999). Antidepressants drug use in Italy since the introduction of SSRIs: National trends, regional differences and impact on suicide rates. *Social Psychiatry and Psychiatric Epidemiology, 34*, 152–156.

Bertrand, M., Duflo, E., & Mullainathan, S. (2004). How much should we trust differences-in-differences estimates? *Quarterly Journal of Economics*, 249–275.

Carlsten, A., Waern, M., Ekedahl, A., & Ranstam, J. (2001). Antidepressant medication and suicide in Sweden. *Pharmacoepidemiology and Drug Safety, 10*, 525–530.

Cheng, A. T. A. (1995). Mental illness and suicide. *Archives General Psychiatry, 52*, 594–603.

Gunnel, D., & Ashby, D. (2004). Antidepressants and suicide: What is the balance of benefit and harm? *British Medical Journal, 329*, 34–38.

Hahn, J. (1997). A note on the efficient semiparametric estimation of some exponential panel models. *Econometric Theory, 13*, 583–588.

Hall, W. D., Mant, A., Mitchell, P. B., Rendle, V. A., Hickie, I. B., & McManus, P. (2003). Association between antidepressant prescribing and suicide in Australia, 1991–2000: Trend analysis. *British Medical Journal, 326.*
Isacsson, G. (2000). Suicide prevention – A medical breakthrough? *Acta Psychiatrica Scandinavica, 102,* 113–117.
Isacsson, G., Boethius, G., & Bergman, U. (1992). Low level of antidepressant prescription for people who later commit suicide: 15 years of experience from a population based drug database in Sweden. *Acta Psychiatrica Scandinavica, 85,* 444–448.
Isacsson, G., Holmgren, P., Wasserman, D., & Bergman, U. (1994). Use of antidepressants among people committing suicide in Sweden. *British Medical Journal, 308,* 506–509.
Isometsä, E. T., Henriksson, M. M., Aro, H. M., Heikkinen, M. E., Kuoppasalmi, K. I., & Lönnqvist, J. K. (1994). Suicide in major depression. *American Journal of Psychiatry, 151,* 135–142.
Khan, A., Khan, S., Kolts, R., & Brown, W. A. (2003). Suicide rates in clinical trials of SSRIs, other antidepressants, and placebo: Analysis of FDA reports. *American Journal of Psychiatry, 160,* 790–792.
Kézdi, G. (2002). *Robust standard error estimation in fixed-effects panel models.* Mimeo: University of Michigan.
Ludwig, J., & Marcotte, D. (2004). Anti-depressants, suicide and drug regulation. *Journal of Policy Analysis and Management, 24*(2).
Osgood, D. W. (2000). Poisson-based regression analysis of aggregate crime rates. *Journal of Quantitative Criminology, 16,* 21–43.
Rihmer, Z. (2001). Can better recognition and treatment of depression reduce suicide rates? A brief review. *European Psychiatry,, 16,* 406–409.
Wooldridge, J. M. (1999). Distribution-free estimation of some nonlinear panel data models. *Journal of Econometrics, 90,* 77–97.

PART II:
SOCIAL INTERACTIONS

CHOICE, SOCIAL INTERACTION AND ADDICTION: THE SOCIAL ROOTS OF ADDICTIVE PREFERENCES☆

Ole-Jørgen Skog

ABSTRACT

It is argued that addicts, as people in general, are forward-looking and that they try to make the best of what they have got. However, this does not imply that they are fully rational. Cognitive defects, instabilities in preferences, and irrationalities in the form of wishful thinking and dynamical inconsistency play an important role in addictive behaviours. These "imperfections" in people's rationality may not have very large consequences in the case of ordinary goods, but their effect can be dramatic in relation to addictive goods. In the first part of the paper, the rational addiction theory and the empirical evidence that have been presented in support of the theory is reviewed. Regarding the conventional tests of the theory by econometric methods, it is argued that the tests are misguided, both theoretically and methodologically. Furthermore, it is claimed that the definition of addiction implicit in the rational addiction

☆ Prepared for presentation at the *24th Arne Ryde symposium on the economics of substance use*, Lund, Sweden, August 13–14, 2004.

theory is unrealistic, and that the theory makes unrealistic assumptions about human nature. Some empirical evidence for these claims is reviewed. It is concluded that although the theory has its virtues, it faces serious problems and must be rejected in its original form. Secondly, the socio-cultural embeddedness of addictive behaviours, and the social roots of individual preferences, are discussed. These issues are more or less ignored in rational addiction theory. It is argued that we cannot expect to obtain a proper understanding of many addictive phenomena, unless they are seen in their proper socio-cultural context.

1. THE NEO-CLASSICAL ECONOMIC APPROACH TO ADDICTION

Economic theory treats addiction as a type of habit-formation. According to Gary Becker, addictive consumption stands out from more benign habits, mainly by being so strong as to be destabilising (Becker & Murphy, 1988; Becker, 1992).

The basic idea underlying Becker's theory of addiction is this: Due to certain properties of addictive drugs, there is a consumption threshold, or a point of "no return", so that consumers at higher levels become trapped. As long as the consumer stays below the critical threshold, he is safe. Occasional sprees will be followed by regression back to the safe level. However, if at some stage, the consumer's long-term consumption level should happen to exceed the critical threshold, he will gravitate towards even higher consumption levels; i.e. the state of addiction.

In Becker's theory, this higher consumption level is inferior to consumption levels below the threshold, according to the agent's own utility calculation. Hence, in the state of addiction, the consumer is worse off. However, according to the theory, the consumer is unable to return to his optimal consumption level because this requires a temporary set-back (e.g. due to withdrawal symptoms, etc.), and he is not sufficiently motivated by the prospects of future improvements. Therefore, given his own myopia and his consumption career, he will prefer to continue at the high consumption level (cf. Skog, 1999).

The concept of a threshold plays a very crucial role in this theory. Becker and Murphy (1988) seem to imply that this threshold is an attribute of the addictive substance itself, and that it does not vary much across individuals. This follows from their claim that the theory predicts a bimodal distribution of the consumers. If the threshold should vary considerably across individuals (and/or within individuals over time), bimodality could not be expected.

Becker and Murphy also predict that addiction stops "only through cold turkey". A gradual "maturing out of addiction" should not be a common phenomenon, according to this view. However, strictly speaking, "cold turkey" does not follow from the theory's premises, unless the threshold is a fixed property of the addictive substance. If the threshold is variable across socio-economic contexts and stages of the consumption career, "maturing out" of the type often observed (Heather & Robertson, 1981; Pattison, Sobell, & Sobell, 1977; Nordström & Berglund, 1987) could easily follow from this theory (Skog, 1999). Therefore, even this prediction suggests that the threshold is held by Becker and Murphy to be fairly stable.

In Becker's theory, the habit-formation process is described by the consumer's consumption capital. This is mainly an aggregate measure of past consumption history. The consumer's current preferences are affected by his consumption capital and a high capital implies a taste for high consumption. Furthermore, the consumption capital changes gradually when the consumer's instantaneous consumption changes. The rate of change in the consumption capital is described by the depreciation rate. If the consumption capital adjusts itself quite rapidly, the theory would not predict "cold turkey". Hence, the "cold turkey" prediction seems to suggest that Becker and Murphy tacitly assume that depreciation is a slow process.

In addition to these causal mechanisms, the theory assumes that addictive behaviour is volitional behaviour. Becker and Murphy (1988) assume that the consumers are forward-looking, rational utility maximizers with stable preferences. In a stable environment and with full information, these agents would never enter the state of addiction, as this is an inferior state for the consumer. According to the theory, entry could occur, either due to a life crisis (Becker & Murphy, 1988), or in the absence of full information, when the consumer takes a calculated risk (Orphanides & Zervos, 1995). This assumption clearly sets the theory apart from traditional disease theories of addiction.

I have argued elsewhere (Skog, 2000) that the traditional disease theory of addiction (e.g. Jellinek, 1960; Keller, 1972), which conceives the addict as unable to choose, is neither internally consistent nor empirically realistic. From this point of view, Becker's voluntaristic theory is an improvement. Addictive behaviour must be understood as intentional behaviour, and the agents should be conceived as more or less forward-looking. The theory brings the agent's future-orientation into focus as a risk factor. It predicts that consumers who are more forward-looking will have a lower risk, while myopic agents who are less motivated by the future will have a larger risk for becoming addicted. This is probably correct, and of considerable importance.

However, the hypothesis that consumers are fully rational maximizers with stable preferences, is much more problematic, as Becker himself seem to have acknowledged in his Nobel lecture (Becker, 1996). It is probably true that people in general, and addicts in particular, tries to make the best of what they have got. However, cognitive defects (Kahneman & Tversky, 2000), instabilities in preferences (Skog, 1997) and irrationalities in the form of wishful thinking (Wagenaar, 1988; Elster, 1999) and dynamical inconsistency (Ainslie, 1992), probably plays an important role in addictive behaviours. These "imperfections" in people's rationality may not have large consequences in the case of ordinary goods, but their effect can be dramatic in relation to addictive goods.

On the following pages I shall address some of these issues more closely. First, I shall discuss economists' alleged testing of the theory of rational addiction by econometric methods. I shall argue that these attempts are misguided, both theoretically and methodologically. Second, I shall discuss the definition of addiction implicit in the theory, and the lack of realism in the theory's assumptions about human nature. In this section I will also present some empirical evidence which is quite different from the conventional econometric tests. I shall argue that the theory faces serious problems, and must be rejected in its original form. Lastly, I shall discuss some issues that are more or less ignored in "rational addiction" theory, namely the socio-cultural embeddedness of addictive behaviours and the social roots of individual preferences. I will argue that we cannot expect to obtain a proper understanding of addictive phenomena, unless they are seen in their proper socio-cultural context.

2. THE ECONOMETRIC TESTING THE "RATIONAL ADDICTION" THEORY

Since the "rational addiction" theory conceives addiction as a strong habit, it follows that present consumption is affected by present, as well as past prices (Becker & Murphy, 1988; Becker, Grossman, & Murphy, 1992). Past prices should affect present consumption due to a feedback mechanism via the consumption capital: Last years prices affected last year's consumption, which affects the consumption capital, which affects present consumption.

This delayed effect of price change means that conventional econometric approaches (cf. Edwards et al. (1994) for a review regarding alcohol) may have underestimated the effects of price change, by focusing exclusively on the concurrent effect.

The theory also predicts that the forward-looking addict will adjust her consumption in advance, when anticipating a future price change. If the agent anticipates that prices will go up in the future, she is expected to start reducing her consumption immediately, and if a reduction is anticipated, she is expected to increase her consumption (Becker & Murphy, 1988).

So far, empirical tests of the rational addiction theory have focused on the prediction that (anticipated) future price changes affect current consumption (e.g. Becker, Grossman, & Murphy, 1994; Chaloupka, 1991; Gruber & Köszegi, 2001; Keeler, Hu, Barnett, & Manning, 1993). However, there are both theoretical problems with the hypothesis itself, and some severe methodological difficulties with the econometric approach.

Regarding the theoretical status of the anticipation hypothesis, one faces three problems. First, anticipation effects of one sort or another would be predicted by *any* choice theory which assumes that the agents are forward-looking. In particular, Gruber and Köszegi (2001) have demonstrated that hyperbolic discounters would act the same way. Hence, an empirical demonstration of anticipation effects is no proof for "*rational* addiction". At best, it is only evidence for people being forward-looking.

Second, the following fact has been overlooked. The theory predicts that addicts should be less forward-looking than non-addicted consumers, since a high rate of time discounting (myopia) is a risk factor for addiction, while a low rate of discounting is a protective factor. Since the discount rate strongly affects the anticipation effect, the theory predicts that addicts should be *less* influenced by anticipated future price changes than ordinary consumers, not *more*. Therefore, an empirical demonstration of anticipation effects is no proof for "rational *addiction*". In aggregate data, anticipation effects could first and foremost indicate that *non-addicts* are forward-looking. For this reason, anticipation effects cannot serve as an empirical test for the rational addiction theory. A possible exception to this would be drugs where the prevalence of addicts are very large, and the selection effect therefore minimal. Tobacco consumption might be an example. However, for most other drugs, the prevalence of addicts is fairly low, and the mechanism outlined above would be highly relevant.

Third, the anticipation effect requires that the consumers are in fact able to correctly anticipate future price changes. In many cases, this information will not be available to the consumers, and few of the studies reporting anticipation effects have actually demonstrated that consumers knew in advance. Gruber and Köszegi (2001) have taken this problem seriously, and present some less fragile evidence for tobacco. However, as noted above, tobacco may be quite exceptional among the addictive drugs. In the near future, forthcoming analyses of recent Danish, Swedish and Finnish experiences regarding the effects of anticipated, European Union (EU) induced price reductions, etc. may shed more light on the issue for alcohol (Room, 2004). This will offer an opportunity for a more rigorous testing of the anticipation effect. The project will also allow us to test if anticipation effects, provided they exist at all, is present among the heavy consumers, as the theory predicts.

Regarding methodological issues, econometric studies in this field have typically failed to deal with the autocorrelation problem in a satisfactory way (Skog, 1999). In general, both price and consumption series are strongly autocorrelated, and this will easily induce spurious correlation between present consumption and past and future prices. In order to avoid the problem, one needs to take these autocorrelations into consideration, either by filtering the series or by using an ARIMA specification or both. In fact, Keeler et al. (1993) failed to find effects of future prices when the trend was included in the model. Furthermore, Gruber and Köszegi (2001) demonstrate that the anticipated price effects previously reported by Becker et al. (1994) disappear when adequate controls for autocorrelation are made in their data. However, Gruber and Köszegi (2001) do present some less fragile evidence for anticipation effects in the case of cigarettes.

Auld and Grootendorst (2002) shed light on these methodological difficulties by estimating the rational addiction model for ordinary, non-addictive commodities, such as milk, eggs and oranges, and obtain anticipation effects of the type interpreted as indicative of "rational addiction" by economists. In a Monte Carlo simulation, they also demonstrate that spurious results of this sort are likely to obtain in the presence of strong autocorrelation, and that time series analysis will often be insufficient to differentiate rational addiction from autocorrelation in the consumption series.

In conclusion, the evidence for anticipation effects, which is considered the hallmark of "rational addiction", is far from convincing. Furthermore, even if such evidence were abundant, it would not be evidenced for *"rational addiction"*; it would at most suggest some sort of addiction-like habit-formation in forward-looking consumers. Econometric studies are simply not the right way of testing the theory of "rational addiction".

3. THE RATIONAL CHOICE CONCEPT OF ADDICTION

Implicit in the idea of a fixed threshold is the idea that addiction is an either/or phenomenon. Below the threshold you are not addicted, while above it, you are. However, today most experts would say that addiction comes in all degrees (e.g. Edwards, 1982). A dichotomy may sometimes be convenient for practical reasons, for instance when deciding whether or not to initiate treatment. Thus, a diagnostic and statistical manual of mental disorders, DSM IV (1994), defines a cut-off at three or more symptoms (out of seven) having been present during the last 12 months. However, this (more or less arbitrary) cut-off is required by the fact that the intervention is dichotomous (treatment or no treatment), rather than the condition itself being discrete.

The seven DSM-IV criteria are:

1. tolerance;
2. withdrawal;
3. often consuming more than was intended;
4. persistent desire or unsuccessful efforts to cut down;
5. spending a great deal of time with drug-related activities;
6. giving up important social, occupational or recreational activities;
7. continuing consumption despite physical or psychological harm which the agent know is caused by his or her abuse.

All the symptoms listed may be present in degrees. Some individuals may experience very high degrees of tolerance, while others have less tolerance to the same substance; some may experience violent withdrawal symptoms, while others experience milder symptoms, and the desire and unsuccessful efforts to cut down may vary considerably across individuals, to mention just three examples. Clearly, addiction is really a continuous concept, going from very mild habit-formation without big problems, to nearly irresistible urges with severe medical, psychological and social consequences, and with all intermediate forms being present in large numbers.

One should therefore question the whole construct of a destabilizing, fixed threshold in Becker's model. For sure, the typical addict will have progressed gradually over a period of time, but not all cases progress to very high levels. Many stop at intermediate levels, and others progress to very high levels, only to reduce their intake again, while still others fluctuate widely over prolonged periods. In fact, consumers typically distribute themselves along the consumption scale in fairly smooth, but highly dispersed way. No bimodality is found. Fig. 1 reproduces distributions from general population surveys of drinking in a high consumption (France) and a low consumption (Norway) culture. These unimodal curves are quite typical for what we normally observe in empirical data (Skog, 1980b, 1985).

Moreover, the consumption pattern of alcohol-dependent consumers is not at all stable over time (Polich, Armor, & Braiker, 1980; Fillmore & Midanik, 1984; Skog & Duckert, 1993). In fact, their consumption fluctuates strongly from one year to the next, as is illustrated in Table 1. These data obtains from a prospective study of alcoholics treated in an in-patient clinic in Oslo. The mean duration of their drinking problem ($\pm$ standard deviation) was 9 ($\pm$8) years, and clients had a high number of previous alcohol-related hospitalizations, on average 7.2 ($\pm$6.8) times. Moreover, 74% had used Antabuse. (For a more detailed description of these clients, see Duckert, 1988). The patients were followed up annually for 4 years. Table 1 gives the transition matrix between consumption categories from one year to the next, estimated by pooling the three post-treatment transition matrices.

As can be seen from the marginal distribution (right-hand column), a large fraction of these alcoholics occasionally drink fairly moderate amounts during a 1-year period. Furthermore, the transitions to higher levels are

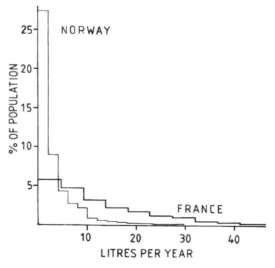

Fig. 1. The Distribution of Alcohol Consumers in France and Norway According Annual Intake. *Source*: Skog (1986).

Table 1. One-Year Transition Matrix (12 Months) for Inpatients' Alcohol Consumption After Treatment. The Figures are Conditional Probabilities, Estimated by Pooling Three 1-Year Transitions (1–2, 2–3 and 3–4 Years After Treatment). Consumptions States are Measured in Average Number of Grams Pure Alcohol per Day.

Old State	New State									
	Abstainer	1–10	11–20	21–40	41–80	81–160	160+	Drop-out	Sum	n^*
Abstainer	**0.33**	0.20	0.03	0.13	0.07	–	0.07	0.17	1.00	30
1–10	0.11	**0.43**	0.20	0.06	0.06	0.07	–	0.07	1.00	54
11–20	0.02	0.25	**0.22**	0.29	0.16	–	–	0.06	1.00	51
21–40	0.03	0.07	0.19	**0.26**	0.23	0.07	–	0.14	0.99	69
41–80	0.03	0.03	0.07	0.19	**0.28**	0.12	0.09	0.20	1.01	69
81–160	0.02	0.02	0.02	0.13	0.19	**0.28**	0.20	0.16	1.02	64
160+	–	–	0.02	0.06	0.06	0.28	**0.30**	0.28	1.00	50
Drop-out	0.01	0.02	0.03	0.02	0.04	0.09	0.05	**0.74**	1.00	159

Source: Skog and Duckert (1993).
*Pooled over three transitions.

typically not explosive, but smooth and gradual. Dramatic changes also occur, but they are not in majority. Most often, clients who at some stage drink at fairly low level will progress to a somewhat higher level, but some will stay put, and others will decrease. Those who are at very high levels at some stage, will typically have decreased their consumption a year later, but normally not by "cold turkey". The typical pattern is a moderate reduction.

In the light of such data, it is difficult to hold on to the idea of fixed threshold and stable preferences. If there is a threshold, it must vary considerably, since the distributions are very skew and fairly smooth. And the large fluctuations observed in alcoholics' drinking, strongly suggests that their preferences are far from stable. In fact, the correlation between consumption in successive years suggests that about half of the inter-individual variations are transient. Furthermore, the correlations die out with increasing time distance only fairly slowly (see Table 2), and this suggests that these alcohol-dependent drinkers fluctuate around very different consumption levels after treatment. This is clearly incompatible with the idea of a fixed threshold.

These large fluctuations in addicts' consumption, and consequently in their revealed preferences, is not at all surprising, in the light of what we now know about addictions (Heather & Robertson, 1981; Marlatt, Demming, & Reid, 1973; Mello & Mendelson, 1965, 1966, 1972). In fact, the "rational

Table 2. Pearson Correlations (After Exclusion of Abstainers and Log-transformation of Consumption Variable), and Spearman Rank Correlations (All Cases) at Different Time-Lags in the In-patient Group. At Lag 1 and 2 Years the Correlations are Averaged Over, Respectively, Three and Two Replications.

	Lag 1 Year	Lag 2 Years	Lag 3 Years
Pearson correlation	0.67	0.61	0.58
Spearman correlation	0.69	0.61	0.60

Source: Skog and Duckert (1993).

addiction" theory's idea of a fixed threshold seems to rely heavily on the old idea of loss-of-control (e.g. Jellinek, 1960). The difference is that the biological loss-of-control mechanism in the classical model is replaced by a hedonistic mechanism in Becker's version.

Traditionally, the loss-of-control concept was founded on the observation that addicts at some stage wish to discontinue, but nevertheless they continue heavy drinking the next day, week or month. Although the observation may be correct, the interpretation that this suggests that they are not masters of their own actions, is hardly acceptable.[1] A more reasonable interpretation is that these consumers are highly ambivalent, suffering under strong, but incompatible motives. They both wish to consume and to abstain. Sometimes the abstention motive has the upper hand, on other times the consumption motive is the winner. Under this interpretation, strong fluctuations in consumption are to be expected.

Furthermore, the very existence of self-control measures like Antabuse implies that the consumer knows from experience that his own preferences tend to fluctuate. In periods were the abstention motive is in charge, the consumer wishes to control his own future choices, as he anticipates that his consumption motives may become dominant at times. To take Antabuse is to set up a causal machinery that will reduce the likelihood of giving into these consumption motives. These motivational fluctuations are probably not only typical for addicts. Most of us suffer from the same problem, but with less dramatic consequences.

The "rational addict" of economic theory is not a real addict. The whole idea that addicts can be conceived as fully rational, forward-looking utility maximizers with stable preferences is unrealistic. Such an agent always does what is best, according to his own utility calculus. He has no motive for changing his consumption behaviour and should not struggle to cut back. If a rational addict thinks that it is best to cut back, he will cut back. In the opposite case, he will simply continue. There is no room for ambivalence and struggling with oneself in standard rational choice theory. Yet, the very idea of addiction is intimately tied to these concepts (Skog, 2003). In particular, the "rational addiction" theory has no room for typical addiction-related phenomena, such as repeated remission and relapse.

However, this does not imply that addiction is unavailable to economic theory in general, only that the economic addiction theory needs some serious fixing. The problem is not the idea that addicts are forward-looking and trying to make the best of what they have got. As we have already seen, part of the problem is the idea that their preferences are stable, and that there is a fixed threshold. The remaining problem, which I shall now turn to, is the idea that addicts (and people in general) are fully rational.

A very important type of irrationality is wishful thinking, or the self-serving bias. People tend to believe all sorts of things, not because they have good reasons for believing them, but because they wish the world to be that way. In relation to addictive substances it has been observed that smokers believe that the risk of lung cancer is lower than non-smokers believe (Viscusi, 1992). (However, both tend to overestimate the actual risk.) This may be due to a selection mechanism, as those who have low estimates are more likely to start smoking or to a cognitive dissonance (a self-servicing bias of the type "since I smoke, it cannot be very dangerous") or both. More direct evidence regarding self-serving bias has been reported by McKenna (1990), demonstrating that individual smokers tend to believe that they are less likely than the average smoker to suffer health problems due to smoking.

Studies of compulsive gamblers have also uncovered irrational belief-formation. In games where there is a 50% chance of winning, some gamblers believe that after a run of five or six losses, the likelihood of winning has increased. Others make the opposite mistake, and believe that the likelihood of winning has gone down (Wagenaar, 1988). Another mechanism is driven by the "psychology of a near win". Even in games of pure chance, gamblers interpret outcomes similar to the one they had betted on, as confirmation that they were on to something (op. cit.). The tendency to transform losses into "near wins", can obviously produce very biased expectations. A further indication that gamblers are victims of irrational beliefs, as Elster (1999) notes, is the very existence of the Monte Carlo Revue Scientifique, which logs successive outcomes at roulette.

A Norwegian general population survey of gambling behaviour produced revealing results (Lund & Nordlund, 2003). The subjects were asked a series of questions about their own gambling habits, as well as about their beliefs regarding the chances of winning. On the basis of the former questions one could classify people according to gambler types. Table 3 reproduces the responses of the subjects on the latter questions in different groups of gamblers. All five questions signify irrational beliefs of one sort or another, and a disturbingly high percentage of the pathological gamblers subscribe to such beliefs. Frequent, non-pathological gamblers are victims of the same type of wishful thinking, but to a somewhat smaller extent. And even in the rest of the populations, irrational beliefs are not uncommon. Compared to the latter group, pathological gamblers (approximately 1.5% of the population) are approximately three times as likely to hold these beliefs. Presumably, this difference is due to selection, since believers are more at risk. However, such beliefs could also be augmented during the gambling career, for instance by cognitive dissonance reduction.

In addition to irrational belief-formation, weakness of the will in the form of dynamic inconsistency, e.g. due to hyperbolic discounting (Ainslie, 1992;

Table 3. Beliefs about Gambling in the General Population and among Pathological Gamblers Norway. Percent that Agree with Different Statements in a Population Survey.

Statement	Percent Agreeing among			
	Pathological Gamblers ($n = 72$)	Frequent Gamblers ($n = 533$)	Rest of the Population ($n = 4,677$)	Total ($n = 5,282$)
In the long run, I will win more than I lose	25.4	15.6	9.4	10.2
I can influence the outcome through things I do or think while playing	42.0	19.8	13.1	14.2
I often feel that I will have better winners luck than I normally have	71.8	32.7	19.8	21.8
The longer bad luck has persisted, the bigger becomes the chance of soon winning	41.4	25.2	13.8	15.3
It is likely that at some time, I will win a big prize	58.3	38.8	17.0	19.8

Data from Lund and Nordlund (2003).

Vuchinich & Simpson, 1998; Bretteville-Jensen, 1999) or fluctuating time preferences (Skog, 1997), probably plays a crucial role in the addictions. Dynamic inconsistency means that the agent does not act as he or she intended, and this implies that the core idea in "rational addiction" theory is invalid.

Lastly, rational addiction theory assumes that the agent makes his choice on the basis of realistic information about the possible effects of his consumption choices. In particular, the theory assumes that the inexperienced agent actually knows how an addictive craving will feel like, and how unpleasant the harmful consequences of excessive use will be. This is obviously unrealistic. As Walt Whitman has put it:

> "None know – none can know, but they who have felt it – the burning, withering thirst for drink, which habit forms in the appetite of the wretched victim of intoxication."
> Whitman ([1842] 1929, p. 148)

However, the problem an inexperienced person will have at understanding in advance how enslavements feels, and more generally in understanding how it feels to be a person with different preferences compared to the preferences one actually has at present, is only one side of the issue. Another side is the problem of retaining a fresh and realistic memory of strong motives actually experienced in the past. George Loewenstein (1999) has argued that people in general tend to have a biased memory of visceral motives, typically underestimating their strength. If this is correct, it would be quite difficult for a person with strong outbursts of visceral motives to plan ahead, for instance by setting up realistic defence strategies to prevent himself from giving into these outbursts. Combining this with dynamic inconsistency and self-serving biases, we end up with a very different picture of addiction.

In conclusion, a realistic theory of addiction will have to abandon quite a lot of the assumptions on which rational addiction theory is built. What remains is the idea that the agent is more or less forward-looking, trying to make the best of what he has got, according to his own valuations.

4. CULTURE AND PREFERENCE FORMATION: OUTLINE OF A MODEL

Economic theory normally takes the consumers' preferences for granted, and do not ask where they come from. In "rational addiction" theory, certain preference changes are explicitly modelled, namely that consumption breeds appetite. However, no external environment is modelled in this theory, except economic factors such as prices. The addict is in consequence conceived as a "Robinson Crusoe". In order to obtain a firmer understanding of who are at risk and how people develop addictive preferences we obviously need to consider the socio-cultural context where these preferences are formed.

Our likes and dislikes are socio-cultural products, they are shaped and reshaped in social interaction. Therefore, individual risks and choices should depend strongly on the social and cultural environment. This has implications, both for exit from and entry into addictive states. Regarding exist, an individual can be severely addicted in one context, suffering under an irresistible urge for continued heavy consumption, but not in another context, where the circumstances are different and the costs of continued indulgence unacceptable to him. Lee Robins' (1993) study of Vietnam veterans offers a stunning illustration of this fact. In her sample, 45% of the soldier had used opiates, and 20% had developed dependence during their stay in Vietnam. Knowing that they would be tested before returning to the U.S.A., about half of them had managed to stop on their own, while the remaining half had a positive urine test. A year after their return, only 5% of those who had been dependent was still dependent, and same was true 3 years after the return. A few were occasional users with no signs of dependence, but many were abstinent. A dramatic change in socio-cultural context made the "impossible" possible.

Weakness of the will and ambivalence are important components of addiction, cf. items 3 and 4 on the DSM-IV list; i.e. consuming more than one intended, and having tried to cut back, and failed. In fact, Heather (1998) argues, convincingly, to the effect that item 4 on the list is a sine qua non of addiction. A very strong, but unstable conflict between abstention and consumption motives would typically characterize this state of addiction. However, the relative strength of these motives would clearly depend on the circumstances. In one context, the negative consequences of continued indulgence could become so strong that the consumer finds them unacceptable, and he succeeds in quitting, at least for a while. Under other circumstances, the same consumer may not have very strong reasons for holding back – say because he has lost his family, friends and job, and feels he no longer has anything to live for (cf. Skog, (2003), for a fuller discussion). In short, the actual choices made by people who are strongly addicted, will obviously be influenced by the socio-cultural context in which they live. And people who are only moderately addicted are probably even more sensitive to circumstances. Hence, trying to understand addictive behaviour outside any social context, as "rational addiction" theory invites us to, is meaningless.

Concerning entry, the likelihood that an individual shall consume a drug at all, and to consume enough to experience real problems of the sort listed among the DSM-IV criteria, strongly depends on environmental factors, including social norms, cultural rules and traditions, and the consumption behaviour of others. The same individual could develop a preference for abstention, infrequent drinking, frequent drinking or excessive drinking, depending on the cultural environment he or she is socialized into. Comparisons between drinking cultures with highly different consumption levels has revealed that the whole distribution of consumers according to intake is typically shifted, when we move from low to high consumption cultures (Skog, 1985). The phenomenon is illustrated in Fig. 2, which suggests that individual consumption preferences are strongly influenced by the culture in which they are socialized. The typical light drinker (say, represented by the 25th percentile) drinks considerably more in the "wet"-drinking cultures of Southern Europe, than in the "dryer" cultures of Northern Europe. The same applies to the typical moderate drinker (represented by the 50th percentile) and the heavier drinkers (represented by the 90th or the 95th

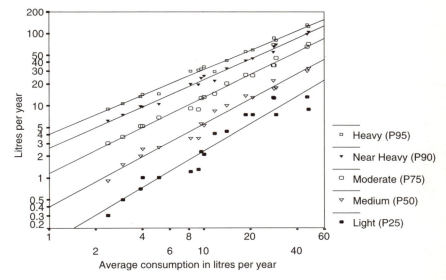

Fig. 2. Relationship between Average Consumption and the Consumption Level of Selected Drinking Groups (Defined by Percentiles), in 21 Population Surveys. The Straight Lines are Least Square Regressions. Logarithmic Scales. *Source*: Skog (1985).

percentile). However, for the latter groups, the dependence on the overall level of consumption (as measured by the slope of the regression) is note quite as strong as in the case of the former groups.

A comparison of the hazard rates (also called "consumption containment rates", cf. Taylor, 1979) corresponding to these consumption distributions, elaborates the latter observation, and reveal some interesting properties. The hazard rate is defined as:

$$h(x) = \frac{f(x)}{1 - F(x)}$$

where f and F denotes the probability density and the cumulative probability function, respectively. Although the hazard rates are very different at low consumption levels in high and low consumption cultures, respectively, they appear to be fairly similar at high consumption levels (Skog, 1993). The curves displayed in Fig. 3 attempt to describe the overall pattern observed in the data.

The hazard rate at a certain consumption level can be interpreted as a measure of the tendency of consumers who have reached that level, to

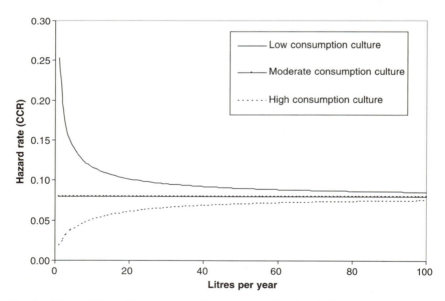

Fig. 3. Hazard Rate (Consumption Containment Rate) at Different Consumption Levels in Typical Low, Moderate and High Consumption Cultures.

remain at this level (as opposed to progressing to even higher levels). The large intercultural differences observed at low consumption levels tell us that at low and moderate consumption levels, cultural factors have a very strong impact on individual preferences and actual drinking habits. At these levels, the tendency to progress varies strongly across cultures. However, at very high consumption levels, the cultural differences are much smaller. Hence, when a consumer has reached high consumption levels, the likelihood of proceeding to even higher levels appear to be less sensitive to the cultural context. At this level, the addiction mechanisms might have stronger effects on consumption choices.

However, it should be noted that although the hazard rates at high levels are similar across cultures, the *proportion* of the consumers that reach these high levels are quite different across cultures. In high consumption cultures, a much higher fraction of the population reaches high levels due to the collective displacement of the whole population along the consumption scale.

An interpretation of these observations might be the following. An individual's preferences for drinking are to a large extent formed by extant drinking habits and traditions in the individual's socio-cultural environment. People who are socialized in a wet environment are more likely to have their drinking fostered, and a larger fraction of the population will reach a consumption level where the level of dependence is no longer insignificant. At these levels, the risk of progressing to even higher levels is less influenced by (but not independent of) the drinking culture, and more dependent on individual factors, including the degree of dependence. For instance, the moderating effect of moderate drinking peers may gradually become less influential as the consumer progresses towards higher levels.

The consumer's current consumption choice, which we denote Y, thus ought to be seen as a function of a long series of factors, including the socio-cultural environment. We let S denote the level of drinking in his subculture.[2] Second, we have general push factors, i.e. internal and external causal factors that shape the individual's current preferences, as well as external opportunities and constraints. We let P denote these push factors, which includes taste, values, economic resources, physiological and psychological make-up, social roles and norms, prices, availability of drug in question, etc. Some of these stimulate and others restrain his consumption. Third, we have pull factors, i.e. the forward-looking, intentional part, which we denote F.[3] These factors include the positive outcomes the agent tries to obtain, and the negative consequences he tries to avoid. His (rational or irrational) beliefs about the likelihood of winning (in the case of gambling) and beliefs about the risk of experiencing harm (in the case of drugs) belong to this category. Lastly, his consumption history forms his habits and induces weak or strong dependence, and we let H denote a suitable measure of this stock variable (which corresponds to Becker's consumption capital).[4] His present consumption choice ought to be a function of all these factors, $Y = f(S, P, F, H)$. Both the consumption levels in his sub-culture, S, and the consumption history, H, ought to have a positive impact on Y, while the push and pull factors are mixtures of positive and negative factors.[5]

As was noted earlier, addictions come in degrees, it is not an either/or phenomenon. An addicted person finds it difficult to abstain, or significantly reducing his or her consumption. The stronger the addiction, the more difficult it is. For most addicts, entry is probably a slippery slope, rather than rational choice. Wishful thinking and myopia prevents him from seeing the full picture during the early stages of the process. Some will realize the dangers early enough to prevent further progression, others at much later stages. There is no reason to assume that there is a fixed point of no return, and consequently no need to model one, as the consumer could end up at any consumption level, depending on the relative strength of factors pulling in different directions.

5. SOME IMPLICATIONS FROM THE MODEL: THE SOCIAL ROOTS OF ADDICTIVE PREFERENCES

The model outlined above could be used as a starting point for a more detailed analysis of the phenomenon of dependence, and in particular the slippery slope into addiction, as well as the struggle to get out, with relapse and continued struggle. However, I shall not pursue this issue here, and will instead focus on a few issues related to the social mechanisms.

Let us first note that the positive impact of the consumption level in the sub-culture on individual's consumption implies that wet cultures are expected to have a higher number of consumers at high levels. Since the likelihood of dependence increases strongly with consumption level (Edwards et al., 1994), we would in effect expect an increasing number of both moderately and severely addicted consumers as the overall level of consumption in society increases.

As was already pointed out, the impact of sub-culture on the individual consumer (df/dS, or the parameter β in the linear approximation) could be a decreasing function of the consumer's level of dependence, and therefore also a decreasing function of consumption level. However, the relationship between β and consumption level is probably also influenced by a selection mechanism. Some people are quite strongly integrated into their sub-culture, and are therefore strongly influenced by this sub-culture. Others are more socially isolated, and less influenced by their sub-culture. These differences exist prior to the development of dependence. The more strongly people are influenced, the more homogenous the group will be with respect to consumption level, i.e. the smaller will be the variance of the consumption distribution. For simplicity, assume that we have split the population in two, according to the individual consumers' level of integration. Those who are weakly influenced by their sub-culture would typically be more spread out along the consumption scale than the strongly integrated, as outlined in Fig. 4.

This mechanism implies that consumers who are weakly influenced by their sub-culture could be expected to dominate both at high and low consumption levels, while those who are more strongly influenced should dominate at intermediate consumption levels. In consequence, an inverted U-shaped relationship should be expected between consumption level and social integration. This effect should be present, independently of the dependence mechanism mentioned earlier. In Fig. 4, the average consumption level of weakly and strongly integrated consumers are similar. If one of these population segments, e.g. the strongly integrated consumers, drinks more than the other, the resulting relationship would become asymmetrical. However, we would still expect an inverted U-shape, although skew. If the

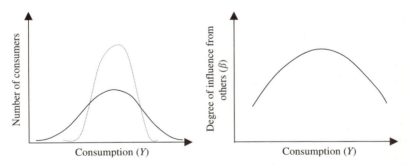

Fig. 4. Left: Distribution of Strongly (Dotted) and Weakly (Solid) Integrated Individuals According to Consumption Level. Right: Implied Relationship between The Degree to Which the Drinker Is Influenced by Others in Their Sub-culture and the Drinkers Consumption Level.

strongly integrated on the average tend to drink more, the right-hand branch of the curve would be smaller and less pronounced.

Relationships of this type have been reported in the literature. A study of Swedish military conscripts (Leifman, Kühlhorn, Allebeck, Andreasson, & Romelsjö, 1993) found that several different indicators of social isolation had a U-shaped relationship to consumption level. Both heavy drinkers and abstainers/very light drinkers reported higher levels of isolation than the moderate drinkers. Since socially isolated individuals can be expected to be less influenced by their sub-culture than socially well-integrated individuals, this result is in line with the prediction.

Similar results are evident in data from a Norwegian health survey, reported in Table 4. Both abstainers/light drinkers and frequent drinkers reported feelings of loneliness more often than drinkers at intermediate levels. The abstainers and very light drinkers report feelings of loneliness more than twice as often as the reference group (drinking 2–3 times per month), and the most frequent drinkers report this nearly twice as often. This relationship is still present after controlling for gender and age, although somewhat less pronounced. The abstainers and very light drinkers report feelings of loneliness about 40% as often as the reference group, and the most frequent drinkers report this about 60% more often.

In conclusion, the higher levels of social isolation often observed among alcohol-dependent consumers, are probably both an effect of a selection mechanism and a causal effect of excessive drinking. The weakly integrated have a higher likelihood of drinking in excess of their culture's norm due to weak informal social control (mechanism no. 1), and the process of becoming addicted would further reduce their integration (mechanism no. 2).

Furthermore, it follows from the sub-culture argument that some drinkers should end up at a high consumption level in spite of being strongly socially integrated, simply because they are integrated into a very wet sub-culture (mechanism no. 3). Hence, the importance of social isolation as a risk factor should not be exaggerated. Although the consumption career of these heavy "social drinkers" gradually could lead to a reduction in their social integration, they would not necessarily end up as social isolates.

Still another mechanism would be that the consumer moves away from his old moderate-consuming sub-culture, and into one with a higher consumption level. There are basically two ways of handling a large discrepancy between one's personal level of drinking and that in one's sub-culture: Either reducing one's own consumption level or pulling back from this sub-culture's sphere of influence. The last strategy can be obtained either by seeking isolation (letting β become reduced) or by seeking a new social

Table 4. Prevalence of Feelings of Loneliness in Different Alcohol Consumption Groups. Logistic Regression Analysis.

	Model 1				Model 2			
	b	SE (b)	Wald	P	OR	b	SE (b)	Wald	P	OR
Abstainer	1.088	0.134	65.6	<0.001	2.970	0.345	0.145	5.7	0.017	1.411
Less than once per month	0.729	0.140	27.1	<0.001	2.073	0.337	0.144	5.4	0.020	1.400
About once per month	0.381	0.158	5.8	0.016	1.464	0.246	0.160	2.4	0.125	1.279
Reference group (2–3 times per month)	–	–	–	–	1.000	–	–	–	–	1.000
About once per week	0.215	0.158	1.9	0.173	1.240	0.172	0.160	1.1	0.284	1.187
Several times per week	0.619	0.173	12.7	<0.001	1.856	0.482	0.178	7.3	0.007	1.619
Age (years over 18)	–	–	–	–	–	0.029	0.002	165.9	<0.001	1.029
Gender (females = 1)	–	–	–	–	–	0.843	0.084	101.6	<0.001	2.324
Constant	−2.723	0.118	536.0	<0.001	0.066	−4.345	0.164	698.4	<0.001	0.013
−2LL		5,117.1					4,847.7			
Hosmer–Lemeshow		–					8.2, $d.f.=8$, $P=0.419$			

Data from the Norwegian Health Survey (1985), $n = 7,674$.
SE: standard error; OR: odds ratio.

network with drinking habits more in line with one's own habits; i.e. seeking a higher S (mechanism no. 4).

The last social mechanism I should like to mention is drug consumption as a substitute for social contact, i.e. a kind of self-medication for loneliness (mechanism no. 5).[6] A particular version of this mechanism might be relevant for explaining relapse. Since treatment means opportunities for socializing, and end of treatment means less socializing, the lonely addicts may use drugs as a substitute for socializing after treatment. From this point of view it is not surprising that lonely addicts are often observed to relapse fairly quickly (Skog, 1990; Vuchinich & Tucker, 1996). However, at the other end of the spectrum, addicts who are integrated into a wet network also have an elevated risk of relapse.

There are in effect several social mechanisms that need to be considered in theories of addiction, and some of these are reciprocal (for instance nos. 1 and 2, as well as 3 and 4). These mechanisms are summarized in Fig. 5. Additional complexity derives from the fact that a high consumption level over time (H) influences both the level of dependence (γ), the addict's evaluation of risks and his time preferences (i.e. the motivational force of future consequences, F), as well as numerous push factors. The result is a rather complex causal structure that is not easily fitted into the formal models of neo-classical economics. This does not mean that economic theory has little to offer in relation to addiction. It only means that some theoretical rigor may have to be sacrificed for the sake of realism.

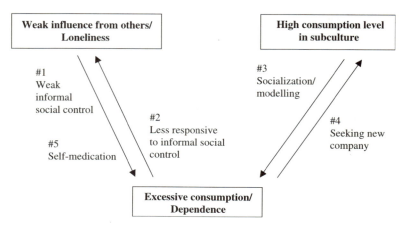

Fig. 5. Five Social Mechanisms Connecting Excessive Consumption/Dependence and the Consumer's Social Environment.

6. CONCLUSION

Gary Becker's theory of rational addiction is probably one of the most important social science contribution to the theory of addiction in recent years, not because it offers a correct description and analysis of addiction, but because it introduced a fruitful way of looking at the phenomenon. The theory in its original form is clearly inadequate, by assuming too much rationality, and by having a somewhat simplistic conception of the phenomenon of addiction. However, the general approach clearly has the potential of being developed into a more realistic, albeit less parsimonious theory.

Economic theories of addiction need to address the following issues, and to make the necessary adjustments. Some of these are not violations of the rational choice paradigm itself, but refutations of conventional addendums to this paradigm (e.g. stable preferences). Others are clearly violating the rational choice paradigm, although not the idea of forward-looking agents who are choosing freely according to their own appetites and constraints:

Addiction comes in degrees, from light through moderate to very high. It should not be modelled as an either/or phenomenon. The idea of a distinct, destabilizing threshold is probably not realistic.

People's vulnerability probably varies a lot. Among different individuals with the same consumption career, some would be severely addicted, while others would hardly show signs of addiction. This heterogeneity needs to be modelled in order to avoid highly unrealistic predictions.

Addictive preferences are typically not stable over time. They tend to fluctuate strongly, in response to environmental factor, due to cognitive defects (e.g. hyperbolic discounting) and due to sheer psychic turbulence. Economic theory will miss the very essence of addiction, the addicts' struggles and relapses, unless these instabilities are taken into consideration.

Economists' attempts at testing the rational addiction theory via econometric models will probably prove unproductive. Most theories conceiving addiction as choice would allow for anticipation effects of one sort or another. Furthermore, non-addicts are likely to be more future-oriented than addicts, due to selection effects. The important testing ground for choice theories lies elsewhere.

Self-serving belief formation probably plays a very important role in the case of addictive substances. This irrationality needs to be studied most carefully, as it clearly would have particularly devastating consequences for consumer's goods that are positive in the short run, but potentially harmful in the long run.

In addition to self-serving bias, both dynamic inconsistencies and the problem of knowing in advance how life as an addict feels, makes it unreasonable to model these choices as long-term plans for the entire consumption career. A more modest model is needed, where current choices are allowed to be influenced by beliefs about the future, past consumption behaviour, but also the numerous other factors influencing real people's consumption choices.

In particular, the embeddedness of individual consumers in their social and cultural context must be acknowledged. Individuals' consumption behaviour are strongly interdependent, and drug-taking behaviour is typically conformist behaviour. The likelihood that any given individual shall engage in this sort of behaviour and the extent to which he is doing it, very much depends on what other individuals are doing.

Whether or not a consumer is in a state of addiction may strongly depend on the social circumstances. Addiction means that the agent finds it difficult to abstain or to curtail his consumption, but these difficulties will typically be highly dependent on the social context (cf. Robins' Vietnam veterans.)

The relationship between the level of socializing and level of consumption is complex. Just as loneliness under certain circumstances may foster addiction, so may strong integration into a heavy consuming sub-culture. And addiction may bring about social isolation, or a shift into another sub-culture.

NOTES

1. An empirical test of this claim could be this: If the (immediate) consequences of continued consumption became painful enough, all (or practically all) should be able to resist their craving.

2. The level of consumption in the consumer's sub-culture might be defined as a weighted average of the consumption levels in his social network, where the weights p_{ij} indicate the relative importance of other consumers ($p_{ii} = 0$):

$$S_i = \sum_{j=1}^{N} p_{ij} Y_j, \quad \text{where} \quad \sum_{j=1}^{N} p_{ij} = 1$$

It is well documented empirically that individual drinking is influenced by the drinking behaviour of peers (for reviews, cf. Skog, 1980a; Quigley & Collins, 1999). A model of this type has been postulated to explain the collective differences between drinking cultures described in Fig. 2. The social interaction theory proposes that the phenomenon is explained by diffusion mechanisms in social networks (Skog, 1979, 1980a, 1985).

3. Both *P* and *F* should be conceived as vectors of a number of variables, some of which have a positive (e.g. economic resources, hedonistic motives), while others have a negative (e.g. prices, fear of harmful effects) impact on consumption.

4. A suitable measure of an individual's drinking history might be:

$$H(t) = \delta Y(t-1) + (1-\delta)H(t-1)$$

where δ is the depreciation rate. In equilibrium, $H = Y$.

5. If consumption is measured on a logarithmic scale, a local approximation to this function could be:

$$Y = \alpha + \beta S + \gamma H + \pi P + \varphi F + \varepsilon$$

where ε is a random "error". The parameter β measures the effect of the sub-culture on the consumer, while γ measures the effect of habit (degree of dependence). However, this it not meant to imply that β and γ are constant and independent of the person's consumption career (see the text). In more realistic versions, non-linearities would have to be modelled. The push and pull factors are vector products.

6. Rachlin (2000) has focused on this particular mechanism, but the fact that his analysis ignores all the other mechanisms outlined above, restrict the value of his analysis.

REFERENCES

Ainslie, G. (1992). *Picoeconomics*. Cambridge: Cambridge University Press.
Auld, M.C., & Grootendorst, P. (2002). *An empirical analysis of milk addiction*. Unpublished manuscript.
Becker, G. (1996). *Accounting for tastes*. Cambridge, MA: Harvard University Press.
Becker, G. S. (1992). Habits, addictions, and traditions. *Kyklos*, 45, 327–346.
Becker, G. S., & Murphy, K. M. (1988). A theory of rational addiction. *Journal of Political Economy*, 96, 675–700.
Becker, G. S., Grossman, M., & Murphy, K. M. (1992). Rational addiction and the effect of price on consumption. In: G. Loewenstein & J. Elster (Eds), *Choice over time* (pp. 361–370). NY: Russel Sage Foundation.
Becker, G. S., Grossman, M., & Murphy, K. M. (1994). An empirical analysis of cigarette addiction. *American Economic Review*, 84, 396–418.
Bretteville-Jensen, A. L. (1999). Addiction and discounting. *Journal of Health Economics*, 18, 393–407.
Chaloupka, F. (1991). Rational addictive behavior and cigarette-smoking. *Journal of Political Economy*, 99, 722–742.
Diagnostic and statistical manual of mental disorders (4th ed.). (1994). Washington, DC: American Psychiatric Association.
Duckert, F. (1988). Recruitment to alcohol treatment – A comparison between male and female problem drinkers recruited to treatment in 2 different ways. *British Journal of Addiction*, 83, 285–293.
Edwards, G. (1982). *The treatment of drinking problems*. NY: McGraw-Hill.
Edwards, G., Anderson, P., Babor, T., Casswell, S., Ferrence, R., Giesbrecht, N., Godfrey, C., Holder, H., Lemmens, P., Mäkelä, K., Midanik, L., Norström, T., Österberg, E.,

Romelsjö, A., Room, R., Simpura, J., & Skog, O.-J. (1994). *Alcohol policy and the public good*. Oxford: Oxford University Press.

Elster, J. (1999). Gambling and addiction. In: J. Elster & O.-J. Skog (Eds), *Getting hooked: Rationality and addiction* (pp. 208–234). Cambridge: Cambridge University Press.

Fillmore, K. M., & Midanik, L. (1984). Chronicity of drinking problems among men – A longitudinal-study. *Journal of Studies on Alcohol, 45*, 228–236.

Gruber, J., & Köszegi, B. (2001). Is addiction "rational"? Theory and evidence. *Quarterly Journal of Economics, 116*, 1261–1303.

Heather, N. (1998). A conceptual framework for explaining drug addiction. *Journal of Psychopharmacology, 12*, 3–7.

Heather, N., & Robertson, I. (1981). *Controlled drinking*. London: Methuen.

Jellinek, E. M. (1960). *The disease concept of alcoholism*. New Brunswick, NJ: Hillhouse Press.

Kahneman, D., & Tversky, A. (2000). *Choices, values, and frames*. New York: Cambridge University Press/Russel Sage Foundation.

Keeler, T. E., Hu, T.-W., Barnett, P. G., & Manning, W. G. (1993). Taxation, regulation, and addiction: A demand function for cigarettes based on time-series evidence. *Journal of Health Economics, 12*, 1–18.

Keller, M. (1972). On the loss-of-control phenomenon in alcoholism. *British Journal of Addiction, 67*, 153–166.

Leifman, H., Kühlhorn, E., Allebeck, P., Andreasson, S., & Romelsjö, A. (1993). Antecedents and covariates to a sober lifestyle and its consequences. *Social Science and Medicine, 41*, 113–121.

Loewenstein, G. (1999). A visceral account of addiction. In: J. Elster & O.-J. Skog (Eds), *Getting hooked: Rationality and addiction* (pp. 235–264). Cambridge: Cambridge University Press.

Lund, I., & Nordlund, S. (2003). *Pengespill og pengespillproblemer i Norge*. Oslo: SIRUS.

Marlatt, G. A., Demming, B., & Reid, J. B. (1973). Loss of control drinking in alcoholics: An experimental analogue. *Journal of Abnormal Psychology, 81*, 233–241.

McKenna, F. A. (1990). Heuristics or cognitive deficits: How should we characterize smoker's decision making. In: D. M. Warburton (Ed.), *Addiction controversies* (pp. 261–270). Chur, Switzerland: Harwood.

Mello, N. K., & Mendelson, J. H. (1965). Operant analysis of drinking patterns of chronic alcoholics. *Nature, 206*, 43–46.

Mello, N. K., & Mendelson, J. H. (1966). Experimental analysis of drinking behavior of chronic alcoholics. *Annals of New York Academy of Sciences, 133*, 828–845.

Mello, N. K., & Mendelson, J. H. (1972). Drinking patterns during work contingent and noncontingent alcohol acquisition. *Psychosomatic Medicine, 34*, 139–164.

Nordström, G., & Berglund, M. (1987). A prospective-study of successful long-term adjustment in alcohol dependence – Social drinking versus abstinence. *Journal of Studies on Alcohol, 48*, 95–103.

Orphanides, A., & Zervos, D. (1995). Rational addiction with learning and regret. *Journal of Political Economy, 103*, 739–758.

Pattison, E. M., Sobell, M. B., & Sobell, L. C. (1977). *Emerging concepts of alcohol dependence*. New York: Springer.

Polich, J. M., Armor, D. J., & Braiker, H. B. (1980). *The course of alcoholism: Four years after treatment*. Santa Monica, CA: Rand Corp.

Quigley, B. M., & Collins, R. L. (1999). The modeling of alcohol consumption: A meta-analytic review. *Journal of Studies of Alcohol, 60*, 90–98.

Rachlin, H. (2000). *The science of self-control.* Cambridge, MA: Harvard University Press.

Robins, L. N. (1993). Vietnam veterans' rapid recovery from heroin addiction: A fluke or normal expectation? *Addiction, 88*, 1041–1054.

Room, R. (2004). *Tsunami or ripple? Studying the effects of current Nordic alcohol policy changes.* Unpublished manuscript.

Skog, O.-J. (1979). *Modeller for drikkeatferd.* SIFA-report no. 32. Oslo: National Institute for Alcohol Research.

Skog, O.-J. (1980a). Social interaction and the distribution of alcohol consumption. *Journal of Drug Issues, 10*, 71–92.

Skog, O.-J. (1980b). Is alcohol consumption lognormally distributed? *British Journal of Addiction, 75*, 169–173.

Skog, O.-J. (1985). The collectivity of drinking cultures. A theory of the distribution of alcohol consumption. *British Journal of Addiction, 80*, 83–99.

Skog, O.-J. (1986). The wetness of drinking cultures: A key variable in epidemiology of alcoholic liver cirrhosis. *Acta Medica Scandinavica, Suppl, 703*, 157–184.

Skog, O.-J. (1990). Alcohol in a social network perspective: Implications for epidemiology. *Alcologia, 2*, 13–21.

Skog, O.-J. (1993). The tail of the alcohol consumption distribution. *Addiction, 88*, 601–610.

Skog, O.-J. (1997). The strength of weak will. *Rationality and Society, 9*, 245–271.

Skog, O.-J. (1999). Rationality, irrationality, and addiction – Notes on Becker and Murphy's theory of addiction. In: J. Elster & O.-J. Skog (Eds), *Getting hooked: Rationality and addiction* (pp. 173–207). Cambridge: Cambridge University Press.

Skog, O.-J. (2000). Addict's choice. *Addiction, 95*, 1309–1314.

Skog, O.-J. (2003). Addiction – Definitions and mechanisms. In: N. Heather & R. Vuchinich (Eds), *Choice, behavioural economics and addiction.* New York: Pergamon Press.

Skog, O.-J., & Duckert, F. (1993). The development of alcoholics' and heavy drinkers' consumption: A longitudinal study. *Journal of Studies on Alcohol, 54*, 178–188.

Taylor, C. (1979). A method for describing variability in alcohol consumption levels. *British Journal of Addiction, 74*, 57–66.

Viscusi, K. (1992). *Smoking.* Oxford: Oxford University Press.

Vuchinich, R. E., & Simpson, C. A. (1998). Hyperbolic temporal discounting in social drinkers and problem drinkers. *Experimental and Clinical Psychopharmacology, 6*, 292–305.

Vuchinich, R. E., & Tucker, J. (1996). Alcohol relapse, life events and behavioral theories of choice: A prospective analysis. *Experimental and Clinical Psychopharmacology, 4*, 19–28.

Wagenaar, W. A. (1988). *Paradoxes of gambling behavior.* London: Lawrence Erlbaum.

Whitman, W. ([1842] 1929). *Franklin Evans or the inebriate.* NY: Random House.

THE SPREAD OF DRUG USE: EPIDEMIC MODELS OR SOCIAL INTERACTION?

Hans O. Melberg

ABSTRACT

This chapter argues that models trying to explain the spread of drug use should not be based on standard epidemiological models developed to describe the spread of infectious diseases. The main weaknesses of the standard model are the lack of attention to micro-foundations and the inappropriateness of several of its assumptions in the context of drug use. An approach based on mechanisms and social interaction is argued to provide a promising alternative to the standard approach. To illustrate this, a model of the spread of drugs based on two mechanisms has been developed (observational learning and social stigma). Lastly, some of the difficulties in testing and deriving policy implications in these models are discussed.

1. INTRODUCTION

It is sometimes claimed that drug use is contagious. In the words of a former high-ranking Norwegian police officer:

> Every new drug abuser lures or persuades about 3–4 of his acquaintances to try the drug. Each of these cause 3–4 others join and so on, thus creating an increase like a geometric pattern: 3–9–27–72 and so on.
>
> Quoted and translated from Hauge (2000, p. 241)

Related to this view is the argument that the spread of drug use can be analysed using standard epidemic models used to analyse the spread of diseases. As one of the first contributors to the scholarly literature on the subject wrote:

> If drug abuse is seen as a practice that is transmitted from one person to another, it can be considered for operational purposes, as a contagious illness.
>
> de Alarcón (1969, p. 17)

Faced with the epidemic model of drug use one might ask several questions. Is drug use really contagious and is this an important question? If it appears to be contagious, what are the mechanisms behind its contagious nature? What are the policy implications of using a contagion model? And, finally, is it possible to model and test these mechanisms empirically?

On the first question I shall argue that the term "contagious" is misleading, and that using standard epidemic models originally developed to describe the spread of infectious diseases as a method for analysing the spread of drugs can produce counterproductive policy conclusions. The main cause of the problem is the lack of attention to *micro-foundations* and a related acceptance of several assumptions in the standard model, which are inappropriate when applied to drug use. On a more positive note, I argue that an approach based on mechanisms and social interaction is a better alternative than the epidemic approach. The difference is important because once we focus on social interaction we are forced down to the micro-level – thinking about the mechanisms that create the appearance of an epidemic.

After criticising existing models, I attempt to be more constructive by discussing how mechanisms of social interaction may help to explain the level of drug use in a society. Two mechanisms are discussed and modelled in detail. The first mechanism is *observational learning*: Before deciding whether or not to use drugs each generation is assumed to observe and learn about the dangers and attractions of drugs from current users. The second mechanism relies on the dynamics of *social stigma*: In the same way that the stigma of divorce is reduced when many people get divorced, one might view the social stigma of using drugs as a decreasing function of the number of people using drugs. After presenting the formal model and exploring some of its properties, I move on to policy implications and the possibility of empirical testing of the model. The argument in this section is that the difficulty of testing the aggregate implications of the mechanisms should not lead to the pessimistic conclusion that no empirical testing is possible. To establish the relevance of a mechanism, it is also possible to examine the behavioural assumptions that go into the theory directly either through experiments or observations. This may render the existence of a proposed mechanism more convincing, but it does not necessarily lead to a clear policy recommendation since different mechanisms have contradictory effects and this makes it difficult to judge the overall net effect of policy changes.

2. DRUG USE AND CONTAGIOUSNESS

Clearly drug use is not contagious in the same sense as measles, the flue, cholera and other diseases we label "contagious". Admittedly we sometimes use the term contagious about behaviour and not only bacteria and viruses that spread. For instance, laughter and yawning are sometimes said to be contagious. However, these phenomena have a more involuntary character than taking drugs for the first time. Yawning is largely a muscle reflex while starting to use drugs, as argued by Skog (2000), is at least in some sense the result of a choice. This distinction seriously weakens the analogy purportedly existing between drug use and contagious diseases.

Most researchers who describe drug use as contagious do not use the term literally. For instance, in one of the earliest references to contagious drug use in the economics literature the author writes: "We can also think of them [heroin users] as potential carriers of a contagious malady" (Seagraves, 1973, p. 279). The argument here is not that drug use is literally contagious, but that it can be profitably analysed as if it were a contagious disease, using the tools and models of standard epidemic research. Hence, those who build models of drug use based on epidemic models cannot be criticised for arguing that drug use literally is contagious. However, one might still argue that it is unfortunate to use terminology that may easily confuse the public and policy-makers into thinking that drugs are in fact contagious in the traditional sense of the term. There is some evidence that this confusion has affected policy. For instance, research on the contagiousness of drugs has been used to justify claims that heroin addiction is "just about as contagious and just about as deadly as the bubonic plague", and that harsh action should be taken against drug users (General Lewis W. Walt, Head of the Task Force on World Narcotics Traffic, testifying before Congress in 1972, referring to research by de Alarcón and quoted in Weimer (2003, p. 273)).

Be that as it may, the main point of this chapter is not to examine the unfortunate choice of words. Although important enough, the arguments against this practice have been made a long time ago; see Drucker and Sidel (1974) and Jacobs (1976) for early criticism of borrowing epidemiological words and concepts, and the implications that followed. Instead, the present focus is to question even the "as if" analysis, i.e. whether the analogy between the spread of drugs and the spread of diseases is such that the models used to analyse one can be used to analyse the other. Before such an evaluation can take place, however, it is necessary to take a short detour into standard theories of diffusion in epidemic theory.

In the following section I shall briefly present one of the most common approaches used for diseases that are transmitted from person to person, ignoring models used to describe diseases that are transmitted indirectly (e.g. by water contamination); see Hethcote (2000) or Sattenspiel (1990) for an overview of the literature on the spread of infectious diseases. I shall then review the literature on the application of these models to the spread of drugs. The aim of the presentation at this point is mainly descriptive.

2.1. The SIR Model

In a standard deterministic epidemic model a person at some point in time (t) can be in one of the three compartments – susceptible (S), infected (I) and recovered (R). The names of the compartments give the model its shorthand name – the SIR model. One could extend the model to include births (with and without passive immunity) and a compartment for individuals who are exposed but not yet infective. Often, however, modellers ignore birth and assume a constant population size with no immigration or emigration.

After specifying the compartments, the next step is to say something about the transmission dynamics, i.e. the factors governing the transfer of people between the compartments. One may, for instance, assume that a fixed proportion (γ) of the infected recover during the course of each time period:

$$\frac{dR}{dt} = \gamma I \tag{1}$$

The number of new people becoming infected is often assumed to follow the mass–action principle. This was first suggested by Hamer (1906) and it states that the number of new cases is a quotient (β) of the number of susceptibles divided by the number of infectives in the population. All the new infectives are derived from the susceptibles, so in each time period the size of this group decreases:

$$\frac{dS}{dt} = -\beta SI \qquad (2)$$

Once we know the inflow to the recovered and the outflow from the susceptibles, it is easy to work out the change in the number of infected. From the susceptibles we must add all those who have been infected in the time period, but there is also an outflow since some infectives are assumed to recover each time period:

$$\frac{dI}{dt} = \beta SI - \gamma I \qquad (3)$$

After specifying the transmission dynamics, we can solve the system (analytically or by simulation) and thereby get an impression of the factors that govern the spread of the disease, its threshold level and the effect of policy interventions, such as vaccination or isolation, and provide explanations for different outcomes in different countries. One may also extend the model to include more compartments; for instance, to distinguish between men and women or drug users and non-drug users in a model of the spread of human immunodeficiency virus (HIV). One could also introduce other kinds of complications, such as using a stochastic instead of a deterministic frame. In short, the SIR model has proved to be a flexible tool that can be extended to cover many different diseases and assumptions.

2.2. Application of the Standard Models to the Spread of Drug Use

Although the model above is meant to describe infectious diseases, some researchers in the drug field have suggested that similar reasoning can be used to model the spread of drug use. One of the first to focus explicitly on the apparently contagious nature of drug use, even before it was mentioned briefly by Seabright, was de Alarcón (1969). From all known drug users between the ages of 15 and 20 who had sought treatment at the Crawley Psychiatric Service in 1967, he obtained the date and place of the first heroin dose, the name of the person who reportedly had initiated the user to the drug and whom they themselves had initiated. Based on these data ($N = 58$), de Alarcón found, first, that the use of heroin was not initiated by aggressive pushers from London. Instead it started with "local boys who had acquired the habit whilst visiting or living in another town" (de Alarcón, 1969, p. 20). Moreover, from the web of named initiators, he concluded that some users appeared to be much more contagious than others (see B4, B8, A3 and A8 in Fig. 1).

de Alarcón's contribution was the first of several articles and books in the 1970s that described drug use as if it were a contagious illness (Dole, 1973; DuPont, 1971, 1973; DuPont & Greene, 1973; Hughes & Crawford, 1972, 1974; Hunt & Chambers, 1976; Jonas, 1972, 1973). These contributions were mainly verbal and descriptive, trying to estimate prevalence and incidence, and tracing the lines of contagion between individuals and places or to identify various epidemic outbreaks in time and space.

One of the weaknesses with de Alarcón's article and the other articles from this period is that they do not discuss the causal role of the initiator. In the case of measles and other contagious diseases it makes sense to say that a person was infected because he came into contact with somebody who was infected. Although recent research has revealed a new infectious agent (prions), the mechanism of transmission for most diseases are well understood and works through familiar agents like "viruses, bacteria, protozoa and helminthes (worms)" (Hethcote, 2000). In the case of drug addiction it is much less clear whether it makes sense to say that the encounter with the initiator was causally decisive. It is impossible to become sick with cholera

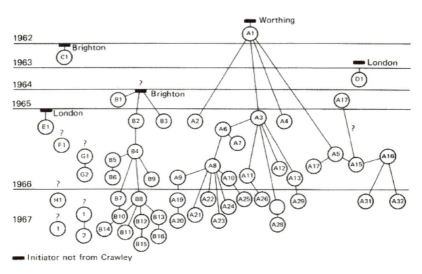

Fig. 1. de Alarcón's Illustration of the Spread of Heroin Use among Individuals in Crawley.

unless one is infected by somebody else; there are many possible alternative and complementary reasons behind taking drugs other than meeting an initiator. Thus, removing the virus or the initiator produces a guaranteed outcome when it comes to traditional diseases (no infection occurs), but not in the case of drug use. If being causally important is defined counterfactually in the sense that the outcome would be different had the encounter not happened, then drug use and cholera are very different.

Later contributions on the spread of drug use followed up on the verbal suggestion that drug use was contagious and created more formal models. For instance, Mackintosh and Stewart (1979) present a mathematical model of the spread of drugs based on a model developed for the spread of infectious diseases. They are mainly concerned with the effects of removing some of the infectious agents or early intervention to prevent the number of infectious agents to grow beyond a point where only massive intervention is effective. They do not, however, provide any micro-foundations and they can therefore be subject to the same criticism as de Alarcón.

The first to combine rigorous modelling of micro-foundations within a revised SIR-model to explain the spread of drug use was Hoppensteadt and Murray (1981). They modelled individuals' response to a drug as a function of the drug dose and the number of free receptors in the brain (which are bound by the drug). They furthermore assumed that the cure rate depended on age (older people are more likely to exit the user group) and, interestingly, that the infectiousness of a user depended on the drug reaction – "the greater the drug reaction, the more infectious is a user" (Hoppensteadt & Murray, 1981, p. 83). They did not, however, discuss why infectiousness should be related to drug reaction or exactly how or why drug use is transmitted from person to person.

One might argue that the omission is not significant since there are many obvious ways in which the link could be explained. Take, for instance, the common suggestion referred to in my introduction, i.e. existing users "lure or persuade" non-users. When asked why they should do so, one response could be the financial gains the existing user could receive as a pusher for the new user. This is how it has been interpreted in a model by Billiard and Dayananda (1993). In their model, which builds on Hoppensteadt and Murray (1981), a fraction of users is labelled "pushers" and it is this group that is assumed to be infectious. Although this is an advance compared to prior chapters in terms of providing a story to justify the transmission mechanism, it does not discuss the possibility of using alternative mechanisms for explaining how drugs spread from one individual to another. It is important to reflect on this, because, as I shall argue below, the standard explanation can produce misleading policy implications. Furthermore, one reason why the models are misleading is that they do not pay enough attention to the micro-foundations behind the aggregate relationships.

In what way can the standard disease model produce misleading implications? Usually when something is contagious we – (1) eliminate or reduce whatever is contagious; (2) isolate the agent carrying the infectious disease until she is treated and (3) immunise people who are not affected (vaccination). This focus is clearly illustrated by the articles on the spread of drugs. For instance, Mackintosh and Stewart (1979) focus explicitly on "the effect of removal policies" suggesting that:

> Those individuals who have affected others could be removed by such techniques as compulsory closed-ward treatment, immunisation with long-acting antagonists like cyclazocide, or, as a last resort, imprisonment.
>
> Mackintosh and Stewart (1979, p. 302)

Similarly, Hoppensteadt and Murray are concerned about the threshold above which a drug epidemic will result. From their expression of the threshold, it follows that to reduce the possibility of an epidemic we should be "increasing the cure rate" or "decreasing the individual's response, say, through education or chemical treatment" (Hoppensteadt & Murray, 1981, p. 87). This line of reasoning is by no means dead. For instance, the British newspaper *The Independent* recently reported that Professor David Nutt, "a leading government drug advisor" in the U.K., was in favour of a vaccination plan under which "doctors would immunise children at risk of becoming smokers or drug users with an injection" (Goodchild & Bloomfield, 2004). Thus, the focus and the implications from the models are very much in line with that of traditional diseases – to reduce the susceptibility of the population (vaccination or immunisation) and to isolate the contagious agents.

To see why the policy implication mentioned above may be problematic, consider the suggestion that the crack epidemic in the 1980s in the U.S.A. subsided when potential users observed the devastating effects the drug had on previous users (Musto, 1987). There is no room for this in a standard contagion model because it assumes that interaction is always negative in the sense that existing users always recruit new users. Musto, on the other hand, suggests that existing users sometimes deter potential users. Moreover, if the deterring effect is dominant, isolating existing users may *increase* the number of new users as opposed to decreasing it as implied by standard contagion models. Thus, it seems as if we have a case where analogical reasoning may lead us astray and we would be better off avoiding the term contagion and instead refer to social interaction that may go both ways (positive and negative).

In addition to potentially counterproductive policy recommendations, the analogy with contagious diseases also leads to a misplaced focus in basic academic research. Some of the main questions in the study of contagious diseases are focused on calculating the threshold beyond which an epidemic will occur, estimating the reproductive number and determining the length of the period of infectiousness and the natural or biological history of the infectious agent. Building on this analogy drug researchers have spent time and effort estimating the length of time a user remains infectious (i.e. introduces new users to drugs) and estimating the number of users which would result in the start of an epidemic. In contrast, little of the research on modelling the spread of drug use has focused on how incentives affect the spread of drugs. For instance, when many people use drugs one might expect that the stigma attached to drugs decreases, thus leading even more people to use drugs.

2.3. What Went Wrong?

The idea that observing drug users might deter some individuals from getting started, instead of infecting them, was absent in all the models discussed above. This is rather surprising given the ease by which we could find an example of the opposite effect. It is less surprising when we remember that the standard models usually operate at an aggregate level with standard assumptions about how to model the spread of a disease. The standard models do not start by asking exactly *how* people influence each other and the aggregate equations are not derived explicitly from decision processes at the individual level. Instead the standard models just assume that a disease will spread when susceptibles meet infectives. Thus, when drug researchers borrowed epidemic models they did not ask how people were linked. As Mackintosh and Stewart (1979, p. 300) explicitly admit: "We are not considering here, any more than in conventional models of infection, the behavioural variables which influence conversion of the 'susceptible' to a receptive state..."

3. AN ALTERNATIVE APPROACH

The aim of this section is to exemplify an alternative approach to modelling the spread of drug use. The nature of this approach follows logically from the criticism made in the previous sections. It should, first of all, start by asking how people influence each other, i.e. it should have micro-foundation based on mechanisms of social interaction. Second, the mechanisms should include both the possibility that current drug users attract new users, as well as the possibility that they scare some away from using drugs. Third, the mechanisms should be able to generate the various aggregate patterns that we observe, i.e. patterns that sometimes look like a classic epidemic with rapidly increasing drug use, a peak and then a decrease. Before going further into the details, however, I shall deal with two general issues about the alternative approach. First, some might argue against the three demands made above. Second, given the emphasis placed on "social interaction" there is a need to define this term more precisely.

3.1. Do We Need Micro-foundations?

Some might argue that it is not necessary to satisfy all three properties in an alternative approach. For instance, building on previous models by Everingham and Rydell (1994), and others, Behrens et al. (2002) have created a model, which "reconcile the competing tendencies of users to both promote and deter initiation..." (Behrens, Caulkins, Trangler, & Feichtinger, 2002, p. 920). Although this is almost the same general idea that is behind the approach that I propose, there is one important difference. In their framework "drug users' behaviour is governed by flow rates estimated from population-level historical data, not deduced from individual-level models of utility maximization..." (Behrens et al., 2002, p. 924). Specifically, they assume that the aggregate equation describing the number of new initiators per time period (I) is a function of the number of light users (L) and a decaying memory of former heavy users (E):

$$I(L, E) = \tau + sLe^{-qE/L} \qquad (4)$$

"where τ is the rate of 'spontaneous initiation', s, the annual rate at which light users attract non-users when reputation is benign and q, the constant which measures the deterrent effect of heavy use" (Behrens et al., 2002, p. 923). Hence, while Behrens et al. create a model that satisfies the second and third demands, it does not formalise how people interact at the micro-level to produce the aggregate equations.

It is perfectly possible and sometimes even desirable to avoid the complexities introduced by micro-foundations. For instance, Behrens et al. (2002) want to explore the optimal control policy in a situation where

The Spread of Drug Use

drug use both deters and attracts, and that potential users rely on fading memories to estimate the dangers of using drugs. To do so they need empirical estimates of the aggregate parameters and there is less of a need to justify the link between the aggregate and the individual. In general, from the perspective of prediction and policy it may be perfectly legitimate to operate at the aggregate level. For instance, aggregate models describing the spread of influenza are claimed to be very successful and useful in the sense that they can be used to determine the amount of medication necessary in an area at a given point in time.

However, predictive success on an aggregate level should not be confused with explanatory success. Moreover, even if prediction and policy implications are the main purposes of the model, it may still be dangerous to dispense with micro-foundations altogether. As an illustration of the problem, consider the following example: One of the main conclusions in the literature on optimal control theory and the spread of drug use is that intervention is highly effective in the beginning of an epidemic, but less so at its peak (Behrens et al., 2002). The obvious reason behind this is that early intervention will prevent the spread to many new cases while later in the epidemic the increasingly visible bad effects of the drug deters many susceptibles. At this point intervention will have less of an effect, since there are fewer susceptibles in the population and the bad consequences is deterrence enough in itself. The conclusion seems to jump logically from the aggregate pattern of diseases: Clearly, it must be better to intervene and stop the spread in the beginning before it starts to grow!

It is, however, possible to construct a micro-foundation with similar aggregate patterns, but with different policy conclusions. Imagine, for instance, that the decision to use drugs is influenced by a combination of curiosity and a desire to be non-conformist or to rebel against social norms. Those who are curious would in this case try out a new drug. Heavy early intervention by the authorities could bolster the reputation of the drug as the drug of the anti-conformists as well as bringing it to the attention of many more, thus intensifying its attractiveness for some and causing usage to increase even further. After some time the drug might lose its novelty appeal and the bad consequences of the drug become more visible. Once these effects are known it might justify intervention without automatically being labelled as unjustified imposition of old moralistic norms by potential users. At this point intervention might not generate the backlash that an early intervention would.

The point of the above remarks is not to suggest a more plausible explanation than the one presented in Behrens et al. (2002), but to illustrate the importance of micro-foundations for policy implications. The same aggregate pattern might be explained with different micro-level mechanisms and these mechanisms in turn have different policy implications with respect to the desirability of early intervention. Hence, instead of working at the aggregate level with borrowed epidemic models we should focus on social interaction. By so doing we are forced to think about the mechanisms linking individual behaviour and its aggregate consequences. It is the nature of these links that generate policy decisions and if we simply assume the link to be of the standard disease type we are easily led to potentially wrong conclusions.

3.2. Social Interaction

What does it mean to base an approach on social interaction? There are several definitions of social interaction in economics. In a recent contribution, Brock and Durlauf (2001, p. 235) write that:

> By social interactions, we refer to the idea that the utility or payoff an individual receives from a given action depends directly on the choices of others in the individual's reference group, as opposed to the sort of dependence which occurs through the intermediation of markets.

Although preference interaction of this sort may be very important, the definition seems too narrow. For instance, it excludes social interaction in the form of learning.

A much broader definition is presented by Manski (2000). In an overview of social interaction in economics he defines and lists three general types of social interaction:

> Agents interact through their chosen actions. An action chosen by one agent may affect the actions of other agents through three channels: constraints, expectations, and preferences.
>
> Manski (2000, p. 119)

In the case of drug use, the availability of drugs may be an example of the first (a user moving into a drug-free neighbourhood may remove the availability constraint for others); learning about the effects of drugs (positive and negative) from existing users may be an example of how other agents' actions may influence your expectations; and if many of my friends use drugs it may change my own preferences on whether or not to use drugs.

Schelling (1998) defines a mechanism as a hypothesis that seeks to explain something in terms of two types of interaction:

> I propose that...a social mechanism is a plausible hypothesis, or set of plausible hypotheses, that could be the explanation of some social phenomena, the explanation being in terms of interactions between individuals and other individuals, or between individuals and some social aggregate.
>
> Schelling (1998, pp. 32–33)

Changing lanes when the next car is less than 5 feet away is an example of individual-to-individual interaction. Adjusting your speed to the average speed is an example of interaction between the individual and a social aggregate. Schelling's work shows that this approach has the potential to produce original and convincing explanations of social phenomena that are considered to be paradoxical. The classic example being Schelling's now well-known explanation of why neighbourhoods are so segregated when people seldom state that they want to live in completely segregated neighbourhoods.

Manski's and Schelling's typologies of social interaction may be combined (see Fig. 2) and this is useful for several reasons. First of all it is a convenient classification devise that allows us to organise our knowledge. Second, the figure can be used to suggest new avenues of research. If a general approach has blank spots in terms of the model, one might suspect that it has ignored potentially important mechanisms and try to explore these avenues.

3.3. Exemplifying the Approach

In this section I shall provide a detailed example of a model built on the alternative approach described above. I will first of all formalise the micro-foundations I want to explore. Based on the micro-foundations, I then create a macro-model of the level of drug use in a society and explore some of its properties. The aim is not to present a comprehensive analysis of all kinds of mechanisms, but to illustrate the general approach by exploring two different mechanisms in the same model.

The two mechanisms I shall explore are social learning and social stigma dynamics. The intuitive idea is that before deciding whether or not to

	Constraints	Expectations	Preferences
Individual to individual	1	2	3
Individual to social	4	5	6

Fig. 2. Typology of Social Interaction.

experiment with drugs people are influenced by the social stigma and the perceived risk associated with drug use. The model is framed in terms of individual-to-social interactions, i.e. it is assumed that people are influenced by the aggregate values found by summing over all individuals. In terms of Fig. 2, the model exemplifies an analysis within categories 5 and 6. It should also be noted that there have been some previous contributions related to these categories. For instance, Moene (1999) has modelled the effect of a desire to conform on drug use and there is a relatively large body of literature on observational learning in economics (Bikhchandani, Hirschleifer, & Welch, 1998). Although both mechanisms have been examined separately, there are no models of both mechanisms together in the context of drug use.

In a model of the kind presented below it would be impossible to present results on changes in all kinds of parameters and assumptions, and a choice was made to focus on two issues. First, given the emphasis on epidemics in this chapter it was interesting to examine whether the model could generate patterns that resembled a drug epidemic. Second, it was decided to examine the effect of increased spending on treatment both because this is an important topic in itself, but also because this is an area in which the disease-based model was criticised for providing potentially misleading advice. Treatment can be viewed as one way of isolating drug users and in the standard disease model this would always reduce the number of infectives. The question then becomes whether the effect is the same in the model below.

3.3.1. Micro-foundations
Assume that each individual (i) who turns 18 years old in time period (t) decides whether to use drugs based on a comparison of his expected utility of using drugs [$EU_{it}(D)$] and the expected utility if he chooses to abstain from drugs [$EU_{it}(A)$]. The underlying assumption is that the behaviour is influenced by some kind of calculation, as opposed to behaviour based purely on emotions or norms. The choice is assumed to be risky in the sense that there is a probability of becoming addicted:
    Use drugs if:

$$EU_{it}(D) > EU_{it}(A) \tag{5}$$

What are $EU_{it}(D)$ and $EU_{it}(A)$? The last, $EU_{it}(A)$, is assumed to be a constant. To work out $EU_{it}(D)$ we need to consider the possible consequences of experimenting with drugs. For the sake of simplicity I shall assume that there are only two possible outcomes for individuals who experiment with drugs. Either they have a junkie career (unhappy) or they have a yuppie career (happier than a junkie). This assumption is meant to capture the fact that not all individuals who experiment with drugs end up as stereotypical junkies. In fact, only a very small minority of drug experimenters end up as junkies.

The two possible outcomes of experimenting with drugs – becoming a yuppie or a junkie – result in certain payoffs. A very simple way of formalising this would be to say that U_{it}^J is the total (discounted) sum of utility you receive if you end up as a junkie (for individual i at time t) while U_{it}^Y is the total sum of utility if you end up as a yuppie. Note that U_{it}^J does not represent annual utility as a junkie. It represents the *total* (discounted) sum of utilities if it turns out that experimenting with drugs makes you a junkie for whatever time horizon the person has. The formulation is agnostic about whether the time period is considered to be the rest of your life or whether the agent is myopic to the extent that he only considers the possibilities next year. If the interpretation is "life", then it may include some years as a yuppie, some years as a junkie and then, finally, some years as a non-user (treated or natural recovery/matured out). The same goes for U_{it}^Y. It does not only include years as a happy drug user, but also years as a non-user after being a "happy user".

The individual does not know whether he will end up as a junkie or a yuppie, so when working out the expected utility of experimenting with drugs, he or she has to estimate the probability of ending up as a junkie. One way of doing so would be to use the current share of junkies (j) in the population relative to the share of yuppies (y) as an input in the estimation of how likely you believe it is that you will end up as a junkie: $p_{it}(j, y)$. It is as if the individual looks around and if he sees relatively few junkies compared to the yuppies, and then he or she concludes that the danger of becoming a junkie must be quite small.

Finally, in order to capture the effects of social stigma, I introduce a moral cost of experimenting with drugs (m). One might think about this as the cost of doing something that many people dislike. A stigma parameter like this should vary depending on the number of people who engage in the activity. For instance, when few people got divorced, the associated stigma was large, but in a situation when divorce is common the stigma is lower. Hence, the stigma associated with drugs is assumed to depend on the share of people that use drugs, i.e. the share of junkies (j) and yuppies (y) in the population. Moreover, individuals are assumed to differ to the extent they care about the stigma or moral cost associated with drugs. Each person has a parameter (θ_i) that indicates the degree to which they are sensitive to social stigma. This parameter has a cumulative density function described by $F(\theta)$

and we may also include negative values of θ_i to allow for the possibility that some people enjoy deviating from the majority.

Altogether then, the expected utility of experimenting with drugs for an individual (i) at a point in time (t) is the utility he will receive in the two possible outcomes (junkie career or yuppie career) multiplied by their respective expected probabilities and adjusted for individual sensitivity to social stigma. The probabilities depend on the share of junkies relative to the share of yuppies, and stigma is a function of the share of drug users (yuppies and junkies):

$$EU_{it}(D) = p_{it}(j,y)U_{it}^J + (1 - p_{it}(j,y))U_{it}^Y - \theta_i m_t(j,y) \qquad (6)$$

One might argue that the formulation so far ignores many issues that are central to addiction. For instance, I do not explicitly model discounting which many people argue is an important phenomenon when trying to explain addiction. I do not deny the importance of discounting, but the current focus is on something else, namely the effects of interaction through observational learning and social stigma. I want to isolate this and I do not want to bring in more complications than necessary.

So far all I have is a very general formulation of the decision problem. What I want, however, is an expression of the aggregate result – the share of drug users of the total population and how it changes – if people make their decisions based on the micro-foundation just described. This requires several assumptions, both in terms of simplifying assumptions and in terms of more substantial assumptions about the mechanisms of aggregation.

In order to make it easier to get analytic results, I now make the following simplifying assumptions:

$p_{it} = p_t \quad \forall i$ (everybody uses the same probability of becoming a junkie)
$U_{it}^{(\cdot)} = U^{(\cdot)} \forall it$ (the utility of ending up as a junkie, a yuppie or an abstainer is the same for everybody at all times)

This means that everybody uses the same probability of becoming a junkie and that the utility of ending up as a junkie or as a yuppie is the same for everybody at all times. The decision problem for the individual is then reduced to comparing U^A to the following expression:

$$EU_{it}(D) = p_t(j,y)U^J + (1 - p_t(j,y))U^Y - \theta_i m_t(j,y) \qquad (7)$$

Assume a fixed population. In each time period, the individuals can select one of two actions – to experiment with drugs or not. They make this decision based on the micro-foundation described above. In equilibrium there is no incentive to change strategy, so for the individual at the margin the expected utility of using drugs must be equal to the utility of not using drugs:

$$EU(D) = U^A \tag{8}$$

Substituting Eq. (7) into Eq. (8) gives

$$p_t(j,y)U^J + (1 - p_t(j,y))U^Y - \theta_i m_t(j,y) = U^A \tag{9}$$

Solving this for θ_i gives the level of sensitivity to social stigma that makes the marginal individual indifferent between experimenting and not experimenting with drugs:

$$\theta_i^* = \frac{p_t(j,y)U^J + (1 - p_t(j,y))U^Y - U^A}{m_t(j,y)} \tag{10}$$

Or, in plain language, there are some people who will choose to experiment with drugs (those who are least sensitive to social stigma, i.e. $\theta < \theta^*$), and some people who will not experiment with drugs ($\theta > \theta^*$). Hence, one might use the cumulative density function of θ to indicate how many in the new generation chooses to experiment with drugs; $F(\theta)$ then gives the share of the new generation that takes up the habit. To avoid corner solutions where everybody or nobody uses drugs, I assume that the other parameters are such that $F(\theta^*)$ is never zero or one.

3.3.2. Macro-implications: Epidemics and Effects of Treatment?

To find this year's share of yuppies or junkies in the population we simply start from last year's share and add those who begin and subtract those who quit. The share of the new generation that decides to experiment with drugs in period t is given by $F(\theta_t^*)$. Each time period some individuals also leave the yuppie group for a variety of reasons: They just quit drugs, they die or they become junkies. Hence:

$$y_t = y_{t-1} + \beta_1 F(\theta_t^*) - \beta_2 y_{t-1} \tag{11}$$

where β_1 is the share of the new generation out of the whole population and β_2 represents the share of yuppies who leave the group every year for various reasons.

By analogy, there is an inflow into to the junkie group since a share of the yuppies is assumed to become junkies every time period (δ_1), and a share of the junkies leaves the group due to death, treatment or natural recovery (δ_2):

$$j_t = j_{t-1} + \delta_1 y_{t-1} - \delta_2 j_{t-1} \quad (12)$$

Define equilibrium as a situation where the number of junkies and yuppies is stable from year to year and recall that $F(\theta_t^*)$ depends on the share of junkies and yuppies (see Eq. (10)). This implies that every year the inflow must be equal to the outflow which means that the following must be true in equilibrium:

$$y^* = \frac{\beta_1}{\beta_2} F\left(\frac{p(j^*, y^*) U^J + (1 - p(j^*, y^*)) U^Y - U^A}{m(j^*, y^*)}\right) \quad (13)$$

$$j^* = \frac{\delta_1}{\delta_2} \frac{\beta_1}{\beta_2} F\left(\frac{p(j^*, y^*) U^J + (1 - p(j^*, y^*)) U^Y - U^A}{m(j^*, y^*)}\right) \quad (14)$$

The solution above indicates the possibility of multiple equilibria if some of the equations are non-linear [$p(\cdot)$, $F(\cdot)$ or $m(\cdot)$]. We then have a system of non-linear simultaneous equations and depending on the precise functions and parameter values such a system may have multiple solutions. For instance, in the case with a uniform distribution it was verified analytically that the system had two solutions. The mathematical solution is quite long so it is omitted here but it is available from the author upon request. This is interesting in itself, but the number of possible equilibria is not the main focus in this chapter. The key questions are how the number of drug users will develop over time and how treatment will affect this level. Analytical solutions of the type above say little about out-of-equilibrium behaviour and nothing about the case when there is no equilibrium. Hence, in order to further examine the macro-implications of observational learning and social stigma, it was decided to use agent-based modelling. In this type of modelling one uses a computer program to simulate a world in which agents act on the proposed micro-foundations. One disadvantage of the approach is that the details of the model are less transparent because it is often more difficult to read and follow programming code as opposed to mathematical models. However, the approach has been applied widely in the field of social interaction and it also has several advantages (Axelrod & Tesfatsion, forthcoming): Agent-based modelling makes it easy to examine the dynamics of a system by tracking the aggregate variables over time, it does not require the existence of equilibrium to be analysed, it is easy to combine many different mechanisms in one model, and it avoids some of the mathematical complexities that arise in analytical modelling. Given these advantages and that one of the main purposes with the investigation is to explore the dynamics of the system, it was decided to use agent-based modelling.

In order to simulate the aggregate effects of the micro-mechanisms and get a feel for how the number of junkies and yuppies could evolve over time, it is necessary to make some assumptions about the functional form of the relationships and the parameter values. Assume, for instance, that we start from a situation described in Table 1. Each time period the new generation has to make up their minds about whether to experiment with drugs or not. They do so using the general micro-foundation described above, but with the following more specific assumptions.

First, each of the 100,000 individuals in the computer simulation is randomly assigned a value for their sensitivity to social stigma from a normal distribution with mean 2 and standard deviation 1. This implies that some individuals will have negative values, i.e. they enjoy deviating from the majority:

$$\theta \sim N(2, 1) \qquad (15)$$

Second, when forming expectations about the risk of becoming a junkie, the individuals in the new generation look at the current ratio of junkies to drug users. This may be a plausible description of how some people form their expectations, but one should note that they might improve their estimates by

Table 1. Starting Values for the Simulation[a].

Variable	Initial Value
Yuppies (y)	6.0%
Junkies (j)	0.7%
Total share of drug users in population (d)	6.7%
Population size	100,000
Size of new generation (= deaths every time period)	2,000
Share of yuppies that become junkies each time period	0.03
Share of yuppies that quit each time period	0.10
Share of junkies that quit each time period	0.03
Excess mortality for junkies (each time period)	0.03
Utility from junkie career	0
Utility from yuppie career	10
Weight placed on moral stigma	5
Utility from abstaining from drugs	4

[a]The program uses a random procedure to assign initial values and deaths, so there might be small variations in the shares of individuals assigned to be junkies and yuppies. The variations will be small because the population is large (100,000 individuals) which means that random variations tend to cancel out.

also using past information, not just the current share of junkies:

$$p_t = \frac{j_{t-1}}{j_{t-1} + y_{t-1}} \qquad (16)$$

Third, moral stigma is assumed to decrease linearly with the number of drug users. One might question the realism of this assumption. If a majority become drug users, the stigma is negative which implies that there is a social pressure to use drugs. For some substances, like alcohol, it may be plausible that the majority exerts a pressure towards use. There might be some similar mechanisms for drug use, but it could be weaker. In any case, little is known about the precise functional form of the moral cost of using drugs and the assumption can easily be changed in a computer simulation:

$$m_t(j, y) = 0.5 - (j_{t-1} + y_{t-1}) \qquad (17)$$

The results from some simulations using the assumptions in Table 1 and the functional forms presented above are illustrated in Figs. 3–5. The figures show, first of all, that the micro-foundations described above can generate a wide variety of aggregate patterns. For instance, Fig. 3 is consistent with the general pattern of epidemics, while Fig. 4 – based on the same values as in Fig. 3 except that there is an increase in the assumed utility of being a yuppie from 10 to 20 – shows a more stable development. The sluggishness in Fig. 3 is partly caused by lagged learning: It takes time before potential users observe the damaging effects of the drugs because it takes time for yuppies to become junkies.

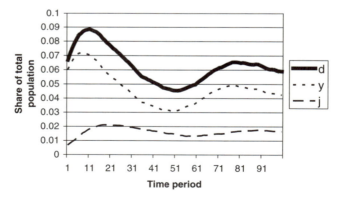

Fig. 3. Computer Simulation Results: Benchmark (Values As Specified in the Table of Initial Values).

The Spread of Drug Use

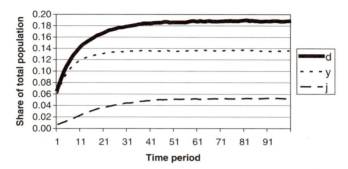

Fig. 4. Computer Simulation Results of Increasing the Utility of a Yuppie Career (from 10 to 20).

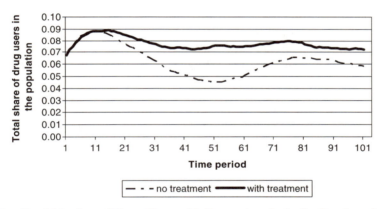

Fig. 5. Total Number of Drug Users with Parameters As in the Benchmark Case But Increasing the Exit Rate of Junkies from 3% to 6% (e.g. Increasing Treatment).

Second, increasing treatment may be viewed as increasing the exit rate from the junkie group. It is interesting to examine this because this chapter has argued that social interaction is important to determine the effect of treatment on the number of drug users in society. Fig. 5 shows that observational learning may reduce this effect, even to the extent that we have more drug users in a world with treatment than one without it. A higher exit rate from the junkie group reduce the number of junkies and hence the fear of becoming a junkie. This, in turn, makes more people willing to experiment with drugs, thus increasing the general share of drug users in society under the assumptions used to construct Fig. 5.

Third, further simulations experimenting with changes in some of the parameters confirm the impression that the mechanisms of observational learning and social stigma were capable of generating many types of aggregate patterns. For instance, experimenting with different assumptions about the other parameters showed that the introduction of treatment did not always increase the number of drug users. In short, depending on the assumptions made, the mechanisms generated stable patterns and instable patterns, it generated situations in which increased treatment reduced the total number of drug users as well as situations in which the number of drug users increased.

Observational learning and social stigma are only two mechanisms out of a large number of variables and mechanisms that affect the use of drugs. Hence, there would be little point in spending much effort to fine tune or calibrate the simulated model in order to generate results that look quantitatively like the observed level of drug use in society. There is no use in finding the parameter values that will make an obviously oversimplified model fit the real world. The aim was to explore the qualitative nature of two mechanisms, and the conclusion is that the mechanisms can generate both apparent epidemics and stable patterns of drug use as well as higher and lower total numbers of drug users as a result of increased treatment. The application also shows the power of agent-based modelling as a tool for exploring the implications of different micro-foundations. It would, for instance, be much easier to add more mechanisms and explore the consequences of different functional forms in such a simulations compared to a more analytic approach.

3.4. Discussion and Empirical Relevance

One might wonder what we gain by exploring a formal mechanism in this way. It is not an attempt to explain drug addiction, in general, so its utility as an explanatory model is, at best, partial. What we have are some more or less plausible assumptions about individual behaviour and the model helps to derive the aggregate consequences of these. These aggregate consequences are not immediately obvious so in this sense it may be worthwhile to engage in formal modelling of mechanisms. If it turns out that the model captures a mechanism that is empirically important, the model may, for instance, help to explain increases and decreases in the level of drug use in a society and why some communities seem stuck in a "high-use" situation while others are locked in a "low-use" situation.

In addition to its explanatory potential, the model may also have some novel policy implications. Unlike the standard models, marginalising or isolating the heavy-drug users may be counterproductive in the model proposed in this chapter since if they were isolated they would no longer deter potential users from experimenting with drugs. Instead, one might interpret the model to suggest that the visibility of users should be *increased* in order to reduce the aggregate level of drug use. Thus, when the police decided to break up the central gathering point of heavy-drug addicts in Norway, it may reduce the deterrence effect from observing the bad effects of drugs. This is very relevant in Norway since the main gathering point is downtown in the centre of Oslo, very close to the main railway station, thus making it visible to a great number of people.

The implication, however, is not very strong in the sense that it depends heavily on the relative strength of the various links. Even if high visibility could increase the belief that drug use is harmful, it could also reduce the belief that drug use is limited to a small group of people. Observing a large group of users everyday might lead some to think that drug use is more common than it really is, and that the authorities do not consider it dangerous enough to intervene. This, in turn, could imply that some youths try drugs in part because they wrongly believe that it is a common thing to do. Unless we have good empirical evidence on the relative strength of the links, we are led to the conclusion that we can use knowledge of mechanisms to explain ex post, but not to predict or design policies (Elster, 1998). This example also illustrates the usefulness of including both stigma and learning in the same model since the problem would not arise if only one of the mechanisms were included.

Would it be possible to gather empirical evidence necessary to evaluate the net effect of the various links and test the various models? One of the main problems of testing theories of social interaction, as discussed by Manski (2000), is the so-called "reflection problem". For instance, when students in a neighbourhood behave similarly it is statistically often very difficult to distinguish whether they do so because they face the same environmental circumstances or whether they influence each other more directly (peer pressure and so on). Of course, there are ways in which we might test whether models are in general agreement with the facts. One stylised fact about drug use is that it tends to differ greatly between different geographic areas, more so than can be explained by variables like unemployment, urbanisation and income differences. For instance, Melberg and Alver (2003) report that a regression with 16 variables believed to influence or be related to drug-related expenditures only explained 44% of the variation in the per capita expenditures between the 432 municipalities included in the study (the variables included unemployment, income, broken homes, age structure, death rates and a measure for urbanisation). This seems to indicate that a model with multiple equilibria is at least compatible with some key facts since in such models two otherwise similar municipalities may have very different levels of drug use due to historical good fortune or misfortune (hysterese). However, being compatible with the facts is not very convincing evidence for a specific theory since there are many possible mechanisms that could generate the same aggregate pattern. Rather than looking at aggregate data, therefore, one might be better off trying to explore the empirical plausibility of the micro-foundations that go into the model.

It is easy to find evidence of the type that friends of drug users often use drugs. For instance, Guo, Hill, Hawkins, Catalano, and Abbott (2002) and Andrews, Tildesley, Hops, and Li (2002) both show that peers influence each other even after controlling for a number of other possible confounders. These studies, however, do no control for the selection effects or simultaneity bias. However, even after controlling for selection effects, using a two-stage probit regression model and the method of instrumental variables, Lundborg (2005) still finds that peers have significant effects on substance use.

Ideally, to investigate the mechanisms of peer influence one would like to conduct social experiments, but for natural reasons few controlled experiments have been done on peer influence and illegal drugs. There has, however, been extensive research on the extent to which the amount of alcohol consumed is influenced by the introduction of another person (heavy or moderate drinker, male or female, high or low status). The results from these experiments strongly suggest that people are influenced by their peers (Quigley & Collins, 1999). The same is true in studies of smoking and even those that control for selection effects in observational data conclude that although the peer effect is reduced, it is still statistically significant (Gaviria & Raphael, 2001). However, the mere existence of a peer group effect does not tell whether this is due to a desire to conform, a stigma effect, an effect of learning or some other mechanism at the individual level.

On the question on the specific mechanisms, as opposed to whether there is overall effect, there is some evidence that estimates of the risk of drugs are important for the decision to experiment. For instance high-school teenagers have been asked about perceived dangers of different drugs and in some cases this is seen to correlate well with a reduction in the incidence of that drug (Johnston, 1991). There are also studies, which show that those with high-risk estimates are more likely to avoid smoking than those with low-risk estimates (Viscusi, 1991).

Although suggestive and supportive of the empirical relevance of the mechanisms modelled in the last part of this chapter, the evidence relies too much on correlation to be used as strong evidence for the existence of a causal relationship of the type explored in this chapter. The best that can be said is that the correlations at least do not appear to contradict the assumptions on which the model is built. Little can be said about the relative importance of the different mechanisms and more research is needed in this area.

There are many possible extensions to the model developed in this chapter. Within the model individuals are assumed to be influenced by everybody else. It is as if they observe all the other individuals and what they are doing at all times. A much more realistic formulation would be to let people interact more locally in small groups. Instead of observing the number of junkies in the total population, they would observe the number of junkies within their small groups. And, instead of being influenced by a desire to conform (or deviate) to the whole population, they could be influenced mainly by the members of the group to which they belong. Localising the social interaction mode in this way would produce a much more realistic model, but one of the main conclusions would remain (i.e. the existence of multiple equilibria and the importance of the visibility of the bad effects of drugs).

4. CONCLUSION

Several formal models on the spread of heroin and other drugs have used standard epidemic models as their starting point. In these models a drug user is always contagious in the sense that he spreads the habit when he interacts with friends. The obvious policy conclusion would then be to isolate the contagious individual in order to reduce the spread. One weakness with this line of argument is that people are linked by assumption instead of explicit modelling of mechanisms. The model does not say exactly *how* drug use is contagious. Once this is taken into account we discover that sometimes drug use may deter as much as it attracts. Observing a friend die from heroin use may sometimes scare friends away from continued use, but hanging out in a group where there is no social stigma attached to drug use (indeed, there may be a pressure to conform to use) has the opposite effect. Formal modelling and computer simulation show that these mechanisms can generate a variety of aggregate patterns.

ACKNOWLEDGEMENTS

I am grateful to Jonathan P. Caulkins, Karl Ove Moene, Ole J. Røgeberg, Ole-Jørgen Skog, Jo Thori Lind and Jörgen Weibull who all made valuable comments that led to substantial improvements. I am also grateful to the

Arne Ryde Foundation and the participants at the *Arne Ryde symposium* for the opportunity to present and discuss this chapter.

REFERENCES

Andrews, J. A., Tildesley, E., Hops, H., & Li, F. (2002). The influence of peers on young adult substance use. *Health Psychology*, *21*(4), 349–357.

Axelrod, R., & Tesfatsion, L. (forthcoming). A guide for newcomers to agent-based modeling in the social sciences. In: K. L. Judd & L. Tesfatsion (Eds), *Handbook of computational economics, Vol. 2: Agent-based computational economics*. Amsterdam: North-Holland.

Behrens, D. A., Caulkins, J. P., Trangler, G., & Feichtinger, G. (2002). Why present-oriented societies undergo cycles of drug epidemics. *Journal of Economic Dynamics and Control*, *26*, 919–936.

Bikhchandani, S., Hirschleifer, D., & Welch, I. (1998). Learning from the behavior of others: Conformity, fads, and informational cascades. *Journal of Economic Perspectives*, *12*(3), 151–170.

Billiard, L., & Dayananda, P. W. A. (1993). Drug addiction – Pushers generated from the addicts. *Biomedical Journal*, *35*(2), 227–244.

Brock, W. A., & Durlauf, S. N. (2001). Discrete choice with social interactions. *Review of Economic Studies*, *68*, 235–260.

de Alarcón, R. (1969). The spread of heroin abuse in a community. *Bulletin on Narcotics*, *21*(3), 17–21.

Dole, V. P. (1973). Heroin addiction – An epidemic disease. *Harvey Lectures*, *67*, 199–211.

Drucker, E., & Sidel, V. W. (1974). The communicable disease model of heroin addiction: A critique. *American Journal of Drug and Alcohol Abuse*, *1*(3), 301–311.

DuPont, R. L. (1971). Profile of a heroin-addiction epidemic. *New England Journal of Medicine*, *285*(6), 320–324.

DuPont, R. L. (1973). Coming to grips with an urban heroin addiction epidemic. *Journal of the American Medical Association*, *223*(1), 46–48.

DuPont, R. L., & Greene, M. H. (1973). The dynamics of a heroin addiction epidemic. *Science*, *181*(101), 716–722.

Elster, J. (1998). A plea for mechanisms. In: P. Hedström & R. Swedberg (Eds), *Social mechanisms* (pp. 45–73). Cambridge: Cambridge University Press.

Everingham, S. S., & Rydell, C. P. (1994). *Modelling the demand for cocaine*. Santa Monica, CA: RAND.

Gaviria, A., & Raphael, S. (2001). School-based peer effects and juvenile behavior. *Review of Economics and Statistics*, *83*(2), 257–268.

Goodchild, S., & Bloomfield, S. (2004). Children to get jabs against drug addiction. *The Independent on Sunday*, *25*(July).

Guo, J., Hill, K. G., Hawkins, J. D., Catalano, R. F., & Abbott, R. D. (2002). A developmental analysis of sociodemographic, family, and peer effects on adolescent illicit drug initiation. *Journal of the American Academy of Child and Adolescent Psychiatry*, *41*(7), 838–845.

Hamer, W. H. (1906). Epidemic diseases in England. *Lancet*, *1*, 733–739.

Hauge, R. (2000). Har narkotikapolitikken spilt fallitt? *Nordisk tidsskrift for kriminalvitenskap*, *87*(3), 241–245.

Hethcote, H. W. (2000). The mathematics of infectious diseases. *Society for Industrial and Applied Mathematics Review, 42*(4), 599–653.
Hoppensteadt, F. C., & Murray, F. C. (1981). Threshold analysis of a drug use epidemic model. *Mathematical Biosciences, 53*, 79–87.
Hughes, P. H., & Crawford, G. A. (1972). A contagious disease model for researching and intervening in heroin epidemics. *Archives of General Psychiatry, 27*(2), 149–155.
Hughes, P. H., & Crawford, G. A. (1974). The high drug use community: A natural laboratory for epidemiological experiments in addiction control. *American Journal of Public Health, 64*, 11–15.
Hunt, L. G., & Chambers, C. D. (1976). *The heroin epidemics: A study of heroin use in the United States, 1965–1975*. New York: Spectrum Publications.
Jacobs, P. E. (1976). Epidemiology abuse: Epidemiological and psychosocial models of drug abuse. *Journal of Drug Education, 6*(3), 256–271.
Johnston, L. D. (1991). Toward a theory of drug epidemics. In: L. Donohew, H. E. Sypher & W. J. Bukoski (Eds), *Persuasive communication and drug abuse prevention* (pp. 93–131). Hillsdale, NJ: Lawrence Erlbaum Associates.
Jonas, S. (1972). Heroin utilization. A communicable disease? *NY State Journal of Medicine, 72*(11), 1292–1299.
Jonas, S. (1973). Communicable-disease theory of heroin addiction. *New England Journal of Medicine, 288*(8), 421–422.
Lundborg, P. (forthcoming). Having the wrong friends? Peer effects in adolescent substance use. *Journal of Health Economics*.
Mackintosh, D. R., & Stewart, G. T. (1979). A mathematical model of a heroin epidemic: Implications for control policies. *Journal of Epidemiology and Community Health, 33*, 299–304.
Manski, C. F. (2000). Economic analysis of social interactions. *Journal of Economic Perspectives, 14*(3), 115–136.
Melberg, H. O., & Alver, Ø. O. (2003). *Rus og psykiatri i inntektssystemet for kommunene*. Oslo: Statens Institutt for Rusmiddelforskning.
Moene, K. O. (1999). Addiction and social interaction. In: J. Elster & O. J. Skog (Eds), *Getting hooked: Rationality and addiction* (pp. 30–46). Cambridge, UK; New York: Cambridge University Press.
Musto, D. F. (1987). *The American disease: Origins of narcotic control*. New York: Oxford University Press.
Quigley, B. M., & Collins, R. L. (1999). The modeling of alcohol consumption: A meta-analytic review. *Journal of Studies on Alcohol, 1*, 90–98.
Sattenspiel, L. (1990). Modeling the spread of infectious disease in human population. *Yearbook of Physical Anthropology, 33*, 245–276.
Schelling, T. (1998). Social mechanisms and social dynamics. In: P. Hedström & R. Swedberg (Eds), *Social mechanisms* (pp. 32–44). Cambridge: Cambridge University Press.
Seagraves, J. A. (1973). Discussion. *American Economic Review, 63*(2), 278–279.
Skog, O. J. (2000). Addicts' choice. *Addiction, 95*(9), 1309–1314.
Viscusi, W. K. (1991). Age variations in risk perceptions and smoking decisions. *The Review of Economics and Statistics, 73*(4), 577–588.
Weimer, D. (2003). Drug-as-a-disease: Heroin, metaphors, and identity in Nixon's drug war. *Janus Head, 6*(2), 260–281.

STRUCTURAL ESTIMATION OF PEER EFFECTS IN YOUTH SMOKING

Brian Krauth

ABSTRACT

This chapter outlines a new approach to measuring peer influence on the choice of a young person to smoke cigarettes. The methodology is based on estimating an equilibrium discrete choice model in which the relative benefit to smoking is increasing in the fraction of peers who smoke. In contrast to much of the literature, this structural model allows for positive correlation in observable and unobservable characteristics between peers. The structural approach has been applied to estimating close friend peer effects in Canada, California, and the U.S.A. in general. In all three settings, I find that close friend smoking is substantially less influential than is generally found by previous studies.

1. INTRODUCTION

This chapter outlines a new approach to measuring peer influence on the choice of a young person to smoke cigarettes. The consensus in the youth smoking literature is that peers are quite influential (Tyas & Pederson,

1998), yet much of this consensus has been developed using simple reduced form econometric models in which peer behaviour is treated as an exogenous variable. Researchers have been aware of serious identification problems with the reduced form approach for some time. Manski (1993) provides a detailed discussion of these identification problems in the general context of measuring social influences on behaviour. As Manski notes, using reduced form methods to estimate peer effects yields upwardly biased estimates due to *sorting* and *simultaneity*. Sorting is the tendency of individuals to form groups with others who are similar to themselves. Simultaneity arises because young people both influence and are influenced by the other members of their peer group; as a result, any structural interpretation of reduced form coefficients will be subject to simultaneous equations bias.

The methodology introduced here is based on estimating an equilibrium discrete choice model in which the relative benefit to smoking is increasing in the fraction of peers who smoke. In contrast to much of the literature, this structural model allows for sorting, in the form of non-zero correlation in observable and unobservable characteristics among peers. Simultaneity is also accounted for, by using an equilibrium model and treating peer behaviour as an endogenous variable. This structural approach has been used to estimate close friend peer effects in Canada (Krauth, 2005a), California (Krauth, 2004), and the U.S.A. as a whole (Krauth, 2005b). All three of these papers find that close friend smoking is substantially less influential than is generally found by previous studies.

This short chapter aims to provide a brief overview of the methodology and findings, and to place the results in the context of the literature on peer effects in youth smoking to a greater extent than is possible with any of the original papers. Section 2 provides an overview of the structural model, and Section 3 provides an overview of the results and a comparison to previous results in the literature. Section 4 provides a discussion of the strengths and weaknesses of this method relative to others, and suggests directions for future research.

2. MODEL

This section briefly outlines the structural model. Krauth (2005b) describes the model in greater detail, provides more extensive justification for key modeling assumptions, and discusses identification and estimation. The model features a large population of youth arranged into peer groups. Each young person chooses whether to smoke or not based on the relative perceived benefit from smoking, which is a function of his or her own observed and unobserved characteristics, aggregate factors such as prices, and the fraction of peer group members that smoke.

Peer groups are indexed by $g \in \{1, 2, 3, \ldots\}$, and the individuals within group g are indexed by $i \in \{1, 2, \ldots, n_g\}$. The size of peer group g, denoted by n_g, is exogenous and can vary across groups. Member i of group g chooses to smoke ($s_{i,g} = 1$) or not ($s_{i,g} = 0$), and has the utility function $u_{i,g}(s_{i,g}; \mathbf{s}_g)$ where $\mathbf{s}_g$ is a vector describing the choice of all members of group g, and:

$$u_{i,g}(1; \mathbf{s}_g) - u_{i,g}(0; \mathbf{s}_g) = \alpha + \beta x_{i,g} + \lambda z_g + \gamma \bar{s}_{i,g} + \varepsilon_{i,g} \qquad (1)$$

where $x_{i,g}$ is a vector of individual observed characteristics, z_g is a vector of aggregate factors such as prices, $\varepsilon_{i,g}$ is an idiosyncratic unobserved term, and:

$$\bar{s}_{i,g} \equiv \frac{1}{n_g - 1} \sum_{j \neq i} s_{j,g} \qquad (2)$$

is the average choice of peers.

Given preferences, it is assumed that each peer group plays the lowest-smoking Nash equilibrium of the complete-information static game defined by the players, strategies, and payoffs described above. The low-smoking equilibrium of the static game can alternatively be interpreted as the steady state of a dynamic game with an initial condition of "all non-smokers" and a myopic best reply updating rule. In any case, Monte Carlo results in Krauth (2005b) suggest that for small to moderate peer effects, the choice of the equilibrium selection rule is not critical.

Sorting is accommodated in the model by allowing for a reduced form correlation in both observed and unobserved individual characteristics. Specifically, individual-level characteristics are assumed to take on a multivariate normal distribution across individuals such that:

$$\begin{aligned} corr(\beta x_{i,g}, \beta x_{j,g}) &= \rho_x \quad \forall i \neq j \\ corr(\varepsilon_{i,g}, \varepsilon_{j,g}) &= \rho_\varepsilon \quad \forall i \neq j \\ corr(\beta x_{i,g}, \varepsilon_{j,g}) &= 0 \quad \forall i, j \end{aligned} \qquad (3)$$

As in many discrete choice models, the parameters of the incremental utility function are identified only up to a normalization, so we normalize such that $\varepsilon_{i,g} \sim N(0, 1)$. Although the model is formally identified without further restrictions, non-parametric identification requires one additional substantive restriction on the model. The baseline restriction used is given by:

$$\rho_\varepsilon = \rho_x \qquad (4)$$

This restriction is similar to the one used by Altonji, Elder, and Taber (2005) to identify the effect of attending a Catholic school while accounting for selection into Catholic school on unobservable characteristics. In other words, Eq. (4) states that the within-peer-group correlation in unobserved individual characteristics is equal to the correlation in observed characteristics. The intuition behind this assumption is that it will hold in expected value if the observed characteristics are a random subset of all individual characteristics. If the characteristics that econometricians observe are more salient to potential friends as well, then ρ_x is likely to provide an upper bound on ρ_ε. A conservative lower bound on ρ_ε is zero; in other words, friends will be at least as similar in unobserved characteristics as randomly selected pairs of youth, so the model is also estimated under the interval restriction:

$$\rho_\varepsilon \in [0, \rho_x] \tag{5}$$

Point estimates of the model parameters are not non-parametrically identified under the interval restriction (5), but informative bounds on parameters can be identified.

Finally, the studies described here are based on individual-level data in which the respondent's own smoking is derived from a self-report, and the smoking of his or her peers is derived from the respondent's own report. It is well known in the smoking literature that young people understate their own smoking and often overestimate peer smoking. By construction, this equilibrium model implies an equal unconditional expectation of own smoking and peer smoking. To account for the empirical fact of differential reported rates of own smoking and peer smoking, the basic model must be supplemented with a simple behavioural model of reporting. Specifically, I assume that young people who smoke falsely claim to be non-smokers with probability p_r, and that otherwise reporting is truthful. While this model is obviously an oversimplification of the issues discussed in the literature (Norton, Lindrooth, & Ennett, 2003), it represents a first step.

3. RESULTS AND COMPARISON WITH LITERATURE

Table 1 reports the findings of earlier studies of peer effects in youth smoking. For purposes of comparison across a variety of functional forms, results are translated into something approaching a common scale using simple thought experiment. Consider a representative individual whose observable characteristics imply a conditional probability of being a self-reported

Table 1. Results from Studies Using Reduced Form and Instrumental Variables (IV) Methods[a].

Study	Identifying Restriction	Model Type	Peer Effect Marginal	Peer Effect Incremental (%)
Wang et al. (1995) U.S. age 14–18, TAPS Peer group: Same-sex friends	$\bar{s}$ exogenous	Logit	–	36.0–52.8
Norton Lindrooth and Ennett (1998) U.S. grade 8, DARE study Peer group: Elementary school	$\bar{s}$ exogenous IV ($\bar{x}$ exogenous)	Probit	0.93 0.96	29.4 30.5
Alexander, Piazza, Mekos, and Valente (2001) U.S. grade 7–12, Add Health Peer group: School	$\bar{s}$ exogenous	Logit	0.88	29.5
Gaviria and Raphael (2001) U.S. grade 10, NELS Peer group: School	$\bar{s}$ exogenous IV ($\bar{x}$ exogenous)	LPM LPM	0.16 0.16	4.0 3.9
Lloyd-Richardson et al. (2002) U.S. grade 7–12, Add Health Peer group: Three best friends	$\bar{s}$ exogenous	Logit	–	24.1
Norton et al. (2003) North Carolina grade 9 Peer group: Three best friends	$\bar{s}$ exogenous	LPM	0.53	13.2
Illinois grade 5–6 Peer group: School	$\bar{s}$ exogenous	LPM	0.40	9.9
Powell, Tauras, and Ross (2003) U.S. grade 9–12 Peer group: School	$\bar{s}$ exogenous IV ($\bar{x}$ exogenous)	Probit Probit	0.56 0.54	13.9 13.5
Clark and Lohéac (2004) U.S. grade 7–12, Add Health	Lagged $\bar{s}$ exogenous			
Peer group: Same grade	No school effects School effects	Probit Probit	0.14–0.17 −0.02–0.07	3.8–4.6 −0.4–1.8
Peer group: Close friends	School effects	Probit	0.15–0.17	3.9–4.4
Lundborg (2005) Sweden, age 12–18	$\bar{s}$ exogenous,	Probit	0.18	4.5

Table 1. (*Continued*)

Study	Identifying Restriction	Model Type	Peer Effect Marginal	Incremental (%)
Peer group: Classmates	$\bar{s}$ exogenous, school effects	Probit	0.17	4.3
	IV, school effects	Probit	0.47	11.8
Kawaguchi (2004) U.S. grade 4–12, NLSY97 Peer group: School	Perceived $\bar{s}$ exogenous	Probit	0.29	7.9

[a]See text for details.

smoker of 20%, and who has no peers that smoke. For this representative individual, I calculate and report both the "marginal peer effect" and the "incremental peer effect." The marginal effect is simply the partial derivative of the representative individual's probability of smoking with respect to the rate of smoking among peers. The incremental effect is the percentage point change in the representative individual's probability of smoking in response to a one friend (for studies of close friend effects) or 25% (for studies of peer effects at the classroom level or above) change in the number of peers who smoke. In close friend studies with variable numbers of friends, the representative individual is taken as having four close friends. Marginal effects are not calculated for two studies (Wang, Fitzhugh, Westerfield, & Eddy, 1995; Lloyd-Richardson, Papandonatos, Kazura, Stanton, & Niaura, 2002) of close friend peer effects in which peer behaviour is represented using dummy variables for "one friend smokes," "two friends smoke," etc.

As Table 1 shows, these studies are varied both in methodology and in the peer group under analysis. Some studies focus on close friend peer effects, while others consider much larger peer groups, such as schools and neighbourhoods. In addition, the peer effect is identified in some cases with a reduced form model in which peer behaviour is treated as exogenous, and in some cases with an alternative method aimed at accounting for sorting and/or simultaneity. These alternative methods include an instrumental variables (IV) approach in which group characteristics are used as instruments for group behaviour, the use of lagged peer behaviour as an explanatory variable, and the incorporation of school-level fixed effects. Despite this variety of approaches, the consensus in these studies is clear: Peer smoking exerts a strong influence on the decision of a young person to smoke. The estimated peer effect is quite large in many of these studies, and is usually statistically significant. Out of the peer effect estimates reported in Table 1, only Gaviria and Raphael's IV estimate and Clark and Lohéac's estimated classroom peer effects with school fixed effects fail to be statistically significant at the 5% level. Another issue to note in Table 1 is that all four studies using the IV approach produce IV estimates that are as large as the corresponding reduced form estimates.

Table 2 reports key results for three recent studies using the structural approach. In addition to peer behaviour, the empirical models include standard covariates in the smoking literature such as age, sex, race/ethnicity, fixed effects for year and geography, parental/sibling/teacher smoking, employment, disposable income, and exposure to advertising and classroom information about tobacco. For each of these studies, estimates for three different models are reported: A simple reduced form probit model that treats peer smoking as exogenous, the structural model under the assumption of random peer selection ($\rho_\varepsilon = 0$), and the structural model under the assumption of equal correlation in observable and unobservable characteristics ($\rho_\varepsilon = \rho_x$). Taken together, the two structural estimates

Table 2. Results from Studies Using Structural Methods[a].

Study	Identifying Restriction	Sorting Effect (ρ_ε)	Peer Effect (γ) Marginal	Peer Effect (γ) Incremental (%)
Krauth (2004)	$\bar{s}$ exogenous	–	0.78	16.6
California age 14–17, 1994–2002 CYTS	$\rho_\varepsilon = 0$	–	0.34	9.2
Peer group: Close friends	$\rho_\varepsilon = \rho_x$	0.55	0.05	1.3
Krauth (2005b)	$\bar{s}$ exogenous	–	0.53	15.6
U.S. age 15–19, 1993 TAPS	$\rho_\varepsilon = 0$	–	0.42	11.8
Peer group: Four best friends	$\rho_\varepsilon = \rho_x$	0.62	0.06	1.4
Krauth (2005a)	$\bar{s}$ exogenous	–	0.63	18.3
Canada age 15–19, 1994 YSS	$\rho_\varepsilon = 0$	–	0.36	9.3
Peer group: Close friends	$\rho_\varepsilon = \rho_x$	0.24	0.26	6.6

[a]See text for details.

provide consistent bounds on the peer effect under the relatively weak restriction that $\rho_\varepsilon \in [0, \rho_x]$.

The findings of all three studies reported in Table 2 are roughly consistent. The reduced form estimates suggest a fairly strong peer effect. This result is in accordance with the previous literature employing similar reduced form approaches. In contrast, estimates from the structural model with random peer selection imply a peer effect, which is 50–75% as large as the reduced form model estimate, while estimates from the structural model with equal correlation in observable and unobservable characteristics imply a peer effect, which is only 8–36% as large. The differences between reduced form and structural estimates are larger in the two U.S. studies than in the Canadian study, largely because the Canadian youth have lower estimated within-group correlation in characteristics. In all three studies the structural estimates are well below previous estimates of close friend effects. This finding suggests that one should be quite skeptical of reduced form estimates of peer effects.

4. DISCUSSION

The structural models developed in this research programme incorporate two important features missing from most previous studies, simultaneity and sorting, at a cost of a somewhat simplistic behavioural model. One clear advantage of a reduced form approach is that it is far easier to allow for a more complex picture of peer influence to develop. This section discusses interpretation of findings and directions for future research in the context of this more complex picture.

First, the empirical work so far using the structural model described in Section 2 has only considered the influence of close friends. As such, the results are not necessarily inconsistent with the findings of earlier researchers using IV methods that school-level peer effects are relatively strong. It is also likely that the bias from reduced form estimation is lower for school-level effects than for close friend effects: Simultaneity bias decreases in the number of group members, and it is likely that the backgrounds and preferences of close friends are more highly correlated than are classmates. The structural model described in this chapter can be directly applied to the estimation of school-level peer effects; research in progress (joint with Lisa Powell, using the data set from Powell et al., 2003) does so. The extension of the structural approach to a dynamic setting in which individuals are influenced by different types of peers is conceptually straightforward. More problematic is the possibility of social influences operating at a much larger scale than the school or neighbourhood. For example, the substantial variation in smoking rates across ethnicities, across genders within different ethnic groups, and across states and regions, suggests that shifts in social norms may occur at a high level of aggregation. Unfortunately, shifts in social norms are difficult to track entirely from behaviour, and economists have long been reluctant to trust purely attitudinal data.

Second, the structural model has little to say on the mechanisms by which close friend behaviour may be influential. Candidate mechanisms include the provision of information on the costs and benefits of smoking, the formation of localized social norms or social identities which are friendly or unfriendly to smoking, modelling, and imitation, or simple externalities (e.g., smoking alone is less pleasant than smoking with a friend). Previous studies have attempted to untangle these mechanisms using focus groups and survey answers to attitudinal questions (Nichter, Vukovic, Quintero, & Ritenbaugh, 1997), but the findings from this approach are affected by substantial endogeneity issues, and must be regarded as suggestive rather than definitive. One possible solution is to infer mechanisms from the patterns of influence. For example, Kobus (2003) notes that smoking among relatively wide friendship groups is associated with higher rates of smoking initiation, while best friend smoking is associated with higher rates of smoking maintenance. This finding suggests that initiation is driven by forces of information, social norms, and social identity, while maintenance is driven by a more direct utility spillover between smokers.

Third, the structural model assumes that the ultimate source of peer influence is the peers' own smoking behaviour. Norton et al. (2003) argue that young people respond less to the actual behaviour of their peers than to their own-often inaccurate-perceptions of that behaviour. This idea, along with substantial evidence that young people systematically overestimate the drinking, smoking, and drug use of others, has led to several campaigns to provide more accurate information about the prevalence of these activities among youth. Other researchers have argued for the importance of the existence of close friends, as well as their behaviour. Social network analysts (e.g., Ennett & Bauman, 1993) have found that position in the social network matters. In particular, young people who are relatively isolated in the network are more likely to smoke than those who are well-integrated in that network. Unfortunately, answers to these questions are particularly difficult to identify because perceptions and social position both affect and are affected by behaviour.

5. CONCLUSION

Initial findings from the application of structural methods to the estimation of close friend peer effects on youth smoking are clear. Close friends are markedly less influential than indicated by previous findings. This is partly because much of the earlier literature ignores the propensity of young people to form relatively homogeneous peer groups, and partly because it ignores the simultaneity implied by bidirectional peer influence.

At the same time, the structural model of behaviour used so far has been simplistic in comparison to a number of earlier studies. Multiple peer types, dynamics, and more detailed mechanisms of influence all remain to be incorporated into this approach. Given that adjusting for sorting and simultaneity using the structural approach yields such different answers in such a simple setting, it is likely that doing so may also provide new findings in a more detailed setting.

ACKNOWLEDGEMENTS

I have received helpful commentary on this work from seminar audiences at Western Washington University, and from a number of conference participants, especially Ole-Jørgen Skog, my discussant Rosalie Pacula, the referees, and editors of this volume. All errors are mine.

REFERENCES

Alexander, C., Piazza, M., Mekos, D., & Valente, T. (2001). Peers, schools, and adolescent cigarette smoking. *Journal of Adolescent Health, 29*, 22–30.

Altonji, J. G., Elder, T. E., & Taber, C. R. (2005). Selection on observed and unobserved variables: Assessing the effectiveness of Catholic schools. *Journal of Political Economy, 113*(1), 151–184.

Clark, A. E., & Lohéac., Y. (2004). "It wasn't me, it was them!" Social influence in risky behavior by adolescents. Working paper, DELTA.

Ennett, S. T., & Bauman, K. E. (1993). Peer group structure and adolescent cigarette smoking: A social network analysis. *Journal of Health and Social Behavior, 34*, 226–236.

Gaviria, A., & Raphael, S. (2001). School-based peer effects and juvenile behavior. *Review of Economics and Statistics, 83*(2), 257–268.

Kawaguchi, D. (2004). Peer effects on substance use among American teenagers. *Journal of Population Economics, 17*, 351–367.

Kobus, K. (2003). Peers and adolescent smoking. *Addiction, 98*, 37–55.

Krauth, B. V. (2004). Peer and selection effects on youth smoking in California. Working paper, Simon Fraser University.

Krauth, B. V. (2005a). Peer and selection effects on smoking among Canadian youth. *Canadian Journal of Economics, 38*(3).

Krauth, B. V. (2005b). Simulation-based estimation of peer effects. Working paper, Simon Fraser University. *Journal of Econometrics* (forthcoming).

Lloyd-Richardson, E. E., Papandonatos, G., Kazura, A., Stanton, C., & Niaura, R. (2002). Differentiating stages of smoking intensity among adolescents: Stage-specific psychological and social influences. *Journal of Consulting and Clinical Psychology, 70*(4), 998–1009.

Lundborg, P. (2005). Having the wrong friends? Peer effects in adolescent substance use. *Journal of Health Economics* (forthcoming).

Manski, C. F. (1993). Identification of endogenous social effects: The reflection problem. *Review of Economic Studies, 60*(3), 531–542.

Nichter, M., Vukovic, N., Quintero, G., & Ritenbaugh, C. (1997). Smoking experimentation and initiation among adolescent girls: Qualitative and quantitative findings. *Tobacco Control, 6*, 285–295.

Norton, E. C., Lindrooth, R. C., & Ennett, S. T. (1998). Controlling for the endogeneity of peer substance use on adolescent alcohol and tobacco use. *Health Economics, 7*, 439–453.

Norton, E. C., Lindrooth, R. C., & Ennett, S. T. (2003). How measures of perception from survey data lead to inconsistent regression results: Evidence from adolescent and peer substance use. *Health Economics, 12*, 139–148.

Powell, L. M., Tauras, J. A., & Ross, H. (2003). Peer effects tobacco control policies and youth smoking behavior. Working paper, University of Illinois, Chicago.

Tyas, S. L., & Pederson, L. L. (1998). Psychosocial factors related to adolescent smoking: A critical review of the literature. *Tobacco Control, 7*, 409–420.

Wang, M. Q., Fitzhugh, E. C., Westerfield, R. C., & Eddy, J. M. (1995). Family and peer influences on smoking behavior among American adolescents: An age trend. *Journal of Adolescent Health, 16*, 200–203.

PART III:
MARKETS

TRENDS IN WINE CONSUMPTION IN NORWAY: IS DIFFUSION THEORY APPLICABLE?

Ingeborg Rossow

ABSTRACT

The study aimed at assessing whether diffusion theory may be applicable to explain the increasing trends in consumption of table wine in Norway over a four-decade period. Data comprised a series of eight cross-sectional surveys from 1962 to 1999 in national samples of adults. The results indicated that diffusion theory might in part be applicable to explain the trends in wine consumption in Norway. Thus, early adopters were characterized by high social status and being more "cosmopolite". Yet, the typical S-shaped curve for adoption rate was not found, nor the expected association between wine consumption and social network.

1. INTRODUCTION

In Norway the consumption of wine has traditionally constituted a minor fraction of the total alcohol consumption. This is despite the fact that Norway's trade agreements with wine-producing countries like Spain, Portugal and France in the 1920s, and further on implied import of wine to balance fish export. In 1960 the wine sales constituted 7% of the total alcohol sales in litres of pure alcohol in Norway. Since then total alcohol consumption has increased by 70%. Sales of spirits are reduced by more than a third, sales of beer are doubled and sales of wine have increased by over 600%. If we look more specifically at the sales of table wine (usually with an alcohol content around 10–12%), we find that in 1960 only one-third of the wine sales (in pure alcohol) was table wine, the remaining two-thirds were fortified wines. Thus, in 1960 table wine constituted around 2% of the total alcohol sales (in litres of pure alcohol). In 2002 table wine constituted 25% of total alcohol sales and 96% of total wine sales. Sales of table wine (in litres of pure alcohol per adult inhabitant) thus increased by a factor of 18 from 1960 to 2002 (Fig. 1). Divergent trends in beverage-specific alcohol sales are rather prominent over the past two decades. Whereas beer sales have increased by 20%, sales of spirits are reduced by 50% and sales of table wine have increased by 200% (Fig. 1).

During the same period (1980–2000) the prices of alcoholic beverages (adjusted for consumer index) have varied to a far lesser extent. Real prices

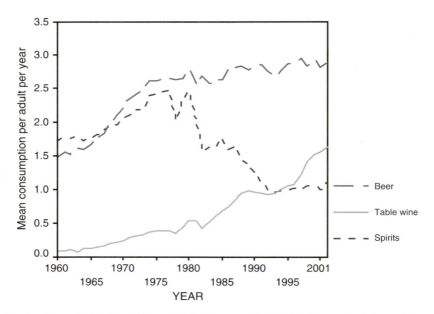

Fig. 1. Recorded Sales of Beer, Table Wine and Spirits in Norway in Litres of Pure Alcohols per Adult Inhabitant (>15 years) per Year.

for table wine and beer have increased by approximately 20% and 35%, respectively, whereas the real prices for spirits have increased by 10% (Bye, 2003). Recent analyses of the association between prices and sales of alcoholic beverages in Norway showed that for the period 1996–2003, through which sales of red wine were doubled, the price elasticity for red wine was very small and statistically insignificant, whereas the price elasticities for beer, fortified wine and spirits were all around −0.6 and statistically significant (Alver, 2004). This is contrary to previous analyses where estimates of price elasticities have been found to vary around −1 for wine and spirits, when analysing the periods 1960–1974 and 1974–1991 in Norway (Horverak, 1977; Strand, 1993).

The availability of both wine and spirits in Norway has increased since 1960. This is due to an increase in number of monopoly outlets for wine and spirits, and an increasing urbanization of the Norwegian population. The availability of beer has also increased due to an increase in number of retail outlets, and increased urbanization. A significant increase in bars, cafes and restaurants for on-premise sales of alcohol has furthermore contributed to an increased availability of all alcoholic beverages. Consequently, there are probably other important factors than price and availability to which the significant differential trends in sales of spirits, beer and wine in Norway may be attributed. Such other factors that may have influenced our demand for wine comprise the significant increase in travels abroad (and thereby exposure to, for instance, wine cultures in southern European countries); a significant increase in wine journalism; increased availability of wine in bag-in-box, and that wine consumption seems to have come into fashion.

Although wine is a product that has been imported to and consumed in Norway for centuries, the consumption has been quite modest and probably confined to a small fraction of the population. Hamran (2001) noted that in the first half of the 20th century consumption of table wine (often Bordeaux wines) was reserved for the few and accompanied festive meals, whereas consumption of fortified wines (mostly port) was more widespread and served the purpose of intoxication. In the 1950s and 1960s some books launched the message that wine was not solely a snobbish thing for the few, rich and knowledgeable, but rather a product that could be enjoyed by everyone, at an affordable price and without any specific knowledge about wines (Hamran, 2001). Thus, one may argue that consumption of wine, and in particular table wine, has represented a novelty for most Norwegians as recently as in the 1950s and 1960s and that wine consumption, particularly with meals, was a cultural innovation. Consequently, the strong increase in wine consumption and presumably also strong increase in the proportion of wine consumers in Norway may fit the model of diffusion of innovation (Rogers, 2003).

Innovation is defined as an idea, practice or object that is perceived as new to an individual (or another unit of adoption) (Rogers, 2003). Diffusion is the process through which a perceived new idea spreads via certain communication channels over time among the members of a particular social system (Haider & Krebs, 2004). The diffusion process tends to imply a cumulative rate of the innovation that forms an S-shaped curve, i.e. an initial slow increase followed by a rapid increase and then a small increase and levelling off (Ferrence, 2001). According to Rogers (2003) innovations have, amongst others, a relative advantage over alternative products or behaviours, they are compatible with existing values, and have impact on social relations. The adoption of the innovation depends on characteristics of the society (social norms and social statuses) as well as the individuals (personality, attitudes and communication behaviours) (see Haider & Krebs, 2004; Rogers, 2003). Thus, those who adopt the innovation at an early stage of the diffusion process (innovators, early adopters) are more likely to be oriented towards, and communicating with societies, cultures and individuals outside their own social system. Moreover, they tend to have a higher social status and to be more innovative (Rogers, 2003). Thus, empirical studies have found that compared to later adopters early adopters tend to:

- have more years of formal education;
- have a higher social status and income;
- have more social participation and larger social networks;
- be more cosmopolite (i.e. oriented outside one's own social system);
- be more exposed to mass media communication (Rogers, 2003).

This model of diffusion of innovation has been applied to topics in diverse areas and across a variety of academic disciplines (Haider & Krebs, 2004). In the alcohol and drug area, there are, however, a rather small number of studies that have applied diffusion theory (see Ferrence (1994, 2001) for a thorough review). In her review Ferrence (2001) has included only two studies on alcohol consumption, both addressing shifts in beverage preferences (Sulkunen, 1989; Hupkens et al., 1993). Sulkunen (1989) studied household data on beverage specific consumption in France from 1965 to 1979. During this period wine consumption decreased significantly, whereas consumption of beer and spirits increased. By analysing data separately for social class indicators Sulkunen found that these trends appeared to have been adopted by the middle class first, and was then followed by lower social groups. Hupkens et al. (1993) examined whether adoption of "new" (or increasingly popular) beverage types differed by gender, age and education in European Community countries. They found that people with high education level tended to drink the "new" beverage types more frequently compared to people with low education level, whereas the opposite was true with respect to consumption of "traditional" beverage types. A recent literature search (ISI, ETOH, MedLine) on alcohol and diffusion theory revealed some additional studies with relevance to diffusion of prevention programmes and treatment, but none that addressed consumer behaviour.

The present study attempts to broaden the empirical basis with respect to the applicability of diffusion theory in relation to trends in beverage-specific alcohol consumption by addressing the significant increase in wine consumption in Norway in recent decades. Obviously, all aspects of diffusion theory will not (and cannot) be tested empirically in the present analyses, yet characteristics of the innovation; rate of adoption and some characteristics of early and late adopters will be addressed. Thus, if diffusion theory is applicable:

1. Wine consumption in Norway in the post-war period would be characterized by the typical attributes of innovations, i.e. relative advantage, compatibility, lack of complexity, trialability and observability.
2. The rate of adoption would reflect an increased use of mass media as communication channel.
3. Wine consumption would have spread from a small to a larger fraction of the population.
4. The early adopters of wine consumption would be characterized by:
    having more years of formal education,
    having a higher income,
    having larger social networks,
    being more cosmopolite,
    being more exposed to mass media communication.

The first two hypotheses can be empirically illuminated by Hamran's (2001) historic analyses of wine consumption in Norway in the 20th century and Horverak's (in press) analyses of wine journalism in Norway.

1.1. Attributes of Wine Consumption in Norway in Recent Decades

According to Hamran (2001) the Norwegian health authorities have throughout the post-war period aimed at turning people's beverage preferences towards lower alcohol content drinks. Thus, table wine has been promoted as a better choice than spirits. Over the past 10–15 years much media attention has been paid to the beneficial effects of (particularly red) wine on heart disease. Thus, wine consumption has over the years most probably been conceived of as having a relative advantage to spirits and being compatible with prevailing values and beliefs. In the 1950s and 1960s wine was promoted as a beverage to be consumed without any specific knowledge about wine districts, grape varieties, vintages, etc. and the wine and liquor monopoly launched their own blended brand of red table wine (simply called "red wine") at a (relatively) low price. Thus, one may argue that lack of complexity had also become a new feature of wine consumption. In 1988 bag-in-box wine was launched on the Norwegian market. This packaging implies that it may be easier to have a glass or two of wine compared to opening a bottle of wine, and bag-in-box wine now constitutes half of the wine sales in Norway. Much of the striving for simplicity around wine consumption seemed to dominate the 1950s, 1960s and 1970s, whereas with the economic boom in the 1980s consumption of more expensive wines, knowledge about wines and private wine clubs came into fashion. The selection of table wines at the Norwegian market became larger and comprised to a larger extent wines from other countries and areas than those which had traditionally dominated the market (e.g. France, Spain and Italy). One may argue that several aspects of wine consumption (for instance selecting an appropriate wine with a meal, tasting and commenting on the wine, etc.) have a symbolic value, indicating taste and cultural capital. These aspects are easily observable in social contexts, and seem to have become more valued and fashionable over the last one or two decades.

1.2. Mass Media As a Communication Channel

Alcohol advertising was banned in Norway in 1975. It is not clear whether or to what extent wine was advertised in the media until 1975. In the early 1980s a few newspapers started regular columns with wine journalism, probably in response to a growing interest in and consumption of wine, and the extent of wine journalism in Norway has increased significantly since then (Horverak, in press). At present most newspapers have their own wine columns reporting on new wines, results of wine tasting, recommendations of good buys, good choices with various dishes, etc. Moreover, television programmes on cooking may also recommend particular wines or brands to supplement the meal. In a market free of alcohol advertising, wine reviews in the media may thus serve as marketing (Horverak, in press), and recent analyses of the association between wine reviews in the newspapers and wine sales have shown that the consumers to a large extent act in concordance with the recommendations (Horverak, in press).

2. DATA AND METHODS

The latter two hypotheses are put to empirical tests by statistical analyses based on a series of cross-sectional population surveys that cover wine consumption and characteristics of the wine consumers.

2.1. Population Surveys

These comprise national surveys in the Norwegian adult population for the years 1962, 1966, 1973, 1979, 1985, 1991, 1994 and 1999. Sampling, data collection procedures and questions were identical in these eight surveys. The samples were drawn in a three-stage manner with municipalities as first-stage units and households as second-stage units. From each household one person, above 15 years of age and with the most recent birthday, was interviewed face-to-face. Subjects who were not willing to participate, not available in their homes, or for other reasons were non-responders, were replaced by a person from a neighbouring household. Data were collected by structured personal interviews undertaken by a national opinion poll. The net samples comprised around 2,000 persons in each survey, except 1962 ($n = 3,954$) and 1994 ($n = 2,752$). The samples were weighted so as to represent the age, gender and area of residence distribution in the total adult population. Nevertheless, it is likely that heavy drinkers are under-represented in these samples.

The respondents were asked whether they had had any alcoholic drinks in the past year, and if so, they were asked how many times during the past 12 months they had had beer, wine and spirits, respectively. Data on gender, age, level of education, household income, marital status, urban/rural dwelling, and travel time to the nearest wine and spirits monopoly outlet were also collected. For the years 1979 through 1999 information was obtained on whether the respondents had travelled abroad during the past 12 months.

2.2. Operationalizations

Wine consumption may be conceived of as an innovation in several respects. In this study two dichotomous measures have been applied – any consumption of wine in the past 12 months, and a frequency of wine consumption corresponding to at least monthly consumption. It can be assumed that the adoption of these behaviours displays different cumulative adoption rates, and that the proportion drinking wine at least once a year is larger than the proportion drinking wine monthly at all time points. Characteristics of early adopters were operationalized in the following ways.

2.2.1. Social Status

- More years of formal education – college or university education.
- Higher income – being in the 5th quintile of household income.
- High cultural capital – being in the 5th quintile on a cultural capital sum-score[1].

2.2.2. Communication Behaviour

- Larger social networks – being in the 5th quintile on a social network sum-score[2].
- Being more cosmopolite – having been abroad in the past year[3] and living in Oslo.
- More exposed to mass media communication – being in the 5th quintile on a sum-score on number of hours per week reading books and newspapers.

Previous studies have found generally no or inconsistent association between early adoption of an innovation and age. However, a dichotomous variable on age (<50 years versus older) was included in the present analyses. Travel time to the nearest wine and spirits outlet was assumed to be a potential confounder of the associations between early adopter characteristics and wine consumption, and a dichotomous measure (<30 min back and forth versus longer time) was included in multivariate analyses.

3. RESULTS

3.1. Changes in Wine Consumption and Characteristics of Wine Drinkers

Data from the eight population surveys showed that the proportion of respondents reporting to have consumed wine during the past 12 months increased substantially from 1962 to 1999, i.e. from 47% to 86%.

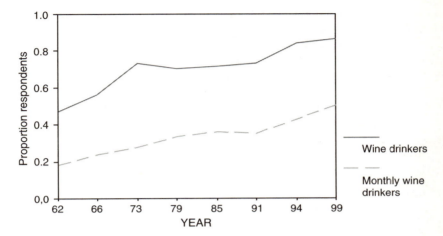

Fig. 2. Proportion of Survey Respondents Reporting to have Consumed Wine in the Previous Year (Full Line) and to Have Consumed Wine At Least Monthly (Broken Line).

Correspondingly, the proportion reporting at least monthly wine consumption increased from 18% in 1962 to 47% in 1999 (Fig. 2). The mean annual reported frequency of wine drinking increased by more than three-fold from 6 times a year in 1962 to 20 times a year in 1999. Over the same period the average travel time to the nearest wine and spirits outlet decreased significantly, and the proportion spending less than 30 min back and forth increased from 24% to 53%.

3.1.1. Social Status Characteristics

The proportions of wine drinkers and of monthly wine drinkers were both significantly higher among those with university or college education, those in the highest-income quintile, those living in Oslo and those under 50 years of age (Table 1). The question as to whether these differences had diminished with an increasing cumulative adoption rate was tested by interaction terms in logistic regression models. The differences in proportions of wine drinkers and monthly wine drinkers between respondents in Oslo and elsewhere diminished over the years (in terms of statistically significant interaction terms in multivariate models[4]). However, no other diminishing differences were found. Based on data only from the 1991 survey a higher proportion of wine drinkers and of monthly wine drinkers was also found among those in the 5th quintile on the cultural capital score (Table 1).

Table 1. Proportion of Respondents Who Had Wine in the Past 12 Months and Proportion Who Had Wine as Frequently as At Least Once a Month, by Survey Year (Decade) and Social Status and Demographical Characteristics.

	Wine in Past 12 Months				Wine At Least Monthly			
	1960s	1970s	1980s	1990s	1960s	1970s	1980s	1990s
All (%)	50	72	72	85	20	29	36	43
Education (%)								
High	77	88	87	92	43	60	55	61
Low	48	70	67	82	18	26	29	35
Income (%)								
High	69	87	88	94	34	52	58	65
Low	47	69	70	84	17	25	31	39
Cultural capital (%)								
High			88				59	
Medium/low			69				28	
Age (%)								
<50	56	78	79	89	23	34	40	55
50+	38	58	58	77	15	21	25	38
Dwelling (%)								
Oslo	66	84	86	89	35	54	56	54
Elsewhere	47	70	70	84	18	25	33	40

Logistic regression models of the likelihood of having had wine in the past year and the likelihood of having had wine at least monthly were estimated by applying model fit criteria for variable inclusion. The models show (Table 2) that the likelihood of wine drinking and monthly wine drinking increased significantly over the years, also when social status (high education and high income), demographic characteristics (age and dwelling) and travel costs were adjusted for.

3.1.2. Communication Behaviour

The proportions of wine drinkers and of monthly wine drinkers were both significantly higher among those who had been abroad in the preceding 12 months (Table 3). The differences in proportions of wine drinkers and monthly wine drinkers between those who had and those who had not been abroad did however not diminish, nor did they increase over the years (in terms of statistically significant interaction terms in multivariate models).

Table 2. Associations between Survey Period, Socio-economic and Demographical Characteristics and Likelihood That Respondents Had Had Wine in the Past 12 Months and Had Wine At Least Monthly.

	Wine Past 12 Months		Wine At Least Monthly	
	Regression Coefficient	Odds Ratio	Regression Coefficient	Odds Ratio
Period	0.046 (0.002)	1.047***	0.027 (0.002)	1.027***
High education	0.771 (0.067)	2.16***	0.799 (0.046)	2.22***
High income	0.136 (0.012)	1.15***	0.150 (0.009)	1.16***
Living in Oslo	0.493 (0.065)	1.64***	0.460 (0.051)	1.59***
<50 years	0.721 (0.042)	2.06***	0.345 (0.042)	1.41***
Low travel costs	0.256 (0.043)	1.29***	0.332 (0.039)	1.39***
Constant	3.36 −(0.147)		−3.55 (0.141)	

Multivariate logistic regression analyses. Adjusted regression coefficients, standard errors in parentheses, adjusted odds ratios and levels of statistical significance.
***$p<0.001$.

Table 3. Proportion of Respondents Who Had Wine in the Past 12 Months and Proportion Who Had As Frequently As At Least Once a Month by Survey Year (Decade) and Indicators of Communication Behaviour.

	Wine in Past 12 Months			Wine At Least Monthly		
	1970s	1980s	1990s	1970s	1980s	1990s
Abroad (%)						
Yes	82	88	91	45	51	52
No	63	61	76	27	24	28
Large social network (%)						
Yes			87			41
No			85			43
High mass media exposure (%)						
Yes		76			45	
No		72			33	

No significant differences were found between those with large social networks and others, whereas a significantly higher proportion of monthly wine drinkers was found among those with high mass media exposure as compared to others.

Table 4. Associations between Social Status, Demographical Characteristics and Indicators of Communication Behaviour and Likelihood that Respondents had Wine in the Past 12 Months and had Wine at least Monthly.

	Wine Past 12 Months		Wine At Least Monthly	
	Regression Coefficient	Odds Ratio	Regression Coefficient	Odds Ratio
Been abroad	0.046 (0.002)	1.047***	0.462 (0.109)	1.59***
High education	0.686 (0.138)	1.99***	0.528 (0.115)	1.70***
High income	0.071 (0.036)	1.07*	0.173 (0.027)	1.19***
Living in Oslo			0.365 (0.151)	1.44*
High cultural capital	0.677 (0.179)	1.97***	0.777 (0.131)	2.18***
<50 years	0.663 (0.122)	1.94***		
Low travel costs			0.460 (0.115)	1.58***
Constant	−0.16 (0.11)		−1.76 (0.11)	

Multivariate logistic regression analyses. Adjusted regression coefficients, standard errors in parentheses, adjusted odds ratios and levels of statistical significance. Analyses based on data only from the 1991 survey.
*$p<0.05$.
***$p<0.001$.

Logistic regression models of having had wine in the past year and of having had wine at least monthly were estimated with respect to indicators of communication behaviour. The indicator of large social network did not contribute significantly to model fit for either innovation variable, whereas having been abroad was significantly associated with both dependent variables in multivariate models (Table 4).

4. DISCUSSION

The question as to whether diffusion theory is applicable when addressing the trends of wine drinking in Norway over the past four decades, depends first of all on whether wine drinking can be considered an innovation in this respect. Indeed, wine drinking was not at all an entirely new idea, yet one may argue that the launching of simple, un-snobbish wines that were preferable to spirits in the 1950s and 1960s may have changed the ways in which most people conceived of wine drinking and thereby implied a *re-invention* of wine drinking (Rogers, 2003). Moreover, wine drinking seems to fit well the criteria of an innovation in terms of relative advantage, compatibility, lack of complexity and observability.

Looking at the adoption rates of the innovations(s), we do, however, not find the typical S-shaped curve when applying the two operationalizations of wine drinking as an innovation. The proportion of wine drinkers was relatively high (50%) in the 1960s, and displayed a relatively steep increase in the 1960s, after which the increase slowed down. The proportion of monthly wine drinkers was far lower at the beginning of the observation period, but displayed a steady increase over the four-decade period. Despite a frequent, versatile and positive presentation of wine in the mass media over the last 15–20 years, there are no clear indications that this has fuelled the adoption rate of wine drinking as operationalized in the present study.

The associations between social status indicators and wine drinking are much in line with the predictions of diffusion theory. Hence, early adopters (the monthly wine drinkers) were significantly more often found among those with high social status, i.e. those with college or university education, those in the highest income groups and those who scored highest on cultural capital. That wine consumption is more frequent in higher social status groups is long well documented in Nordic studies (Saglie, 1994; Rossow & Træen, 1995; Mortensen, Jensen, Sanders, & Reinisch, 2001).

The associations between indicators of communication behaviour and wine drinking were in part in accordance with the predictions. "Cosmopoliteness" was associated with wine drinking and wine drinkers, and monthly wine drinkers were more often found among those who had been abroad in the previous year as well as among residents of the Norwegian capital, Oslo. A positive association between frequent exposure to books and newspapers and monthly wine drinking was found, whereas no association between a social network indicator and annual wine drinking was found.

The empirical analyses thus seem to imply that diffusion theory to some extent, although not fully, may be applicable when attempting to explain the trend in wine consumption in Norway in the latter half of the 20th century.

NOTES

1. The sum score was based on three variables on frequency of having visited opera/theatre, classical music concerts and art exhibitions/museums in the previous year. Only obtained in the 1991 survey.
2. The sum score was based on three variables: Frequency of visiting friends, number of friends/neighbours that were frequently visited and an indicator of loneliness. The sum score was only obtained in the surveys in 1994 and 1999.

3. This was obtained for the surveys in 1973, 1979, 1985, 1991, 1994 and 1999.
4. Interaction terms are not reported but available from the author on request.

REFERENCES

Alver, Ø. (2004). *Om pris og etterspørsel etter alcohol I Norge* [*On prices and demand for alcoholic beverages in Norway.*] SIRUS-rapport nr 4/2004. Oslo: Norwegian Institute for Alcohol and Drug Research.

Bye, E.K. (Ed.) (2003). *Rusmidler i Norge 2003*. [*Intoxicants in Norway 2003.*] Oslo: Norwegian Institute for Alcohol and Drug Research.

Ferrence, R. (1994). Diffusion of innovation as a model for understanding population change in substance use. In: G. Edwards & M. Lader (Eds), *Addiction: Processes of change* (pp. 189–201). New York, NY: Oxford University Press.

Ferrence, R. (2001). Diffusion theory and drug use. *Addiction*, 96, 165–173.

Haider, M., & Krebs, G. L. (2004). Forty years of diffusion of innovations: Utility and value in public health. *Journal of Health Communication*, 9(Suppl 1), 3–11.

Hamran, O. (2001). *Vinlandet. Vin i Norge 1920—2000*. [*The wine country. Wine in Norway 1920–2000.*] Oslo: Samlaget.

Horverak, Ø. (1977). *Etterspørselen etter brennevin og vin i Norge. En analyse av sammenhengen mellom omsatt kvantum og priser på brennevin og vin. [The demand for spirits and wine in Norway. An analysis of the association between sales and prices of spirits and wine].* Oslo: Norwegian Institute for Alcohol and Drug Research.

Horverak, Ø. (in press). Wine journalism – Marketing or consumer's guide?

Hupkens, C. L. H., Knibbe, R. A., & Drop, M. J. (1993). Alcohol consumption in the European community: Uniformity and diversity in drinking patterns. *Addiction*, 88, 1391–1404.

Mortensen, E. L., Jensen, H. H., Sanders, S. A., & Reinisch, J. M. (2001). Better psychological functioning and higher social status may largely explain the apparent health benefits of wine – A study of wine and beer drinking in young Danish adults. *Archives of Internal Medicine*, 161, 1844–1848.

Rogers, E. M. (2003). *Diffusion of innovations* (5th ed.). New York: Free Press.

Rossow, I., & Træen, B. (1995). *På kafe i Norge. Om kafebruk, alkoholbruk og livsstil.* [*On visiting public drinking places, alcohol consumption and life style.*] Oslo: Norwegian Institute for Alcohol and Drug Research.

Saglie, J. (1994). *Norske drikkekulturer: Geografi, sosial bakgrunn, livsstil og tilgjengelighet.* [*Norwegian drinking cultures: Geographical distribution, social background, life style and availability.*] Oslo: Norwegian Institute for Alcohol and Drug Research.

Strand, M.M. (1993). *Pris- og inntekstselastisiteter for brennevin og vin.* [*Price- and income elasticities for spirits and wine.*] Masters thesis, University of Oslo, Oslo.

Sulkunen, P. (1989). Drinking in France 1965–1979. *An analysis of household consumption data. British Journal of Addiction,*, 84, 61–72.

AN INVESTIGATION OF THE EFFECTS OF ALCOHOL POLICIES ON YOUTH STDs

Michael Grossman, Robert Kaestner and Sara Markowitz

ABSTRACT

The purpose of this chapter is to examine the role of alcohol policies in reducing the incidence of sexually transmitted diseases (STDs) among youth. Previous research has shown that risky sexual practices (e.g., unprotected sex and multiple partners) that increase the risk of contracting an STD are highly correlated with alcohol use. If alcohol is a cause of risky sexual behaviour, then policies that reduce the consumption of alcohol may also reduce the incidence of STDs. In this chapter, we examine the relationship between alcohol policies (e.g., beer taxes and statutes pertaining to alcohol sales and drunk driving) and rates of gonorrhea and acquired immune deficiency syndrome (AIDS) among teenagers and young adults. Results indicate that higher beer taxes are associated with lower rates of gonorrhea for males and are suggestive of lower AIDS rates. Strict drunk driving policies in the form of zero tolerance laws may also lower the gonorrhea rate among males under the legal drinking age.

1. INTRODUCTION

When compared to older adults, teenagers and young adults are particularly at risk for contracting a sexually transmitted disease (STD). Incidence rates of chlamydia and gonorrhea, the two most common reportable STDs, are the highest among American teenagers and young adults. In 2002, chlamydia incidence was 297 per 100,000 population for persons of all ages, 1,483 for teenagers, and 1,610 for young adults (Centers for Disease Control and Prevention (CDC), 2003). Similar age disparities are found for gonorrhea, with incidence rates per 100,000 population of 125, 476, and 593, respectively. Moreover, approximately half of all new human immunodeficiency virus (HIV) infections in the U.S.A. occur among people under age 25 years (CDC, 2002). These statistics make clear that teenagers' sexual behaviours are adversely affecting their health and development.

The high rates of STDs and risky sexual practices of teens have motivated researchers to look for causes of these behaviours. Numerous studies have shown a positive association between substance use and risky sexual practices.[1] For example, Graves and Leigh (1995) show that young adults who drink heavily are more likely to be sexually active and to have multiple partners, and those who are heavy drinkers are also less likely to use condoms. Similar evidence also comes from Strunin and Hingson (1992), and Fergusson and Lynskey (1996) who show that alcohol use by teenagers is associated with unprotected intercourse. Regrettably, all of these sexual behaviours have been shown to increase the risk of contracting STDs (Laumann, Gagnon, Michael, & Michaels, 1994).

The policy implications of this research are important. If alcohol consumption causes youth to engage in unsafe sexual practices, then reductions in alcohol consumption will also reduce the negative outcomes associated with unsafe sex. On the other hand, if alcohol consumption is simply correlated with risky sexual behaviour, then (exogenous) reductions in consumption would have no effect on teens' risky sexual behaviours. Therefore, policies that are known to affect alcohol consumption can be used to identify indirectly the effect of such consumption on risky sexual behaviours and STDs. In fact, many studies have shown that alcohol consumption is responsive to changes in alcohol prices (see, for reviews, Leung & Phelps, 1993; Cook & Moore, 2000). Studies focusing specifically on youth consumption also show a responsiveness to policies pertaining to availability, such as the minimum legal drinking age (Grossman, Chaloupka, Saffer, & Laixuthai, 1994; Moore & Cook, 1995; Grossman, Chaloupka, & Sirtalan, 1998) and zero tolerance laws (Carpenter, 2004).

In this chapter, we examine the relationship between STD rates and prices and policies pertaining to the consumption of alcohol. This research strategy makes use of the known relationship between alcohol control policies and alcohol consumption to indirectly study the effect of alcohol consumption on risky sexual behaviour and STDs. More importantly, we provide evidence on the effect of policy tools that legislators can use to affect teen and young adult behaviour.

2. PREVIOUS RESEARCH

While the bulk of the existing research on substance use and risky sex describes a positive correlation between these behaviours, researchers have just begun to examine the causal nature of the substance use-risky sex link. To establish causality, it is essential to address the non-random nature of substance use and risky sexual behaviour. Economists have taken the lead in this area. Recent studies by economists have attempted to go beyond simply measuring the correlation by using methods that account for non-random selection. The results of these studies are mixed. Alcohol use has been reported to lower contraception use among young women (Kaestner & Joyce, 2001) and teens of both genders (Sen, 2002; Grossman & Markowitz (2004)), and to increase the probability of having sex (Sen, 2002). By contrast, heavy alcohol use and drunkenness appear to have no causal impacts on the probabilities of having sex among teens (Rees, Argys, & Averett, 2001; Sen, 2002; Grossman & Markowitz (in press); Grossman, Kaestner, & Markowitz (2004)) or using protection among young females (Rees et al., 2001; Sen, 2002). However, Rees et al. (2001) find that drunkenness may lead to a lower probability of contraception use among males. The mixed nature of these findings is not easily reconciled by theoretical considerations and a recent study by Rashad and Kaestner (2004) calls into question the validity of the methods used to obtain estimates reported by Rees et al. (2001) and Sen (2002). Therefore, the question of the causal relationship between teen alcohol use and risky sex remains largely unanswered.

Very little research has examined the causal relationship between alcohol or drug use on outcomes of risky sexual practices. Kaestner and Joyce (2001) examine the effects of substance use on the probability of unintended pregnancy. They find that among whites, alcohol use increases the likelihood of unintended pregnancy while drug use has no statistically significant effects. They also find that substance use is statistically unrelated to unintended pregnancy for blacks and Hispanics. Dee (2001) reaches an alternate conclusion in his study on changes in the minimum legal drinking age and childbearing among teens and young adults. Using a panel of state-level data across time, he finds evidence that reductions in alcohol consumption encouraged by higher drinking ages reduced the childbearing rates of blacks, while having an uncertain effect on childbearing rates of whites. The discrepancy in the conclusions between Dee's study and that of Kaestner and Joyce (2001) may arise because of differences in the outcomes studied (childbearing rates versus unintended pregnancies), time period under consideration (1977–1992 versus 1984 and 1988), and unit of observation (state versus individual). It is clear, however, that much is still unknown about the relationship between alcohol consumption and teenage sexual behaviours and outcomes.

Three other studies have analysed the relationship between alcohol and risky sexual behaviours indirectly by examining the relationships between alcohol control policies and STDs, another outcome of risky sexual behaviours. This approach relates the exogenous determinants of alcohol consumption (i.e., public policies such as the excise tax on beer) directly to STD rates. Causal relationships are inferred since the only way that these policies should affect STD rates directly is through reduced consumption and risky sexual practices.

Chesson, Harrison, and Kassler (2000) show that gonorrhea and syphilis rates fall as the state beer or liquor tax rises. To obtain these estimates, Chesson et al. (2000) use a time series of state-level data for the year 1981 through 1995 and controls for state and year effects. The results stated above apply to persons of all ages, young adults, and male teenagers. In addition, Chesson et al. (2000) report that increases in the minimum legal drinking age lower the gonorrhea rate for youths age 15–19 years.

Scribner, Cohen, and Farley (1998) report a negative relationship between gonorrhea rates and alcohol outlet density among urban residential census tracts in New Orleans in 1995. However, it is unknown whether this relationship is causal, or whether the effects reflect a correlation with other neighbourhood and individual characteristics. For example, people with a taste for multiple risky behaviours may be clustered in high outlet density neighbourhoods.

Lastly, Carpenter (2005) examines the effect of zero tolerance laws for under-age drunk driving in reducing gonorrhea rates over time. Zero tolerance laws are associated with reduced alcohol consumption among teens (Carpenter, 2004), and therefore might also affect other outcomes associated with alcohol consumption. Indeed, Carpenter finds that the adoption of zero tolerance laws are associated with a reduction in gonorrhea rates for white males ages 15–19 years, although the results are mixed for white females and are statistically insignificant for black males and females.

This chapter adds to the existing literature by examining the impact of alcohol prices on gonorrhea and *acquired immune deficiency syndrome* (AIDS) rates for teenagers and young adults. In its basic structure, this chapter is similar to that of the study by Chesson et al. (2000), whose primary focus is the impact of beer and liquor taxes on the determinants of gonorrhea and syphilis rates among people of all ages. Our chapter differs, however, in a number of respects. First, our sample consists only of youth, and includes an analysis of AIDS, which is more prevalent than syphilis.[2] Second, our data on gonorrhea rates extend over a longer and more recent time period. Third, along with the price of alcohol, we include a number of other alcohol regulatory variables. The inclusion of drunk driving laws and a measure of alcohol availability are other novel aspects of this chapter. Lastly, our estimation strategy differs somewhat from that of Chesson et al. (2000). Details are described in the next section.

3. METHODS

The empirical specification is based on the notion that risky sexual behaviours may lead to the contraction of an STD. Alcohol consumption may contribute to the contraction of the STD because of its effect on risky sexual behaviour. Therefore, the exogenous determinants of alcohol use are hypothesized to reduce STD rates through decreased consumption. The regression model is specified as follows:

$$\ln(\text{STD}_{jt}) = \alpha_0 + \alpha_1 P_{jt} + \alpha_2 X_{jt} + \alpha_3 \gamma_j + \alpha_4 \tau_t + \varepsilon_{jt} \quad (1)$$

Eq. (1) specifies that the natural logarithm of the STD rate (STD) for a gender and age group in an area (*j*) at a point in time (*t*) is a function of area alcohol regulatory variables (P_{jt}), other characteristics of the population of the area (X_{jt}), area effects (γ_j), year effects (τ_t), and an error term. The vector of coefficients on P_{jt} will show whether alcohol policies influence STD rates. Given the strong evidence mentioned above linking alcohol policies to consumption, we assume that any estimated effects of the policies work through a reduction in consumption. After accounting for area characteristics and time trends, there is little reason to believe that substance use policies may affect STD rates in any other way except through changes in consumption.

The estimation of AIDS rates entails an added difficulty in that the cases are reported to public health officials only after the individual has developed symptoms of AIDS. This may occur many years after the initial transmission of the HIV virus.[3] Given this lag, the alcohol regulatory variables should be matched to the date of initial viral transmission rather than the date of diagnosis. Unfortunately, it is not possible to match each case with the infection date. Instead we use the average length of time between transmission of the HIV virus and symptomatic AIDS infection, which is 8 years (Bartlett & Gallant, 2003). The equation for AIDS therefore includes an 8-year lag of all the independent variables:

$$\ln(\text{AIDS}_{jt}) = \alpha_0 + \alpha_1 P_{jt-8} + \alpha_2 X_{jt-8} + \alpha_3 \gamma_j + \alpha_4 \tau_{t-8} + \varepsilon_{jt}. \quad (2)$$

Two problems may arise in estimating Eqs. (1) and (2). First, the residuals may be serially correlated if there exists unobserved state-specific time-varying factors. Persistent discrepancies in state reporting practices or screening programmes might cause the error terms to be correlated across time within a state. Bertrand, Duflo, and Mullainathan (2004) show that this is an especially serious problem when independent variables are positively correlated over time because they change infrequently. For example, dichotomous policy variables may change only once in the sample period. Thus, we adopt the Bertrand et al. (2004) correction for serial correlation by computing robust standard errors that allow for clustering by area (state for gonorrhea, Metropolitan Statistical Areas (MSAs) for AIDS).

The second problem arises if the incidence rate of communicable diseases depends on the past incidence or prevalence of the disease. This suggests that the lagged STD rate should be included in the equations.[4] Nickell (1981), Baltagi (2001), and others show that the coefficient of the lagged-dependent variable is inconsistent in a fixed-effects model applied to a panel even if the disturbance term is serially uncorrelated. The reason is that in the standard fixed-effects estimation procedure the lagged-dependent variable is correlated with the error term which includes the mean error. This inconsistency will translate to the coefficients of other regressors that are correlated with the lagged-dependent variable.

To address this problem, we adopt alternative methods to account for the lagged-dependent variable. The first is a reduced form equation which replaces the lagged STD rate with some of its determinants, and the second directly includes the lagged STD rate. The reduced form ordinary least square (OLS) equations include lagged beer taxes and per cent dry as additional regressors. For gonorrhea only one lag is included (year $t-1$). Further lags proved to be statistically insignificant and are omitted because they do not contribute to the models. For AIDS, we include two lags of the beer tax (years $t-9$ and $t-10$) since these prove to be jointly statistically significant in the models. Further lags of the beer tax are insignificant, as is the second lag of the per cent dry, which is omitted.

Models that include a lagged-dependent variable apply two methods: OLS and a first-difference two-stage least squares (FD2SLS) estimator (Baltagi, 2001). The OLS estimates are inconsistent but the FD2SLS may encounter problems due to random measurement error in the regressors. Inconsistencies due to this phenomenon are exacerbated by taking first differences, and may be particularly apparent when AIDS is considered as there is uncertainty as to the timing of the initial infection and the corresponding alcohol regulatory variables. The FD2SLS estimator is constructed by taking first differences of all variables and thereby eliminating area fixed effects. The lagged first-differenced STD rate ($STD_{jt-1} - STD_{jt-2}$) is correlated with the first-differenced residual ($\varepsilon_{jt} - \varepsilon_{jt-1}$) since STD_{jt-1} is correlated with ε_{jt-1}. Hence, the second lag of STD (STD_{jt-2}) is employed as an instrument for the lagged first difference ($STD_{jt-1} - STD_{jt-2}$). Baltagi (2001) indicates that the second lag is highly correlated with the lagged difference in most applications, yet it is uncorrelated with the error term ($\varepsilon_{jt} - \varepsilon_{jt-1}$) since future shocks have no impacts on lagged values of the dependent variable.[5]

When considering STDs, it is questionable as to what is the appropriate lagged STD rate. If a disease is contracted through heterosexual sex then the lagged STD rate for the opposite sex may be appropriate. The opposite would hold when homosexual sex is a mechanism of transmission (particularly when AIDS among males is considered). Additionally, a 1-year time lag may also be too long a period to correctly identify which gender's lagged STD rate is appropriate. Therefore, two models of lagged STD rates are considered. One contains the lagged-dependent variable, which is gender specific (columns 3 and 5 in the tables), and the other includes the lagged total rate for both genders (columns 4 and 6). Since the lagged total rate includes the lagged-dependent variable, both models are still estimated by FD2SLS.

Our empirical approach differs in part from the one taken by Chesson et al. (2000) because they include the lagged-dependent variable as an exogenous regressor. We treat it as endogenous. As shown in the Section 5 below, the treatment of the lagged-dependent variable can significantly influence the results.

4. DATA

Gonorrhea and AIDS are currently on the list of nationally notifiable diseases. A notifiable disease is one for which "regular, frequent, and timely information regarding individual cases is considered necessary for the prevention and control of the disease" (CDC, 2000a). Public health officials at state health departments and officials at the CDC determine which diseases are nationally notifiable. Each state, however, has the authority to determine which diseases are reportable, and reporting is mandated only at the state level. Reporting to the CDC is voluntary, although all states typically participate.

The data used in this study was collected from state health departments and was provided to the CDC through the National Electronic Telecommunications System for Surveillance (NETSS). Reports for gonorrhea include the date of diagnosis, state of residence at diagnosis, age at diagnosis, and gender. AIDS reports include date of diagnosis, age, gender, and residence for people living in MSAs with populations of 500,000 or more.

The annual number of reported cases of gonorrhea are available from the CDC beginning in 1981. Incident rates from 1981 to 2001 are calculated by gender for teens ages 15–19 years and young adults ages 20–24 years. To create the rates, the number of reported cases in each state for each gender–age group is divided by the corresponding population of persons in that age category.

AIDS data for 103 large MSAs are available annually beginning in 1982 and are currently available through 2001. The data collected are for diagnosed cases of AIDS, and not cases of HIV. The case definitions were modified in 1985, 1987, and 1993 to incorporate a broader range of indicator diseases and to include results of HIV tests. The data used in this chapter contain all cases meeting the 1993 surveillance definition, the broadest definition (see CDC, 1992, for details on the definition). Incident rates are created by gender for people diagnosed with AIDS at ages 20–29 and 30–34 years. Using the average 8-year time period between initial viral transmission and the development of symptomatic AIDS, these individuals most likely contracted the disease between the ages of 12–21 and 22–26 years, respectively, thus providing a sample of teenagers and young adults. The population of the relevant age group in the MSA is used as the denominator in calculating the rate.

Since the FD2SLS models use the second lag of the dependent variable as an instrument, the first year of observation in these regressions is 1983 for gonorrhea and 1984 for AIDS. In order to keep the sample consistent and to allow for comparisons across the models, we exclude the first 2 years of data from all OLS models. The final sample size is 950 for gonorrhea and 1854 for AIDS.[6] Excluding these beginning years makes little difference to the OLS results.

Several variables are used to measure state-level alcohol regulations. First, the real (1982–1984 = 1) state and federal excise tax on a gallon of beer measures the price of alcohol. Beer taxes come from the Beer Institute's *Brewers Almanac*. The tax on beer is chosen because beer is the most popular alcoholic beverage among youths. Second, the percentage of each state's population living in counties dry for beer in each of the years is included. These data come from the Beer Institute's *Brewers Almanac* (various years). With larger percentages of populations living in dry counties, travel time to obtain alcohol increases, adding to the full price of alcohol. If alcohol consumption contributes to risky sexual practices, then it is expected that policies which make obtaining alcohol more costly will reduce STDs.

The other measures of alcohol regulation are indicators for the presence of blood-alcohol concentration (BAC) laws. These laws make it illegal per se to drive with a BAC greater than a certain level. In 1981, 14 states had a BAC law of 0.10 or higher. In 1983, Oregon and Utah were the first states to pass a BAC law of 0.08. By 2000, almost all states passed BAC laws, with 20 states having 0.08 as the legal limit. Beginning in the mid-1980s, states also began enacting "zero tolerance" laws for under-age drinking and driving. These laws typically set the BAC for under-age drinkers at 0.02 or less. Federal legislation passed in 1995 encouraged all states to pass zero tolerance laws by allowing for the withholding of federal highway funds. By 1998, all 50 states plus the District of Columbia had a zero tolerance law in effect.

Three indicators for BAC laws are included: A dichotomous indicator for a BAC law of 0.10 or higher, a dichotomous indicator for a BAC law of 0.08 or higher, and a dichotomous indicator for the presence of a youth zero tolerance law. For states in which the laws become effective at some point during the year, fractional values are used to represent the percentage of the year under which the law was in effect. Youth and young adults living in states with more stringent BAC laws face a higher full price of alcohol relative to youth living in less stringent states because the probability of being charged with drunk driving increases. Thus, it is expected that stricter BAC laws will reduce alcohol consumption and possibly reduce STDs.

Each model includes a number of other state-level variables to capture additional factors which may influence the gonorrhea or AIDS rate. These variables include the unemployment rate, real income per capita, the percentage of the population living in rural areas (gonorrhea only), and the percentage of the population 25 years and over that has obtained a bachelor's degree. The percentage of each state's population identifying with certain religions (Mormon, Southern Baptist, Protestant, and Catholic) is also included. Lastly, all models include area and time dummies. The area dummies will help to capture any unobserved time-invariant area effects which may influence STD rates and may be correlated with the alcohol control policies. Time dummies are included to capture secular trends.

The state-level variables are appended to the AIDS data based on the state or states represented by the MSA. Where a MSA crosses state lines, the variables are taken as a population weighted average from the relevant states. In the case of the dichotomous laws related to drunk driving, the MSA is assigned values from the state with the largest population in the MSA.

5. RESULTS

Figs. 1 and 2 show national gonorrhea and AIDS rates by age group and gender. Among youth, gonorrhea rates have shown a distinct downward trend over time, while AIDS rates peaked in the early 1990s, and have decreased since. Gonorrhea rates may be under-reported by as much as 50%; however, the long history of reporting provides for a good indication of the true trends in the disease (CDC, 2000b). It is uncertain as to whether the under-reporting of diseases will present a problem for the multivariate estimation. If the under-reporting is random and is uncorrelated with the included variables, the estimated coefficients will not be biased. However, if there exists systematic reporting errors that are not captured by the state dummies, then biases may occur.

Table 1 shows the average gonorrhea and AIDS rates along with the summary statistics for the alcohol regulatory variables and the area characteristics. Young females ages 15–19 years have the highest average gonorrhea rate at 457 per 100,000 population. This average is closely followed by the rates for males and females ages 20–24 years at 456 and 376 cases per 100,000 population, respectively. Young males ages 15–19 years have the lowest reported rates of 332 cases per 100,000 population. The average AIDS rates are much lower than that of gonorrhea. The average male AIDS rate per 100,000 population are 14.95 and 37.35 for those ages 20–29, and 30–34 years, respectively, while the corresponding rates for females are 4.42 and 7.90, respectively.

Tables 2–7 show the results of the impact of the alcohol regulatory variables on gonorrhea and AIDS rates for males and females by age group. Six regression models are presented in each table. The first is a simple OLS, the second is an OLS with lagged alcohol regulatory variables, the third and

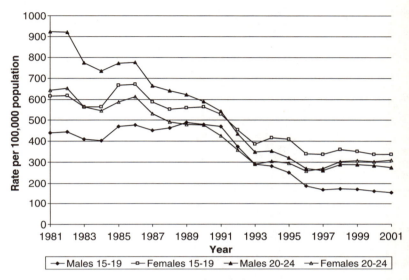

Fig. 1. National Gonorrhea Rates, 1981–2001.

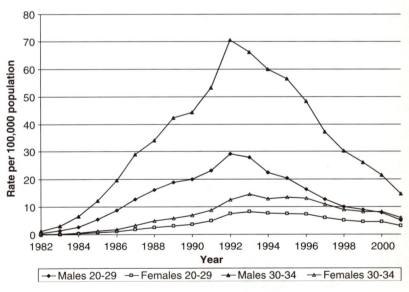

Fig. 2. New AIDS Cases per 100,000 Population, 1982–2001.

Table 1. Summary Statistics.

Variable	Definition	Mean, Standard Deviation (Gonorrhea Sample: States)	Mean, Standard Deviation (AIDS Sample: MSAs)
Male gonorrhea rate, ages 15–19 years (log rate)	Gonorrhea rate for males ages 15–19 years per 100,000 population ages 15–19 in state	331.81, 524.99 (5.08, 1.36)	
Male gonorrhea rate, ages 20–24 years (log rate)	Gonorrhea rate for males ages 20–24 years per 100,000 population ages 20–24 years in state	456.13, 566.75 (5.56, 1.19)	
Female gonorrhea rate, ages 15–19 years (log rate)	Gonorrhea rate for females ages 15–19 years per 100,000 population ages 15–19 years in state	456.69, 485.58 (5.64, 1.13)	
Female gonorrhea rate, ages 20–24 years (log rate)	Gonorrhea rate for females ages 20–24 per 100,000 population ages 20–24 years in state	376.46, 338.30 (5.49, 1.09)	
Male AIDS rate, ages 20–29 years (log rate)	AIDS rate for males ages 20–29 years per 100,000 population ages 20–29 years in MSA		14.95, 13.82 (2.22, 1.24)
Male AIDS rate, ages 30–34 years (log rate)	AIDS rate for males ages 30–34 years per 100,000 population ages 30–34 years in MSA		37.35, 36.26 (3.14, 1.24)
Female AIDS rate, ages 20–29 years (log rate)	AIDS rate for females ages 20–29 years per 100,000 population ages 20–29 in MSA		4.42, 6.60 (0.40, 1.83)

Table 1. (Continued)

Variable	Definition	Mean, Standard Deviation (Gonorrhea Sample: States)	Mean, Standard Deviation (AIDS Sample: MSAs)
Female AIDS rate, ages 30–34 years (log rate)	AIDS rate for females ages 30–34 years per 100,000 population ages 30–34 years in MSA		7.90, 12.09 (0.77, 2.12)
Real beer tax (log real beer tax)	Real state and federal excise tax per gallon of beer	0.49, 0.14 (−0.75, 0.27)	0.54, 0.23 (−0.69, 0.37)
Per cent dry	Percentage of state population living in counties that are dry for beer	4.09, 9.49	4.28, 7.87
0.10 BAC law	Dichotomous variable that equals 1 if per se illegal to drive with a BAC of 0.10 or greater	0.74, 0.43	0.60, 0.48
0.08 BAC law	Dichotomous variable that equals 1 if per se illegal to drive with a BAC of 0.08 or greater	0.16, 0.36	0.04, 0.19
Zero tolerance law	Dichotomous variable that equals 1 if state has a zero tolerance law for youth under-age drinking and driving	0.43, 0.49	0.11, 0.30
Unemployment	Unemployment rate	5.75, 2.02	6.90, 1.91
Real income	Per capita income, adjusted for inflation	145.19, 25.25	136.06, 20.89
Per cent rural	Percentage of state population living in rural areas	30.04, 15.19	Not Applicable

Table 1. (*Continued*)

Variable	Definition	Mean, Standard Deviation (Gonorrhea Sample: States)	Mean, Standard Deviation (AIDS Sample: MSAs)
College degree	Percentage of state population 25 years and older that has graduated from a 4-year college	21.37, 5.05	18.07, 3.95
Mormon	Percentage of state population Mormon	2.98, 10.09	1.47, 6.74
Southern Baptist	Percentage of state population Southern Baptist	7.11, 9.90	7.79, 9.48
Protestant	Percentage of state population Protestant	21.65, 9.87	19.73, 7.61
Catholic	Percentage of state population Catholic	19.19, 12.66	20.48, 12.80

Note: Means for independent variables used in the AIDS regressions are lagged 8 years.

fourth include the lagged-dependent variable or the lagged total rate treated as exogenous, and the fifth and sixth are the FD2SLS estimates with the lagged-dependent variable or lagged total rate. All standard errors are adjusted for clustered by state, and all estimates are weighted by the relevant population.

The dependent variables are all in log form, as is the beer tax so that elasticities are directly estimated. In the early years of the AIDS data, some MSAs have no reported cases of AIDS. This occurs in 6% of the male sample and 25% of the female sample. In these cases, a small value (1 in 2 million) is used so that logs can be taken. This value is chosen to ensure that the zero cases will be represented by the smallest value possible in the data. Note that using unlogged AIDS rates as the dependent variable yields results very similar to those presented below. There are no zeros in the gonorrhea data.

Table 2. Gonorrhea, Males Ages 15–19 Years.

	OLS (1)	Lagged OLS (2)	Lagged-Dependent Variable OLS (3)	Lagged Total Rate OLS (4)	Lagged-Dependent Variable FD2SLS (5)	Lagged Total Rate FD2SLS (6)
Lagged male gonorrhea rate			0.639 (25.14)		0.464 (2.35)	
Lagged total rate				0.710 (25.42)		0.588 (2.22)
Log beer tax	−0.471 (−2.02)	−0.355 (−1.07)	−0.278 (−3.06)	−0.427 (−4.75)	−0.467 (−2.34)	−0.441 (−2.10)
Lag log beer tax		−0.128 (−0.64)				
Per cent dry	−0.025 (−1.54)	−0.003 (−0.22)	−0.010 (−1.30)	−0.013 (−1.64)	0.014 (0.79)	0.017 (0.89)
Lag per cent dry		−0.026 (−1.77)				
0.10 BAC law	−0.005 (−0.05)	0.003 (0.03)	−0.034 (−0.72)	0.032 (0.68)	0.135 (1.48)	0.126 (1.38)
0.08 BAC law	−0.145 (−1.03)	−0.138 (−0.95)	−0.077 (−1.30)	0.018 (0.30)	0.175 (1.63)	0.181 (1.63)
Zero tolerance law	−0.083 (−1.50)	−0.082 (−1.49)	−0.071 (−2.63)	−0.071 (−2.66)	−0.084 (−2.66)	−0.074 (−2.41)
Unemployment	−0.039 (−1.49)	−0.040 (−1.54)	−0.011 (−1.34)	−0.018 (−2.21)	0.006 (0.41)	0.006 (0.45)
Real income	0.015 (2.58)	0.015 (2.60)	0.006 (3.36)	0.007 (3.79)	0.002 (0.53)	0.003 (0.78)
Per cent rural	0.031 (1.69)	0.030 (1.65)	0.010 (1.65)	0.016 (2.58)	0.005 (0.31)	0.008 (0.54)
College degree	0.002 (0.24)	0.002 (0.24)	−0.0003 (−0.04)	−0.002 (−0.30)	0.003 (0.41)	0.003 (0.34)
Per cent Mormon	0.033 (0.58)	0.034 (0.58)	0.031 (0.83)	−0.04 (−1.10)	−0.016 (−0.47)	−0.026 (−0.95)
Per cent Southern Baptist	0.03 (0.96)	0.033 (1.02)	0.014 (0.76)	0.017 (0.91)	−0.025 (−1.12)	−0.019 (−0.81)
Per cent Protestant	−0.037 (−2.26)	−0.036 (−2.20)	0.003 (0.42)	0.004 (0.52)	0.019 (1.98)	0.017 (1.76)
Per cent Catholic	−0.043 (−1.49)	−0.043 (−1.49)	−0.011 (−1.52)	−0.017 (−2.47)	−0.032 (−2.13)	−0.026 (−1.36)
F-test: Beer tax, lag beer tax		2.89 [0.065]				
F-test: Per cent dry, lag per cent dry		1.67 [0.199]				
R^2	0.928	0.928	0.958	0.959	−	−

Note: t-statistics in parentheses, P-values in brackets, and intercept not shown. Standard errors are clustered by state. All models include state and year dummies and are weighted by the state population. $N = 950$.

Table 3. Gonorrhea, Males Ages 20–24 Years.

	OLS (1)	Lagged OLS (2)	Lagged-Dependent Variable OLS (3)	Lagged Total Rate OLS (4)	Lagged-Dependent Variable FD2SLS (5)	Lagged Total Rate FD2SLS (6)
Lagged male gonorrhea rate			0.635 (24.18)		0.649 (2.83)	
Lagged total rate				0.663 (24.41)		0.656 (2.40)
Log beer tax	−0.411 (−2.12)	−0.410 (−1.28)	−0.237 (−2.79)	−0.310 (−3.66)	−0.378 (−2.20)	−0.368 (−2.08)
Lag log beer tax		0.004 (0.02)				
Per cent dry	−0.044 (−1.98)	−0.024 (−1.45)	−0.021 (−2.60)	−0.023 (−2.92)	0.016 (0.71)	0.017 (0.80)
Lag per cent dry		−0.024 (−1.54)				
0.10 BAC law	0.018 (0.17)	0.026 (0.24)	−0.042 (−0.92)	−0.0003 (−0.01)	0.101 (1.08)	0.110 (1.16)
0.08 BAC law	−0.015 (−0.11)	−0.004 (−0.03)	−0.042 (−0.74)	0.022 (0.38)	0.105 (1.00)	0.118 (1.10)
Zero tolerance law	−0.066 (−1.25)	−0.065 (−1.22)	−0.044 (−1.72)	−0.054 (−2.11)	−0.029 (−1.08)	−0.03 (−1.09)
Unemployment	−0.047 (−2.22)	−0.049 (−2.33)	−0.016 (−2.02)	−0.022 (−2.87)	0.025 (1.74)	0.023 (1.59)
Real income	0.017 (2.94)	0.017 (2.98)	0.008 (4.45)	0.008 (4.29)	0.002 (0.35)	0.002 (0.37)
Per cent rural	0.029 (1.45)	0.028 (1.42)	0.012 (1.93)	0.013 (2.12)	0.011 (0.63)	0.010 (0.57)
College degree	0.013 (1.20)	0.013 (1.20)	0.004 (0.52)	0.004 (0.62)	0.002 (0.24)	0.0002 (0.03)
Per cent Mormon	0.097 (1.97)	0.095 (1.89)	0.061 (1.67)	0.021 (0.57)	0.044 (2.32)	0.044 (2.30)
Per cent Southern Baptist	0.058 (1.28)	0.060 (1.30)	0.028 (1.47)	0.026 (1.38)	−0.0002 (−0.01)	−0.005 (−0.19)
Per cent Protestant	−0.024 (−1.34)	−0.024 (−1.38)	0.008 (1.06)	0.006 (0.90)	0.022 (2.37)	0.019 (1.97)
Per cent Catholic	−0.049 (−1.90)	−0.049 (−1.87)	−0.013 (−1.88)	−0.018 (−2.63)	−0.012 (−0.96)	−0.012 (−0.76)
F-test: Beer tax, lag beer tax		2.49 [0.093]				
F-test: Per cent dry, lag per cent dry		2.03 [0.143]				
R^2	0.916	0.916	0.95	0.95	–	–

Note: *t*-statistics in parentheses, *P*-values in brackets, and intercept not shown. Standard errors are clustered by state. All models include state and year dummies, and are weighted by the state population. $N = 950$.

Table 4. Gonorrhea, Females.

	OLS (1)	Lagged OLS (2)	Lagged-Dependent Variable OLS (3)	Lagged Total Rate OLS (4)	Lagged-Dependent Variable FD2SLS (5)	Lagged Total Rate FD2SLS (6)
Ages 15–19 years						
Lagged female gonorrhea rate			0.700 (29.23)		0.548 (2.88)	
Lagged total rate				0.704 (28.43)		0.53 (2.28)
Log beer tax	0.027 (0.12)	−0.004 (−0.01)	−0.052 (−0.66)	0.070 (0.88)	0.060 (0.28)	0.066 (0.31)
Lag log beer tax		0.040 (0.15)				
Per cent dry	−0.010 (−0.54)	0.010 (0.67)	−0.002 (−0.28)	0.002 (0.22)	0.025 (1.79)	0.024 (1.68)
Lag per cent dry		−0.024 (−1.85)				
0.10 BAC law	−0.156 (−1.78)	−0.149 (−1.66)	−0.082 (−2.00)	−0.120 (−2.90)	0.121 (1.62)	0.130 (1.74)
0.08 BAC law	−0.334 (−2.56)	−0.323 (−2.50)	−0.122 (−2.34)	−0.173 (−3.28)	0.169 (1.75)	0.175 (1.87)
Zero tolerance law	−0.038 (−0.71)	−0.036 (−0.68)	−0.030 (−1.30)	−0.026 (−1.11)	0.010 (0.25)	0.001 (0.01)
F-test: Beer tax, lag beer tax		0.02 [0.984]				
F-test: Per cent dry, lag per cent dry		1.87 [0.164]				
Ages 20–24 years						
Lagged female gonorrhea rate			0.643 (24.47)		0.455 (2.11)	
Lagged total rate				0.655 (23.48)		0.589 (2.53)
Log beer tax	−0.045 (−0.21)	−0.132 (−0.44)	−0.048 (−0.57)	0.055 (0.63)	−0.044 (−0.23)	0.004 (0.02)
Lag log beer tax		0.108 (0.43)				
Per cent dry	−0.031 (−1.39)	−0.006 (−0.39)	−0.013 (−1.61)	−0.01 (−1.21)	0.024 (1.26)	0.026 (1.29)
Lag per cent dry		−0.028 (−1.95)				
0.10 BAC law	−0.118 (−1.30)	−0.108 (−1.15)	−0.088 (−1.91)	−0.136 (−2.92)	0.137 (1.59)	0.124 (1.43)
0.08 BAC law	−0.224 (−1.62)	−0.208 (−1.48)	−0.116 (−2.01)	−0.188 (−3.19)	0.139 (1.25)	0.131 (1.26)

Table 4. (Continued)

	OLS (1)	Lagged OLS (2)	Lagged-Dependent Variable OLS (3)	Lagged Total Rate OLS (4)	Lagged-Dependent Variable FD2SLS (5)	Lagged Total Rate FD2SLS (6)
Zero tolerance law	−0.013 (−0.26)	−0.010 (−0.20)	−0.020 (−0.75)	−0.002 (−0.06)	0.031 (0.84)	0.031 (0.83)
F-test: Beer tax, lag beer tax		0.11 [0.894]				
F-test: Per cent dry, lag per cent dry		1.91 [0.159]				

Note: t-statistics in parentheses, P-values in brackets, and intercept not shown. Standard errors are clustered by state. All models include state characteristics (unemployment, income, education, religion), state, and year dummies, and are weighted by the state population. $N = 950$.

5.1. Gonorrhea

In regards to the male gonorrhea rates for both age groups, a striking result arises that all models in Tables 2 and 3 show a negative and statistically significant coefficient on the beer tax (the beer tax and lagged beer tax are jointly significant in the lagged models, although at the 10% level). From the simple OLS models, a 10% increase in the average state excise tax on beer will reduce the gonorrhea rate by 4.7% for males ages 15–19 years and by 4.1% for males ages 20–24 years. Models including the lagged tax rate give similar estimates.

The magnitude of these effects fall slightly by a range of 6–10% from the OLS in columns 1 and 2 to the FD2SLS estimates in columns 5 and 6. When the lagged total rate is included (column 6), a 10% increase in the average state excise tax on beer will reduce the gonorrhea rate by 4.4% for males ages 15–19 years and by 3.7% for males ages 20–24 years. Estimates are slightly larger when the lagged dependent variable is included. This decrease in the elasticity is not surprising since the tax effect is calculated holding the lagged gonorrhea rate constant. That is, it represents a short-run effect which only lets tax influence the current STD rate. A long-run effect can be calculated by dividing the tax coefficient by one minus the coefficient on the lagged gonorrhea rate. For males in both age groups, the long-run elasticity is −1.1 based on the estimates in column 6.

Table 5. AIDS, Males Ages 20–29 Years.

	OLS (1)	Lagged OLS (2)	Lagged-Dependent Variable OLS (3)	Lagged Total Rate OLS (4)	Lagged-Dependent Variable FD2SLS (5)	Lagged Total Rate FD2SLS (6)
Lagged male AIDS rate			0.185 (4.04)		0.102 (1.53)	
Lagged total rate				0.224 (4.90)		0.153 (2.11)
Log beer tax	−0.513 (−2.92)	−0.245 (−0.90)	−0.434 (−2.74)	−0.41 (−2.61)	−0.203 (−1.12)	−0.204 (−1.11)
First lag log beer tax		0.104 (0.40)				
Second lag log beer tax		−0.711 (−6.58)				
Per cent dry	0.024 (1.53)	0.026 (0.98)	0.022 (1.72)	0.022 (1.75)	0.005 (0.14)	0.006 (0.18)
Lag per cent dry		−0.003 (−0.14)				
0.10 BAC law	0.017 (0.24)	−0.001 (−0.01)	0.019 (0.33)	0.023 (0.44)	0.127 (1.11)	0.133 (1.11)
0.08 BAC law	0.021 (0.19)	−0.052 (−0.46)	0.012 (0.14)	0.021 (0.23)	0.106 (0.72)	0.107 (0.70)
Zero tolerance law	0.028 (0.47)	0.029 (0.49)	0.029 (0.58)	0.035 (0.72)	0.049 (0.86)	0.053 (0.93)
Unemployment	0.082 (3.86)	0.075 (3.52)	0.068 (3.90)	0.066 (3.90)	0.055 (2.71)	0.054 (2.61)
Real income	0.01 (2.63)	0.008 (2.05)	0.009 (2.85)	0.009 (2.61)	0.005 (0.72)	0.004 (0.62)
College degree	−0.193 (−6.19)	−0.186 (−6.29)	−0.162 (−5.82)	−0.156 (−5.69)	−0.077 (−2.28)	−0.077 (−2.29)
Per cent Mormon	0.06 (1.69)	0.105 (3.06)	0.068 (2.12)	0.077 (2.46)	−0.06 (−0.72)	−0.069 (−0.84)
Per cent Southern Baptist	0.035 (0.58)	0.019 (0.34)	0.03 (0.62)	0.024 (0.53)	−0.048 (−0.48)	−0.046 (−0.46)
Per cent Protestant	0.039 (1.53)	0.035 (1.39)	0.032 (1.50)	0.03 (1.46)	0.029 (0.96)	0.027 (0.92)
Per cent Catholic	−0.056 (−3.22)	−0.057 (−3.38)	−0.041 (−3.10)	−0.036 (−2.93)	−0.059 (−2.00)	−0.056 (−1.89)
F-test: Beer tax, lag beer tax		23.66 [0.000]				
F-test: Per cent dry, lag per cent dry		1.15 [0.322]				
R^2	0.833	0.837	0.84	0.842	0.214	0.19

Note: t-statistics in parentheses, P-values in brackets, and intercept not shown. Standard errors are clustered by MSA. All independent variables are lagged 8 years. All models include MSA and year dummies, and are weighted by the MSA population. $N = 1,854$.

Table 6. AIDS, Males Ages 30–34 Years.

	OLS (1)	Lagged OLS (2)	Lagged-Dependent Variable OLS (3)	Lagged Total Rate OLS (4)	Lagged-Dependent Variable FD2SLS (5)	Lagged Total Rate FD2SLS (6)
Lagged male AIDS rate			0.233 (5.07)		0.264 (4.25)	
Lagged total rate				0.247 (5.27)		0.276 (4.43)
Log beer tax	−0.315 (−2.49)	−0.054 (−0.30)	−0.248 (−2.67)	−0.223 (−2.37)	0.06 (0.46)	0.071 (0.55)
First lag log beer tax		0.071 (0.40)				
Second lag log beer tax		−0.655 (−6.74)				
Per cent dry	0.019 (0.97)	0.019 (0.64)	0.016 (1.07)	0.017 (1.13)	−0.007 (−0.28)	−0.003 (−0.10)
Lag per cent dry		−0.00002 (−0.0008)				
0.10 BAC law	0.004 (0.05)	−0.013 (−0.17)	0.005 (0.08)	0.011 (0.19)	0.084 (0.96)	0.088 (0.99)
0.08 BAC law	0.034 (0.28)	−0.035 (−0.29)	0.041 (0.46)	0.052 (0.59)	0.197 (1.83)	0.203 (1.88)
Zero tolerance law	−0.036 (−0.74)	−0.036 (−0.72)	−0.037 (−0.97)	−0.032 (−0.85)	0.005 (0.09)	0.003 (0.05)
Unemployment	0.061 (3.48)	0.055 (3.18)	0.046 (3.59)	0.045 (3.44)	0.019 (0.90)	0.019 (0.88)
Real income	0.002 (0.62)	−0.0002 (−0.05)	0.002 (0.67)	0.001 (0.45)	−0.003 (−0.48)	−0.003 (−0.48)
College degree	−0.147 (−5.61)	−0.139 (−5.53)	−0.104 (−4.77)	−0.104 (−4.76)	0.001 (0.05)	−0.001 (−0.07)
Per cent Mormon	0.051 (1.14)	0.094 (1.99)	0.048 (1.46)	0.053 (1.55)	0.035 (0.40)	0.036 (0.41)
Per cent Southern Baptist	0.084 (1.35)	0.068 (1.10)	0.054 (1.12)	0.057 (1.11)	−0.101 (−0.85)	−0.103 (−0.86)
Per cent Protestant	0.064 (2.66)	0.06 (2.53)	0.049 (2.58)	0.049 (2.61)	0.045 (1.70)	0.046 (1.70)
Per cent Catholic	−0.079 (−3.64)	−0.079 (−3.72)	−0.055 (−3.59)	−0.053 (−3.51)	−0.047 (−1.76)	−0.045 (−1.71)
F-test: Beer tax, lag beer tax		20.09 [0.000]				
F-test: Per cent dry, lag per cent dry		0.45 [0.641]				
R^2	0.841	0.844	0.853	0.854	0.078	0.083

Note: t-statistics in parentheses, P-values in brackets, and intercept not shown. Standard errors are clustered by MSA. All independent variables are lagged 8 years. All models include MSA and year dummies, and are weighted by the MSA population. $N = 1,854$.

Table 7. AIDS, Females.

	OLS (1)	Lagged OLS (2)	Lagged-Dependent Variable OLS (3)	Lagged Total Rate OLS (4)	Lagged-Dependent Variable FD2SLS (5)	Lagged Total Rate FD2SLS (6)
Ages 20–29 years						
Lagged female AIDS rate			0.155 (4.20)		0.15 (2.70)	
Lagged total rate				0.155 (2.83)		0.012 (0.18)
Log beer tax	−0.362 (−1.67)	0.309 (0.89)	−0.31 (−1.61)	−0.291 (−1.41)	0.044 (0.11)	0.038 (0.10)
First lag log beer tax		−0.333 (−0.63)				
Second lag log beer tax		−0.816 (−4.77)				
Per cent dry	−0.009 (−0.86)	−0.033 (−1.72)	−0.006 (−0.68)	−0.01 (−0.97)	−0.003 (−0.10)	−0.008 (−0.29)
Lag per cent dry		0.027 (1.20)				
0.10 BAC law	−0.039 (−0.27)	−0.067 (−0.46)	−0.041 (−0.34)	−0.034 (−0.25)	−0.033 (−0.21)	−0.052 (−0.34)
0.08 BAC law	−0.252 (−1.00)	−0.38 (−1.51)	−0.259 (−1.21)	−0.252 (−1.07)	−0.157 (−0.59)	−0.167 (−0.65)
Zero tolerance law	−0.071 (−0.73)	−0.082 (−0.85)	−0.06 (−0.73)	−0.066 (−0.71)	0.096 (0.70)	0.083 (0.68)
F test: Beer tax, lag beer tax		7.96 [0.000]				
F-test: Per cent dry, lag per cent dry		1.66 [0.195]				
Ages 30–34 years						
Lagged female AIDS rate			0.086 (2.43)		0.019 (0.36)	
Lagged total rate				0.163 (3.30)		−0.037 (−0.56)
Log beer tax	−0.946 (−3.66)	0.509 (1.01)	−0.863 (−3.52)	−0.886 (−3.66)	0.859 (1.37)	0.846 (1.36)
First lag log beer tax		−1.401 (−2.26)				
Second lag log beer tax		−0.657 (−3.35)				
Per cent dry	−0.071 (−2.96)	−0.047 (−1.43)	−0.064 (−2.79)	−0.072 (−3.08)	−0.004 (−0.09)	−0.005 (−0.11)

Table 7. (Continued)

	OLS (1)	Lagged OLS (2)	Lagged-Dependent Variable OLS (3)	Lagged Total Rate OLS (4)	Lagged-Dependent Variable FD2SLS (5)	Lagged Total Rate FD2SLS (6)
Lag per cent dry		−0.025 (−0.78)				
0.10 BAC law	−0.073 (−0.45)	−0.106 (−0.66)	−0.062 (−0.41)	−0.068 (−0.45)	0.243 (1.32)	0.235 (1.25)
0.08 BAC law	−0.114 (−0.45)	−0.257 (−1.00)	−0.111 (−0.47)	−0.102 (−0.42)	0.102 (0.37)	0.095 (0.35)
Zero tolerance law	0.015 (0.11)	0.013 (0.09)	0.019 (0.15)	0.018 (0.14)	0.125 (0.75)	0.125 (0.76)
F-test: Beer tax, lag beer tax		17.15 [0.000]				
F-test: Per cent dry, lag per cent dry		4.26 [0.017]				

Note: t-statistics in parentheses, P-values in brackets, and intercept not shown. Standard errors are clustered by MSA. All independent variables are lagged 8 years. All models include state characteristics (unemployment, income, education, religion), MSA and year dummies, and are weighted by the MSA population for the age group. $N = 1,854$.

Both the long-run and short-run tax effects presented here are larger than those found by Chesson et al. (2000) who do take into account the endogeneity of the lagged gonorrhea rate.[7] The coefficients presented in column 3 and 4 of Tables 2 and 3 demonstrate that the treatment of the lagged dependent variable matters. For example, the short-run tax effect for males ages 20–24 years is 37% smaller and the long-run tax effect is 40% smaller when the lagged dependent variable is treated as exogenous (compare columns 3 and 5). Due to the bias in the OLS models with lagged dependent variables, the remaining discussion of the results will focus primarily on the OLS models in columns 1 and 2, and the FD2SLS models in columns 5 and 6.

The availability of alcohol, as measured by the percentages of the population living in dry counties, does not appear to be important in lowering male gonorrhea rates. The same can be said for the drunk driving laws. Neither the 0.10 BAC law nor the 0.08 BAC law has an effect on gonorrhea rates for males, although zero tolerance laws, which are aimed at drivers under the legal drinking age, are associated with a decrease in the gonorrhea rate of males ages 15–19 years. Using the results from the FD2SLS estimates, teenage males living in states with a zero tolerance law have lower gonorrhea rates (by 7–8%) than those in states without such a law.

For brevity, Table 4 contains only the results of alcohol regulatory variables on the female gonorrhea rates for the two different age groups. Here, none of the alcohol regulatory variables that affect male rates are effective in lowering the female rates. The coefficients on the beer tax are statistically insignificant and the sign switches depending on the model. A similar statement can be made for the coefficients on per cent dry. Estimates associated with the BAC laws are mixed, and the inconsistent signs and levels of significance suggest that no firm conclusions can be made and further research is warranted.

5.2. AIDS

Tables 5 and 6 show the results of the impact of the alcohol regulatory variables on AIDS rates for males ages 20–29 and 30–34 years, respectively. The OLS models in columns 1–2 show negative and statistically significant effects of the beer tax on AIDS rates. For the younger males, the estimates in column 1 yield a tax elasticity of –0.51, which increases to –0.85 if the lags of the tax are included. The magnitudes are smaller for the older males, with elasticities of –0.32 and –0.64 in columns 1 and 2, respectively. For the younger males, the tax coefficients are negative but are not statistically significant in the FD2SLS models. Here, the magnitudes are smaller than in the OLS models. The short-run elasticity is –0.20, and the long-run elasticity is about –0.24. For older males, the FD2SLS coefficients are statistically insignificant and positive. Note that the coefficients on the lagged AIDS rates in all male models are small in magnitude (columns 3–6). This provides some evidence that a 1-year lag in the AIDS rate does not contribute much to this model and the OLS models in columns 1 and 2 may be the preferred specifications.

Results for the female AIDS rates in Table 7 are similar to those for males in that the beer tax coefficients are negative and statistically significant in the OLS models, but these results do not hold in the FD2SLS models. Again, the coefficients on the lagged AIDS rates are small in magnitude and in the FD2SLS models, only one coefficient of the four is statistically significant. In regards to the drunk driving laws and the per cent dry, none of these alcohol policies are associated with decreased AIDS rates for youth of both genders. The one exception is that states with larger percentages of the population living in dry counties have a lower AIDS rate among females ages 30–34 years. Here, every 1% increase in the per cent living in dry counties is associated with a 0.07% decrease in the AIDS rate. Note that this result pertains only to the OLS models in columns 1–4.

It is somewhat surprising that the lagged AIDS rate does not have much of an influence on the current AIDS rate for both males and females. It is possible that the model is mis-specified and that the 1-year lag is inappropriate, particularly given the difficulties in tracking the timing of HIV infection. Models were tested with a 2-year lag and results remained similar. Recall also that biases due to random measurement error in the alcohol variables will be exacerbated in the first-differences models, possibly making these estimates unreliable. Given these problems, we treat the AIDS results as suggestive and not definitive. Clearly, further research is needed.

6. DISCUSSION

One important risk factor in determining risky sexual behaviours among youth is alcohol consumption. Given the strong link between alcohol use and risky sexual practices, this chapter seeks to determine whether policies designed to reduce the consumption of alcohol may succeed in reducing rates of STDs among youth as well. The results of multivariate regressions indicate that higher beer taxes and the presence of zero tolerance laws are associated with reductions in the male gonorrhea rates, although other alcohol policies such as BAC laws and dry counties appear to have no effects. The results also suggest that AIDS rates may be reduced with higher beer taxes, although this result is not robust to the FD2SLS models which include the lagged AIDS rate. Future research should focus on a similar study of HIV rates, rather than AIDS cases, where the alcohol control variables can be matched more closely to the risky sexual act and the appropriate date of transmission.

In addition to the problems with matching the alcohol control variables to the transmission date of HIV, there are some other limitations to this research that must be considered. First, this research does not provide much policy guidance on ways to reduce gonorrhea rates for females. This is certainly a direction for future research. Second, by 1999, all states had enacted zero tolerance laws, and now these laws are no longer a viable policy tool which can be used to further reduce the teenage male gonorrhea rate. Third, while the state dummies help capture time-invariant state-level factors which may be correlated with alcohol policies and STDs, time-variant factors may still remain in the error term and have the potential to bias the results. However, it is difficult to predict the direction of any such bias.

The results in the chapter presented here suggest that male gonorrhea rates, and by inference, the sexual behaviours that put males at risk for contracting STDs, can be reduced through the manipulation of alcohol policies that reduce alcohol consumption. To place these results in the broader context of the existing literature, recall that firm conclusions regarding the nature of the causal relationship between risky sexual behaviours and alcohol consumption are still in question. However, two results appear to be prevalent in this literature regarding teenage behaviours: The first is that alcohol use lowers contraception use, particularly for males, and the second is that alcohol use appears to have no causal impact on the probability of having sex. If these conclusions are true, then the notion that gonorrhea and AIDS rates may be reduced with policies such as higher beer taxes or strict drunk driving laws is in line with the consensus findings, as STDs are preventable by both abstinence and contraception in the form of condoms. It is highly plausible that alcohol control measures reduce alcohol consumption, increase condom usage, and thereby reduce the transmission of STDs. These links allow for the observed negative relationship between some alcohol regulatory variables and STD rates.

NOTES

1. For a review of this literature see Leigh and Stall (1993), and Donovan and McEwan (1995).

2. Chlamydia is also a very common STD; however, data on state-level rates have only been available for most states since 1996. In addition, screening and treatment programmes that are primarily directed towards women lead to reporting biases (CDC, 2000b). Given the short-time period and biases in the reported data, chlamydia rates are not analysed in this chapter.

3. By contrast, gonorrhea has an incubation period of less than a week.

4. The omission of the lagged STD rate can also lead to serial correlation in the error term.

5. The coefficients on the second lags of the dependent variables are negative and statistically significant in the first stages of all models presented in the tables below. However, the magnitudes of these coefficients are much smaller for gonorrhea than AIDS. For example, the coefficient on the second lag of the male gonorrhea rate for ages 15–19 years is –0.03, with a standard error of 0.01. In the AIDS regressions for males ages 20–29 years, the coefficient is –0.33 with a standard error of 0.015.

6. Georgia, Idaho, Indiana, Massachusetts, and Tennessee have missing data for gonorrhea in a few years.

7. Chesson et al. (2000) present partial elasticities (the percentage change in the gonorrhea rate for a $1.00 change in the beer tax) for youth. Converting their estimates to elasticities using the mean tax rate existing during their sample period, the tax elasticities for males ages 15–19 and 20–24 years are –0.36 and –0.32, respectively.

ACKNOWLEDGEMENTS

Funding for this research was provided by grant number DA12692-03 from the National Institute on Drug Abuse to the National Bureau of Economic Research. The authors would like to thank Jeff DeSimone, Hope Corman, Jody Sindelar, Will Manning, and seminar participants at iHEA, University of South Florida and the *24th Arne Ryde symposium on the economics of substance use* for helpful comments. This chapter has not undergone the review accorded official NBER publications; in particular, it has not been approved by the Board of Directors. Any opinions expressed are those of the authors and not those of NIDA or NBER.

REFERENCES

Baltagi, B. H. (2001). *Econometric analysis of panel data*. England: John Wiley and Sons.
Bartlett, J. G., & Gallant, J. E. (2003). *Medical management of HIV infection*. Baltimore: Johns Hopkins University.
Beer Institute. (various years). *Brewers' Almanac*. New York: United States Brewers Foundation.
Bertrand, M., Duflo, E., & Mullainathan, S. (2004). How much should we trust differences-in-differences estimates? *Quarterly Journal of Economics, 119*(1), 249–275.
Carpenter, C. (2004). How do zero tolerance drunk driving laws work? *Journal of Health Economics, 23*(1), 61–83.
Carpenter, C. (2005). Youth alcohol use and risky sexual behavior: Evidence from underage drunk driving laws. *Journal of Health Economics, 24*(3), 613–628.
Centers for Disease Control and Prevention. (1992). 1993 revised classification system for HIV infection and expanded surveillance case definition for AIDS among adolescents and adults. *Mortality and Morbidity Weekly Report, 41*(no RR17;001).
Centers for Disease Control and Prevention. (2000a). Summary of notifiable diseases, United States, 2000. *Mortality and Morbidity Weekly Report, 49*.
Centers for Disease Control and Prevention. (2000b). *Tracking the hidden epidemics, trends in STDs in the United States 2000*. Atlanta, GA: U.S. Department of Health and Human Services, Centers for Disease Control and Prevention.
Centers for Disease Control and Prevention. (2002). *Young people at risk: HIV/AIDS among America's youth*. Atlanta, GA: U.S. Department of Health and Human Services, Centers for Disease Control and Prevention.

Centers for Disease Control and Prevention. (2003). *Sexually transmitted disease surveillance, 2002.* Atlanta, GA: U.S. Department of Health and Human Services, Centers for Disease Control and Prevention.

Chesson, H., Harrison, P., & Kassler, W. J. (2000). Sex under the influence: The effect of alcohol policy on sexually transmitted disease rates in the U.S. *Journal of Law and Economics, 43*(1), 215–238.

Cook, P. J., & Moore, M. J. (2000). Alcohol. In: A. J. Culyer & J. P. Newhouse (Eds), *Handbook of health economics,* (Vol. 1B, pp. 1629–1673). New York: North-Holland.

Dee, T. (2001). The effects of minimum legal drinking ages on teen childbearing. *Journal of Human Resources, 36,* 823–838.

Donovan, C., & McEwan, R. (1995). A review of the literature examining the relationship between alcohol use and HIV-related sexual risk-taking in young people. *Addiction, 90*(3), 319–328.

Fergusson, D. M., & Lynskey, M. T. (1996). Alcohol misuse and adolescent sexual behaviors and risk taking. *Pediatrics, 98,* 91–96.

Graves, K. L., & Leigh, B. L. (1995). The relationship of substance use to sexual activity among young adults in the United States. *Family Planning Perspectives, 27,* 18–33.

Grossman, M., Chaloupka, F. J., Saffer, H., & Laixuthai, A. (1994). Effects of alcohol price policy on youth: A summary of economic research. *Journal of Research on Adolescence, 4,* 347–364.

Grossman, M., Chaloupka, F. J., & Sirtalan, I. (1998). An empirical analysis of alcohol addiction: Results from the monitoring the future panels. *Economic Inquiry, 36*(1), 39–48.

Grossman, M., Kaestner, R., & Markowitz, S. (2004). Get high and get stupid: The effect of alcohol and marijuana use on teen sexual behavior. *Review of the Economics of the Household, 2,* 413–441.

Grossman, M., & Markowitz, S. (in press). I did what last night?! Adolescent risky sexual behaviors and substance use. *Eastern Economic Journal.*

Kaestner, R., & Joyce, T. (2001). Alcohol and drug use: Risk factors for unintended pregnancy. In: M. Grossman & C. Hsieh (Eds), *The economic analysis of substance use and abuse: The experience of developed countries and lessons for developing countries.* UK: Edward Elgar Limited.

Laumann, E. O., Gagnon, J. H., Michael, R. T., & Michaels, S. (1994). *The social organization of sexuality: Sexual practices in the United States.* Chicago: The University of Chicago Press.

Leigh, B. C., & Stall, R. (1993). Substance use and risky sexual behavior for exposure to HIV, issues in methodology, interpretation and prevention. *American Psychologist, 48*(10), 1035–1044.

Leung, S. F., & Phelps, C. E. (1993). 'My kingdom for a drink …?' A review of the price sensitivity of demand for alcoholic beverages. In: G. Bloss & M. Hilton (Eds), *Economic and socioeconomic issues in the prevention of alcohol-related problems.* U.S. Government Printing Office, 1993.

Moore, M. J., & Cook, P. J. (1995). Habit and heterogeneity in the youthful demand for alcohol. NBER Working Paper no. 5152.

Nickell, S. J. (1981). Biases in dynamic models with fixed effects. *Econometrica, 49*(6), 1417–1426.

Rashad, I., & Kaestner, R. (2004). Teenage sex, drugs and alcohol use: Problems identifying the cause of risky behaviors. *Journal of Health Economics, 23*(3), 493–503.

Rees, D. I., Argys, L. M., & Averett, S. L. (2001). New evidence on the relationship between substance use and adolescent sexual behavior. *Journal of Health Economics, 20*(5), 835–845.

Scribner, R. A., Cohen, D. A., & Farley, T. A. (1998). A geographic relation between alcohol availability and gonorrhea rates. *Sexually Transmitted Diseases, 25*(10), 544–548.

Sen, B. (2002). Does alcohol-use increase the risk of sexual intercourse among adolescents? Evidence from the NLSY97. *Journal of Health Economics, 21*(6), 1085–1093.

Strunin, L., & Hingson, R. (1992). Alcohol, drugs, and adolescent sexual behavior. *International Journal of Addictions, 27*, 129–146.

CAN WE MODEL THE IMPACT OF INCREASED DRUG TREATMENT EXPENDITURE ON THE U.K. DRUG MARKET?

Christine Godfrey, Steve Parrott, Gail Eaton, Anthony Culyer and Cynthia McDougall

ABSTRACT

This chapter introduces a simulation model to estimate the social costs of problem drug misusers in England and Wales, and how policies to increase the number of drug users in treatment may impact on both social costs and government expenditure. Consequences are divided into five domains – health, crime, social care, work, and driving. Social costs are estimated to be between £12 and £12.3 billion, and the total cost of government expenditure is around £3.5 billion. Increases in the numbers in treatment, are estimated to reduce social costs across a 5-year period by between £3.0 and £4.4 billion.

1. INTRODUCTION

Although evidence is difficult to compile to inform drug policy making, governments have, in any case, been generally reluctant to base their strategies on empirical research findings. Policies have been more influenced by moral opinions rather than research evidence (e.g., Reuter, 2001). The application of economics and the use of modelling techniques can add value both by using the limited available data to explore policy options and also to suggest where future research may be most likely directed to yield the greatest benefit for informing policy decisions.

Evidence has accumulated on the cost-effectiveness of treatment for problematic drug users both compared to doing nothing and also compared to other drug policies such as enforcement strategies (Rydell & Everingham, 1994; Cartwright, 2000). Problem users, although small in number, are known to be responsible for a large proportion of drug-related problems in society. Increasing numbers in treatment may therefore be one means of reducing population levels of drug-related problems.

Drug policy in the U.K. has always been generally set in a pragmatic fashion responding to perceived problems and allowing innovative interventions, such as the introduction of needle exchange schemes in response to the spread of human immunodeficiency virus (HIV) among injecting drug users. There were attempts to assess the role of treatment in the range of tools available in a drug strategy in the mid-1990s, and research was commissioned which generated some U.K. data on the outcomes of routine treatment (Gossop, Marsden, & Stewart, 2001). Partly in response to the results of this research and partly from a concern with levels of drug-related crime, the government announced a major increase in spending on treatment in their 2000 spending review and the consequential policy of "treatment works" seems to be set to continue with further increases in treatment expenditure announced in 2002. Although this may suggest that U.K. Governments are amenable to an evidence-based policy approach, no explicit modelling of the expectations of such a policy were published with this policy announcement.

The purpose of this chapter is to examine a simple model of the impact of changing the number of problem drug misusers in treatment in England and Wales (two of the four countries of the U.K.) on the social costs of drug misuse. This research was initially commissioned by the U.K. Anti-Drugs Co-ordination Unit in order to explore, not only, whether more explicit economic models could be constructed but, whether they would yield information that was credible and that might be used by policy makers. The focus of the analyses was on social costs of health, crime, social care, work, and driving related problems of those users taking drugs subject to the highest and most restrictive classification in the U.K. Public finance implications in the same areas were also considered. The so-called "class A" drugs of these analyses include heroin, cocaine, crack cocaine, methadone, ecstasy, Lysergic acid diethylamine (LSD), and magic mushrooms and amphetamine prepared for injecting. While an attempt was made to be as inclusive as possible of all the costs associated with this drug use, data and research availability restricted the coverage.

Some of the research and policy background to the project are explored in the next section. The model and results from some simple simulations are set out in the third section of the chapter. The limitations of the model and potential for further development are explored in the final section.

2. BACKGROUND

A range of different modelling techniques has been employed in attempts to understand the spread of drug use numbers and problems. In a recent project designed to explore the range of models available and how they may inform EU policy making, the various techniques were reviewed (Godfrey, Wiessing, & Hartnoll, 2001). Two basic groups of modelling techniques were found, broadly divided into statistical and dynamic models (Wiessing, Hartnoll, & Rossi, 2001). In general, the statistical models were inductive and data driven with limited number of explicit theoretical assumptions. The aim was to test hypotheses and the models were static. At the other extreme dynamic models were deductive and theory driven with more explicit assumptions generating hypotheses containing a number of dynamic and feedback loops. Most of the models found in this project had been constructed by epidemiologists, mathematicians, and social scientists – but excluding economists.

A few dynamic models of drug markets have been published. These have been focused on simulating the cost-effectiveness of alternative policy alternatives, often including a dynamic element. However, there have been no attempts to build more complex models of systems such as those constructed for simulating community alcohol policies (Holder, 1998). In particular researchers at RAND conducted a number of different studies; for example, Rydell and Everingham (1994) and Caulkins, Rydell, Everingham, Chiesa, and Bushway (1999). A schematic version of the Rydell and Everingham (1994) study of the cocaine market is shown in Fig. 1. Extensions of this model were undertaken by Behrens, Caulkins, Tagler, Haunschmied, and Feichtinger (1999). One extension included the hypothesis that drug users "infect" non-users and that this infection may depend on the perceived costs of this use. Increased treatment could reduce these perceived costs and alter the time path of the epidemic. The results suggest that increasing

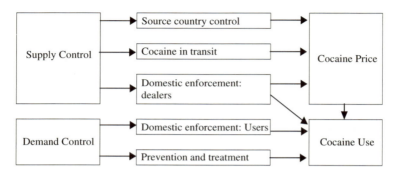

Source: Rydell and Everingham (1994)

Fig. 1. Schema of Rydell and Everingham Model. *Source:* Rydell and Everingham (1994).

treatment at the start of an epidemic could be counter-productive in the aim of reducing the total number of users over time.

The advantage of more complex models is the direct modelling of the market. The implications are driven by the number of users, in most models divided into light and heavy users with different social cost weights attached. In the Rydell and Everingham (1994) model, crime costs were assumed to be proportional to expenditure on drugs and productivity costs proportional to consumption levels. Simulation of changes in social costs from such models is dependent on the quality of the cost data as well as many of the other key parameters. The models, while logically simple, sometimes seem like black boxes. For many countries there are insufficient data to populate them. As always, of course, policy makers find it easier to accept models when their implications are in line with a favoured policy direction, than when results run contrary to it.

Examples of research results and economic modelling, which directly influence policy are therefore limited. There are some simple models that are readily understandable and that gain ownership from policy makers given the right political conditions but there are manifest pitfalls for researchers attempting more complex analyses, especially if they yield results that are not supported by the political climate of the time.

Certain factors favoured some experimentation with model building explicitly directed at policy makers (rather than as an academic exercise) in the U.K. The U.K. Treasury reviews all public expenditure in detail every 2 years. These Comprehensive Spending Reviews (CSR) require each government department to state the outcomes expected from the public money they demand over the following 4-year period. The departmental claims are mediated by the Treasury and the broad allocations of funds that result from the exercise are published. The exercises are becoming more sophisticated. In parallel with this process, governmental use of economic evaluation techniques has expanded. Treasury guidelines suggest a social perspective, should be taken in evaluating policies (HM Treasury, 2003). It is clear that this policy has made government departments nationally more aware of "value for money" criteria and therefore, more inclined to seek economic evidence to support spending bids.

Following the CSR, departments publish more detailed plans within the agreed broader spending projections. In the 2000 CSR, a more detailed breakdown of the planned allocation of funds between the four different components of the drug policy at the time was published (see Table 1). These four components were – treatment, policies directed at preventing drug use among young people, specific community initiatives especially directed at reducing drug-related crimes, and availability controls directed at reducing the supply of drugs. The money allocated to these different components was planned to increase in all four areas although the proportionate increase in treatment expenditure was much larger than for availability controls so that, by 2003/2004, 40% of all expenditure would be on treatment compared to 38% on availability. Further increases in expenditure were announced after the 2002 CSR, the total now at £1,026 million in 2002/2003 to increase to £1,500 million in 2005/2006. The focus for this increased expenditure was on more treatment and more expenditure on criminal justice interventions in order to get people into treatment. New targets were set in the updated drugs strategy and there was a target to increase the participation of drug users in treatment from the 100,000 baseline of 1998 by 55% by 2004 and 100% by 2008, with expenditure for treatment rising from

Table 1. Projected Government Expenditure on Drugs Policy, 2000 CSR.

Group/£ Million (% of Total in Year)	2000/2001	2001/2002	2002/2003	2003/2004
Treatment	234 (34)	328 (38)	377 (40)	401 (40)
Young people	63 (9)	90 (10)	97 (10)	120 (12)
Community	45 (6)	79 (9)	80 (9)	95 (10)
Availability	353 (51)	373 (43)	376 (40)	380 (38)
Total	695 (100)	870 (100)	931 (100)	996 (100)

Source: HM Treasury (2000).

£503 million in 2003/2004 to £573 million in 2004/2005. This presents an opportunity for an evaluation of the potential impact of the increase in treatment expenditure on drug markets in England and Wales.

3. CONSTRUCTION OF THE MODEL AND DATA SOURCES

After the 2000 CSR, a project was commissioned by the Home Office principally to estimate the social costs of class A drug use in England and Wales but with a subsidiary aim to explore the potential for constructing models that could explore how the social costs and public finance burden might change if there were changes in policies. Class A drugs in England and Wales include heroin, cocaine, crack cocaine, methadone, ecstasy, LSD and magic mushrooms, and amphetamine prepared for injecting.

The proposed simple model was based first on a classification of the different types of drug user and estimates of the number of users in each group. The division of users was principally determined by a mixture of expected costs attached to each type combined with behavioural factors. The second part of the model was concerned with determining the consequences associated with each type of user. This required knowledge of the link between the drug use of that type with particular consequences and identifying a means of quantifying the number of consequences occurring in a given time period. The final step was to apply values to each identified consequence. Providing unit costs of each consequence then allowed a simulation of costs to be made by varying the parameters of the model.

That is:

$$C = \sum_{i=1}^{I} C_i = \sum_{i=1}^{I} n_i (\sum_{j=1}^{J} \bar{e}_{ij} v_j)$$

where C is the cost of drug use; i denotes the types of drug user, $i = 1, \ldots, I$; C_i is the cost from drug users of type I; n_i is the number of drug users of type I; j denotes the type of consequence, $j = 1, \ldots, J$; $\bar{e}_{ij}$ denotes the mean number of units of consequence j for drug users of type i; v_j is the value of one unit of consequence j.

This model was initially seen as static, yielding costs in one time period. However, by determining different flows of drug users of different types with different rates of consequences through time, then this simple model can be extended to simulate different policy changes. For this project, the main change considered was the increasing numbers of problem drug users in treatment.

The next stage of the project was to explore the international research literature and empirical studies of England and Wales in order to find estimates to use with the model. Further details of the initial review are given in Culyer, Eaton, Godfrey, Koutsolioutsos, and McDougall (2001). Full details of the data used and assumptions made in constructing the baseline model are given in Godfrey, Eaton, McDougall, and Culyer (2002). While a lot of research evidence was reviewed for the parameters in the model as detailed in these publications, the main effectiveness evidence for treatment was taken from special analyses of the National Treatment Outcome Research Study (NTORS) as detailed below (Gossop, Marsden, & Stewart, 1998). Further details of the economic analyses of this survey, as applied in the new analyses presented here, are available in Godfrey, Stewart, and Gossop (2004).

Drug users in the baseline model were assumed to be in one of three groups – young recreational users; older regular users and problem users. Older users (aged 25 or older) having very irregular use were considered to have only very marginal impact and were included with non-users. Within the young recreational users, it was thought there would be a sub-group of young people with enhanced risks of becoming problem users. Several divisions among problem users were considered. Initially, it was thought useful to distinguish between injecting and non-injecting users because of the number of increased health risks with injecting behaviour. However, much of the data for making such a distinction were not available at the time of the study (Godfrey et al., 2002).

Data on the numbers of drug users in different groups were drawn from several sources. Some data were available from population surveys for estimating the numbers of young recreational users and older regular users. From these surveys it was assumed, for heroin and cocaine users, that half were non problematic and half problematic despite there being but limited evidence for this assumption. Population surveys are known grossly to underestimate the number of problem users. Frischer, Hickman, Kraus, Mariani, and Wiessing (2001) had suggested a number of different methods for estimating this population from routinely available data. Updating the Frischer et al. (2001) methods, an estimate of 337,500 problem users was calculated (Godfrey et al., 2002). This was higher than the 250,000 used in policy briefings at the time, a figure for which no source was available. Further research is currently under way using capture/recapture techniques to provide more reliable estimates capable of being updated on a regular basis. For the purposes of simulation, the total number is important only in estimating total costs; it does not affect changes in social cost that arise from changing the numbers in treatment. The simulations are based on changes in numbers in treatment irrespective of the baseline numbers.

Consequences were divided into five types – health, crime, social care, work, and driving. One version of the model was used to estimate the resource costs of drug use, including elements for the victim costs of crime and drug-related deaths as well as the resources used in public sector response to drug use such as health services and criminal justice costs. A second version combined public sector resource costs with estimates of benefits claimed by drug users.

Even with limited types of consequence and broadly defined groups of drug users, it proved difficult to find reliable data. There were some data on population levels of consequences for young recreational users and older regular uses but no means of linking the observed levels of consequences with the prevalence of drug use (Culyer et al., 2001). The simulations did not involve any changes to the number of users or consequences for these two types of users and therefore this part of the wider model is not considered further here. More data were available for the consequences of problem drug use.

One of the major policy initiatives at this period was to increase treatment places for problem users. In order to simulate the impact of this policy it was necessary to determine the different costs attaching to different users by treatment status. The main source of data was the NTORS (Gossop et al., 1998). NTORS had a longitudinal, prospective cohort design, which recruited 1,075 entrants to treatment from purposely, sampled 54 representative drug treatment agencies in England between March and July 1995. Data were available for a range of variables for up to 2 years before the beginning of the treatment episode at the time of sampling. Follow-up questions were conducted at 12 months and 24 months after the beginning of the sample. Economic analyses of these data have been published (Godfrey et al., 2004). The results of this study in the U.K. have provided similar results to the wider international economic literature on the cost benefits of drug treatment (Cartwright, 2000). However, like many of the US large illicit drug treatment studies, NTORS was an observational study with no control group and some care is needed in attributing the total changes in social costs to the treatment episode alone.

We thought that the best estimate of the social costs of those problem drug users not in treatment was in the data collected about the period prior to entry into the NTORS study. The follow-up data from 1 year would give an estimate of the initial impact of treatment and the 24-month follow-up data, covering the 12–24-month period, gives an estimate of the costs for the second and subsequent years after entry to treatment. The new treatments in this period were primarily community rather than residentially based. Data for the simulations were based on those who initially received either methadone detoxification or methadone maintenance at the time of the NTORS initial sample.

The problem drugs using group is therefore divided into three groups in the simulations. Changing numbers in these groups each year combined with the associated cost by treatment status yields the results for the simulations. In every year of the simulation, the new problem drug users taking up treatment move from the out-of-treatment group to the in-treatment group. Further analysis of the NTORS data suggested that 5% of users who entered treatment were drug free after 1 year and in the following year had no further addiction treatment. We assumed that, this 5% represented those who left the class A drug using population and that they generated no external costs. While the numbers are small, the assumption of no additional treatment cost for this group may cause some overestimation of the effects of treatment – some users will have continued health problems and some may not cease all criminal activities. In the second year of the simulation, some additional problem drug users may enter the in-treatment group and those that entered the previous year, less than 5% (or different proportion in sensitivity analyses) who became drug free, move to the group that have been in treatment for more than 1 year.

The simulations used the assumption, that the baseline problem drug using population was stable, although not necessarily made up of the same individuals: Incoming numbers of problem drug users and outgoing numbers without any new treatment places would be equal, with the proportions in and out of treatment remaining the same. These limited dynamics were driven by a lack of data. The resulting conceptually limited model had, however, the advantage of being simple and easy to demonstrate to policy makers. It also provided a means of setting out the research requirements for building more complex dynamic models.

One complication arose in estimating criminal justice costs. In the NTORS study, respondents were asked both about the offences they committed and their contact with different parts of the criminal justice system. In previous research, Brand and Price (2000) had estimated the unit costs per type of offence using the expectation of being arrested, tried and punished (Brand & Price, 2000). These unit cost values were calculated from evidence on all offenders rather than drug-related offenders and are therefore dependent on the two groups having similar propensities for arrest and once arrested, for punishment. An alternative method would have been to use actual data on arrests and punishments, and other contacts with criminal justice agencies. However, the data on contact with criminal justice agencies at any period of time tend to relate to more distant offences than those committed at the time period of questioning. In practice, data using actual criminal justice contacts from the NTORS study yielded a total criminal justice cost for problem drug users of £2,374 million (this method is referred to as Method 1 in the results section). Based on the offence data, the estimated criminal justice costs were £2,634 million (this is Method 2 in the results section). The difference between the two estimates is £260 million. The implications of using the different methods for simulating the impact of additional treatment expenditure are considered below.

4. RESULTS

The numbers of individuals in different drug groups are shown in Table 2. The largest group is those over 25 who use class A drugs, the older regular users. The drugs used by this group were mainly LSD and magic mushrooms. Only 218,000 were estimated to have taken ecstasy in the last month. 148,000 were estimated to have used cocaine. Even a small underestimate of the amount of problems associated with these patterns of use could have a major impact on the total baseline social cost estimates. However, in this particular set of simulations the number of people in this group was assumed to stay the same.

Various consequences and their unit values for problem drug users are shown in Table 3. All the averages from the treatment sample did not fall after treatment. Some health care consequences will rise because health problems are more likely to be picked up and treated while drug users are still in contact with treatment agencies. Although, similarly the average number of acquisitive crime offences falls in the first year after entering treatment, there is an increase for some crimes in the second year. The 5-year follow-up data indicated that most outcomes maintained this pattern, there was little change in outcome measures between the 2- and 5-year follow-up period (Gossop et al., 2001).

Combining the number of drug users with the rates of problems for that type of user and the cost of the consequences yields the total social cost figures. The basic model for the year 2000 for all users is given in Table 4 using Method 1 for the criminal justice costs. Total social costs comprise health service costs, criminal justice costs, the victim costs of crime, premature deaths and social welfare expenditure of childcare. Governmental

Table 2. Estimated Number of Class A Drug Users England and Wales, 2000.

Type of User	Estimated Number
Young recreational users	399,000
Older regular users	1,091,000
Problem drug users of which:	337,350
Out of treatment	224,900
In treatment less than 1 year	56,225
In treatment more than 1 year	56,225
Total	1,827,350

Source: Godfrey et al. (2002).

Table 3. Number of Events and Values per Event for Selected Consequences.

Type of Consequence/ Average Number of Events	Out of Treatment	In Treatment Less than 1 Year	In Treatment More than 1 Year	Value of Each Event, £2,000
Health				
GP visits	3.6	5.6	6.8	18
A&E visit	0.7	0.6	0.8	282
Inpatient days	1.75	2.8	2.4	223
Out-patient mental health	1.3	0.8	1.6	50
Inpatient mental health	1.5	0.4	2.0	144
Criminal justice system (CJS) Costs				
Drug arrests	0.3	0.8	0.4	3,551
Acquisitive crime arrest	1.35	1.6	0.4	1,346
Stay in police cell night	2	1.2	0.8	69
Court appearances	2.2	1.4	1.2	699
Prison days	36	34	39	68.96
Offences				
Shoplifting	16.6	5.2	4.0	20 (CJS) 80 (victim)
Burglary	1.2	0.3	0.4	470 (CJS) 1,830 (victim)
Robbery	0.3	0.1	0.3	1,400 (CJS) 3,300 (victim)
Fraud	3.8	0.9	1.5	196 (CJS) 891 (victim)

Source: Godfrey et al. (2002).

Table 4. Total Costs of Class A Drug Users, 2000, £ in 000s.

	Problem Drug Users	Young Recreational Users	Older Regular Users	Total
Health	£347,137	£2162	£2402	£351,701
Crime (all)	£10,556,410	£3766	£3766	£10,563,943
Deaths	£997,760	£22,884	£0	£1,020,644
Childcare	£63,073	£0	£0	£63,073
Total social costs	£11,964,380	£28,813	£6,169	**£11,999,361**
Crime (CJS only, Method 1)	£2,366,175	£3,766	£3,766	£2,373,707
Benefits	£735,615	£0	£0	£735,615
Total government expenditure	£3,512,000	£5,928	£6,168	**£3,524,096**

Source: Godfrey et al. (2002).

expenditure is the sum of health care costs, criminal justice costs, childcare expenditure, and the estimate of unemployment benefits related to drug use. Total social costs were estimated to be £12 billion, using Method 1 for criminal justice costs, £12.3 billion using Method 2 for criminal justice expenditure. The average social cost (including transfers) per class A drug user was estimated to be £6,567, with a total government expenditure of £1,929 per user (using Method 1). The costs are dominated by crime costs. Problem users have much higher costs per user (£35,466 for social costs, £10,410 government expenditure) than young recreational users (£72 social costs, £7.5 government expenditure) and older regular users (£3 social costs, £3 government expenditure).

A more detailed breakdown of the costs per user is given in Table 5. This illustrates the different time pattern of costs. Health care costs rise after entering treatment both in the first year and subsequent year. Victim costs of crime fall dramatically in the first year after treatment then rise slightly in the second year but are still well below the pre-treatment data.

The different methods of estimating criminal justice expenditure yield different time profiles. Estimates using Method 1 suggests that drug users have more contact with the criminal justice system after entering treatment than in the period before treatment. This may reflect delays in the criminal justice system or that it is contact with this system that had prompted a treatment episode. In contrast, Method 2 which is based on the expected cost per offence committed shows a large fall once users enter the treatment system. However, in reality, as Method 1 potentially suggests, the "savings" in the drop in criminal offences may take more than one period to be realised.

Table 5. Breakdown of Cost per Problem Drug Users By Type of Cost As Used in the Simulation Model, £ in 2000.

	Out of Treatment	In Treatment Less than 1 Year	In Treatment More than 1 Year
Health costs	956	1,072	1,277
Victim costs of crime	30,827	8,893	13,464
CJS costs Method 1	7,037	8,397	5,538
CJS costs Method 2	9,036	5,260	5,308
Cost of premature deaths	2,957	2,957	2,957
Cost of childcare	187	187	187
Unemployment benefit payment	2,198	2,144	2,144

The simulation model did not directly include changes in drug treatment expenditure. Problem drug users in the U.K. enter and leave treatment agencies a number of times in any time period. In 2 years, prior to entering the NTORS study, 80% of participants had some addiction treatment. The participants in the NTORS study also took up treatment other than the NTORS index treatment in the 2 years following the start of this index treatment. It was important to factor in both the cost of the additional treatment episodes in the simulation model but also to include other treatment problem drug users may take-up during this period. To do this figures from the NTORS study were again used.

Using data from the economic analysis of NTORS (Godfrey et al., 2004) we estimated that, in the year prior to intake, problem drug users would on average consume approximately £2,614 of treatments such those provided by as street agencies, needle exchanges, other substitute prescribing, residential rehabilitation or hospital inpatient care. This was taken as the unit value for those problem drug users not in treatment in any year of the simulation. In the year following entry into the NTORS programme, those receiving treatment in the community received about £1,861 of NTORS treatment and £1,988 of other treatment, a total of £3,849. The NTORS index treatment costs are assumed to represent the new "additional" treatment in the simulation model. From NTORS, in the second year following treatment, only 37% remained in the index community treatment. On average, this amounted to £925 direct treatment costs for each problem drug user in the second year after entering treatment. There was an average expenditure of £2,324 per problem drug user on other addiction treatment in this second year. Adjusting the treatment expenditure costs for the loss of numbers in the second year gives a total treatment cost of £3,421 per problem drug user, still lower than the 1-year figure, and a net increase of £807 over the pre-NTORS treatment level.

Combining the various estimates, the simulation model generated the results shown in Table 6.

The final table shows the results of simulating the impact of increasing the numbers of problem drug users entering into a new treatment episode by about 10,000 per year. The impacts run for a 5-year period. All other factors are assumed to remain constant. New entrants to treatment move from the "out of treatment group" to the "in treatment less than a year" group. This is the total predicted effect in year 1. In the second year, 5% of the entrants from the previous year, leave the problem drug using population, 95% move into the group "in treatment more than 1 year" and then the same people are assumed to stay in this group for all subsequent years. The new entrants in year 2 of the simulation move through treatment groups in the same way as those that entered in year 1. In other words as the simulation continues, overall the problem drug using group as a whole gets smaller as 5% leave after completing 1 year of treatment. More and more problem drug users move through the group "in treatment less than 1 year" and then remain in the group "in treatment more than 1 year".

The simulations performed were designed to test the sensitivity of the model to different assumption about the numbers entering the treatment system and the numbers who may leave the problem drug using population altogether. The first simulation examines the impact of the same new numbers (10,000) entering for each of 5 years. It is assumed that there is a 5% effectiveness rate, that is, 5% of the new entrants loss leave the problem

Table 6. Costs Per Problem Drug User from Simulation Model.

	Out of Treatment	In Treatment Less than 1 Year	In Treatment More than 1 Year
Total social costs (CJS Method 1)	41,964	21,506	23,453
Total social costs (CJS Method 2)	43,963	18,369	23,223
Public finance (CJS Method 1)	10,378	11,800	9146
Public finance (CJS Method 2)	12,377	8,663	8,916
Treatment costs	2,614	3,849	3,421

drug using population after the first year in treatment. The second simulation has the same number of entrants into treatment but the effectiveness rate is increased to 10%. In the third simulation, a different time pattern of entrants to treatment is assumed based on an assumption that there is a backlog of problem drug users who wish to enter treatment but it may prove more difficult to attract problem drug users into treatment in each successive year. Hence it is assumed more new people could be attracted in the first year but successive years would see a drop in new entrants. For this simulation 15,000 entered in the first year, 13,000 in the second year, 11,000 in the third year, 9,000 in the fourth year and 7,000 in the fifth year with a 5% effectiveness rate. The fourth simulation is this same reducing number of new entrants but with the higher 10% effectiveness rate. Finally, a simulation is undertaken where it is assumed that the treatment policy being pursued both increases the numbers of entrants to treatment, from 10,000 in the first year by an extra 1,000 each year, giving 14,000 in year 5 but also increases the effectiveness rate from 5% for the first year cohort by 1% per year, rising to 8% when the fourth year cohort have finished their first year of treatment in the fifth year of the simulation.

The model estimates were generated over a 5-year calendar period. This was taken to mirror the type of calculations of both social cost changes and public finance implications over a CSR exercise. However, this implies that only 1 year's data from the last cohort entering into the simulation in year 5 is taken into account. Savings that may accrue from them leaving the drug using population or staying in treatment for more than 1 year are not included. The total changes in social costs and public expenditure including the additional costs of treatment are given in Table 7. The results are undiscounted costs over the 5-year period.

Overall those leaving the problem drug using group over the 5-year period are modest in all simulations, ranging from 5,000 (Simulation 1) to 13,000 (Simulation 4). Simulation 3 produced the highest number of additional treatment years, and hence the highest additional treatment cost. Simulation 4 had the largest social cost saving compared and the largest public expenditure saving using Method 2 for criminal justice expenditure.

5. DISCUSSION

We have outlined a simulation model for investigating the impact of public programmes designed to increase the number of problem drug users receiving treatment on social costs and government expenditure over a

Table 7. Simulated Changes in Costs (Pounds in Million) from Increasing Numbers in Treatment, 2000.

	Simulation 1 (10,000 per Year, 5% Effectiveness)	Simulation 2 (10,000 per Year, 10% Effectiveness)	Simulation 3 (Decreasing Numbers in Treatment, 5% Effectiveness)	Simulation 4 (As Simulation 3, 10% Effectiveness)	Simulation 5 (Increasing Number in Treatment and Increasing Effectiveness)
Total social costs (Method 1)	2,991	3,109	3,680	3,837	3,513
Total social costs (Method 2)	3,470	3,586	4,250	4,406	4,076
Public finance (Method 1)	98	144	140	66	131
Public finance (Method 2)	576	621	711	770	681
Additional treatment costs	138	134	168	162	161
Net savings in TCS (1)	2,853	2,974	3,512	3,674	3,352
Net savings in TCS (2)	3,331	3,452	4,083	4,243	3,915
Net savings in PF (1)	−41	9	−27	−96	−30
Net savings in PF (2)	438	487	543	608	519

5-year period. The model forecasts that increases of the sort envisaged for the U.K. are likely to reduce social costs of drug misuse substantially from £12 billion estimated to exist in 2002. The first simulation, for example, yields an estimate of the social costs in 2007 of £9.4 (at 2002 prices) billion. The total social saving across the 5 years of simulation varies between £3.0 and £4.4 billion depending on the simulation. Increases in the number of problem drug users in treatment is, however, not cost neutral in terms of public expenditure, adding additional spending of between £134 and £168 million. This excludes the additional expenditures that would be incurred if the additional numbers treated were to be recruited through criminal justice interventions like arrest referral schemes rather than through them presenting themselves voluntarily.

If the pattern of criminal justice expenditure is similar to that actually experienced in the NTORS study, public expenditure will peak in the year in which problem drug users enter a treatment episode. If it is assumed that criminal justice expenditure will eventually fall following the pattern of offences (Method 2), public expenditure savings is predicted to be over £400 million in every simulation.

The numbers estimated to cease being class A drug users through additional treatment is relatively modest in all simulations, the highest being 13,000 out of the estimated total of 337,350. From other analysis of the NTORS study it was found about 42% were regularly using heroin at the 2-year follow-up point compared to 80% at intake, and 13% were regularly using non prescribed methadone at the 2-year follow-up point compared to 31% at intake. Regular crack use at intake was 12%, which fell to about 6% at the 2-year point although, unlike other class A drugs, consumption had risen to 10% at the 4–5-year follow-up interview (Gossop et al., 2001). More detailed data on consumption would be useful for estimating the impact of changes in consumption in a fuller simulation model. No direct access to the NTORS data is available.

There are a number of obvious extensions to the model. We would have liked to have data on the general trends in overall prevalence and on the movement of users between user groups. Problem drug users cause very large costs compared to all other drug users and it is important to understand the factors influencing the movement between groups. Further knowledge of such drug use patterns would enable the building of a more comprehensive and dynamic model to simulate the impacts of a wider range of policy options.

We have estimated point estimates only. Our model is heavily dependent on the NTORS study rather than a systematic review of several studies, let alone a meta-analysis. A follow-up study of NTORS is currently being planned and these data plus new and regular estimates of prevalence of drug use will make further extension of the model possible. The assumption that parameters remain constant even when the proportion of drug users were within the treatment system is rising is an over strong assumption. It can be expected that the characteristics of the drug users attracted into treatment may change. We did not conduct sensitivity analysis on this point because it is not clear whether this would increase or decrease the overall effectiveness of treatment. Users with shorter and less chaotic patterns of use may be better able to get treatment places than others. On the other hand, it may be that the services have to work harder to attract the more chaotic users to fill their treatment places. The model currently cannot examine the character of the services on which the planned increase in treatment expenditure is best spent. The overall effectiveness and cost-effectiveness of the various services is likely to vary substantially, both across the services and for different intensities of each.

These results, despite their imperfections, nonetheless represent a first attempt to model the impact of enhanced treatment programmes on the social costs of drug use in England. It has been possible to simulate potential changes in social costs with data from a sample of drug users who had experienced a new episode of treatment and had on average reduced both their use and costs they imposed on the rest of society. The model is in an Excel spreadsheet form, which means it can be easily updated as new data on prevalence, values and effects become available. It is also possible to add new impacts of drug use and link these to prevalence figures as new research becomes available.

ACKNOWLEDGEMENTS

Funding for the project on which this chapter is based was provided by the Home Office, U.K. The views expressed in this chapter are those of the authors and do not necessarily reflect those of the Home Office. The authors are grateful to Professor Mike Gossop and Duncan Stewart for the additional data provided from the NTORS drug treatment study for this research.

REFERENCES

Behrens, D., Caulkins, J., Tagler, G., Haunschmied, J., & Feichtinger, G. (1999). A dynamic model of drug initiation: Implication for treatment and drug control. *Mathematical Biosciences, 159,* 1–20.
Brand, S., & Price, R. (2000). *The economic and social cost of crime.* Home Office Research Study 217, Economic and Resource Analysis Research Development and Statistics Directorate. London: Home Office.
Cartwright, W. S. (2000). Cost-benefit analysis of drug treatment services: Review of the literature. *Journal of Mental Health Policy and Economics, 3,* 11–26.
Caulkins, J., Rydell, P., Everingham, S., Chiesa, J., & Bushway, S. (1999). *An ounce of prevention: A pound of uncertainty.* Drug Policy Research Center, Santa Monica, CA: RAND.
Culyer, A., Eaton, G., Godfrey, C., Koutsolioutsos, H., & McDougall, C. (2001). *Economic and social cost of substance misuse in the United Kingdom: Review of the methodological and empirical studies of the economic and social costs of illicit drugs.* York: Centre for Criminal Justice Economics and Psychology, University of York.
Frischer, M., Hickman, M., Kraus, L., Mariani, F., & Wiessing, L. (2001). A comparison of different methods for estimating problematic drug misuse in the Great Britain. *Addiction, 96,* 1465–1476.

Godfrey, C., Eaton, G., McDougall, C., & Culyer, A. (2002). *The economic and social costs of class A drug use in England and Wales, 2000*. Home Office Research Study 249. London: Home Office.

Godfrey, C., Stewart, D., & Gossop, M. (2004). Economic analysis of costs and consequences of drug misuse and its treatment: Two year outcome data from the National Treatment Outcome Research Study (NTORS). *Addiction, 99*, 697–707.

Godfrey, C., Wiessing, L., & Hartnoll, R. (2001). *Modelling drug use: Methods to quantify and understand hidden processes*. EMCDDA Scientific Monograph Series, No. 6. EMCDDA, Lisbon.

Gossop, M., Marsden, J., & Stewart, D. (1998). *NTORS at one year: The National Treatment Outcome Research Study: Changes in substance use, health and criminal behaviors at one year after intake*. London: Department of Health.

Gossop, M., Marsden, J., & Stewart, D. (2001). *NTORS after Five Years: Changes in substance use, health and criminal behaviour during the five years after intake*. London: London Addiction Centre.

HM Treasury. (2000). *Spending review 2000: Prudent for a purpose: Building opportunity and security for all*. London: HMSO.

HM Treasury. (2003). *The green book: Appraisal and evaluation in central government*. London: HMSO.

Holder, H. (1998). *Alcohol and community: A systems approach to prevention. International Research Monographs in the Addictions*. Cambridge: Cambridge University Press.

Reuter, P. (2001). Why does research have so little impact on American drug policy? *Addiction, 96*, 373–376.

Rydell, C., & Everingham, S. (1994). *Controlling cocaine: Supply versus demand programs*. Drug Policy Research Center, Santa Monica, CA: RAND.

Wiessing, L., Hartnoll, R., & Rossi, C. (2001). Epidemiology of drug use at macro level: Indicators, models and policy making. In: Godfrey, C., Wiessing, L., & Hartnoll, R. *Modelling drug use: Methods to quantify and understand hidden processes*. EMCDDA Scientific Monograph Series, No. 6. Lisbon: EMCDDA.

TOBACCO CONTROL POLICIES AND YOUTH SMOKING: EVIDENCE FROM A NEW ERA

John A. Tauras, Sara Markowitz and John Cawley

ABSTRACT

This chapter examines the impact of cigarette prices, taxes, and tobacco control policies on youth and young adult smoking propensity and intensity in the U.S. during the years 1997–2001, a period characterized by significant changes in cigarette prices and tobacco control policies. Employing a fixed effects technique, we find a strong negative impact of cigarette prices and taxes on youth and young adult smoking prevalence and conditional demand. Moreover, we find purchase, use, and possession laws to be inversely related to youth and young adult smoking prevalence.

INTRODUCTION

Recent government interventions designed to reduce smoking in the U.S.A. can be traced back to the 1964 Surgeon General's report on the harmful effects of smoking. This public education campaign was followed by the requirement that warning labels appear on packs of cigarettes, bans on cigarette broadcast advertising, and state-initiated bans and restrictions on smoking in public places. Laws establishing minimum ages for tobacco possession and sale have also been enacted, and federal legislation in 1996 reinforced these state laws. Increases in the federal and state excise tax rates have occurred periodically, and these taxes have proven to be one of the most powerful weapons in the anti-smoking advocate's arsenal (U.S. Department of Health and Human Services (USDHHS), 2000).

A new era of tobacco control emerged as a result of the 1998 Master Settlement Agreement (MSA) between 11 major tobacco companies and 46 states. The plaintiffs sued the tobacco industry to recoup Medicaid costs for the care of persons injured by tobacco use. The suit alleged that the companies had violated antitrust and consumer protection laws, conspired to withhold information about adverse health effects of tobacco, manipulated nicotine levels to maintain smoking addiction, and conspired to withhold lower-risk products from the market. The companies settled and agreed to pay $206 billion to states over 25 years. The settlement also included new restrictions on marketing and promotion, and established funds to support anti-smoking research and advocacy efforts. Immediately following the November 1998 MSA agreement, major tobacco companies such as Phillip Morris and R.J. Reynolds raised wholesale prices by $0.45 to finance the payments. This increase was in addition to four price increases earlier in 1998 (Capehart, 1999).

In the wake of the MSA, states have been able to take advantage of prevailing anti-tobacco sentiment as an opportunity to dramatically increase excise taxes. Since 1998, 38 states (including Washington, DC) raised their excise tax rates at least once; never before have so many states raised cigarette taxes in a comparable period of time. The current average state excise tax is $0.74, more than double the 1997, pre-settlement, value of $0.35 per pack. Even Tennessee and Georgia, tobacco-producing states that traditionally have resisted raising taxes, have recently increased the tax rate on cigarettes.

This chapter takes advantage of the significant variation in cigarette prices and taxes in the post-MSA era to provide new estimates of the price elasticity of demand for cigarettes among youth. Pinning down the correct elasticity of demand is vital to inform public policy and to determine optimal tax rates. For example, in 1998, Congress considered a federal tax increase of $1.10 per pack, in part to reduce teenage smoking. A *New York Times* article highlighted the debate surrounding the tax increase, and cited vastly different estimates of the demand elasticity from the U.S. Treasury Department and researchers at Cornell University (Meier, 1998).

Most prior studies on the determinants of cigarette demand have employed cross-sectional data. A limitation of cross-sectional data is that one cannot easily control for unobserved, individual-level, time-invariant heterogeneity. However, many unobserved factors are potentially very important when examining cigarette demand. For example, it would be ideal to control for individual factors such as sentiment towards tobacco, attitudes about health risks, time preference, genetic disposition, differences in addictive susceptibility, etc. It is quite likely that these unobserved factors are correlated with some regressors that capture observed heterogeneity. If the unobserved effect is correlated with some included covariates, econometric techniques that do not account for the unobserved effect will yield biased estimates of the included variables. This chapter uses a two-way fixed effects estimation technique to control for time-invariant individual-level unobserved heterogeneity and individual-invariant year-specific unobserved heterogeneity. The estimates from this technique are robust to the potential correlation between the unobserved individual effect and the explanatory variables included to capture the observed heterogeneity.

While numerous studies have estimated youth price elasticities of demand for cigarettes, no study that controls for unobserved individual heterogeneity has been published, nor have any published studies used data from the post-MSA era, which is characterized by frequent and large price changes. One of the difficulties with conducting any demand study is that there must be sufficient variation in prices. The post-MSA era provides us with ample variation.

This chapter is the first study to investigate the impact of cigarette prices and tobacco control policies on youth and young adult smoking propensity and intensity during the late 1990s through early 2000s; a period characterized by unprecedented changes in smoking policies. If the organizations funded by the MSA have been successful in achieving their goals of tobacco education, prevention, and cessation, the resulting changes in the prevailing attitudes towards smoking may have altered the shape of the demand curve by youths. New estimates of the price elasticity of demand are warranted.

PREVIOUS LITERATURE

A number of previous studies have examined the impact of price or tax increases on cigarette smoking by youth and young adults. Using a variety of different data sets, time periods and age groups, the majority of these studies find that higher cigarettes prices will lower the probability of being a smoker and the frequency of smoking conditional on being a smoker. The

Cragg (1971) two-part model has been the most commonly used technique to estimate the total price elasticity which is calculated by summing the participation and frequency elasticities. A comprehensive review can be found in Chaloupka and Warner (2000), so only a brief summary of elasticities are reported here for reference.[1] The earliest study of teenage smoking was conducted by Lewit, Coate, and Grossman (1981) who estimate the price elasticity of demand for adolescents 12–17 years old. They find participation and frequency elasticities of −1.20 and −0.25, respectively. They report a total price elasticity of −1.44, indicating that youth smoking is fairly responsive to price. Using Monitoring the Future (MTF) data from the early 1990s, Chaloupka and Grossman (1996) estimate the participation and frequency elasticities for adolescents in 8th, 10th, and 12th grade. They calculate a participation elasticity of −0.675 and a total price elasticity of −1.31. Evans and Huang (1998) use the MTF surveys from 1977 to 1992 and 1985 to 1992 to estimate participation elasticities of −0.20 and −0.50 for the two time periods, respectively. They do not calculate the frequency elasticity conditional on being a smoker.

Two recent studies have used teenage smoking data from the early and mid-1990s. First, Gruber and Zinman (2001) examine data from 1991 to1997 and find prices to be an important determinant of smoking participation and frequency among older teens (high-school seniors). However, the price coefficients are statistically insignificant when younger teens (9–11th graders) are considered. Second, Ross and Chaloupka (2003) use data from 1996 along with six different measures of cigarette prices. Their preferred specifications yield a total price elasticity of −0.67 when the state average price is used and −1.02 when an average perceived price is used.

Studies of older youths also generally find negative price effects on smoking, but the magnitude tends to be smaller than that of teenagers. Grossman, Coate, Lewit, and Shakotoko (1983) estimate the overall price elasticity of demand to be −0.76 for 17–24 year olds. Evans and Farrelly (1998) estimate the participation and frequency price elasticities of −0.58 and −0.22, respectively for 18–24 year olds, implying a total elasticity of −0.80. Using the 1993 Harvard College Alcohol Survey, Chaloupka and Wechsler (1997) find the participation and frequency elasticities to be −0.526 and −0.729, respectively for 18–22 year olds, yielding a total elasticity of −1.26. Czart et al. (2001) use the 1997 version of the Harvard College Alcohol Survey and find an average estimated participation elasticity of −0.26 and conditional demand elasticity of −0.62. However, using the rational addition model of Becker and Murphy (1998), and Chaloupka (1991) finds that the overall price elasticity for young adults ages 17–24 years is very small in magnitude and not statistically significant.

DeCicca et al. (this volume) examine smoking participation decisions of respondents in their mid 1920s. Baseline estimates show that participation is responsive to current taxes, but this result disappears when past taxes are added. They conclude that the baseline results reflect the effect of past taxes on past smoking decisions. Their chapter is also significant because it discusses the potential bias from failing to account for past prices when the measure of participation includes both past initiators and quitters.[2]

Much of the empirical literature investigating the impact of non-price-based anti-smoking policies, such as clean indoor air laws, demonstrates that such restrictions have negative effects on teenage smoking at all levels of smoking. Chaloupka and Grossman (1996) conclude that strong restrictions on smoking in public places significantly reduce both the prevalence and average consumption of cigarette smoking by adolescents. Chaloupka and Wechsler (1997) report similar findings among college students. Tauras and Chaloupka (2001) show that stronger restrictions on smoking in private worksites will increase the probability of cessation among young adult females, while Tauras (2004) shows that statewide restrictions on smoking in private worksites and any public place other than restaurants will increase the probability of smoking cessation by all young adults.

Wasserman, Manning, Newhouse, and Winkler (1991) examine cigarette demand by teenagers, as well as adults. Using an index of restrictions on smoking along with price, they find statistically insignificant price effects for both age groups, although stricter restrictions on smoking do reduce the demand for cigarettes. Further, exclusion of the smoking restriction index in the adult sample results in statistically significant price elasticities that are similar to those found in other studies of adults. A similar exercise is not performed for the sample of adolescents; therefore, it is unknown if the inclusion of the smoking restriction index influences the price effects for teenagers.

To summarize, a majority of the previous studies conducted on the determinants of youth and young adult cigarette demand has found both smoking propensity and intensity to be inversely related to cigarette prices. This chapter attempts to validate this finding by exploiting within-individual variation in cigarette prices employing longitudinal data during a period characterized by unprecedented changes in cigarette prices.

DATA

This chapter uses data from the National Longitudinal Survey of Youth 1997 Cohort (NLSY97). The NLSY97 is a nationally representative sample of 9,022 youths aged 12–16 years as of December 31, 1996. The first wave was conducted in 1997, with follow-ups in 1998, 1999, 2000, and 2001. The age range of this panel (12–22) covers the ages at which many smokers experiment with cigarettes and escalate their dose patterns in the uptake process (i.e. increase the number of cigarettes smoked and increase the amount of nicotine extracted per cigarette) until stable daily patterns of cigarette use and nicotine blood concentration are established (U.S. Department of Health and Human Services (USDHHS), 1988).

Each year, the respondents were asked about their current smoking. These data were used to construct two dependent variables: An indicator for current smoking and, for current smokers, average number of cigarettes smoked monthly. The first measure, participation in current smoking, is a dichotomous indicator equal to one for respondents who indicated that they smoked cigarettes in the 30 days prior to the survey and is equal to zero otherwise. The second measure, average smoking among current smokers, is a continuous measure of monthly cigarette consumption based on the number of days each smoker smoked in the past 30 days multiplied by the average number of cigarettes smoked per day on days smoked.

Table 1 shows that 26.14% of the observations are current smokers. The average consumption among current smokers was 199.32 cigarettes per month (approximately 6.64 cigarettes per day).

In our regression models, the following characteristics of the youth and family are included as regressors: Age, age squared, education category (less than high school, high school diploma, attended college, college graduate, enrolled in high school; reference category), marital status (married and not married; reference category), youth income (which includes earned income and allowances from parents), household size, family structure (child lives with no parents, child lives with a step parent, child lives with one parent, and child lives with both parents; reference category), an indicator that equals one if the child does not identify with a religion, and a dichotomous indicator of work status. Table 1 shows means and standard deviations for these variables.

To control for unobserved heterogeneity over time, time fixed effects are included in each regression. That is, a dichotomous indicator for each year of data was created (1998, 1999, 2000, 2001, and 1997; reference category). The time fixed effects are included in each regression allowing the intercept to differ across the different years of data collection.

Several tobacco control variables were merged with the survey data. Cigarette price and tax data were obtained from the annual Tax Burden on Tobacco. Until 1999, the Tobacco Institute published state-level cigarette

Table 1. Descriptive Statistics.

Variable	Mean	Standard Deviation
Current Smoker	0.26	0.44
Average consumption among smokers	199.32	250.57
Real price	1.58	0.342
Real state tax	0.249	0.160
Purchase, use, possession index	1.56	1.024
Smoke-free air index	17.88	12.834
Youth access index	16.38	6.90
Age (years)	16.76	2.167
Age squared	285.544	72.450
Real income	2,238.21	4,664.381
Work	0.547	0.498
Dropout	0.094	0.293
High school degree	0.102	0.302
In college	0.152	0.359
College degree	0.0002	0.015
Married	0.019	0.135
Household size	4.29	1.630
Step parents	0.124	0.330
One parent	0.286	0.452
No parent	0.132	0.338
1998	0.202	0.402
1999	0.198	0.399
2000	0.194	0.396
2001	0.188	0.391

prices and taxes. Since then, Orzechowski and Walker (2001) have published the data. The prices are weighted averages for a pack of 20 cigarettes as of November 1 of each year and are inclusive of state level excise taxes applied to cigarettes but are exclusive of local cigarette taxes. We employ average yearly state prices and taxes in the analyses. The prices are computed by subtracting state and federal excise taxes from the current year's November price, previous year's November price, and future year's November price, and weighting the pre-tax prices accordingly to create a pre-tax price for 1 calendar year. Then the appropriate average federal tax and average state tax for each year were added back to the yearly average pre-tax price. Both the cigarette prices and taxes were deflated by the national Consumer Price Index published by the Bureau of Labor Statistics (1982–1984 = 100). Finally, based on the state of residence or the location of the respondent's college, when applicable, the cigarette prices and taxes are merged in with the survey data.

We also control for three measures of state tobacco regulations in all models. The first is an index ranging from 0 to 3 that records the presence of state laws barring youth possession, use, and/or purchase of tobacco. The second captures the overall magnitude of state level policies on smoke-free air. It is an index that ranges from 0 to 51 and reflects the presence and level of state laws requiring smoke-free air in various types of establishments and facilities.[3] These two measures were created for Project ImpacTeen by Gary Giovino and colleagues at the Roswell Park Cancer Institute. The third measure captures the extensiveness and comprehensiveness of state policies aimed at reducing youth access to tobacco products. It is an index that ranges from 0 to 31 that reflects the presence and severity of youth access laws; these youth access laws concern minimum purchase age, restrictions on packaging, photo identification requirements, clerk intervention during sales, restrictions on vending machines, restrictions on free samples, penalties to retailers who sell to minors, random inspections, and statewide enforcement. This index was developed by Alciati et al. (1998) for the National Cancer Institute and updated by Gary Giovino and colleagues at the Roswell Park Cancer Institute for Project ImpacTeen.

METHODS

We estimate a two-part model of cigarette demand, based on a model developed by Cragg (1971), in which smoking participation and frequency conditional on participation are estimated separately. We employ a two-way fixed effects estimation technique to control for time-invariant individual-level unobserved heterogeneity and individual-invariant unobserved heterogeneity over time. In particular, we estimate the following model for each dependent variable:

$$Y_{it} = X_{it}B + \alpha_i + \lambda_t + + u_{it} \qquad (1)$$

where X is a vector of explanatory variables that varies across time (t) and individuals (i), α_i the unobserved individual-specific effect, λ_t unobserved time-specific effect, and u_{it} the idiosyncratic error that changes across t as well as i. We estimate an individual-demeaned equation using pooled ordinary least squares (OLS) techniques to remove the unobserved individual effect prior to estimation. Specifically, the individual-specific average is subtracted from each observation for both the dependent and independent variables (including the time fixed effects) prior to estimation.

After considerable diagnostic testing, the fixed effects approach described above is preferred to both a simple pooling technique (that does not sweep away the individual-level heterogeneity) and a random effects approach. In particular, an *F*-test rejects the null hypothesis that the individual-fixed effects are jointly equal to zero implying that individuals do not share a common intercept. Moreover, the estimates from the pooled OLS approach are markedly different from those obtained from the fixed effects approach that yields consistent estimates. These findings suggest that the pooled OLS estimator suffers from omitted variable bias and are not robust in the presence of unobserved time-invariant individual-level heterogeneity.

Choosing between the fixed effects approach and the random effects approach depends on whether or not the individual effect is correlated with the explanatory variables. While the fixed effects technique will produce consistent estimates regardless of the correlation between the individual effect and the explanatory variables, the random effects technique will provide inconsistent estimates if the individual effect is correlated with any of the explanatory variables. A test proposed by Hausman (1978) was employed to compare the two estimators. Under the null hypothesis, both the random effects and the fixed effects are consistent, and the random effects technique is more efficient. Under the alternative hypothesis, the fixed effects approach is still consistent, but the random effects approach is inconsistent. The Hausman test rejects the null in favour of the alternative implying that the fixed effects approach is preferred.

Finally, since the prices, taxes, and policies are merged with the surveys by state and year, the standard errors of the estimates are cluster corrected on state and year using a robust method of calculating the variance covariance matrix developed by Huber (1967).

RESULTS

Estimates from the smoking prevalence equations and the conditional cigarette demand equations are presented in Table 2. We estimate two models of each outcome. The only difference between them is that the first includes cigarette price (but not excise tax) as a regressor and the second includes excise tax (but not cigarette price). The model specifications that include cigarette prices are comparable to most of the prior studies on cigarette demand and assume that consumers' choices to purchase cigarettes are determined by cigarette prices. The model specifications that include taxes are

Table 2. Smoking Demand Equations.

Variable	Smoking Prevalence Model 1	Smoking Prevalence Model 2	Average Consumption by Smokers Model 1	Average Consumption by Smokers Model 2
Real price	−0.052 (−2.20)	—	−63.499 (−2.67)	—
Real state tax	—	−0.061 (−2.33)	—	−72.448 (−2.68)
Purchase, use possession index	−0.008 (−3.57)	−0.008 (−3.62)	3.548 (0.92)	3.588 (0.93)
Smoke-free air index	0.0007 (1.51)	0.001 (1.48)	−0.323 (−0.47)	−0.354 (−0.51)
Youth access index	0.0003 (−0.46)	0.0004 (−0.52)	0.052 (0.05)	0.019 (0.02)
Age (years)	0.063 (4.16)	0.064 (4.17)	185.574 (9.95)	185.662 (9.96)
Age squared	−0.002 (−4.71)	−0.002 (−4.72)	−5.220 (−9.68)	−5.219 (−9.69)
Real income	0.000 (−0.87)	0.000 (−0.87)	0.001 (1.61)	0.001 (1.61)
Work	0.004 (0.87)	0.004 (0.97)	10.004 (1.90)	9.943 (1.89)
Dropout	0.044 (5.15)	0.044 (5.15)	27.051 (3.17)	26.934 (3.13)
High school degree	0.016 (2.50)	0.016 (2.50)	35.241 (4.41)	35.195 (4.40)
In college	0.002 (0.34)	0.002 (0.35)	28.576 (3.31)	28.665 (3.33)
College degree	0.089 (1.09)	0.090 (1.10)	81.763 (1.77)	81.540 (1.79)
Married	−0.093 (−6.07)	−0.093 (−6.06)	−25.479 (−1.98)	−25.499 (−1.99)
Household size	0.000 (0.08)	0.000 (0.09)	−2.244 (−1.00)	−2.211 (−0.98)
Step parents	0.012 (1.08)	0.012 (1.08)	8.937 (0.62)	8.734 (0.61)
One parent	0.018 (2.06)	0.018 (2.05)	22.777 (2.02)	22.566 (2.00)
No parent	0.009 (1.01)	0.009 (1.00)	29.616 (2.74)	29.458 (2.73)
1998	0.078 (7.71)	0.073 (7.51)	34.698 (2.37)	29.217 (2.09)
1999	0.138 (7.31)	0.119 (7.99)	80.986 (3.42)	56.424 (2.83)
2000	0.177 (6.68)	0.148 (7.31)	121.056 (3.70)	85.085 (3.17)
2001	0.217 (6.78)	0.185 (7.14)	143.996 (3.68)	103.882 (3.12)
Price/tax elasticity	−0.311	−0.058	−0.516	−0.090
N	40,563	40,563	10,641	10,641

Note: Asymptotic *t*-statistics are in parentheses. The critical values for the *t*-statistics are 2.58 (2.33), 1.96 (1.64), 1.64 (1.28) at the 1%, 5%, and 10% significance levels, respectively, based on a two-tailed (one-tailed) test.

important for policy-maker because taxes are the policy lever that governments can pull to effectively increase cigarette prices.

Cigarette Price and Tax Results

The real price of cigarettes has a negative and significant impact on the number of youth and young adults who smoke and average level of smoking among those who smoke. The estimated smoking prevalence price elasticity of demand and conditional price elasticity of demand are −0.311 and −0.516, respectively. These estimates imply that a 10% increase in the real price of cigarettes will decrease the number of adolescent and young adult smokers by approximately 3.1% and reduce the average number of cigarettes smoked by adolescent and young adult smokers by 5.2%. The estimated total price elasticity of demand, −0.827, is comparable to the −0.89 total price elasticity estimated by Lewit and Coate (1982) for individuals aged 20–25 years; it is smaller in absolute value than the −1.44 total price elasticity of demand estimated by Lewit et al. (1981) for individuals aged 12–17 years and falls within the range −0.67 to −1.02 reported by Ross and Chaloupka (2003). However, the estimated total price elasticity is significantly larger (in absolute value) than the consensus estimate for adults (−0.4) and is consistent with the notion that an inverse relationship exists between age and the price elasticity of cigarette demand. Similarly, the real state excise tax on cigarettes has a negative and significant impact on both smoking propensity and intensity. The estimated tax elasticities of smoking prevalence and conditional demand are −0.058 and −0.090, respectively. The estimated strong inverse relationship between cigarette prices and taxes, and adolescent and young adult smoking should be of interest to policy-makers interested in decreasing the future burden of tobacco-related disease.

Other Tobacco Control Policies

We find a negative and significant relationship between smoking prevalence and the purchase, use, and possession (PUP) index in both of the equations that were estimated. The estimates from the prevalence equations were used to perform simulations that predict smoking prevalence rates under alternative assumptions about the magnitude of state level PUP laws holding all other covariates at their mean levels. Table 3 provides predicted probabilities of smoking prevalence when the PUP index is alternately set to: The

Table 3. PUP Simulations.

	Predicted Smoking Prevalence			
	Mean PUP	Minimum PUP	Maximum PUP	Percentage Decrease from Minimum to Maximum
Model 1 (price)	26.23	27.47	25.09	8.66
Model 2 (tax)	26.23	27.49	25.07	8.80

minimum value in the sample, the mean of sample, and the maximum value in the sample. Varying the PUP index from its minimum value of zero to its maximum of value of three decreases the predicted probability of smoking prevalence in Model 1 from 27.47 to 25.09, a decrease of 8.7%. The predicted probabilities of smoking prevalence employing the estimates from Model 2 are virtually identical to those estimated in Model 1.

Unlike the strong negative impact of PUP laws on smoking prevalence, we find no evidence that PUP laws affect the average number of cigarettes smoked by adolescent and young adult smokers. Moreover, we find smoke-free air laws and youth access laws to be insignificant determinants of smoking decisions of youth and young adults. These insignificant findings may, however, be due in part to a lack of variation. In particular, only 11.7% and 29.4% of states made changes to their smoke-free air laws and youth access laws during the time under investigation. Since a small fraction of individuals change states of residence during the time under investigation, it is likely that a lack of variation in policies within states causes the estimates for these variables to be poorly determined (i.e. large standard errors).

Other Explanatory Variables

Age has a positive and significant impact on both smoking prevalence and average consumption among smokers. The relationship between age and smoking is estimated to be concave, suggesting that smoking is increasing in age, but at a decreasing rate. Individuals who drop out of high school or whose highest level of schooling is a high school degree are significantly more likely to smoke and smoke more on average than are individuals who are currently attending high school. Moreover, smokers who are currently attending college smoke significantly more cigarettes on average than smokers who are currently enrolled in high school, controlling for age. Individuals who are married are significantly less likely to smoke than those who are single. Individuals who live with one parent are significantly more likely to smoke and smoke more on average than individuals who live with both parents. Furthermore, smokers who do not live with their parents smoke significantly more on average than do smokers who live with both parents.

DISCUSSION

This chapter examines the influence of cigarette prices and other tobacco control policies on smoking prevalence and average consumption by youth and young adult smokers. It employs within-individual variation in both dependent and explanatory variables from nationally representative longitudinal surveys to identify the demand equations. This chapter is the first to estimate the demand elasticity among a panel of youths during the late 1990s and early 2000s; a period characterized by unprecedented changes in cigarette prices and smoking policies.

The results are consistent with that of the previous literature and clearly indicate that increases in cigarette prices decrease both smoking prevalence and conditional cigarette demand. The estimated price elasticities suggest that a 10% increase in cigarette prices will reduce the total number of cigarettes consumed by approximately 8.3%. Slightly more than half of the impact of price will be due to a reduction in average smoking by youth and young adults with the remainder of the effect on reduced smoking prevalence. In addition, stronger PUP laws were found to decrease smoking prevalence by youth and young adults. These findings should be of particular interest to policy-makers contemplating the use of public policy to curb smoking among America's youth.

NOTES

1. The literature on smoking initiation among youth is not summarized here. See Cawley, Markowitz, and Tauras (2004) for a review.
2. The sample used in our paper is much younger than that of DeCicca et al. and likely contains fewer quitters.
3. The index of state laws regarding smoke-free air is calculated as the following: [(restaurants × 2) + (recreational facilities × 2) + (cultural facilities × 2) + (shopping malls × 2) + (public schools × 2) + (private schools × 2) + (private worksites) + (health

facilities) + (public transit)]. For a complete description of how the individual components were coded, see the ImpacTeen web site at: http://www.impacteen.org/ATODData/Tobacco/TCpolicyandprevcodebook081903.pdf

ACKNOWLEDGEMENTS

The authors would like to thank Michael Grossman, Damien de Walque, and conference participants for helpful comments and suggestions. The authors would also like to thank Tomas Rinkunas and Stavros Tsipas for excellent research assistance.

REFERENCES

Alciati, M. H., Frosh, M., Green, S. B., Brownson, R. C., Fisher, P. H., Hobart, R., Roman, A., Sciandra, R. C., & Shelton, D. M. (1998). State laws on youth access to tobacco in the United States: Measuring their extensiveness with a new rating system. *Tobacco Control, 4*, 345–352.
Becker, G. S., & Murphy, K. M. (1998). A theory of rational addiction. *Journal of Political Economy, 96*, 675–700.
Capehart, T. (1999). Cigarette price increase follows tobacco pact. *Agricultural Outlook, January/February*, 8–10.
Cawley, J., Markowitz, S., & Tauras, J. A. (2004). Lighting up and slimming down: The effects of body weight and cigarette prices on adolescent smoking initiation. *Journal of Health Economics, 23*(2), 293–311.
Chaloupka, F. J. (1991). Rational addictive behavior and cigarette smoking. *Journal of Political Economy, 99*, 722–742.
Chaloupka, F.J., & Grossman, M. (1996). *Price, tobacco control policies, and youth smoking.* Working Paper no. 5740. NBER Working Paper.
Chaloupka, F. J., & Wechsler, H. (1997). Price tobacco control policies and smoking among young adults. *Journal of Health Economics, 16*, 359–373.
Chaloupka, F. J., & Warner, K. E. (2000). The economics of smoking. In: A. J. Culyer & J. P. Newhouse (Eds), *Handbook of Health Economics* (pp. 1539–1627). Netherlands: North-Holland, Elsevier Science.
Cragg, J. G. (1971). Some statistical models for limited dependent variables with application to the demand for durable goods. *Econometrica, 39*(5), 829–844.
Czart, C., Pacula, R. L., Chalopuka, F. J., & Wechsler, H. (2001). The impact of prices and control policies on cigarette smoking among college students. *Contemporary Economic Policy, 19*(2), 135–149.
Evans, W. N., & Farrelly, M. C. (1998). The compensating behavior of smokers: Taxes, tar, and nicotine. *RAND Journal of Economics, 29*(3), 578–595.
Evans, W. N., & Huang, L. X. (1998). *Cigarette taxes and teen smoking: New evidence from panels of repeated cross sections.* Working Paper. Department of Economics, University of Maryland, Maryland, U.S.A.

Grossman, M., Coate, D., Lewit, E. M., & Shakotoko, R. A. (1983). *Economic and other factors in youth smoking*. Final Report. National Science Foundation.

Hausman, J. (1978). Specification tests in econometrics. *Econometrica*, *46*, 1251–1271.

Huber, P. J. (1967). The behavior of maximum likelihood estimates under non-standard conditions. *Proceedings of the fifth Berkeley symposium on mathematical statistics and probability*, *1*, 221–233.

Lewit, E. M., & Coate, D. (1982). The potential for using excise taxes to reduce smoking. *Journal of Health Economics*, *1*, 121–145.

Lewit, E. M., Coate, D., & Grossman, M. (1981). The effects of government regulations on teenage smoking. *Journal of Law and Economics*, *24*, 545–569.

Meier, B. (1998). Politics of youth smoking fueled by unproven data. *New York Times*, May 20.

Orzechowski, W. P., & Walker, R. (2001). *Tax burden on tobacco*. Arlington, VA: Orzechowski and Walker.

Ross, H., & Chaloupka, F. J. (2003). The effect of cigarette prices on youth smoking. *Health Economics*, *12*, 217–230.

Tauras, J. A. (2004). Public policy and smoking cessation among young adults in the United States. *Health Policy*, *68*(3), 321–332.

Tauras, J. A., & Chaloupka, F. J. (2001). Determinants of smoking cessation: An analysis of young adult men and women. In: M. Grossman & C. -H. Hsieh (Eds), *The economic analysis of substance use and abuse: The experience of developed countries and lessons for developing countries*. Cheltenham, UK: Edward Elgar Publishing.

U.S. Department of Health and Human Services. (1988). *The health consequences of smoking: Nicotine addiction. A Report of the Surgeon General*. Rockville, MD: U.S. Department of Health and Human Services, Public Health Service, Center for Disease Control, Center for Chronic Disease Prevention and Health Promotion, Office on Smoking and Health.

U.S. Department of Health and Human Services. (2000). *Reducing tobacco use. A report of the surgeon general*. Atlanta, GA: U.S. Department of Health and Human Services, Centers for Disease Control and Prevention, Center for Chronic Disease Prevention and Health Promotion, Office on Smoking and Health.

Wasserman, J., Manning, W. G., Newhouse, J. P., & Winkler, J. D. (1991). The effects of excise taxes and regulations on cigarette smoking. *Journal of Health Economics*, *10*, 43–64.

THE FIRES ARE NOT OUT YET: HIGHER TAXES AND YOUNG ADULT SMOKING

Philip DeCicca, Don Kenkel and Alan Mathios

1. INTRODUCTION

In recent policy discussions, the conventional wisdom is that adolescent smoking is substantially more tax- or price-responsive than adult smoking.[1] In a previous study, we used data from the first three waves of the National Education Longitudinal Study (NELS) to estimate the impact of taxes and prices on smoking initiation during adolescence (DeCicca, Kenkel, & Mathios, 2002). Contrary to the conventional wisdom, we found weak or nonexistent tax/price effects in our models of the onset of adolescent smoking between 1988 and 1992. In this study, we use data from the 2000 wave of NELS, when most respondents were about 26 years old. Although cigarette prices increased by almost 40% in real terms between 1992 and 2000, smoking prevalence among the NELS respondents also increased from 18% to 23%, about the same increase observed in other cohorts over these ages.

Following the standard approach, we use the 2000 wave of NELS to estimate an empirical model of smoking participation at a point in time. However, we exploit the longitudinal nature of NELS to make several important extensions to previous research on the economics of smoking. First, because we know respondents' previous states of residence, we can explore the role of past taxes. As is discussed in more detail below, when taxes are serially correlated the approach used in most previous studies yields estimates of the impact of current taxes on current smoking participation that are biased away from zero. This problem is exacerbated by the fact that the standard approach (as applied to U.S. data) relies on tax variation across states for identification. If taxes are correlated with unmeasured anti-smoking sentiment at the state level, the standard approach is again biased towards finding strong tax effects. In fact, when we estimate a benchmark model that takes the standard approach, we obtain the standard result. In probit models current cigarette taxes are negatively and statistically significantly associated with smoking participation in 2000. We next include in our model both the tax the young adult faced in 1992 and the current tax. We find that only the 1992 tax is statistically significantly associated with smoking participation in 2000.

Our second main extension to previous research is to exploit a new source of identifying variation by focussing on young adults who face different cigarette taxes because they moved to a different state between 1992 and 2000. When the sample is restricted to movers, the estimated relationship between current taxes and smoking participation becomes weak and statistically insignificant.

In Section 2, we discuss our empirical specification in more detail and compare it to the standard approach. Section 3 provides an overview of the data, while Section 4 presents our econometric approach to handle attrition before the last wave of the NELS. Sections 5 and 6 present our main results, and Section 7 is a brief conclusion.

2. EMPIRICAL SPECIFICATION OF A SMOKING PARTICIPATION EQUATION

A standard approach to study cigarette demand uses cross-sectional data to estimate a two-part model, where the first part is a model of smoking participation, and the second part analyses consumption conditional upon participation (e.g., Wasserman, Manning, Newhouse, & Winkler, 1991). However, current smoking participation reflects initiation and cessation decisions made over many years, so modelling smoking participation as a function of current prices is fundamentally mis-specified. Consider the relationship between the probability of smoking participation (S) at age t and the conditional probabilities of initiation (I) and cessation (Q)

at age t:

$$S_t = I_t(1 - S_{t-1}) + (1 - Q_t)S_{t-1} \tag{1}$$

Recursively substituting for S, the right-hand side of Eq. (1) can be expressed in terms of I_t, Q_t, I_{t-1}, Q_{t-1}, I_{t-2}, Q_{t-2}, ..., I_0, where I_0 is smoking initiation at the earliest relevant age (e.g., age 14). In a myopic addiction model where initiation and cessation decisions at age t reflect the current price faced at age t, Eq. (1) implies an empirical model of smoking participation of the general form:

$$S_t = G(\gamma_0 + \gamma_1 P_t + \gamma_2 P_{t-1} + \gamma_3 P_{t-3} + \cdots) \tag{2}$$

In Eq. (2) the other (non-price) determinants of smoking participation have been suppressed for simplicity. Eq. (2) can be thought of as a reduced-form smoking participation equation from an addiction model.[2] The exact specification of Eq. (2) is complicated and depends upon simplifying assumptions.[3] The general point for the empirical models to be estimated is that current smoking participation should be modelled as a function of the relevant history of prices (P_t, P_{t-1}, P_{t-2}, ...). Assuming $G()$ is the standard normal cumulative distribution function implies the probit model. Below we estimate probit models of young adult smoking participation that take a step towards the correct specification.

In a correctly specified model, the estimated coefficient β_t on P_t would capture the impact of current price on current initiation and cessation decisions:[4]

$$\beta_t = \frac{\partial S_t}{\partial P_t} = \left[\frac{\partial I_t}{\partial P_t}\right](1 - S_{t-1}) - \left[\frac{\partial Q_t}{\partial P_t}\right]S_{t-1} \tag{3}$$

As the standard approach focuses on smoking participation, the separate effects of price on initiation and cessation are not identified.

However, most empirical models of smoking participation fail to include past prices. To the extent current and past prices are serially correlated, this creates an omitted variables bias in the resulting price-elasticity estimates. In the U.S.A., most of the variation in cigarette prices is driven by state-excise tax policy. During times when tax policies are not frequently revised, cigarette prices will tend to be very serially correlated.[5] In this situation the current price of cigarettes tends to proxy for the history of prices. As a result, the estimated effect of the current price on current smoking participation tends to reflect the effects of past prices on initiation and cessation decisions. Put differently, the resulting price-elasticity estimate roughly corresponds to a long-run price-elasticity, reflecting long-standing differences in prices across states.[6]

Not only does the political process tend to create serial correlation in cigarette prices, it also raises the possibility that prices will be correlated with other, hard-to-observe determinants of adolescent smoking. In an analysis of state cigarette taxes from the 1920s through the 1970s, Warner (1982, p. 483) concludes that: "The fluctuations in new-tax activity do not appear to have occurred randomly. To the contrary, they correspond closely to the evolution of public concerns about the link between cigarette smoking and illness..." As evidence supporting this hypothesis, he points out that from 1921 to 1952 tobacco-producing states and other states taxed cigarettes similarly; but as public awareness of the smoking-and-health issue grew, other states were much more likely to increase cigarette taxes than were the tobacco states. Similarly, Hunter and Nelson (1992) estimate an empirical political economy model of state tobacco taxes from 1946 to 1989. Their results suggest that states increased cigarette taxes in response to a shift in the public's demand for anti-smoking policies.

To further explore this issue, DeCicca, Kenkel, Mathios, and Shin (2004) develop an empirical measure of state-level anti-smoking sentiment during the 1990s. The simple correlation between the measure of anti-smoking sentiment and current prices increased from 0.53 in 1992 to 0.59 in 2000. It seems likely that anti-smoking sentiment will be an important determinant of adolescent smoking; for example, parents can have a strong influence through channels such as restrictions on smoking at home (Hersch, 1998; Wakefield et al., 2000; Powell & Chaloupka, 2005). In empirical demand models that do not adequately control for the influence of anti-smoking sentiment, its correlation with cigarette taxes or prices creates potentially serious omitted variables bias in estimates of tax- or price-responsiveness.[7] DeCicca et al. (2004) explore these issues empirically by including a measure of state anti-smoking sentiment in the standard cross-sectional specification. The results show two consistent patterns: State anti-smoking sentiment is an important influence on youth smoking participation; and after controlling for differences in state anti-smoking sentiment, the price of cigarettes has a weak and statistically insignificant influence on smoking participation.

The upshot is that in a standard model of smoking participation, the current cigarette price tends to proxy for the entire history of prices and anti-smoking sentiment the individual has faced. The resulting price-elasticity estimates are biased regardless of whether they are interpreted as applying to the short- or long-run. In the empirical work below, we first explore the extent of this bias, and second develop an empirical strategy to yield reliable estimates of the short-run price-elasticity of smoking participation.

3. DATA

3.1. Overview of NELS

The NELS began in 1988 as a nationally representative survey of U.S. eighth graders. Since this initial wave there have been four follow-up surveys – in 1990, 1992, 1994, and the most recent coming in 2000 when most sample members were 25 or 26 years old. While the interval before the 2000 wave is relatively long, NELS retained approximately two-thirds of the respondents to the 1992 wave.[8] More precisely, of the 19,220 respondents to the 1992 wave, 12,144 are included in the 2000 wave. In Section 4 we discuss our econometric approach to the attrition issue in more detail.

3.2. Key Variables

Table 1 presents descriptive statistics for the key variables used in the analysis. Our measure of smoking participation is based on responses to a question about the number of cigarettes smoked per day. Legitimate responses include – zero, less than one, one to five, six to ten, one-half to two packs (10–40 cigarettes), and more than two packs (41 or more cigarettes) per day. In the 2000 data, 75.3% report being non-smokers, 1.3% smoking less than one cigarette per day, 6.4% one to five, 7.0% six to ten, 9.3% eleven to forty, and 0.7% report smoking more than two packs per day. For the analyses that follow, we collapse this information into a dichotomous smoking participation measure. We include the relatively small number of individuals who report smoking less than one cigarette per day with non-smokers, because this likely includes those with very little attachment to daily smoking.

The key explanatory variable of interest is the cigarette excise tax. Cigarette taxes were merged to the data on the basis of state of residence information in the appropriate year.[9] There does not seem to be a consensus among researchers about whether to use cigarette taxes or prices in empirical models of smoking participation. Arguments in favour of the use of taxes include: Prices may be subject to market-level endogeneity and so may be higher in areas with higher demand; and taxes are the directly

Table 1. Sample Means and Standard Deviations, by State Moving Status.

	Full Sample	Stayers	Movers
Daily smoker	0.227 (0.419)	0.238 (0.426)	0.187 (0.390)
State cigarette tax (2000)	47.603 (31.575)	47.851 (31.468)	46.676 (31.963)
State cigarette tax (1992)	27.333 (11.675)	27.336 (11.762)	27.322 (11.347)
Male	0.476 (0.499)	0.471 (0.499)	0.495 (0.500)
White	0.692 (0.461)	0.638 (0.468)	0.759 (0.428)
Black	0.094 (0.291)	0.098 (0.297)	0.078 (0.268)
Hispanic	0.131 (0.337)	0.149 (0.356)	0.063 (0.243)
Other race	0.083 (0.275)	0.078 (0.268)	0.100 (0.300)
Born in 1972	0.049 (0.213)	0.055 (0.225)	0.027 (0.159)
Born in 1973	0.290 (0.448)	0.298 (0.451)	0.261 (0.436)
Born in 1974	0.650 (0.461)	0.638 (0.468)	0.695 (0.428)
Born in 1975	0.011 (0.102)	0.009 (0.093)	0.017 (0.128)
Test score	51.480 (10.098)	50.294 (9.781)	55.916 (10.027)
Northeast	0.174 (0.379)	0.176 (0.381)	0.167 (0.373)
Midwest	0.248 (0.432)	0.264 (0.441)	0.187 (0.390)
South	0.359 (0.480)	0.350 (0.477)	0.392 (0.488)
West	0.219 (0.414)	0.209 (0.407)	0.254 (0.436)
N	11,326	8,933	2,393

Notes: The first column presents statistics for individuals who lived in same state in 1992 and 2000 (stayers) and also for those who changed states between these years (movers). Summary statistics in the second column include only stayers and those in the third column include only movers. Samples correspond to those used to generate model estimates.

manipulable policy tool. We use taxes in our empirical models, and use the results to calculate the implied price-elasticity. To calculate the price-elasticity from the tax-elasticity, we assume that taxes are fully passed through to prices.

3.3. Analysis Sample

As noted above, the fourth follow-up of NELS includes 12,144 individuals. Restricting to those with complete smoking and relevant state of residence information in 1992 and 2000 reduces sample size slightly to 11,326, or about 93% of fourth wave respondents. This number represents the maximum number of cases in our 2000 cross-sectional models. All specifications include controls for gender, race, year of birth, region, and the respondent's composite score on from standardized tests in reading and mathematics. Missing data on the covariates race (53 cases), year of birth (317 cases), and test score (202 cases) reduces the available sample for complete case analysis to 11,350. We follow our earlier work and use conditional mean imputation to fill in missing values for these covariates. Hence, our overall analysis sample consists of the above-mentioned 11,326 individuals with smoking and state information in 1992 and 2000. In all cases, differences between the results we present and those generated by complete case analysis are trivial.

4. PANEL ATTRITION

As discussed above, despite the efforts by the NELS staff to follow respondents, there was about 37% attrition between the 1992 and 2000 waves. In this section, we present the results of a simple test for attrition bias, and then discuss the econometric approach we use in response to the attrition problem.

To test for attrition bias, we estimate a model of smoking participation in 1992 as a function of a dummy variable indicating future attrition, as well as other explanatory variables. The statistical significance of the coefficient on the attrition dummy provides a simple test for attrition bias (Verbeek & Nijman, 1992). The estimated coefficient is positive and statistically significant, suggesting that controlling for other observable differences, respondents who eventually attrite from the sample were more likely to smoke in 1992. To further explore this, we estimate a second specification that includes an interaction term between the attrition indicator and cigarette taxes. The interaction term is not statistically significantly different from zero, suggesting that in 1992 future attriters and non-attriters were similarly tax-responsive. This is somewhat re-assuring, given the focus of this chapter on estimating tax-responsiveness. However, the basic specification test results suggest that attrition is a potential problem.

In the empirical work below, to allow for attrition we use the inverse probability weighted (IPW) estimator suggested by Wooldridge (2002a). The first step to implement the IPW estimator is to estimate a probit model of sample retention between 1992 and 2000 as a function of observable characteristics in 1992. The inverse of the fitted probabilities from this model are then used as weights when estimating the models of 2000 smoking participation reported below in Section 5. Intuitively, the IPW estimator corrects for sample attrition by placing more weight on observations from respondents who are similar to those who attrite. Technically, Wooldridge

(2002a) shows that the estimator is consistent under the assumption of selection on observables. Although the assumption of selection on observables may not necessarily hold, it should be stressed that the observables can include endogenous variables, such as lagged values of the dependent variable (Moffit, Fitzgerald, & Gottschalk, 1999). In our case, smoking participation in 1992 is included as an explanatory variable in the model of retention between 1992 and 2000, and hence reflected in the sample weights.

5. THE ROLE OF PAST TAXES IN MODELS OF YOUNG ADULT SMOKING PARTICIPATION

In this section, we explore modifying the standard cross-sectional model of smoking participation in light of the dynamics of smoking behaviour. From Eq. (2), the correct specification of a model of smoking participation includes the relevant history of cigarette taxes or prices. For our model of young adult smoking participation in 2000, this approach would require including measures of taxes at least back to 1988. Given the serial correlation in taxes within each state, this set of variables would be highly multicollinear. As a step towards this specification, we instead use the 1992 tax rate as a proxy for all past taxes.

Tables 2A and 2B present the results from two specifications. The first baseline model is the standard (mis-)specification, where 2000 smoking participation is modelled as a function of the 2000 tax rate and characteristics of the individual. The second model adds the 1992 tax rate. The results for the baseline model are consistent with other studies: The 2000 tax rate is negatively and statistically significantly associated with a lower probability of smoking participation. The implied price-elasticity is −0.6, very much in line with the consensus based on previous cross-sectional studies (CBO, 1998; U.S. Department of the Treasury, 1998). However, when the 1992 tax rate is included in the model, the estimated coefficient on 2000 taxes is only one-fifth as large as in the baseline specification, and it loses statistical significance. In contrast, 1992 taxes have a strongly negative and statistically significant association with smoking participation in 2000. Put differently, the results suggest that the variable that is typically omitted from the standard specification of models of smoking participation (past taxes) is much more important than the variable that is typically included (current taxes).

Table 2A. Probit Coefficients from 2000 Smoking Participation Model, Current and Past Taxes.

	Current Tax	Past and Current Tax
State cigarette tax (2000)	−0.00133 (2.41)	−0.00026 (0.49)
State cigarette tax (1992)	—	−0.0045 (3.1)
Male	0.14499 (5.31)	0.14653 (5.44)
Black	−0.53197 (11.70)	−0.54031 (11.74)
Hispanic	−0.38551 (7.41)	−0.36473 (6.74)
Other race	−0.26702 (5.69)	−0.26372 (5.58)
Birth year 1972	0.16109 (2.86)	0.16907 (3.03)
Birth year 1973	0.10781 (3.24)	0.11026 (3.31)
Birth year 1975	0.00263 (0.02)	0.00614 (0.05)
Test score	−0.02171 (9.93)	−0.02195 (10.11)
Northeast	0.24800 (5.53)	0.26441 (6.16)
Midwest	0.24059 (5.24)	0.25483 (6.03)
South	0.06529 (1.31)	0.08418 (1.81)
Implied price-elasticity 2000	−0.610	−0.119
Implied price-elasticity 1992	—	−1.137
N	11,326	11,326

Notes: Price-elasticities are calculated by multiplying tax-elasticities by the ratio of average price to average tax. In 1992, this ratio was 7.151 and in 2000, this ratio was 7.445. Absolute values of *t*-ratios in parentheses. Standard errors adjusted for non-independence of observations within states.

The impact of controlling for past taxes in Table 2 is particularly striking given that there was more within-state variation in cigarette taxes over this time period than has often been the case. For example, from 1984 to 1992 – the 8-year period prior to the period we study – 42 states increased their cigarette tax, but the average nominal increase among these states was only 10.8 cents.[10] In contrast, from 1992 to 2000 – the period we study – although only 29 states raised cigarette taxes, the average real increase among these states was 26.6 cents, nearly two and a half times larger than that over the earlier period. Over all states, regardless of whether or not they increased, the average nominal tax increased from 15.6 to 25.69 cents from 1984 to 1992, while it increased from 25.69 to 41.96 cents from 1992 to 2000. In real terms, the latter increase is nearly twice as large as the former (7.45 cents versus 13.26 cents). Compared to the period 1992–2000, in periods with little new tax activity past and current taxes will be more highly correlated. When data from such periods are used to estimate models that omit past taxes, the

Table 2B. Probit Coefficients from 2000 Smoking Participation Model, Current and Past Taxes, Corrected for Attrition.

	Current Tax	Past and Current Tax
State cigarette tax (2000)	−0.0015 (2.72)	−0.00041 (0.75)
State cigarette tax (1992)	—	−0.00451 (3.04)
Male	0.15224 (5.69)	0.15385 (5.83)
Black	−0.52455 (11.84)	−0.53266 (11.85)
Hispanic	−0.39314 (7.7)	−0.37195 (6.95)
Other race	−0.26194 (5.21)	−0.25843 (5.1)
Birth year 1972	0.15792 (2.89)	0.16594 (3.06)
Birth year 1973	0.11043 (3.31)	0.11273 (3.36)
Birth year 1975	0.01443 (0.12)	0.01747 (0.15)
Test score	−0.02154 (9.97)	−0.02143 (10.15)
Northeast	0.25326 (5.64)	0.2695 (6.29)
Midwest	0.2421 (5.19)	0.25689 (6.00)
South	0.06138 (1.24)	0.0811 (1.73)
Implied price-elasticity 2000	−0.678	−0.183
Implied price-elasticity 1992	—	−1.126
N	11,326	11,326

Notes: Price-elasticities are calculated by multiplying tax-elasticities by the ratio of average price to average tax. In 1992, this ratio was 7.151 and in 2000, this ratio was 7.445. Absolute values of *t*-ratios in parentheses. Standard errors adjusted for non-independence of observations within states.

resulting estimates of the impact of current taxes on current smoking participation may be even more biased than is apparent in Table 2.

Two previous studies also find that current smoking participation is a function of past cigarette taxes. In one set of models, Gruber and Zinman (2001) use Vital Statistics Natality data on the smoking behavior during pregnancy by women aged 24 and older. They find that the tax the women faced when they were 14–17 years old is statistically significantly associated with their later smoking during pregnancy. In contrast to our results in Table 2, however, even after controlling for past taxes Gruber and Zinman (2001) find that are current taxes are statistically significantly associated with current smoking. In fact, Gruber and Zinman find that current taxes are quantitatively more important than past taxes: The implied price-elasticity of smoking participation during pregnancy with respect to current taxes is −0.6, compared to the implied price-elasticity with respect to past taxes of only −0.06. The contrast with our results may partly stem from the fact that the women in the Natality sample are on average older than respondents to the NELS 2000 wave. As a result, Gruber and Zinman consider a longer time span between past and current taxes than we do (about 20 years versus 8 years). Glied (2002) uses data from repeated waves of the National Longitudinal Survey of Youth 1979. She finds that even after controlling for current taxes, "taxes at age 14 remain a potent predictor of smoking behaviour 5–13 years later" (Glied, 2002, p. 129). Glied notes that her results in general show that current taxes reduce current smoking, but she does not report the estimated coefficient on current taxes or the implied price-elasticity. Based on the results of Gruber and Zinman, Glied, and Table 2, it is hard to draw definitive conclusions about the relative importance of past and current taxes. However, all three sets of results are consistent with the key point of Eq. (2) – that current smoking participation should be modelled as a function of the relevant history of prices or taxes.

The results in Table 2 shed light on the problems with the standard specification of models of smoking participation, but because of the limitations that remain they should not be viewed as definitive estimates of the tax-responsiveness of young adult smoking. The estimated coefficient on the measure of current (2000) taxes from the model that includes 1992 taxes is not subject to as much bias from omitting the past tax variables, to the extent 1992 taxes proxy for the entire relevant history of taxes. But there still may be bias to the extent current and past taxes are correlated with unobserved current and past state anti-smoking sentiment. DeCicca et al. (2004) find that controlling for anti-smoking sentiment, current prices or taxes have little or no impact on current smoking participation in 1992. This tends to suggest that the estimated impact of 1992 taxes on smoking participation in 2000 may also tend to reflect past anti-smoking sentiment rather than a true tax-responsiveness.

Before turning to our new approach to break the correlation between current taxes and the past, Table 3 presents results from additional specifications of the smoking participation model. One way to motivate our probit model of smoking participation is to adopt the random utility model proposed by McFadden (1974).[11] In that model, unless personal attributes have different effects on utility in each state, they do not enter the indirect utility comparison directly (Amemiya, 1981). However, they can enter indirectly, for example, through the marginal utility of income (which determines the impact of taxes on the indirect utility comparison). In the context of our model, this specification of the random utility approach implies that personal attributes – gender, race, year of birth, region and the respondent's

Table 3. Probit Coefficients from 2000 Smoking Participation Model, Taxes Interacted with Personal Attributes.

	Only Interactions	Interactions and Main Effects
State cigarette tax (2000)	0.01088 (3.4)	−0.00918 (1.92)
Male		0.18498 (3.93)
Male * tax	0.00186 (3.13)	−0.00087 (1.28)
Black		−0.5582 (9.07)
Black * tax	−0.00798 (5.55)	0.00051 (0.31)
Hispanic		−0.34366 (3.26)
Hispanic * tax	−0.0058 (4.14)	−0.00083 (0.37)
Other race		−0.27199 (2.36)
Other race * tax	−0.0035 (4.7)	0.00008 (0.06)
Birth year 1972		0.17667 (1.71)
Birth year 1972 * tax	0.00254 (2.27)	−0.00096 (0.35)
Birth year 1973		0.02721 (0.46)
Birth year 1973 * tax	0.00226 (2.92)	0.00178
Birth year 1975		−498355 (2.11)
Birth year 1975 * tax	0.00254 (2.43)	0.00823 (3.02)
Test score		−0.02748 (8.85)
Test score * tax	−0.00028 (4.56)	0.00012 (1.85)
Northeast		0.07932 (0.73)
Northeast * tax	0.00351 (8.19)	0.00237 (1.74)
Midwest		0.11281 (1.07)
Midwest * tax	0.00402 (6.62)	0.00199 (1.36)
South		−0.07993 (0.72)
South * tax	0.00043 (0.36)	0.00274 (1.31)
N	11,326	11,326

Notes: Absolute values of t-ratios in parentheses. Standard errors adjusted for non-independence of observations within states.

composite score on from standardized tests in reading and mathematics – should only enter the model in interaction with the cigarette tax variable.

The first column of Table 3 presents results from a probit model where personal attributes only enter in interaction with taxes; the second column presents results where personal attributes enter directly as well as interactions. In the second column, many of the personal attributes are statistically significant determinants of smoking participation, even after controlling for their effects in interaction with taxes. One interpretation of their significance is that it provides evidence of state dependence (addiction), where the effects of personal attributes on utility are different depending on smoking status. Another interpretation is that the results indicate that our model is mis-specified: Apparently the individuals sampled have a basic bias in favour or against smoking independent of the transition probabilities we focus on.

Apart from their relevance to the random utility model, the Table 3 results are also useful to explore whether tax-responsiveness varies with personal attributes. The results provide evidence that younger respondents who were born in 1975 are less tax-responsive than those in the baseline group born in 1974. The results also suggest that respondents with higher scores on standardized tests are less tax-responsive.[12]

6. COMPARING MOVERS AND STAYERS

The standard specification yields biased estimates of the impact of current taxes on smoking participation to the extent taxes are serially correlated within states, and to the extent taxes are correlated with state anti-smoking sentiment. Another approach to break the correlation between current taxes and past taxes/anti-smoking sentiment is to focus on those respondents who changed their state of residence. In this section, we estimate separate models of smoking participation for movers and stayers, to compare the tax sensitivity of those who switched their state of residence between 1992 and 2000 to those who did not.

Given this strategy, a natural question relates to differences between these two groups. Table 1 contains several comparisons of movers and stayers. In particular, note that the levels of taxes in both 1992 and 2000 are virtually identical for the two groups. This suggests that respondents' movement across states is largely orthogonal to taxes. To the extent that this is true, comparisons of movers and stayers should provide improved estimates of tax-responsiveness, relative to the traditional cross-sectional model. While taxes are unrelated to mover or stayer status, there exist other, non-trivial differences between stayers and movers. As seen in Table 1, movers are less likely to smoke, more likely to be white, and are perhaps more academically inclined, as the average test score for this group is roughly one-half of one standard deviation higher than their non-mover counterparts. On the surface, these differences suggest college attendance may be a prime reason for state moving.

The models of smoking participation for movers and stayers are presented in Tables 4A and 4B. For comparison purposes, Tables 4A and 4B also repeat the baseline model from Table 2. Table 4A presents results from conventional maximum likelihood probit models. Table 4B presents results of probit

Table 4A. Probit Coefficients from 2000 Participation Model, by State Moving Status.

	Full Sample	Stayers	Movers
State cigarette tax	−0.00133 (2.41)	−0.00153 (2.77)	−0.00045 (0.37)
Male	0.14499 (5.31)	0.13948 (4.23)	0.17825 (3.17)
Black	−0.53197 (11.70)	−0.55088 (10.89)	−0.42862 (3.91)
Hispanic	−0.38551 (7.41)	−0.37470 (6.72)	−0.47112 (4.15)
Other race	−0.26702 (5.69)	−0.32302 (6.09)	−0.06528 (0.57)
Birth year 1972	0.16109 (2.86)	0.19054 (3.25)	−0.06756 (0.30)
Birth year 1973	0.10781 (3.24)	0.10457 (2.98)	0.13048 (1.91)
Birth year 1975	0.00263 (0.02)	0.04013 (0.35)	−0.07407 (0.30)
Test score	−0.02171 (9.93)	−0.01935 (8.08)	−0.02799 (6.57)
Northeast	0.24800 (5.53)	0.25906 (5.61)	0.17198 (1.57)
Midwest	0.24059 (5.24)	0.26523 (5.56)	0.07359 (0.85)
South	0.06529 (1.31)	0.08258 (1.56)	−0.01506 (0.18)
Implied price-elasticity	−0.610	−0.692	−0.214
N	11,326	8,933	2,393

Notes: The first column corresponds to models that include both individuals who lived in same state in 1992 and 2000 (stayers) and those who changed states between these years (movers). Models in the second column include only stayers and those in the third column include only movers. Price-elasticities are calculated by multiplying tax-elasticities by the ratio of average price to average tax. In 2000, this ratio was 7.445. Absolute values of *t*-ratios in parentheses. Standard errors adjusted for non-independence of observations within states.

models that use the IPW estimator to allow for sample attrition. In general, the results are not very sensitive to the IPW correction for attrition bias.

The results in Tables 4A and 4B reveal that the strong effect of 2000 taxes in the baseline model is driven by the relationship between smoking participation and taxes in the sub-sample of respondents who did not change their state of residence. In the sub-sample of movers, the estimated coefficient on taxes is much smaller and loses statistical significance. Other than the tax effect, the results for most of the other explanatory variables are very similar across the sub-samples. The region indicator variables are an exception: They are not strongly related to smoking participation in the sub-sample of state movers. This pattern is actually somewhat similar to the result for taxes, because it suggests that the individual's current region of residence (which may tend to capture anti-smoking sentiment) is not important for those young adults who have moved.

Given the differences between movers and stayers shown in Table 1, are there reasons to expect, a priori, that their tax-responsiveness varies as in

Table 4B. Probit Coefficients from 2000 Participation Model, by State Moving Status, Corrected for Attrition.

	Full sample	Non-Switchers	Switchers
State cigarette tax	−0.00150 (2.72)	−0.00166 (2.93)	−0.00078 (0.66)
Male	0.15224 (5.69)	0.14744 (4.55)	0.18314 (3.30)
Black	−0.52455 (11.84)	−0.53995 (10.99)	−0.43192 (3.88)
Hispanic	−0.39314 (7.70)	−0.38121 (6.95)	−0.48935 (4.33)
Other race	−0.26194 (5.21)	−0.31574 (5.66)	−0.06189 (0.53)
Birth year 1972	0.15792 (2.89)	0.18794 (3.33)	−0.07599 (0.33)
Birth year 1973	0.11403 (3.31)	0.10542 (3.02)	0.14087 (2.12)
Birth year 1975	0.01443 (0.12)	0.06194 (0.52)	−0.09023 (0.37)
Test score	−0.02154 (9.97)	−0.01920 (8.19)	−0.02793 (6.53)
Northeast	0.25326 (5.64)	0.26486 (5.64)	0.17679 (1.66)
Midwest	0.24210 (5.19)	0.26801 (5.51)	0.07556 (0.86)
South	0.06138 (1.24)	0.07995 (1.49)	−0.02602 (0.31)
Implied price-elasticity	−0.678	−0.739	−0.369
N	11,326	8,933	2,393

Notes: Estimates corrected for attrition as in Wooldridge (2002b). The first column corresponds to models that include both individuals who lived in same state in 1992 and 2000 (non-switchers) and those who changed states between these years (switchers). Models in the second column include only non-switchers and those in the third column include only switchers. Price-elasticities are calculated by multiplying tax-elasticities by the ratio of average price to average tax. In 2000, this ratio was 7.445. Absolute values of *t*-ratios in parentheses. Standard errors adjusted for non-independence of observations within states.

Tables 4A and 4B? As we note above, some of the differences suggest that moving may be related to college attendance. This suggest the movers may be more future oriented, which may have implications for their tax-responsiveness.[13] Some empirical patterns in the NELS data partially support this idea. Both intuition and the theory of rational addiction suggest that present-oriented people are potentially more addicted to harmful goods than future-oriented people (Becker & Murphy, 1988). If so, stayers should be more addicted than movers. In the data, although stayers are more likely to smoke, conditional on smoking stayers are only slightly more likely to smoke at least half a pack a day (43% versus 39%). To begin to explore the role of time preference further, we tried using years of completed schooling as an alternative proxy for time preference. When we extend our probit model of smoking participation to include years of schooling and its interaction with tax, we find that people with more schooling are less tax-responsive (results not reported but available upon request).[14] However, controlling for schooling and its interaction with tax does not have much of an effect on the estimated coefficient on the mover/tax interaction; that is, we continue to find evidence that movers are less tax-responsive than stayers. An interesting direction for future work is to conduct additional theoretical and empirical analysis of the relationships between time preference, moving status, and tax-responsiveness.

7. CONCLUSIONS

Looking at our results as a whole, they suggest that the standard specification of a smoking participation model yields misleading evidence on the impact of higher taxes on young adult smoking. Although the smoking participation price-elasticity implied by the baseline model is consistent with previous estimates, it appears to mainly reflect the impact of past taxes on past smoking behaviour. When we control for past taxes, or look at respondents who face a different tax rate in 2000 because they moved to a new state, we find little evidence that current smoking participation is responsive to current taxes.

Our results shed new light on the correct specification of empirical models of smoking participation in general, not just for models of youth or young adult smoking. An important area for future research is to more fully explore the distinctions between smoking initiation, cessation, and participation. The first econometric studies that use cross-sectional microdata on individual smoking behaviour were published over 20-years ago (e.g., Lewit, Coate, & Grossman, 1981; Lewit & Coate, 1982). These studies were an important advance over studies that use aggregate data on tobacco sales, because they can decompose the impact of an influence like tax into its impact on smoking participation plus its impact on the conditional demand by smokers. The richer longitudinal microdata now available provides the opportunity to further decompose smoking participation into a series of initiation and cessation decisions. This decomposition can motivate studies that focus on initiation and cessation per se, but as shown in this chapter it also has important implications for the correct specification of the standard model of smoking participation.

NOTES

1. For example, the 2000 Surgeon General's Report concludes that: "The price of tobacco products has an important influence on the demand for tobacco products,

particularly among young people." (USDHHS, 2000, p. 359; emphasis added.) Similarly, a World Health Organization Report concludes that: "Price increases on tobacco products are one of the most effective means of reducing cigarette smoking. Studies show that a price increase of 10% results in a 2.5–5% smoking reduction in the short run and possibly up to 10% in the long run, if prices are increased to keep pace with inflation. *Young people may reduce their smoking at two to three times the rate of older people."* (Gilbert and Cornuz, 2003; emphasis added.)

2. To clarify our terminology: What we term the structural smoking participation equation includes prior smoking status as an endogenous explanatory variable (because of addiction); what we term the reduced-form smoking participation equation includes the determinants of prior smoking status (e.g., the history of prices) as additional explanatory variables. The structural participation equation is analogous to the linear difference equation derived by Becker, Grossman, and Murphy (1994), where current cigarette consumption is a function of past and future cigarette consumption, the current price of cigarettes, and shift variables. Most studies of rational addiction focus on estimating this structural equation, although the reduced-form equation of current consumption as a function of current, past, and future prices has also been estimated (e.g., Gruber & Kosegi, 2000). Most rational addiction studies also use a continuous measure of smoking. However, Kan and Tsai (2001), and Contoyannis and Jones (2001) estimate structural models of cessation as functions of the level of past smoking. Gilleskie and Strumpf (2000), and Auld (2004) estimate structural models of youth smoking initiation.

3. DeCicca et al. (2004) discuss in more detail the specification of smoking initiation, cessation, and participation equations.

4. For ease of discussion Eq. (3) assumes that the linear probability model is used to estimate the determinants of smoking participation. Most previous studies use probit or logit, so the estimated marginal effect of price on participation is the appropriate transformation of the probit or logit coefficient.

5. Bertrand, Duflo, and Mullainathan (2002), and Helland and Tabarrok (2004) make a similar point in their demonstrations that serial correlation can cause serious problems in inference (deflated standard errors) in difference-in-difference estimates of policy effects.

6. The interpretation of previous price-elasticity estimates as corresponding to the long run is implicit in some earlier studies. But it is inconsistent with the way price-elasticity estimates are often used in policy discussions. During the debate that preceded the 1998 Master Settlement Agreement with the tobacco industry, a consensus emerged that the price-elasticity of adolescent smoking participation was around −0.7 (e.g., CBO, 1998; U.S. Department of the Treasury, 1998). In policy discussions this estimate was often intuitively described as meaning that for every 10% increase in price, the adolescent smoking participation rate would immediately drop by 7%. The predicted effects of policy proposals in testimony before Congress (Harris, 1998) and the U.S. Department of the Treasury, (1998) essentially use price-elasticity estimates in the same way; that is, assuming −0.7 is the short-run rather than the long-run price-elasticity.

7. The CDC (1998), Gruber (2000), and Gruber and Zinman (2001) use data from repeated cross sections, and include state dummies (state fixed effects) to control for unobservable state-level influences on youth smoking. Of course, this strategy does

not address the possibility that within-state variation in cigarette taxes is correlated with within-state variation in anti-smoking sentiment. In addition, both the CDC (1998) and Gruber (2000) adopt the standard mis-specification that fails to account for the role of past prices in smoking participation. As will be discussed below in more detail, Gruber and Zinman (2001) use data on maternal smoking reported on birth statistics to estimate demand models that include both current and past taxes, and control for state fixed effects.

8. NELS staff made special efforts to locate prior respondents for the 2000 wave. These measures included the use of marketing databases and, when possible and necessary, state motor vehicle registries. Additional efforts were made to locate those inherently more difficult to find (e.g., individuals in the military and those incarcerated at time of survey).

9. Given the timing of fourth follow-up interviewing, which occurred between January and September 2000, only one state, New York, presents problems in assigning the appropriate tax rate. New York increased its cigarette tax from 56 to 111 cents, effective March 1, 2000. In previous work with NELS data, we assigned tax based on respondent date of interview, but this information is not available in the fourth follow-up. Since the majority of interviewing occurs after this increase, and since it was announced long before January 2000, we assign a tax of 111 cents to New York residents.

10. We use the CPI-U, defined over all items, as a deflator.

11. We thank Peter Zweifel for suggesting this approach.

12. Cawley, Markowitz, and Tauras (2004) find that the price-responsiveness of smoking is greater for adolescent males than for adolescent females. In Table 3 there is evidence that young adult males are slightly more tax-responsive than females, but the coefficient is not statistically significant at conventional levels. In Table 3 we present the estimated probit coefficients on the various interaction terms. These should be viewed with caution because in a probit model the interaction effect is not the same as marginal effect of the interaction term, and depends on all the covariates in the model (Ai & Norton, 2003).

13. We thank Michael Grossman for pointing this out. Becker, Grossman, and Murphy (1991, Note 3) show that under what they argue is a plausible condition, more future-oriented people will be less price-responsive. The condition involves second and cross-partial derivatives of the utility function. In other words, it requires that "The increase in S [the addictive stock] has a larger effect on its marginal utility than does the increase in c [current consumption]."

14. Similarly, in Table 3 above respondents who scored more highly on standardized tests appear to be less tax-responsive. Kim (2005) analyses the relationships between schooling, time preference, and smoking in more detail.

ACKNOWLEDGEMENTS

We received useful comments from Michael Grossman, Peter Zweifel, and other participants at the *Lund symposium on the economics of substance abuse*, Lund, Sweden, August 12–13, 2004. Comments welcome. All remaining errors remain our responsibility.

REFERENCES

Ai, C., & Norton, E. C. (2003). Interaction terms in logit and probit models. *Economics Letters, 80,* 123–129.

Amemiya, T. (1981). Qualitative response models: A survey. *Journal of Economic Literature, 19,* 1483–1536.

Auld, C. (2004). Causal effect of early initiation on adolescent smoking patterns. *Canadian Journal of Economics* (forthcoming).

Becker, G. S., & Murphy, K. M. (1988). A theory of rational addiction. *Journal of Political Economy, 96*(4), 675–700.

Becker, G. S., Grossman, M., & Murphy, K. M. (1991). Rational addiction and the effect of price on consumption. *American Economic Review/Papers and Proceedings, 81*(2), 237–241.

Becker, G. S., Grossman, M., & Murphy, K. M. (1994). An empirical analysis of cigarette addiction. *American Economic Review, 84*(3), 396–418.

Bertrand, M., Duflo, E., & Mullainathan, S. (2002). *How much should we trust differences-in-differences estimates?* NBER Working Paper No. 8841.

Cawley, J., Markowitz, S., & Tauras, J. (2004). Lighting up and slimming down: The effects of body weight and prices on adolescent smoking initiation. *Journal of Health Economics, 23*(2), 293–311.

Centers for Disease Control [CDC]. (1998). Responses to increase in cigarette prices by race/ethnicity, income, and age groups – United States, 1976–1993. *Morbidity and Mortality Weekly Report, 47*(29), 605–609.

Congressional Budget Office [CBO]. (1998). *The proposed tobacco settlement: Issues from a federal perspective.* CBO Paper, April.

Contoyannis, P., & Jones, A. (2001). Addiction, and adjustment costs: An empirical implementation. In: M. Grossman & C. R. Hsieh (Eds), *The economic analysis of substance use and abuse* (pp. 61–83). Edward Elgar.

DeCicca, P., Kenkel, D. S., & Mathios, A. D. (2002). Putting out the fires: Will higher taxes reduce the onset of youth smoking? *Journal of Political Economy, 110*(1), 144–169.

DeCicca, P., Kenkel, D. S., & Mathios, A. D. (2004). *Cigarette taxes and the transition from youth to adult smoking: Smoking initiation, cessation, and participation.* Working Paper, Department of Policy Analysis & Management, Cornell University.

DeCicca, P., Kenkel, D. S., Mathios, A. D., & Shin, J. (2004). *Youth smoking, taxes, and antismoking sentiment.* Working Paper, Department of Policy Analysis & Management, Cornell University.

Gilbert, A., & Cornuz, J. (2003). *Which are the most effective and cost-effective interventions for tobacco control?* Copenhagen: World Health Organization's Regional Office for Europe's Health Evidence Network.

Gilleskie, D., & Strumpf, K. (2000). *The behavioral dynamics of youth smoking.* NBER Working Paper No. 7838.

Glied, S. (2002). Youth tobacco control: Reconciling theory and empirical evidence. *Journal of Health Economics, 21,* 117–135.

Gruber, J. (2000). *Youth smoking in the U.S.: Prices and policies.* NBER Working Paper 7506.

Gruber, J., & Kosegi, B. (2000). *Is addiction 'rational'? Theory and evidence.* NBER Working Paper 7507.

Gruber, J., & Zinman, J. (2001). Youth smoking in the United States: Evidence and implications. In: J. Gruber (Ed.), *Risky behavior among youths: An economic analysis* (pp. 69–120). Chicago and London: The University of Chicago Press.

Harris, J. E. (1998). *Economic analysis of proposed legislation*. Memorandum prepared at the request of the staff of Senator Kent Conrad, Chair, Senate Democratic Task Force on Tobacco. January 21.

Helland, E., & Tabarrok, A. (2004). Using placebo laws to test "more guns less crime". *Advances in Economic Analysis & Policy*, 4(1), Article 1.

Hersch, J. (1998). Teen smoking behavior and the regulatory environment. *Duke Law Review* pp. 1143–1170.

Hunter, W. J., & Nelson, M. A. (1992). The political economy of state tobacco taxation. *Public Finance/Finances Publiques*, 47(2), 214–228.

Kan, K., & Tsai, W.-D. (2001). Rational cessation and re-initiation of cigarette smoking: Evidence from Taiwan. In: M. Grossman & C.-R. Hsieh (Eds), *Economic analysis of substance use and abuse*. Northampton, MA: Edward Elgar.

Kim, S. (2005). *Endogenous time preference and addiction*. Ph.D. dissertation, The City University of New York, New York.

Lewit, E., & Coate, D. (1982). The potential for using excise taxes to reduce smoking. *Journal of Health Economics*, 1, 121–145.

Lewit, E., Coate, D., & Grossman, M. (1981). The effects of Government Regulation on teenage smoking. *Journal of Law and Economics*, 24, 545–573.

McFadden, D. L. (1974). Conditional logit analysis of qualitative choice analysis. In: P. Zarembak (Ed.), *Frontiers in econometrics* (pp. 105–142). New York: Academic Press.

Moffit, R., Fitzgerald, J., & Gottschalk, P. (1999). Sample attrition in panel data: The role of selection on observables. *Annales D'Economie et de Statistique*, 55–56.

Powell, L. M., & Chaloupka, F. J. (2005). Parents, public policy, and youth smoking behavior. *Journal of Policy Analysis and Management*, 24(1), 93–112.

U.S. Department of the Treasury. (1998). *The economic costs of smoking in the United States and the benefits of comprehensive tobacco legislation*. Washington, DC: U.S. Department of the Treasury.

U.S. Department of Health and Human Services [USDHHS] (2000). *Reducing tobacco use: A report of the surgeon general*. Atlanta, Georgia: U.S. Department of Health and Human Services, Centers for Disease Control and Prevention, National Center for Chronic Disease Prevention and Health Promotion, Office on Smoking and Health.

Verbeek, M., & Nijman, T. (1992). Testing for selectivity bias in panel data models. *International Economic Review*, 33(3), 681–703.

Wakefield, M. A., Chaloupka, F. J., Kaufman, N. J. et al. (2000). *Do restrictions on smoking at home, at school and in public places influence teenage smoking?* ImpacTeen Research Paper Series, no. 3.

Warner, K. E. (1982). Cigarette excise taxation and interstate smuggling: An assessment of recent activity. *National Tax Journal*, 35, 483–490.

Wasserman, J., Manning, W. G., Newhouse, J. P., & Winkler, J. D. (1991). The effects of excise taxes and regulations on cigarette smoking. *Journal of Health Economics*, 10, 43–64.

Wooldridge, J. M. (2002a). *Inverse probability weighted M-estimators for sample selection, attrition, and stratification*. Centre for Microdata Methods and Practice working paper no. CWP 11/02.

Wooldridge, J. M. (2002b). *Econometric analysis of cross section and panel data*. Cambridge: The MIT Press.

COUPONS AND ADVERTISING IN MARKETS FOR ADDICTIVE GOODS: DO CIGARETTE MANUFACTURERS REACT TO KNOWN FUTURE TAX INCREASES?

Dean R. Lillard and Andrew Sfekas

ABSTRACT

We develop and test a pricing model for a monopolist that sells an addictive good. The model illustrates the conditions under which a monopolist lowers the price he charges youth when a future tax is imposed. Using household survey data, we investigate whether individuals use "cents-off" coupons in a way consistent with the price discrimination implied by the model. We find evidence that all smokers, not just the young, are more likely to use coupons prior to a tax increase if they are exposed to more advertising. With our data we cannot test whether cigarette manufacturers selectively offer youth price discounts in other ways.

1. INTRODUCTION

In most studies of cigarette demand, researchers assume that cigarette manufacturers do not have market power. That is, no firm has enough market share to significantly influence the market price. In a market as highly concentrated as the cigarette industry, this assumption may be inappropriate. In 2003, three firms accounted for about 80% of all cigarettes sold in the U.S. With the merger of RJ Reynolds and Brown & Williamson in October of 2003, two firms now account for 80% of sales.

Evidence from empirical studies of the cigarette market suggests that regulatory barriers give cigarette manufacturers some market power within states. Keeler, Hu, Barnett, Manning, and Sung (1996) find that there is some evidence that cigarette makers can vary the price they charge in different states and that market concentration helps determine the degree of pricing power that cigarette makers can exercise. Such price discrimination is possible in cigarette markets because the federal government forbids buying cigarettes in one state and selling them in another. Sumner (1981) also finds evidence that supports the hypothesis that cigarette manufacturers have market power. He finds that in states that recently raised cigarette taxes the average price of cigarettes raises by more than the amount of the tax increase. A tax pass through of more than one is predicted by a monopoly-pricing model. However, a later study by Ashenfelter and Sullivan (1987) finds that monopoly models do not predict pricing behaviour in cigarette markets.

The question of whether cigarette manufacturers are able to set prices matters for reasons beyond the simple issue of non-competitive behaviour because cigarettes deliver nicotine – a substance that has been shown to be addictive.

Two theoretical studies discuss how price-setting behaviour varies when the good being sold is addictive. Showalter (1999) shows that a monopolist sets the current price of an addictive good by trading off current loss of profits against future profits that result from increased future consumption of new addicts. The implication flows from a model in which consumers are assumed to be myopic (i.e., they do not consider the future consequences of their behaviour), but the monopolist is rational. To maximize discounted profits, the monopolist sets a lower price for an addictive good than he does for a non-addictive good. In a model of rational consumption of addictive goods, Becker, Grossman, and Murphy (1994a) use a fairly general consumer utility function to show that, under some circumstances, the current price of an addictive good will rise when future taxes increase.

The above two strands of literature establish first that cigarette manufacturers may have market power to set prices (within states) and that the pricing behaviour of a monopolist selling an addictive good varies with whether consumers are myopic or forward-looking rational actors.

What these studies have not done is to recognize that a monopolist selling an addictive good has strong incentives to price discriminate in favour of young (non-addicted) consumers. Neither Showalter (1999) nor Becker, Grossman, and Murphy (1994a) model showed how the incentive to price discriminate changes when a monopolist selling an addictive good faces a future tax increase.

In this chapter we model and empirically investigate one of the many ways that cigarette manufacturers can selectively market their products: The issuance of price discount coupons. Consumers who receive these coupons can use them to purchase cigarettes at a price lower than the retail price.

Coupons could affect demand in several different ways. Manufacturers may target coupons at current smokers to encourage them to switch brands, or to encourage them to remain with the same brand. Alternatively, manufacturers may target coupons at light smokers to encourage them to smoke more or at non-smokers to encourage them to start smoking. This chapter examines this second possibility, that manufacturers use coupons to encourage new smokers.

2. THEORETICAL MODEL

This section lays out a basic theoretical model to highlight the conditions under which a monopolist will issue coupons in the face of a future increase in taxes. We assume that a monopolist offers discount coupons in order to price discriminate among groups with different price elasticities of demand. The monopolist discriminates between two groups – old consumers and young consumers. As old consumers live for only one period, the monopolist has no incentive to change the price he charges them when he knows that taxes will go up in the next period. Young consumers live for two periods. If taxes are expected to increase in the next period, the monopolist will change the price he charges young consumers in period 1 if doing so maximizes his profits.

The basic framework is a model in which a single representative consumer lives for two periods. Let the consumer purchases quantities be Q_1 and Q_2 in periods 1 and 2, respectively. The monopolist chooses prices P_1 and P_2, and faces constant marginal costs C_1 and C_2.

We incorporate addiction into the model in the usual way, by specifying the consumer's demand in period 2 as a function of the price in period 2 and the quantity consumed in period 1:

$$Q_2 = Q_2(P_2, Q_1) \tag{1}$$

where $\partial Q_2/\partial P_2 < 0$, $\partial Q_2/\partial Q_1 > 0$, $\partial^2 Q_2/\partial P_2^2 \leq 0$ and $\partial^2 Q_2/\partial Q_1^2 < 0$. The derivative of quantity demanded in period 2 with respect to the quantity demanded in period 1 measures the addictive nature of the good. The higher is the quantity demanded in period 2 for a given increase in period 1, the more addictive is the good.

Following Becker and Murphy (1988), we allow consumers to be forward looking, that is, they pay attention to the fact that smoking more now will cause them to smoke more later. Studies by Chaloupka (1991), Gruber and Koszegi (2001), and Keeler, Marciniak, and Hu (1999) provide empirical evidence to support the assumption that consumers are forward looking.

The consumer's demand in period 1 is a function of the price in period 1 and the price in period 2:

$$Q_1 = Q_1(P_1, P_2) \tag{2}$$

where $\partial Q_1/\partial P_1 < 0$ and $\partial Q_1/\partial P_2 \leq 0$. If $\partial Q_1/\partial P_2$ is strictly less than 0, the consumer is forward looking because a higher future price reduces current consumption.

The monopolist's second-period profit-maximization problem is:

$$\max_{P_2} Q_2(P_2, Q_1)(P_2 - C_2) \tag{3}$$

With some assumptions, it is possible to define implicit functions for P_2^*, Q_2^*, and π_2^*, the second-period optimal values for price, quantity, and profits, respectively. The implicit functions can be defined in terms of the parameter C_2 and first-period quantity Q_1. The derivatives with respect to cost are $\partial P_2/\partial C_2 > 0$, $\partial Q_2/\partial C_2 < 0$, and $\partial \pi_2/\partial C_2 < 0$. The derivatives with respect to Q_1 are all positive.

In the first period, the monopolist solves the profit-maximization problem:

$$\max_{P_1} Q_1(P_1, P_2)(P_1 - C_1) + \lambda \pi_2(Q_2(P_2, Q_1), P_2, C_2) \tag{4}$$

where λ is the monopolist's discount rate.

The first-order condition (FOC) is:

$$Q_1 + \frac{\partial Q_1}{\partial P_1}(P_1 - C_1) + \lambda \left(\frac{\partial \pi_2}{\partial Q_2}\right)\left(\frac{\partial Q_2}{\partial Q_1}\right)\left(\frac{\partial Q_1}{\partial P_1}\right) = 0 \tag{5}$$

When the good is not addictive, that is when demand is not linked across periods, $\partial Q_2/\partial Q_1 = 0$ and the above expression simplifies to the standard one-period profit-maximizing FOC.

However, as Showalter (1999) shows, when a good is addictive, the optimum quantity sold in the first period will be higher, and the price will be lower, than in the case where demand is not linked between periods. If no new consumers enter, the price in period 2 must be higher than the price in period 1 because the monopolist could raise the price to the one-period profit-maximizing level and have higher profits than if the monopolist kept prices at the period 1 level.

The goal of the above model is to show how price in period 1 changes when the monopolist knows that a tax will be imposed (or raised) on cigarettes in period 2. We treat the tax as equivalent to an increase in C_2, the period 2 cost. Taking the total differential of the FOC for first-period profit maximization with respect to P_1 and C_2 and rearranging terms yields:

$$\frac{dP_1}{dC_2} = -\frac{(A)+(B)+(C)+(D)+(E)+(F)+(G)+(H)+(I)}{2\frac{\partial Q_1}{\partial P_1} + (P_1 - C_1)\frac{\partial^2 Q_1}{\partial P_1^2} + \lambda \frac{\partial^2 \pi_2}{\partial Q_1^2}\left(\frac{\partial Q_1}{\partial P_1}\right)^2 + \lambda \frac{\partial \pi_2}{\partial Q_1}\frac{\partial^2 Q_2}{\partial P_1^2}} \quad (6)$$

where the terms (A)–(I) are given by:

$$(A) = \frac{\partial Q_1}{\partial P_2}\frac{\partial P_2}{\partial C_2} < 0$$

$$(B) = (P_1 - C_1)\frac{\partial^2 Q_1}{\partial P_1 \partial P_2}\frac{\partial P_2}{\partial C_2} > 0$$

$$(C) = \lambda \frac{\partial^2 \pi_2}{\partial Q_2^2}\frac{\partial Q_2}{\partial Q_1}\frac{\partial Q_1}{\partial P_1}\frac{\partial Q_2}{\partial P_2}\frac{\partial P_2}{\partial C_2} < 0$$

$$(D) = \lambda \frac{\partial^2 \pi_2}{\partial Q_2^2}\left(\frac{\partial Q_2}{\partial Q_1}\right)^2 \frac{\partial Q_1}{\partial P_1}\frac{\partial Q_1}{\partial P_2}\frac{\partial P_2}{\partial C_2} < 0$$

$$(E) = \lambda \frac{\partial^2 \pi_2}{\partial Q_2 \partial P_2}\frac{\partial Q_2}{\partial Q_1}\frac{\partial Q_1}{\partial P_1}\frac{\partial P_2}{\partial C_2} > 0$$

$$(F) = \lambda \frac{\partial^2 \pi_2}{\partial Q_2 \partial C_2}\frac{\partial Q_2}{\partial Q_1}\frac{\partial Q_1}{\partial P_1} > 0$$

$$(\text{G}) = \lambda \frac{\partial \pi_2}{\partial Q_2} \frac{\partial^2 Q_2}{\partial Q_1 \partial P_2} \frac{\partial Q_1}{\partial P_1} \frac{\partial P_2}{\partial C_2} \leqslant 0$$

$$(\text{H}) = \lambda \frac{\partial \pi_2}{\partial Q_2} \frac{\partial^2 Q_2}{\partial Q_1^2} \frac{\partial Q_1}{\partial P_1} \frac{\partial Q_1}{\partial P_2} \frac{\partial P_2}{\partial C_2} < 0$$

$$(\text{I}) = \lambda \frac{\partial \pi_2}{\partial Q_2} \frac{\partial Q_2}{\partial Q_1} \frac{\partial^2 Q_1}{\partial P_1 \partial P_2} \frac{\partial P_2}{\partial C_2} > 0$$

The denominator is the second-order condition with respect to P_1. At the optimum, this should be negative.

The sign of the numerator depends on the nature of the addictive relationship, on whether consumers are forward looking, and on the relative magnitudes of the terms (A)–(I) that remain after one adopts a particular assumption on these two relationships.

When consumers are myopic they do not consider the second-period price they will face when they decide how much to consume in the first period. Thus, $\partial Q_1 / \partial P_2 = 0$. In this case, terms (A) = (B) = (D) = (H) = (I) = 0.

In the most general formulation shown above, the numerator depends on the relative magnitudes of the positive and negative terms. That is, the sign of the total differential depends on whether (A) + (C) + (D) + (G) + (H) is greater than or less than (B) + (E) + (F) + (I) in absolute value.

Term (A) captures the effect of an increase in C_2 on first-period profits through its direct effect on first-period demand. It reflects the forward-looking behaviour of consumers who lower their demand in anticipation of higher future prices.

Terms (B) and (I) capture the effect of an increase in C_2 on first-period profits through its effect on the slope of the first-period demand with respect to the first-period price.

Together, terms (C), (D), (E), and (F) capture how an increase in C_2 affects first-period profits through the effect of that change on the marginal profitability of a unit sold in period.

Finally, terms (G) and (H) capture how an increase in C_2 affects first-period profits through the effect of that change on the relationship between second-period consumption and first-period consumption.

The sign of the total derivative cannot be established without knowing the relative magnitudes of the above terms. Becker, Grossman, and Murphy (1994b) derive quantity demanded from a Cobb–Douglas function for a representative consumer. Their derived demand functions are:

$$Q_1 = a_1 P_1^{-\varepsilon_1} P_2^{-g\gamma} \tag{7}$$

$$Q_2 = a_2 P_2^{-\varepsilon_2} Q_1^{\gamma} \tag{8}$$

where $\varepsilon_1 > 0$, $\varepsilon_2 > 0$, and $0 \leqslant \gamma < 1$.

With these demand functions, the total effect of the additional terms is ambiguous. The term $(\partial Q_1/\partial P_2)(\partial P_2/\partial C_2)$ is negative, but the other two additional terms are positive. Thus, the net effect of an increase in second-period costs on first-period price could be in either direction.

The monopolist will lower the price charged to young (less-addicted) consumers if the absolute magnitude of the negative terms above exceed the absolute magnitude of the positive terms. In general the monopolist is more likely to lower the first-period price when consumers are more forward looking (terms (A), (C), (D), and (H)), if the slope of the first-period demand relative to first-period price does not vary much with respect to an increase in the second-period price (terms (B) and (I)), if the second-period marginal profits from second-period sales do not change much when second-period costs or price increase (terms (E) and (F)), and when the addictive nature of the good does not vary when second-period price changes (term (G)).

Under these conditions and if the manufacturer is able to use coupons to price discriminate, the model implies that the manufacturer will target coupons at the group that should receive the lower price – younger consumers. When the future tax changes, manufacturers should respond by adjusting the number or amount of price discount coupons offered to younger consumers.

3. DATA AND METHODS

The theoretical model predicts that an increase in taxes in period 2 will lower the price charged to younger consumers in period 1 only under certain conditions. However, it is possible to make some testable predictions. First, if firms can price discriminate between older and younger smokers, they will charge the younger smokers a lower price. Additionally, they will change the price for younger smokers when the next-period tax increases, but leave the price for older smokers unchanged. We will test the price discounting implication by using an individual-level data set to determine whether individuals are more likely to use coupons just prior to a cigarette tax increase.

While we do not have data on prices paid by smokers, their smoking history, or the intensity of their smoking habit, we do have data on whether smokers use coupons to buy tobacco products. We estimate the probability that a smoker uses tobacco discount coupons as a function of current and future taxes and as a function of cigarette advertising to which he or she is exposed.

Under the conditions described above, a future tax increase will cause manufacturers to issue more discount coupons in selective ways in the months leading up to the tax increase. We include a measure of cigarette advertising in our analysis for two reasons. First, manufacturers might use advertising to deliver coupons directly to their target audience.[1] Second, advertising may raise general demand for cigarettes and thereby raise the probability that an individual uses a coupon.

In Table 1, we report summary statistics for the data we draw from several sources. The data on state tax rates come from the *Tax Burden on Tobacco*, which was formerly published by the Tobacco Institute, and is now published by Orzechowski and Walker. Individual-level data come from the *National Consumer Survey* of the *Simmons Survey of Media and Markets: Choices II (NCS)*. The NCS contains individual-level information on coupon use, demographic information, smoking status, magazine readership, and state of residence. Our data are drawn from the following surveys – fall 1995, spring 1996, spring and fall 1997, spring and fall 1998, and fall 1999.

Our advertising data comes from the Smoking Cessation Advertisements Database (SCADS). The SCADS database, collected and archived at Cornell University, consists of advertising appearing in 27 popular magazines and 2 physician journals during the period January 1985 through May 2002. The magazines included in the SCADS database were drawn from a list of 182 magazine titles. A magazine was included if it was one of the ten magazines most frequently read in 1999 by people with pre-selected demographic characteristics (age, gender, race, education, and income). Readership rankings for each magazine were constructed using survey information on demographics and magazine readership of the approximately 20,000 consumers included in the *NCS*. The readers of the 27 magazines in the SCADS sample comprise about 60% of national magazine readers.

Included in the SCADS database are 10 weekly, 2 bi-weekly, and 17 monthly magazines contributing a total of 13,497 individual magazine issues over the sampling period. The database contains digital copies of all advertisements for smoking, smoking cessation, and smoking-related public service announcements appearing in the SCADS magazine sample.

Using these data we calculate the fraction of the last four issues of each magazine that each respondent has read. We do so for the magazines that are in both the Simmons and SCADS data sets. We then assume that this

Table 1. Summary Statistics for Coupon Model.

	Full Sample	Smokers Only
Per cent use coupons for tobacco products	0.102	0.298
	(0.302)	(0.457)
Current tax (6 month average)	0.269	0.264
	(0.137)	(0.134)
Future tax increase (6 month average)	0.007	0.006
	(0.036)	(0.034)
Per cent female	0.550	0.550
	(0.497)	(0.498)
Per cent white	0.873	0.875
	(0.333)	(0.331)
Per cent black	0.078	0.084
	(0.268)	(0.277)
Per cent married	0.618	0.530
	(0.486)	(0.499)
Per cent divorced	0.099	0.151
	(0.299)	(0.358)
Per cent widowed	0.065	0.056
	(0.246)	(0.230)
Per cent separated	0.023	0.035
	(0.150)	(0.183)
Age	45.622	42.759
	(15.830)	(14.295)
Per cent unemployed	0.032	0.047
	(0.176)	(0.213)
Household income/1000	6.594	5.830
	(4.939)	(4.459)
Highest grade completed	13.778	13.013
	(2.487)	(2.232)
Ads exposed to (annual)	1.187	1.295
	(1.233)	(1.328)
Number of observations	62,478	13,848

fraction proxies for the fraction of issues of each magazine the respondent has read over the past year. We label this fraction Ads_{ijt} where the subscripts denote respondent i in state j in year t. We know, from our SCADS data, exactly how many cigarette advertisements appeared in each magazine over the course of the sample year. Using these data we calculate the number of advertisements to which a respondent was potentially exposed in each year. We first multiply the fraction of issues of each magazine the respondent read times the number of advertisements that appeared in each magazine over the previous year. We then sum across all magazines in the SCADS sample. The resulting sum is our measure of potential exposure to smoking-related magazine advertisements.

Table 1 contains the summary statistics for the coupon-use model. The summary statistics show that about 10% of everyone in the sample and 30% of smokers use coupons for tobacco products. The sample population has a higher percentage of whites than the U.S. population. The full sample and the smokers-only sample are similar in terms of education, race, and gender. Smokers in this sample have somewhat lower incomes, are less likely to be married, are younger, and are more likely to be unemployed than the full sample. Smokers also see slightly more ads.

We note that our dependent variable, whether a person used a coupon to buy tobacco products, is a composite variable that results from both a decision by a firm and from a decision by an individual. Manufacturers decide whether to offer a "cents-off" coupon and to whom the coupons will be targeted. These decisions by firms affect the probability that an individual is exposed to a "cents-off" coupon. Given that an individual receives (or has the chance to use) a "cents-off" coupon, he or she then decides whether or not to use it. As our data are measured only at the individual level, the coefficients in our models on individual demographic characteristics will mix the above two processes. Consequently, the coefficients can only be interpreted in terms of the net effect of each variable on coupon usage. For example, consider how to interpret the coefficient on demographic variables. Our model predicts that, under the above stated conditions, a monopolist should charge a lower price to younger smokers, so younger individuals should be more likely to use coupons. However, younger individuals might find using coupons more costly to use than do older smokers, so the supply effect is not identified. Instead, we observe the net association between age and the probability of coupon use.

The changes in coupon use in response to future tax increases should be identifiable as supply effects. The manufacturer should change the supply of coupons prior to a tax increase. Except for hoarding, the consumer has no additional incentive to use coupons, and certainly no incentive not to use them.

4. RESULTS

To test our predictions, we estimate probit models of the probability that an individual uses a "cents-off" coupon for tobacco products. The empirical model can be specified as:

$$\tilde{Y}_{ijt} = \beta_0 + \beta_1 Tax_{j,t+1} + \beta_2 Ads_{ijt} + \beta_3 Age_{ijt} + \beta_4 Age_{ijt} * Ads_{ijt}$$
$$+ \beta_5 Age_{ijt} * Tax_{j,t+1} + X_{ijt}\gamma + \varepsilon_{ijt} \qquad (9)$$

$$Y_{ijt} = 1 \quad \text{if } \tilde{Y}_{ijt} > 0$$
$$Y_{ijt} = 0 \quad \text{otherwise}$$

where i is the individual, j is the state, and t is the time period.

We estimate the model for two groups of respondents – the entire sample and smokers only. Table 2 presents the results of this analysis.

In our analysis we specify the current tax as the average real tax rate for the current month and previous 5 months. The measure of future taxes (size of future tax increase) is the average of the next 6 months minus the current tax variable. Female, white, black, married, divorced, separated, widowed, and unemployed are indicator variables.

The results show several patterns of use. First, whites are more likely than other races to use coupons, and blacks are less likely. Household income is negatively associated with coupon use. Women are more likely to use coupons than men.

Younger individuals are less likely to use coupons for tobacco than older individuals. This association is not consistent with the idea of offering less-addicted individuals a lower price. However, as mentioned above, this association is probably a mix of the individual's decision to use a coupon and the firm's decision to offer it.

We estimate three additional specifications of the basic model to examine whether coupons are being used to segment the market between more-addicted and less-addicted consumers. We first interact age with the future tax. Our model suggests that the coefficient on this interaction term should be negative and significant. In the results shown in Table 2, the coefficient on the interaction between age and future taxes is positive but not statistically different from zero. We also interact the advertising in youth-oriented magazines with the future tax to see if advertising in those magazines raises the probability that younger use coupons to buy tobacco. This interaction was also insignificant.

Our data do not identify the source of the tobacco coupon used. It is possible that coupons directed at newer smokers would be more likely to show up in magazines than in other sources. Model 3 includes two more interactions – age with cigarette ad exposure, and age with future tax and ad

Table 2. Probit Models of Probability of Coupon Use.

	All Respondents			Smokers Only		
Current tax	−0.096**	−0.096**	−0.096**	−0.185*	−0.185*	−0.186*
	(0.023)	(0.023)	(0.023)	(0.079)	(0.079)	(0.079)
Size of future tax increase	−0.138**	−0.167	−0.170	−0.210	−0.251	−0.244
	(0.044)	(0.115)	(0.116)	(0.154)	(0.416)	(0.417)
Respondent female	0.001	0.001	0.001	0.065**	0.065**	0.065**
	(0.002)	(0.002)	(0.002)	(0.008)	(0.008)	(0.008)
Respondent white	0.025**	0.025**	0.025**	0.050*	0.050*	0.050*
	(0.005)	(0.005)	(0.005)	(0.020)	(0.020)	(0.020)
Respondent black	−0.027**	−0.027**	−0.027**	−0.107**	−0.107**	−0.108**
	(0.006)	(0.006)	(0.006)	(0.021)	(0.021)	(0.021)
Respondent married	−0.002	−0.002	−0.002	0.052**	0.052**	0.052**
	(0.004)	(0.004)	(0.004)	(0.012)	(0.012)	(0.012)
Respondent divorced	0.017**	0.017**	0.017**	0.020	0.020	0.020
	(0.005)	(0.005)	(0.005)	(0.015)	(0.015)	(0.015)
Respondent widowed	0.004	0.004	0.005	0.006	0.006	0.005
	(0.006)	(0.006)	(0.006)	(0.021)	(0.021)	(0.021)
Respondent separated	0.011	0.011	0.011	0.016	0.016	0.016
	(0.008)	(0.008)	(0.008)	(0.024)	(0.024)	(0.024)
Respondent's age	0.009**	0.009**	0.009**	0.023**	0.023**	0.022**
	(0.000)	(0.000)	(0.001)	(0.002)	(0.002)	(0.002)
Age squared	−0.0001**	−0.0001**	−0.0001**	−0.0002**	−0.0002**	−0.0002**
	(0.000)	(0.000)	(0.000)	(0.000)	(0.000)	(0.000)
Unemployed	0.029**	0.029**	0.029**	0.021	0.021	0.021
	(0.007)	(0.007)	(0.007)	(0.019)	(0.019)	(0.019)
Household income	−0.003**	−0.003**	−0.003**	−0.006**	−0.006**	−0.006**
	(0.000)	(0.000)	(0.000)	(0.001)	(0.001)	(0.001)
Highest grade completed	−0.015**	−0.015**	−0.015**	−0.014**	−0.014**	−0.014**
	(0.000)	(0.000)	(0.000)	(0.002)	(0.002)	(0.002)
Ad exposure/100	0.007**	0.007**	0.009**	0.008*	0.008*	−0.004
	(0.001)	(0.001)	(0.003)	(0.003)	(0.003)	(0.010)
Age* size of tax increase		0.001	0.000		0.001	0.002
		(0.002)	(0.003)		(0.009)	(0.009)
Age* ad exposure			−0.000			0.000
			(0.000)			(0.000)
Age* exposure* tax increase			0.000			−0.001
			(0.001)			(0.002)
Observations	62,478	62,478	62,478	13,848	13,848	13,848

*, **, and *** indicate statistical significance at <10%, <5%, and <1% levels, respectively. Standard errors in parentheses. All models contain state and year effects.

exposure. The effect is insignificant, so the results do not support the hypothesis that manufacturers target coupons in this way.

Overall, the empirical evidence suggests that younger consumers are less likely to use "cents-off" coupons to buy tobacco products. We find evidence that, rather than raising the probability of coupon use, a higher future tax lowers the probability that an individual uses coupons. We find no difference in the propensity to use coupons of younger and older consumers who face a future tax increase. Since observed coupon use results from decisions by manufacturers to issue and target coupons, and from decisions by individuals to use or not use those coupons, our findings leave open the question of whether manufacturers use "cents-off" coupons to price discriminate in response to a future tax increase.

5. CONCLUSION

This chapter explored whether a monopolist who sells an addictive good and who faces a future tax increase will choose to price discriminate in favour of younger (less-addicted) consumers. Our model predicts that, under certain conditions, he will. In general, the empirical analysis of "cents-off" coupon use data do not support the predictions of the theory. Although our empirical results show that all consumers and all smokers are more likely to use coupons when they are exposed to more advertising, there is no evidence that the average (young or old) consumer uses coupon more in response to future price increases.

This lack of correlation could occur either because there is truly no association or because even these data are too noisy to identify the association. For example, the survey data we use does not identify the exact date that questions were answered. Therefore, we cannot know exactly what tax to assign each individual. We have adopted the most conservative assumption – that answers were given at the end of each sample period. In future work we will explore whether the results are sensitive to this assumption. We also note that coupons are not the only method of price discrimination. For example, manufacturers also offer price discounts that do not require coupons. Our analysis does not consider alternative forms of price discrimination. Thus, it is still possible that manufacturers change the prices for younger consumers when future taxes increase.

Future research should attempt to determine whether manufacturers use other types of price discrimination to increase smoking among younger individuals. The future investigation will require high-quality price data that allows researchers to track price changes geographically and over short periods of time. In particular, researchers need access to data that measure prices actually paid at a level of geographic aggregation lower than a state. Most researchers do not have access to such high-quality data. Instead most researchers use data aggregated (usually averaged) at the state level.[2] High-quality price data are necessary, however, because, if manufacturers do price discriminate, they are likely to do so in sub-markets in a given state. Consequently, averaging of prices within a given state is likely to mask any price discrimination.

NOTES

1. For example, a manual search of selected Marlboro and Belair advertisements in an archive of cigarette advertising uncovered coupons offering free packs of cigarettes only for Marlboro cigarettes. The coupons were included in advertising in August and September 1989. The coupons were attached to advertisements that appeared in Cosmopolitan, People, Playboy, Rolling Stone, and Sports Illustrated.

2. Auld and Grootendorst (2004) illustrate how aggregate data can lead to spurious estimates by estimating a model of rational addiction for milk.

ACKNOWLEDGEMENTS

This research is part of a larger smoking cessation research project underway at Cornell University. That project is funded by NIH/NCI grant (5 R01 CA94020, 4/20/02–3/31/06). This chapter would not have been possible without the help and cooperation of our project colleagues at Cornell University – Rosemary Avery, Donald Kenkel, Alan Mathios, and the team of undergraduate research assistants on the smoking cessation research team. The chapter has benefitted from the thoughtful comments of Sören Höjgård and participants at the *24th Arne Ryde symposium*. We also received helpful comments from Mark Showalter, Phil DeCicca, Alan Mathios, and Donald Kenkel. We thank Eamon Molloy for expert research assistance. All errors that remain we blame on each other.

REFERENCES

Ashenfelter, O., & Sullivan, D. (1987). Nonparametric tests of market structure: An application to the cigarette industry. *The Journal of Industrial Economics, 35*(4), 483–498.

Auld, M. C., & Grootendorst, P. (2004). An empirical analysis of milk addiction. *Journal of Health Economics, 23*(6), 1117–1133.
Becker, G. S., & Murphy, K. M. (1988). A theory of rational addiction. *The Journal of Political Economy, 96*(4), 675–700.
Becker, G. S., Grossman, M., & Murphy, K. M. (1994a). An empirical analysis of cigarette addiction. *The American Economic Review, 84*(3), 396–418.
Becker, G. S., Grossman, M., & Murphy, K. M. (1994b). *An empirical analysis of cigarette addiction.* NBER Working Paper no. w3322.
Chaloupka, F. (1991). Rational addictive behaviour and cigarette smoking. *The Journal of Political Economy, 99*(4), 722–742.
Gruber, J., & Koszegi, B. (2001). Is addiction "rational"? Theory and evidence. *The Quarterly Journal of Economics, 116*(4), 1261–1303.
Keeler, T. E., Hu, T.-W., Barnett, P. G., Manning, W. G., & Sung, H.-Y. (1996). Do cigarette producers price-discriminate by state? An empirical analysis of local cigarette pricing and taxation. *Journal of Health Economics, 15*, 499–512.
Keeler, T. E., Marciniak, M., & Hu, T.-W. (1999). Rational addiction and smoking cessation: An empirical study. *The Journal of Socio-Economics, 28*, 633–643.
Showalter, M. H. (1999). Firm behaviour in a market with addiction: The case of cigarettes. *Journal of Health Economics, 18*, 409–427.
Sumner, D. A. (1981). Measurement of monopoly behaviour: An application to the cigarette industry. *The Journal of Political Economy, 89*(5), 1010–1019.

PART IV: POLITICS

SYMBOLISM AND RATIONALITY IN THE POLITICS OF PSYCHOACTIVE SUBSTANCES

Robin Room

ABSTRACT

Psychoactive substances take on many symbolic meanings, and thus the politics of psychoactive substances has featured symbolic elements, or value-based rationality, alongside and often dominating instrumental rationality. Drawing particularly on the work of Joseph Gusfield and Nordic scholars, the chapter considers the symbolic dimension in the politics of substance use, even in Nordic countries celebrated for their societal commitment to knowledge-based policymaking, and its effects on the interplay of science and policy.

INTRODUCTION

The present chapter considers, particularly in a Nordic context, the place of symbolism and symbolic action in the politics of psychoactive substances. In addition to the use-values derived from their physical properties (Mäkelä, 1983), it is argued, psychoactive substances take on many symbolic meanings in daily life. Some of the properties of psychoactive substances which lie behind their symbolic power at both the personal and the political level are considered. The chapter then considers several analyses of symbolism and rationality, and their relationship in the politics of psychoactive substances: Gusfield's classic analysis of the U.S. temperance movement as a "symbolic crusade", and more recent analyses of the symbolic dimension in the Nordic politics of substance use. Drawing on a recent analysis by Boudon, and in keeping with Gusfield's interpretation, it is argued that values-based rationality must be considered alongside instrumental rationality in understanding human actions. As Boudon points out, values-based or prescriptive belief systems often incorporate instrumental statements, so that science-based arguments are often used in values-based as well as in instrumentally oriented policy arguments. Some implications of this for the interplay of value-based and consequentialist arguments are considered, with examples from the Swedish policy context.

THE SYMBOLIC POWER OF PSYCHOACTIVE SUBSTANCE USE

The use or non-use of psychoactive substances, and the manner, amount, and history of use, have carried strong symbolic meaning throughout human history. Use often carries positive associations and symbolism. Mere mention of the word "champagne", for instance, conjures up an image of celebration and luxury, even in those who have never drunk the beverage. In pre-industrial times, access to psychoactive substances was often limited to the powerful or the wealthy, so that use of them, and particularly copious use, became a mark of high status, as in the courts of the early modern Russian czars (Smith & Christian, 1984). At the opposite end of the scale, abstaining from a drug can also carry strong symbolic meaning. Abstaining from alcohol, for instance, is a mark of faithful adherence for Muslims and for some Christian denominations. For a working-class man to be an abstainer in 19th-century Britain, Harrison (1971) noted, was a signal of ambition, that he wanted his children to get ahead in the world, and similar themes can be found today, in such places as Papua New Guinea (Room, 1983) and in some immigrant groups (Gordon, 1978).

On the other hand, use or heavy use of psychoactive substances often carries a negative and derogated symbolic meaning. In the U.S.A. in 1900, for instance, to be seen drinking would immediately threaten a middle-class woman's respectability, and the idea that being seen with a drink in her hand threatened a woman's reputation survived well after that (Room, 1991). In recent decades, politicians shy away from admitting use of an illicit drug, even long in the past, because of what the use would be taken to mean. In terms of heavy use, drinking or drug use patterns become the defining characteristics of the person when such terms as "drunkard" or "dope fiend" are applied. To call the person instead "dependent" or an "addict" or "substance abuser" may be to shift to a medicalized or semi-medicalized terminology, but it is not clear that the symbolic meaning and the associated stigma changes much. Thus both alcoholism and drug addiction ranked near the top, in terms of the degree of social disapproval or stigma reported by informants on 18 different characteristics, in nearly all of the 14 countries in a World Health Organization (WHO) study – in all but two countries, for instance, above being "dirty and unkempt"; in all but three being a drug addict was reported to be more disapproved or stigmatized than having a criminal record for burglary (Room, Rehm, Trotter II, Paglia, & Üstün, 2001, p. 276). Conversely, non-use of a drug, or opposition to its use, can also carry a negative symbolism, as in the Australian term "wowser" (Dunstan, 1974).

Cultural attitudes towards different psychoactive substances have varied greatly from one place and time to another (Courtwright, 2001), and the nature, valence, and strength of their symbolic import have varied at least as much.

BEHIND THE SYMBOLIC POWER OF SUBSTANCES

We may ask, what is it about the use of psychoactive substances which makes them often so symbolically powerful? First, psychoactive substances are valued physical goods. Their status as physical goods renders them subject to commodification, and indeed globalization in use and trade. Given their positive valuation, possession and use is often a symbol of power and domination (Morgan, 1983), or at least of access to resources beyond subsistence.

Second, using psychoactive substances is a behaviour, and very often a social behaviour. Drinking or drug use thus is often a performance in front of others, and what we use and how is infused with symbolic meanings. Looking at a few advertisements for legal substances reminds us of this, since advertisers seek to attach positive symbolization to their product. "Blow some my way", says the woman to her date as he lights his cigarette (http://tobaccodocuments.org/pollay_ads/Ches01.01.html#images) in a

1926 Chesterfield ad. "I am a Canadian" is the punchline of a series of advertisements in 2000 (http://www.coolcanuckaward.ca/joe_canadian.htm) for a beer that wrapped itself in the national colours. Use of the substances socially means that the use also often serves to demarcate the boundaries of inclusion and exclusion in a social grouping (Room, 1975).

Third, psychoactive substance use is a peculiarly intimate behaviour, in that the substance is taken into the body. Use is thus potentially fateful; the substance has the potential to contaminate, whether the contamination is defined in terms of poison, infection, sin, or spirit possession. Like other substances taken into the body (foods, drinks, medicines, body fluids), there are thus many normative prescriptions and taboos about psychoactive substances, again creating a fertile field for symbolization. The symbolic meanings are complex and mixed.

Fourth, more patently than other substances taken into the body, psychoactive substances have the power to affect behaviour – (to change mood, to affect motor coordination and judgement, to intoxicate) – and to take one out of oneself, even to the extent that the substance may be seen as possessing the user, submerging the true self (Room, 2001). This quality is both positively valued and feared, and even the terms used regarding the substances often have a double edge. Keane (2002, pp. 14–15), quoting Derrida, points out the ambiguity of the Greek word *pharmakon*, meaning both poison and cure. In the same vein, the words "drug" and "intoxication" also have both positive and negative connotations, depending on the context. "The distinctions between medicine and poison, good drug and bad, are unstable and complex", Keane notes; "good nicotine in the form of patches and gums is used to treat addiction to bad nicotine found in cigarettes." On the positive side, besides their use as medicines, psychoactive substances are often used in religious rituals and experiences, lending them another world of symbolic meaning. In many cultural circumstances, intoxication is positively valued as a recreational or social experience, and English and other languages are extraordinarily rich in symbolic language to describe intoxicated states (Levine, 1981).

On the other hand, behaviour when intoxicated is seen as less predictable, and often as potentially dangerous. The effect of the substance is seen as making the intoxicated person less amenable to reason, to social norms, and to laws. These expectations, and along with them the behaviour while under the influence of the substance, vary between cultures (MacAndrew & Edgerton, 1969). The stronger the perceptions of disinhibition, the more potentially fearsome the power of the intoxicated person is seen as being. Again, the perceptions become infused with symbolism. The desire to constrain intoxication accounts for much of the moral loading that surrounds psychoactive substance use in most societies (Room et al., 2001).

Fifth, psychoactive substances are seen as potentially causing addiction or, to use the current technical term, dependence. The core meaning of addiction is that the substance has enslaved the user, that she/he has lost the ability to control whether and how much of the substance is used. In the ordinary understanding of addiction, there is also a second, associated loss of control, over one's life – that the user's life has "become unmanageable", in the words of the First Step of Alcoholics Anonymous. Again, the addiction concept is subject to cultural variation (Room et al., 1996; Schmidt & Room, 1999), and indeed has a history, becoming a common understanding of habitual heavy substance use only in the 19th century (Levine, 1978; Ferentzy, 2001). Addiction is, of course, surrounded by a heavy penumbra of symbolism, mostly negative.

There are, then, multiple properties of psychoactive substances underlying their symbolic power. This power is expressed in our everyday lives – in the symbolism of tobacco and alcohol advertisements, in how we behave while and after using, in what others expect from us and in how our actions while and after using are evaluated. The symbolic powers of psychoactive substances have also made them a prime arena for political action. Political movements for substance control have relied heavily on emotive symbolization, from the attack on "demon rum" in the temperance era to denunciations of drugs as a global "scourge" in the era of the modern "war on drugs" (Room, 1999).

SYMBOLISM, RATIONALITY, AND PATHOLOGY IN POLITICAL ACTION

Forty years ago, the sociologist Joseph Gusfield (1963) published an interpretation of the American temperance movement, entitled *Symbolic crusade: Status politics and the American temperance movement*. In terms of the history of alcohol and for that matter of other psychoactive substances, the temperance movement may be seen as the most important political movement of the last 200 years. Yet, at the time Gusfield was writing, the temperance movement had been thoroughly discredited in U.S. intellectual life for 30 years. To his contemporaries, as Gusfield puts it in his Introduction, "such a movement seems at once naïve, intolerant, saintly, and silly" (p. 1).

At the level of social movements and politics, Gusfield's book may be seen in its way as a parallel effort to the current efforts of microeconomists in the tradition of Becker and Murphy's (1988) theory of rational addiction; that is, he wanted to explicate a way in which the apparently irrational could be understood as a kind of rationality.

Gusfield sets up two foils for his interpretation. One is an interpretation of history in terms of economic and class determinants, which sees politics in terms of "the conflict between the material goals and aspirations of different social groups" (p. 17). This is the materialist model which is the common heritage of, say, Marxist analysis, welfare economics, and mainline political science. Since political science, as much as economics, has tended to operate in terms of the presumption of rationality, political scientists had generally not paid much attention to "the possible political consequences of drug use", perhaps "out of a commitment to a rationalist view of politics", as Stauffer (1971) remarked in 1971.

The second "major model of political motivation", Gusfield proposes, "reflects a view of politics as an arena into which 'irrational' impulses are projected" – a view, as he notes, which is "drawn from clinical psychology" (p. 177), and which had been used by others to describe movements like the American temperance movement. This could be regarded as the equivalent at the political level of a psychopathological model, just as an addiction conceptualization is an expression of that model at the individual level. "Unlike instrumental action, which is about conflicts of interest", Gusfield adds, "the substance of political struggles in expressive politics is not about anything because it is not a vehicle of conflict but a vehicle of catharsis – a purging of emotions through expression".

Against these two models, Gusfield proposes a third model as a frame for understanding the temperance movement, in terms of "symbolic action". Symbolic action, he argues, "is a major way in which conflicts in the social order are institutionalized as political issues. Groups form around such issues, symbols are given specific meaning, and opposing forces have some arena in which to test their power and bring about compromise and accommodation if possible" (p. 182). He adds:

> we live in a human environment in which symbolic gestures have great relevance to our sense of pride, mortification and honor. Social conflicts and tensions are manifested in a disarray of the symbolic order as well as in other areas of action. Dismissing these reactions as "irrational" clouds analysis... (p. 183).

Gusfield does not see the three models as mutually exclusive. In the context of the American temperance movement, he sees the model of symbolic action as particularly linked to status conflicts within American society, offering a way to "help us understand the implications of status conflicts for political actions and, vice versa, the ways in which political acts affect the distribution of prestige". Most social movements, he adds, "contain a mixture of instrumental, expressive, and symbolic elements" (p. 180).

ANALYSES OF THE SYMBOLIC DIMENSION IN THE NORDIC POLITICS OF SUBSTANCE USE

The symbolic dimension remains important in the politics of substance use today, in Nordic countries as elsewhere. This is illustrated in several analyses of Nordic discourse and policy about psychoactive substances. The analysis by Nils Christie and Kettil Bruun (1996; see also Bruun & Christie, 1985) of Nordic drug policies starts from the strong stands and actions Nordic countries have taken against illicit drugs – out of all proportion to actual problems from the drugs, as compared to problems from alcohol, tobacco, and psychoactive medicines, for instance. Illicit drugs, they argue, are a "suitable enemy" for the modern state. The campaign against drugs then becomes a unifying symbolic crusade. Christie and Bruun (1996, pp. 57–58) outline the qualities needed for a suitable enemy for the modern state. Among the qualities noted are that the enemy should not be associated with a powerful group in the society, and that the problem and those associated with it should be capable of being presented as dangerous and even diabolical. As Tham (1995) notes, Christie and Bruun argue that "drug abusers are ideal when out-groups as well as someone to blame social problems on are needed; they are young and sometimes oppositional; they represent no powerful interests; and controlling them leaves the majority of inhabitants unaffected". Suitable enemies are those which can never be entirely beaten, Christie and Bruun add, and it should not be too clear whether things are getting better or worse. They also argue that the fight against drugs serves as a distraction from problems such as unemployment and poverty, on which it is much more difficult for the state to find consensus (p. 18). In contrast, alcohol, tobacco, and coffee are unsuitable as enemies: The interests supporting them are strong; "they occupy central positions both nationally and internationally. They are met with sympathy in wide circles. And they are capable of carrying on an offensive fight against everyone that wants to get them under control". For the state, then, they would be "strong enemies, dangerous enemies, unsuitable enemies" (Bruun & Christie, 1985).

Drawing on the analyses both of Gusfield and of Christie and Bruun, Henrik Tham (1995) argues that, in the case of Sweden, after 1980 the fight against drugs took on the character of a "national project". Moral values were central to the argument; for instance, one actor puts forward "the working-class values of order, solidarity, conscientiousness, honour, and decent behaviour" as the antithesis of drug use. The ideal of "a drug-free society", still the official goal of Swedish drug policy, is, Tham notes, in itself "an expression of an absolute moral philosophy". The ideal and associated policies were presented as representing a consensus of "the people", with those opposed to the policies "depicted as not belonging to 'the people'". In line with this theme, "another consistent theme", Tham found, "is that drugs come from abroad and are alien to Sweden". All in all, Tham argues, "the powerful and widespread reaction against drugs in Sweden... can...be seen as a means for reinforcing a national identity". In a period when Sweden's autonomy has been weakened by all that went with joining the European Union, and in which "Sweden has become less 'provincial' due to immigration, a more open economy, foreign travel, and television, ... the struggle against drugs has been broadened into a more general national project for the defense of 'Sweden'".

In contrast to the analyses of drug policy, analyses of the present-day Nordic discourse about alcohol policy have tended to identify the strongest symbolic elements in the discussion as coming from the opposite political tendency, from the arguments for less restrictive alcohol controls. Thus Olsson (1990) found that, while those arguing for stricter controls used a rationalistic discourse, all facts and figures, the other side's arguments were more phenomenological, and often appealed to a "dream of a better order", an alternative Swedish social order where:

> alcohol still has a central role, but the drama has been removed, with the negative consequences of alcohol believed to be minimized. The continental drinking culture is the theme of this dream, nourished by the shame felt about what is felt to be the dominating drinking culture in our society, which is characterized by heavy drinking, drunkenness, and violence. The dream picture goes along probably with a general unhappiness with "what is" and a longing for what "is not" but "could be" (Olsson, 1990).

SYMBOLISM AND RATIONALITY

Implicit in these analyses of Nordic political discourse on alcohol and drugs is an idea very close to the central proposition in Gusfield's analysis of the classic American temperance movement – that we are dealing with frames and arguments which have their own logic, but it is not the logic of instrumental rationality. The appeal to a symbolic dimension in the argument – to the goal of a drug-free society, or to an ideal of Apollonian drinking – might, in fact, be seen as a signal that we have broken out of the bounds of the world of instrumental rationality – out of the world of *homo œconomicus* and his brethren in political science and sociology, in other words.

Social scientists have returned in recent years to the question of how to bring into the analytical frame aspects of human behaviour that seem to fall outside the boundaries of instrumental rationality. One answer, exemplified by Becker and Murphy's (1988) analysis of "rational addiction", is to show that even the apparently quintessentially irrational can indeed be fitted into a frame of instrumental rationality. Another, exemplified by analyses in terms of "bounded rationality" (Jones, 1999), acknowledges the many departures from rational choice models in actual political behaviour, but interprets the departures primarily in terms of the actor's limited information – "the limitations of humans to comprehend and act on inputs from the environment" – or cognitive failure in the face of the "fundamental complexity of the environment" (Jones, 1999).

Discussing recent literature on the role of ideas as well as self-interest in politics and policy-making, John Campbell (2002) pushes further beyond the limits of "rational choice theory" (RCT), as it is often called in sociology. He notes discussions of the influence on decisions of normative frameworks – "taken-for-granted assumptions about values, attitudes, and other 'collectively shared expectations'"; in this sense, he continues, "policy-makers operate according to a logic of moral or social appropriateness, not a logic of consequentiality ... Normative beliefs may be so strong that they override the self-interests of policy makers". Identities, that is, "historically constructed ideas that individuals and organizations have about who they are vis-à-vis others ... may also affect policy-making". He notes the implications of some analyses that "under at least some conditions ideas may matter substantially more than interests", but suggests that "a more fruitful approach would ask how ideas and interests interact", avoiding "the pitfalls of the old idealist versus materialist debate about the nature of public policy-making".

In a more fundamental departure from the RCT frame, Raymond Boudon (2003) proposes that RCT is a special case of a more general rationality "which is not exclusively instrumental". The goals of human action, Boudon argues, extend beyond instrumental rationality to include "symbolic rewards, prestige, symbolic distinctions", and the premises for action are often religious and ethical beliefs. This position, Boudon argues, picks up the thread of Max Weber's analysis of two forms of rationality, instrumental

(*Zweckrationalität*), and axiological (values-based, *Wertrationalität*); he notes that it is also compatible with some of Adam Smith's analyses. As Boudon summarizes his argument:

> social action generally depends on beliefs; ...as far as possible, beliefs, actions and attitudes should be treated as rational, or more precisely, as the effect of reasons perceived by social actors as strong; ...reasons dealing with costs and benefits should not be given more attention than they deserve...
> People's actions are understandable because they are moved by reasons. But these reasons can be of several types. Action can rest on beliefs or not; the beliefs can be commonplace or not; they can be descriptive or prescriptive.

In Boudon's view, there are "no general criteria of the strength of a system of reasons". Whether beliefs are "scientific" or "ordinary", and whether they are "prescriptive" or "descriptive", "a system of reasons can be stronger or weaker than another and we can explain why; ...but the truth and rationality are comparative, not absolute notions".

The examples of systems of beliefs Boudon chooses for illustration of processes of change, however, all have a consequential element in them, and this is the element which becomes falsified in the example. For instance, he argues, "the argument 'capital punishment is good because it is an effective threat against crime' became weaker" when it was shown that the abolition of capital punishment did not increase the crime rates. Boudon offers no general discussion of how axiological reasons become stronger or weaker, although examples elsewhere in the article suggest that general social and structural conditions can be determinative.

A crucial point for our purposes in Boudon's argument is that "cognitive reasons ground prescriptive as well as descriptive beliefs in the mind of individuals", so that there usually is a greater or smaller cognitive element in a prescriptive belief system. Indeed, a "prescriptive or normative conclusion can be derived from a set of...statements that are all descriptive, except one".

Boudon also notes in passing that "irrationality should be given its right place. Tradition and affective actions also exist".

SYMBOLIC POLITICS AND CONSEQUENTIAL KNOWLEDGE

Boudon's analysis thus ends up with much the same tripartite division as Gusfield's in *Symbolic crusade* concerning the grounds of political action. Besides the irrational, which neither Gusfield nor Boudon emphasize, there is social action which is materialist or instrumental, and social action which is symbolic or values-based.

But some nuances can be added to this analysis. While they can be analytically distinguished, symbolic or values-based action may also be instrumental in its purpose. Gusfield's analysis of symbolic action in *Symbolic crusade* is primarily organized around status politics: In his account, struggles over temperance in the late 19th-century U.S. were above all about the distribution of prestige or social honour between status groups in the population. Social status may not have a cash worth in itself, but in a wider sense it is certainly a sought-after good, so that the symbolic action Gusfield analyses can be viewed as instrumental even if it is not materially oriented. Further, although Gusfield argues strongly, and with good sociological precedents, that social "class and status make up two analytically separate orders of social structure", he acknowledges that in the long run there is mutual influence between the two dimensions. This implies that a symbolic fight for status in the long run may have material implications. On the other hand, to interpret the U.S. temperance movement's symbolic fight only in terms of material and class interests (e.g., Rumbarger, 1989) is in my view too reductionist.

Boudon's analysis offers a step forward in understanding the place and interplay of symbolism and rationality in the politics of psychoactive substances. His point about the place of cognitive arguments in prescriptive belief systems aptly characterizes a recurring phenomenon. The classic 19th-century temperance movement may indeed have been a "symbolic crusade", but science and scientific arguments were very important to the cause. Scientific research was often emphasized, and the Women's Christian Temperance Union's efforts in the schools were on behalf of what was called "scientific temperance instruction" (Zimmerman, 1999). Science was put to use in buttressing what was fundamentally a value-based cause.

Another analysis by Gusfield (1984), this time of the cultural politics of drinking–driving issues in the modern U.S.A., makes this point for a later period, emphasizing the extent to which the consequentialist arguments, and the scientific enterprise itself, are subordinated to the taken-for-granted framing of the issue. Gusfield was struck, early in his work on drinking–driving issues, by how "all the parties with whom I came in contact – police, offenders, judges, officials – were locked into a consciousness of drinking–driving which narrowly shut out possible alternative conceptualizations and solutions" (p. 6). Crucial to this consensus was the role of "scientific knowledge". "Science, scientific pronouncements, technical programs, and technologies appear as supports to authority, and counterauthority, by giving to program or policy the cast of being validated in nature, grounded in a neutral process by a method which assures both certainty and accuracy" (p. 28). Gusfield's book therefore studies the field of drinking–driving in terms of the rhetoric and dramaturgy of its use of science.

As noted above, the symbolic powers of psychoactive substances make them a recurrent arena for value-based politics. But, picking up on Boudon's point, even value-oriented arguments about psychoactive substances have many consequentialist assertions included in them, and in modern times these assertions often take on and wear the mantle of science. This does not in itself discredit the science; the creditability of the science is appropriately judged by a set of standards outside the political frame. But it does put in the foreground the issue of the relation between science and policy.

SCIENCE AND THE NORDIC POLITICS OF SUBSTANCE USE

In relative terms internationally, the Nordic countries are paragons of pragmatism in politics and of a societal commitment to knowledge-based social policies. Far away in California, I remember speculating with Ron Roizen some years ago about why Nordic alcohol sociologists seemed to pay relatively little attention to Joe Gusfield's work. Our theory was that maybe his work was of limited interest in a Nordic context because Nordic law-making seemed to be so rational and instrumental, with little room for symbolism.

In relative terms, there may have been something to our theory, but closer experience has taught me that symbolism and value-based political action play an important role at least in Swedish policy-making on psychoactive substances. However, the priority on values as a base for policy is tempered by another strong societal value – a commitment to evidence-based policy-making. Research findings do matter in the Swedish policy debate, for instance, to an extent that can often be surprising for a native English speaker.

There can, however, be ironic corollaries of this in value-laden policy areas like psychoactive substances policies. Researchers may find that there is a strong expectation that they will stay within the fences. For instance, a recent debate article by researchers who had questioned the premises of a campaign for no drinking at all by pregnant women drew a response that was incredulous that such an argument could come from publicly-funded researchers: "...to attempt to belittle the problem and criticize that someone tries to do something about it is extremely noteworthy. When [the critique] comes from representatives of a state-financed alcohol research center it is naturally yet more remarkable" (Heilig & Rågsjö, 2004). Another strategy to avoid unwelcome research findings can be to avoid commissioning studies which it is suspected might produce them. To a considerable extent, this was the situation with Swedish social research on illicit drugs until a couple of years ago. As Lenke and Olsson (2002) summarized the situation then, "researchers and other drug policy experts were in many ways placed in intellectual quarantine". Given the strong moral-political loading, "the incentives for experts to try to introduce relevant facts into the debate are rather limited. One consequence is that public awareness slowly withers away, and anything can be presented as a fact in the debate without the risk of scrutiny". The first thaw of the Swedish ice-jam on drug policy issues was signalled when the drugs coordinator, Björn Fries, came into office and set about commissioning research, remarking that the politicians had been making decisions on drug issues on the basis of too little data.

Commissioning research may also be a way to postpone the debate or decision between two conflicting paths; the extraordinary Swedish controlled social experiment on the effects of Saturday opening of liquor stores (Norström & Skog, 2003) can be seen in this light. As Kettil Bruun (1973) once put it, "research could be seen as a modern instrument of debate on policy, primarily on the alternative means derived from the same basic values, rather than on alternative goals". In his view, Bruun continued, "social research produces arguments rather than logical conclusions regarding policy and action...The big decisions will always be taken primarily on the basis of values – the small, but still important ones might, however, be improved by social research".

In the longer run, though, science often plays a subversive role, undermining the current governing image of a psychoactive substance and its problems. The strongest influence of science is thus often outside the immediate political moment, in changing the *gestalt*, the fundamental frame of understanding. The rise of what is called in Sweden the "total consumption model" for understanding the dynamics of rates of alcohol problems is one such example of a research-led change in *gestalt*, which undercut the governing image of alcohol problems in terms of alcoholism, for instance in the U.S.A. (Room, 1984). Another such is the ongoing neuroscience-driven change in our understanding of psychoactive substances. Recognition that "the neural pathways that psychoactive substances affect are also those which are affected by many other human behaviours, including eating a meal, having sex, and gambling for money", that "in this sense, the use of psychoactive substances...is one part of the spectrum of human behaviours which potentially bring pleasure or avoid pain" (WHO, 2004, p. 241), must tend in the long run to bring a normalization in our view of the substances.

CONCLUSION

To do research in the psychoactive substance field, I have argued, is to work in an arena laden with symbolism. If public funds support our research, the motivation for funding us is almost always to find solutions, at least in the long run, to what are seen as serious social and health problems. Our science is thus necessarily value-laden, if only in the choices of research issues on which to focus. But our duty as scientists, as I would see it, is to try in our research to see and write beyond these circumstances of our funding. It is not only a matter of producing better research, but also of being more useful in the long run to our societies.

Our research findings when published become public property. But there are "multiple realities through which Science may be construed", as Gusfield (1981, p. 107) puts it. Boudon's analysis reminds us that our research findings, apart from any immediate consequentialist usefulness, also often become elements in value-based arguments. And, he argues, these rationalist findings can become the means for strengthening or weakening arguments for value-based policies.

To understand the politics of psychoactive substances, it is certainly relevant to consider the empirical research and to study its role in the arguments for and against particular policies. But my main conclusion is that this is not enough. To restrict our field of attention to rational action and argument is to miss crucial parts of the reality of the politics of psychoactive substances. In a heavily symbolic arena, where deep personal and societal values are at stake, we must develop paradigms of research which bring the taken-for-granted assumptions and the values into the object-field of the research.

ACKNOWLEDGEMENTS

Prepared for presentation at the *24th Arne Ryde symposium on the economics of substance use*, Lund, Sweden, August 13–14, 2004. Thanks to Kaye Fillmore, Klaus Mäkelä, and Ron Roizen for their comments.

REFERENCES

Becker, G. S., & Murphy, K. M. (1988). A theory of rational addiction. *Journal of Political Economy*, 96, 675–700.
Boudon, R. (2003). Beyond rational choice theory. *Annual Review of Sociology*, 29, 1–21.
Bruun, K. (1973). Social research, social policy, and action. In: *The epidemiology of drug dependence: Report on a conference.* EURO 5436 IV. Copenhagen: WHO Regional Office for Europe.
Bruun, K., & Christie, N. (1985). Unsuitable enemies. *The Globe* (Oslo) 2/1985 (June), pp. 18–20.
Campbell, J. L. (2002). Ideas, politics, and public policy. *Annual Review of Sociology*, 28, 21–38.
Christie, N., & Bruun, K. (1996). *Den gode fiende: Narkotikapolitikk i norden* (2nd ed.; 1st ed., 1985). [*The suitable enemy: Drug policy in the Nordic countries.*] Oslo: Universitetsforlaget.
Courtwright, D. (2001). *Forces of habit: Drugs and the making of the modern world.* Cambridge, MA: Harvard University Press.
Dunstan, K. (1974). *Wowsers: Being an account of the prudery exhibited by certain outstanding men and women in such matters as drinking, smoking, prostitution, censorship and gambling.* Sydney: Angus and Robertson.
Ferentzy, P. (2001). From sin to disease: Differences and similarities between past and current conceptions of chronic drunkenness. *Contemporary Drug Problems*, 28, 363–390.
Gordon, A. J. (1978). Hispanic drinking after migration: The case of Dominicans. *Medical Anthropology*, 2, 61–84.
Gusfield, J. R. (1963). *Symbolic crusade: Status politics and the American temperance movement.* Urbana, etc.: University of Illinois Press, 3rd printing of paperback, 1972.
Gusfield, J. R. (1984). *The culture of public problems: Drinking–driving and the symbolic order (first published 1981).* Chicago: University of Chicago Press.
Harrison, B. (1971). *Drink and the Victorians: The temperance question in England 1825–1872.* Pittsburgh: University of Pittsburgh Press.
Heilig, M., & Rågsjö, K. (2004). Var tionde gravid har alkoholproblem. [Every tenth pregnant woman has an alcohol problem.] *Dagens Nyheter* July 14, 4.
Jones, B. D. (1999). Bounded rationality. *Annual Review of Political Science*, 2, 297–321.
Keane, H. (2002). *What's wrong with addiction?* Melbourne: Melbourne University Press.
Lenke, L., & Olsson, B. (2002). Swedish drug policy in the twenty-first century: A policy model going astray. *Annals of the American Association of Political and Social Science*, 582, 64–79.
Levine, H. G. (1978). The discovery of addiction: Changing conceptions of habitual drunkenness in America. *Journal of Studies on Alcohol*, 39, 143–174.
Levine, H. G. (1981). The vocabulary of drunkenness. *Journal of Studies on Alcohol*, 42, 1038–1051.
MacAndrew, C., & Edgerton, R. (1969). *Drunken comportment.* Chicago: Aldine.
Mäkelä, K. (1983). The uses of alcohol and their cultural regulation. *Acta Sociologica*, 26, 21–31.
Morgan, P. (1983). Alcohol, disinhibition, and domination: A conceptual analysis. In: R. Room & G. Collins (Eds), *Alcohol and disinhibition: Nature and meaning of the link* (pp. 405–420). Rockville, MD: National Institute on Alcohol Abuse and Alcoholism Research Monograph No. 12, DHHS Publication No. (ADM) 83-1246.

Norström, T., & Skog, O.-J. (2003). Saturday opening of alcohol retail shops in Sweden: An impact analysis. *Journal of Studies on Alcohol, 64,* 393–401.
Olsson, B. (1990). Alkoholpolitik och alkoholens fenomenologi: Uppfattningar som artikulerats i pressen. (Alcohol policy and the phenomenology of alcohol: Opinions expressed in the press). *Alkoholpolitik, 7,* 184–194.
Room, R. (1983). Alcohol as an issue in Papua New Guinea: A view from the outside. In: M. Marshall (Ed.), *Through a glass darkly: Beer and modernization in Papua New Guinea* (pp. 441–450). Boroko, Papua New Guinea: IASER Press.
Room, R. (1984). Alcohol control and public health. *Annual Review of Public Health, 5,* 293–317.
Room, R. (1991). "Should I surrender?" – Women's drinking and courtship in American movies. Presented at the *Annual meetings of the American Psychological Association,* San Francisco, August 16. http://www.bks.no/surrendr.htm.
Room, R. (1999). The rhetoric of international drug control. *Substance Use and Misuse, 34,* 1689–1707.
Room, R. (2001). Intoxication and bad behaviour: Understanding cultural differences in the link. *Social Science and Medicine, 53,* 189–198.
Room, R., Janca, A., Bennett, L. A., Schmidt, L., & Sartorius, N., with 15 others. (1996). WHO cross-cultural applicability research on diagnosis and assessment of substance use disorders: An overview of methods and selected results [with comments and a response]. *Addiction, 91,* 199–230.
Room, R., Rehm, J., Trotter II, R. T., Paglia, A., & Üstün, T. B. (2001). Cross-cultural views on stigma, valuation, parity and societal values towards disability. In: T. B. Üstün, S. Chatterji, J. E. Bickenbach, R. T. Trotter II, R. Room, J. Rehm & S. Saxena (Eds), *Disability and culture: Universalism and diversity* (pp. 247–291). Seattle, etc.: Hogrefe & Huber.
Rumbarger, J. J. (1989). *Profits, power and prohibition: American alcohol reform and the industrializing of America, 1800–1930.* Albany, NY: State University of New York Press.
Schmidt, L., & Room, R. (1999). Cross-cultural applicability in international classifications and research on alcohol dependence. *Journal of Studies on Alcohol, 60,* 448–462.
Smith, R. E. F., & Christian, D. G. (1984). *Bread and salt: A social and economic history of food in Russia.* Cambridge: Cambridge University Press.
Stauffer, R. B. (1971). *The role of drugs in political change.* New York: General Learning Press.
Tham, H. (1995). Drug control as a national project: The case of Sweden. *Journal of Drug Issues, 25,* 113–128.
WHO. (2004). *Neuroscience of psychoactive substance use and dependence.* Geneva: World Health Organization.
Zimmerman, J. (1999). *Distilling democracy: Alcohol education in America's public schools, 1880–1925.* Lawrence: University Press of Kansas.

WHAT DOES IT MEAN TO DECRIMINALIZE MARIJUANA? A CROSS-NATIONAL EMPIRICAL EXAMINATION

Rosalie L. Pacula, Robert MacCoun, Peter Reuter, Jamie Chriqui, Beau Kilmer, Katherine Harris, Letizia Paoli and Carsten Schäfer

ABSTRACT

Although frequently discussed as a singular policy, there is tremendous variation in the laws and regulations surrounding so-called decriminalization policies adopted by Western countries, with many jurisdictions adopting depenalization policies rather than policies that actually change the criminal status of cannabis possession offences. This paper provides a discussion of the liberalization policies being adopted in Western countries, highlighting distinct elements about particular policies that are important for proper analysis and interpretation of the policies. It then discusses some of the environmental factors that also shape these policies, and hence influence their potential impact, using data from the U.S.A. as a particular example. The results clearly show that researchers should be careful conducting intra- or international comparisons of policies because important aspects of these policies are frequently ignored.

Although widely used in discussions regarding alternative cannabis policy regimes, the term decriminalization to date has gone largely undefined in the international policy arena. The term literally implies a removal in the criminal status of cannabis possession offences; however, numerous countries and sub-jurisdictions that are recognized as having decriminalized cannabis in fact merely reduce the penalties associated with possession of specified amounts. Hence, the term cannabis depenalization has evolved in the scientific literature as a more useful term for describing the diversity in liberalizing policies that have arose across and within countries (e.g. MacCoun & Reuter, 2001). Decriminalization, nonetheless, remains a common term used in policy discussions and debates.

The ubiquitous use of the term decriminalization does more than obscure meaningful policy differences that exist across countries; it has led to the development and interpretation of policy research that is myopically focused on evaluating the impact of a single dichotomous indicator that is inconsistently defined within and across countries (MacCoun & Reuter, 2001; Pacula, Chriqui, & King, 2003). Thus, it is not surprising that the literature does not provide a clear, consistent conclusion regarding the impact of decriminalization on cannabis use, its harmful consequences, and arrests when these different studies are in fact evaluating different policies.

Although all developed countries today prohibit in some fashion the possession, cultivation, distribution and/or sale of cannabis and cannabis products, the countries differ in the types of behaviours that are allowed, the resources devoted to enforcing the laws, the penalties that are imposed on those who break these laws, and their citizens' knowledge of these policies. Variations in laws, how they are enforced, and the penalties imposed together determine the policy and, when combined with the public's understanding of the policy, the possible impact on behaviour (MacCoun, 1993). Hence, those interested in evaluating the impact of specific policies like cannabis decriminalization need to consider more than just the law and a simple binary label for its penalty structure. They must at the very least also consider how and to what degree specific policies get enforced in relevant jurisdictions.

This paper begins by describing the statutory varieties of liberalization of cannabis laws that have been adopted in Western countries, highlighting for a few countries a distinct element that influences how the policy is interpreted and implemented. We then discuss some of the environmental factors that also shape these policies and influence their potential impact, in particular enforcement and knowledge of the laws. We demonstrate using data from the U.S.A. that differences in statutory laws may not translate into differences in outcomes because of offsetting environmental factors (enforcement and/or perception of law), not because the legal differences have no effect. By discussing both the legal and environmental factors related to these policies, we hope to better inform researchers interested in evaluating the economic and behavioural impacts of cannabis policy across different jurisdictions and encourage them to be more specific about what exactly is being evaluated and how.

1. DECRIMINALIZATION: A FORM OF DEPENALIZATION

Decriminalization and depenalization are both terms that represent a range of policies targeting cannabis users in countries where the *supply* of cannabis for the purpose of recreational use is statutorily prohibited.[1] Hence, these policies do not relate to how the suppliers of cannabis get treated in specific countries. They only differentiate how those caught in possession (with the intent to use) get treated.[2]

Just as apples are a type of fruit, decriminalization is a specific type of depenalization policy. In this paper, depenalization refers to any policy that reduces the penalties associated with possession or use of cannabis. The penalties that get reduced can be criminal or civil in nature. For example, policies that retain the criminal status of possession offences but remove or reduce the amount of incarceration imposed as a penalty would be examples of depenalization policies. On the other hand, decriminalization, refers specifically to depenalization policies that change the criminal status of possession offences from that of a crime to that of a non-criminal offence. As penalties are usually graduated with the severity of crime, a change in the criminal status of an offence will also imply a reduction in the level and type of penalties imposed with that offence, which is why decriminalization policies may be viewed as a special form of depenalization policies.

There are two methods of using statutory law to reduce the burden of enforcement of cannabis possession prohibitions both on the criminal justice system and on arrested cannabis users:[3]

1. Eliminate the criminal penalties, while still retaining cannabis possession as a criminal offence, for example with respect to civil or administrative rights. This is depenalization.
2. Eliminate the criminal status of the offence itself, automatically removing the possibility of incarceration as a penalty. This is decriminalization.

Depenalization reduces the burden of processing individual arrestees only to the extent that jail time was actually imposed previously. Decriminalization may do more to lower costs by reducing the processing costs, since civil offences can usually be dealt with more expeditiously and with fewer procedural protections. Legal changes do not always have the intended effect because of what are referred to as "net-widening" effects. For example, both South Australia and the U.K. experienced an increase in the number of cannabis-involved arrests and citations after they reduced the criminal status of the drug, causing a rise in system costs associated with processing these cases under the alternative system.

In addition to differential costs borne by the government, there are significant differences in costs imposed on users by these two methods of depenalization. Even if the specific penalties imposed on users in each of these two situations were structured identically (e.g. a fine of $1,000 and no jail time), the first method retains the criminal status of the offence while the second option (true decriminalization) does not. The importance of a criminal charge depends on the jurisdiction. In some jurisdictions, criminal charges can influence an individual's ability to obtain and/or retain work, student loans, and public assistance; hence decriminalization can substantially reduce the personal cost associated with getting charged with possession offences. In other, more rehabilitative jurisdictions, criminal charges do not impose these sort of additional personal burdens, but they still might influence one's rights travelling to jurisdictions that are more punitive in nature.[4]

2. MODELS OF DEPENALIZATION

There are a variety of different depenalization models that have been adopted in developed countries. Even within specific countries, important variations to the model exist. Many countries have adopted a policy of "partial depenalization," in which the penalties for use offences vary on the basis of the quantity of cannabis involved and the number of prior arrests of the individual. For example, first-time offenders who are caught in possession of small amounts of cannabis might receive civil penalties while those caught in possession of larger quantities or who are repeat offenders may face criminal charges. Variants of this policy are seen in Australia, Germany, and the U.S.A. Other countries have adopted a policy of "full decriminalization," where the simple possession or use of cannabis for personal consumption is not a crime regardless of the number of prior offences. In these countries, offences remain illegal but have civil (or administrative) sanctions, typically involving mandatory treatment and a fine. Examples of European countries that have adopted policies of full decriminalization include Italy (since 1975, although it was re-criminalized from 1990 to 1993), Spain (since 1983), and Portugal (since 2001).[5] The Netherlands represents the single biggest outlier to cannabis policy models experimented with thus far, as it is the only country that has allowed a retail (but not wholesale) market to develop. Even in this case, however, the retail market is strictly regulated and stiff penalties remain for individuals caught in possession of large quantities of the substance.

2.1. Australia

Since 1986, the goal of Australia's national drug strategy has been to "minimize the harmful effects of drugs on Australian society" (Blewett, 1987, p. 2). Efforts to achieve this goal include the provision of education, a significant expansion of treatment, and the collection of national data on drug use and drug-related harms (Bammer, Hall, Hamilton, & Ali, 2002). In the Australian Federal system, states and territories are responsible for enacting criminal legislation and implementing drug policies while the Federal government can influence national policy by tying funding for drug programmes to compliance with broadly agreed national goals. Consequently, there has been no uniform approach to harm minimization and several Australian states and territories have experimented with their own policies (Bammer et al., 2002).

Since the mid-1980s, four Australian territories have replaced the criminal penalties associated with minor cannabis offences with administrative fines, if the fines are paid within a specified amount of time (referred to as expiation). South Australia was the first to adopt the Cannabis Expiation Notice (CEN) system in 1987. In 1992 and 1996, the Australian Capital Territory and Northern Territory, respectively, adopted similar systems (Ali et al., 1999). Western Australia has just recently made the change in 2003.[6] Under the CEN, possession of up to 100 g of cannabis, 20 g of cannabis resin, or equipment for consuming cannabis are all treated as minor cannabis offences that are punishable by a small fine ranging from Australian $50 to $150. If this fee is paid within 30–60 days, there are no criminal proceedings and no offence is recorded. Failure to pay the fine leads to criminal proceedings and may result in imprisonment (Bammer et al., 2002).

Another unique aspect of the Australian policy is that the cultivation of a small number of plants was included in the category of "minor cannabis offences" in order to allow users to obtain cannabis without resorting to the black market. For example, South Australia initially allowed up to 10 plants to be grown for personal consumption, but this quantity was later reduced to just three plants. The prohibition against home cultivation of larger than statutory amounts is still enforced as is evidenced by a rise in the number of such cannabis offences detected (Christie, 1999).

2.2. Germany

As opposed to its Australian and U.S. counterparts, the German federal government is exclusively responsible for enacting criminal laws. German states (the *Länder*) are merely in charge of implementing them. Nonetheless, in Germany there remains a considerable degree of heterogeneity in the handling of cannabis possession offences across states. In Germany, this variance results from the different interpretation and implementation of several provisions within the Act on Narcotics (*Betäubungsmittelgesetz*, hereinafter BtMG), the Code of Criminal Procedure (*Strafprozeßordnung*), and the Act on Juvenile Courts (*Jugendgerichtsgesetz*) that empower prosecutors and courts to dismiss criminal proceedings involving consumption-related drug offences under certain conditions.[7]

The provision most frequently used to dismiss consumption-related drug offences is Section 31a BtMG, which was introduced by the German Parliament in 1992 and partially depenalized consumption-related drug offences by giving public prosecutors the authority to decide when to prosecute defendants charged with consumption-related drug offences even though it retained the criminality of offences involving the mere possession of these drugs. In 1994, the Federal Constitutional Court reviewed Section 31a BtMG and ruled that criminal cases involving the possession, purchase, or import of small amounts of cannabis for "occasional private use and if there is no danger to third parties" must be dismissed because the prosecution of such offences would amount to excessive state intervention and thus seriously infringe upon the constitutional principle of proportionality. It further required the German states to develop and implement consistent non-prosecution policies so as to not infringe on the basic rights of equal treatment under the law.

Despite this ruling, the German states are far from having developed and implemented a uniform policy of non-prosecution with respect to cannabis offences. A consensus has not been reached by the individual states, and thus considerable regional differences continue to exist. Several northern and middle states (Hamburg, Hesse, Lower-Saxony, North Rhine-Westphalia, and Schleswig-Holstein among others) have adopted guidelines or recommendations requiring or allowing the non-prosecution in cases involving 10–15 g of cannabis and, in Schleswig-Holstein, up to 30 g of cannabis. In contrast, the southern states and several eastern ones (such as Baden-Württemberg, Bavaria, Saxony-Anhalt, and Thuringia) have issued more restrictive guidelines, ruling that prosecutor's offices and courts can only dismiss cases involving less than 6 g of cannabis. The more liberal states also allow dismissals for repeat offenders, whereas conservative states usually rule out this possibility or allow dismissals only in exceptional circumstances. Some states (such as Mecklenburg-West Pomerania) have issued no such guidelines so far (Schäfer & Paoli, 2004; see also Körner, 1996).

2.3. Portugal

Upon the recommendation of the Commission for a National Drug Strategy (CNDS) in 1998, the Portuguese Parliament and Council of Ministers decriminalized the simple possession and use of cannabis, along with all other drugs, in July 2001. This decision was based on a broad policy of harm reduction that aims to reduce the harms to the drug-using individual as well as to society.

A central element of this harm reduction strategy was the declaration that drug users were not to be cast out of society as criminals or pariahs, but were to be fully integrated members of society (van het Loo, van Beusekom, & Kahan, 2002). This was demonstrated by the complete separation of drug offenders from the criminal justice system. If the police stop someone for using or possessing cannabis they do not arrest them. Instead they issue a citation to appear before the city's administrative committee, a three-person administrative body consisting of two medically qualified and one legal member. This committee decides on a course of action based on the evidence of the case, including the severity of the offence, the type of drug used, whether the use was public or private, if the person is an addict, whether the use is occasional or habitual and the personal circumstances of the user (van het Loo et al., 2002). The possible sanctions range from the suspension of individual rights (such as revocation of a professional license, a driver's license, or a ban on where the individual might travel) to fines. Sanctions can be removed or reduced after completion of voluntary treatment (van het Loo et al., 2002). Critics of the

Portuguese policy claim that the police and criminal justice system is simply being replaced by a new system. Only time will tell if the system that is implemented realizes the intentions of the policy makers.

2.4. The Netherlands

The Netherlands is the only country that has successfully experimented with a reduction in penalties for possession *and sale* of small amounts of cannabis. In 1976 a formal written policy of non-enforcement made the possession and sale of up to 30 g of cannabis *de facto* legal even though the Netherlands technically retained its prohibitionist policy against cannabis (Korf, 2002). The policy basically stated that prosecutors and police would refrain from enforcing the law in those cases where the quantity possessed or sold did not exceed 30 g. They would also tolerate the sale of these small amounts in coffee shops (MacCoun & Reuter, 2001). By not enforcing the prohibition in these cases, the Dutch government in effect sanctioned the creation of a retail cannabis market. They continue to aggressively enforce the prohibition against the sale, distribution, and trafficking of larger quantities of cannabis. They also prohibit the cultivation of cannabis for personal or industrial/commercial use.

In the 10 years after 1976, a series of formal and informal guidelines emerged that effectively regulate the *de facto* retail cannabis market. These regulations prevent coffee shops that sell cannabis products from the following – (1) advertising these products, (2) selling hard drugs, (3) selling cannabis to minors, (4) selling amounts greater than the legally specified quantity, and (5) allowing public disturbances (MacCoun & Reuter, 2001). In the 1990s, a licensing system was created that enables the government to limit the number and location of coffee shops, and hence to control where cannabis can be sold. In 1995, the formal non-enforcement policy was modified to reduce the quantity of cannabis that can be legally sold and/or possessed to 5 g (Korf, 2002). Thus the Dutch policy has allowed a retail cannabis market to develop as a result of non-enforcement of the law while maintaining a statutory prohibition on cannabis use and supply.

2.5. The U.S.A.

Even though the U.S. federal government treats marijuana possession as a criminal offence, the vast majority of marijuana possession cases are tried in state courts and hence are subject to state, not federal, law (Ostrom

& Kauder, 1999).[8] Therefore distinctions in state drug laws are important for understanding how marijuana offenders are treated in the U.S.A. Although it is commonly recognized that 11 U.S. states reduced the criminal penalties associated with possession of small amounts of marijuana during the late 1970s, recent analyses of state legal statutes shows that by 1989 many more states had reduced the penalties associated with minor marijuana possession offences, with 43 states and the District of Columbia allowing offenders to circumvent statutorily imposed jail time through diversion programmes (Pacula et al., 2003).

To more clearly demonstrate the complicated legal differences across U.S. states, we show in Table 1 information on decriminalization policy and statutory penalties in effect as of January 2001 for first time marijuana possession offenders caught in possession of small amounts of marijuana for all 50 states and the District of Columbia.[9] As in the other countries, each state uniquely defines what it means by "small amounts," and the laws described here are those associated with the first quantity trigger (smallest amount referred to in the state law). In column I, we identify those states that are widely recognized as decriminalized states in 2001 based largely on policies enacted during the 1970s (MacCoun & Reuter, 2001). In column II, we identify those states that reduced the criminality of minor marijuana possession offences by changing the criminal status of these offences to a non-criminal offence in their state law. When we compare states in columns I and II, we see that as of January 2001 15 states actually remove the criminal status of minor possession offences, seven of which are not formally recognized as decriminalized states. Furthermore, four states that are widely recognized as having decriminalization statutes (Alaska, Arizona, California and North Carolina) maintain the status of marijuana possession offences as a criminal charge.

In some of the U.S. states, a minor marijuana possession charge can also be removed through a formal process called expungement. Provided that the offender successfully completes mandated punishment for the offence, such as payment of a fine, drug education, treatment, or community service, then the charge is erased (or "expunged") from the individual's public record as if the crime never occurred. Column III identifies the 19 states that, as of January 2001, allowed for the possible expungement of minor marijuana possession offences committed by adults. Again, we see by comparing columns I and III that many of the states that have expungement provisions are not known as decriminalized states.

Table 1 demonstrates the problem of using a label like "decriminalization" to describe policy differences across jurisdictions, particularly within

Table 1. Recognized U.S. State Policies and Statutory Law as of January 2001.

State	I Recognized Decrim State	II Non-Criminal Status Offence	III Expunge Charge upon Completed Sentence	State	I Recognized Decrim State	II Non-Criminal Status Offence	III Expunge Charge upon Completed Sentence
AL				MT			
AK	Yes			NE	Yes	Yes	
AZ	Yes			NV			
AR				NH			
CA	Yes	Yes		NJ		Yes	Yes
CO	Yes	Yes		NM			Yes
CT			Yes	NY	Yes	Yes	
DE				NC	Yes		Yes
DC			Yes	ND			Yes
FL			Yes	OH		Yes	
GA				OK			Yes
HI			Yes	OR	Yes	Yes	
ID				PA			
IL				RI			Yes
IN				SC			Yes
IA				SD			
KS			Yes	TN			Yes
KY			Yes	TX			
LA				UT			
ME	Yes	Yes		VT		Yes	Yes
MD		Yes		VI			Yes
MA		Yes		WA			
MI				WV			
MN	Yes	Yes	Yes	WI		Yes	Yes
MS	Yes	Yes	Yes	WY		Yes	
MO							
				Total number of states	11	15	19

the U.S.A. today. Without a firm understanding of the legal environment in which these policies are enacted, or recognition of how the legal environment changes over time, it is easy to misunderstand policies as they are written, let alone how they are implemented. Future researchers interested in evaluating U.S. depenalization policy, for example, need to construct a more accurate representation of state statutory differences than those used in the past. Further, given the power of the judicial system in some jurisdictions, it is important to also consider the extent to which these laws have been shaped by the judicial systems through sentencing guidelines, assignment of discretionary authority, and case law. As is evident in the case of Germany, prosecutorial discretion has become increasingly more important in recent years than prior to 1992. There is similar evidence that prosecutorial discretion is important in the U.S.A. at least among youth, where prosecutors can decide for themselves whether to formally prosecute minor marijuana offenders (Terry-McElrath & McBride, 2004).

3. THE ROLE OF ENFORCEMENT

Of course, one must also consider the environment in which these policies are enacted in order to fully understand the implementation of the policy. The enforcement of these policies by police can either reinforce or counter the intentions of the statutory laws. As was discussed previously, although the Netherlands has a law prohibiting the use and sale of cannabis, they also have a formal policy of non-enforcement that creates an environment where small *de facto* legal markets can exist. However, most jurisdictions do not have formal enforcement policies such as these, and hence inconsistencies between written law and law enforcement are not as easily identifiable. Nonetheless, they have important implications for understanding the potential impact written law could have on behaviour, an issue we are beginning to carefully examine in several European countries. A simple look at the enforcement of marijuana laws in the U.S.A. provides some interesting insights, however, regarding the importance of understanding enforcement when evaluating the effect of policies.

The number of marijuana possession arrests in the U.S.A. more than doubled between 1992 and 1998, accounting for 38% of all drug arrests by 1998 (Federal Bureau of Investigation, FBI, 2001). Over the same period the National Household Survey on Drug Abuse shows that the prevalence of marijuana use in the general population (ages 12 years and older) rose very slightly from 7.9% in 1992 to 8.6% in 1998 (Substance Abuse and Mental

Health Services Administration (SAMHSA), 2001). Critics of U.S. policies argue that the enormous increase in marijuana possession arrests is the result of a law enforcement crackdown on non-violent drug offenders (Thomas, 1999; Gettman, 2000). Such a claim seems to be substantiated by the fact that of the 1,579,466 drug arrests in the U.S.A. in 2000, 5.6% were for marijuana sales or cultivation and 40.9% were for simple possession (FBI, 2001).[10] However, as reported previously, several U.S. states adopted policies that removed the criminal status of marijuana possession offences since. Hence, if these statutory changes in law did indeed reflect a real policy change that was uniformly enforced by law enforcement, one would not expect marijuana possession arrests to be as high in states decriminalizing possession of marijuana than those that did not. Further, we would not expect arrests to have risen as much in decriminalized states.

We examine the association between marijuana possession arrests and state statutory policy by linking statutory penalty data from our legal analysis of state statutes over the years 1991 through 2000 to arrest data collected by the FBI's Uniform Crime Report (UCR). The UCR system provides information on the number of crimes reported to the police in specific crime categories each year for every police jurisdiction in the U.S.A. Arrests are also reported by criminal offence. Data is collected on a monthly basis from approximately 17,000 law enforcement agencies and jurisdictions, although the crime and arrest data are not always complete from every agency. Each year, the Intra-university Consortium of Political and Social Research (ICPSR) generates county-level arrest and crime estimates from the incomplete agency data collected by the FBI and makes these data available to the public.[11] While the shortcomings of these data are well documented (e.g. O'Brien, 1985), they remain the only source of geographically disaggregated crime and arrest data in the U.S.A. The biggest limitation of the UCR arrest data is that they only report the arrest for the most serious crime committed. Hence, the data cannot be used to identify the total number of individuals arrested for specific charges because not all charges are reported in the data.[12] However, the data remain useful for analyses such as these where the interest is cases where the most serious offence was marijuana possession.

Table 2 reports the per capita marijuana possession arrest rate for each state for select years during the 1991–2000 time period as well as the per cent change in per capita arrest rates during selected years. Due to significant reporting problems in UCR, we do not include information for Florida, Illinois, Kansas, or Montana. States that have statutorily lowered the criminal status of marijuana possession offences involving small amounts of

Table 2. Marijuana Possession Arrests per 10,000 Residents.

	1991	1993	1995	1996	1998	2000	% Change 1991–1995	% Change 1995–2000	% Change 1991–2000
AL	11.898		33.651	42.885	52.347	52.592	182.8	36.0	342.0
AK	21.834	22.282	48.677	46.037	78.736	52.285	122.9	6.9	139.5
AZ	39.861	65.721	94.740	105.407	100.721	98.582	137.7	3.9	147.3
AR	18.811	26.537	49.825	61.565	64.381	53.192	164.9	6.3	182.8
CA	18.387	30.014	45.840	51.400	52.942	50.436	149.3	9.1	174.3
CO	23.412	51.197	82.132	78.622	80.505	92.143	250.8	10.9	293.6
CT	15.129	38.881	70.221	70.239	69.167	59.881	364.2	−17.3	295.8
DE	17.176	9.923		68.554	60.459	88.759			416.8
DC	17.284	28.350	82.908				379.7		
GA	11.978	28.196	51.171	59.699	79.293	64.513	327.2	20.7	438.6
HI	37.551	40.745	62.943	57.745	57.883	45.135	67.6	−39.5	20.2
ID	18.102		63.176	62.877	66.448	61.160	249.0	−3.3	237.9
IN	13.044	15.075	39.796	46.364	59.338	62.022	205.1	35.8	375.5
IA			30.243	37.605	47.834	53.718		43.7	
KY	28.610								
LA	15.629	25.386	59.016	66.557	69.223	76.953	277.6	23.3	392.4
ME	16.474	23.652	49.123	59.698	60.957	71.351	198.2	31.2	333.1
MD	21.780	38.049	82.430	81.712	96.462	102.624	278.5	19.7	371.2
MA	16.885	18.649	46.146	46.446	41.453	44.229	173.3	−4.3	161.9
MI	10.720	19.680	35.242	35.524	37.953	36.961	228.8	4.6	244.8
MN	11.139	20.871	45.479	45.128	58.846	61.862	308.3	26.5	455.3
MS			55.054	68.024	72.197	70.049		21.4	
MO	20.191	29.591	49.960	56.534	60.491	61.165	147.4	18.3	202.9
NE	29.558	35.789	65.036	72.635	81.670	95.241	120.0	31.7	222.2
NV				68.777	72.548	71.782			
NH	20.813	32.753		72.682	90.666	86.824			317.2
NJ	22.678	41.072	83.563	84.111	78.854	73.094	268.5	−14.3	222.3
NM	20.104	21.770	82.034	80.132	62.376	54.321	308.0	−51.0	170.2
NY	20.629	37.325	71.223	79.033	111.995	139.755	245.3	49.0	577.5
NC	22.828	27.867	48.547	58.382	66.291	61.745	112.7	21.4	170.5
ND			29.435	31.473	40.352	43.522		32.4	
OH	11.689	16.897	37.215	48.061	48.834	54.262	218.4	31.4	364.2
OK	19.964	30.220	50.804	51.975	70.156	75.704	154.5	32.9	279.2
OR	24.439	33.059	62.080	74.375	57.469	60.898	154.0	−1.9	149.2
PA	7.926	12.575	25.345	27.617	36.125	41.738	219.8	39.3	426.6
RI	18.346	39.585	65.548	53.252	68.797	67.496	257.3	2.9	267.9
SC			65.641	74.814	83.979	85.175		22.9	
SD	8.867	31.846	66.442	78.012	74.770	89.416	649.3	25.7	908.4
TN					40.780	52.081			
TX	22.807	40.247	66.304	74.905	75.053	72.730	190.7	8.8	218.9
UT	23.585	44.741	68.578	70.013	60.299	60.552	190.8	−13.3	156.7
VT	10.617		19.310	3.004	12.980	28.148	81.9	31.4	165.1

Table 2. (*Continued*)

	1991	1993	1995	1996	1998	2000	% Change 1991–1995	% Change 1995–2000	% Change 1991–2000
VA	14.084	25.944	54.592	65.037	58.079	47.113	287.6	−15.9	234.5
WA	15.748	24.694	44.262	53.967	57.307	64.485	181.1	31.4	309.5
WV	9.142	11.866	25.898	32.349	33.752	30.352	183.3	14.7	232.0
WI	19.251	31.808	66.519	73.626			245.5		
WY	14.756	22.759	51.407	57.844	100.541	93.579	248.4	45.1	534.2
AVG	16.249	28.865	49.609	53.843	56.859	56.708	201.2	14.6	264.4

marijuana to a non-criminal offence are indicated with shading.[13] The states that are written using bolded text are those commonly recognized as having adopted a decriminalization policy, but whose statutes still retain possession offences as a misdemeanor (i.e. criminal) offence. The average across all states are reported at the bottom of the table for each column.

There are a number of things to note from Table 2. First, by examining the last row, one can see that there was a 264.4% increase in marijuana possession arrests across all states and that the vast majority of this increase occurred between 1991 and 1995. Second, in 1991 there was not a huge amount of variation in the number of arrests per capita. Although there were some states with relatively low arrest rates (e.g. Pennsylvania and South Dakota) and those with relatively high rates (e.g. Hawaii and Arizona), the difference in arrest rates per capita between the highest and lowest state was only slightly larger than 30 arrests per capita. If we look at arrest rates in 2000, we see that the level of arrests across states has gotten substantially larger. Now the difference between the state with the lowest arrest rate (Vermont) and that with the highest arrest rate (New York) is nearly four times what it was in 1991, or 110 arrests per 10,000 people.

A particularly important feature of Table 2 is that states that have eliminated the criminal status of possession offences involving amounts of one ounce or less of marijuana (highlighted in gray) do not have systematically lower arrests per capita than those states retaining the criminal status. Indeed, several of the states, including New York and Louisiana, have larger per capita arrest rates in most years than the national average across states. Further, the increases in arrest rates during the 1991–1995 time period and the 1991–2000 time period is substantially larger than the national average for many of these states. This is further demonstrated in Fig. 1, where arrests in states without criminal charges for marijuana possession amounts

What Does it Mean to Decriminalize Marijuana

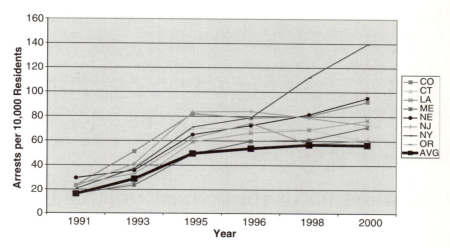

Fig. 1. Marijuana Possession Arrests in 8 of 14 U.S. States With No Criminal Charge for Small Amounts of Marijuana.

are graphed against the average total arrests for all states. Here it is easier to see that more than half of the states that do not consider small marijuana possession offences a criminal offence still have per capita arrest rates greater than the national average and they still experience a significant increase in arrests during the 1992–1995 time period.

There are at least two alternative interpretations of these data. First, it may be the case that the UCR marijuana possession arrest data do not generally reflect individuals in possession of small amounts of marijuana. If this is indeed the case, then these may not be the appropriate data for evaluating this sort of small policy difference across states. However, such an interpretation also implies that the rise in arrests during the 1990s does not reflect a crackdown on people caught in possession of only small amounts of marijuana as suggested by critics of the current policies. A second interpretation of these data is that the enforcement of marijuana laws today is not highly correlated with the criminal status of marijuana possession offences. States that have removed the criminal status of marijuana or adopted a widely recognized decriminalization policy during the 1970s do not have systematically lower rates of arrest and they experienced increases in possession arrests at rates comparable to that of the other states, with some significantly higher (e.g. New York, Minnesota, Connecticut, and

New Jersey) and some significantly lower (Vermont, North Carolina, Arizona, and California). Given that arrests rates do not appear to be correlated with statutory penalties,[14] it might not be surprising to find that statutory penalties have little effect on individual cannabis use behaviour. However, recent studies do find a consistent and statistically significant effect of these penalties on consumption behaviour in the manner consistent with a deterrent effect even after controlling for enforcement (DeSimone & Farrelly, 2003; Pacula et al., 2003; Williams, Pacula, Chaloupka, & Wechsler, 2004). It is not clear, in light of what we now know about enforcement, why this is the case.

4. KNOWLEDGE OF THE SEVERITY OF PENALTIES: A LOOK AT THE U.S.A.

Of course, in order for any policy to have a deterrent effect on behaviour, people must be aware of and understand the policy (both the law and its enforcement). In theory, any deterrent effect of levels of cannabis sanctioning should be mediated by citizens' perceptions of their certainty and severity.[15] Various lines of evidence suggest that citizens may have distorted or biased beliefs about sanctioning threats (see MacCoun, 1993), but very little work has been done to empirically investigate whether this is true with respect to drug laws.

Given recent information collected as part of the National Survey on Drug Use and Health (NSDUH), it is now possible to investigate this issue in the U.S.A. The NSDUH is an annual national household survey of the non-institutionalized U.S. population 12 years and older conducted by the SAMHSA. It is the primary source of information on the prevalence of use of illegal drugs for the U.S. population. Since 1999, approximately 70,000 individuals have been interviewed each year across the U.S.A. with at least 900 respondents in each of the 50 states. Great care is taken to ensure that information on illicit drug use is accurately reported. For example, the questions on illicit drug use are self-administered through a computer assisted interview survey, no names are used or collected during the interview, and interviews are conducted in private settings away from other people in the household.[16]

In 2001, the NSDUH included questions for the first time pertaining to the individual's knowledge of state marijuana laws. All individuals taking the survey were asked, "What is the maximum legal penalty in (state of residence) for first offence possession of an ounce or less of marijuana for your own use?" Possible responses were – (1) a fine, (2) probation, (3) community service, (4) possible prison sentence, (5) mandatory prison sentence, and (6) Do not know. Information on the weighted fraction of the state sample reporting specific penalties were aggregated to the state level and made available to us by the Office of Applied Studies (OAS) at SAMHSA.

To these state aggregated data we merged information on each state's statutory penalties associated with possession of *one ounce* of marijuana for first-time offenders. The penalties again represent laws in effect as of January 1, 2001, and include the minimum and maximum jail term, minimum and maximum fine, conditional discharge provisions, and expungement provisions for the lowest two quantity trigger amounts, which capture amounts of one ounce or less for all states.[17] The conditional discharge variable reflects instances where compliance with the specified conditions leads to a dismissal of charges.

The first column of Table 3 presents the fraction of the state population reporting a particular maximum penalty across all states, regardless of the state's actual penalties. On average we see that nearly one-third of the population do not know what the maximum penalty is for marijuana possession offences in their state and another third believe that possible or mandatory jail is the maximum offence. Note that 6% of the population reports that mandatory jail is the maximum offence for possession of an ounce of marijuana though no U.S. state requires a mandatory jail time for low-level marijuana possession offences.

To evaluate whether individuals understood the maximum penalty for possession of marijuana in their state, we differentiated states based on their statutory provision of jail sentences. We first separated states based on whether they were recognized in the literature as having a decriminalization policy ("decrim") or not ("non-decrim"). Although we showed in Table 1 that these policies do not reflect actual differences in the criminal status of marijuana offences, it may be the case that the mere label that has been applied to these states for the past 25 years might generate a greater awareness of the state's actual penalties for those living within these states. If people living in decriminalized states were actually aware of this labelled policy (i.e. that a violation was *not* subject to criminal penalties), then we would expect that they would be less likely to report jail as the maximum penalty and more likely to report fines or community service as the maximum penalty than people living in non-decrim states. The findings in the second and third columns of Table 3 show that this is indeed the case, as people living in so-called decriminalized states are statistically less likely to report jail as the maximum penalty and more likely to report fines as the

Table 3. Reported Maximum Penalty for Possession of One Ounce of Marijuana: Aggregated State-Level Data from the 2001 NSDUH.

	Full Sample	Decrim	Non-Decrim	P-Value	No Record or No Jail	Other	P-Value
Number of observations	51	12	39		22	29	
Maximum penalty							
Fine	0.151	0.199	0.136	0.000***	0.167	0.138	0.009***
Jail	0.326	0.307	0.331	0.076*	0.261	0.264	0.709
Mandatory jail	0.063	0.058	0.064	0.211	0.059	0.066	0.054*
Probation	0.134	0.121	0.138	0.029**	0.126	0.140	0.067*
Community service	0.073	0.070	0.074	0.528	0.075	0.072	0.527
Don't know	0.317	0.303	0.321	0.145	0.312	0.320	0.496

Notes: Each cell represents the fraction of the weighted state-sampled population reporting that the specific penalty is the maximum penalty associated with first-time marijuana possession offences for amounts less than an ounce of marijuana.
Significance is denoted as follows:
*indicates significance at the 10% level (two-tailed test).
**indicates significance at the 5% level (two-tailed test), and
***indicates significance at the 1% level (two-tailed test)

maximum penalty. However, the actual magnitude of these differences is extremely modest and nearly 30% of people living in a so-called decriminalized state still report jail as the maximum penalty imposed.

One explanation for this small difference in reported penalties is that we have misclassified people based on decriminalization status, as several other states have also eliminated jail time for possession offences (Pacula et al., 2003). So, in the second part of Table 3 we show differences in the fraction of the state population reporting specific penalties for states in which the jail times have been removed as a penalty (either by a change in the criminal status or a reduction in penalties) and those that do not. Again we find that individuals living in states that have statutorily removed jail sentences as penalties for possession of up to an ounce of marijuana are less likely to report jail as the mandatory penalty and more likely to report fines as the maximum penalty. However, again we see that the actual difference in knowledge across states is small.

Another explanation for the very small difference in knowledge of laws may have to do with the fact that recent changes in these penalties are not widely publicized in the press or other venues; hence, only those interested in obtaining this information search it out. Relevant evidence suggesting that this might indeed be the case comes from Johnston, O'Malley, and Bachman's (1981) report on decriminalization in the 1970s. Using the Monitoring the Future Survey of high-school seniors, they examined responses to an item asking, "Which best describes the law IN YOUR STATE regarding marijuana? Possession in private of an ounce or less of marijuana (by an adult) is... (a) a criminal offence, carrying a possible jail sentence, (b) a criminal offence, carrying a possible fine, but not a jail sentence, (c) a non-criminal offence, like a traffic ticket, carrying a small fine and no criminal record at all, (d) not a legal offence at all, (e) I do not know if the offence is criminal, but I know it carries a fine, and (f) I do not know." In the data reported by Johnston et al. (1981) it appears that in the 1970s many high-school seniors were aware of their state's marijuana laws, as those living in decriminalized states generally reported that jail was not a probable penalty by 1980 regardless of when the policy passed. In the early decriminalization adoption states, only 14% (1976) to 16% (1980) of citizens believed marijuana possession carried a possible jail sentence. In the late decriminalization adoption states the proportion of citizens holding this belief dropped precipitously, from 58% in 1976 to 18% by 1980. Overall, these results suggest that more people were aware of their state penalties in 1980 than today. Why? One possibility is that it is the publicity surrounding a change in law, rather than the law's actual enforcement, that produces differences in citizen perceptions by state. Another possibility, again not mutually exclusive, is that there has been erosion over time in what may have been, in the 1970s, a real policy change. Indeed, research in other policy areas have shown that the impact of a policy is usually seen within a 1–3-year period following the policy's adoption/effectiveness date (MacCoun, 1993; Ross, 1976). Given that many of the depenalization policies examined here occurred well before 2001, time may have decayed people's knowledge or awareness of the laws.

5. CONCLUSIONS

This chapter provides important insights regarding the range of cannabis depenalization policies that can be observed in Western countries and provides a framework in which policy analysts and makers should consider and compare specific policies. Decriminalization, which literally means an elimination of the criminal status of minor cannabis possession offences, is but one form of depenalization. The ubiquitous application of the term "decriminalization" to describe a range of policies has, however, obscured from the debate and analysis meaningful policy differences that exist across countries both in the laws and their enforcement. Although numerous Western countries have adopted policies that reduce the penalties associated with minor cannabis possession offences, the extent to which criminal charges are removed, reduced penalties apply to all offenders, and "minor" is precisely defined, varies substantially from country to country as well as within jurisdictions in the same country, as we showed for Germany and the U.S.A. Further, the extent to which those enforcing the laws (police and prosecutors in particular) influence the interpretation and implementation of these policies is largely unknown for most countries and cannot always be interpreted from official statistics on arrests. Finally, rarely has consumer knowledge of these laws been considered when evaluating the magnitude of the effect of these policies.

Without a careful understanding of these nuances within each country and how they differ across countries, it is unclear what can be gained from analyses attempting to evaluate the impact of them. Even in the U.S.A., new research is needed that more accurately evaluates real differences across the states in terms of the legal status of possession offences, how these laws are enforced and interpreted by police and prosecutors, how these differences get translated into arrest patterns, and how these differences in laws and their enforcement are perceived by citizens. Only then we can hope to accurately assess the real impact of a policy change on the primary outcomes of interest – consumption and harms. Strides are being made within particular countries to better understand these issues, but much work remains.

NOTES

1. Although the Netherlands is recognized as having a partially legal cannabis market, their statutory law still prohibits the sale, cultivation, and distribution of cannabis. The details of this policy are explained later in the document.

2. Some countries do differentiate penalties imposed on those caught possessing cannabis and those caught using it.

3. Of course, it is also possible to reduce the burden through regulatory law, case law, or sentencing guidelines. Adopting a policy of non-enforcement, such as that adopted in the Netherlands, is an example of how to change the policy without using statutory law.

4. A conviction for cannabis possession in another country can lead to denial of a U.S. visa, for example.

5. All three countries have decriminalized all psychoactive substances, not just cannabis.

6. Other states in Australia have retained the criminal status of these minor cannabis offences, although diversion to education and treatment are now the most common outcome for first offenders in all states.

7. In Germany, the federal law does not distinguish cannabis from other illegal drugs. In practice, however, consumption-related offences are handled (and dismissed) differently depending on the type of the substance involved.

8. In the U.S.A., marijuana is by far the most common form of cannabis product consumed for recreational purposes, and most statistics and statutes refer explicitly to marijuana. Hence, for consistency we will use the term marijuana when discussing U.S.A. data or laws.

9. The statutory data were collected through original legal research by experts at The MayaTech Corporation for the purposes of this project.

10. It is interesting to note that the fraction of drug arrests involving marijuana sales or cultivation did not change much during the 1992–1998 time period when marijuana possession arrests took off (FBI, 2001).

11. As ICPSR changed their method for imputing missing values in 1994, it was necessary to develop our own method for imputing missing information that could be consistently applied for the full time period. Our algorithm is based on the "coverage indicator" (CI) developed by the ICPSR in 1994 to measure the integrity of the arrest data provided by the FBI. Each county has a score ranging from 0 to 100, with 100 denoting that arrest information for all agencies in the county. First, we calculated the lowest possible CIs for counties pre-1994. Second, we imputed annual arrest information for counties that *could* be below a CI threshold of 30. This was done for every year from 1990 to 2000. The imputed data are based on the estimates provided by counties (above this threshold) with similar populations and within the same state. We then summed all county-level arrests to generate state-level arrest rates (number of arrests per 10,000 residents) for marijuana possession offences in each state from 1991 through 2000. Alternative imputation strategies were also considered and evaluated. Although differences exist in the level of arrests generated by each of these methods, trends in these arrests over time were incredibly consistent. Information on how this imputation strategy compared to alternative methods is available from the authors upon request.

12. Indeed a recent evaluation of charges in Baltimore City revealed that only one-half (56%) of all marijuana possession charges in this area were cases where the marijuana possession charge was the most serious offence according to the FBI hierarchy of crimes (Reuter et al., 2000).

13. Specific definitions of "small amount" varies substantially across states from 10 g to over 1 lb.

14. Multivariate regression analyses that examine the relationship between statutory penalties and state arrest rates (and growth in arrest rates), controlling for the economy and unobserved fixed effects support the general finding that the level and rates of increase in arrest rates over time are not significantly correlated with state penalty variables.

15. We refer here to general deterrence; sanctions may also influence cannabis use through incapacitation, specific deterrence, price effects, availability effects, and stigma effects (see MacCoun, 1993; MacCoun & Reuter, 2001).

16. Further information about survey methodology is available at www.oas.samhsa.gov/nhsda/2k1nhsda/PDF/cover.pdf.

17. Illinois is the only state in which the penalty for possession of an ounce of cannabis is captured in a higher quantity trigger (trigger no. 3). In this one case we collected additional information so that we can reflect the penalties in place in all states for amounts involving one ounce of marijuana.

ACKNOWLEDGEMENTS

Research presented in this paper was supported by grants from the National Institute on Drug Abuse (R01DA12724) and the Robert Wood Johnston Foundation to RAND. We gratefully acknowledge research assistance from Jeremy Arkes. The opinions in this paper reflect those of the authors and not their respective institutions.

REFERENCES

Ali, R., Christie, P., Lenton, S., Hawks, D., Sutton, A., Hall, W. D., & Allsop, S. (1999). *The social impacts of the Cannabis expiation notice scheme in South Australia. Summary report presented to the Ministerial Council on Drug Strategy*, National Drug Strategy Monograph (Vol. 34). Canberra: Commonwealth Department of Health and Aged Care.

Bammer, G., Hall, W. D., Hamilton, M., & Ali, R. (2002). Harm minimisation in a prohibition context: Australia. *Annals of the American Academy of Political and Social Sciences, 58*, 80–93.

Blewett, N. (1987). *National campaign against drug abuse: Assumptions, arguments and aspirations*. Canberra: Australian Government Publishing Service.

Christie, P. (1999). *Cannabis offences under the cannabis expiation notice scheme in South Australia*. National Drug Strategy Monograph (Vol. 35). Canberra: Commonwealth Department of Health and Aged Care.

DeSimone, J., & Farrelly, M. C. (2003). Price and enforcement effects on cocaine and cannabis demand. *Economic Inquiry, 41*(1), 98–115.

Federal Bureau of Investigation. (2001). *Crime in the United States 2000*. Uniform Crime Reports. Washington, DC: U.S. Department of Justice.

Gettman, J. (2000). *Part one: County level arrest data 1995–1997*. National Organization for the Reform of Cannabis Laws Research Brief.http://www.norml.org/facts/arrestreport/index.html.

Johnston, L.D., O'Malley, P.M., & Bachman, J.G. (1981). *Cannabis decriminalization: The impact on youth 1975–1980*. Monitoring the Future Occasional Paper no. 13. Institute for Social Research, University of Michigan, Ann Arbor, Michigan.

Korf, D. J. (2002). Dutch coffee shops and trends in cannabis use. *Addictive Behaviors, 27*(6), 851–866.

Körner, H. (1996). Die Entpoenalisierung und die Entkriminalisierung von Cannabiskonsumenten mit geringen Cannabismengen zum Eigenkonsum. *Deutsche Vereinigung für Jugendgerichte und Jugendgerichtshilfen, 3,* 232–241.

MacCoun, R. J. (1993). Drugs and the law: A psychological analysis of drug prohibition. *Psychological Bulletin, 113,* 497–512.

MacCoun, R., & Reuter, P. (2001). *Drug war heresies: Learning from other vices, times and places.* Cambridge: Cambridge University Press.

O'Brien, R. (1985). *Crime and victimization data.* Beverly Hills, CA: Sage.

Ostrom, B., & Kauder, N. (1999). Drug crime: The impact on state courts. *National Center for State Courts Caseload Highlights, 5*(1). Available online at http://www.ncsonline.org/D_Research/csp/Highlights/DrugsV5%20No1.pdf

Pacula, R.L., Chriqui, J.F., & King, J. (2003). *Decriminalization in the United States: What does it mean?* National Bureau of Economic Research Working Paper no. 9690 (NBER), Cambridge, USA.

Reuter, P., Hirschfield, P., & Davies, C. (2000). Assessing the crack-down on marijuana in Maryland. Unpublished manuscript, University of Maryland.

Ross, H. L. (1976). The neutralization of severe penalties: Some traffic law studies. *Law and Society Review, 10,* 403–413.

Schäfer, C., & Paoli, L. (2004). Zwischenbericht zur Untersuchung "Drogenkonsum und Strafverfolgungspraxis", unpublished progress report submitted to the German Federal Ministry of Health and Social Security. January.

Substance Abuse and Mental Health Services Administration. (2001). *Summary of findings from the 2000 National Household Survey on Drug Abuse.* Washington, DC: Department of Health and Social Services.

Terry-McElrath, Y. M., & McBride, D. C. (2004). Local implementation of drug policy and access to treatment services. *Crime and Delinquency, 50*(1), 60–67.

Thomas, C. (1999). Cannabis arrests and incarceration in the United States. *FAS Drug Policy Analysis Bulletin, 7*(June), 5–7.

van het Loo, M., van Beusekom, I., & Kahan, J. P. (2002). Decriminalization of drug use in Portugal: The development of a policy. *Annals of the American Academy of Political and Social Science, 582,* 49–63.

Williams, J., Pacula, R. L., Chaloupka, F. J., & Wechsler, H. (2004). Alcohol and cannabis use among college students: Economic complements or substitutes? *Health Economics, 13*(9), 825–843.

ECONOMIC PERSPECTIVES ON INJECTING DRUG USE

David E. Bloom, Ajay Mahal and Brendan O'Flaherty

ABSTRACT

Injecting drug use (IDU) has traditionally been seen as a law enforcement problem and a stain on society. With the emergence of human immunodeficiency virus (HIV)/acquired immune deficiency syndrome (AIDS), however, the discourse on IDU has widened to include crucial public health and human rights concerns. Economic analysis, too, has much to contribute to the policy debate. By examining the costs and benefits of drug use from the perspective of injecting drug users, economic analysis can shed light on the problem of IDU and the transmission of HIV among users. This chapter also presents new results on the economic analysis of needle exchange programmes.

1. INTRODUCTION

Injecting drug use (IDU), when addressed at all, has for long been dealt with purely as a law enforcement problem. Its links with crime and its image as a stain on society have dominated policy debates (MacCoun & Reuter, 2002). Law and order approaches to IDU have had varying success; some have curbed the practice while others have made little impact, with suppliers and consumers finding other means of reaching each other. In the past, the drain on resources has been the major outcome of unsuccessful policies. More recently, human immunodeficiency virus (HIV)/acquired immune deficiency syndrome (AIDS) has emerged as an additional cost of IDU practices that involve the sharing of needles and syringes. IDU with HIV-infected injecting equipment is a highly effective means of HIV transmission, and ill-thought-out policies to control the former today run the risk of increasing the latter.

The emergence of HIV/AIDS has opened up the discourse on IDU, which is now increasingly seen as more than just a crime issue, since it also poses significant public health challenges and brings up human rights concerns. For instance, traditional crime-focussed approaches to addressing HIV among drug users have led to human rights abuses, some of which, such as the imprisonment of HIV-positive injecting drug users in the Indian state of Manipur in the early 1990s, have attracted worldwide attention (Sarkar et al., 1993). Perhaps of even greater concern is the recognition that IDU is a major channel for transmission of the virus in many countries and, since drug users have sex with non-drug users, it also acts as a bridge for HIV to cross into the mainstream population. Governments have therefore been forced to revise their stance on the issue. While many remain wary of providing services and information to individuals they see as criminals, some policy-makers have begun to bring users into the social services fold as part of multi-pronged HIV-prevention strategies (MacCoun & Reuter, 2002).

While public health and human rights aspects of IDU are obviously crucial, economic analysis also has much to contribute to the policy debate. During the last decade, economists have enhanced greatly our understanding of the HIV/AIDS epidemic by focussing on its economic dimensions – its economic impacts, its roots such as economic deprivation, or tools to evaluate alternative policy interventions, such as cost–benefit and cost-effectiveness analyses. A particularly fruitful area of research has been economists' contributions to behavioural models that describe HIV transmission among sex workers and subsequently into the general population (Kremer, 1996; Philipson & Posner, 1993). Economic research has also focussed on drug markets and drug use, characterized by significant theoretical and empirical contributions, especially in the field of drug addiction (Becker & Murphy, 1988; Grossman & Chaloupka, 1998; Saffer & Chaloupka, 1999). It is somewhat surprising then to find that there are relatively few economic analyses that focus on understanding the behaviour patterns of people who inject drugs and share needles and syringes, and how that behaviour links to HIV transmission. It is this gap that the chapter proposes to address.

In thinking about the ways in which economic analysis can contribute to the understanding of IDU and HIV transmission, we adopt the following strategy for this chapter. Section 2 describes the scale of IDU worldwide and HIV infection among injecting drug users to highlight the extent of the policy challenge. Section 3 examines possible interventions for reducing the harmful impacts of IDU and looks in particular at how an economic perspective, which takes into account incentives for injecting, can help. Section 4 concludes this chapter.

2. IDU AND HIV/AIDS: HOW BIG IS THE PROBLEM?

2.1. How Widespread is IDU?

According to the United Nations Office on Drugs and Crime (UNODC) (an organization whose name reflects the overwhelming policy emphasis on the links between drugs and crime), there are 13 million injecting drug users worldwide (UNODC, 2004). Users tend to be young men in their twenties and thirties who are usually unmarried and often from poor backgrounds (Riehman, 1996). Those that are employed work in low-skilled jobs. Injecting drug users are highly mobile, often travelling within their own countries and abroad to obtain or sell drugs or look for employment. A 1994 World Health Organization (WHO) study found that large proportions of users had recently injected outside their home cities, with many of these episodes involving needle sharing (WHO, 1994).

Detailed and up-to-date statistics on IDU are patchy, in part because, being illegal and covert, it is a difficult practice to measure. A recent United Nations review of 130 countries estimated that South and Southeast Asia hosts the highest number of injecting drug users (see Table 1).

In terms of the proportion of the population injecting drugs, Asia, where heroin is the main drug injected, and Latin America, where cocaine is more popular, have the highest rates among developing countries, with Africa only recently seeing increases in use (Riehman, 1996). Most countries have a share of injecting drug users in their total population that is below 1%, although Eastern European countries such as Russia and Estonia (each with 2%) and Poland (1.5%) have higher shares. In Asia, 1.5% of Malaysians inject drugs, while India and China, where the share of injecting drug users in the total population is estimated to be around 0.1%, nevertheless have over a million users each (Aceijas, Stimson, Hickman, & Rhodes, 2004).

Table 1. Number of Injecting Drug Users by Region of the World.

Region	Number of Injecting Drug Users (Millions)
South and Southeast Asia	3.3
Eastern Europe and Central Asia	3.2
East Asia and Pacific	2.3
North America	1.4
Western Europe	1.2
South America	1.0
Middle East and North Africa	0.4
Oceania	0.2
Caribbean	0.02
Sub-Saharan Africa	0.009

Source: UNODC (2004), Map 2, p. 47.

In the West, Spain has more than 1% of its population injecting drugs, with the corresponding estimate for the U.S.A. at around 0.5%.

The prevalence of IDU has shot up in some low- and middle-income countries in recent years. In Russia and India, for example, there are thought to be 20 times more injecting drug users today than in 1990 (although rates in Russia have recently stabilized) (United Nations Development Programme (UNDP), 2004). Globalization has contributed to this growth. Improved transport and communications networks have made it easier for drugs to be moved. Drug trade routes have therefore shifted and expanded, and previously untapped markets have been exposed to hard drugs for the first time. In large swathes of Asia, IDU was relatively unheard of until the 1980s; Southern India, for example, was only exposed to injection-quality heroin when young people began to migrate there from Manipur in the northeast. West African states such as Nigeria and Cote d'Ivoire, meanwhile, have recently become stops on international heroin trafficking routes. Both South Asia and West Africa have seen sharp rises in IDU (Stimson & Choopnaya, 1998). Institutional breakdown, such as the collapse of health and drug control systems in Russia, is a further factor behind the increases, and the greater availability of plastic syringes as countries have become more open to foreign-produced medical supplies may also have had an effect.

In some areas, on the other hand, IDU has stabilized or declined in recent years. After a clampdown on opium growing in Afghanistan in 2001, IDU rates fell in the countries of the former Soviet Union (although with the rapid resurgence of poppy growing in Afghanistan, rates may well be rising again). In Western Europe, moreover, IDU has been declining steadily in the past decade (UNODC, 2004).

2.2. IDU and HIV

Sharing unsterilized needles is a very effective means of transmitting HIV. HIV enters a population of injecting drug users either via users from other areas or sexually active individuals who also inject drugs. In New York, for example, HIV is thought to have crossed into the IDU population from men who have sex with men (Des Jarlais & Friedman, 1998). Once established, the virus can spread quickly. Needle sharing is common among users, sterilization of equipment is rare. Unprotected sex between those who inject drugs provides further opportunities for the virus.

The number of countries where HIV transmission among injecting drug users occurs has more than doubled, to 114, since 1992 (UNDP, 2004). At this time, an estimated 3.3 million injecting drug users are infected with HIV – one in 12 of all existing infections. In Eastern Europe, Asia, and Latin America in particular, infection through IDU accounts for a significant proportion of all HIV cases.

The UN Reference Group on HIV/AIDS Prevention and Care among Injecting Drug Users estimates that 41 countries have HIV prevalence among users of over 5% (Aceijas et al., 2004). Disparities between and within regions are large, with Asian drug users, for example, especially hard hit by AIDS. Data on infection rates among users are patchy and can differ wildly from study to study. The UN Reference Group review estimates rates of between 10% and 40% in Malaysia, for example, and 37–63% in Myanmar. High HIV rates in the IDU population have also been reported in Latin America and parts of Western Europe (see Table 2), while some countries, such as Hong Kong and Singapore, have very low levels of infection.

Once HIV enters an IDU population, it can quickly ravage it. Infection rates among users in New York City rose from 10% to around 50% between 1978 and 1982. After HIV penetrated the IDU population in Manipur, India, in 1982, infection rates hit 60% within 6 years. In Odessa, Ukraine, they hit 30% within a year and in Bangkok, Thailand, 40% within 2 years (UNODC, 2004). Infection rates in Bangkok and other previously hard-hit areas, such as Russia and Poland, have now stabilized, but the risk of HIV crossing from injecting drug users into the mainstream population remains.

HIV is transmitted from users to non-users through unprotected sex. Many injecting drug users are sexually active and there is some evidence that they use condoms less frequently than non-users (Riehman, 1996). In a 1994

Table 2. HIV Infection among Injecting Drug Users in Asia, Latin America, and Western Europe.

Regions/Countries	Estimates of HIV Infection among Injecting Drug Users
Asia	
China	0–80%
India	1–68%
Indonesia	15–47%
Malaysia	10–40%
Myanmar	37–63%
Latin America	
Argentina	19–39%
Brazil	28–42%
Puerto Rico (San Juan only)	42–55%
Uruguay	8%
Western Europe	
France	14–19%
Italy	10–66%
Portugal	14%
Spain	15–66%

Source: Aceijas et al. (2004).

study carried out in Rio de Janeiro, the WHO found that 70% of users reported never using condoms with casual partners, although of course behaviour may have changed since. In Bangkok, 45% never used them (WHO, 1994). Studies in India also indicate lower rates of condom use among those who inject drugs (Kumar, Aggarwal, & Kumar, 1996).

Whether HIV among injecting drug users is transmitted to the general population, of course, depends on the amount of unprotected sex they have with non-users. Sexual intercourse is a less efficient means of transmitting the virus than sharing needles, so the non-IDU individuals most likely to be at risk are those who have sex with users on a regular basis. Prisoners and clients of sex workers may be the most likely conduits from users to the mainstream population, along with long-term partners of drug users.

Many injecting drug users go into sex work in order to finance their habit, an obvious way in which economics enters the equation between HIV and IDU (UNODC, 2004, p. 51). Some sex workers, moreover, inject drugs to relieve stress. A U.S. study found that 70% of female users and 56% of male users had had sex in return for money or drugs (Rothenberg et al., 2000).

Studies in Europe and Asia have also found overlap between the two practices. People who have unprotected sex with sex workers are therefore vulnerable to HIV infection.

IDU is also common in prisons. Due to the constraints in such settings, sharing needles is widespread. Sexual intercourse between prisoners (mostly men) occurs frequently, and since anal sex is a more effective transmission route than other types of intercourse, HIV rates tend to be higher inside than outside prisons (UNODC, 2004). Adding IDU to the mix puts prisoners and those they come into contact with at even greater risk. According to UNODC, "After the prisoner's release, the virus is spread via sexual transmission to sexual partners, and via needle sharing to other injecting drug users . . . These prison populations constitute a significant risk factor for the diffusion of HIV" (UNODC, 2004).

Unprotected sex with sex workers or individuals whose sexual history is not known, of course, is risky whether or not that individual is an injecting drug user. If sex workers do not contract HIV from needle sharing, they may well contract it through intercourse. It is the efficiency with which needle sharing disseminates the virus that adds an extra element of risk to relationships with injecting drug users and makes them a likely route for the virus to enter the general population. In the U.S.A., infection rates among injecting drug users' partners rose steadily through the 1990s (Morbidity and Mortality Weekly Report (MMWR), 1996). In Yunnan Province, China, where 49% of married male users in a study were HIV-positive, 10% of their non-IDU wives were also infected. None of the couples used condoms (Zheng et al., 1994). The study authors estimated an annual transmission rate of 6.4% per person.

Sharing needles therefore poses serious threats to both injecting drug users and mainstream populations. HIV has a disproportionate effect on those who inject drugs compared to the rest of society. In the U.S.A., 36% of HIV-positive women and at least 23% of men are thought to be injecting drug users (less than 1% of the overall population injects drugs) (Centers for Disease Control and Prevention (CDC), 2002). In Western Europe, 10% of new infections in 2002 occurred through IDU, and in Eastern Europe 41% (European Centre for the Epidemiological Monitoring of AIDS, 2003). In parts of the developing world outside Africa, injecting drug users represent an even higher proportion of infections – in Malaysia, 77% of people living with HIV/AIDS are injecting drug users, and in China and Vietnam around two-thirds of infected individuals inject drugs (Aceijas et al., 2004).

IDU is likely to become a less important mode of HIV transmission once the virus takes hold in the mainstream population, with sexual intercourse taking over as the main transmission channel. Unprotected sexual intercourse between users and non-users, however, remains an effective way for the virus to bridge the two population groups.

2.3. Policy Challenges

Clearly, IDU poses threats to societies as well as practitioners. As indicated above, users can act as a bridge for HIV to cross over into the mainstream population if they have unprotected sex with non-IDU partners, a phenomenon that constitutes a negative externality, if the latter are uncompensated (Philipson & Posner, 1993). Similarly, HIV-positive female users may also transmit the virus to their children during childbirth and while breastfeeding. As well as the obvious harm in terms of poor health and loss of life, this may have significant economic costs for societies, which have to divert resources to HIV/AIDS treatment and also lose many productive individuals to the virus (HIV/AIDS primarily affects people of working age) (Bloom et al., 2004).

A different type of public health and economic problem is associated with increased levels of crime that often accompany IDU. This association is not surprising since sustaining a drug habit is expensive, and the difficulty of combining repeated IDU with the need to finance the habit forces many users to turn to crime. For instance two-thirds of people arrested in Britain test positive for drugs, while in Holland half of all petty crimes are committed by users of hard drugs such as heroin and cocaine. The British Home Office estimated that drug-related crime costs the country over $7 billion per year (*Economist*, 2002). Drug-related crime also diverts resources from other law and order matters, increasing the risk of broad social breakdown.

The crime problems associated with injected drugs are not limited to the places where drugs are used, as is best illustrated by drug-producing countries such as Colombia and Afghanistan. Poverty and lack of social cohesion, and law and order promote suitable conditions for the growth and manufacture of drugs. The latter, in turn, creates further societal divisions (from petty crime to full-scale war) and hinders development efforts. The prospects of entire societies are therefore threatened. Sanctions against countries that produce drugs can also have negative effects. Sanctions deepen poverty, hunger, and unemployment, and force more individuals to resort to illegal means of making a living. They also distract the sanctioning countries' attention from other issues. The National Commission on Terrorist Attacks upon the United States (2004) found that customs officers and law enforcement agencies were more preoccupied with preventing illegal drugs entering the country than with the threat of terrorism.

IDU, then, poses complex challenges to societies. The long-recognized links with crime remain important, but the emergence of HIV/AIDS has added a new dimension to drug use and requires new approaches from policy-makers. Traditional law and order solutions may now have the unintended consequences of worsening a country's AIDS problem. These and other interventions to reduce IDU will be discussed in Section 3 of this chapter.

3. IDU: ECONOMICS OF BEHAVIOUR AND INTERVENTION

This section focuses on the contribution of economic analysis to policy thinking about HIV transmission among injecting drug users. The centrepiece of the economic approach is to view individual behaviour as being "rational" in the sense of being more or less determined by a comparison of the benefits and costs to the individual of each action that is being contemplated, and that the plan is consistent over time (Becker & Murphy, 1988). The section is divided into two parts. The first introduces a simple framework of individual behaviour that sheds light on the circumstances in which individuals would choose injection over other methods of drug consumption. The second uses the insights of this framework, along with the economic analysis of drug and needle markets, to highlight the potential efficacy of various policy interventions currently being used to address the HIV epidemic.

3.1. Individual Behaviour

IDU is an efficient way of achieving a high. By entering the bloodstream and the brain faster than drugs that are inhaled, injected drugs produce both a more immediate and more satisfying rush. Since the invention of the hypodermic syringe in 1850 allowed drugs to be administered intravenously, heroin, cocaine, and amphetamines have been the most commonly injected drugs worldwide, although many other drugs can also be injected.

To understand how economists perceive the decision to inject, consider an individual who seeks to obtain the maximum possible satisfaction (or utility). This individual regards increased highs from drug consumption as enhancing utility (along with other consumable items such as food), but recognizes the fact that increased drug consumption at any given point in time affects his utility not just at the current time, but potentially also in future time periods by increasing his "tolerance" levels to increased quantities of the drug.

He cannot, however, consume infinite amounts of food and drugs, owing to the budgetary constraint that he faces. The individual's problem is: How much of drugs (leading to highs) and how much food should he consume? A specific example of this decision-making process in action is the rational addiction framework adopted in the influential work of Becker and Murphy (1988), in which an individual seeks to maximize lifetime utility subject to a lifetime budget constraint.

In the context of the preceding framework, it immediately follows that, all else the same, if there is *no* discomfort from needles and needle prices are sufficiently low, the individual will always prefer to use the most effective mode of drug intake, that is, injection. This is because he can always replicate the high produced by an alternative mode of drug intake while spending less on the drug. Interestingly, the behavioural framework described in the previous paragraph can provide a straightforward justification for why access to injection equipment can lead to increased use of drugs. In particular, a key result in the rational addiction literature in economics is that decreases in the unit prices of drugs can lead to their increased and persistent consumption in the long run (Becker & Murphy, 1988). Given that injection drug use is more efficient, increased access to injection equipment is equivalent to a reduced price for obtaining a high, with the implication that IDU will lead to increased levels of drug consumption, both in the present and in the long run.

The increased benefit obtained from injecting rather than smoking drugs raises the question of why some users choose not to inject. This requires expanding upon the theoretical framework of rational addiction discussed above to allow for a number of negative consequences associated with IDU. Several negative consequences exist. IDU can cause great harm to those who practise it by enhancing dependency. Since this increases tolerance to a drug, users need larger doses to achieve a high, which heightens the risk of overdose. Dependency also impairs concentration on day-to-day tasks, making it difficult to work and forcing many to turn to criminal means of obtaining funds to buy further fixes, which may also impose disproportional costs on the drug user (Iversen, 2001).

Injecting drug users also face the risk of infection with HIV or hepatitis. Many users share needles, for reasons of scarcity, camaraderie, or fear of arrest for needle or drug possession. Studies in Rio de Janeiro, India, and China have found that the majority of users regularly share syringes (Riehman, 1996). If needles are improperly cleaned, traces of blood may remain on them and infections can be easily transmitted between users. McCoy and Inciardi (1995) have found that, in settings where 10% of injecting drug users are infected with HIV, a user shooting up with a shared needle three times a day is very likely to use an infected needle within 7 days.

The opprobrium of society is another major negative effect of IDU. Unlike smoking, injection leaves visible scars on the body. It also requires visits to pharmacies or other stores to buy equipment. As well as being stigmatized by their peers, therefore, injecting drug users are also more likely to be arrested than those who smoke. In many countries, too, health services, legal systems, and other state bodies discriminate against those who inject drugs.

The preceding framework for individual drug injecting behaviour can readily accommodate a scenario providing for the sharing of injecting equipment, as should be obvious from the discussion above. In particular, the greater is the full cost of owning a personal needle (or a new needle) relative to the expected cost of a shared needle (including the expected cost of HIV infection from sharing), the greater the likelihood will be of the individual sharing injecting equipment.

It should be emphasized in this connection that the full cost of a personal needle is not just the market price of the needle at a pharmacy: Black market needle prices will typically be higher when needles cannot be purchased without a prescription. Moreover, the (expected) costs of carrying a personal needle would also go up if possessing injecting equipment without a prescription is considered illegal, or when the chance of being arrested for drug possession, or being otherwise harassed by the police, increases with needle possession. This last possibility would also adversely affect the frequency with which injecting drug users would buy drugs, potentially lowering their opportunity of buying drugs at the best prices. Sharing would, of course, lower the likelihood of a given individual being caught with injecting equipment during a random police check, by reducing the requirement for every injecting drug user to carry his own needle.

The expected cost of infection from sharing a used needle would be small if the individual making the decision already knows himself to be HIV-positive with a high degree of certainty. In contrast, if the individual is HIV-free, the expected cost of being infected is likely to be high.

3.2. Interventions in IDU

The central problems of IDU are needle sharing and drug dependency. Needle sharing may result in HIV and hepatitis infection among users and, via sexual contact with them, non-users. Drug dependency causes physical and psychological problems for users, increases the risk of overdose and premature death, reduces employment prospects and therefore quality of life, and drives many users to crime.

Worldwide responses to these two root problems are ranged across a broad legal spectrum, with outright criminalization (of drug production, sale, and possession; and needle sale and possession) at one end, and legalization at the other. So far, no country has tried outright legalization, though some have legalized parts of the IDU tool kit while treating leniently those that remain illegal (MacCoun & Reuter, 2002).

3.3. Criminalization

As with the other methods employed to tackle the problems of IDU, outright criminalization can have positive, neutral, or negative effects. At the level of production, Afghanistan's ban on opium poppy production in 2001 and reduced production in Myanmar and Laos cut IDU in Central, South, and Southeast Asia in 2002, for example (UNODC, 2004) (although even here the long-term effects are uncertain as poppy growing has recently recovered in Afghanistan).

Efforts by the U.S.A. to stop cocaine production in South America, however, have merely served to destabilize countries, such as Colombia, and shift the industry to other parts of the region, such as Peru, without reducing the availability of drugs in the U.S. Gang warfare over control of distribution networks within the U.S.A., meanwhile, continues to take a heavy social toll. Even where law enforcement efforts are successful in targeting the production of drugs that can be injected, they may, at least until production shifts to other areas, drive up drug prices. When such efforts are successful, users can then obtain a smaller quantity of drugs for their money and therefore need to gain satisfaction from a smaller amount, or spend more money. If the rational drug user of the previous subsection was initially smoking/inhaling drugs, he might find injecting, which provides a more immediate and more enduring high than the other intake options, an attractive option, if the benefits minus the risks (expected cost) from IDU exceed the net benefits from smoking/inhalation.

If sharing is the cheaper of the two injecting options (sharing versus owning a personal needle) an even lower cost is possible by sharing needles, although the individual's risk of HIV infection, of course, goes up. It is important to note that sharing would be the preferred mode for injecting drugs, when the "full" price of owning a personal needle is high for the reasons mentioned previously (illegality of possessing a needle, potential for getting caught for drug possession when possessing a needle) and the expected cost of injecting with an infected needle is low. Individuals infected with HIV, or those that foresee sharing frequently in their "careers", might be expected to have relatively lower expected costs of sharing injecting equipment and, therefore, will prefer sharing now when injecting drugs.

At the level of consumption, in India, for example, efforts to clamp down on heroin use in the 1980s were successful in curbing heroin injection but unsuccessful in changing injecting behaviour, as users injected synthetic opiates instead (Riehman, 1996). Criminalization of sale and consumption also has the effect of driving IDU off the streets and into prisons in many countries, where the imperative to share needles is increased, rationalized in the individual utility maximization framework as an increase in the full cost of obtaining new needles. In 1994, the WHO recommended that drug policies switch their focus from law enforcement to public health and socially based approaches (WHO, 1994).

A parallel can be drawn between the criminalization of IDU and methods to curtail sex work. Like drug use, sex work has long been treated as a crime and dealt with purely by law enforcement. In Asia, for example, where the sex work industry blossomed in the 1960s and 1970s, initial responses took the form of arrests or even execution of sex workers and pimps. Since the industry and the abuses that tarnished it continued unabated, however, policy makers were forced to look for new solutions. This search became more urgent with the advent of HIV/AIDS, as sex work was now linked to an unusually serious public health problem – one that goes far beyond concerns about syphilis and gonorrhea. In recent years, Asian governments have worked through brothel madams to improve working conditions for their employees and through non-governmental groups to transmit health messages and promote alternative employment opportunities for young women. In Thailand, where drug dealers continue to be executed, sex work has been decriminalized.

Some governments have begun to take a similar approach in their response to IDU. Several countries have attempted to improve the conditions within which IDU takes place. Some have done this by relaxing laws, with countries such as Turkey legalizing needle sale and possession. A broader perspective, incorporating public health and economic considerations, has also begun to make inroads into drug policy.

3.4. A Broader Perspective

Although legalizing needle sale and possession stops short of complete decriminalization of drug possession and use, it is a tacit acknowledgement that eradicating the practice is beyond governments' capabilities; if those who want to can access drugs (and they find many ingenious ways of doing so), they will use them, and if they use them it is better that they use them safely. Legalization of needle sale increases availability and therefore lowers the market price of needles. Perhaps even more significantly, it reduces the full cost of carrying a personal needle, which includes the monetary cost as well as the cost resulting from legal sanctions related to carrying injecting equipment on one's person. Thus, users who would otherwise rent needles at shooting galleries or share needles in a group may now find it worthwhile to purchase and carry their own needle. Users concerned about infection, therefore, or who place a premium on needle sharpness (old needles are blunter than new ones) may switch to buying new needles from legal outlets such as pharmacies.

Research conducted for this chapter has found that legalization of needle sale has a positive impact similar to that of needle exchange programs (NEPs) on reducing HIV infection. As the theoretical model that is the basis for our findings provides identical conclusions for the case of needle legalization and NEPs, we will provide a fuller explanation of our results during the discussion on the impact of NEPs below.

The above theoretical conclusions are borne out by studies. After needle sale was legalized in the U.S. state of Connecticut in 1992, for example, needle sharing is reported to have decreased from 71% to 15% within 3 years (Span, 1996).

For needle legalization to be fully effective, law enforcement agencies need to be included in discussions about enforcement. Legalizing needles does not mean legalizing drugs, and police have been known to search and arrest people purchasing needles from pharmacies on suspicion of drug possession (Stimson, 1988). If injecting drug users cannot be sure they will be able to purchase needles freely, legalization is likely to have little or no effect on needle sharing because its effect on the extent of needle sharing depends on how legalization of needle possession/purchase by injecting drug users can lower the carrying costs of needles.

3.5. Strategy on Provision of Drugs to Users

Given that the illegality of drug possession, and the associated risk of arrest and incarceration is a major factor in the sharing of needles, an alternative approach to reaching drug users might be to supply small amounts of drugs for consumption purposes to inject in settings that are relatively free from such risk. These methods may have benefits other than reduction in transmission of HIV. In Switzerland, for example, daily heroin doses are provided to users, and crime and drug-related deaths have declined as a consequence. While IDU remains officially illegal, police do not intervene in the heroin programme (*Economist*, 2003). Such radical approaches remain uncommon, although Britain also supplied heroin to users until the 1960s.

Alternatively, one may offer other drugs to reduce dependency that are cheaper and may appeal to drug addicts as a substitute – treatment with methadone is becoming more widespread (MacCoun & Reuter, 2002). Methadone, which is a synthetic narcotic, reduces heroin withdrawal symptoms and frees users from craving for the drug, because its effects on the body last several hours longer than those of heroin, and it has a high similar in many respects to that of heroin. Due to these features, methadone offers the potential of reducing the optimal injection frequency of drug users, and therefore reducing the incidence of HIV in injecting drug user populations. As it is also cheaper than heroin and is legal when prescribed by a licenced provider (e.g., in the U.S.A.), it likely reduces the carrying cost of injecting equipment, thereby making needle sharing less desirable, in addition to reducing the incentives for crime. Moreover, methadone clinics provide methadone orally, so that IDU is likely to decline even further. When combined with counselling, methadone can be an effective "cure" for heroin dependency. Studies in Hong Kong and New York have found that users attending methadone clinics that provide methadone were to a large extent protected from HIV infection, while other research has found that methadone treatment is a cost-effective way of reducing needle sharing, crime, and drug-related deaths (Riehman, 1996; Marseille et al., 2002).

3.6. Promotion of Bleach and NEPs

Bleach distribution and NEPs focus on the second major problem posed by IDU, needle sharing. By bleaching used syringes, it has been suggested, needle-sharing users can reduce the risk of hepatitis and HIV infection. Unfortunately, bleach is not readily available in countries where it is not used as a disinfectant in homes, however, and its effectiveness is disputed (Chitnis, Chitnis, Patil, & Chitnis, 2002). Even if it was effective as an HIV-disinfectant, bleaching provides no incentives to reduce sharing of injecting equipment in a regime where needles and drug possession are subject to severe penalties. It may be, though, more effective than doing nothing, particularly when bleach is supplied to users through outreach campaigns that also provide information and advice (Abdala, Gleghorn, Carney, & Heimer, 2001).

NEPs are a more effective and increasingly common method of tackling needle sharing. Like bleach promotion programmes, they are often combined with outreach work, frequently with former users providing advice on safe needle and syringe use and counselling. As with methadone programmes, successful NEPs can bring health service providers closer to injecting drug users and provide an opportunity to wean users off drugs altogether.

NEPs' principal goal, however, is to cut HIV infection. The traditional view is that they do this by replacing old needles with new ones, thereby reducing the proportion of contaminated needles in circulation, and so reducing the likelihood of a shared needle being HIV-infected. Making clean, sharp needles available at a low price has the added effect of diminishing the need to share needles. NEPs have been implemented in a variety of settings, from Britain and the Netherlands in Western Europe, to Nepal and Thailand in Asia, to Brazil, Canada, and the U.S.A. in the Americas. How they work varies – some are legal and supported or run by governments, while others are illegal and run solely by non-governmental organizations. In some Western European countries, syringes can be purchased or exchanged at vending machines (Lurie et al., 1993). Programmes in other settings, however, operate covertly.

A review for the Centers of Disease Control and Prevention of NEPs in the U.S.A., Canada, the Netherlands, and Britain observed that NEPs did not limit themselves to needle exchange activities. Most of them provided condoms to clients, as well as advice on HIV and other health matters. They also referred clients to public health services including methadone programmes and HIV counselling and testing. However, drug treatment facilities are typically not set up to cope with large numbers of regular referrals from NEPs, so many users end up on long waiting lists for treatment. NEPs, the reviewers concluded, are not sufficiently integrated into public health systems for a needle exchange-drug treatment nexus to function effectively.

Research into the effectiveness of NEPs in reducing HIV-infection rates has shown little by way of direct evidence of NEPs on HIV-transmission reduction. However, indirect evidence has been considered quite compelling on this score. In New Haven, Connecticut, the fraction of infected needles returned to the city's NEP declined from 67% to 40% after the programme was introduced, and there was a decline in needle-sharing rates, although HIV infection itself was not measured (Kaplan, Khoshnood, & Heimer, 1994). The aforementioned CDC review found no clear correlation between NEPs and decreased infection rates, but it did confirm the New Haven findings of reductions in needle sharing and therefore risk behaviour, after the introduction of NEPs. In smaller-scale studies, although the overall balance is positive, the extent of the effect is disputed and, of course, varies from programme to programme and from country to country. Based on studies of risk reduction, Lurie and associates found that the lifetime medical cost of treating an individual infected with HIV was at least 10 times the annual financial cost of operating an NEP, thus pointing to the large gains possible from NEPs (Lurie et al., 1993). In Hamilton, Canada, the local NEP was forecast to prevent 24 cases of HIV infection in 5 years, with a ratio of cost savings to costs of 4 : 1, given the significant gains in avoided treatment costs (Gold, Gafni, Nelligan, & Millson, 1997).

3.7. Evaluation of NEPs in an Economic Framework

Economists can contribute significantly to the understanding of the working of NEPs and their effectiveness on HIV transmission. Almost all of the existing work assessing the impact of NEPs on HIV transmission is based on epidemiological models that pay little attention to the determinants of behaviour regarding the type of needle (new versus old) and the extent of needle sharing, the numbers and types of needles exchanged at an NEP, and the average number of times a needle is used. The prevailing approach has been to treat the likelihood of being injected by a HIV-contaminated needle as being determined by a probability distribution independent of an individual injector's decision to share or not. In this view, "sorting" among injectors and needles is purely random: Infected needles are neither more nor less likely to get matched with infected people than non-infected needles are; and the converse is true as well. The key assumption is that an individual's beliefs about his expected likelihood of HIV infection would have no influence on what sort of needle he uses. This assumption appears not to be supported in studies of other modes of HIV transmission (see Philipson & Posner, 1993, p. 69), or in empirical studies of IDU behaviour (Desenclos, Papaevangelou, & Ancelle-Park, 1993; Magura et al., 1989). If positive matching of the sort suggested in these studies occurs among injecting drug users, it is likely that existing estimates of NEP effectiveness may be misleading.

To see why sorting can potentially be important for assessing NEPs, consider a polar case of sorting. Suppose there are two groups of injecting drug users, a safe group, and a risky group. Members of the safe group know that they are HIV-negative, know everyone in the group is HIV-negative, and share only among themselves. The members of the risky group of injecting drug users know they are HIV-positive, know everyone in the group is HIV-positive, and share only among their group. Then changes in the needle infection rate recorded in the literature may reflect only changes in the rate at which the two groups hand needles into the NEP. The falling needle infection rate indicates only that the safe group is becoming relatively more numerous among those who turn in needles either, for instance, because knowledge about the NEP is disseminating more quickly among this group, or because the safe group finds it optimal to turn needles over more quickly than the risky group. In either case, the fall in the needle infection rate would have no bearing whatsoever on the spread of HIV.

Similarly, existing models treat needle exchanges very much like "mosquito nets" that randomly net-contaminated (or uncontaminated) needles, and replace them with uninfected new needles. But injecting drug users are likely to choose which needles to turn in and when to turn them in. Thus one would expect the least desirable and therefore the oldest needles to be the ones most likely turned into NEPs (i.e., discarded). One immediate consequence is that the needles that are turned into NEPs will have higher contamination rates than of the "average" needle being used by drug injectors. That would suggest that analyses using needle infection rates among needles turned into NEPs are based on "terminal" needle infection rates and not "average" needle infection rates; and so will give an inaccurate estimate of HIV-transmission rates.

It should also be added that most current epidemiological models for IDU and HIV take as given that NEP needles would exchange one for one with the existing stock of needles, leaving their overall supply unchanged. If as we would expect, there is a black market flow of needles that responds to the NEP intervention, the attractive results claimed in existing studies may not hold up; for instance, about 30% of the needles the New Haven NEP collected were from non-programme sources. Most existing analyses cannot say whether reductions in flows of needles from those other sources offset, or more than offset, the NEP flows. If there were a reduction in needle flows from alternative sources that fully offset the added flow from an NEP, the NEP would accomplish nothing.

In work undertaken for this chapter we modelled IDU behaviour in different settings that allowed for optimizing behaviour by injecting drug users and the existence of markets for needles. In the model, a drug user makes a decision on whether to rent an old needle, to rent a new needle for injecting drugs, or opt for smoking, abstaining, or carrying one's own needle in a utility maximization framework. The model allowed for both new and old needles, and for the fact that needles have finite life spans. The model and its variants were used to analyse several different policies that have been proposed for reducing the spread of HIV among injecting drug users, such as

NEPs, legalization of needle sales, and harsher penalties for sale and possession. This chapter also reviewed epidemiological models currently used to assess NEPs and compared their results with our model's calculations.

The major conclusion of our work is that standard epidemiological models underestimate the HIV-reducing effects of NEPs. The underestimation results because previous models are constructed to consider only the impact of changes in "circulation times" and on needle contamination rates, and not the effects of NEPs on users' choices between using clean needles and sharing them, i.e. sorting effects. Table 3 presents simulation results for an IDU community of the impact of alternative sized NEPs, and with varying elasticities of supply of new needles in the black market (Bloom, Mahal, & O'Flaherty, 2004; Table 1). It also assesses effectiveness (in terms of changes in HIV-incidence rates) of alternatively sized NEPs using a behavioural perspective, and compares these findings to calculations based on standard epidemiological models that do not allow for endogenously determined behaviour (e.g., Kaplan & O'Keefe, 1993).

Several features of the results in Table 3 are worthy of note. First, increases in the size of NEP and the needle supply elasticity parameter ε (easing of supply conditions) are associated with lower average needle infection rates, lower percentage of shared injections, lower average number of times a needle is used, and ultimately lower HIV incidence. Second, these results provide, we believe, a convincing explanation, based on rational behaviour, of the empirical findings of reduced sharing, reduced number of times a needle is used and the like, as observed by several authors on the subject (Lurie et al., 1993). Third, the average and the terminal needle infection rates need not move in the same direction and that findings based on terminal needle infection rates may lead to erroneous conclusions, and make NEPs to appear to be less effective than they actually are.

Most current model-based assessments of NEPs rely on terminal needle infection rates to calculate effects of NEPs on HIV incidence. These models, for reasons mentioned above, also ignore the sorting effect of an NEP and so usually underestimate its beneficial effect, in percentage terms, even if they had used the average needle infection rate for their calculations of incidence. This can be directly observed from Table 3, which presents HIV-incidence estimates from standard epidemiological models, using average needle infection rates, and compares them to incidence rate calculations that account for behaviour response. Ignoring the sorting effect meant that the standard models underestimate, in percentage terms, the effect of NEPs on HIV incidence in Table 3. Using the terminal needle for calculating HIV-incidence rates would only accentuate these biases.

Table 3. The Impact of NEP on Needle Reuse, Sharing and HIV Transmission: An Illustrative Calculation.

	\multicolumn{5}{c}{NEP SIZE (Needles As Share of Total Number of IDU)}
	0.00	0.05	0.10	0.20	0.40
Supply elasticity of needles, $\varepsilon = 0$					
Number of times needle used	16.7	9.1	6.3	3.8	2.2
Average needle infection rate (%)	53.6	52.5	51.2	48.2	44.3
Terminal needle infection rate (%)	57.3	59.7	61.8	63.3	59.0
Shared injections (% of total)	94.0	89.0	84.0	74.0	46.0
HIV incidence (behavioural) per 1,000,000 drug users	151.4	133.2	115.6	84.5	41.3
HIV incidence (standard) per 1,000,000 drug users	161.1	149.6	137.6	114.1	76.5
Supply elasticity of needles, $\varepsilon = 0.2$					
Number of times needle used	8.5	6.0	4.7	3.2	2.0
Average needle infection rate (%)	52.3	51.0	49.6	46.9	44.0
Terminal needle infection rate (%)	60.1	62.0	63.0	62.8	57.7
Shared injections (% of total)	88.2	83.4	78.6	69.0	49.8
HIV incidence (behavioural) per 1,000,000 drug users	130.3	113.5	97.9	71.4	34.9
HIV incidence (standard) per 1,000,000 drug users	147.7	136.1	124.6	103.5	70.1
Supply elasticity of needles, $\varepsilon = 0.5$					
Number of times needle used	3.6	3.1	2.8	2.3	1.7
Average needle infection rate (%)	47.6	46.6	45.7	44.5	43.9
Terminal needle infection rate (%)	63.1	62.6	61.7	59.6	55.0
Shared injections (% of total)	71.9	68.0	64.0	56.0	39.9
HIV incidence (behavioural) per 1,000,000 drug users	78.8	68.9	60.0	44.7	22.4
HIV incidence (standard) per 1,000,000 drug users	109.6	101.4	93.7	79.8	56.0

Source: Authors' calculations using starting data from existing studies for New York, New Haven, and elsewhere. Shared needles = $(N/(N+O))100$ where N = new needle users, O = old needle users; ε = supply elasticity of new needles in the black market.

3.8. Summing Up

The various analyses above suggest that effectiveness of individual programmes is likely to depend on a range of factors, but reaching injecting drug users with some type of programme is obviously critical if health is to improve. Legal constraints and police harassment may deter users from accessing programmes, which highlights the importance of involving other sectors in NEP planning. Where users, moreover, do not perceive a need to use new needles (e.g., if they and many of their peers are already infected with HIV or lack knowledge of infection risks), they are unlikely to attempt to make use of programmes whatever the police impediments or absence thereof. Education efforts, possibly using peer educators, will be vital in such cases, while incentives such as free drug provision or even cash are likely to be needed to reach the most reluctant users.

Devising an effective NEP is a complex task, particularly when support from the state is weak or absent. Inadequate funding of programmes hampers efforts, leaving NEPs bereft of well-trained staff and reliable equipment supplies. In the developed world, opposition to NEPs among voters and local communities is likely to limit funding, but in developing countries resources are often scarce regardless of which policies are seen as desirable. Some governments are unable to afford needles for medical use, for example, and therefore have a hard time explaining their use in NEPs. In such circumstances, means of supplying needles other than from the public purse will have to be considered. Legalization of sale, which gives the private sector responsibility for distribution and for attracting customers, may be an effective alternative (or complement) to NEPs. International HIV-prevention programmes may also be a valuable source of supplies.

All these potential obstacles mean that NEPs are unlikely to be wholly effective at preventing HIV transmission. Overcoming them is likely to require a more comprehensive strategy, involving bleach distribution, education programmes, and treatment for dependency, as well as needle exchange. Legalization of needle sale and possession should also be considered by policy makers.

4. CONCLUSIONS

In conclusion, no single approach is likely to effectively address the key IDU-related problems of drug dependency and needle sharing. Criminalization has failed to wipe out IDU, and programmes involving bleaching, needle exchange, or peer education work best when complemented by efforts in other areas.

By clarifying the underpinnings of behaviours at risk for HIV infection, economic analysis has also contributed to understanding the complexity of the mechanisms associated with the transmission of HIV and served to underline the points of the previous paragraph. The hallmark of economists' approach to explaining individual and organizational behaviour is the explanation of that behaviour based on an assessment of potential benefits, relative to its costs, and this framework for explaining behaviour turns out to be extremely useful in providing policy insights.

Harsh policies focussed on arresting drug users for drug and needle possession that are often the focus of national drug policies increase the attractiveness of sharing needles with the unintended consequence of increased risk of HIV transmission, a problem in the realm of public health and human rights. Similarly, policies focussed solely on restraining the supply side of drugs can lead to rising drug prices that may in turn contribute to increasing the attractiveness of injecting drugs, again with a potential role for public health. Relying on methadone programmes to wean injecting drug users away from heroin may simply promote a different form of drug dependency, unless accompanied by strict oversight and counselling, which will require a cooperative, rather than an antagonistic stance towards the drug-using community.

Given the combination of policies that are needed for effectiveness, involving multiple stakeholders in IDU strategies is particularly important. Outright legalization of injectable drugs is politically impossible in most countries, but public health efforts need the support of law enforcement agencies if they are to reach drug users and function effectively. Involving communities in tackling the problem is also important, as local opposition, often fuelled by the media, can block NEPs and other approaches. A public health-oriented approach to IDU would benefit from attempting to change public perceptions about drug users. Informing the media and communities of the reality of dependency and the effectiveness of programmes to prevent it may build momentum towards de-stigmatizing the issue, thus enabling policy makers to address it with less fear of political repercussions.

Injecting drug users are not the only ones with responsibility for preventing HIV from crossing into the mainstream population. Those who have sex with them are also a logical target for interventions, be they casual or long-term partners or sex workers and their clients. Information and education campaigns aimed at these non-IDU stakeholders may be an effective means of countering the difficulty of reaching injecting drug users themselves.

Multiple approaches involving multiple stakeholders, then, appear the most promising way forward for IDU interventions. Successful programmes tend to combine needle exchange with other interventions such as education, condom distribution, or referral to health services. They also enlist support from law enforcement agencies and public health practitioners. The problems posed by IDU have no simple solutions, but political awareness and a broad perspective on both methods and target audiences is likely to reward those attempting to limit the damage it causes.

ACKNOWLEDGEMENTS

The authors acknowledge the assistance of Om Lala, Larry Rosenberg, and Mark Weston in the preparation of this chapter.

REFERENCES

Abdala, N., Gleghorn, A., Carney, J., & Heimer, R. (2001). Can HIV-1-contaminated syringes be disinfected? Implications for transmission among injecting drug users. *Journal of Acquired Immune Deficiency Syndromes, 28*(5), 487–494.

Aceijas, C., Stimson, G., Hickman, M., & Rhodes, T. (2004). Global overview of injecting drug use and HIV infection among injecting drug users. *AIDS, 18*(17), 2295–2303.

Becker, G., & Murphy, K. (1988). A theory of rational addiction. *Journal of Political Economy, 96*(4), 675–700.

Bloom, D., Mahal, A., & O'Flaherty, B. (2004). *The economics of needle use and reuse.* Draft. Boston, MA: Harvard School of Public Health.

Bloom, D., Mahal, A., Rosenberg, L., Sevilla, S., Steven, D., & Weston, M. (2004). *Asia's economies and the challenge of AIDS.* Manila: Asian Development Bank.

Centers for Disease Control and Prevention (CDC). (2002). *HIV/AIDS surveillance report.* Atlanta, GA: CDC.

Chitnis, V., Chitnis, D., Patil, S., & Chitnis, S. (2002). Hypochlorite (1%) is inefficient in decontaminating blood containing hypodermic needles. *Indian Journal of Medical Microbiology, 20*(4), 215–218.

Des Jarlais, D., & Friedman, S. (1988). HIV infection among persons who inject illicit drugs: Problems and prospects. *Journal of Acquired Immune Deficiency Syndromes, 1,* 267–273.

Desenclos, J., Papaevangelou, G., & Ancelle-Park, R. (1993). Knowledge of HIV serostatus and preventive behavior among European injecting drug users. *AIDS, 7*(10), 1371–1377.

Economist (2002). It's all in the price. London, June 6.

Economist (2003). Just say maybe. London, April 3.

European Centre for the Epidemiological Monitoring of AIDS. (2003). *HIV surveillance in Europe.* Paris: Institut de Veille Sanitaire.

Gold, M., Gafni, A., Nelligan, P., & Millson, P. (1997). Needle exchange programs: An economic evaluation of a local experience. *Journal of the Canadian Medical Association, 157*(3), 255–262.

Grossman, M., & Chaloupka, F. (1998). The demand for cocaine by young adults: A rational addiction approach. *Journal of Health Economics, 17*(4), 427–474.

Iversen, L. (2001). *Drugs: A very short introduction.* Oxford, UK: Oxford University Press.

Kaplan, E., & O'Keefe, E. (1993). Let the needles do the talking! Evaluating the new haven needle exchange. *Interfaces, 23*(1), 7–26.

Kaplan, E., Khoshnood, K., & Heimer, R. (1994). A decline in HIV-infected needles returned to New Haven's needle exchange program: Client shift or needle exchange? *American Journal of Public Health, 84*(12), 1889–1891.

Kremer, M. (1996). Integrating behavioral choice into epidemiological models of the AIDS epidemic. *Quarterly Journal of Economics, 111*(2), 549–573.

Kumar, S., Aggarwal, O., & Kumar, N. (1996). Prevalence of HIV related high risk behavior among drug abusers in a re-settlement colony in Delhi. Abstract no. Tu.C.2511. *XI international conference on AIDS*, Vancouver, Canada.

Lurie, P., Reingold, A., Bowser, B., Chen, D., Foley, J., Guydish, J., Kahn, J., Lane, S., & Sorensen, J. (1993). *The public health impact of needle exchange programs in the United States and abroad* (Vol. 1). San Francisco, CA: University of California.

MacCoun, R., & Reuter, P. (2002). The varieties of drug control at the dawn of the twenty-first century. *Annals of the American Academy of Political and Social Sciences, 582*(1), 7–19.

Magura, S., Grossman, J., Lipton, D., Siddiqi, Q., Shapiro, J., Marion, I., & Amann, K. (1989). Determinants of needle sharing among intravenous drug users. *American Journal of Public Health, 79*(4), 459–462.

Marseille, E., Morin, S., Collins, C., Summers, T., Coates, T., & Kahn, J. (2002). *Cost-effectiveness of HIV prevention in developing countries*. San Francisco, CA: Center for HIV Information, HIV Insite. http://hivinsite.ucsf.edu/InSite?page=kb-authors&doc=kb-08-01-04

McCoy, C., & Inciardi, J. (1995). *Sex, drugs, and the continuing spread of AIDS*. Los Angeles: Roxbury Publishing Company.

Morbidity and Mortality Weekly Report (*MMWR*). (1996). Continued sexual risk behavior among HIV-seropositive, drug-using men – 1993. *45*, 392–398.

National Commission on Terrorist Attacks Upon the United States. (2004). *The 9/11 commission report: Final report of the National Commission on Terrorist Attacks upon the United States*. College Park, MD: National Archives and Records Administration. http://www.9-11commission.gov

Philipson, T., & Posner, R. (1993). *Private choices and public health: The AIDS epidemic in an economic perspective*. Cambridge, MA: Harvard University Press.

Riehman, K. (1996). *Injecting drug use and AIDS in developing countries: Determinants and issues for policy consideration*. Working paper, World Bank, Policy Research Department, Washington, DC.

Rothenberg, R., Long, D., Sterk, C., Pach, A., Potterat, J., Muth, S., Baldwin, J., & Trotter, R. (2000). The Atlanta Urban Networks Study: A blueprint for endemic transmission. *AIDS, 14*, 2191–2200.

Saffer, H., & Chaloupka, F. (1999). The demand for illicit drugs. *Economic Inquiry, 37*(3), 401–411.

Sarkar, S., Das, N., Panda, S., Naik, T., Sarkar, K., Singh, B., Ralte, J., Aier, J., & Tripathy, S. (1993). Rapid spread of HIV among drug injectors in north-eastern states of India. *Bulletin on Narcotics, 1*(6), 91–105.

Span, P. (1996). Needle exchanges inject controversy in AIDS prevention. *Washington Post*, July 16, A1.

Stimson, G. (1988). Injecting equipment exchange schemes in England and Scotland. In: R. Battjes, & R. Pickens (Eds), *Needle sharing among intravenous drug abusers: National and international perspectives.* NIDA Research Monograph No. 80. Public Health Service, Washington, DC.

Stimson, G., & Choopanya, K. (1998). Global perspectives of drug injecting. In: G. Stimson, D. Des Jarlais & A. Ball (Eds), *Drug injecting and HIV infection: Global dimensions and local responses.* London: University College of London Press.

United Nations Development Programme (UNDP). (2004). You and AIDS portal: Injecting drug use. http://www.youandaids.org/themes/InjectingDrugUse.asp

United Nations Office on Drugs and Crime (UNODC). (2004). World drug report. Geneva: UNODC.

World Health Organization (WHO). (1994). *Multi-city study on drug injecting and risk of HIV infection: A report prepared on behalf of the WHO International Collaborative Group.* Geneva: WHO, Program on Substance Abuse.

Zheng, X., Tian, C., Choi, K., Zhang, J., Cheng, H., Yang, X., Li, G., et al. (1994). Injecting drug use and HIV infection in Southwest China. *AIDS, 8,* 1141–1147.

MODELS PERTAINING TO HOW DRUG POLICY SHOULD VARY OVER THE COURSE OF A DRUG EPIDEMIC

Jonathan P. Caulkins

ABSTRACT

The goals of this chapter are three-fold: (1) to outline some broad empirical regularities concerning how drug problems evolve over time, (2) to sketch some plausible mechanisms for ways in which aspects of that variation might be endogenous, and (3) to review two classes of dynamic models of drug use that have implications for how policy should vary over a drug epidemic.

1. INTRODUCTION TO STATE DYNAMICS MODELLING

"Drug use and associated problems vary dramatically over time, so drug policy should too." I have made that statement often to policy-makers in the U.S.A. and abroad. The most common reaction is, "That's obvious, but I'd never thought of it before."

When I observe that drug use and problems vary dramatically over time, I actually mean to suggest something more than what those words literally imply, but the most concise form of the statement involves jargon not familiar to some policy-makers. The technically more accurate and interesting observation is that drug problems appear to be dynamic not only in the sense that they change but also in the sense of being characterized by non-linearity and feedback. That is, the systems dynamics seem to be (at least partially) *endogenous*.

For some readers no further explanation is needed, and they can proceed directly to the next section. For others a few words of clarification may be helpful. The dominant paradigm in traditional quantitative analysis of drug-related issues focuses on levels of interrelated variables. It assumes that when one vector of "independent" variables X has a particular set of values, then another vector of "dependent" variables Y will be determined by the level of those independent variables via a relationship such as:

$$Y = f(X). \tag{1}$$

Sometimes the model is primarily descriptive. Sometimes policy-makers can control some of Y's predictors. We might distinguish controllable factors by calling them u and writing $Y = f(X; u)$. Then the effects or perhaps even the cost-effectiveness of an intervention might be assessed by "comparative statics".

Of course this is a superficial characterization. Models can get much more complicated, particularly when trying to empirically estimate relationships (i.e., determine the functional form of $f()$ and parameterize it), notably when one has multiple-dependent variables (i.e., Y is a vector), some of which also influence other Y's so:

$$Y = f(X, Y; u) \tag{1'}$$

where Y is a vector. A classic example is when Y includes both price and market quantity. Nevertheless, the focus is on predicting levels of the dependent variable, with changes in Y coming from changes in the right-hand side variables.

A different paradigm focuses on explaining not the level of the variables of interest (Y) but rather their rates of change, and, in its elementary forms, dispenses with the distinction between X and Y. Its classic starting equation is customarily written as:

$$\dot{X} = f(X), \tag{2}$$

where the dot superscript denotes the derivative with respect to time. Note that with this paradigm there is no intrinsic notion of a single "level" of the left-hand side variable. True one can solve (numerically if not analytically) the system of differential equations to find $X(t)$, and $X(t)$ describes how the level of the state variables evolve over time. However, there is no particular reason to expect that $X(t)$ will ever stop moving. For example, the simple undamped, two-state harmonic oscillator familiar from high-school physics class cycles forever. Furthermore, even in models for which $X(t)$ can approach a stable ("steady state") level, great attention is paid to the dynamic transition to that steady state (the "transient response") and to the possibility that different steady states can be approached depending on one's starting position (so-called "state dependence").

Just as with the previous paradigm, one can augment the purely descriptive models (Eq. (2)) with some controls u:

$$\dot{X} = f(X; u), \qquad (2')$$

and evaluate the efficiency of those controls. The evaluation is not called "comparative statics" because the control u itself varies over time (i.e., $u = u(t)$), so one seeks to find the "optimal" dynamic policy ($u^*(t)$) (Feichtinger & Hartl, 1986; Léonard & Long, 1992). As the transient response is central, one typically focuses on the discounted present value (denoted J) over some (possibly infinite) planning horizon, computing:

$$J(u) = \int e^{-rt}(V(X) - c(u))\, dt$$

such that

$$\dot{X} = f(X; u)$$

where r is the planner's discount rate. The net (present-valued) benefit of changing from (dynamic) policy $u_0(t)$ to $u_1(t)$ is $J(u_1) - J(u_0)$. This state-dynamics paradigm is valuable when addressing the question motivating this chapter, "How should policy vary over the course of a drug epidemic?"

2. STYLIZED FACTS CONCERNING HOW DRUG USE AND PROBLEMS EVOLVE OVER TIME

2.1. Evolution of Drug-Related Indicators in the Absence of Variation in Control

Several observations can be made about how drug problems evolve over time. The most basic is that they can change very rapidly (Caulkins, 2001).

Much has been made of the dramatic increases and reductions in violence in the U.S.A. over the past four decades, but the prevalence of cocaine use has varied far more rapidly and dramatically than have measures of crime, such as homicide rates. Likewise, illicit drug initiation varies much more than does initiation of licit drugs. As estimated by the National Household Survey of Drug Abuse (Johnson, Gerstein, Ghadialy, Choy, & Gfroerer, 1996), between 1962 and 1992, the ratios of the maximum to minimum numbers of initiates per year into regular alcohol and cigarette use were a little over 2 : 1. For marijuana the ratio was about 15 : 1; for cocaine it was almost 150 : 1. Drug prices have also varied dramatically over time (Office of the National Drug Control Policy (ONDCP), 2004).

Indeed, drug-related measures can change more quickly and in more fundamental ways than do socio-economic indicators, such as the unemployment rate, the number of youth (in absolute terms or relative to the number of adults), or drug control spending. Thus static linear models based on these explanatory variables cannot easily explain all of the variation in drug indicators (Weatherburn & Lind, 1997; Caulkins, 2001). To be sure, some drug-related indicators vary more modestly over time, particularly those associated with endemic use of drugs in mature markets. The statement here is only that drug use *can* change much more quickly, not that it always does.

The second key observation is that the variation upwards may not only be rapid (large first derivative with respect to time), but also increasing at an increasing rate (positive second derivative). Such convexity on the upswing is clear in trends in indicators such as marijuana initiation and cocaine-related emergency room mentions.

If change stems from a single exogenous shock to a linear system, the adjustment dynamics classically follow a decaying exponential approach to the new equilibrium. That can yield rapid change if the adjustment rate coefficient is large, but at a decreasing, not an increasing rate.

Alternately, convexity can stem from a positive feedback loop. As the state increases, it triggers greater increases in its rate of increase. A common explanation of positive feedback for substance use is "contagious" spread of use as existing users introduce the drug to their friends, acquaintances, and relatives.

Obviously contagion here is metaphorical. Drug use can spread human immunodeficiency virus (HIV), hepatitis C virus (HCV), tuberculosis (TB), and various other pathogenic diseases, but there is not a physical pathogen for drug use itself. Nevertheless, dependence is a well-defined medical condition that, with some probability, evolves as a consequence of use. In this sense, the use state is parallel to being infected, and dependence is parallel to having the disease. Furthermore, business practice and research literature have long recognized that new product adoption can be modelled with the same tools epidemiologists use to study true contagious diseases (e.g., Bass, 1969; Bass et al., 1994, 2000, 2001). It is not clear why marketing diffusion models should not also be a useful component of aggregate models of drug use. Some economists might object to drug diffusion models that do not explicitly model consumer choice within a utility maximization framework (Melberg, 2004). Note, though, that with a few exceptions (e.g., Horsky, 1990), the diffusion models in the marketing literature for licit goods do not do so (cf. Mahajan, Muller, & Wind, 2000).

The mechanisms by which a user might "infect" a non-user are diverse and include role modelling, peer pressure, enhancing availability, instruction (e.g., in the mechanics of drug preparation and injection), altering perceptions of norms, and classic testimonial or "word of mouth" advertising effects. Sometimes current users may seek to profit (Furst, Herrmann, Leung, Galea, & Hunt, 2004). However, often the interactions are more social than profit-oriented. More than half of past-year marijuana users report most recently obtaining marijuana for free and, more than half reported having given away or shared some of their most recent acquisition (Caulkins & Pacula (in submission)).

Although some positive feedback from current use to initiation is widely accepted (Agar & Wilson, 2002), what is less clear is whether "contagious spread" is the only such positive feedback, or whether there are others, such as enforcement swamping or learning by doing (possibilities discussed further below).

Time series cannot increase at increasing rates forever and still remain finite. So another rather obvious observation is that something eventually slows the spread of a drug. Drug epidemic models begin to diverge in their interpretations of what acts as a brake. Some focus on negative reputation effects (Musto, 1999; Behrens, Caulkins, Tragler, Haunschmied, & Feichtinger, 1999, 2000; Behrens et al., 2002). For others it is depletion of the population susceptible to initiation (e.g., Rossi, 1999, 2001; Almeder, Caulkins, Feichtinger, & Tragler, 2001, 2004). For still others (e.g., Tragler, Caulkins, & Feichtinger, 2001), there are "diminishing returns" to infectivity. Which class of models one prefers may depend in part on some additional observations.

The third observation about trajectories of drug use is that they often decline after peaking. In other words, the initial surge "overshoots" its longer-term levels. The extent of overshoot depends on the drug and measure. The number of past-year users of marijuana and cocaine in the

U.S.A. both fell by roughly 50% from their peaks.[1] Measures of total demand and consequences of use tend to fall later, if at all. For example, estimates of total demand for cocaine fell by about one-third between the late 1980s and 2000 (Everingham & Rydell, 1994; Caulkins, Behrens, Knoll, Tragler, & Zuba, 2004). Notably, drug-related emergency room mentions for many substances (heroin, cocaine, marijuana) have risen more or less continually since 1980 (SAMHSA, 1996), presumably in part because users' health deteriorates as they get older and have used longer. On the other hand, post-peak declines for particular drugs have exceeded 50%. Examples include paregoric arrests in Detroit in the 1960s (Lerner, 1966), Drug Abuse Warning Network (DAWN) emergency department mentions for phencyclidine (PCP) and diazepam (Substance Abuse and Mental Health Services Administration (SAMHSA), 1996), and heroin overdoses in Australia during the recent heroin drought (Weatherburn, Jones, Freeman, & Toni, 2003).[2]

Drug prevalence tends to overshoot its final level on the upswing. Sometimes there is also a tendency to undershoot on the downside, past the peak, that is, for a drug use measure to first increase, then decrease, then increase again before stabilizing. Series that are provocative in this regard are the Monitoring the Future Survey's long-term trends in drug use among youth (Johnston, O'Malley, & Bachman, 2002). Details vary by drug, but the broad trend is dramatic increases in the 1970s, substantial declines in the 1980s through 1992, with a rebound through the rest of the 1990s and stabilization or perhaps further declines since 2000. Fig. 1 illustrates this pattern from 1975 to 2001.[3]

There is less evidence of post-peak undershoot in use among the general population. That is not surprising. Use among youth is essentially a measure of a flow (initiation), whereas use among the general population is the stock to which that flow contributes. Household use is effectively an integrator of youthful use (in the sense of mathematical integration, not in the sense of coordinating diverse activities). Oscillations in a flow are damped by such integration.

Undamped oscillation leads to indefinite cycling. Looking over a broad sweep of history, Musto (1999) observes alternating periods of greater and lesser drug use. A cycle of quiescence, rapid escalation, plateau, and gradual decline has been observed for various drugs, including powder cocaine in the late 19th and early 20th century (Spillane, 1998) and crack more recently (Golub & Johnson, 1997). However, there are no quantitative, drug-related time series that show clear evidence of long-term, undamped oscillation for illicit drugs, in part because the time series are too short. Perhaps the time series most suggestive of minimal damping is heroin-related hospital

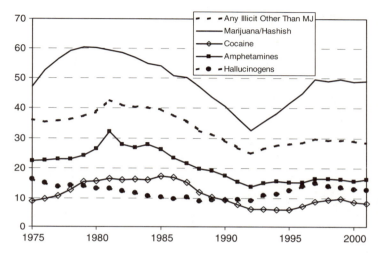

Fig. 1. Broad Trends in Lifetime Prevalence of Use Among High School Seniors, a Measure of Recent Initiation, Is Increases in the 1970s, Declines in the 1980s Through 1992, with a Rebound and Perhaps Stabilization Since.

admissions in Italy, assembled in Fig. 2 from Marotta (1992) and Preti, Miotto, and DeCoppi (2002).

To reiterate: There is clear evidence of overshoot for many substances, there is evidence of post-peak undershoot for some substances, and a few series hint of further oscillation, with the possibility of more such evidence as time series lengthen.

Another observation is that drug-related indicators can follow stable, multi-year trends for 10 or more years. Fig. 1 is an example. These long-term trends are not always obviously correlated with fluctuations in the business cycle, which does not imply that macroeconomic conditions do not influence use. Weatherburn and Lind (1997) suggest a state dynamics model in which offences are a lagged, non-linear response to economic conditions. However, the stable trends in drug indicators do not appear to be merely a linear contemporaneous symptom of trends in other variables. Mathematically, this suggests that the time constants governing stabilization are fairly long. In particular, they are measured in years not weeks or months.

A final observation concerning endogenous dynamics is that some, but not all variation seems to be explained by variation in prices. A considerable literature has established an inverse causal relationship between price and

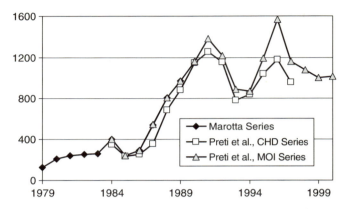

Fig. 2. Trends in Unintentional Drug Overdose Deaths in Italy Show Some Signs of Ongoing Oscillation.

use even for addictive substances. (See Chaloupka & Pacula, 2000; Grossman, 2004, for reviews.) However, there are also instances of substantial variation in use that is not known to be correlated with price (e.g., PCP). Furthermore, for cocaine in the 1980s, both initiation and prevalence fell at the same time prices dropped sharply. That positive correlation cannot be attributed to declining demand; overall demand was relatively stable as declining demand from light users was offset by increasing demand from heavy users (Everingham & Rydell, 1994; Caulkins et al., 2004).

2.2. The Effect of Policy Variation on the Evolution of Drug-Related Indicators

Nothing has been said yet about variation in drug control efforts. In principle all variation in drug indicators might stem from variation in policy. Indeed, politicians and pundits tend to use drug indicators as a simple "score card" for evaluating policy performance. If drug use is low, it is inferred that drug policy has been successful. Conversely, if drug use is high, it is evidence of policy failure.

It is difficult to defend this reasoning empirically. There appear to be some correlations between particular policy actions or events and short-term response, such as disruptions of cocaine supply and retail prices in 1989/1990 and 1995 affecting prices and emergency department (ED) visits (Crane, Rivolo, & Comfort, 1997), regulation of methamphetamine precursors affecting hospital admissions in the 1990s (Cunningham & Liu, 2003), and (with less agreement in the literature) marijuana decriminalization increasing use (e.g., Model, 1993). However, there are many more instances in which drug-related indicators vary without an associated change in policy or even move in ways contrary to what one would expect based on that policy. MacCoun and Reuter (2001) make this observation with respect to inter-country variation among developed nations at the macro level.

This is easy to understand with respect to demand-side interventions. They simply are not that powerful, and their effects are delayed and/or diffuse over time. For example, even model school-based drug prevention programmes reduce lifetime illicit drug use for participants by single digit percentages (Caulkins, Rydell, Everingham, Chiesa, & Bushway, 1999; Caulkins, Pacula, Paddock, & Chiesa, 2002, 2004).

With respect to treatment, Rydell and Everingham (1994) modelled cocaine treatment entry as leading to a 13% chance of leaving heavy use, with two-thirds of those leaving being vulnerable to relapse. Manski, Pepper, and Petrie (1999) sharply criticized even that as potentially too optimistic. Opiate treatment might be more effective, but the volume of opiate treatment in the U.S.A. has been stable for extended periods so it becomes part of the background, not a driver of variation.[4]

Thus, variation in demand-side interventions has not been driving variation in drug use. A better image might be that policy variation rides on larger waves of endogenous variation in drug use, presumably having some real but secondary effects on the overall course of the epidemics. The same may also be true of supply control efforts, even in the U.S.A., which invests by far the most in efforts to restrict supply.

Source country control efforts rarely have any discernable effect on opiate supplies in first world markets.[5] Even for cocaine, whose production is more concentrated and which has long been the focus of aggressive U.S. efforts, total areas under coca cultivation did not begin to decline until 2002 (United Nations Office on Drugs and Crime (UNODC), 2004).[6]

Interdiction is credited with occasional short-term disruption of cocaine markets (Crane et al., 1997), but drug markets adapt rapidly (Reuter, Crawford, & Cave, 1988), so relative to decade-long trends, the effects are more like blips than long-term drivers. Creating such blips may still be worthwhile; the point here is simply that they are ephemeral.

There has been a dramatic expansion in drug enforcement since 1980 within the U.S.A. Of the resulting ten-fold increase in imprisonment, 90–95% is directed at people involved in drug distribution (Sevigny &

Caulkins, 2004). Roughly two-thirds has been directed at cocaine, with about 10% each for heroin, methamphetamines, and marijuana. Nevertheless, prices of cocaine, heroin, and methamphetamines have fallen dramatically over the last 25 years. Marijuana prices rose initially in the 1980s, but then fell substantially in the 1990s; ironically, marijuana arrests in total and per user rose sharply in the 1990s.

In short, for the major drugs in the U.S.A., dramatic increases in supply control are juxtaposed with sharply declining prices. There are ways of explaining this puzzle without dismissing the basic premise of Reuter and Kleiman's (1986) "risks and prices" equilibrium model. For example, risk-compensation rates (e.g., the monetary compensation demanded per expected year in prison) could have fallen sharply. Still, the simpler conclusion is that supply control efforts are not particularly effective at constraining supply sufficiently to greatly alter patters of use.

There are two important caveats to the generalization that variation in supply control does not appear to have decisively affected drug-use trends. First, enforcement may have aborted some epidemics altogether. Such non-events are intrinsically hard to document or disprove. Second, except perhaps for marijuana, there is little solid empirical basis for estimating the effects of a dramatic regime change like legalization.

2.3. Summary

To summarize what these observations imply for the behaviour of a dynamic model of the evolution of drug use. *Models of drug epidemics and drug control should be able to account for the rapid spread of drugs at an increasing rate, overshoot, and damped oscillation, with some ambiguity as to how strong the damping is. Furthermore, they should be able to account for stable multi-year trends that may be partially but not fully explained by variations in prices or the business cycle. Programmes and policies can alter the course of a drug "epidemic", but short of a regime change, it is the exception not the rule when these interventions dramatically alter the course an established drug epidemic.*

This review of the stylized facts concerning variation in macro, drug-related indicators suggests that an important part of that variation is driven by internal structures (as with predator-prey models). Hence, the next section explores a few conjectures concerning endogenous dynamics that might generate such variation.

3. SOURCES OF NON-LINEARITY AND FEEDBACK IN DRUG SYSTEMS

Caulkins (2001) reviews some potential sources of endogenous non-linear feedback in drug systems. Four of the most important and interesting from an economic perspective are described here in somewhat more formal terms.

3.1. Enforcement Swamping

Drug market participants, like most living things generally, respond to incentives. One may or may not be inclined to presume that the response is "optimal" either in a bounded or an absolute sense, depending in part on one's disciplinary leanings. However, merely assuming there can be some response in the same direction as would be predicted by a rational actor model is not a strong assumption.

One important incentive for drug market participants is the risk of enforcement. This risk is driven by the *intensity* of enforcement, that is, by the amount of effort expended by enforcement agencies relative to the number of people participating in the sanctioned activity, not by the absolute amount or level of enforcement effort.

This point is important enough to reinforce with a (simplified) numerical example. Suppose that marijuana possession arrests are primarily of marijuana users, not distributors. (In reality they include arrests for possession with intent to distribute, but those cannot be separated in available national data.) In the U.S.A. such arrests averaged about 350,000 per year in the early 1980s, but fell in the late 1980s to about 260,000 by 1990. That does not mean the arrest risk for marijuana users fell during the 1980s. The number of people self-reporting past-year marijuana use in the National Household Survey fell from about 32 million in the early 1980s to about 20 million in 1990, so the number of possession arrests per 100 users stayed roughly stable at about 1.2 per 100. In contrast, the large increase in marijuana arrests during the 1990s (reaching 648,000 in 2000) combined with a modest 10% decline in the number of past-year users nearly tripled the arrest risk to 3.5 per 100.

Responses to changes in enforcement risk can include reducing the frequency of offending and/or displacing the activity to another location, mode of operation, drug, or time of day (Caulkins, 1992). Thus, increased enforcement pressure can reduce the number of offenders who are subject to that pressure.

Together these two simple observations combine to create a feedback effect which Mark Kleiman has dubbed "enforcement swamping" (Kleiman, 1993). Suppose the number of market participants is reduced for exogenous reasons, such as expansions in treatment or prevention. A smaller market facing the same quantity of enforcement yields a larger enforcement risk. That increased risk makes drug market activity less appealing, which might induce others to exit the market, which further intensifies enforcement pressure. Depending on the specific circumstances, this feedback could "tip" the market to a new, lower-level equilibrium or merely amplify the effect of the original demand-control intervention (Caulkins et al., 1999, 2002).

The multiplier effect can work in either direction and can be stimulated by a change in the level of enforcement, not just by an exogenous shock. Suppose the number of drug arrests or the amount of incarceration were reduced, for example, for budgetary reasons. That reduced risk makes it more appealing for others to join the market; their joining further dilutes enforcement. Depending on the specific circumstances, this feedback effect could "tip" the market to a new, higher-level equilibrium or it could merely amplify the effect of the original reduction in enforcement.

In symbols, if we let X denote the number of participants in some drug-related activity and v stands for the amount of enforcement directed at those individuals, then a more formal way of capturing these ideas is to write:

$$\dot{X} = f(X, v/X)$$

or some variant that does not explode as X approaches zero (reflecting, e.g., increased search cost for police as the number of targets thins). Dynamic feedback via enforcement swamping has been incorporated into models of both local drug markets (Caulkins, 1993; Baveja, Batta, Caulkins, & Karwan, 1993; Baveja, Caulkins, Liu, Batta, & Karwan, 1997; Naik, Baveja, Batta, & Caulkins, 1996; Kort, Feichtinger, Hartl, & Haunschmied, 1998) and aggregate markets (e.g., Rydell & Everingham, 1994; Rydell, Caulkins, & Everingham, 1996; Tragler et al., 2001; Caulkins, Dworak, Feichtinger, & Tragler, 2000; Knoll & Zuba, 2004).

3.2. Individual Demand is a Function of Past Levels of Consumption

Economics is careful to distinguish consumption from demand, where the latter denotes a schedule or relationship between consumption and price. For many goods, the quantity consumed varies over time with shifting supply but the demand curve is stable or, if it varies at all, it varies because of exogenous factors.

For drugs, the demand curve may depend not only on exogenous factors but also on past consumption because of at least three distinct mechanisms – intoxication, tolerance, and dependence. The last of these is still commonly referred to in the economics literature as "addiction" so that term will be used here. This idea is captured in spirit if not in detail by models following Becker and Murphy (1988) that include the stock of (perhaps discounted) an individual's past consumption as part of his or her current state. It is not necessary to review the considerable resulting literature here. It suffices to observe that a variety of rich behaviours and opportunities for empirical estimation emerge from this insight.

Note, though, that in reality intoxication, tolerance, and addiction might best be modelled by three separate stocks, not just one, since they have different time constants of decay. This can be seen by thinking of these three states in binary terms and noting that individuals can be found in any one of the resulting eight possible states. Someone who has never used a substance is neither intoxicated, nor tolerant, nor addicted (0,0,0). Someone who has used steadily for many years without interruption could well be intoxicated, tolerant, and addicted (1,1,1). Someone can clearly be intoxicated without being tolerant or dependent; for alcohol that would describe someone who abstained until they reached the legal drinking age but then binged on their 21st birthday. Likewise, inasmuch as addiction is a chronic relapsing disease that reflects long-term physical changes in the brain, not merely the presence of the intoxicant, someone who has become dependent but then remains abstinent for a year (e.g., in prison) would be dependent but neither intoxicated nor tolerant (0,0,1). Indeed, drug-dependent individuals exiting prison can be prone to overdose death precisely because they mistakenly presume they are still as tolerant as they were when they last used. If that dependent ex-inmate uses a non-lethal amount, they would be intoxicated and dependent, but not tolerant, etc.

Details vary by substance, but roughly, the half-life of decay of the intoxication stock is measured in hours. For tolerance the corresponding half-life is measured in days or perhaps weeks, and for addiction it is measured in years, decades or some might argue is so long relative to human life spans as to be best thought of as not decaying at all.

All three states (or stocks of past consumption) can affect current demand. One image of dependence is that it reduces overall utility but increases the marginal utility of drug consumption and, hence, increases demand. Thus, drug consumption is reinforcing in an economic as well as a psychologic sense.

Tolerance could also have a reinforcing effect (users often seek increasing doses to achieve the same subjective experience), but it might also have the opposite effect if it reduces the marginal benefit of a given amount of consumption.

Intoxication can affect consumption decisions directly by clouding judgment or by altering preferences or rates of inter-temporal trade-offs. There can also be non-linearities. If one drink is good and another is better, that does not mean one will enjoy 10 even more. Indeed, one may not be conscious for the potentially pleasant part of consuming 10 drinks and wish one were unconscious for the delayed consequences.

Addiction and positively reinforcing effects of tolerance can create a positive feedback. Suppose supply increases, which has no immediate effect on the demand curve, but would increase consumption. For a conventional good, that would be the end of the story. But for drugs, that increase in consumption can subsequently lead to an increase in demand, which increases consumption still further, which increases demand, and so on. Whether this positive feedback pushes the market to some qualitatively different equilibrium or merely amplifies the effect of the original shift in supply depends on the particular circumstances.

These demand-amplifying effects are not unique to drugs. Some goods have an "acquired taste" (opera is a common example); others are subject to private network externalities. Nevertheless, the existence of other exceptions to the standard notion of stable demand does not undermine the importance of this feedback for drugs.

3.3. Learning by Doing

Learning by doing is the analogue with respect to supply of addiction and tolerance with respect to demand. The supply curve describes how much suppliers would be willing to sell as a function of the market price. It is often thought of as varying only in response to exogenous factors, but learning by doing can make the supply curve itself a function of past production.

Learning by doing refers to the idea that the supply curve is directly affected by the cost of production, and production costs decline as suppliers gain experience. Learning by doing is by no means unique to drugs. It occurs with many emerging industries, famously the electronic calculator whose prices collapsed as production volumes spurred innovation. However, Kleiman (1989) has suggested that "learning by doing" could be a significant factor in drug markets. Even though drug use has occurred for millennia, the modern illicit drug markets are relatively new. High-volume cocaine production is about 30-year olds.

One can distinguish at least two types of learning by doing – industry-wide learning that benefits all producers equally and intra-organizational learning that is private information. If all learning is industry-wide, then the production cost schedule is a function simply of the integral of historical consumption. The potential power of learning-by-doing effects can be illustrated easily for this case. The possibility that some or all learning becomes proprietary information makes things more complicated, but also opens interesting possibilities concerning how enforcement might affect prices. Some ideas along those lines will be introduced qualitatively below, but first consider the possibility that industry-wide learning by doing might help explain the great 1980s paradox of declining cocaine prices despite increasing enforcement stringency.

The U.S. cocaine market is highly competitive, so it may not be unreasonable to assume price equals marginal cost because free entry bids away excess rents. In the business literature, it is common to model unit production costs as following a power law with respect to cumulative production to date. Hence, it is of interest to see whether a power-law learning-by-doing model of marginal costs can mimic historical price series.

Caulkins et al. (2004) estimate U.S. cocaine demand from 1972 to 2000. Their series can be extended to 2003 by assuming initiation was stable for the additional 3 years.[7] ONDCP (2004) provides estimates of retail powder cocaine prices from 1981 to 2003. Given a short-term or per-capita elasticity of demand, the demand series can be converted into an estimated consumption series. The overall elasticity of demand for cocaine is not known with any precision but may be around 1 (Caulkins et al., 1997; Grossman, 2004). Very little is known about the relative magnitude of its constituent parts, but some past analyses have assumed the short-term elasticity is half the long-run elasticity (e.g., Rydell & Everingham, 1994; Rydell et al., 1996), so we will use a figure of 0.5 here.

The power-law learning curve model has two parameters, in addition to a scaling factor: (1) the exponent and (2) the assumed cumulative level of consumption before 1981. Minimizing the sum of the squared differences between annual cocaine prices and modelled unit production costs with respect to these two parameters yields an excellent fit (see Fig. 3). The resulting parameters are borderline plausible. The best-fitting cumulative consumption through 1980 is about one-third greater than what the Caulkins et al. (2004) series would imply for 1972–1980. Given the rapid growth of cocaine use in the 1970s, it is not implausible that use during the 1970s could be about triple use in preceding decades. The exponent of −0.83 is larger (in absolute value) than is typical of industrial applications. It implies a

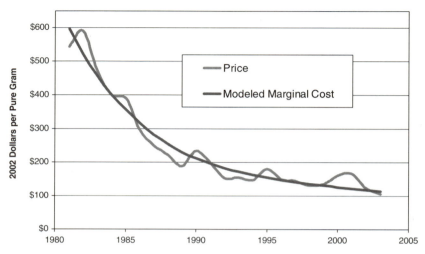

Fig. 3. Modelled Marginal Cost for a Simple Power-Law Learning Curve Model Can Reproduce the Dramatic Collapse in U.S. Cocaine Prices During the 1980s.

"learning slope" of 56%, whereas slopes of 70–100% are typical of industrial applications.[8]

Note what this exercise has and has not done. It does not offer a realistic let alone a validated model of the evolution of U.S. cocaine prices. Notably, it ignores completely enforcement's role in determining prices. The objective of this exercise was much simpler. It merely sought to illustrate the idea that learning by doing could plausibly be important. Even if we use a learning-by-doing slope of 75% (implying an exponent of -0.42), learning-by-doing effects in an industry-wide learning model could easily have generated a 56% decline in price between 1981 and 2003.

Now consider how enforcement might interact with a learning-by-doing effect if some or all of the learning is proprietary knowledge to a particular organization. If an organization that is far up the learning curve were destroyed and replaced by a new and naive supplier, enforcement might drive up production costs and, hence, prices not only because of risk-compensation effects but also by destroying tacit knowledge. Thus, enforcement-induced turn-over among drug suppliers could help keep prices high. On the other hand, if there is heterogeneity across organizations in their cumulative learning and prices are set by the least experienced (highest-cost) providers, then fluctuations in enforcement risk for infra-marginal suppliers may have no effect on prices. (Taylor et al., in submission, explore in detail a variety of peculiar consequences that heterogeneity in marginal production costs has on enforcement's effect on prices.)

Finally, note that regardless of whether learning is industry-wide or intra-organizational, if suppliers change operating procedures in response to a new law enforcement tactic, those changes could raise production costs even if the efforts at "avoidance" are successful and there are no arrests or incarceration (cf. Reuter et al., 1988). The "push-down, pop-up" nature of drug markets' adaptation to law enforcement is sometimes viewed as demonstrating the futility of drug law enforcement. However, if the renewed activity pops up in a mode of operation that forces suppliers to "reset" their position on the learning-by-doing curve, enforcement could have a positive effect on drug prices, at least in the short run, even if the markets are not eradicated.

To summarize, learning by doing can create positive feedback. The more that is sold, the more efficient suppliers become. The more efficient suppliers become, the lower prices will be, and lower prices induce greater consumption which leads to further learning by doing, and so on. To date this possibility has not commonly been incorporated in quantitative models of drug epidemics.

3.4. Initiation is a Function of Current Levels of Use

As noted above, drug use is often described as being "contagious" because initiation rates can be positively influenced by the current prevalence, or level, of use. The metaphor of a drug "epidemic" is commonly used precisely because of this tendency for current users to "recruit" new users.

However, the feedback from current use to initiation is not necessarily all positive. Musto (1999) argues that knowledge of the possible adverse effects of drug use can act as a deterrent or brake on initiation. He hypothesizes that drug epidemics eventually die out when a new generation of potential users becomes aware of the dangers of drug abuse and, as a result, does not start to use drugs. Whereas many light users work, uphold family responsibilities, and generally do not manifest adverse effects of drug use, many heavy users are visible reminders of the dangers of using addictive substances. Hence, one might expect large numbers of heavy users to suppress initiation into drug use, particularly if that hard drug use is visible (e.g., the user remains on the street rather than being sequestered in a far-off long-term residential treatment facility) and has visible consequences (such as homelessness or acquired immune deficiency syndrome (AIDS)).

The adverse consequences of drug use take time to develop. Hence, Musto's hypothesized negative feedback is a lagged effect. Early in a drug epidemic, current users might amplify initiation, even if later on they suppress it. This "Musto" dynamic has been observed by others (e.g., Egan, 1999), and has been investigated in detail in a series of papers co-authored by Doris Behrens (Behrens et al., 1999, 2000, 2002), which are detailed below. Parallel mechanisms appear in models in other contexts, such as the spread of sexually transmitted diseases (e.g., Velasco-Hernandez, Brauer, & Castillo-Chavez, 1996).

4. MODELS OF ENDOGENOUS FEEDBACK IN DRUG SYSTEMS

There are two classes of state dynamics models of drug-related phenomena – those with many states and those with few. Approaches with many states include systems dynamics (Levin, Roberts, & Hirsch, 1975; Homer, 1993a, b), compartmental models (e.g., Rossi, 1999, 2001), and distributed parameter (partial differential equation) models (e.g., Almeder et al., 2004). These models manifest complicated behaviours that offer interesting and sometimes counter-intuitive suggestions for how policy ought to evolve over the course of an epidemic. However, they are often too large to address analytically, and so are typically run as simulations. Furthermore, they require estimation of a large number of parameters, which is a challenge when studying illicit activity.

Models in the second class use fewer states (typically one to four). They are simpler and more stylized, but generate more qualitative insights and are more likely to include explicit dynamic optimal control. This section focuses on two groups of these models ("A" models and "LH" models).

4.1. "A" Models with a Single Type of User

Tragler pioneered a line of research (Tragler et al., 2001; Caulkins et al., 2000; Mautner, 2002; Grosslicht, 2002; Moyzisch, 2003; Zeiler, 2004) in which a steady state number of users ($\hat{A}$) emerges when quitting at a constant per capita rate balances initiation which is an increasing but concave function of use. Uncontrolled dynamics take the form:

$$\dot{A} = kA^\alpha - \mu A$$

so there is a stable steady state at $\hat{A} = (k/\mu)^{(1-\alpha)}$. A one-state continuous time model cannot generate over-shoot and/or undershoot, but in other respects it has been satisfactorily calibrated to the U.S. cocaine and Australian heroin epidemics.

Tragler et al. (2001) use this framework to explore inter-temporal dynamic tradeoffs between investing in treatment that accelerates outflow from use and price-raising enforcement that reduces initiation, suppresses per capita use by existing users, and increases quit rates.

The modelling of enforcement's effect on price is motivated by enforcement swamping as described above. Caulkins et al. (1997) show that when distribution costs are additively linear in three components – costs that are proportional to the quantity delivered, costs that are proportional to the value of drugs delivered, and costs that are proportional to the level of enforcement and when free entry bids away rents so revenues just equal total distribution costs, then price is linear in the ratio of enforcement to market volume. Tragler et al. (2001) use the number of users as a measure of market size, so:

$$p(A(t), v(t)) = d + ev(t)/(A(t) + \varepsilon)$$

where $v(t)$ is enforcement spending and ε is a small constant that avoids division by 0. This form implies a floor on prices even when dedicated drug enforcement goes to 0 reflecting Reuter's (1983) "structural consequences of product illegality" and/or background enforcement (e.g., from patrol officers) that would exist even if there were no dedicated drug enforcement agents. However, as the number of users goes to 0, this price function can be made almost arbitrarily large. Since enforcement targets are hard to find when there are few users, Tragler et al. (2001) impose a lower bound on the number of users.

The objective is assumed to be minimizing a discounted weighted sum of control spending and consumption, with various constraints placed on spending to reflect practical and political limits on what policies can realistically be implemented.

Analysis of the model yields a number of interesting conclusions. The most basic is that traditional static discussions of the merits of various drug control interventions (e.g., claiming that treatment is better than enforcement or vice versa without reference to the stage of the epidemic) may be overly simplistic. Even this simple model yields optimal solutions that substantially vary the mix of interventions over time.

In particular, when decision-makers recognize a new drug problem, the model suggests they should decide immediately whether to "eradicate" use (drive it to minimum levels) or just moderate its growth towards a high-volume equilibrium. There are three necessary conditions for eradication to be optimal. First, initiation must be an increasing function of prevalence so that eradication pays dividends by short-circuiting a positive feedback loop. Second, it must be early enough in the epidemic that the level of use is below a critical threshold. Finally, it must be politically feasible to direct very substantial resources towards the problem even though the problem is still relatively small. If any of these conditions is not satisfied, then accommodation may be preferred.

If eradication is pursued, it is optimal to move quickly and decisively, using massive levels of both enforcement and treatment. If accommodation is pursued, then initially most energies should be directed towards enforcement. Treatment spending starts small and should grow roughly proportionally with the number of users. Enforcement should also grow roughly linearly in the number of users, but with a large intercept and so over time treatment should receive a greater and greater share of the drug control budget. As the ratio of enforcement effort to market size declines, prices fall. Thus, according to this model, it can be optimal to have prices decline precipitously as the number of users grows. Drug prices did decline sharply in the U.S.A. during the 1980s. Often that price collapse is thought of as a disaster, but a price collapse is not necessarily inconsistent with optimal management of a drug epidemic.

If eventually initiation declines (e.g., because the drug acquires a bad reputation), treatment spending should decline as the problem abates, but relatively smoothly. In contrast, once the drug has lost its attraction to potential users, the value of enforcement's ability to keep prices high diminishes and enforcement could be cut more aggressively.

The eradication/accommodation threshold is quite interesting. Fig. 4 updates one from Tragler et al., (2001), using a slightly larger exponent on endogenous initiation in light of Grosslicht's (2002) findings. The horizontal axis depicts the number of users and the vertical axis shows optimal annual control spending (in thousands of dollars). A so-called Dechert–Nishimura–Skiba threshold (labeled A_{DNS}) occurs when the number of users is about 1.3 million (Skiba, 1978; Dechert & Nishimura, 1983). If the initial number of users is below this threshold, the optimal strategy is to use massive levels of enforcement and treatment to reduce use to the minimal level. Otherwise, it is optimal to let use grow towards a positive equilibrium. This finding of a sharp choice between eradication and accommodation is consistent with analyses of the impact of enforcement on local drug markets (e.g., Caulkins, 1993; Baveja et al., 1993, 1997; Naik et al., 1996; Kort et al., 1998).

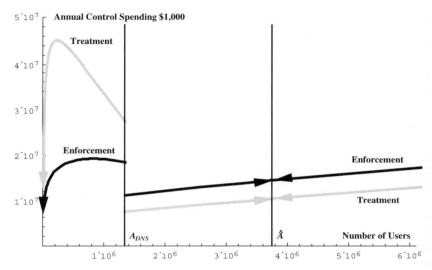

Fig. 4. DNS-Threshold in a Tragler et al. (2001) "A" Model Separating Initial Numbers of Users for Which the Optimal Strategy Is Eradication vs. Accommodation.

These "A" models demonstrate that enforcement swamping can generate "tipping models" that view explosions in use as instances of "tipping" from the low- to the high-level equilibrium. Implications for policy are two-fold. First, policy-makers should strive to prevent the system from tipping from low to high levels of use. Second, modest interventions are unlikely to have dramatic effects, but a massive intervention might tip the system back to a low-level equilibrium, at which point the intervention could be cut back dramatically without having use return to its high levels.

Variations of this basic model have been pursued adapting it to the Australian heroin epidemic, including drug market revenues in the objective, and considering other policy instruments, such as drug courts (Caulkins et al., 2000). One implication of the latter model is that policy prescriptions can be sensitive not only to the overall elasticity of demand (a point long realized) but also to its composition. In these models, the overall elasticity has three components reflecting effects on per capita use, initiation, and cessation. When drug spending is part of the objective (e.g., as a surrogate for drug-related crime), price-raising enforcement's appeal in the long run depends importantly on how much of that overall elasticity stems from the short-run component.

4.2. LH models

4.2.1. LH Model with Scripted Initiation

Everingham and Rydell (1994), Everingham, Rydell, and Caulkins (1995) made a key contribution by developing a two-state Markov model of cocaine demand (Fig. 5). They parameterized the model for the U.S. and differentiated between light ($L(t)$) and heavy ($H(t)$) users, with parameters a, b, and g representing the annual rate at which light users quit, light users escalate to heavy use, and heavy users quit, respectively.[9] This simple descriptive model captured the broad trends of the U.S. cocaine epidemic though 1992, and with updated parameters (Caulkins et al., 2004), continues to do so at least through 2000.

Several insights emerge from this model. For example, most (roughly 86%) of those who try cocaine do not escalate to heavy use, but those who do persist in heavy use for about $1/g \approx 12$ years. Given average annual consumption in excess of 100 g per year and social costs of \$215 per gram consumed (Caulkins et al., 2002), the social cost associated with the residual career of a typical heavy cocaine user in the U.S.A. is on the order of \$200,000, even with discounting. Hence, even treatment programmes with quite modest success rates in terms of relapse can be cost-effective (Caulkins, 2004).

Since heavy users' consumption rates are much higher than for light users,[10] expected lifetime consumption per initiation (roughly 225–475 g, Caulkins et al., 1999) is dominated by a very large expected consumption given escalation to heavy use multiplied by a small probability of escalating. Indeed, many users never proceed beyond "very light" use (Caulkins, 1997), so the median social cost per cocaine career could be close to 0.[11] These sharp contrasts between light and heavy users are a principal justification for employing a two-state "LH" modelling framework.

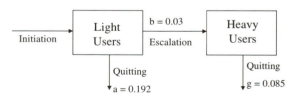

Fig. 5. Everingham and Rydell's (1994) Light and Heavy User Model with Flow Rates Updated by Caulkins et al. (2004).

4.2.2. LH Models with Endogenous Initiation

Everingham and Rydell's (1994) original model was used to describe past trends and project a baseline counterfactual for policy analysis purposes (Rydell & Everingham, 1994), but initiation was scripted, not modelled explicitly. Behrens et al. (1999) converted the model into continuous time and incorporated feedback from the current prevalence to initiation. In particular, they included an endogenous model of initiation in which some initiation was "spontaneous" (e.g., because of immigration) but most occurred through interactions with current light users.

In equations:

$$\dot{L} = I(L, H) - (a+b)L \quad L(0) = L_0$$
$$\dot{H} = bL - gH \quad H(0) = H_0$$
$$I(L, H) = initiation$$

In keeping with Musto's (1999) arguments described above, Behrens et al. (1999, 2000) had the drug's reputation moderate the rate at which light users recruit new initiates. In particular, reputation was modelled as a negative exponential function of the relative number of current heavy and light users. This did an excellent job of reproducing the successive peaks of the U.S. cocaine epidemic, with initiation peaking first, then light users, then total users, and finally heavy users.

Two strands of subsequent work generalized this approach to endogenous initiation. The first responds to a problem with the pure LH model, namely that removing a heavy user (either naturally or through treatment) immediately and entirely erases all of that individual's contribution to the drug's negative reputation. In reality, memories can persist. This problem can be avoided by introducing a third state variable that explicitly represents knowledge of past use and making the negative exponential reputation term reflect the ratio of this third state to light users. Behrens et al. (2002) took a step in this direction by introducing the decaying memory of ever-heavy users, denoted by the variable E, with state dynamics:

$$\dot{E} = bL - \delta E$$

The major drawback of this LHE approach is that three individuals who use heavily for one day, one year, and one decade, respectively, all contribute the same amount to the memory of heavy use. An alternative bases reputation on memory of the number of person-years spent in heavy use. Behrens et al. (in submission) introduce a different third state representing decaying memory of heavy users' years (denoted Y) and let this new state serve as the deterrent in the reputation function. The flow into this state is the number of current heavy users (H). The outflow is a simple exponential decay governed by a memory parameter (δ). When this parameter is small, memories of drug abuse are long-lived; when δ is large, memory of heavy users' years of use and associated problems dissipates rapidly. This extension is referred to as the LHY model.

The second strand of subsequent work on endogenous initiation continued to base negative reputation on current heavy users (H), but considered other functional forms. Winkler, Caulkins, Behrens, & Tragler (2004) and Knoll and Zuba (2004) suggest that the negative exponential term over-estimates heavy users' ability to deter initiation, particularly late in an epidemic. Winkler et al. generalized the original Behrens et al. model by placing a floor under reputation. Specifically:

$$I(L, Y) = \tau + L \max\left\{B, s \ \exp\left(-q\frac{H}{L}\right)\right\}$$

where:

τ = number of innovators per year,
s = annual rate at which light users attract non-users,
q = constant which measures the deterrent effect of heavy use,
B = floor on infectivity per light user.

Knoll and Zuba (2004) searched a range of alternate functional forms and concluded that:

$$I(L, H) = \varepsilon L - \delta H + \phi \exp(\psi H/L)$$

fit U.S. cocaine data better from 1988 on.

All variants of the LH model yield some consistent suggestions for policy that stem from the following dynamic. If current light users recruit additional initiation and, with a lag, light users escalate to a heavy use state that suppresses initiation, then (1) initially initiation is driven by a powerful positive feedback and (2) merely delaying individuals' initiation early in the epidemic (even if initiation is not permanently prevented) can bring lasting benefits. Merely slowing down the positive feedback until the lagged negative feedback cycle kicks in can bring substantial, lasting benefits, reducing the total and peak numbers of people who ever use and who use heavily.

An implication explored in depth by Winkler et al. (2004), is that the cost-effectiveness of prevention programmes varies dramatically over the course of an epidemic. They can benefit from an enormous "social multiplier effect" (cf. Caulkins et al., 1999, 2002) early in the epidemic, even if later on their cost-effectiveness is mediocre.

This means school-based prevention programmes customized to a particular drug epidemic cannot possibly be deployed when they would be most effective against that particular epidemic. That is, one cannot hope to see early warning signs of the next epidemic, design a curriculum around that particular threat, and deploy it in time to strike that epidemic when prevention is most cost-effective.[12] Instead, prevention programmes that are generic with respect to the specific epidemic (perhaps even generic with respect to delinquency generally) should be implemented on an ongoing basis. They can be a cost-effective way of making a modest difference to an endemic problem and "cheap insurance" against the worst ravages of a possible, new future epidemic that would approach too quickly to allow for customized prevention response.

Treatment is also incapable of responding decisively to the early explosive growth stages of an epidemic for two reasons. First, in those early stages, most users are light users who do not have a medically treatable condition. Second, treatment's effects are diffuse over time (cf. Caulkins et al., 1997). Many dependent users require multiple treatment episodes to stop. Furthermore, since residual drug use careers span a decade or longer, even for those who achieve permanent abstinence immediately upon their first treatment, the direct effects of successful treatment are spread over many years.

With LH models, treatment's greatest contributions come late in the epidemic, when consumption is dominated by heavy users. Inasmuch as heavy users deter initiation, reducing their numbers could be a double-edged sword, bringing immediate benefits but possibly allowing initiation to rise. Indeed, in the original LH model, pursuing treatment aggressively enough to increase the baseline outflow rate from heavy use by about 50% replaces damped oscillation towards the interior focus with a limit cycle, implying recurrent epidemics, with each cycle characterized first by many light users and few heavy users and then later by having demand dominated by heavy use.[13]

Law enforcement, in contrast, has unique capacity to focus its effects on the present. That is obvious for the incapacitation effects of shorter sentences, but deterrent effects also manifest around the time arrest is threatened. This counter-intuitive point is best understood by considering an extreme hypothetical example. Suppose it were credibly announced that starting today, all convicted drug offenders would be sentenced to life in prison without parole. Presumably that would affect the number of drug users, sellers, prices, and quantities sold and consumed.

Now suppose that later it were credibly and broadly announced that sentences were going back to their previous lengths. The people arrested in the intervening month would still be in prison for life. However, those who had not yet been caught could pretty much go back to doing things as they had before. The fact that sentences had once been very long is of no direct consequence to them, even though those arrested during that month might still be in prison for decades to come. So, the deterrence effects, however big or small, are concentrated around the time of arrest. Enforcement's market shaping potential is likewise available in the short run (Caulkins, 2002).

What is less clear is whether enforcement can target the light users who drive the positive feedback loop. Knoll and Zuba (2004) took a step towards trying to investigate the relative advantages of enforcement directed at the markets serving light users vs. markets serving heavy users. However, data and computational challenges forced them to focus only on the period from 1988 on, after the explosive growth stage of the cocaine epidemic had passed, so much remains to be investigated.

To some extent secondary prevention blends the best of what primary prevention and enforcement offer (Winkler et al., 2004). Its effects are more proximate than those of conventional school-based prevention because it works with people around the time of initiation (indeed, slightly after). Furthermore, by definition and design, secondary prevention focuses on users before they escalate to heavy use.

In summary, the LH models suggest that drug policy ought to evolve over the course of an epidemic as follows. "Enforcement's greatest contributions to reducing use are likely to come early in an epidemic, when demand is growing rapidly because of contagious spread of use. Secondary prevention that induces current light users to quit may also be particularly effective at this time. Treatment in contrast is likely to make its greatest contributions later, in the endemic stage. Enforcement's role later in the epidemic might more usefully be focused on reducing heavy use and/or reducing harms per unit of drugs sold and used. Finally, school-based prevention should be done on an ongoing basis, not timed to the ebb and flow of particular epidemics.

5. SUMMARY

Drug use and associated phenomena change rapidly over time, raising important questions about how drug policy should adapt to such change. In particular, drug use changes much more rapidly than do macro-level measures of social conditions, and in ways unlike simple linear adjustment dynamics to exogenous shocks. For example, drug use often initially increases at an increasing rate (convex growth) and then overshoots its long-run stable levels. These observations suggest that drug-use dynamics are driven by endogenous not just exogenous factors.

Taking into consideration the special nature of drug markets, drug use, and the spread of use suggests a number of possible, non-linear dynamic feedback effects that could be important. Four were reviewed here to give a flavor of these dynamics.

These empirical and theoretical considerations suggest that when studying drug problems, traditional methods can usefully be complemented by dynamic models adapted from epidemiology and mathematical biosciences. When these "stocks and flows" models are embedded within an optimal dynamic control framework, the results suggest that drug policy ought to evolve over the course of a drug epidemic. This elementary idea should not be surprising and, indeed, strikes most policy-makers as eminently sensible. Since the scope and nature of drug problems change dramatically over the course of an epidemic cycle, the policy response ought likewise to evolve over time.

The stocks and flows models can be divided into those with a relatively small number of states and those with many (sometimes infinitely many) states. Some prominent results concerning two types of the former models were reviewed – one-state "A" models and two or more state "LH" models. Both deserve further investigation, and there are other, substantially different classes of epidemic models yet to be investigated. Dynamic modelling of the cost-effectiveness of drug control interventions over an epidemic cycle is an important but under-studied area of research that has direct and important implications for drug policy.

NOTES

1. The number of cocaine users fell from 12 million or so in the mid-1980s to less than 6 million by the late 1990s. The number self-reporting marijuana use in the National Household Survey fell from 33 million in 1979 to 18 million in the mid-1990s.

2. Weatherburn et al. (2003) likewise describe a 36% decline in heroin expenditures despite marked price increases and a roughly 50% decline in the percentage of arrestees testing positive for opiates.

3. PCP is an outlier inasmuch as it fell more sharply and has rebounded less. Inhalants are another outlier, with trends that are negatively correlated with every other drug. Inhalants are also the only substance that is not illegal per se, since the inhaled substances have legitimate household uses.

4. For example, the period from 1992 to 2001 is thought of as a period of increasing heroin use, yet according to TEDS data (analysed on line) the number of people in treatment for heroin or other opiates did not decline. It grew modestly, by an average of less than 6% per year.

5. Exceptions are the Turkish opium ban which, in conjunction with the breaking of the French connection, contributed to a heroin drought in the U.S.A. in the early 1970s and the Taliban's opium eradication campaign in Afghanistan, which appears to have affected prices in European markets (Pietchmann, 2004).

6. Peruvian production began to fall in the mid-1990s and Bolivian production in the late 1990s, but until recently expansion in Colombia made up the difference. U.N. and U.S. government figures are slightly different but tell the same basic story.

7. Most demand comes from existing users, not new initiates, so demand in 2001–2003 is relatively insensitive to initiation in those years.

8. The "slope" in a standard per unit learning-by-doing model is the unit production cost after doubling volume relative to the earlier per unit production cost. For example, if the 1st unit cost $100 to produce and the second cost $80, then that would be a "slope" of 80%. One hundred percent slope implies no learning. Slopes of less than 100% imply learning effects.

9. The original model had a flow (f) from heavy back to light use. Subsequent variants eliminated this flow and increased parameter g accordingly for practical reasons (f and g could not be separately identified) and theoretical reasons (former heavy users using lightly have a different expected future trajectory of use than do first-time light users). Likewise, escalation is now interpreted as excluding one-time binges of frequent use that are not sustained. For a fuller explanation, see Behrens et al. (1999).

10. Everingham and Rydell suggested a ratio of 7.25:1 for "heavy" vs. "light users". Abt analysts estimate that "chronic" users spend about six times as much per capita as do "occasional" users (ONDCP, 2001).

11. Among NHSDA respondents aged 35 or older (hence, likely to have completed cocaine use), about half report using on fewer than a dozen days in their life. Since there are many such people (∼14 million) relative to the number of heavy users, even if all current heavy users were missed by the NHSDA, the median number of days of use would not be dramatically higher.

12. To see this, consider when a cocaine-prevention curriculum would have to have been developed for the U.S. cocaine epidemic. Cocaine initiation peaked in the late 1970s, and the median age of cocaine initiation is 21.5 years (Johnson et al., 1996). Since school-based prevention programmes often target 13- or 14-year olds, the programmes would have had to have been in schools in the late 1960s and early 1970s. It takes time to design a programme, budget funds, and scale it up nationally, so the prevention initiative would have to have been started at least by the mid- if not early 1960s. However, recognition of the severity of the U.S. cocaine epidemic was not widespread until the early to mid-1980s. Detecting an epidemic in its early stages is hard enough; let alone predicting its arrival 15 years ahead of time.

13. Cycles are less likely to emerge in the LHE and LHY models or with reputation forms other than negative exponentials.

ACKNOWLEDGEMENTS

This research was partly financed by the Robert Wood Johnson Foundation Substance Abuse Policy Research Program and benefits from collaborations with various colleagues, particularly at the Vienna Institute of Technology.

REFERENCES

Agar, M. H., & Wilson, D. (2002). Drugmart: Heroin epidemics as complex adaptive systems. *Complexity*, 7(5), 44–52.
Almeder, C., Caulkins, J. P., Feichtinger, G., & Tragler, G. (2001). An age-specific multi-state initiation models: Insights from considering heterogeneity. *Bulletin on Narcotics*, 53(1), 105–118.
Almeder, C., Caulkins, J. P., Feichtinger, G., & Tragler, G. (2004). An age-structured single-state initiaton model – Cycles of drug epidemics and optimal prevention programs. *Socio-Economic Planning Sciences*, 38(1), 91–109.
Bass, F. M. (1969). A new product growth model for consumer durables. *Management Science*, 15(5), 215–227.
Bass, F. M., Gordon, K., Ferguson, T. L. & Githens, M. L. (2001). DIRECTV: Forecasting diffusion of a new technology prior to product launch. *Interfaces*, 31(3), Part 2 or 2, S82–S93.
Bass, F. M., Jain, D., & Krishnan, T. (2000). Modeling the marketing mix influence in new product diffusion. In: Handbook of new product diffusion models (Chapter 5).
Bass, F. M., Krishnan, T. V., & Jain, D. C. (1994). Why the bass model fits without decision variables. *Marketing Science*, 13(3), 203–223.
Baveja, A., Batta, R., Caulkins, J. P., & Karwan, M. H. (1993). Modeling the response of illicit drug markets to local enforcement. *Socio-Economic Planning Sciences*, 27(2), 73–89.
Baveja, A., Caulkins, J. P., Liu, W., Batta, R., & Karwan, M. H. (1997). When haste makes sense: Cracking down on street markets for illicit drugs. *Socio-Economic Planning Sciences*, 31(4), 293–306.
Becker, G. S., & Murphy, K. M. (1988). A theory of rational addiction. *Journal of Political Economy*, 96(4), 675–700.
Behrens, D. A., Caulkins, J. P., Tragler, G., Haunschmied, J. L., & Feichtinger, G. (1999). A dynamical model of drug initiation: Implications for treatment and drug control. *Mathematical BioSciences*, 159, 1–20.
Behrens, D. A., Caulkins, J. P., Tragler, G., Haunschmied, J., & Feichtinger, G. (2000). Optimal control of drug epidemics: Prevent and treat – but not at the same time. *Management Science*, 46(3), 333–347.
Behrens, D., et al. (2002). Why present-oriented societies undergo cycles of drug epidemics. *Journal of Economic Dynamics and Control*, 26(6), 919–936.
Caulkins, J. P. (1992). Thinking about displacement in drug markets: Why observing change of venue isn't enough. *The Journal of Drug Issues*, 22(1), 17–30.

Caulkins, J. P. (1993). Local drug markets' response to focused police enforcement. *Operations Research*, *41*(5), 848–863.
Caulkins, J. P. (1997). How prevalent are 'very light' drug users? Federation of American Scientists'. *Drug Policy Analysis Bulletin*, *3*, 3–5.
Caulkins, J. P. (2001). The dynamic character of drug problems. *Bulletin on Narcotics*, *53*(1), 11–23.
Caulkins, J. P. (2002). *Law enforcement's role in a harm reduction regime*. Crime and Justice Bulletin Number 64. New South Wales Bureau of Crime and Justice Research.
Caulkins, J. P. (2004). Drug policy: Insights from mathematical analysis. In: M. L. Brandeau, F. Sainfort & W. P. Pierskalla (Eds), *Operations research and healthcare: A handbook of methods and applications* (pp. 297–332). Boston: Kluwer Academic Publishers.
Caulkins, J. P., Behrens, D. A., Knoll, C., Tragler, G., & Zuba, D. (2004). Modeling dynamic trajectories of initiation and demand: The case of the US cocaine epidemic. *Health Care Management Science*, *7*(4), 319–329.
Caulkins, J. P., Dworak, M., Feichtinger, G., & Tragler, G. (2000). Drug enforcement and property crime: A dynamic model. *Journal of Economics*, *71*(3), 227–253.
Caulkins, J. P., Pacula, R., Paddock, S., & Chiesa, J. (2002). *School-based drug prevention: What kind of drug use does it prevent?* Santa Monica, CA: RAND.
Caulkins, J. P., Pacula, R., Paddock, S., & Chiesa, J. (2004). What we can – and can't – expect from school-based drug prevention. *Drug and Alcohol Review*, *23*(1), 79–87.
Caulkins, J. P., & Pacula, R. (in submission). Marijuana markets: Inferences from reports by the household population.
Caulkins, J. P., Rydell, C. P., Everingham, S. S., Chiesa, J., & Bushway, S. (1999). *An ounce of prevention, a pound of uncertainty: The cost-effectiveness of school-based drug prevention program*. Santa Monica, CA: RAND.
Caulkins, J. P., Rydell, C. P., Schwabe, W. L., & Chiesa, J. (1997). *Mandatory minimum drug sentences: Throwing away the key or the taxpayers' Money?* MR-827-DPRC, RAND, Santa Monica, CA.
Chaloupka, F. J., & Pacula, R. L. (2000). Economics and anti-health behavior: The economic analysis of substance use and abuse. In: W. Bickel & R. Vuchinich (Eds), *Reframing health behavior change with behavioral economics* (pp. 89–111). Hillsdale, NJ: Lawrence Earlbaum Associates.
Crane, B. D., Rivolo, A. R., & Comfort, G. C. (1997). *An empirical examination of counterdrug interdiction program effectiveness*. Alexandria, Virginia: Institute for Defense Analysis.
Cunningham, J. K., & Liu, L. M. (2003). Impacts of federal ephedrine and pseudoephedrine regulations on methamphetamine-related hospital admissions. *Addiction*, *98*, 1229–1237.
Dechert, W. D., & Nishimura, K. (1983). A complete characterization of optimal growth paths in an aggregated model with a non-concave production function. *Journal of Economic Theory*, *31*(2), 332–354.
Egan, T. (1999). A drug ran its course, then hid with its users. *New York Times*, September 18.
Everingham, S. S., & Rydell, C. P. (1994). *Modeling the demand for cocaine*. Santa Monica, CA: RAND.
Everingham, S., Rydell, C. P., & Caulkins, J. P. (1995). Cocaine consumption in the US: Estimating past trends and future scenarios. *Socio-Economic Planning Sciences*, *29*(4), 305–314.
Feichtinger, G., & Hartl, R. (1986). *Optimale kontrolle ökonomischer prozesse – Anwendungen des maximumprinzips in den wirtschaftswissenschaften*. Berlin: deGruyter.

Furst, R. T., Herrmann, C., Leung, R., Galea, J., & Hunt, K. (2004). Heroin diffusion in the mid-Hudson region of New York State. *Addiction, 99*, 431–441.

Golub, A. L., & Johnson, B. D. (1997). *Crack's decline: Some surprises across U.S. cities.* Research in Brief, Washington, DC: National Institute of Justice.

Grosslicht, F. (2002). *Optimal dynamic allocation of prevention and treatment in a model of the Australian heroin epidemic.* Masters Thesis at the Technical University of Vienna.

Grossman, M. (2004). *Individual behaviors and substance abuse: The role of price.* Plenary Address given to the *24th Arne Ryde symposium on economics of substance abuse*, Lund University, Lund Sweden, August 13–14.

Homer, J. B. (1993a). A system dynamics model for cocaine prevalence estimation and trend projection. *The Journal of Drug Issues, 23*(Spring), 251–279.

Homer, J. B. (1993b). Projecting the impact of law enforcement on cocaine prevalence: A system dynamics approach. *The Journal of Drug Issues, 23*, 281–295.

Horsky, D. (1990). A diffusion model incorporating product benefits, price, income, and information. *Marketing Science, 9*(Fall), 343–385.

Johnson, R. A., Gerstein, D. R., Ghadialy, R., Choy, W., & Gfroerer, J. (1996). *Trends in the incidence of drug use in the United States, 1919–1992.* Washington, DC: US Department of Health and Human Services.

Johnston, L. D., O'Malley, P. M., & Bachman, J. G. (2002). *Monitoring the future: National survey results on drug use, 1975–2001. (NIH Publication No. 02-5106).* Bethesda, MD: National Institute on Drug Abuse.

Kleiman, M. A. R. (1989). *Marijuana: Costs of abuse, costs of control.* Westport, CT: Greenwood Press.

Kleiman, M. A. R. (1993). Enforcement swamping: A positive-feedback mechanism in rates of illicit activity. *Mathematical and Computer Modeling, 17*, 65–75.

Knoll, C., & Zuba, D. (2004). *Dynamic models of the US cocaine epidemic: Modeling initiation and demand and computing optimal controls.* Ph.D. thesis, Technical University of Vienna, Vienna, Austria.

Kort, P. M., Feichtinger, G., Hartl, R. F., & Haunschmied, J. L. (1998). Optimal enforcement policies (crackdowns) on an illicit drug market. *Optimal Control Applications & Methods, 19*, 169–184.

Léonard, D., & Long, N. V. (1992). *Optimal control theory and static optimization in economics.* Cambridge: Cambridge University Press.

Lerner, A. M. (1966). The abuse of paregoric in Detroit Michigan (1956–1965). *Bulletin on Narcotics, 3*, 13–19.

Levin, G., Roberts, E. B., & Hirsch, G. B. (1975). *The persistent poppy: A computer-aided search for heroin policy.* Cambridge, MA: Ballinger Publishing Company.

MacCoun, R. J., & Reuter, P. (2001). *Beyond the drug war: Learning from other times, places, and vices.* New York: Cambridge University Press.

Mahajan, V., Muller, E., & Wind, J. (2000). *New-product diffusion models.* Boston, MA: Kluwer Academic Publishers.

Manski, C. F., Pepper, J. V., & Petrie, C. V. (Eds) (1999). *Assessment of two cost-effectiveness studies on cocaine control policy.* Washington, DC: National Academy Press.

Marotta (1992). Drug abuse and illicit trafficking in Italy: Trends and countermeasures 1979–1990. *Bulletin on Narcotics, 1*, 15–22.

Mautner, K. (2002). *A dynamic one-state two-control optimization model of the current Australian heroin problem.* Masters thesis, Technical University of Vienna, Vienna, Austria.

Melberg, H. O. (2004). *The spread of drug use: Epidemic models or social interaction?* Mimeo.
Model, K. E. (1993). The effect of marijuana decriminalization on hospital emergency room drug episodes: 1975–1978. *Journal of the American Statistical Association, 88*, 737–747.
Moyzisch, F. (2003). *Sensitivity analysis in a one-state three-control model of the US cocaine epidemic.* Masters thesis, Institute for Econometrics, Operations Research, and Systems Theory. Vienna Institute of Technology, Vienna, Austria.
Musto, D. (1999). *The American disease.* New Haven, CT: Yale University Press.
Naik, A. V., Baveja, A., Batta, R., & Caulkins, J. P. (1996). Scheduling crackdowns on illicit drug markets. *European Journal of Operational Research, 88*, 231–250.
Office of National Drug Control Policy (ONDCP). (2001). *What America's users spend on illegal drugs.* Washington, DC: The White House.
Office of National Drug Control Policy. (2004). *The price and purity of illicit drugs: 1981 through the second quarter of 2003.* Washington, DC: The White House.
Preti, A., Miotto, P., & DeCoppi, M. (2002). Deaths by unintended illicit drug overdose in Italy, 1984–2000. *Drug and Alcohol Dependence, 66*, 275–282.
Reuter, P. (1983). *Disorganized crime: The economics of the visible hand.* Cambridge, MA: MIT Press.
Reuter, P., & Kleiman, M. A. R. (1986). Risks and prices: An economic analysis of drug enforcement. In: M. Tonry & N. Morris (Eds), *Crime and justice: An annual review of research*, Vol. 7. Chicago, IL: University of Chicago Press.
Reuter, P., Crawford, G., & Cave, J. (1988). *Sealing the borders: The effects of increased military participation on drug interdiction.* Santa Monica, CA: RAND.
Rossi, C. (1999). Estimating the prevalence of injection drug users on the basis of Markov models of the HIV/AIDS epidemic: Applications to Italian data. *Health Care Management Science, 2*, 173–179.
Rossi, C. (2001). A mover–stayer type model for epidemics of problematic drug use. *Bulletin on Narcotics, 53*(1), 39–64.
Rydell, C. P., & Everingham, S. S. (1994). *Controlling cocaine. Supply Versus demand programs.* Santa Monica, CA: RAND.
Rydell, C. P., Caulkins, J. P., & Everingham, S. S. (1996). Enforcement or treatment: Modeling the relative efficacy of alternatives for controlling cocaine. *Operations Research, 44*(6), 687–695.
Sevigny, E., & Caulkins, J. P. (2004). Kingpins or mules? An analysis of drug offenders incarcerated in federal and state prisons. *Criminology and Public Policy, 3*(3), 401–434.
Skiba, A. K. (1978). Optional growth with a convex–concave production function. *Econometrica, 46*, 527–539.
Spillane, J. (1998). Did drug prohibition work? Reflections on the end of the first cocaine experience in the United States, 1910–45. *Journal of Drug Issues, 28*(2), 517–538.
Substance Abuse and Mental Health Services Administration. (1996). *Historical estimates from the drug abuse warning network: 1978–1994 estimates of drug-related emergency department episodes.* Washington, DC: US Department of Health and Human Services.
Tragler, G., Caulkins, J. P., & Feichtinger, G. (2001). Optimal dynamic allocation of treatment and enforcement in illicit drug control. *Operations Research, 49*(3), 352–362.
United Nations Office on Drugs and Crime. (2004). *2004 world drug report.* Vienna, Austria: Oxford University Press.

Velasco-Hernandez, J. X., Brauer, F., & Castillo-Chavez, C. (1996). Effects of treatment and prevalence-dependent recruitment on the dynamics of a fatal disease. *IMA Journal of Mathematics Applied to Medicine and Biology, 13*, 175–192.

Weatherburn, D., Jones, C., Freeman, K., & Toni, M. (2003). Supply control and harm reduction: Lessons from the Australian heroin 'Drought'. *Addiction, 98*, 83–91.

Weatherburn, D., & Lind, B. (1997). On the epidemiology of offender populations. *Australian Journal of Psychology, 49*(3), 169–175.

Winkler, D., Caulkins, J. P., Behrens, D., & Tragler, G. (2004). Estimating the relative efficiency of various forms of prevention at different stages of a drug epidemic. *Socio-Economic Planning Sciences, 38*(1), 43–56.

Zeiler, I. (2004). Prevention, treatment, and law enforcement in an optimal control model of cocaine use in the USA. Masters thesis, Technical University of Vienna, Vienna, Austria.

ECONOMIC EVALUATION OF RELAPSE PREVENTION FOR SUBSTANCE USERS: TREATMENT SETTINGS AND HEALTH CARE POLICY

Tetsuji Yamada, Chia-Ching Chen and Tadashi Yamada

ABSTRACT

Evaluating the prevention, intervention, and treatment programme is critical to understanding the decision-making behaviour of substance abusers. The study interweaves behavioural health economics with the extended PRECEDE–PROCEED Model and examines the effectiveness of treatment settings for substance users in New Jersey Drug and Alcohol Abuse Treatment (13,775 samples). The study also identifies the factors that are associated with substance users' recurrence to the treatment centre. The results concluded that educational attainment, counselling services from health care providers, mental agency services, and detoxification treatments have a significant impact on preventing relapse behaviour.

1. INTRODUCTION

The use and abuse of alcohol and drugs generates problems for educational attainment, health and health care utilization, social welfare, criminal justice, and the community. Drug and alcohol abuse has a significant impact on society, especially in the allocation of resources for local, state, and federal governments. *Healthy People* 2010, states that substance abuse remains a major public health problem (U.S. Department of Health and Human Services, 2000). The health economic theory applies concepts and principles of behavioural economics to study substance use. A large body of literature has analysed and examined the effect/influence of substance use on children's behaviours (Chatterji & Markowitz, 2000), educational attainment (Yamada, Kendix, & Yamada, 1996; Chatterji, 2003), human capital formation (Pacula, Ringel, & Ross, 2003), crime/arrest (Cuellar, Markowitz, & Libby, 2003; Pacula & Kilmer, 2003), traffic accidents caused by drunken drivers, (Chaloupka, Saffer, & Grossman, 1993; Yamada, Yamada, & Karmakar, 2000; Carpenter, 2004), and rational addiction behaviours (Grossman & Chaloupka, 1998; Grossman, Chaloupka, & Sirtalan, 1998). In these literatures, demand theory has been successfully applied to understand decision-making health behaviour. Studies on behavioural economics facilitate health interventions (i.e., informal and formal health education, government interventions, *i.e. drug enforcement, tax policy and regulations*, and health/medical treatment) that reduce alcohol and drug abuse.

Research on substance use and relapse prevention has extended broadly to primary care settings. Friedmann, Saitz, and Samet (1998), and Samet, Friedmann, and Saitz (2001) highlight the potential benefits of creating health care systems that incorporate primary care and mental health care services for relapse prevention. More recently, there is increasing evidence to suggest that cognitive–behavioural intervention and psychotherapy with pharmacotherapy play a key role in treating alcohol and drug abusers (Currie, Clark, Hodgins, & El-Guebaly, 2004; Schmitz, Stotts, Sayre, DeLaune, & Grabowski, 2004; Yen, Wu, Yen, & Ko, 2004). Other academic disciplines, including sociology, psychology, and epidemiology, have also studied substance use behaviour. The social epidemiology of alcohol and drug abuse considers social factors that influence the population distribution of substance use behaviour. A large quantity of work has investigated the relation between social factors (i.e., alcoholics anonymous social network and social support), and substance cessation and relapse (Weitzman & Kawachi, 2000; Kaskutas, Bond, & Humphreys, 2002; McCrady, Epstein, & Kahler, 2004). Although identifying social factors is important to determine substance use behaviours, the prevention, intervention, and treatment need a coherent, comprehensive, and continuous effort. Alcohol/drug abuse has an important influence on the financing and delivery of health care, educational achievement, personal behaviours, social welfare, and criminal activities. Relapses by substance users need to become central issues of concern to those trying to improve public health.

The objectives of this chapter are: (1) to evaluate the effectiveness of treatment settings for substance users and (2) to investigate the factors that are associated with substance users' recurrence, namely relapse, to the treatment centre. The chapter proceeds as follows. First, treatment modes and relapse behaviours will be discussed, and then empirical framework will be described. After presenting empirical results, the final section offers conclusions and discussions.

2. TREATMENT MODES AND RELAPSE BEHAVIOURS

Many substance users, who are admitted to treatment programmes, have experienced prior admissions and relapse behaviours. There is an increased risk of relapse when a situation poses a threat to an individual's sense of control. Relapse is related to two decision-making behaviours – intra-personal determinants and interpersonal environmental determinants that refer to a relapse episode related to a behavioural change that may either encourage or discourage the continuation of the behaviour.

Intra-personal determinants include the personal motivation to change behaviours based on subjective knowledge, attitudes, beliefs, perceived values, perceived needs, perceptions, religion, ethnicity, cultural background, etc., which Green and Kreuter (2004) defined as predisposing (PR) factors. Interpersonal determinants involve both "formal" and "informal" relationship of social influences that lead to changing health behaviours. A "formal" relationship refers to a relationship between health care providers and patients, and an "informal" relationship refers to one between families and friends.

The concepts of interpersonal determinants of decision-making behaviours have been developed in prevention, intervention, and treatment settings for alcohol/drug abusers. Successful prevention programmes will take a comprehensive approach to the problems by creating supportive environments that improve social capital (Bolin, Lindgren, Lindström, & Nystedt, 2003), that is, a social network and community that foster the individual's commitment to an alcohol- and drug-free lifestyle. Intervention and treatment programmes are an important part of public health policy because they help prevent the relapse of substance use and are designed to improve the quality of life for alcohol/drug abusers. During intervention, formal and informal education provide the knowledge and information that help create an environment that promotes, restores, or establishes a healthy lifestyle. For example, a community-based social welfare/public policy, regulations, rules, laws, health care services/facilities, and availability of health care resources are intervention tools. Green and Kreuter (2004) explicitly denoted these interventions and treatment settings as reinforcing and enabling (EN) factors in their theoretical behavioural framework. The framework will be discussed in the next section.

On the other hand, the relapse of alcohol/drug abuse is attributable to various characteristics (e.g., market and non-market goods for health investment) that influence good health, namely health stock (Grossman, 2003). The health capital (HC) factors involve education, income level, age, marital status, etc. (Kaestner, 1998). In addition, marital status and family structure also influence personal behaviours (Grossman, 1972a, b). By theoretically developing Grossman's model, Jacobson (2000), and Bolin, Jacobson, and Lindgren (2001, 2002a, b) further extended health-related behaviours that are derived from common family preference as a health producer. Various components, as well as the amount of time invested in health within the family/individual would influence an individual's health behaviour. Kaestner (1998) and Pacula, Ringel, and Ross (2003) also state that drug use is associated with severe poverty (i.e., loss of job). In turn, the abuse of alcohol/drugs affects human capital development and decreases HC factors. Years of education represent the human capital that is related to HC factors (Grossman, 2003). Informal/formal education may prevent the relapse of alcohol/drug abuse. Human capital will facilitate or hinder an alcohol/drug abuser's motivation to change their conduct. Availability of health knowledge, health information, and informal/formal health education are all crucial to efficiently reducing relapse through behavioural change.

3. EMPIRICAL FRAMEWORK

This study incorporates intra-personal and interpersonal determinants with our extended PRECEDE–PROCEED Model (the extended PP Model), and embodies the patient's preparation, action, and maintenance stages in which relapse behaviours are attributable to HC, PR, RE, and EN factors of the

Economic Evaluation of Relapse Prevention for Substance Users   435

extended PP Model in Fig. 1 (Miller & Pollnick, 1991; Green & Kreuter, 2004). The original PP Model has the goals to explain health-related behaviours and environments, and to design and evaluate the interventions (Green & Kreuter, 2004). The model emphasizes that health and health risks are caused by multiple factors. The PP framework for planning is funded on the disciplines of epidemiology; the social, behavioural, and educational sciences; and health administration.

This study modified and extended the third and fourth phases of the original PP Model, and hypothesizes that the extended PP Model is able to explain the relapse behaviour of alcohol/drug abusers. In Fig. 1, Phases 1–5 shows the assessment of the extended PP Model. Phase 4 shows four categories of influential factors. The focus of this study is to evaluate these influential factors that are related to process evaluation and impact evaluations.

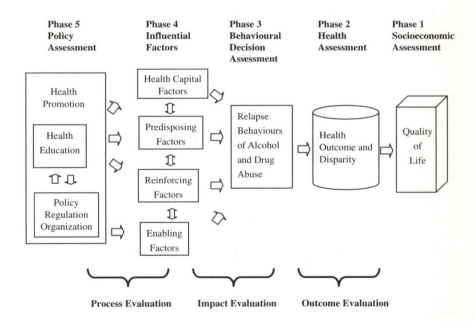

Source: Green, L.W., & Kreuter, M.W. (2004). *Health Program Planning: An Educational and Ecological Approach* (4th ed.). New York: McGraw-Hill.

Fig. 1.   Extended PP Model for Relapse Behaviour.

The basic estimation equation for relapse behaviour is:

$$\text{RELAPSE}_i = \beta_0 + \beta_1 \text{HC}_i + \beta_2 \text{PR}_i + \beta_3 \text{RE}_i + \beta_4 \text{EN}_i + \beta_5 \text{SU}_i + \varepsilon_i \quad (1)$$

where $i = 1, \ldots, k$, and ε is an unobserved error, generally assumed to satisfy $E(\varepsilon|\text{HC, PR, RE, EN, SU}) = 0$. The estimation equation postulates that the relapse behaviour, (RELAPSE) depends on HC and PR factors. This study assumes that health is measurable and interpretable as HC factors (see theoretical implication by Jacobson, 2000; Bolin et al. 2001, 2002a, b; and its empirical application by Bolin et al., 2003). The RE factors include some intervention factors that policy/programme planners claim influence relapse behaviour, legal and, correction-related programmes, and a welfare/social network. EN factors comprise the eligibility of health insurance, and the availability of treatment, facilities, and human resources (DeVoe, Fryer, Phillips, & Green, 2003). SU stands for types of abuse and the intensity of the use.

There are three issues to be considered for the estimation – specification, exogeneity/endogeneity, and sample selection of admitted patients for the treatment. A person's limited market value along with a low income may encourage illegal market activities since there is a low full price (i.e., including direct price costs, indirect costs, and opportunity costs) of illegal drug activities (Kaestner, 1998). Unemployment may increase social pressure and available leisure time for alcohol/drug use. Thus, income level is negatively associated with relapse and positively associated with joblessness. The covariance and the correlation between income level and unemployment status are negatively related. The economic theory underlying the discussion above implies that the estimated coefficient on income level would be an upward biased estimate of the true impact of income, as long as the unemployment variable is omitted. For the specification test, the likelihood ratio test ($\lambda = 19.54$, $\chi^2 = 3.84146$) and Ramsey's RESET (regression specification error test) test ($F = 56.446$) are significant at the 5% level. Therefore, our conclusion is to reject the restricted regression. By using the TSP (time series processor) programme, heteroskedasticity is corrected using the Eicker–White procedure.

Variables of the household income and educational levels are also concerns for the same specification issue. The variable of education represents the health knowledge related to alcohol/drug abuse. Thus, a person with a higher educational level is less likely to engage in risky behaviour. The household income represents an opportunity cost with a market value of human capital. An increase in income level is generally associated with a decrease in alcohol/drug abuse because of the high costs caused by risky activities. It is theoretically logical to think that excluding a variable of educational level would lead to the misspecification of a regression model in this study.

For exogeneity/endogeneity tests, alcohol and drug use have an adverse influence on human capital development, which in turn, causes an increase in poverty, lower earnings, and unemployment. The state of poverty that stems from having a low income and being unemployed, may cause alcohol/drug use. The study of relapse behaviour, by applying the extended PP Model, requires exogeneity/endogeneity tests for household income and unemployment status. These statuses are related to readmission to the alcohol/drug treatment in this study. Concerning the tests for exogeneity/endogeneity, Granger's causality exogeneity test ($F = 0.16340 < 1.69$) shows that the test of the hypothesis is not rejected and that the variables of income and unemployment can be treated exogenously. For the purpose of this study, the endogeneity test was also examined. The residuals of income and unemployment reduced forms are included in the structural form. The study used employment counselling as an instrument variable. The results of "t" statistics for the coefficient of residuals ($t = 0.584$ for income) and ($t = 0.306$ for unemployment) in the structural form imply that the income and unemployment variables are exogenous.

In a sample selection of admitted patients, an individual patient with a heavily addictive personality has a high probability of being admitted to a treatment service, regardless of the provided financial resources such as Medicaid, special funding from the community, and state and federal reimbursement sources (i.e., General Drug Addiction Services Funding, Drug Court, Residential Community Release Programme, Direct County Funding, etc.). On the other hand, slightly- or moderately-addicted alcohol/drug abusers, who are referred to treatment facilities or programmes by their family, friends, or an addiction service and who are facing financial difficulty, may not be admitted for treatment. In this situation, the data of this study only includes persons who are admitted by treatment health care providers.

3.1. Source of Data

The New Jersey Drug and Alcohol Abuse Treatment (here after NJDAAT) was conducted by the Division of Addiction Services (DAS), New Jersey Department of Health and Senior Services. The data for this study includes substance abuse behaviour, geographic distribution, and the socio-demographic characteristics of patients in the New Jersey treatment population.

Drug abuse treatment agencies throughout the New Jersey State submit reports on treatment admissions and discharges to the DAS for each treatment admission from October 2002 to February 2004. Detail characteristics of the treatment population, such as age, sex, race/ethnicity, and county of residence are reported. Other social characteristics include marital status, living arrangement, employment status, and legal status. Information about the substance abuser's behaviour includes the primary, secondary, and tertiary drug use, the route of administration of the drug, age at admission, and the age when he/she first used the primary drug. The original sample consists of 18,128 individuals who were admitted to treatment services. The study focuses on people who are of age 13 years or older. Outliers of data samples, such as negative ages and negative income, are omitted from observations due to the missing data resulted in a final sample size of 13,775 individuals. The main dependent variable is patients who are admitted to receiving treatment services for alcohol/drug use addiction. Table 1 presents the definition of the variables and their descriptive statistics.

4. EMPIRICAL RESULTS

By using the data of the NJDAAT, this study interweaves health economic theory with an extension of the extended PP Model to analyse relapse behaviours that are shown in Fig. 1. The study examines how the influential policy/programme affects the relapse of alcohol/drug abusers in order to implement effective settings and also analyses how the influential policy/programme on alcohol/drug abusers with effective settings for addicted patients could prevent the relapse behaviour of alcohol/drug abusers.

Table 2 presents the regression results of alcohol/drug readmission for treatment for all ages by the probit estimation approach. The cohort estimations for age groups (years): (14–19), (20–29), (30–39), (40–49), and (50+), use the same specifications as Table 2, and the results of different age cohorts are available upon request. The coefficients for other age cohorts are generally consistent and have the expected signs.

Higher education attainment in HC factors is one of the important inputs to improving the health status of alcohol/drug abusers. Acquiring health education increases one's health knowledge, attitude, and motivation to obtain health-risk information and health services. It also prevents previous alcohol/drug abusers from relapsing during the action and maintenance stages (Miller & Pollnick, 1991). The variable of a college education shows that alcohol/drug abusers who receive a degree have a 1.8 percentage point

Table 1. Definition of the Variables and Descriptive Statistics ($n = 13{,}775$).

Variables	Definition	Mean	Standard Deviation
Dependent variable			
Readmission	DV = 1 for a patient readmitted to the same agency or different agency; 0 otherwise	0.064	0.244
HC factors			
Household income	Household annual income of patients ($)	8,921.814	18,877.420
Unemployed	DV = 1 for a patient who is unemployed; 0 otherwise	0.546	0.497
Junior high school	DV = 1 for a patient who is a junior high school graduate; 0 otherwise	0.393	0.488
Senior high school	DV = 1 for a patient who is a senior high school graduate; 0 otherwise	0.568	0.495
College	DV = 1 for a patient who is a college/university graduate; 0 otherwise	0.039	0.194
Age 14–19	Patient who is between 14 and 19 years of age	0.066	0.250
Age 20–29	Patient who is between 20 and 29 years of age	0.272	0.445
Age 30–39	Patient who is between 30 and 39 years of age	0.307	0.461
Age 40–49	Patient who is between 40 and 49 years of age	0.263	0.440
Age 50+	Patient who is 50 years old and over	0.092	0.289
Marital status	DV = 1 for patient who is married; 0 otherwise	0.141	0.348
Family structure	Number of members in patient's family	2.124	1.854
PR factors			
Gender	DV = 1 for a patient who is a male; 0 for female	0.693	0.461
Caucasian	DV = 1 for a patient who is a Caucasian; 0 otherwise	0.582	0.493
African-American	DV = 1 for a patient who is an African-American; 0 otherwise	0.347	0.476
Child tobacco stopping	DV = 1 for a patient who is age 19 and below, and wants to stop using tobacco or cut down from his/her current tobacco use; 0 otherwise	0.022	0.146

Table 1. (*Continued*)

Variables	Definition	Mean	Standard Deviation
RE factors			
Legal enforcement	DV = 1 for a patient who has a legal problem (i.e., case pending, drug court, probation, parole, etc.); 0 otherwise	0.533	0.499
Self-help	DV = 1 for a patient who is self-help referred to the hospital; 0 otherwise	0.358	0.479
Family	DV = 1 for a patient who is referred to the hospital by a family member; 0 otherwise	0.080	0.271
Addiction service	DV = 1 for a patient who receives addiction service referred by a treatment programme, county drug, or alcohol coordinator to the hospital; 0 otherwise	0.080	0.272
Welfare service	DV = 1 for a patient who receives welfare/social service referred by human services department or substance abuse initiative to the hospital; 0 otherwise	0.090	0.287
Correction programme	DV = 1 for a patient who receives a correction-related programme referred by federal court, municipal court, family, etc.; 0 otherwise	0.218	0.413
Mental health	DV = 1 for a patient who receives mental health referred by a mental health screening centre or mental health provider/clinic, etc.; 0 otherwise	0.035	0.183
EN factors			
Alcohol counselling	DV = 1 for a patient who receives alcohol counselling; 0 otherwise	0.288	0.453
Drug counselling	DV = 1 for a patient who receives drug counselling; 0 otherwise	0.492	0.500
Psychologic counselling	DV = 1 for a patient who receives psychologic counselling; 0 otherwise	0.249	0.433
Detoxication by hospital	DV = 1 for detoxication hospitalization; 0 otherwise	0.099	0.299
Detoxication by residential	DV = 1 for detoxication-free-standing/ sub-acute residential; 0 otherwise	0.134	0.340

Table 1. (Continued)

Variables	Definition	Mean	Standard Deviation
Short-term residential	DV = 1 for short-term medically monitored residential treatment; 0 otherwise	0.184	0.387
Standard treatment	DV = 1 for standard/traditional outpatient treatment level of care; 0 otherwise	0.384	0.486
Detoxication for outpatient	DV = 1 for detoxication treatment for an outpatient; 0 otherwise	0.018	0.132
Outpatient maintenance	DV = 1 for maintenance treatment for an outpatient; 0 otherwise	0.108	0.310
Halfway house	DV = 1 for halfway house, transitional care, or non-traditional treatment programme; 0 otherwise	0.020	0.140
Medicaid	DV = 1 for a patient with Medicaid; 0 otherwise	0.177	0.381
Employer financing	DV = 1 for a patient with employer financing; 0 otherwise	0.160	0.367
County financing	DV = 1 for a patient with direct county/ youth service commission financing; 0 otherwise	0.169	0.375
Primary substance abuse			
Primary alcohol	DV = 1 for a patient with primary alcohol abuse; 0 otherwise	0.279	0.448
Primary marijuana	DV = 1 for a patient with primary marijuana abuse; 0 otherwise	0.127	0.333
Primary cocaine	DV = 1 for a patient with primary cocaine abuse; 0 otherwise	0.066	0.249
Primary crack	DV = 1 for a patient with primary crack abuse; 0 otherwise	0.081	0.273
Heroin with mental	DV = 1 for a patient with heroin abuse and a mental problem; 0 otherwise	0.097	0.296
Alcohol with mental	DV = 1 for a patient with alcohol abuse and a mental problem; 0 otherwise	0.063	0.243
Heroin intensity use	DV = 1 for a patient who uses heroin 3–6 times per week; 0 otherwise	0.338	0.473
Alcohol intensity use	DV = 1 for a patient who uses alcohol 3–6 times per week; 0 otherwise	0.145	0.352
Child alcohol/drug intensity use	DV = 1 for a child (age 19 and below) who uses alcohol/drug 3–6 times per week; 0 otherwise	0.030	0.170

Table 2. Results of Alcohol/Drug Readmission for Treatment: All Ages (Probability).

Variables	Marginal	Estimate	Standard Error	P-value
Intercept	−0.250	−2.891	0.300	(0.000)
HC factors				
Household income	−0.338E−07	−0.391E−06	0.117E−05	(0.739)
Unemployed	−0.018	−0.210	0.045	(0.000)
Junior high school	−0.004	−0.049	0.046	(0.287)
College	−0.018	−0.210	0.094	(0.025)
Age 20–29	0.061	0.711	0.226	(0.002)
Age 30–39	0.051	0.592	0.230	(0.010)
Age 40–49	0.057	0.660	0.232	(0.004)
Age 50+	0.057	0.665	0.238	(0.005)
Marital status	0.001	0.017	0.064	(0.787)
Family structure	−0.005	−0.058	0.014	(0.000)
PR factors				
Gender	−0.003	−0.032	0.047	(0.495)
Caucasian	0.033	0.383	0.126	(0.002)
African-American	0.047	0.547	0.131	(0.000)
Child tobacco stopping	0.030	0.351	0.240	(0.144)
Reinforcing factors				
Legal enforcement	−0.002	−0.026	0.046	(0.572)
Self-help	0.039	0.456	0.074	(0.000)
Family	0.037	0.431	0.093	(0.000)
Addiction service	0.015	0.174	0.100	(0.083)
Welfare service	0.036	0.422	0.100	(0.000)
Correction programme	0.003	0.034	0.091	(0.713)
Mental health	−0.038	−0.436	0.162	(0.007)
EN factors				
Alcohol counselling	−0.012	−0.136	0.063	(0.031)
Drug counselling	−0.005	−0.059	0.058	(0.307)
Psychologic counselling	−0.025	−0.293	0.117	(0.012)
Detoxication by hospital	−0.051	−0.588	0.218	(0.007)
Detoxication by residential	−0.083	−0.956	0.195	(0.000)
Short-term residential	0.130	1.503	0.152	(0.000)
Standard treatment	0.020	0.235	0.152	(0.123)
Detoxication for outpatient	−0.065	−0.756	0.373	(0.043)
Outpatient maintenance	−0.002	−0.029	0.169	(0.866)
Halfway house	0.100	1.162	0.179	(0.000)
Medicaid	−0.012	−0.135	0.070	(0.053)
Employer financing	0.012	0.140	0.065	(0.031)
County financing	0.046	0.527	0.052	(0.000)

Table 2. (Continued)

Variables	Marginal	Estimate	Standard Error	P-value
Substance abuse				
Primary alcohol	−0.053	−0.610	0.105	(0.000)
Primary marijuana	−0.033	−0.383	0.109	(0.000)
Primary cocaine	−0.041	−0.476	0.116	(0.000)
Primary crack	−0.064	−0.746	0.109	(0.000)
Heroin with mental	0.033	0.378	0.129	(0.004)
Alcohol with mental	0.006	0.067	0.156	(0.665)
Heroin intensity use	−0.014	−0.157	0.074	(0.033)
Alcohol intensity use	0.040	0.465	0.096	(0.000)
Child alcohol/drug intensity use	0.036	0.418	0.227	(0.065)
Number of observations	13,775			
Schwarz B.I.C.	2368.48			
Log likelihood	−2158.80			
R^2	0.300838			
Sum of squared residuals	578.276			
Condition index	58.046			

Note: Standard errors computed from analytic first and second derivatives (Eicker–White). The result of age cohorts (years): 14–19, 20–29, 30–39, 40–49, and 50+, are available upon request to the first author.

lower relapse rate than senior high-school graduates (i.e., an omitted variable). An implication of the result is that not only formal education but also informal education in the community level are important to reducing relapse behaviour.

In PR factors, African-Americans and Caucasians in Table 2 show that they seem to have a higher relapse behaviour than other ethnicities (omitted variable). The results also display ethnic/racial differences of motivational behaviour (Rapp, Li, Siegal, & DeLiberty, 2003). If policy makers and/or programme planners are able to recognize these ethnic/racial differences, they can more effectively prevent the relapse behaviour of alcohol/dug abusers by implementing health intervention that is directed to target populations.

For RE factors, the function of the legal institutional development of drug court, probation, and parole would discourage substance abuse activities. However, the variable of legal enforcement in Table 2 is unexpectedly not statistically significant. The key policy variables in this analysis are referred agencies for alcohol/drug-addicted patients. The negative relationship between readmission and the referred mental health agency produces a very interesting result, and implies that there is a higher probability of reducing relapse behaviour through a mental agency. Reducing mental problems could possibly be an effective way to preventing the relapse behaviours of alcohol/drug abusers.

The positive signs of "Self-Help," "Family," "Addiction Service," and "Welfare Service," imply that the risk of relapse is greater for alcohol/drug abusers referred by self-help, family, and an institution than for those who are referred by medical service providers (i.e., hospitals and clinics). The results suggest that the importance of facilitating the health intervention, which targets self-motivation and family support, is critical for relapse prevention. It also implies that health intervention planners must examine the social network, such as Alcoholics Anonymous and Drug/Narcotics Anonymous in order to identify the most promising strategy to amend relapse behaviour. Addiction service, welfare service, and correction programmes require more efficient solid structures with good operative management to prevent people from relapsing. Poor and/or inept policies may lead to poor implementation or miss-conceptual management of operation. The lack of a social support network would increase relapse behaviour.

The EN factors, which include alcohol, drug, and psychologic counselling, inversely affect relapse behaviour. Alcohol and psychologic counselling are negatively and statistically significant, as shown in Table 2. If an increase in counselling services is negatively associated with relapse behaviour, then a decrease in relapse is caused by a rise in the health status of alcohol/drug abusers. This indicates that there is an increase in their HC factors. Providing counselling service programmes could significantly reduce alcohol/drug abuse. By providing these services, the relapse rate of alcohol/drug abusers would significantly decrease and there would be an overall improvement to their health condition. Human capital development with a better health status raises the market value of alcohol/drug abusers and increases their earnings. A rise in economic opportunity cost would discourage alcohol/drug abusers. Furthermore, a proper coordination of psychologic counselling with the aforementioned variable of a mental referred agency in RE factors would also be an effective intervention to prevent or to reduce the relapse of alcohol/drug abusers.

A better external counselling environment that involves accessibility, availability, quality, and quantity of counselling services for alcohol/drug abusers is essential because it would make it easier for them to carry out desirable healthy behaviour. When the primary focus of treatment is on informal education that is intended to change the behaviour of alcohol/drug abusers, it may involve an in-policy and regulatory approach, and an array of activities to mobilize local resources. An effective counselling programme for relapse prevention calls for process and impact evaluation in order to continue to benefit the alcohol/drug abusers through the community-based educational health intervention. Additionally, the cost-benefit/effective analysis is especially important when evaluating the effectiveness of counselling programmes.

Additional important key policy variables are the treatment settings in the EN factors, which are located in Table 2. The regression results of detoxication treatment provided by hospitals and residences are on an outpatient basis, and are negatively and statistically significant. This indicates that these treatments are more effective than long-term residential treatment (i.e., an omitted variable). On the other hand, based on the positive regression results, the treatment provided by the short-term residence and halfway house is less effective than the treatment provided by long-term residence programmes. This suggests that detoxication treatment is the most advantageous treatment programme for alcohol/drug abusers to motivate a behavioural change. Although the approach that the present study uses is different from Maisto et al. (2001), the result is congruent with their findings. Maisto et al. found that standard care is less effective than brief advice that is provided to low-dependent drinkers. However, the present study implies that when an alcohol/drug abuser is admitted to an outpatient alcohol/drug abuse treatment programme, the decisions made by the administrators or interviewers play a key role in motivating the patient's behavioural change. There are a variety of treatment selections for users of substances, such as alcohol, cocaine, crack, heroine, and marijuana. In addition, the steps that could be taken for the outpatient-based alcohol/drug abuse treatment include – standard treatment (standard/traditional outpatient or intensive outpatient), outpatient detoxification (methadone or non-methadone), and outpatient maintenance. Appropriate and accurate decisions should be implemented with care in order to reduce health care costs and also raise the efficiency of treatment since addiction is related to primary, secondary, and tertiary substance uses.

Health care coverage is a major issue in alcohol/drug abuse treatment. In Table 2, the regression result for Medicaid is negatively and statistically significant. This finding is surprising and unexpected. One cause for this result may be that Medicaid alcohol/drug patients are treated as effectively when compared to uninsured-addicted patients (an omitted variable). Another possible reason could be that alcohol/drug abusers with Medicaid tend to have fewer, shortened, and lower treatment units due to the restricted government reimbursement, which utilizes a managed care method. A third possible explanation could involve the fact that uninsured alcohol/drug-addicted patients are given different reimbursement sources (block grants, substance abuse initiatives, criminal justice, drug-court residential, public assistance, community funding, etc.) because of their inability to pay for the treatment services. The positive results of financing sources from employer and county are puzzling because alcohol/drug abusers have a higher relapse behaviour than those who are uninsured or who are Medicaid patients. DeVoe et al. (2003) stated that the receipt of services is strongly and positively associated with the types of health insurance. The results of financing the treatment for alcohol/drug abusers would need to be a topic of further study to clarify the relapse behaviour and the treatments in this field.

For substance abuse in Table 2, primary alcohol, marijuana, cocaine, and crack users are less likely to relapse compared to heroin users (an omitted variable), with marginal rates ranging from -3.3 to -6.4 percentage points. These negative results are generally consistent through different age cohort groups (the results of other age cohorts are available upon request.). Heroin users with mental problems have a higher probability of relapsing than other substance abusers. The results reveal that the addiction caused by heroin users with mental problems is attributable to a stronger relapse impact than other drugs. Thus, mental treatment is an important, effective, and practical treatment when it comes down to preventing and reducing the relapse behaviour of alcohol/drug abusers. The results imply that carefully coordinated institutional settings by medical and social agencies are required.

5. CONCLUSIONS AND DISCUSSIONS

Heavily addicted substance users demand a greater quantity of treatment than those individuals with less dependency. In other words, a person, who is heavily addicted to alcohol and/or drugs, would have a greater need to utilize health care resources. Targeting relapsed alcohol/drug abusers would be a more logical policy to effectively reducing health care costs. Thus, the importance of relapse prevention and intervention should not be underestimated.

Evaluating the prevention, intervention, and treatment programme is critical to understanding the decision-making behaviour of substance abusers. Many patients have experienced prior admissions to the treatment programme. Why? Using the NJDAAT, the present study interweaves behavioural health economics with the extended PP Model. Alcohol/drug abusers who have completed a college education have lower relapse behaviour than those who are senior high-school graduates, which emphasizes the importance of the HC factors. For intra-personal determinants, African-Americans in the PR factors have a higher relapse behaviour than

Caucasians and other ethnicities, which highlight the importance of implementing health prevention and intervention to a socio-culturally targeted population of substance abusers.

Interpersonal determinants (RE and EN factors) show clear-cut results. Regarding the RE factors, it is critical for policy makers to facilitate health intervention that targets self-motivation and family support. This study points out that health intervention planners must examine social network community-based mental health educational programmes in order to identify the most promising strategies to amend relapse behaviour. For EN factors, accessible and quality-oriented counselling services for substance users are essential for them to carry out desirable healthy behaviours. An effective counselling programme stems from the medically networked community-based health intervention (i.e., alcohol, drug, and mental counselling). Another major finding in EN factors is that when compared to other treatments, there is a significant impact on decreasing the relapse behaviour through detoxication treatments, which include inpatient, outpatient, and residence-based programmes. Many relapse behaviours of substance users have different characteristics. Heroin substance users with mental problems show the highest relapse behaviour among alcohol and other illicit drug users. Reducing mental health problems with addiction treatment could be a practical and effective means for reducing relapse behaviours.

This study has its limitations. First, due to the availability of the data, the study focuses on a cross-sectional study, which only includes the readmission and newly admitted substance abusers. Future study would merge the discharge data with the present admission data to extend an analysis such as a duration approach, which allows examining the duration of addiction period and its cost/resource analysis for relapse behaviours. Second, this study does not differentiate the unemployed, full-time, and part-time substance abusers. About 50% of the samples in this study are unemployed. Future studies should focus on abusers' unemployment status and their relapse behaviours. Third, to understand the characteristics of different drug abuse, future studies could be conducted to characterize the different types of addiction. This may lead to clarify the utilization of health care resources by different types of substance users.

ACKNOWLEDGEMENTS

We are grateful to anonymous referees for their valuable suggestions, insights, and recommendations. This chapter is much improved because of their excellent reviews. We are also very grateful to Paul Nystedt and the participants for their comments at the *24th Arne symposium on economics of substance use-individual behaviour, social interactions, markets, and politics* at Lund University, Sweden. We would like to thank Charles J. Crowley, Administrative Analysis Data Processing in the New Jersey Department of Health and Senior Services, DAS, for compiling and providing us with valuable data. We greatly acknowledge the research supports provided by the Research Council of Rutgers University, the State University of New Jersey, U.S.A.; by the Research Funding from Teachers College of Columbia University, U.S.A.; and by the Grant-in-Aid Scientific Research (C), no. 14530042, from Japan Society for the Promotion of Science (JSPS). Finally, we wish to thank James P. Kushwara for his research assistance at Rutgers University, the State University of New Jersey, U.S.A.

REFERENCES

Bolin, K., Jacobson, L., & Lindgren, B. (2001). The family as the health producer – when spouses are Nash-bargainers. *Journal of Health Economics, 20*, 349–362.

Bolin, K., Jacobson, L., & Lindgren, B. (2002a). Employer investments in employee health. Implications for the family as health producer. *Journal of Health Economics, 21*, 563–583.

Bolin, K., Jacobson, L., & Lindgren, B. (2002b). The family as the health producer – When spouses act strategically. *Journal of Health Economics, 21*, 475–495.

Bolin, K., Lindgren, B., Lindström, M., & Nystedt, P. (2003). Investments in social capital – Implications of social interaction for the production of health. *Social Science and Medicine, 56*, 2379–2390.

Carpenter, C. (2004). How do zero tolerance drunk driving laws work? *Journal of Health Economics, 23*, 61–83.

Chaloupka, F. J., Saffer, H., & Grossman, M. (1993). Alcohol-control policies and motor-vehicle fatalities. *Journal of Legal Studies, 22*, 161–186.

Chatterji, P. (2003). *Illicit drug and educational attainment.* NBER Working Paper No. 10045. Cambridge, MA: National Bureau of Economic Research.

Chatterji, P., & Markowitz, S. (2000). *The Impact of maternal alcohol and illicit drug use on children's behavior problems: Evidence from the children of the national longitudinal survey of youth.* NBER Working Paper No. 7692. Cambridge, MA: National Bureau of Economic Research.

Cuellar, A. E., Markowitz, S., & Libby, A. M. (2003). *The relationships between mental health and substance abuse treatment and juvenile crime.* NBER Working Paper No. 9952. Cambridge, MA: National Bureau of Economic Research.

Currie, S. R., Clark, S., Hodgins, D. C., & El-Guebaly, N. (2004). Randomized controlled trial of brief cognitive–behavioural interventions for insomnia in recovering alcoholics. *Addiction, 99*(9), 1121–1132.

DeVoe, J. E., Fryer, G. E., Phillips, R., & Green, L. (2003). Receipt of preventive care among adults: Insurance status and usual source of care. *American Journal of Public Health, 93,* 786–791.

Friedmann, P. D., Saitz, R., & Samet, J. H. (1998). Management of adults recovering from alcohol or other drug problems: Relapse prevention in primary care. *The Journal of American Medical Association, 279,* 1227–1231.

Green, L. W., & Kreuter, M. W. (2004). *Health program planning: An educational and ecological approach* (4th ed.). New York: McGraw-Hill.

Grossman, M. (1972a). On the concept of health capital and the demand for health. *Journal of Political Economy, 80,* 223–255.

Grossman, M. (1972b). *The demand for health: A theoretical and empirical investigation.* New York: Columbia University Press.

Grossman, M. (2003). The human capital model. In: A. J. Culyer, & J. P. Newhouse (Eds), *Handbook of health economics* (3rd ed., pp. 347–408). Amsterdam: Elsevier North Holland.

Grossman, M., & Chaloupka, F. J. (1998). The demand for cocaine by young adults: A rational addiction approach. *Journal of Health Economics, 17,* 427–474.

Grossman, M., Chaloupka, F. J., & Sirtalan, I. (1998). An empirical analysis of alcohol addiction: Results from the monitoring the future panels. *Economic Inquiry, 36,* 39–48.

Jacobson, L. (2000). The family as producer of health – an extended Grossman model. *Journal of Health Economics, 19,* 611–638.

Kaestner, R. (1998). *Does drug use cause poverty?* NBER Working Paper No. 6406. Cambridge, MA: National Bureau of Economic Research.

Kaskutàs, L. A., Bond, J., & Humphreys, K. (2002). Social networks as mediators of the effect of alcoholics anonymous. *Addiction, 97*(7), 891–900.

Maisto, S., Conigliaro, J., McNeil, M., Kraemer, K., Conigliaro, R. L., & Kelly, M. E. (2001). Effects of two types of brief intervention and readiness to change on alcohol use in hazardous drinkers. *Journal of Studies on Alcohol, 62,* 605–614.

McCrady, B. S., Epstein, E. E., & Kahler, C. W. (2004). Alcoholics anonymous and relapse prevention as maintenance strategies after conjoint behavioral alcohol treatment for men: 18-month outcomes. *Journal of Consulting and Clinical Psychology, 72*(5), 870–878.

Miller, W. R., & Pollnick, S. (1991). *Motivational interviewing: Preparing people to change addictive behavior.* New York: Guilford Press.

Pacula, R. L., & Kilmer, B. (2003). *Marijuana and crime: Is there a connection beyond prohibition.* NBER Working Paper No. 10046. Cambridge, MA: National Bureau of Economic Research.

Pacula, R. L., Ringel, J., & Ross, K. E. (2003). *Does marijuana use impair human capital formation?* NBER Working Paper No. 9963. Cambridge, MA: National Bureau of Economic Research.

Rapp, R. C., Li, L., Siegal, H., & DeLiberty, R. N. (2003). Demographic and clinical correlates of client motivation among substance abusers. *Health and Social Work, 28,* 107–115.

Samet, J. H., Friedmann, P., & Saitz, R. (2001). Benefits of linking primary medical care and substance abuse services: Patient, provider, and societal perspectives. *Archives of Internal Medicine, 161,* 85–91.

Schmitz, J. M., Stotts, A. L., Sayre, S. L., DeLaune, K. A., & Grabowski, J. (2004). Treatment of cocaine–alcohol dependence with naltrexone and relapse prevention therapy. *American Journal on Addictions, 13*(4), 333–341.

U.S. Department of Health and Human Services. (2000). *Healthy People 2010* (2nd ed.). Washington, DC: U.S. Government Printing Office.

Weitzman, E. R., & Kawachi, I. (2000). Giving means receiving: The protective effect of social capital on binge drinking on college campuses. *American Journal of Public Health, 90*(12), 1936–1939.

Yamada, T., Kendix, M., & Yamada, T. (1996). The impact of marijuana and alcohol use on high school graduation. *Health Economics, 5*, 77–92.

Yamada, T., Yamada, T., & Karmakar, R. (2000). Determinants of social violence among the youth and their risky health behaviors: Policy implications. *In Violence and Health* (pp. 290–303). World Health Organization, WHO Publication.

Yen, C. F., Wu, H. Y., Yen, J. Y., & Ko, C. H. (2004). Effects of brief cognitive–behavioral interventions on confidence to resist the urges to use heroin and methamphetamine in relapse-related situations. *Journal of Nervous and Mental Disorder, 192*(11), 788–791.